Pride and Prodigies
Studies in the Monsters of the *Beowulf*-Manuscript

*'Then there came from the moor, under the misty slopes,
Grendel approaching: he bore the wrath of God.'*

Monsters and the monstrous, whether from the remote pagan past or the new world of Christian Latin learning, haunted the Anglo-Saxon imagination in a variety of ways. In this series of detailed studies, Andy Orchard demonstrates the changing range of Anglo-Saxon attitudes towards the monstrous by reconsidering the monsters of *Beowulf* against the background of early medieval and patristic teratology and with reference to specific Anglo-Saxon texts.

The immediate manuscript context of the monsters in *Beowulf* is analysed, shedding light on the poet's treatment of the theme of the monstrous and its integration into his work, and a series of parallel discussions consider a range of medieval treatments of the same theme in a variety of analogous texts (all provided with translation) in Latin, Old English, Middle Irish, and Old Icelandic.

The twin themes of pride and prodigies are suggested by tracing changing attitudes towards the concept of pride and establishing a close link between the proud pagan warriors depicted in Christian tradition and the monsters they fight, and with whom they become increasingly identified.

An appendix contains new editions and translations (some for the first time in English) of the *Liber Monstrorum*, *The Letter of Alexander to Aristotle*, and *The Wonders of the East.*

ANDY ORCHARD is the Associate Director of the Centre for Medieval Studies at the University of Toronto.

PRIDE AND PRODIGIES

Studies in the Monsters of the *Beowulf*-Manuscript

ANDY ORCHARD

UNIVERSITY OF TORONTO PRESS
Toronto Buffalo London

Paperback edition published by University of Toronto Press Incorporated 2003
Toronto Buffalo London

First published by D.S. Brewer, Cambridge 1985

ISBN 0-8020-8583-0

Printed on acid-free paper

National Library of Canada Cataloguing in Publication

Orchard, Andy
Pride and prodigies : studies in the monsters of the Beowulf-manuscript / Andy Orchard.

First ed. published: Cambridge ; Rochester, NY : D.S. Brewer, 1995.
Includes bibliographical references and index.
ISBN 0-8020-8583-0

1. Beowulf. 2. Beowulf – Manuscripts. 3. Monsters in literature.
4. Heroes in literature. 5. Pride in literature. I. Title.

PR1587.M65O73 2003 829.3 C2002-905864-3

University of Toronto Press acknowledges the financial assistance to its publishing program of the Canada Council for the Arts and the Ontario Arts Council.

University of Toronto Press acknowledges the financial support for its publishing activities of the Government of Canada through the Book Publishing Industry Development Program (BPIDP).

CONTENTS

FOR MY
MOTHER AND FATHER

PREFACE TO THE REVISED EDITION

Eight years have passed since this book first appeared, and of course much has changed. In presenting this revised edition, I have attempted to correct as many literal errors as I have detected, and I am thankful to those reviewers who helped steer me in the right direction. I am especially grateful to David McDougall of the Dictionary of Old English for his detailed help in this regard, and to Michael Fox and Samantha Zacher for their assistance. Doubtless, errors still remain: the faults still remain mine. There has, of course, been much work done on *Beowulf* and the other texts mentioned here in the intervening period, and it may be helpful to signal just a few relevant works. The most important new tool available is undoubtedly the *Electronic Beowulf*, ed. Kevin S. Kiernan et al., 2 CDs (London, 2000), which has made the *Beowulf*-manuscript accessible to many. Other monographs that have focused on aspects of the texts and monsters mentioned here include Christine Rauer, *Beowulf and the Dragon: Parallels and Analogues* (Cambridge, 2000), and Magnús Fjalldal, *The Long Arm of Coincidence: The Frustrated Connection between 'Beowulf' and 'Grettis saga'* (Toronto, 1998). An indispensible guide to recent *Beowulf* scholarship is likewise provided by Robert E. Bjork and John D. Niles, eds, *A 'Beowulf' Handbook* (Lincoln, NE, 1997). I am happy to say that my own view of *Beowulf* has developed considerably over the years: more recent expressions of my opinions on matters relating to the theme of this book are to be found in 'The Sources and Meaning of the *Liber monstrorum*,' in *I 'monstra' nell'inferno Dantesco: Tradizione e Simbologie*, Atti del XXXIII Convegno storico internazionale, Todi, 13–16 ottobre 1996, ed. E. Menestò (Spoleto, 1997), pp. 73–105, and in *A Critical Companion to 'Beowulf'* (Cambridge, 2003). My father died before the first edition of this book appeared, but my deep debt to him and to my mother, like the dedication, remains.

Andy Orchard

July 2002
Centre for Medieval Studies, Toronto

PREFACE

The six studies in this book seek to consider the motivation and background to the compilation of the *Beowulf*-manuscript, and in particular to address the question of the precise role and meaning both of the ancient monsters who stalk through the sources and of the heroes who battle against them. All five of the texts contained in that manuscript, namely *Judith*, *The Passion of Saint Christopher*, *The Wonders of the East*, *The Letter of Alexander to Aristotle*, and *Beowulf* itself, are examined in turn for the ways in which contrasting worlds and cultures, Latin and Germanic, christian and secular, classical and biblical, are combined and reconciled in a manner so characteristic of the literature of Anglo-Saxon England. In addition, two other sources, the so-called *Liber monstrorum* and the Icelandic *Grettis saga*, both of which have an established and important place in *Beowulf*-studies, are considered in detail for the further clues they offer to the twin themes of pride and prodigies which, I suggest, unite the texts. In order to facilitate reference and (I hope) to stimulate further study I have provided plain texts and translations of three of the less accessible sources, namely *The Wonders of the East*, *Alexander's Letter to Aristotle*, and the *Liber monstrorum*; but it goes without saying that *Beowulf*, the centre of the study, remains the impetus and inspiration for all that follows here. In such a broadly-based discussion, where I have had to consult a wide range of sources in areas which are the proper preserve of other disciplines, I have made enquiries of many friends. Particular thanks are due to Margaret Bridges, Peter Clemoes, Ali Dale, Morgan Dickson, Matthew Driscoll, David Dumville, Michael Lapidge, Sean Miller, Sam Newton, and Erich Poppe. The errors are not theirs. The dedication reflects a deeper and more long-standing debt: a book is poor payment for thirty years of love and life, but this one is meant for my mum and my dad.

Andy Orchard

July 1994
Emmanuel College, Cambridge

ABBREVIATIONS

ASPR	Anglo-Saxon Poetic Records, ed. G. P. Krapp and E. V. K. Dobbie
CCSL	Corpus Christianorum, Series Latina
CLA	E. A. Lowe, *Codices Latini Antiquiores*, 11 vols. and suppl. (Oxford, 1934–71; 2nd ed. of vol. II, 1972)
CSASE	Cambridge Studies in Anglo-Saxon England
CSEL	Corpus Scriptorum Ecclesiasticorum Latinorum
EEMF	Early English Manuscripts in Facsimile (Copenhagen)
EETS	Early English Texts Society
OS	Original Series
NS	New Series
SS	Supplementary Series
MGH	Monumenta Germaniae Historica
AA	Auctores Antiquissimi
PLAC	Poetae Latini Aevi Carolini
PG	Patrologia Graeca, ed. J. P. Migne, 162 vols. (Paris, 1857–66)
PL	Patrologia Latina, ed. J. P. Migne, 221 vols. (Paris, 1844–64)

PRIDE AND PRODIGIES

CHAPTER I

The *Beowulf*-Manuscript

It was Kenneth Sisam who first considered that the *Beowulf*-manuscript may have been compiled on the basis of an interest in monsters which is exhibited by at least four of the five texts it contains; he mused that a medieval cataloguer, seeking to sum up the contents of the manuscript, might well have described it as a 'book of various monsters, written in English' (*Liber de diversis monstris, anglice*).[1] Since then, numerous commentators have accepted and built on Sisam's suggestion, generally in seeking to explain the transmission of *Beowulf*, and the chance preservation of a poem the great literary merits of which have long been recognised.[2] Investigation of the relationship of *Beowulf* to the other texts in the manuscript highlights not only the extraordinary 'beauty and artistry' of the poem,[3] but also the interests of the anonymous compiler in assembling what at first glance might seem an eclectic collection of texts.

Beowulf is uniquely contained in a composite manuscript, now London, British Library, Cotton Vitellius A. xv.[4] It appears that Sir Robert Cotton (1571–1631) himself first bound together the *Beowulf*-manuscript,[5] also known as the Nowell Codex,[6] with a group of four texts written in the twelfth century.[7] The dating of the

1 Sisam, *Studies*, p. 96.

2 See for example, the perceptive comments of Haarder, *'Beowulf': the Appeal of a Poem*, especially pp. 209–34; Sisam, *Studies*, pp. 66–7; Niles, *Beowulf: the Poem and its Tradition*, pp. 3–30; Newton, *The Origins of 'Beowulf'*, pp. 5–7. Examination of the manuscript transmission of related 'monster-texts' reveals a significant degree of clustering; see now Brynteston, '*Beowulf*, Monsters, and Manuscripts', pp. 41–57.

3 The description is that of Lawrence, *'Beowulf' and Epic Tradition*, pp. viii–ix; cf. Brodeur, *The Art of 'Beowulf'*, pp. 1–38.

4 Listed as no. 399 in Gneuss, 'A Preliminary List'; facsimiles of the relevant parts of the manuscript have been produced by Malone, *The Nowell Codex*; Zupitza, *Beowulf*.

5 Some scholars, notably Kiernan, *Beowulf and the Beowulf Manuscript*, pp. 133–150, occasionally use the term '*Beowulf*-manuscript' to refer to a presumed separate codex comprising *Beowulf* alone; no such distinction is implied by my usage.

6 After Laurence Nowell (d. *c.* 1571), who owned the manuscript in 1563, and wrote his name on the top of the first folio of *The Passion of St Christopher*; cf. Newton, *The Origins of 'Beowulf'*, p. 1; Boyle, 'The Nowell Codex and the Poem of *Beowulf*', p. 23; Sisam, *Studies*, p. 62.

7 See further Kiernan, *Beowulf and the Beowulf Manuscript*, pp. 66–70; Gerritsen, 'British Library MS Cotton Vitellius A.XV'; Gerritsen, 'Have with you to Lexington!'.

Beowulf-manuscript itself has been a matter of hot debate; on palaeographical grounds Neil Ker suggested 's. X/XI',[8] but his conjecture has been widely (mis-) interpreted.[9] David Dumville, after the most recent and comprehensive discussion, concludes that: 'it is in the highest degree unlikely that the *Beowulf*-manuscript was written later than the death of Æthelred the Unready (1016) or earlier than the mid-point of his reign (which fell in A.D. 997)'.[10] The present contents of the *Beowulf*-manuscript can be summed up as follows:[11]

1. *The Passion of St Christopher*, incomplete at the beginning (fols. 94r–98r)
2. *The Wonders of the East*, illustrated in colour (fols. 98v–106v)
3. *The Letter of Alexander to Aristotle* (fols. 107r–131v)
4. *Beowulf* (fols. 132r–201v)
5. *Judith*, incomplete at the beginning and end (fols. 202r–209v)

Two scribes, with quite distinctive styles of Insular minuscule script, are responsible for writing all five texts.[12] Scribe A wrote all three of the prose texts preceding *Beowulf*, as well as some three-fifths of the poem, in a hand principally characterised by extending descenders and ascenders, finishing his stint part-way through a page, and indeed in the middle of a half-line (*Beowulf*, line 1939; fol. 172v3 *scyran*).[13] Scribe B completed the poem, 'writing in a rather crude, late Square minuscule script',[14] and was also responsible for the extant portion of *Judith*. As David Dumville has pointed out: 'No other specimen of either scribe's work has ever been discovered; nor have any closely related scribal performances been identified'.[15] Since the beginning of *Judith* is now lost, it has been suggested that the poem did not form part of the original compilation, while the battered condition of the last folio of *Beowulf* might similarly suggest that it was once the final page of the volume.[16]

Sisam went further, arguing on the basis of linguistic evidence that not only *Judith*, but *Christopher* too, were later additions, pointing to the distribution of *io*-spellings

8 Ker, *Catalogue*, pp. 281–2.

9 Cf. Dumville, '*Beowulf* Come Lately', pp. 50–1; Kiernan, *Beowulf and the Beowulf Manu*script, pp. xi and 13–14; Kiernan, 'The Eleventh-Century Origin', p. 10.

10 Dumville, '*Beowulf* Come Lately', p. 63.

11 The foliation given here is that of 1884, which is followed in the facsimile edition by Malone. See further Malone, *The Nowell Codex*, pp. 12–14; Newton, *The Origins of 'Beowulf'*, p. 2; Sisam, *Studies*, p. 65; Boyle, 'The Nowell Codex and the Poem *Beowulf*', p. 24.

12 Dumville, '*Beowulf* Come Lately', p. 50; Boyle, 'The Nowell Codex and the Poem *Beowulf*', pp. 24–5.

13 Boyle, 'The Nowell Codex and the Poem *Beowulf*', p. 32, notes that part of the following word, *moste*, may also have been written by scribe A, who therefore ended his stint not simply in the middle of a half-line, but in the middle of a word! Boyle suggests that: 'perhaps the plain truth is that he had taken ill, and died'.

14 Dumville, '*Beowulf* Come Lately', p. 50; for the characteristics of Square minuscule script, see Dumville, 'English Square Minuscule Script'.

15 Dumville, '*Beowulf* Come Lately', p. 50.

16 Cf. Newton, *The Origins of 'Beowulf'*, p. 2; Sisam, *Studies*, pp. 67–8; Chambers, *'Beowulf': an Introduction*, p. 509; Ker, *Catalogue*, p. 282; Kiernan, *Beowulf Manuscript*, pp. 149–67; Timmer, ed., *Judith*, p. 1.

in the manuscript, where 'normal' late West Saxon has *eo*.[17] Along similar lines, Eric Stanley has highlighted certain linguistic features in *Judith* which are not shared by the other texts in the *Beowulf*-manuscript, together with the presence of some compound forms of late date,[18] and Rypins, Sisam, and Vleeskruyer all note significant spelling-variants which distinguish *Christopher* from the other texts.[19] Wenisch has produced a detailed linguistic analysis suggesting a Mercian origin for both *Judith* and *Christopher*.[20] Conversely, Sisam has argued for a connection between *The Wonders of the East*, *The Letter of Alexander to Aristotle*, and *Beowulf*, on the basis of shared spellings of *u* for *f*, which in a number of cases had been miscopied by scribe A as *n*, and in particular between *The Letter of Alexander to Aristotle* and *Beowulf*, which, alone among the texts of the manuscript, exhibit genitive plural endings in *-o*.[21] As Sisam concludes: 'additions to an existing collection are easiest made at the beginning and end; and prose and verse would be kept apart if *Christopher* were added at the beginning and *Judith* at the end'.[22] The extent to which Anglo-Saxon scribes were concerned to effect such a distinction, however, is less clear in other extant codices.[23] More important, perhaps, is the separation between those texts which are ostensibly secular in content (*The Wonders of the East*, *The Letter of Alexander to Aristotle*, and *Beowulf*) and those in which explicitly religious themes predominate (*The Passion of St Christopher* and *Judith*).

Most recently, moreover, Peter Lucas, following Neil Ker,[24] has argued persuasively that, so far from being the final item in the *Beowulf*-manuscript, as now, *Judith*

17 Sisam, *Studies*, pp. 67 and 92, where Sisam notes that: 'In the *Letter io* is relatively frequent, though it tends to appear in patches — some 66 examples in 50 pages of the manuscript. (*Christopher* has none in 9 pages; *Wonders* 2 in 17; *Beowulf*, first hand, 11 in 87; *Beowulf*, second hand, 115 in 53; *Judith* fragment none in 15 pages).' Cf., however, the careful arguments of Rypins, *Three Old English Prose Texts*, pp. xiv–xxix, as well as the more recent survey by Cameron, Amos, and Waite, 'A Reconsideration of the Language of *Beowulf*'. See now Bately, 'Old English Prose Before and During the Reign of Alfred'. especially pp. 99 and 112–13.

18 Stanley, 'Some Doubts and No Conclusions', p. 198, quoting Dietrich, '*Hycgan* und *hopian*' and Meroney, 'The Early History of *Down* as an Adverb'. On what Stanley perceives as the West-Saxon character of *Judith*, see now, however, Wenisch, '*Judith*: eine westsächsische Dichtung?', pp. 273–300.

19 Sisam, *Studies*, p. 69: '*Christopher* has always (7 times) the spelling *mytty* (*þe*), *mitty*, where *Alexander's Letter*, the only other text in the codex which uses this phrase, has always *mid þy*. *Christopher* has always the spelling *cyninge* (13 times) which ocurs nowhere else in the codex'; cf. Rypins, *Three Old English Texts*, p. xvi. Vleeskruyer, *The Life of St Chad*, pp. 55–6, argues that *Christopher* came from or through Mercia, noting that the text has been 'West-Saxonised' more completely than the texts which follow it in the *Beowulf*-manuscript.

20 Wenisch, *Spezifisch anglisches Wortgut*, pp. 72, 87, and 327–8

21 Sisam, *Studies*, pp. 64, 85 and 94. Sisam's evidence with respect to genitive plural endings in *-o* can be supplemented by reference to the lists given by Cameron, Amos, and Waite, 'A Reconsideration of the Language of *Beowulf*', p. 53.

22 Sisam, *Studies*, p. 68.

23 So, for example, the Vercelli Book, the only other manuscript of any size containing prose and verse

24 Ker, *Catalogue*, p. 282.

originally preceded *The Passion of St Christopher*; he suggests on the basis of both linguistic and palaeographical evidence that 'the *Beowulf* manuscript is a compilation based on two collections, one containing *Judith* and *Christopher* . . . and one containing [*Wonders*], *Alexander's Letter*, and *Beowulf*'.[25] Lucas's conclusions, if accepted, throw into sharp relief Sisam's reservations about including *Judith* in his scheme for the design of the *Beowulf*-manuscript.[26] But if, as Sisam put it, 'Holofernes is no monster',[27] then his behaviour is certainly monstrous, and, as others have pointed out, Judith, like Beowulf, disposes of her incapacitated foe by decapitation.[28] One might well ask why the compiler of the *Beowulf*-manuscript saw fit to combine the more obviously Christian and religious texts of *Judith* and *The Passion of Saint Christopher* with what appears to have been originally a more ostensibly secular collection of wonder-tales. In fact, as we shall see, the twin narratives of *Judith* and *Christopher*, both of which describe wondrous events, introduce important themes and contrasts which recur throughout the *Beowulf*-manuscript, and raise issues still unsettled in the closing lines of *Beowulf*.[29]

Part of the problem of assessing the wider function that *Judith* and *The Passion of Saint Christopher* may have played in the Beowulf-manuscript as a whole lies in their very incompleteness. As it stands, the 350 extant lines of *Judith* correspond to selected passages from the Vulgate Judith XII.10–XVI.1, although the rendering is not always very close.[30] Certainly, something has been lost from the beginning of the poem, which begins in mid-sentence, but the extent of that loss is difficult to determine. B. J. Timmer argued that the section- or fitt-numbers X, XI, and XII, found at lines 15, 122, and 236, indicate that at least eight fitts (and most of the ninth) are lost, presumably corresponding to the first nine or so chapters of the Vulgate account.[31] According to this view, *Judith* represents a portion of what was once a more-or-less complete versification of the biblical book, despite the fact that other extant Old English biblical poems, such as *Genesis A*, *Exodus*, or *Daniel*, all represent selective renderings to differing extents.[32] Against this argument, Rosemary Woolf pointed out that the first three poems of the Junius manuscript are divided into fitts numbered consecutively I to LV, with no fresh numbering for each poem, and therefore the scribe of *Judith* might simply be reproducing mechanically the numeration of his exemplar.[33] Earlier, A. S. Cook, indicating certain parallels of diction at the beginning and end of the extant poem, had likewise argued that little

25 Lucas, 'The Place of *Judith* in the *Beowulf*-Manuscript', p. 474; some of Lucas's arguments were anticipated by Pickles, 'Studies in the Prose Texts of the *Beowulf* Manuscript', pp. 8–10.

26 Sisam, *Studies*, p. 67; cf. Newton, *The Origins of 'Beowulf'*, p. 5.

27 Sisam, *Studies*, p. 67.

28 See further below, p. 157.

29 See further below, pp. 55–7.

30 Cf. Timmer, ed., *Judith*, pp. 14–16 for the corresponding passages from the Vulgate.

31 Timmer, ed., *Judith*, p. 17; a contrasting view is expressed by Chamberlain, '*Judith*: a Fragmentary and Political Poem'.

32 See further Shepherd, 'Scriptural Poetry', pp. 4–9.

33 Woolf, 'The Lost Opening to the *Judith*', p. 170.

was lost.[34] Similar parallels of diction, it might be said, are also found in other Old English biblical poetry, although they do not always signal the beginning and the end of individual poems,[35] but it is true to say that, as we shall see, the extant poem *Judith* demonstrates considerable care and parallelism of structure.[36] On this view, *Judith*, like the Old English *Exodus*, represents a versification of only part of its biblical source.

Whatever the length of the original poem presented in the *Beowulf*-manuscript, the theme of Judith appears to have focused on the victory of the oppressed over the oppressors, and the fatal humiliation of overweening pagan pride.[37] The Vulgate text itself invites just such an interpretation, with its initial florid description of successive kings, and its final quiet praise of the virtuous Jews. Indeed, the opening seven verses of the Vulgate Judith, which supply the implicit context for the extant poem, introduce a number of themes which are echoed elsewhere in the *Beowulf*-manuscript, and deserve quotation in full:[38]

> Arfaxat itaque rex Medorum subiugaverat multas gentes imperio suo et ipse aedificavit civitatem potentissimam quam appellavit Igbathanis. Ex lapidibus quadratis et sectis fecit muros eius in altitudine cubitorum septuaginta et in latitudine cubitorum triginta. Turres uero eius posuit in altitudinem cubitorum centum per quadrum uero earum latus utrumque uicenorum pedum spatio tendebatur posuitque portas eius in altitudine turrium. Et gloriabatur quasi potens in potentia exercitus sui et in gloria quadrigarum suarum. Anno igitur duodecimo regni sui Nabuchodnosor rex Assyriorum qui regnabat in Nineven civitatem magnam pugnavit contra Arfaxat. Et obtinuit eum in campo magno qui appellatur Ragau circa Eufraten et Tigrin et Hyadas in campo Erioch regis Elicorum. Tunc exultatum est regnum Nabuchodnosor et cor eius elatum est.
>
> *Arphaxad therfore, king of the Medes had subdued manie nations to his empire, and he built a most mightie citie, which he called Ecbatanis, of stone squared and hewed: he made walles therof in height seventie cubites, and in breadth thirtie cubites, and the towers therof he made in height an hundred cubites. But each side of them was in foure square twentie foote long, and he made the gates therof according to the height of the towers: and he gloried as mightie in the force of his armie, and in the glorie of his chariotes. In the twelfth yeare of his reigne Nabuchodonosor the king of the Assyrians, who reigned in Niniue the greate citie, fought against Arphaxad, and overcame him in the greate field which is called Ragau, about Euphrates, and Tigris, and Iadason in the field of Erioch the king of the Elicians. Then was the kingdom of Nabuchodonosor exalted, and his heart was elevated.*

34 Cook, ed., *Judith: an Old English Epic Fragment*, p. 7.

35 See especially *Daniel*, lines 149–51 and 735–6, the first and last time that Daniel is mentioned in the poem, Frank, 'Paronomasia', p. 216. For a closely similar practice in Latin by Insular authors, see below, pp. 89–95.

36 See further below, pp. 7–10.

37 See further below, pp. 9–12; cf. the more general comments of Caie, 'The Old English *Daniel*: a Warning against Pride', pp. 1–9, many of which are applicable to *Judith*.

38 All quotations from the Latin Vulgate are taken from Weber, ed., *Biblia sacra iuxta vulgatam versionem*; English translations of the Latin Vulgate are taken from the Douai-Rheims version (1582–1609), revised by Richard Challoner (1749–50).

The martial vigour of the passage, with its evocation of mighty bygone empires won by force of arms, recalls several passages in *Beowulf*, from the portrayal of the success of Scyld on; the sumptuous portrayal of fantastic cities far away echoes similar descriptions in *The Wonders of the East* and *The Letter of Alexander to Aristotle*;[39] Judith's coming humiliation of Holofernes corresponds to the victory of the saintly Christopher over the wicked pagan Dagnus. Seen from the point of view of the opening passage of its source, there seems little reason to doubt the fitting place of *Judith* in the *Beowulf*-manuscript, as Taylor and Salus have indicated.[40] Such links between the texts are all the more intriguing, given the common exegetical interpretation of the opening passage, which sets a tone for the whole biblical account; Hrabanus Maurus, for example, offers the following allegorical interpretation of Arphaxad in his popular *Expositio in librum Judith*:[41]

> Mystice autem per Arphaxad arrogantium typus atque superborum potest exprimi, quorum totus nisus et labor, qui per fastum tumoris atque per elationem mentis agitur, facile in partem spiritualis Nabuchodnosor, id est diaboli, cadit.
>
> *But there can be interpreted mystically in the figure of Arphaxad the type of proud or arrogant people, whose whole toil and effort, which is conducted through the arrogance of pride and the exaltation of the mind, easily falls into the camp of the spiritual Nabuchodnosor, that is, the devil.*

Opinions differ on the question of the direct influence of Hrabanus Maurus on the poet of *Judith*,[42] but it is certainly the case that similar (and derivative) interpretations of the biblical narrative were in circulation in Anglo-Saxon England, as witness the first of the 'multiplicity of figural interpretations of the story of Judith' offered by Ælfric:[43]

39 Cf., for example, the ornate description of the marvellous city of Porus in *The Letter of Alexander to Aristotle* (§ 8, text and translation in Appendix II below): 'After that we entered the royal city of Porus with our weapons. And we saw his hall and his royal quarters. There were golden columns, very great, and mighty, and firm, which were enormously large and tall, of which we counted a tally of four hundred. The walls were also golden, sheathed with gold plates the thickness of a finger. When I wished to see these things more keenly and went further, I saw a golden vineyard, mighty and firm, and its branches hung about the columns. And I was greatly amazed at that. The leaves of the vineyard were of gold, and its tendrils and fruits were of crystal and emerald, and jewels hung among the crystal. His bedrooms and his main chambers were all most highly embellished with precious stones, the gem-stones unions and carbuncles. On the outside they were wrought in ivory, wonderfully white and fair, and posts of cypress and laurel supported them on the outside, and twisted golden props stood within, and there were countless hoards of gold inside and out, and they were manifold and of various kinds. And many jewelled vessels and crystal drinking-cups and golden pitchers were brought forth there. Seldom did we find any silver there.'

40 Taylor and Salus, 'The Compilation of Cotton Vitellius A XV', pp. 199–204.

41 PL 109, cols. 539–92, at cols. 544–5.

42 See, for example, Huppé, *The Web of Words*, pp. 143–4; Berkhout and Doubleday, 'The Net in *Judith* 46b–54a', pp. 632–4.

43 Assmann, ed., *Angelsächsische Homilien und Heiligenleben*, lines 407–17, pp. 114–15; cf. Godden, 'Biblical Literature: the Old Testament', pp. 219–20.

On hire wæs gefylled þæs hælendes gecwyde:
Ælc, þe hine ahefð, sceal beon geeadmet,
and se, þe hine geeadmet, sceal beon ahafen.
Heo eadmod ond clæne and ofercom þone modigan,
lytel and unstrang, and alede þone micclan,
forðan þe heo getacnode untwylice mid weorcum
þa halgan gelaðunge, þe gelyfð nu on God,
þæt is Cristes cyrce on eallum cristenum folce,
his an clæne bryd, þe mid cenum geleafan
þam ealdan deofle of forcearf þæt heafod,
æfre on clænnysse Criste þeowigende.

In her was fulfilled the Saviour's words: 'Everyone who exalts himself shall be humbled, and he who humbles himself shall be exalted'. She, humble and pure, overcame the proud one; small and weak, she cast down the mighty one, because she undoubtedly signified by her actions the holy assembly that believes now in God, that is Christ's church in all Christian people, his one pure bride, who with bold faith cut off the head of the old devil, always in purity serving Christ.

Ælfric's interpretation, building on that of Hrabanus, emphasises the importance of Judith's heroic struggle in a purely Christian context.[44]

But perhaps the most evident feature of the Old English poem *Judith* lies in its polarisation and simplification of the narrative, lending a coherent structure and even symmetry in the Old English which is certainly not present in the Latin original, and which represents a rather sensitive handling of a complex story.[45] We might compare the relative *dramatis personae* in each case. In the Latin, the cast-list reads as follows:

The Jewish side	*The Assyrian side*
Judith, a widow	Holofernes, a captain
An anonymous hand-maid	Vagao, a eunuch servant
Prince Ozias	King Nebuchadnezzar
Joachim, the High Priest	Achior, a Moabite

In the Old English, by contrast, the number of principal characters has been halved; we find the following:

The Jewish side	*The Assyrian side*
Judith	Holofernes, prince and captain
An anonymous hand-maid	An anonymous soldier

44 Cf. Campbell, 'Schematic Technique in *Judith*', p. 164.
45 Cf. particularly Doubleday, 'The Principle of Contrast in *Judith*', pp. 436–41.

The reduction in numbers is not simply to be explained by the partial nature of the extant text, but is quite clearly deliberate.[46] The easy parallelism of the Old English poem is apparent, with two characters named and unnamed from each side, and with rather wild and boorish men signifying the Assyrians, and calm and determined women representing the Jews.[47] Both the anonymous characters have finely-drawn and central functions within the Old English text. Although Judith's hand-maid does appear in the Vulgate, she has here a much-expanded role, whilst the anonymous Assyrian who announces to his people the death of Holofernes and prophesies their doom is an innovation in the Old English, usurping the role from the particular character Vagao in the Vulgate.[48] The whole focus of the Old English poem is thus thrown on the two central named characters,[49] whose roles have themselves undergone subtle modification.

In the Vulgate, Holofernes is very definitely subservient to Nebuchadnezzar his king, whilst in *Judith* Nebuchadnezzar does not appear at all, and the epithets applied to Holofernes are more fitting for a prince.[50] So, from the beginning of the extant poem, he is described as a 'terrifying lord of men' (*egesful eorla dryhten*, line 21); an 'arrogant distributer of treasure' (*swiðmod sinces brytta*, line 30); a 'prince' (*ealdor*, lines 38 and 58); a 'mighty king of men' (*þearlmod ðeoden gumena*, line 66).[51] Interestingly, this last description of Holofernes is repeated verbatim by Judith, in a prayer to God which artfully echoes in its various designations the different epithets given to Holofernes. Within the space of a few short lines God is addressed as 'prince of glory' (*swegles ealdor*, line 88); 'mighty king of men' (*þearlmod þeoden gumena*, line 91); 'mighty Lord' (*mihtig dryhten*, line 92); 'bright-hearted distributer of glory' (*torhtmod tires brytta*, line 93).[52] The parallel phraseology is both striking and disturbing;[53] by such methods the poet aligns Holofernes firmly with the enemies of God, casting him the role of a devil. He is therefore explicitly described as 'diabolical' (*se deofolcunda*, line 61), a 'treaty-breaker' (*wærloga*, line 71), and, more importantly (if anachronistically), as 'hateful to the Saviour' (*Nergende lap*, line 45).[54]

There is, moreover, considerable stress in the Old English poem on the net which

46 Cf. Woolf, 'The Lost Opening to the *Judith*', p. 171.

47 See further Campbell, 'Schematic Technique in *Judith*', pp. 156–8.

48 Doubleday, 'The Principle of Contrast in *Judith*', p. 436.

49 The only other name mentioned in *Judith* is that of the city of the Jews, Bethulia (lines 138 and 326). The central contrast is likewise highlighted by the clustered references to the Jews on the one hand (*Ebreas*, lines 218, 253, 262, and 298; *Ebrisc*, lines 241 and 305), and the Assyrians on the other (*Assiras*, lines 232, 265, and 309)

50 Doubleday, 'The Principle of Contrast in *Judith*', p. 437; cf. Cook, ed., *Judith*, p. xviii; Timmer, ed., *Judith*, p. 12.

51 Cf. Doubleday, 'The Principle of Contrast in *Judith*', p. 437.

52 In the last case the contrast is especially marked, since not only has Holofernes been described earlier as an 'arrogant distributer of treasure' (*swiðmod sinces brytta*, line 30), but only two lines before God is called a 'distributer of glory' (*tires brytta*, line 93), Holofernes is reviled, in a conscious parody of heroic diction, as a 'distributer of murder' (*morðres brytta*, line 90).

53 For other examples of such parallel phraseology, see now Tyler, 'Style and Meaning in *Judith*', pp. 16–18.

54 See further Pringle, '*Judith*: the Homily and the Poem', pp. 92–3.

surrounds Holofernes' bed. The Vulgate speaks simply of a 'canopy' (*conopeum*),[55] and stresses its opulence as an indication of the fabulous wealth of the Assyrians.[56] The Old English poet spends almost nine full lines on a description of the net (lines 46–54), where it is described as a 'fly-net' (*fleohnet*, line 47). Berkhout and Doubleday give pressing reasons for associating the net with the canopy which would cover a heathen idol, suggesting that 'Holofernes becomes by allusion, if not *diabolus* himself, one of his ministers'.[57]

Likewise, the characterization of Judith herself has changed in the Old English poem. In the Vulgate she is described as a loyal 'widow' (*vidua*), and it is her chastity which is stressed in the Vulgate itself, and still more so by later biblical commentators and patristic authorities.[58] So, Ambrose focuses on Judith in his *Liber de viduis*, and she is named as an outstanding exemplum of widowhood and chastity in two brief sermons by pseudo-Augustine, by Jerome, by Aldhelm in his prose *De Virginitate*, and in verse by Prudentius, Dracontius, and (again) Aldhelm.[59] In Ælfric's homily on Judith, which is so often quoted as analogous to the poem for its focus on the nature of the Just War in reference to the battles between the Anglo-Saxons and the Danes,[60] the focus is once again clearly on Judith's 'chastity' (*clænnysse*) and 'widowhood' (*wudewanhad*).[61] In *Judith* itself, by contrast, her chastity or widowhood are scarcely mentioned, and instead we are invited to consider her beauty, courage, and wisdom.[62] She is an 'elf-bright lady' (*ides ælfscinu*, line 14), but she is also a 'blessed maid' (*eadigan mægþ*, line 35); a 'splendid maid' (*torhtan mægþ*, line 43); a 'holy woman' (*halige meowle*, line 56); a 'maid of the creator' (*scyppendes mægþ*, line 78); a 'courageous lady' (*ides ellenrof*, lines 109 and 146); a 'wise lady' (*snoteran idese*, line 55); a 'prudent woman' (*gleawhydig wif*, line 148); a 'shining maid' (*beorhte mægþ*, line 254). If Holofernes is 'hateful to the Saviour' (*Nergende lab*, line 45), then Judith, by contrast, is a 'servant of the Saviour' (*Nergendes þeowen*, line 73).[63]

There are further ways in which the poet has altered his Vulgate source.[64] Unlike the Latin, *Judith* relies on careful structuring and repetition of key phrases, to drive home the basic contrasts which underlie his account.[65] In the Vulgate, Judith is present throughout the riotous banquet, intent on deceiving Holofernes through

55 Judith X.19, XIII.10, XIII.19, XVI.23; in the whole Vulgate, the word *conopeum* is only found in Judith.

56 Again, one might compare the sumptuous descriptions of fabulous and exotic wealth to be found in the *Letter of Alexander to Aristotle*; see above, n. 39.

57 Berkhout and Doubleday, 'The Net in *Judith* 46b–54a', p. 632.

58 Campbell, 'Schematic Technique in *Judith*', pp. 159–64.

59 Pringle, '*Judith*: the Homily and the Poem', p. 84, provides a useful summary.

60 See further Cross, 'The Ethic of War in Old English', pp. 269–82.

61 See further Pringle, '*Judith*: the Homily and the Poem', especially pp. 85–90.

62 Cf. Mushabac, '*Judith* and the Theme of *Sapientia et Fortitudo*'; Kaske, '*Sapientia et fortitudo* in the Old English *Judith*'; Locherbie-Cameron, 'Wisdom as a Key to Heroism in *Judith*'.

63 Cf. Tyler, 'Style and Meaning in *Judith*', p. 18.

64 See further Magennis, 'Adaptation of Biblical Detail in the Old English *Judith*', pp. 331–7.

65 Cook, ed., *Judith*, pp. xxxiv–xlii gives a list of such repeated phrases. See now Tyler, 'Style and Meaning in *Judith*', pp. 16–19.

flattery, and encouraging him to drink;[66] in the Old English poem, by contrast, the wild feasting and boasting are instigated by Holofernes himself, and not until afterwards does he order Judith to be brought in to satisfy his lust. Again, there is nothing in the Latin to parallel the rather grotesque and full description of the beheading of Holofernes, presented in the Old English in rather grisly detail (lines 98–111):[67]

genam ða þone hæðenan mannan
fæste be feaxe sinum, teah hyne folmum wið hyre weard
bysmerlice, and þone bealofullan
listum alede, laðne mannan,
swa heo þæs unlædan eaðost mihte
wel gewealdan. Sloh ða wundenlocc
þone feondsceaðan fagum mece
heteþoncolne, þæt heo healfne forcearf
þone sweoran him, þæt he on swiman læg,
druncen and dolhwund. Næs he dead þa gyt,
ealles orsawle; sloh ða eornoste
ides ellenrof oþre siþe
þone hæðenen hund, þæt him þæt heafod wand
forð on ða flore.

Then she took the heathen man firmly by his hair, and dragged him wretchedly towards her with her hands, and carefully arranged the wicked and hateful man so that she could most easily deal effectively with the wretch. Then that curly-haired girl struck the wicked-minded foe with a decorated sword so that she sliced through half his neck, so that he lay in a daze, drunk and maimed. He was not dead yet, not quite lifeless. The brave women then struck the heathen dog in earnest a second time, so that his head flew off onto the floor.

The utter hopelessness of Holofernes is dwelt upon with an exultation that is almost more shocking than the vivid description of Judith's double blow; the Latin is entirely unadorned by comparison (Judith XIII.10), stating simply that 'she stroke twice upon his necke, and cut off his head' (*et percussit bis in cervicem eius, et abscidit caput eius*).

A further feature of the poem is the additional description of a full-scale battle between the Jews and the Assyrians, where the Vulgate contains no hint of direct combat at all.[68] Finding Holofernes slaughtered, the Assyrians lose heart and flee away in a disorderly mob, and the Jews cut them down as they flee. In the poem, on the other hand, a battle is described vividly and at length (75 lines), including standard Germanic motifs such as the Beasts of Battle,[69] presented in quite a

66 Cf. Doubleday, 'The Principle of Contrast in *Judith*', p. 437.
67 See further below, p. 41.
68 See, for example, Campbell, 'Schematic Technique in *Judith*', pp. 169–72.
69 Cf. Timmer, ed. *Judith*, p. 12; Fry, 'Type-Scene Composition in *Judith*', pp. 100–19; Heinemann, '*Judith* 236–291a: a Mock-Heroic Approach-to-Battle Type Scene', pp. 83–96.

sophisticated way. The lovingly intense description of the battle is likened to the techniques of cinematography by Alain Renoir,[70] whilst others have praised the audio-visual effects of this part of the poem.[71] The point to stress, however, is that there is simply nothing comparable in the Latin. By delaying the discovery of Holofernes' death until the Assyrians have actually been routed, a further change from the Latin, the poet gives himself scope to explore the extent of devastation and desolation experienced by the beaten foe. The Vulgate version is sparse and unemotional; Vagao simply reports the state of the corpse (XIV.16):

> Una mulier Hebraea fecit confusionem in domo regis Nebuchodonosor: ecce enim Holofernes iacet in terra, et caput eius non est in illo.
>
> *One Hebrewe woman hath made confusion in the house of King Nabuchodonosor: for behold Holofernes lyeth upon the ground, and his head is not upon him.*

By contrast, the Old English poet, by delaying the discovery until after the Assyrians have been utterly defeated, and by giving voice to an anonymous soldier, puts a much deeper perspective on both the decapitation and humiliation of Holofernes (lines 275–90):[72]

Þa wearð sið and late sum to ðam arod
þara beadorinca, þæt he in þæt burgeteld
niðheard neðde, swa hyne nyd fordraf;
funde ða on bedde blacne licgan
his goldgifan gæstes gesne,
lifes belidenne. He þa lungre gefeoll
freorig to foldan, ongan his feax teran,
hreoh on mode, and his hrægl somod,
and þæt word acwæð to þam wiggendum,
þe ðær unrote ute wæron:
'Her ys geswutelod ure sylfra forwyrd
toweard getacnod, þæt þære tide ys
[nu] mid niðum neah geðrungen,
þe we [life] sculon losian somod,
æt sæcce forweorðan: her lið sweorde geheawen,
beheafod healdend ure.'

Then one of the soldiers belatedly and tardily became so bold that he bravely ventured into the pavilion, as forced by necessity; he found his lord lying pale on the bed, deprived of his spirit, bereft of life. Immediately he fell cold on the ground, began to tear his hair and clothes alike, troubled in heart, and he uttered these words to the warriors waiting wretchedly outside: 'Here is revealed our own

70 Renoir, '*Judith* and the Limits of Poetry', pp. 145–50.

71 Campbell, 'Schematic Technique in *Judith*', especially pp. 167–70; Huppé, *The Web of Words*, pp. 114–89.

72 Cf. Campbell, 'Schematic Technique in *Judith*', especially pp. 169–70; Pringle, '*Judith*: the Homily and the Poem', pp. 94–5.

> *doom, imminently signalled that the time has drawn near, along with its griefs, when we must perish and fall together in the fray. Here, hacked by the sword, our lord lies beheaded.'*

As in *Beowulf* (lines 2900–3027), the grim death of the lord spells doom for his benighted pagan people, and that doom is enunciated by a single unnamed messenger.

Just as the biblical tale of Judith is presented as a simplified struggle between an overweening prince and a pious captive, albeit an exotic and partly spiritual contest in which the underdog triumphs, so too *The Passion of Saint Christopher* offers a wondrous story of how a proud pagan king is captivated by his humble (and literally canine) Christian prisoner. The evident polarity between Judith and Holofernes exploited so fully in the Old English *Judith* is still starker in the account of the extraordinary dog-headed Christian giant, Christopher, and his struggle against the petulant heathen king, Dagnus.

The Passion of Saint Christopher in the *Beowulf*-manuscript is incomplete, but at least two further accounts are known from Anglo-Saxon England.[73] Another vernacular *Life of Saint Christopher* existed in London, British Library, Cotton Otho B. x,[74] but was all but destroyed in the infamous fire at Ashburnham House in 1731, which damaged much of the Cotton collection, including the *Beowulf*-manuscript. The *Life* begins as follows:[75]

> Menn þa leofestan, on þære tide was geworden, þe Dagnus se cync rixode on Samon þære ceastre, þæt sum man com on þa ceastre se wæs healf-hundisces manncynnes. Ac he ne cuðe nan þingc to þam lyfiendan Gode, ne his naman ne cigde, þe wæs him ætywed fram urum drihtne, þæt he sceolde fulluhte onfon.
>
> *Dearest people, it happened in the time that King Dagnus ruled in the city of Samos, that a certain man came to the city who was of the race of dog-headed folk. But he knew nothing of the living God, nor called on His name, until he was shown by our Lord that he should receive baptism.*

The typical homiletic opening of this *Life*, beginning with the invocation 'most beloved people' (*men þa leofestan*) betrays its didactic purpose as a tale which depicts the redemption of the apparently irredeemable,[76] whether in the form of monstrous 'dog-heads' (also known as *cynocephali* or *conopenae*), noted for their cannibalism,[77] or the pagan King Dagnus, who after imprisoning, torturing, and finally martyring his canine captive is led (quite literally) into the light; the physical blindness with

73 Pickles, 'Studies in the Prose Texts of the *Beowulf* Manuscript', pp. 15–33.

74 Gneuss, 'A Preliminary List', no. 355; Ker, *Catalogue*, pp. 224–9, at p. 226.

75 Cf. Taylor and Salus, 'The Compilation of Cotton Vitellius A XV', p. 201; Pickles, 'Studies in the Prose Texts of the *Beowulf* Manuscript', pp. 19 and 22–5.

76 Pickles, 'Studies in the Prose Texts of the *Beowulf* Manuscript', pp. 22–3.

77 Cf. Friedman, *The Monstrous Races*, pp. 67–74. Similar attention to the fiercesome and bestial nature of dog-heads is given in all the texts presented in the Appendix below; cf. *The Wonders of the East*, § 7; *The Letter of Alexander to Aristotle*, § 29; *Liber monstrorum* I.16 and II.13

which he is afflicted as retribution for his treatment of Christopher is cured at the same time as the psychological darkness of his sinful soul. By contrast, the *Passion of Saint Christopher* in the *Beowulf*-manuscript ends as follows:

> Þæs eadigan Cristoforus wuldorgeworc synd nu lang to asecgane þe dryhten þurh hyne geworhte to herennesse his naman 7 nu oð þyssne dæg wyrcð. For þon þe þær nu blowað 7 growað his þa halgan gebedu 7 þær ys drihtnes hyrnes mid ealre sybbe 7 gefean 7 þær ys gebletsod Crist Godes sunu lyfigendes se rixað mid fæder 7 mid suna 7 mid þam halgan gaste a butan ende. Þyses eac bæd se halga Cristoforus of þære nihstan tide ær he his gast onsende 7 cwæð: 'drihten min god syle gode mede þam þe mine þrowunga awrite 7 þa ecean edlean þam þe hie mid tearum ræde'.
>
> *It would now be too long to tell the marvellous deeds of Saint Christopher which the Lord worked through him in praise of his name, and still works to this day, since there his holy prayers now flourish and grow, and there is obedience to the Lord, with all peace and gladness, and there is blessed Christ, the son of the living God, who rules with the Father and with the Son and with the Holy Spirit, ever without end. Saint Christopher also commanded this the last time before his spirit passed on, and said: 'My Lord God, grant a good prize to him who may write my tortures down, and then eternal reward to those who read them with tears'.*

The first part of this closing peroration, finishing with the familiar words 'ever without end' (*a butan ende*), looks more suited to the end of a homiletic text,[78] and is indeed closely matched by the final words of the *Life of Saint Christopher* in the Otho manuscript,[79] while the *Passion of Saint Christopher* goes on to finish on a note more particularly suited to a reading audience, leading John Pickles to suggest that the two texts are intended for different purposes: one for the pulpit, the other for private meditation.[80]

A further Anglo-Saxon version of the tale of Saint Christopher is given in the *Old English Martyrology*, from which the following passage might be quoted:[81]

> Se com on Decius dagum þæs caseres on þa ceastre þe Samo is nemned of þære þeode þær men habbað hunda heafod ond of þære eorðan on þære æton men hi selfe. He hæfde hundes heafod, ond his loccas wæron ofer gemet side, ond his eagon scinon swa leohte swa morgen steorra, ond his teð wæron swa scearpe swa eofores tuxas. He wæs gode geleaffull on his heortan, ac he ne mihte sprecan swa mon.

78 In the course of a quick survey, I counted no fewer than fourteen homiletic texts containing the sequence *fæder . . . suna . . . halgan gaste . . . a butan ende*; in every single case except that from the *Passion of Saint Christopher* quoted here, the sequence concluded the text.

79 The text in Otho B. x ended as follows: *Forþam þe þær nu blowað 7 growað ða halgan gebedu 7 þær is drihtnes herung mid eallre sibbe 7 gefean and þær ys gebletsod crist þæs lyfigendes godes sunu se rixað mid fæder 7 mid sunu 7 mid þam halgan gaste a butan ende on ecnysse. AMEN.* Cf. n. 78 above.

80 Pickles, 'Studies in the Prose Texts of the *Beowulf* Manuscript', pp. 23–4.

81 Herzfeld, ed., *The Old English Martyrology*, pp. 66–8; Kotzor, ed., *Das altenglische Martyrologium*, II, pp. 68–71. See too Leinbaugh, 'St Christopher and the Old English Martyrology', pp. 434–7.

> *[Christopher] came in the days of the Emperor Decius into the city which is called Samos, from the race where people have dogs' heads and from the land where folk eat each other. He had the head of a dog, and his locks were exceedingly long, and his eyes shone as brightly as the morning-star, and his teeth were as sharp as boar's tusks. He believed in God in his heart, but he could not speak like a man.*

This striking description of Saint Christopher has been considered close to what might be inferred concerning the monster Grendel in *Beowulf*, who is likewise clearly of human shape and man-eating stock, with bright eyes and sharp teeth, whose severed head Beowulf grasps by the (presumably long) hair.[82] Elsewhere in the *Beowulf*-manuscript, most notably in the *Wonders of the East* and the *Letter of Alexander to Aristotle*, we find other descriptions of creatures who share many of the same physical features.[83]

That the extant (and acephalous) *Passion of Saint Christopher* in the *Beowulf*-manuscript does not mention explicitly that he was one of the *cynocephali* is scarcely surprising, since the fact is usually mentioned at the beginning of parallel accounts, but even in the mutilated text in the *Beowulf*-manuscript, he is described as 'twelve fathoms tall' (*twelf fæðma lang*) and 'the worst of wild beasts' (*wyrresta wildeor*), and there seems little doubt that the same dog-headed saint is depicted.[84] In other respects, moreover, the accounts given in Otho B. x and Vitellius A. xv agree substantially for the brief portion of text where they overlap,[85] and both appear close to a number of extant Latin versions of the text, although the actual source-text for *The Passion of Saint Christopher* remains to be identified.[86] The full text in the *Beowulf*-manuscript, however, will have told a tale familiar from numerous Latin versions,[87] which can broadly be summarised as follows:

> In the days of King Dagnus (or Decius) of Samos, one of the *cynocephali*, a giant race of dog-headed cannibals, believes in God, and receives baptism, a human voice, and the name Christopher. He undertakes to visit Samos to convert the heathens, but is spotted en route by a woman who, naturally alarmed, runs screaming to the palace. Christopher is apprehended by the soldiers of King Dagnus, who imprisons Christopher, and attempts to make him apostasise through torture. Dagnus becomes increasingly angy in the face of an implacable Christopher, and successively places a fiery helmet on his head, binds him to a red-hot iron chair, ties him to a tree, and has archers shoot at him, all to no avail. In the last case the arrows hang impotently in the air, but when Dagnus curses Christopher, they fly back and blind the king. Christopher predicts his own peaceful demise the next day, and advises the king to use blood and soil from his grave as a poultice. Christopher dies, and a voice from heaven proclaims

82 See further Newton, *The Origins of 'Beowulf'*, p. 6.

83 Cf. *The Wonders of the East*, §§ 4, 5, 7, 8, 12, 13, 20, 22, and 27; *The Letter of Alexander to Aristotle*, § 29.

84 Rypins, ed. *Three Old English Texts*, pp. 68/19 and 70/5.

85 See n. 79 above.

86 Cf. Pickles, 'Studies in the Prose Texts of the *Beowulf* Manuscript', pp. 17–21.

87 See further Rosenfeld, *Der Hl. Christophorus, seine Verehrung und seine Legende*, especially pp. 3–366.

his piety. Dagnus does as he has been advised, is cured of his blindness, and promptly converts to Christianity, along with his people. Some closing remarks stress Christopher's curative and intercessionary powers.

The Latin *Life of Saint Christopher* derives ultimately from apocryphal accounts of the adventures of the apostles Andrew and Bartholomew,[88] who in their wanderings in Parthia come across a dog-headed cannibal, which the Syriac account describes as follows:[89]

> Now his appearance was exceedingly terrible. He was four cubits in height, and his face was like unto the face of a great dog, and his eyes were like unto lamps of fire which burn brightly, and his teeth were like unto the tusks of wild boar, or the teeth of a lion, and the nails of his hands were like unto curved reaping hooks, and the nails of his toes were like unto the claws of a lion, and the hair of his head came down over his arms like unto the mane of a lion, and his whole appearance was awful and terrifying.

Once again, many of the physical details of this monstrous creature can be matched in the texts of the *Beowulf*-manuscript, particularly *The Wonders of the East*.[90] The creature, who calls himself Abominable, is struck with a profound desire to become a Christian, and does so, being renamed Christianus by Andrew, and acting as their guide in their subsequent adventures. The legend of the dog-headed Christianus strongly influenced later accounts of the saints Mercurius and Christopher, both of whom are associated with *cynocephali*.[91] Such an association is made the more intriguing by the persistent use of this and related terms to apply to unbelievers by a range of patristic authors.[92]

Interest in *cynocephali* in general, and in Saint Christopher in particular, seems to have been expressed in Celtic countries throughout the medieval period. From Ireland we find a detailed account of the saint in the Leabar Breac, including a gloss which reads *Christopher .i. conchend* ('Christopher, that is dog-head'), while the Manx parish of Conchan may take its name from a similar interest in these dog-heads, to judge from the number of local cross-slabs bearing their image.[93] The

88 Cf. Friedman, *The Monstrous Races*, pp. 70–1.

89 The translation is by Budge, *The Contendings of the Apostles*, pp. 173–4.

90 Cf. *The Wonders of the East*, §§ 5, 7, 8, 12, 13, 20, 22, and 27.

91 Cf. Friedman, *The Monstrous Races*, pp. 70–4; Lecouteux, *Les monstres dans la littérature allemande du moyen âge*, II, pp. 27–8.

92 Cf. Friedman, *The Monstrous Races*, pp. 83–7; Lecouteux, *Les monstres dans la littérature allemande du moyen âge*, II, pp. 20–7; Stanford, 'Monsters and Odyssean Echoes', pp. 114–16. See, for example, Tertullian, *Apologeticum* VIII.4 and *Ad nationes* VIII.1 (Dekkers, ed., *Tertulliani Opera*, I, pp. 21 and 101).

93 Fraser, 'The Passion of Saint Christopher', p. 309; Gaidoz, 'Saint Christophe à tête de chien en Irlande et en Russie'; Kermode, *Manx Crosses*, pp. 6, 134–6, plates 22–61; 23–62; 24–64a; Salmon, 'St Christopher in English Medieval Art and Life', pp. 95–6; Murphy, ed., *Duanaire Finn*, p. 27; McNamara, *The Apocrypha in the Irish Church*; Friedman, *The Monstrous Races*, pp. 72–4.

Welsh poem 'Pa gur yv y porthaur?' from the Black Book of Carmarthen casts Arthur in the role of mighty monster-slayer, and the dog-heads as his unfortunate foes:[94]

Arthur ced huar[t]hei
Y guaed gouerei
In neuat Awarnach
In imlat a gurach.
Ew a guant Pen Palach
In atodev Dissethach.
Ym minit Eidin
Amuc a chinbin.
Pop cant id cuitin,
Id cvitin pop cant,
Rac Beduir Bedrydant.
Ar traethev Trywuid
In amuin a Garvluid
Oet guychir y annuyd
O cletyw ac yscuid.

Though Arthur laughed [or ?played],
he caused the/her blood to flow
in Afarnach's hall,
fighting with a witch.
He pierced Cudgel(?) Head
in the dwellings of Disethach.
On the mountain of Edinburgh
he fought with dog-heads.
By the hundred they fell;
they fell by the hundred
before Bedwyr the Perfect [or *Pefect-Sinew].*
On the shores of Tryfrwyd,
fighting with Rough Grey,
furious was his nature
with sword and shield.

Clearly dog-heads were considered suitable quarry for heroic kings, just as they were for the Irish heroes Labraid Swift Hand and Cú Roí, or the Welsh Taliesin;[95] in such Celtic accounts, dating from as early as the eighth century, it is the fierce and martial nature of these dog-heads which is the prime reason for their inclusion. By contrast, a number of Irish martyrologies name (presumably Christian) *conchind* ('dog-heads') for 28 April, the day on which, according to both the Irish texts and the *Old English Martyrology,* Christopher himself was to be commemorated; the Martyrology of Gorman may tacitly acknowledge the apparently contradictory

94 Roberts, ed., 'Rhai o Gerddi', p. 301; the translation is by Sims-Williams, 'The Early Welsh Arthurian Poems', pp. 41–2.

95 Dillon, 'Notes on Irish Words', pp. 249–51.

nature of the *cynocephali* by specifying the commemoration of 'the dog-heads who are harmonious' (*na Conchind bat cuibde*).[96]

The choice of such a bizarre emissary as one of these same dog-heads, whose very humanity had been doubted by Augustine (*De ciuitate Dei* XVI.8) and Isidore (*Etymologiae* XI.iii.15 and XII.ii.32),[97] to fulfil the saintly role is but one of a number of paradoxes consciously exploited by the Latin author of the *Life of Saint Christopher*, and fully reflected by the Old English translator.[98] Just as it is one of the monstrous *cynocephali*, traditionally associated with paganism, who is represented as the champion of Christianity, so too it is Christopher, called by Dagnus 'the worst of wild beasts' (*wyrresta wildeor*),[99] who stays calm and serene, while the king himself becomes progressively wilder and more enraged, as the Old English translator stresses through repetition of the phrase 'then the king grew angry' (*se cyningc þa yrre geworden wæs*).[100] Christopher's taunting of the king to be quick about offering more tortures, since they are sweeter to him than the bee-bread of honey is typical of the topsy-turvy logic of this text,[101] just as the nature of those tortures, namely crowning with a fiery helm and enthronement on a red-hot seat, only serve to emphasise in contrast the regal authority of the Christian captive, and the abject impotence of the pagan king. In the same way, Christopher predicts his forthcoming death as a result of his cruel punishment by proclaiming that only thereby will he receive his just reward, and be 'brought to life' (*geliffæsted*).[102] In such a context, Dagnus' pained question to Christopher about his efforts to convert his people to Christianity appears distinctly ironic:[103]

> Þu wyrresta wilddeor, hu lange dyrstlæcest þu þæt ðu þis folc fram me tyhtest swa þæt him nis alyfed þæt hi minum godum onsecgen?
>
> *You worst of wild beasts, how long do you dare to incite this people from me so that they are not permitted to sacrifice to my gods?*

In Dagnus' eyes, it is Christopher who is the apostate and infidel, whilst the Latin text is still more explicit; Dagnus complains bitterly to Christopher about the sins of the lost souls that the saint has 'led astray':[104]

96 Hughes, 'Irish Litany of Pilgrim Saints', pp. 328–31.

97 By contrast one might compare the learned exchange (Dümmler, ed., MGH Epistolae IV, pp. 155–7) between Ratramnus of Corbie and Rimbert of Hamburg-Bremen, in the course of which Rimbert suggests that *cynocephali* ought to be considered as men rather than beasts, partly on the evidence of Saint Christopher himself. See further Hughes, 'Irish Litany of Pilgrim Saints', p. 330.

98 Cf. Frederick, 'A Reading of the Old English *Life of St Christopher*', pp. 137–48.

99 Rypins, ed. *Three Old English Texts*, p. 70/5.

100 Rypins, ed. *Three Old English Texts*, pp. 68/3–4 and 11; the Latin text has *iratus rex* on both occasions, p. 108/3 and 7.

101 Rypins, ed. *Three Old English Texts*, p. 68/16; the Latin text has *dulciora super mel et favum tormenta tua*, p. 108/10.

102 Rypins, ed. *Three Old English Texts*, p. 73/4.

103 Rypins, ed. *Three Old English Texts*, p. 70/5–7.

104 Rypins, ed. *Three Old English Texts*, p. 108/24–7.

> Fera mala, non tibi sufficiunt peccata animarum, quas errare fecisti, et non permisisti sacrificare diis; sed omnem populum meum traxisti ad te?
>
> *Wicked wild beast, are the sins not enough for you of those souls whom you have caused to err, and have not permitted to sacrifice to the gods; but you have drawn to yourself my entire people?*

For Dagnus, a king disposessed, it is Christopher's arrogance, according to the Old English version (*hu lange dyrstlæcest þu?*), which has alienated the whole nation from the king's own religion (*minum godum*). Indeed, this is but one example of a series in which the Old English translator goes beyond any putative source in making the conflict between Dagnus and Christopher a highly personalised affair for each; a contest, as the author repeatedly makes clear, between 'my god(s)' and 'your god(s)'.[105]

The Passion of Saint Christopher echoes and elaborates some of the thematic contrasts and distinctions to be observed in the Old English *Judith*. Once again the basic polarity between believers and non-believers, and between oppressors and oppressed is examined; once more the proud are humbled. But *The Passion of Saint Christopher* introduces the further distinction to be made between the basically antagonistic worlds of monsters and men, and the merging and mingling to be observed between them.[106] It is this theme which is so fully developed in the three texts which follow in the *Beowulf*-manuscript, each of which can be said to be centrally concerned with monsters, and with the activities of mighty pagan men.

Immediately following *The Passion of Saint Christopher* in the *Beowulf*-manuscript is *The Wonders of the East*, a curious collection giving rather sparse details of some thirty-two marvels, together with illustrations.[107] The wonders depicted in the *Beowulf*-manuscript can be summed up as follows:

§ 1. The colony Antimolima; the island of sheep, and its proximity to Babylon.

§ 2. Rams as big as oxen; the monuments of Alexander the Great.

§ 3. Lentibelsinea, and the red hens, whose touch burns.

§ 4. The shy eight-footed beasts with two heads and fierce eyes, whose touch burns.

§ 5. Hascellentia, and the two-headed snakes with bright eyes.

§ 6. Huge donkeys with horns as big as oxen; snakes called Corsiae with horns as big as rams, whose touch kills, and who hoard pepper.

105 Cf., for example, Rypins, ed. *Three Old English Texts*, pp. 70/12, 70/18, 71/1, 71/4–5, and 72/4.

106 The same kind of distinction is implicit in the *Liber monstrorum*, of course, where *cynocephali* are described alongside both men (I.16) and beasts (II.13); see below, pp. 244–5 and 268–9.

107 For a text and translation, see the Appendix below, pp. 183–203. No fewer than three unpublished doctoral dissertations are devoted to this text: Garrad, 'The Wonders of the East'; Gibb, '*Wonders of the East*'; Knock, 'Wonders of the East'. I have consulted all three dissertations, of which the latest one, by Knock, running to 1074 pages, deserves special mention, for its meticulous documentation of the background and related texts.

§ 7. Dog-people, called Conopenae, with horses' manes, dogs' heads, and fiery breath.

§ 8. Tall people, called Homodubii, with long hair and beards, who eat raw fish.

§ 9. Swift red and black ants as big as dogs, guarding gold which can be taken from them with the help of camels.

§ 10. The colony Locotheo, and its multitude of elephants.

§ 11. White two-faced people fifteen feet tall with red feet and knees, a long nose and black hair, who travel to India to give birth.

§ 12. The land Ciconia, and its shy inhabitants of three colours, twenty feet tall, with lions' manes, and mouths as big as fans, who sweat blood when they run.

§ 13. Big black cannibals called Hostes, with long legs and feet.

§ 14. The Lertices, with donkey's ears, sheep's wool, and bird's feet.

§ 15. Headless people eight feet long and eight feet wide, with their eyes and mouth in their chests.

§ 16. Dragons, a hundred and fifty feet long, as thick as pillars.

§ 17. The shy and soft-voiced Homodubii, human to the navel, and donkey-shaped below, with long bird-like legs.

§ 18. Barbarous people, and their subject kings; the lakes of the Sun and the Moon.

§ 19. Wondrous trees, like laurel and olive.

§ 20. The polyglot cannibalistic Donestre, who lure strangers to their death, and then eat them, except for the head, over which they sit and weep.

§ 21. Shy, light-coloured people fifteen feet tall and ten feet broad, with large heads and fan-like ears, under which they sleep.

§ 22. Island-people, whose eyes shine brightly at night.

§ 23. The temple of iron and brass; the temple of the Sun, and its priest.

§ 24. The golden vineyard, with its huge precious berries.

§ 25. The mighty mountain, with its decent people, and precious gems.

§ 26. Bearded huntresses, with their pet tigers and leopards.

§ 27. Long-haired white women thirteen feet tall, with boar's tusks, camel's feet, donkey's teeth, and ox-tails on their loins; their slaughter by Alexander the Great.

§ 28. The beautiful wild animals called Catini; people who live on raw meat and honey.

§ 29. The hospitable kings, who have subdued many tyrants.

§ 30. The generous people, who give visitors women; Alexander the Great's refusal to kill them.

§ 31. Trees which produce precious stones.

§ 32. Black people called Sigelwara.

The same material is found in a sumptuous later Old English geographical miscellany, London, British Library, Cotton Tiberius B. v, which dates from the middle of the eleventh century, and contains on fols. 78v–87r a Latin text alongside the Old English, together with a further (and much finer) set of illustrations.[108] The Tiberius manuscript preserves a slightly fuller version of the Old English text than the *Beowulf*-manuscript, particularly at the beginning of § 5, but its readings are not to be preferred in all cases;[109] there are sufficient differences between the texts to show that they do not derive directly from a common ancestor, as Paul Gibb has suggested.[110] The Tiberius manuscript also includes five further marvels at the end of the text which have no parallel in the *Beowulf*-manuscript, and can be summed up as follows:

§ 33. The land of vineyards; the ivory couch 306 feet long.

§ 34. The mountain Adamans; the four-footed Gryphon, with a cow's tail, and an eagle's head.

§ 35. The peacock-crested Phoenix, and its nest of cinnamon; its thousand-year life, self-immolation, and resurrection.

§ 36. The fiery mountain, and its black inhabitants

§ 37. The apocryphal story of Iamnes and Mambres.

Four of these wonders (§§ 32–6) are well-attested in analogous compilations, and appear to reflect features of an original collection which are omitted in the *Beowulf*-manuscript rather than additions to the Tiberius text.[111] More intriguing, and more closely parallel to the putative compilation of the *Beowulf*-manuscript, is the compiler's decision, unmatched in analogous collections, to add the apocryphal tale in which Mambres raises his dead brother's spirit from the grave, and hears him offer a stark warning of his future plight, and bewail what he himself had done, in lording it over other sorcerers and standing up to Moses and Aaron. The names of Iamnes and Mambres occur in three other Old English texts, and their figures have been identified in two illuminations in the illustrated Old English Hexateuch British Library, Cotton Claudius B. iv, alongside their depiction in the Tiberius manuscript.[112] The inclusion of the tale at the end of the *Wonders of the East* in the Tiberius manuscript testifies to the readiness of compilers to supplement the tally of marvels in their text, and demonstrates that explicitly pious material might be

108 Gneuss, 'A Preliminary List', no. 373. A facsimile edition with full commentary is provided by McGurk *et al.*, *An Eleventh-Century Miscellany*, with a detailed discussion of the illustrations of the *Wonders* on pp. 99–103. In addition to the other illustrations one might note a detailed *mappa mundi* on fol. 56v which mentions, amongst many others, the *cinocephales* ('dog-heads').

109 See further Knock, 'Wonders of the East', pp. 92–146.

110 Gibb, '*Wonders of the East*', pp. 5–8.

111 See further below, pp. 24–5.

112 Cf. Hall, 'Jamnes and Mambres', pp. 27–9.

included in such a collection, if sufficient thematic links were perceived. One might draw a broad parallel with the inclusion of the overtly Christian narratives of *Christopher* and *Judith* alongside the more obviously secular wonder-tales in the *Beowulf*-manuscript.

The use of necromancy in the tale might of itself have sufficed to warrant its inclusion, but the words of Iamnes are intriguing:

> Þu, broðor, ic naht unrihtlice eom dead, ac soðlice 7 rihtlice ic eom dead 7 Godes dom wið me standeð for þam ðe ic wæs ana wisera þonne ealle oðre dryas 7 ic wiðstod twam gebroðrum Moyses hatte 7 Aaron, þa worhtan þa micclan tacna 7 forebeacnu.
>
> *Brother, I am not unjustly dead, but rightly and justly am I dead, and God's judgement will go against me because I alone was wiser than all the other sorcerers, and I withstood the two brothers called Moses and Aaron, who performed those great portents and signs.*

Iamnes' sin, it might be inferred, was founded at least in part on pride, the same kind of overweening pride, which led, as we shall see, to the downfall of the giants before the Flood, or that of the classical Titans.[113] The Ambrosiaster suggests as much, in its commentary on II Timothy III.8:[114]

> Iannes enim et Mambres fratres erant magi uel uenefici Ægiptiorum, qui arte magiae suae uirtutibus Dei, quae per Moysen agebantur, aemulatione commentitia resistere se putebant. Sed cum Moysis uirtus in operibus cresceret, humiles facti, confessi sunt cum dolore uulnerum Deum in Moyse operatum.
>
> *For Iamnes and Mambres were brothers, magicians or apothecaries of the Egyptians, who thought that they could resist with feigned imitation through the art of their magic the mighty works of God which were being accomplished through Moses. But when the might of Moses in his works proved greater, they were humbled, and confessed, with the pain of their wounds, that it was God that wrought in Moses.*

Nor was the Ambrosiaster's the only such interpretation of the sins of the brothers, as M. R. James has demonstrated;[115] their inclusion as the culmination of a list of marvels and wonders may well spring as much from the monstrous nature of their offences as their magical talents. The suspicion that there is a didactic or homiletic purpose to the addition of the tale of Iamnes and Mambres at the end of a catalogue of wonders is increased by the way in which the Old English version goes beyond the Latin text, by its formulaic repetition of the horrors of Hell (*þær is . . . þær is . . . ne byð . . . ne byð*), and aligns itself with stock descriptions of Hell familiar from numerous Anglo-Saxon homiletic sources.[116]

A still later (twelfth-century) English manuscript, Oxford, Bodleian Library 614,

113 See further below, pp. 100–10.

114 The Ambrosiaster's commentary is printed in PL 17, cols. 45–508. The passage quoted is from col. 494.

115 James, *The Lost Apocrypha of the Old Testament*, pp. 31–8.

116 See further Tristram, 'Stock Descriptions of Heaven and Hell', pp. 102–13.

contains on fols. 36r-48r yet another version of the Latin text of the *Wonders*, which offers a thorough revision in the light of Christian commentary of at least one section of the text,[117] and at the end adds another twelve marvels, not attested in any of the analogous sources, all but two of which wonders derive directly from Isidore's *Etymologiae*.[118] These supplementary *Wonders* can be summarised as follows:[119]

§ 38. The Unicorn (from Isidore, *Etymologiae* XII.ii.12).
§ 39. Mountains of Gold (from Isidore, *Etymologiae* XIV.iii.7).
§ 40. The Chameleon (from Isidore, *Etymologiae* XII.ii.18–19).
§ 41. Brothers who fight an endless battle.
§ 42. The Sciapods (from Isidore, *Etymologiae* XI.iii.23).
§ 43. The Antipodes (from Isidore, *Etymologiae* XI.iii.24).
§ 44. The Hippopods (from Isidore, *Etymologiae* XI.iii.25).
§ 45. Hermaphrodites (from Isidore, *Etymologiae* XI.iii.11).
§ 46. People with large lower lips (from Isidore, *Etymologiae* XI.iii.18).
§ 47. Satyrs (from Isidore, *Etymologiae* XI.iii.21).
§ 48. Parrots (from Isidore, *Etymologiae* XII.vii.24).
§ 49. The accursed dancers.

Gibb demonstrates that both the Latin text and the illustrations of Bodley 614 are drawn straight from those of Tiberius B. v, and that the compiler's few alterations to the Tiberius-text represent an attempt to tidy up some of the more startling of its infelicities.[120] Of more immediate interest are the twelve additional wonders, particularly those which do not derive directly from Isidore, since they demonstrate that the compiler was ready to augment his text not simply from the learned Latin tradition, but also from popular tradition, and in at least one case (§ 41) from native Germanic lore.[121] Such augmentation provides a useful model for the kinds of successive alteration which has been made to the ancestral text even by the compilers of the versions of *Wonders* found in the *Beowulf*- and Tiberius-manuscripts, as comparison with a range of analogous texts demonstrates.

The Anglo-Saxon versions of the *Wonders* derive ultimately from a text represented in mainly continental manuscripts in many different forms,[122] almost all of which

117 Gibb, '*Wonders of the East*', pp. 8–9, demonstrates how the compiler of Bodley 614 has completely revised the description of the Phoenix (§ 35) in the light of Ambrose, *Hexameron* V.79 and Isidore, *Etymologiae* XII.vii.22.

118 These supplementary marvels are printed with a full discussion by James, *The Marvels of the East*, pp. 22–4 and 30–2. For a closely parallel use of Isidore's *Etymologiae*, to provide fantastic material to supplement a Latin text, one might point to the last twenty Anglo-Latin *Enigmata* of Eusebius, most of which derive from Isidore.

119 Cf. James, *Marvels of the East*, pp. 30–2.

120 Gibb, '*Wonders of the East*', pp. 5–8 and 12–13.

121 Cf. Malone, 'An Anglo-Latin Version of the Hjaðningavíg', pp. 38–9.

122 See the detailed discussion by Knock in McGurk *et al.*, *An Eleventh-Century Miscellany*, pp. 88–103.

share a basic epistolary framework, in which either a character variously named Feramen, Feramus, or Fermes writes to the Emperor Hadrian (A.D. 117–38), or a figure called Premo, Premonis, Perimenis, or Parmoenis writes to Hadrian's predecessor, the Emperor Trajan (A.D. 98–116), to report on the many marvels he has witnessed on his travels.[123] All the names of the sender of the letter appear to be variant forms of Pharasmanes, the name of no less than four different Iberian kings in the first and second centuries A.D., at least one of whom is otherwise attested in contact with Hadrian;[124] it seems likely that the variant-forms in P- stem from confusion with the character of Parmenion, who figures prominently in accounts of Alexander the Great, with whom other letters containing fantastic lists are closely associated, as we shall see.[125] Paul Gibb and Ann Knock give a list of such related texts, some of which remain unedited,[126] comprising *The Letter of Fermes to Hadrian*, from Paris, Bibliothèque Nationale, nouv. acq. lat. 1065, fols. 92v–95r (s. ix/x);[127] *The Letter of King Feramen to Hadrian*,[128] represented by four manuscripts, from Italy, Montecassino, Codex Casinensis 391, fols. 82v–84v (s. xi),[129] from Italy, Cava, Codex Cavensis 3, fols. 393r–394v (s. xi/xii),[130] Madrid, Biblioteca Nacional 19, fols. 198v–199r,[131] and Paris, Bibliothèque Nationale, Anc. fond. lat. 7418, fols. 268–270v (s. xiv); *The Letter of Premonis to Trajan*, from the now-lost manuscript Strasbourg, C. IV. 15;[132] *The Letter of Parmoenis to Trajan*, from a now-lost (or unidentified) Leiden manuscript.[133] The popularity of the ancestral text is further attested by the echoes and reflexes of it to be found in other texts, including a translation of a further variant version into Old French, *The Letter of King Perimenis to the Emperor*, from Brussels, Bibliothèque Royal Albert, Ier. MS 14562, fols. 5v–6v (s. xiii).[134] Extensive borrowing from different versions is also found in Gervase of

123 Cf. Knock, 'Wonders of the East', pp. 21–56; McGurk *et al., An Eleventh-Century Miscellany*, pp. 88–9.

124 Knock, 'Wonders of the East', p. 23.

125 See further below, pp. 116–20.

126 Gibb, '*Wonders of the East*', pp. 17–21 and 201–3; Knock, 'Wonders of the East', pp. 147–298.

127 Knock, 'Wonders of the East', pp. 205–18 and 923–32; Omont, ed., 'Lettre á l'empereur Adrien sur les merveilles d'Asie', pp. 509–15, reprinted by Faral, 'La lettre sur les merveilles de l'Inde', pp. 202–15, and James, *Marvels of the East*, pp. 41–50.

128 Knock, 'The Wonders of the East', pp. 933–40, presents a text based on all the available manuscripts.

129 Gibb, '*Wonders of the East*', pp. 200 and 212–43; Knock, 'The Wonders of the East', pp. 221–3.

130 Gibb, '*Wonders of the East*', pp. 200–1; Knock, 'The Wonders of the East', pp. 223–5.

131 Gibb, '*Wonders of the East*', p. 201; Pitra, ed., *Analecta Sacra Spicilegio Solesmensi Parata*, II, p. 647; Knock, 'The Wonders of the East', pp. 226–33.

132 Graff, ed., *Diutiska*, pp. 191–8. Graff dated the manuscript to the eighth or ninth century, although there is no way of checking. James, *The Marvels of the East*, pp. 33–40, and Faral, 'La lettre sur les merveilles de l'Inde', pp. 202–15, reproduced Graff's text; cf. Gibb, '*Wonders of the East*', pp. 202–3; Knock, 'The Wonders of the East', pp. 163–71.

133 Pitra, ed., *Analecta Sacra Spicilegio Solesmensi Parata*, II, pp. 648–9; cf. Gibb, '*Wonders of the East*', p. 203; Knock, 'The Wonders of the East', pp. 147–61.

134 Hilka, ed., 'Ein neuer (altfranzösischer) Text der Biefes über die Wunder Asiens', pp. 98–103;

Tilbury's *Otia Imperialia*,[135] and the (perhaps eighth-century) compilation now known as the *Liber monstrorum de diuersis generibus*, which is itself preserved in no fewer than five manuscripts.[136] The extent of overlap between these related texts, with respect to *The Wonders of the East*, can be seen in the following Table:[137]

Wonders of the East	*Letter of Fermes*	*Letter of Feramen*	*Letter of Premonis*	*Letter of Parmoenis*	Old French version	*Liber monstrorum*
§ 1	III	–	–	I	II–IV	–
§ 2	IV–VIII	§ 1	–	I	IV–VI	–
§ 3	X.1	§ 2	X.1	I	X.1	–
§ 4	X.2	§ 3	X.2	I	X.2	II.10
§ 5	XI.1	§ 4	XI.1	II	XI.1	III.2
§ 6	XI.2–XIII	§§ 5–6	XI.2–XIII	II–III	XI.2–XIII	II.3 + III.6
§ 7	XIV–XVI.1	§ 7	XIV–XVI.1	III	XIV–XV	II.13
§ 8	XVI.1	§ 8	XVI.1	IV	XVI.1	I.18
§ 9	XVI.2	§§ 9–11	XVI.2	IV	XVI.2	II.15
§ 10	XVII.1–2	§ 12	XVII.1–2a	Va	XVII.1–2	II.2 + II.31
§ 11	XVII.3	§ 13	XVII.2b	Va	XVII.3	I.20
§ 12	XVII–3–4	§ 14	XVII.4	Va	XVII.4	II.17
§ 13	–	–	XVII.3	Va–b	XVII.3b	I.33
§ 14	–	–	–	Vb	XVII.4b	II.31
§ 15	XVII.5	§ 15	XVII.5	–	XVII.5	I.24
§ 16	XVII.6	§ 16	XVII.6	Vb	XVII.6	–
§ 17	–	–	XXIV.2	–	XXIV.2	–
§ 18	XXVI.2	–	XXVI.1–2	–	XXVI.1–2	–
§ 19	XXVII.2	§ 22	–	–	XXVI.2b	–
§ 20	–	§ 19	XXVI.3	–	XXVI.3	I.40
§ 21	XXVI.4	§ 20	XXVI.4	–	XXVI.4	I.43
§ 22	–	–	XXVI.5	–	XXVI.5	I.36
§ 23	XXVII.1–2	§ 21	XXVII	–	XXVII.1	–
§ 24	XXVII.2	§ 25	XXVII	–	XXVII.2	–

cf. Gibb, '*Wonders of the East*', p. 203; Knock, 'The Wonders of the East', pp. 173–203.

135 Cf. Faral, 'La lettre sur les merveilles de l'Inde', pp. 202–15; Knock, 'The Wonders of the East', pp. 301–8 and 941–51.

136 For detailed discussion of this text, see further below, pp. 86–115.

137 Cf. the 'Concordance to the Mirabilia' in McGurk *et al.*, *An Eleventh-Century Miscellany*, p. 96. The texts of the *Wonders of the East* and the *Liber monstrorum* matched here are as in the Appendix below, pp. 175–203 and 254–316. For the *Letter of Fermes* see Faral, 'La lettre sur les merveilles de l'Inde', pp. 202–15; for the *Letter of Feramen*, see Gibb, '*Wonders of the East*', pp. 212–43; for the *Letter of Premonis*, see Faral, 'La lettre sur les merveilles de l'Inde', pp. 202–15; for the *Letter of Parmoenis*, see Pitra, ed., *Analecta Sacra Spicilegio Solesmensi Parata*, II, pp. 648–9; for the Old French version, see Hilka, ed., 'Ein neuer (altfranzösischer) Text der Biefes über die Wunder Asiens', pp. 98–103.

Wonders of the East	*Letter of Fermes*	*Letter of Feramen*	*Letter of Premonis*	*Letter of Parmoenis*	Old French version	*Liber monstrorum*
§ 25	XVIII–XIX	–	XVIII–XX	Vc	XVIII–XX	II.30
§ 26	XXI	§ 17	XXI	Vc	XXI	I.22 + II.30
§ 27	XXII	§ 18	XXII	Vc	XXII	I.28
§ 28	–	–	XXIII	–	XXIII	I.26
§ 29	XXIII	–	XXIII	–	XXIII	–
§ 30	XXIII	–	XXIII	–	XXIII	–
§ 31	XXIV.1	–	XXIV.1	–	XXIV.1	–
§ 32	XXIV.1	–	XXIV.1	–	XXIV.1	I.9 + I.30
§ 33	–	§ 24	XXVII	–	XXVII.2	–
§ 34	XXVIII.1	§ 27	XXVIII.1	–	XXVIII.1	–
§ 35	XXVIII.2	§ 28	XXVIII.2	–	XXVIII.2	–
§ 36	XXIX	–	XXVIII.3	–	XXVIII.3	I.30
§ 37	–	–	–	–	–	–

A number of the idiosyncrasies of the Anglo-Saxon *Wonders* will immediately be evident, the first of which is the apparent displacement of *Wonders* §§ 17–24 from the position after § 32 which they occupy in the analogous texts.[138] Almost all the analogues begin with a formal epistolary opening which is entirely absent from the Anglo-Saxon tradition, and none has any parallel for the apocryphal tale of Mambres and Iamnes found in the Tiberius and Bodley texts (but not in the *Beowulf*-manuscript), which is in any case anomalous, being the only clearly pious marvel noted. Gibb's suggestion that the original version of the text which reached Anglo-Saxon England was written with four marvels on each side of a page is an attractive one, which may account for the displacement of eight marvels (§§ 17–24) from their position after § 32, the loss of four marvels (§§ 33–6) plus the supplementary tale of Mambres and Iamnes from the end of the version in the *Beowulf*-manuscript, and perhaps too the loss of the opening sentence of § 5 of the same text, immediately after the first set of four marvels.[139] Against the assumption is the wide variation in the length of description both of individual wonders, and of groups of four marvels.[140]

A wide disparity between texts is also evident upon closer inspection. To take but a single example of a widely-attested wonder, a curious race of people is described in the Latin *Wonders* (§ 11) as follows:

> Nascuntur et ibi homines habentes statura pedum .XV., corpus habentes candidum, duas in uno habentes capite facies, rubra genua, naso longo, capillis nigris; cum tempus gignendi fuerit, suis manibus transferuntur in Indiam et ibi prolem reddunt.

138 Cf. Gibb, '*Wonders of the East*', pp. 10–11.
139 Cf. Gibb, '*Wonders of the East*', pp. 27–8.
140 Cf. Knock, 'The Wonders of the East', pp. 71–2.

There are born in that place men with a height of fifteen feet, having white bodies, two faces on the one head, red knees, long noses, black hair; when it is time for them to give birth, they are transported in their hands to India, and produce children there.

The Old English version of *Wonders of the East* in the *Beowulf*-manuscript differs only in translating a version of the text which presumably read *in nauibus* ('in ships'), as in a number of the related texts,[141] for the curious *suis manibus* ('in their hands'):

> Ðær beoð cende men, hy beoð fiftyne fota lange 7 hy habbað hwit lic 7 twa neb on anum heafde, fet 7 cneowu swyðe reade, 7 lange nosa 7 sweart feax. Þonne hy cennan willað þonne farað hy on scipum to Indeum, 7 þær hyra gecynda in world bringaþ.
>
> *There are people born there, who are fifteen feet tall and have white bodies and two faces on a single head, feet and knees very red, and long noses and black hair. When they want to give birth, they travel in ships to India, and bring their young into the world there.*

The variation between *in nauibus* and *suis manibus* is further compounded in other versions, which have the creatures transformed into birds (reading *in auibus*),[142] or simply omit the relevant phrase.[143] Similarly, the Anglo-Saxon *Wonders of the East* have *capillis nigris* ('with black hair'), with which one might compare the *sweart feax* of both Old English renderings, where other texts read *scapulas nigras* ('black shoulders') or the equivalent.[144] Nor are these the only distinctive variants in what is clearly a complex and convoluted tradition.[145]

Moreover, just as Sisam considered that consecutive items in the *Beowulf*-manuscript might have a thematic connection, so Gibb has argued at length that there are similar parallels which connect successive descriptions of marvels,[146] and it is certainly the case that some of the *Wonders* described do seem to be linked in this way. So, for example, simply concentrating on the first half-dozen wonders depicted, §§ 3 and 4 describe creatures whose touch burns, §§ 4 and 5 describe two-headed creatures with bright eyes, and §§ 5 and 6 give details of mighty serpents. But this technique of concatenation is not absolutely regular throughout the text, and it is equally possible to compare the descriptions of wonders which are not adjacent. To draw examples simply from the sequence §§ 3–6: the burning touch of §§ 3 and 4 is

141 Cf. *Letter of Premonis*: *in nauibus* (§ XVII.2b), or the Old French version *il passent en nes* (XVII.3).

142 Cf. *Letter of Parmoenis*: *transferuntur in auibus* (§ Va); *Letter of Fermes*: *in auibus . . . transfigurantur* (§ XVII.3).

143 Cf. *Letter of Feramen*: § 13, or the relevant passage from the *Liber monstrorum* (I.20). The Old English version of the *Wonders of the East* from the Tiberius-manuscript similarly omits the phrase; cf. below, pp. 190–3.

144 Cf. the Old French *noires espaules* (§ XVII.3); *Letter of Premonis* (§ XVII.2b) and *Letter of Parmoenis* (§ Va): *scapulas nigras*.

145 See the detailed discussion by Knock in McGurk *et al.*, *An Eleventh-Century Miscellany*, pp. 88–103.

146 Gibb, '*Wonders of the East*', pp. 62–6.

echoed in § 6, the bright eyes of §§ 4 and 5 are repeated in § 22, and the donkeys with horns as big as oxen and snakes with horns as big as rams of § 6 (which, it can be argued from the parallel texts in the tradition,[147] may originally have been two separate marvels, themselves concatenated by thematic association), are both matched by the (horned) rams as big as oxen of § 2. Some themes and ideas are repeated several times, and some names figure prominently, particularly those of Babylon (§§ 1, 2 (twice), 5, 6 (twice), and 25) and Alexander the Great (§§ 2, 27, and 30). Both names combine exotic fascination with, in Christian eyes, an air of decadence, degeneracy, and fallen pride that is often associated with outlandish and monstrous figures, as we shall see.[148] Throughout the text, moreover, the *Wonders of the East* stress the mutual mistrust and even open hostility which exists between the twin worlds of monsters and men; the marvellous creatures depicted all either flee at the first sign of people (§§ 4, 12, 17 and 21), or cause harm to anyone who dares approach (§§ 3, 4, 6 and 36), or actively seek men out as prey (§§ 13 and 20).

This technique of placing key themes in a text in apposition is one with which Old English poets, particularly that of *Beowulf*, were fully familiar.[149] The way in which individual marvels in the *Wonders of the East* are occasionally connected in sequence, or contain thematic parallels with other elements of the text, or again, in the case of Iamnes and Mambres of the Tiberius manuscript or the extra marvels of Bodley 614, appear to have been added to an existing body of wondrous lore, provides of itself a useful analogy for the putative compilation of the *Beowulf*-manuscript. Just as *Judith* and the *Passion of Saint Christopher* are connected by the theme of saintly forbearance overcoming regal arrogance, and the *Passion of Saint Christopher* and the *Wonders of the East* are connected by the figure of the half-human, half-monstrous *cynocephali*, so too the *Wonders of the East* and the *Letter of Alexander to Aristotle* are linked by the figure of Alexander the Great, a mighty pagan monster-slayer whose match is famously celebrated in *Beowulf*, which follows the *Letter* in the manuscript. Other connections between texts which are not contiguous, such as the decapitation-motif in both *Beowulf* and *Judith*, or the putative resemblance between Christopher and Grendel, again help to link the contents of the manuscript. But two themes, perhaps best typified by the recurring images of Babylon and Alexander the Great in the *Wonders of the East*, connect the texts, together with analogous material such as the *Liber monstrorum* and the Icelandic *Grettis saga*,[150] all of which uniformly exhibit a twin interest in the outlandish and in the activities of overweening pagan warriors from a distant and heroic past: pride and prodigies. It is the relationship between these key themes, especially as demonstrated in the remaining two texts in the *Beowulf*-manuscript, namely the *Letter of Alexander to Aristotle* and *Beowulf* itself, to which we now turn.

147 See the Table above, pp. 24–5.
148 See further below, pp. 99–105.
149 Cf. Robinson, *'Beowulf' and the Appositive Style*, pp. 60–1.
150 See further below, pp. 86–115 and 140–68.

CHAPTER II

Psychology and Physicality: The Monsters of *Beowulf*

The central importance of the monsters in *Beowulf* has been underlined many times since J. R. R. Tolkien first highlighted their significance, arguing that in the struggles of Beowulf against his various monstrous foes the poet wished to portray the noble image of 'man at war with the hostile world, and his inevitable overthrow in Time'.[1] Kenneth Sisam took a more sanguine view, suggesting that 'the monsters Beowulf kills are inevitably evil and hostile because a reputation for heroism is not made by killing creatures that are believed to be harmless or beneficent – sheep for instance'.[2] Both scholars, however, shared the now-common opinion that the monsters in *Beowulf* are crucial to the very structure of the poem, and in his investigation of larger rhetorical patterns in *Beowulf*, John Niles similarly suggests that the poet produced a complex ring-composition focusing in turn on each of the three main monster-fights, which he characterises as 'the most important events of [the poet's] story'.[3] The same notion is implicit in Dorothy Whitelock's suggestion that the poem 'could easily have been delivered in three sittings'.[4]

Equally important, moreover, is the poet's clear intention to connect each of the three main monster-fights through shared themes and structure. As Sisam has noted, Beowulf's battle with Grendel is a one fall, one submission, and one knock-out bout, whilst the fight with Grendel's mother has quite a different pace.[5] Here we have a two-fall fight, with first the monstrous female, and then the man (quite literally) on

1 Tolkien, 'Beowulf, the Monsters, and the Critics', p. 260.

2 Sisam, *The Structure of 'Beowulf'*, p. 25.

3 Niles, 'Ring Composition and the Structure of *Beowulf*', p. 925; cf. Rogers, 'Beowulf's Three Great Fights', especially pp. 340–3. Others have proposed a much more complex structural patterning, notably Carrigan, 'Structure and Thematic Development in *Beowulf*', especially pp. 49–51; Leyerle, 'The Interlace Structure of *Beowulf*', especially pp. 15–17. For a useful review of suggestions concerning the structure of the poem, see Hume, 'The Theme and Structure of *Beowulf*', pp. 2–5.

4 Whitelock, *The Audience of 'Beowulf'*, p. 20; by comparison, Kemp Malone's rather stately reading of the entire poem, *'Beowulf' (Complete): Read in Old English by Kemp Malone*, 4 discs (Caedmon Records, TC 4001, 1967), takes just over four hours.

5 Sisam, 'Beowulf's Fight with the Dragon', p. 136.

top.[6] Likewise Beowulf tries two swords, and Grendel's mother two weapons also, her cruel knife (*seax*) and her hideous nails. The dragon-fight, by contrast, is in three rounds, clearly marked off by narratorial enumeration of each phase of the attack, as the dragon surges forward a second time (*oðre siðe*, line 2670) and a third (*þriddan siðe*, line 2688).[7] The level of difficulty experienced by Beowulf increases with each battle; Grendel causes comparatively few problems, whilst his mother, whom we are explicitly told had less terrible might (lines 1282–4), very nearly succeeds in killing Beowulf, and the dragon finally proves fatal. There is a commensurate increase in the amount of armoury brought to bear against the male (no weapons), the bestial female (two swords), and the serpent (two swords and a shield), as Beowulf steadily shifts from a primarily defensive role to an aggressive one, motivated to varying degrees in each of his battles by thoughts of glory, vengeance, and treasure.

These structural and thematic links between each of the three main monster-battles are underpinned by further parallels between successive conflicts which bind the individual episodes together. Thus Grendel and his mother are closely connected not simply by the family relationship between the monsters, but by their human shape, their cannibalistic acts, their shared dwelling, and their decapitation. Just as Grendel attacks Heorot by night, and fatally seizes Hondscio, so too does his avenging mother undertake a nocturnal raid to Heorot to carry off Æschere to his doom.[8] In the same way that Beowulf's wrestling-match with Grendel takes place within the confines of the hall, Grendel's mother comes to grips with Beowulf inside her own cavernous guest-hall.[9] Similar narrative parallels connect the episode of Grendel's mother and the dragon; in both it is the monster who initially is the aggrieved party, and who suffers loss; in both the monsters inhabit a waterside home, from which light shines; in both Beowulf requires two blades to despatch his foe; and in both Beowulf is accompanied by a group of retainers, only some of whom prove faithful.

Moreover, despite the clear antagonism between the worlds of monsters and men, there is, as in the *Passion of Saint Christopher* and *Judith* in the same manuscript, something deeply human about the 'monsters'. All are given human attributes at some stage, and the poet even goes so far as to evoke our sympathy for their plight. We might illustrate this first with reference to perhaps the least human of the monsters, the dragon.[10] When the unprovoked theft of treasure from the barrow by an unwelcome visitor is reported, we are presented with events from the dragon's perspective (*Beowulf*, lines 2287–9):

6 See further the analysis of Nitzsche, 'The Structural Unity of *Beowulf*', pp. 293–4.

7 Cf. Sisam, 'Beowulf's Fight with the Dragon', p. 138.

8 Cf. Carens, 'Handscioh and Grendel', pp. 39–45.

9 See further below, p. 30.

10 The dragon is certainly the least human in terms of shape, notwithstanding the often-noted possibility, most fully argued by Tripp, *More about the Fight with the Dragon*, especially pp. 13–17, that, as in a number of Norse analogues, the dragon was originally a man transformed.

þa se wyrm onwoc, wroht wæs geniwad;
stonc ða æfter stane, stearcheort onfand
feondes fotlast

Then the dragon awoke, strife was renewed; he hastened along the rock, the stout-hearted one discovered the footprints of the foe.

Here the stout-hearted one (*stearcheort*) is the dragon and the foe (*feond*) the human plunderer of his hoard. An exact reversal is seen in the dragon-fight itself, in which Beowulf, on the only other occasion in the poem on which the word is used, is described as 'stout-hearted' (*stearcheort*, line 2552), and the dragon is the 'foe' (*feond*, line 2706). In the first instance we see things from the monster's point of view; the dragon is the aggrieved party. In a similar way our sympathy is evoked for Grendel's mother, driven to avenge the killing of her son by motives which would tug at the hearts of any Germanic audience. Her active engagement in the feud contrasts sharply with the passive impotence of other (human) mothers in the poem, notably Wealhtheow and Hildeburh, whose tale is told immediately before that of Grendel's mother herself.[11] Like the dragon, Grendel's mother is seen as (at first) the victim of an unprovoked attack. Twice her journey is described as a 'sorrowful journey' (*sorhfulne sið*, line 1278; *siðode sorhfull*, line 2119), and we are offered the monster's perspective again. In the same way the poet explicitly mentions that Grendel's mother, like Hrothgar and Beowulf, ruled her mere for fifty years before she (like them) suffered at the hands of an unwelcome guest.[12] Her underwater dwelling is described in human, almost homely terms, as a 'roofed hall' (*hrofsele*, line 1515), albeit a hateful dwelling (*niðsele*, line 1513), and as a 'hall' (*reced*, line 1572) whose walls, like those of Heorot itself, were bedecked with weapons.[13] Likewise the dragon inhabits an 'earth-house' (*eorðhus*, line 2232) also described in the same language of the hall (*eorðsele*, lines 2410 and 2515; *eorðreced*, line 2719); the same word *dryhtsele* ('noble hall'), unattested outside *Beowulf*, applies equally to Heorot (lines 485 and 767) and the dragon's lair (line 2320).

But of all the monsters, it is Grendel who is most consistently depicted in human terms, particularly in the constant evocation of exile imagery to describe his plight.[14] He is, as successively fuller descriptions tell us, an 'unfortunate man' (*wonsæli wer*, line 105), a 'man deprived of joys' (*rinc . . . dreamum bedæled*, lines 720–1; cf. line 1275), who 'wretchedly trod the paths of exile in the form of a man' (*earmsceapen / on weres*

11 Cf. Nitzsche, 'The Structural Unity of *Beowulf*', pp. 290–2.

12 See further lines 1498 (Grendel's mother), 1769 (Hrothgar), and 2209 (Beowulf).

13 Cf. the description of the sleeping warriors in Heorot, immediately before the first visit of Grendel's mother: 'they set at their heads war-bucklers, bright wooden shields; there on the bench was easily seen, above each noble a towering helmet, a ringed corselet, a mighty spear' (*setton him to heafdon hilderandas, / bordwudu beorhtan; þær on bence wæs / ofer æþelinge yþgesene / heaþosteapa helm, hringed byrne, / þrecwudu þrymlic*, lines 1242–6). Presumably a similar scene is envisaged in the monster mere, when Beowulf 'saw amongst the armour a victory-blessed sword' (*geseah ða on searwum sigeeadig bil*, line 1557).

14 See further the comments of Baird, 'Grendel the Exile', pp. 378–9; Greenfield, 'The Formulaic Expression of the Theme of "Exile" in Anglo-Saxon Poetry', p. 205; Greenfield, *Hero and Exile*, p. 130.

wæstmum wræclastas træd, lines 1351–2).[15] Twice he is described as *se mansceaða* (lines 712 and 737), in contexts which suggest that the poet may be playing on the two senses of the homographs *man* ('crime', 'wickedness') and *man* ('man'), especially since both terms are twice found linked by alliteration in *Beowulf*, notably on the first occasion on which the word *mansceaða* is employed (lines 110 and 712). Grendel is certainly 'the wicked destroyer', but he is also both 'the destroyer of men', and 'the man-shaped destroyer'.

Hrothgar makes a similar point concerning the human forms of both Grendel and his mother in his first description of them (lines 1345–57):

Ic þæt londbuend, leode mine,
selerædende, secgan hyrde
þæt hie gesawon swylce twegen
micle mearcstapan moras healdan,
ellorgæstas. Ðæra oðer wæs,
þæs þe hie gewislicost gewitan meahton,
idese onlicnes; oðer earmsceapen
on weres wæstmum wræclastas træd,
næfne he wæs mara þonne ænig man oðer;
þone on geardagum Grendel nemdon
foldbuende; no hie fæder cunnon,
hwæþer him ænig wæs ær acenned
dyrnra gasta.

I have heard the locals, my people, hall-counsellors, tell that they saw two such mighty wanderers in the wastes inhabit the moors, alien spirits, of whom one was, so far as they could most easily tell, the semblance of a woman. The other wretched one whom, in past days, dwellers in the land named Grendel, trod exile-paths in human form, except that he was greater than any other man. They did not know of any father, whether any such had been begotten of secret spirits.

The physical manifestation of the wandering Grendel's extraordinary nature is his size: 'he was greater than any other man' (*he wæs mara þonne ænig man oðer*, line 1353); little wonder that in the waterbound lair that Grendel shares with his mother, Beowulf should discover in his time of need a monstrous sword of suitable stature: 'the choicest of weapons, except that it was greater than anyone else could wield in battle-play' (*wæpna cyst / buton hit wæs mare ðonne ænig mon oðer / to beadulace ætberan meahte*, lines 1559–61).[16]

Such a substantial enemy requires a hero of comparable greatness, and it is interesting to note that another third party, the coast-guard, gives his first impression of Beowulf himself in rather similar terms (lines 247–51):

15 The word *earmsceapen* may also be used to describe the dragon at line 2228; cf. Braeger, 'Connotations of *(earm) sceapen*', pp. 327–30.

16 On this giant sword, see further below, pp. 111–12.

Næfre ic maran geseah
eorla ofer eorþan, ðonne is eower sum,
secg on searwum; nis þæt seldguma,
wæpnum geweorðad, næfne him his wlite leoge,
ænlic ansyn.

Never have I seen a mightier noble on earth, a warrior in armour, than is one of you; he is no hall-retainer made worthy with weapons, unless his appearance belies him, his peerless face.

An intriguing number of intimate links between Beowulf and his most famous foe may be suggested. We hear that in one of Grendel's raids on Heorot he had carried off thirty men (lines 122–3);[17] likewise Beowulf is described by Hrothgar as having the strength of thirty men in his hand-grip (lines 379–81), and in escaping from the scene of Hygelac's death he swims away carrying the armour of just this number of men (lines 2361–2).[18] In this same incident Beowulf is decribed as a 'wretched and solitary figure' (*earm anhaga*, line 2368), a term which might well have been used of Grendel, the 'wretch' (*earmsceapen*, line 1351) twice described as a 'solitary traveller' (*angenga*, lines 165 and 449).[19] So, Grendel on his murderous trips to Heorot is described as a 'hall-thegn' (*healðegn*, line 142), just like Beowulf and his men (*healðegnas*, line 719), and in their fighting both Beowulf and Grendel are linked as 'hall-dwellers', equally enraged (*yrre wæron begen, / reþe renweardas*, lines 769–70).[20] The fury experienced by both Beowulf and Grendel is a further factor which links the combatants; Beowulf waits for Grendel's arrival 'furious at heart' (*bolgenmod*, line 709), while the door of Heorot collapses at Grendel's touch 'since he was furious' (*ða (he ge)bolgen wæs*, line 723); it might be noted that precisely the same reason is given for Beowulf's ability to overwhelm Grendel's mother in their first grappling (*þa he gebolgen wæs*, line 1539), and that throughout *Beowulf* the only figures who are described as 'furious' in this way (*gebolgen* or *bolgenmod*) are Beowulf, in each of his three monster-battles (lines 709, 1539, 2401, and 2550), Grendel (line 723), the monsters at the mere (line 1431), the fallen prince Heremod (line 1713),[21] and the dragon (lines 2220 and 2304). Beowulf, moreover, is described on his visit to the home of Grendel's mother as a 'hall-guest' (*selegyst*, line 1545), who in his encounter with the monster is 'despairing of his life' (*aldres orwena*, line 1565), much as Grendel the 'hall-thegn' (*healðegn*, line 142) in Heorot is equally 'despairing of his life' (*aldres orwena*, line 1002).[22] Beowulf fights monsters because only then is he well-matched. When he does face human champions, like the Frankish Dæghrefn,

17 See further lines 1582–3.

18 See Puhvel, *'Beowulf' and the Celtic Tradition*, pp. 82–5, for an argument that the *Beowulf*-poet was influenced in his depiction of these episodes by Irish models.

19 On the description of Grendel as *angenga*, cf. Lapidge, '*Beowulf* and the Psychology of Terror', pp. 381–2.

20 Cf. Brodeur, *The Art of Beowulf*, pp. 231–3; Rosier, 'The Uses of Association: Hands and Feasts in *Beowulf*', p. 8.

21 On whom see further below, pp. 48–53.

22 Cf. Rosier, 'The Uses of Association: Hands and Feasts in *Beowulf*', p. 12.

his methods are distinctly inhuman, one might almost say monstrous; Dæghrefn is simply crushed to death (lines 2498–508).

Again, it has often been noticed that the poet explicitly links Beowulf and the monsters that he fights by the description *aglæca* (or *æglæca*), for which Klaeber offers the creative series of translations 'wretch', 'monster', 'demon', 'fiend', 'warrior', 'hero',[23] and which is used of Grendel (lines 159, 425, 433, 592, 646, 732, 739, 816, 989, 1000, and 1269), his mother (who is described as an *aglæcwif*, line 1259), the dragon (lines 2520, 2534, 2557, and 2905), the sea-monsters (line 556), and Sigemund the dragon-slayer (line 893).[24] In his account of Beowulf's descent into the monster-mere the poet uses the term ambiguously (line 1512), to designate either the monsters inhabiting the mere or (more likely) Beowulf himself, whilst during the description of the dragon-fight the poet speaks in one half-line of Beowulf and the dragon together as *ða aglæcean* (line 2592). Sherman Kuhn has suggested that the word *aglæca*, which occurs perhaps thirty-six times in extant Old English verse, derives from a very early borrowing of the prehistoric form of the Irish *óclach*, *ócláech*, and meant 'fighter', 'warrior'.[25] A perhaps more likely proposed etymology connects the first element of *aglæca* with a Gothic cognate *agis* ('terror', 'fright'), Old High German *egiso*, Old English *ege* and *egesa* ('awe', 'terror'),[26] and the second element with Old English *lacan* ('to move quickly').[27] The meaning of the term would therefore be 'the awe-inspiring one', 'the formidable one',[28] and this sense best answers to the sole example of the word in Old English prose, where Byrhtferth of Ramsey, with no apparent trace of irony, describes the Venerable Bede as *Beda, se aglæca lareow* ('Bede, the awe-inspiring teacher').[29] Whatever the precise connotations of the term, the fact that the poet employs the word to designate not only monsters but monster-slayers clearly underlines the linked contrasts between the worlds of monsters and men which run throughout the poem and the manuscript.

The conflict and comparison between monsters and men is far from being the only such thematic contrast which runs through *Beowulf*; Tolkien believed that the entire structure of the poem was predicated on the contrast between Youth and Age which is so apparent in Beowulf's own biography,[30] and such a technique of apposition, Tolkien argued, is implicit in the very structure of the Old English poetic line.[31] A similar kind of contrast has been perceived in the way in which the explicit action in *Beowulf* is matched by a graphic series of interior conflicts, leading Michael

23 Klaeber, ed., *Beowulf*, p. 298.

24 Cf. Gillam, 'The Use of the Term *æglæca* in *Beowulf* at Lines 813 and 2592', pp. 145–69.

25 Kuhn, 'Old English *aglæca* –Middle Irish *ochlach*', pp. 213–30.

26 Cf. Huffines, 'OE *aglæce*: Magic and Moral Decline', pp. 71–81.

27 Mezger, 'Goth. Aglaiti "Unchastity", OE Aglæc "Distress" ', p. 69; Lotspeich, 'Old English Etymologies', p. 1; Kuhn, 'Old English *aglæca* –Middle Irish *ochlach*', pp. 214–20; Lapidge, '*Beowulf* and the Psychology of Terror', pp. 380–1.

28 Cf. Dobbie, ed., *Beowulf*, p. 160.

29 Crawford, ed., *Byrhtferth's Manual*, p. 74/15; cf. Nichols, 'Bede "Awe-Inspiring" ', pp. 147–8.

30 The contrast is most effectively stressed by Tolkien, 'Beowulf, the Monsters, and the Critics', for example, pp. 271–2.

31 Cf. Tolkien, 'Beowulf, the Monsters, and the Critics', pp. 273–4.

Lapidge to doubt that the poem can really be described as 'heroic' in any traditional sense,[32] while R. E. Kaske, by contrast, in highlighting the central importance in *Beowulf* of what he describes as 'the great heroic ideal of *sapientia et fortitudo*' ('wisdom and strength'),[33] underlines the differences between the physical and the psychological worlds which play such a large part in the poem, and are particularly important in the poet's developing depictions of the monsters.

The justly-celebrated portrayal of Grendel's approach to Heorot, which has been described as a 'hair-raising description of death on the march',[34] introduces just this distinction between the physical and the psychological worlds, as well as illustrating a number of the other contrasts raised, and deserves quotation as a fine example of the poet's art (lines 702–27):[35]

Com on wanre niht
scriðan sceadugenga. Sceotend swæfon,
þa þæt hornreced healdan scoldon,
ealle buton anum. Þæt wæs yldum cuþ
þæt hie ne moste, þa Metod nolde,
se s[c]ynscaþa under sceadu bregdan; –
ac he wæccende wraþum on andan
bad bolgenmod beadwa geþinges.
Ða com of more under misthleoþum
Grendel gongan, Godes yrre bær;
mynte se manscaða manna cynnes
sumne besyrwan in sele þam hean.
Wod under wolcnum to þæs þe he winreced,
goldsele gumena, gearwost wisse,
fættum fahne. Ne wæs þæt forma sið
þæt he Hroþgares ham gesohte;
næfre he on aldordagum ær ne siþðan
heardran hæle, healðegnas fand!
Com þa to recede rinc siðian,
dreamum bedæled. Duru sona onarn,
fyrbendum fæst, syþðan he hire folmum (æthr)an;
onbræd þa bealohydig, ða (he ge)bolgen wæs,
recedes muþan. Raþe æfter þon
on fagne flor feond treddode,
eode yrremod; him of eagum stod
ligge gelicost leoht unfæger.

32 Lapidge, '*Beowulf* and the Psychology of Terror', pp. 373–4.

33 Kaske, 'The Sigemund-Heremod and Hama-Hygelac Passages', p. 489; Kaske, '*Sapientia et Fortitudo* as the Controlling Theme', especially pp. 423–8.

34 Brodeur, *The Art of 'Beowulf'*, p. 90.

35 The passage has been discussed many times; see particularly Brodeur, *The Art of 'Beowulf'*, pp. 88–94; Greenfield, 'Grendel's Approach to Heorot', pp. 275–84; Renoir, 'Point of View and Design for Terror', pp. 154–67; Storms, 'Grendel the Terrible', pp. 427–36; Irving, *A Reading of 'Beowulf'*, pp. 101–3; O'Keeffe, '*Beowulf*, Lines 720b–836', pp. 487–8; Lapidge, '*Beowulf* and the Psychology of Terror', pp. 383–4

> *Then there came in the dark night the shadow-walker stalking. The warriors slept, who ought to hold that gabled hall, all except one. It was known to men that the fiendish [or 'sinful'] destroyer could not drag them under shadows against the Creator's will; but he, vigilant, in malice against the foe, awaited with swollen heart the joining of battle. Then there came from the moors, under misty slopes, Grendel approaching: he bore God's anger; the wicked destroyer intended to ensnare one of mankind in that high hall. He walked under clouds until he could most clearly perceive the wine-building, the gold-hall of men, adorned with plate. That was not the first time that he had sought out Hrothgar's home; but never before nor afterwards in the days of his life did he come upon a harsher fate! Then there came travelling to that building the man deprived of joys. The door promptly sprang apart, secure with forged bands, when he touched it with his hands. The one intent on evil, since he was swollen with rage, tore open the building's mouth. Swiftly after that, the fiend stepped onto the decorated floor, advanced angry in spirit; from his eyes there stood, most like a flame, an unlovely light.*

What is most intriguing about this passage, as Alain Renoir has argued, is the way in which the poet produces a growing sense of terror by offering alternatively the viewpoint of the approaching monster and the waiting warrior.[36] It is important to the purpose of the poem that up to this point we can have no clear idea what Grendel looks like, since nothing in the preceding verses has offered any substantial physical depiction at all; as Michael Lapidge has argued: 'it is because the monster lies beyond our comprehension, because we cannot visualise it at all, that its approach is one of the most terrifying moments in English literature'.[37] Each repetition of *com* (lines 702, 710, and 720) brings Grendel closer, a shadowy figure stalking out of the darkness, away from the misty moors, and up to the hall. A similar method of (in cinematographic terms) zooming in on the subject is employed elsewhere in *Beowulf* to describe the approach of Beowulf and his men both to Denmark, after their sea-voyage (lines 221–3),[38] and to Heorot, after their trip to the monster-mere (lines 1623–44).[39] The same cinematographic technique is employed elsewhere in the *Beowulf*-manuscript, notably in *Judith* (lines 200–35), where the advance of the Jews into battle is ominously depicted by repetition of the word *stopon* (lines 200, 212, and 227).[40]

36 Renoir, 'Point of View and Design for Terror', pp. 160–5.

37 Lapidge, '*Beowulf* and the Psychology of Terror', p. 384.

38 Here the poet describes the successively more detailed view of approaching land from the sailors' point of view, 'they saw land, sea-cliffs shining, steep hills, broad sea-promontories' (*land gesawon, / brimclifu blican, beorgas steape, / side sænæssas*, lines 221–3). The term 'cinematographic' in this context was first suggested by Renoir, 'Point of View and Design for Terror', p. 162.

39 Cf. Rosier, 'The Uses of Association: Hands and Feasts in *Beowulf*', p. 12.

40 Cf. Campbell, 'Schematic Technique in *Judith*', p. 169. The passage in question is discussed with characteristic insight by Renoir, '*Judith* and the Limits of Poetry', pp. 147–8, although, somewhat curiously, the repetition of *stopon* is not discussed.

Grendel is initially depicted here as a 'shadow-walker' (*sceadugenga*, line 703), a description which recalls his earlier portrayal as a 'spirit' (*gast*, cf. line 133) or 'death-shadow' (*deaþscua*, line 160), and his later depiction as an 'alien spirit' (*ellorgast*, line 807).[41] The word may well also signify, as Stanley Greenfield has suggested, 'Grendel's outcast state, as one deprived of God's light';[42] such a state is specified later in the same passage, with the chilling statement that Grendel 'bore God's anger' (*Godes yrre bær*, line 711). Indeed, the emotions of anger and malice are most explicit throughout this passage;[43] the unspoken terror is implicit. But as Grendel comes closer to Heorot, he becomes identified in successively more concrete and corporeal terms. The precise sense of the term *s[c]ynscaþa* (line 707) in this passage is a matter for debate; the alliteration seems to demand the otherwise unattested *scynscaþa*,[44] deriving from the noun *scinna* ('sprite'),[45] and presumably meaning 'demonic foe', a designation which, like his description both earlier and later in the poem as a 'giant' or 'ogre' (*þyrs*, cf. line 426; *eoten*, line 761), identifies Grendel with the wicked creatures of popular germanic legend, but the manuscript clearly reads *synscaþa*, as at line 801, a word which may carry the double sense of 'persistent destroyer' or 'sinful destroyer'.[46] Like *s[c]ynscaþa*, the related term *manscaða* (line 712), which is used in turn of all three of Beowulf's main monstrous foes,[47] carries a clear physical threat, and it is at precisely this point in the passage when we are first made conscious of Grendel's thoughts and impressions: he has intentions (*mynte*, line 712) and perceptions (*gearwost wisse*, line 715; *gesohte*, line 717; *fand*, line 719) of which we are increasingly aware as he approaches the hall. That Grendel is a sentient human(-shaped) being is made still more apparent when he finally reaches Heorot, and is described as a 'man', albeit one 'deprived of joys' (*rinc . . . dreamum bedæled*, lines 720–1). As with his portrayal as a spirit and a sprite in this passage, the depiction of Grendel as a man is not unique; elsewhere he is described with a range of words which align him with men, such as *wer* (line 105), *guma* (lines 973 and 1682), *hilderinc* (line 986), and *hæleþ* (cf. line 2072).[48] What is important here is the effect; the threefold repetition of *com* marks off the passage into individual sections where we are progressively offered the perspective of the external narrator, the monster himself, and the people inside the hall, as Grendel glides closer, becoming ever more physically real and apparent until, ripping open the mouth of the hall in a fitting prelude to his own cannibalistic frenzy,[49] he stands, eyes blazing,

41 Cf. O'Keeffe, '*Beowulf*, Lines 702b–836', p. 486.

42 Greenfield, 'Grendel's Approach to Heorot', p. 280.

43 So in this short passage we learn of the vicious anger of Grendel (*bealohydig*, *gebolgen*, and *yrremod*; lines 723 and 726), Beowulf (*on andan / bad bolgenmod*, lines 708–9), and God (*yrre*, line 711).

44 Dobbie, ed., *Beowulf*, p. 151.

45 Cf. the collocation *scuccum ond scinnum* ('demons and sprites', line 939).

46 Cf. O'Keeffe, '*Beowulf*, Lines 702b–836', p. 485, who points out that 'Grendel is described frequently by words compounded in *sin-* or *syn-*'.

47 Cf. above, pp. 31–3; the term *manscaða* refers to Grendel at lines 712 and 737, to Grendel's mother at line 1339, and to the dragon at line 2514.

48 See further above, pp. 30–1.

49 Irving, *A Reading of 'Beowulf'*, p. 104.

on the decorated floor. What bursts into Heorot is not a nightmare,[50] but a monstrous terror made flesh. As Tolkien notes: 'in *Beowulf* the weight is on the physical side: Grendel does not vanish into the pit when grappled. He must be slain by plain prowess.'[51]

The description of Grendel's approach to Heorot introduces him as a physical character within the poem; previously he had been little more than a shadowy wanderer (*sceadugenga*, line 703), while subsequently we learn much about his physical traits, notably his enormous size (line 1353), so much so that it takes four men to carry his head (lines 1634–9), his steely nails (line 985), his feasting on human flesh and blood (lines 742–5), his habitat (lines 1345–72), and his invulnerability to iron weapons (lines 802–3 and 987–9).[52] Certainly his fight with Beowulf is undeniably physical. The hall is wrecked, joints crack, fingers burst, sinews spring apart, and Grendel, screaming in agony, flees.[53] The syntax and diction of the portrayal of the fight itself is suitably brisk and vivid, and serves to emphasise still further the link between the antagonists; as Katherine O'Brien O'Keeffe notes: 'not only does the poem predicate a connection between Grendel and the men he approaches, but as he comes closer to Beowulf, the language, syntax, and management of perspective in the scene blur the distinction between the two adversaries'.[54]

Grendel and Beowulf meet in an atmosphere in which the distinctions between man and monster have been deliberately obscured, and in a twilight domain where the mark of the assailant is measured as much in terror and anger as in corporeal harm. An identical contrast between the physical and psychological worlds is implicit elsewhere in the poet's depiction of the monsters, for example in Hrothgar's vivid description of the monster-mere (lines 1357–79):

Hie dygel lond
warigeað, wulfhleoþu, windige næssas,
frecne fengelad, ðær fyrgenstream
under næssa genipu niþer gewiteð,
flod under foldan. Nis þæt feor heonon
milgemearces þæt se mere standeð;
ofer þæm hongiað hrinde bearwas,
wudu wyrtum fæst wæter oferhelmað.
Þær mæg nihta gehwæm niðwundor seon,
fyr on flode. No þæs frod leofað
gumena bearna, þæt þone grund wite.
Ðeah þe hæðstapa hundum geswenced,

50 Cf. Lapidge, '*Beowulf* and the Psychology of Terror', pp. 383–5.
51 Tolkien, 'Beowulf, the Monsters, and the Critics', p. 280.
52 Lapidge, '*Beowulf* and the Psychology of Terror', p. 375.
53 One might contrast the very physical aspects of Beowulf's later adversary, the dragon, of which we are made aware long before the combatants clash. See further Sisam, 'Beowulf's Fight with the Dragon', p. 134.
54 O'Keeffe, '*Beowulf*, Lines 702b–836', p. 488.

heorot hornum trum, holtwudu sece,
feorran geflymed, ær he feorh seleð,
aldor on ofre, ær he in wille,
hafelan [beorgan]; nis þæt heoru stow!
Þonon yðgeblond up astigeð
won to wolcnum, þonne wind styreþ,
lað gewidru, oð þæt lyft drysmaþ,
roderas reotað. Nu is se ræd gelang
eft æt þe anum. Eard git ne const,
frecne stowe, ðær þu findan miht
sinnigne secg; sec gif þu dyrre!

They dwell in a secret land, wolf-slopes, windy headlands, dangerous fen-tracts, where the mountain-stream goes down under the headlands' mists, the flood under the ground. It is not far from here in the tally of miles, where that mere stands, over which hang frosty groves, a wood firm-rooted overshadows the water. There one can see each night a dreadful wonder, fire on the flood. No one lives so wise of the sons of men that knows the bottom. Even though a heath-stepper, driven by the hounds, a hart, strong in its horns, may seek the wooded forest, chased from afar, he will give up his life, his spirit on the brink, rather than plunge in to save his head; that is no pleasant place! From there the tumult of the waves rise up dark to the clouds, when the wind stirs up hateful storms, until the sky turns grim, the heavens weep. Now once again is a solution to be sought from you alone. You do not yet know the dwelling-place, the dangerous spot where you can find the sinful creature. Seek if you dare!

The poet adds further details to this picture in a later description of the expedition undertaken to the mere (lines 1408–17):

Ofereode þa æþelinga bearn
steap stanhliðo, stige nearwe,
enge anpaðas, uncuð gelad,
neowle næssas, nicorhusa fela;
he feara sum beforan gengde
wisra monna wong sceawian,
oþþæt he færinga fyrgenbeamas
ofer harne stan hleonian funde,
wynleasne wudu; wæter under stod
dreorig ond gedrefed.

Then the sons of princes passed over steep, rocky, slopes, thin courses, narrow single tracks, unknown paths, precipitous crags, many dwellings of water-monsters; [Beowulf] went on ahead with a few wise companions to view the place: until suddenly he perceived mountainous trees towering over the grey rock, a joyless wood; water stood beneath, bloody and disturbed.

Richard Morris was the first to point out that this combined description is remarkably close to that found in Blickling Homily XVI,[55] where Saint Paul has a vision of Hell:[56]

> Swa sanctus paulus wæs geseonde on norðanweardne þisne middangeard þær ealle wætero niðergewítað 7 he þær geseah ofer ðæm wætere sumne hárne stán 7 wæron norð of ðæm stáne awexene swiðe hrimige bearwas 7 ðær wæron þystrogenipo 7 under þæm stane wæs niccra eardung 7 wearga 7 he geseah þæt on ðæm clife hangodan on ðæm ísgean bearwum manige swearte saula be heora handum gebundne 7 þa fynd þara on nicra onlicnesse heora gripende wæron swa swa grædig wulf 7 þæt wæter wæs sweart under þæm clife neoðan 7 betuh þæm clife on ðæm wætre wæron swylce twelf mila 7 ðonne ða twigo forburston þonne gewitan þa saula niðer þa þe on ðæm twigum hangodan 7 him onfengon ða nicras.
>
> *So Saint Paul was looking at the northern part of this world, where all the waters go down, and he saw there above the water a certain grey rock, and there had grown north of that rock very frosty woods, and there were dark mists, and under that rock was a dwelling-place of water-monsters and wolves; and he saw that on that cliff there hung in those icy woods many black souls, tied by their hands, and their foes, in the guise of water-monsters, were gripping them like greedy wolves, and the water was black underneath that rock, and between that cliff and the water was a drop of twelve miles, and when the branches broke, the souls who hung on those branches went down, and the sea-monsters snatched them.*

That several of the physical features of the home of Grendel and his mother should match those of the Otherworld is scarcely surprising, given the poet's constant identification of Grendel with demonic forces. Elsewhere he is described as a 'fiend in hell' (*feond on helle*, line 101), a 'captive of hell' (cf. *helle hæfton*, line 788), and a 'hellish spirit' (*helle gast*, line 1274); he and his mother are together called 'devils' (cf. *deofla*, line 1680), while Grendel, desperate to escape from Beowulf's clutches, is said to want 'to flee into darkness, to seek the company of devils' (*wolde on heolstor fleon, / secan deofla gedræg*, lines 755–6).[57] Many of Grendel's titles, moreover, recall those of the devil, such as 'enemy of mankind' (*feond mancynnes*, lines 164 and 1276), 'God's opponent' (*Godes andsaca*, lines 786 and 1682), and 'ancient foe' (*ealdgewinna*, line 1776).[58] More importantly, Grendel is called by the poet, although not by the characters in the poem, a 'heathen' (*hæþen*, cf. lines 852 and 986), whose proper domain, in Christian eyes, is hell, as is made plain by the poet's bald statement that 'joyless in the fen-refuge, he laid aside his life, his heathen soul: there hell received him' (*dreama leas / in fenfreoðo feorh alegde, / hæþene sawle; þær him hel onfeng*, lines

55 Morris, ed., *The Blickling Homilies*, pp. vi–vii; the homily in question is in fact no. XVII in Morris's edition, but the fragment which Morris numbers XVI has been identified as a part of his Homily IV, causing a renumbering of Morris's Homilies XVII–XIX as XVI–XVIII. See further the facsimile by Willard, ed., *The Blickling Homilies*, pp. 38–40.

56 For the text, cf. Collins, 'Blickling Homily XVI and the Dating of *Beowulf*', p. 62; for the translation, cf. Malone, 'Grendel and His Abode', pp. 304–5.

57 Cf. Malone, 'Grendel and His Abode', pp. 298–9.

58 Whitelock, *The Audience of 'Beowulf'*, pp. 10–11; Malone, 'Grendel and His Abode', p. 298.

850–2).[59] What makes the association particularly striking are the verbal similarities between the two descriptions in the homily and the poem, which have been noted many times, and might be summarised as follows:[60]

Blickling XVI	*Beowulf*
þær ealle wætero niðergewítað	ðær fyrgenstream . . . niþer gewiteð (lines 1359–60)
ofer ðæm wætere sumne hárne stán	fyrgenbeamas ofer harne stan (lines 1414–15)
of ðæm stáne awexene swiðe hrimige bearwas	ofer þæm hongiað hrinde bearwas (line 1363)
ðær wæron þystrogenipo	under næssa genipu (line 1360)
niccra eardung	nicorhusa fela (line 1411)
7 þæt wæter wæs sweart under þæm clife neoðan	wæter under stod dreorig ond gedrefed (lines 1416–17)

Several scholars have seen a direct literary link between the two passages;[61] debate has continued over whether the *Beowulf*-poet borrowed from the Blickling Homily,[62] or vice versa.[63] Most recently the old notion that both authors were drawing on a third, intermediary, and vernacular source, originally favoured by Klaeber, amongst others,[64] has found increasing support; Charles D. Wright, in the course of a comprehensive discussion, considers a series of minor details in the descriptions in *Beowulf* and Blickling Homily XVI, and concludes that both authors were drawing independently on a vernacular version of the *Visio S. Pauli*.[65] Hildegard Tristram argues that the description in *Beowulf* 'is wholly traditional and probably borrowed from homiletic writings', but considers that the purely descriptive elements have been deliberately separated from their religious context,[66] and Wright concurs, noting of the *Beowulf*-poet that: 'while retaining the essential configuration, he divests particular elements of their explicitly eschatological reference by literalizing them: his "hell" is still in the north, because that is where the Danes live; his frosty trees, bereft of the souls that once were suspended from their branches, are left to

59 Tolkien, 'Beowulf, the Monsters, and the Critics', pp. 278–80.

60 The list derives from Brown, '*Beowulf* and the *Blickling Homilies*', p. 908; cf. Collins, 'Blickling Homily XVI and the Dating of *Beowulf*', p. 65; Wright, *The Irish Tradition in Old English Literature*, p. 119.

61 A notable exception is Peter Clemoes, 'Style as a Criterion', p. 181, who argues against any such direct literary link, preferring instead to see the passages as reflecting oral and memorial traditions based on preached material.

62 Cf. Morris, ed., *The Blickling Homilies*, p. vii; Brown, '*Beowulf* and the *Blickling Homilies*', p. 909.

63 Collins, 'Blickling Homily XVI and the Dating of *Beowulf*', pp. 67–8.

64 Klaeber, 'Die christlichen Elementen im *Beowulf*', pp. 185–7; Klaeber, ed., *Beowulf*, p. 183; Hoops, *Kommentar zum Beowulf*, p. 164.

65 Wright, *The Irish Tradition in Old English Literature*, pp. 116–36, at pp. 133–6. For further indications that the author of *Beowulf* drew on vernacular traditions ultimately drawn from the *Visio S. Pauli*, see further below, pp. 47–51.

66 Tristram, 'Stock Descriptions', p. 111.

"hang" over the water below; and his water-monsters have been exorcised of their demons'.[67] As we shall see, however, this is not the whole story; the poet of *Beowulf* also introduces eschatological elements into his description, albeit providing them with a naturalistic setting.[68]

In a similar way, it has been suggested that the description of the monster-mere can be compared to a vernacular poetic type-scene, fully integrated into Old English verse, which Donald Fry calls the 'Cliff of Death', and which he traces in three other poems, including 'four basic elements: cliffs, serpents, darkness, and deprivation, and occasionally wolves and wind'.[69] As an example of the theme, Fry cites the account from *Judith*, elsewhere in the *Beowulf*-manuscript, of the fate of Holofernes, who is despatched to damnation in the Old English poem immediately upon decapitation, in a scene which has no parallel in the Vulgate account (lines 111–21):

Læg se fula leap
gesne beæftan, gæst ellor hwearf
under neowelne næs ond ðær genyðerad wæs,
susle gesæled syððan æfre,
wyrmum bewunden, witum gebunden,
hearde gehæfted in hellebryne
æfter hinsiðe. Ne ðearf he hopian no,
þystrum forðylmed, þæt he ðonan mote
of ðam wyrmsele, ac ðær wunian sceal
awa to aldre butan ende forð
in ðam heolstran ham, hyhtwynna leas.

The foul trunk lay dead behind, the spirit turned elsewhere under the deep cliff, and was there brought low, tied with torment for ever after, wound round with worms, bound with punishments, cruelly captive in hell-fire after death. He need not hope, enveloped in darkness, that he might pass from there, out of that worm-hall, but he must dwell there for ever henceforth without end in that dark home, bereft of hopeful joys.

The abrupt transition from Holofernes' tent in the midst of a desert plain, to a dark, seething hell of fire and serpents at the bottom of a cliff can be matched by remarkably similar descriptions of hell in *Christ and Satan* (lines 24–32, 89–105, and 132–6).[70] Of course, the account in Blickling Homily XVI demonstrates all of the same elements too, unless the *nicras* which the homily shares with Beowulf are held to be distinct from the more obviously serpentine 'multitude of worm-kin, wondrous sea-dragons' (*wyrmcynnes fela, sellice sædracan*, lines 1425–6) whom Beowulf and his men encounter at the mere.[71] But such an association would only serve to underline

67 Wright, *The Irish Tradition in Old English Literature*, p. 135.

68 See further below, pp. 42–5.

69 Fry, 'The Cliff of Death', p. 215.

70 Fry, 'The Cliff of Death', pp. 216–18.

71 The precise sense of *nicras* is uncertain; apart from *Beowulf* and Blickling Homily XVI the term is only found in the *Letter of Alexander* (§ 15) and in a prose Life of St Margaret

the essential terror of an imaginary and psychological landscape whose different physical features can scarcely be harmonised;[72] Eric Stanley memorably describes the scenery as 'a gallimaufry of devices, each of which is horrific in its associations'.[73]

It is clear that if the poet did borrow part of his conception of the monster-mere from a description of hell as given in a vernacular version of the *Visio S. Pauli*, he has overlaid the original with a number of extra details which lend extraordinary vividness, both physical and psychological, to his own particular depiction. In mentioning that each night a fire is seen on the turbid waters beneath the icy grove, the poet at once goes beyond the *Visio S. Pauli* (and Blickling Homily XVI), and aligns his own picture still further with a number of Insular visions of the Otherworld, where lost souls flit between fire and ice.[74] The particular collocation *fyr on flode* (line 1366) demonstrates further the artistry of the *Beowulf*-poet, who later on in the poem is able to exploit the same alliterative pairing both in his account of Beowulf's descent in the mere itself, when he emerges into the fire-lit hall of Grendel's mother (line 1516), and in Hrothgar's lengthy 'sermon' to Beowulf on his return from the mere, when he is warned of the insecurity of a prosperous earthly life, which can be cut short by a number of unforseen circumstances, including 'fire's grip and flood's surge' (*oððe fyres feng oððe flodes wylm*, line 1762).[75]

Outside *Beowulf*, combined reference to 'fire and flood' is largely restricted to homiletic prose, specifically apocalyptic visions of the end of the world.[76] In poetry the alliterative pair is found in the Paris Psalter (LXV.11), and in the eschatological *Judgment Day II* (line 166, rendering *fluvius ignivomus*),[77] where again the notion of mingled fire and flood seems particularly suited to Judgment Day themes, as, most spectacularly, in the following passage from *Christ III* (lines 972–88):

(Cockayne, ed., *Narratiunculae anglice conscriptae*, p. 39), in both of which texts the required sense seems to be 'hippopotamus'. Cf. Davis, ' "Hippopotamus" in Old English', p. 141; Fry, 'The Cliff of Death', p. 222. See too further below, pp. 234–5, 294–5, and 298–9. Hippopotami were certainly regarded as bestial, rather than serpentine, by the compiler of the *Liber monstrorum* (II.9 and II.17); it is possible that the *Beowulf*-poet meant to make a similar distinction in describing the *sædracan* and *nicras* as 'worms and wild beasts' (*wyrmas ond wildeor*, line 1430).

72 Cf. Klaeber, ed., *Beowulf*, p. 183; Lawrence, 'The Haunted Mere in *Beowulf*', p. 225, who states that 'it is impossible to reconcile all these [aspects of the description] so as to give a single consistent picture of natural scenery'.

73 Stanley, 'Old English Poetic Diction', p. 441; cf. Butts, 'The Analogical Mere', pp. 113–21.

74 Cf. Sims-Williams, *Religion and Literature in Western England*, pp. 243–72; Tristram, 'Stock Descriptions', p. 111.

75 The theme of the multiplicity of things which can cut short one's life is found, for example, in *The Seafarer*, lines 66–71, as well as in an earlier section of Hrothgar's 'sermon' (*Beowulf*, lines 1735–9), although in none of the parallel passages is there any mention of fire or flood, which appear to have been deliberately introduced by the *Beowulf*-poet. See further, Gordon, ed., *The Seafarer*, pp. 42–3.

76 Most notably, of course, in the Old English version of the *Apocalypse of Thomas*, where a 'fiery flood' (*fyren flod*) is mentioned twice; cf. Willard, *Two Apocrypha in Old English Homilies*, pp. 4 and 6, and *Beowulf*, lines 1359 and 2128.

77 See further Caie, *The Judgment Day Theme in Old English Poetry*, pp. 194–5.

Swa se gifra gæst grundas geondseceð;
hiþende leg heahgetimbro
fylleð on foldwong fyres egsan,
widmære blæst woruld mid ealle,
hat, heorogifre. Hreosað geneahhe
tobrocene burgweallas. Beorgas gemeltað
ond heahcleofu, þa wið holme ær
fæste wið flodum foldan sceldun,
stið ond stæðfæst, staþelas wið wæge,
wætre windendum. Þonne wihta gehwylce,
deora ond fugla, deaðleg nimeð,
færeð æfter foldan fyrswearta leg,
weallende wiga. Swa ær wæter fleowan,
flodas afysde, þonne on fyrbaðe
swelað sæfiscas; sundes getwæfde
wægdeora gehwylc werig swelteð,
byrneþ wæter swa weax.

So the greedy spirit searches through the depths; the ravaging flame casts down the high dwellings to the ground through the terror of conflagration; the widely notorious blast, hot and greedy for gore will destroy the whole world. Shattered city-walls will collapse outright; mountains will melt, and high cliffs, which kept the land safe against the floods, firm and stable bulwarks against the waves, the breaking water. Then the death-flame shall take every single creature, beasts and birds; the fire-dark flame shall stalk the land, a seething warrior. Just as water had stirred the floods, then in a sea of fire sea-fishes will scorch; stopped from swimming, every sea-creature will fail and die; the water will burn like wax.

The motif of the burning sea presented here is not very common, but clearly signifies apocalypse; amongst Insular sources its occurrence has been noted in the pseudo-Bede *Collectanea*,[78] as well as in several Irish texts, such as the 'Ochtfæochlach Choluim Chille'.[79] In a number of the prose accounts which link the concepts of fire and flood, the punishing conflagration at the end of the world is explicitly compared to the Flood which previously swept the earth,[80] a notion which may ultimately derive from Luke XVII.26 (*Et sicut factum est in diebus Noe, ita erit in diebus Filii hominis*);[81] Wulfstan makes the point succinctly:[82]

78 Printed by Migne, PL 94, col. 555: *quinta die ardebunt ipsae aquae ab ortu usque ad occasum* ('on the fifth day the very waters shall burn, from their rising until their fall'); Cf. Lapidge and Sharpe, *Bibliography of Celtic Latin Literature*, no. 1257. See further Hill, 'The Old World, the Levelling of the Earth, and the Burning of the Sea', pp. 323–5.

79 Quin, ed., 'Ochtfæochlach Choluim Chille', p. 144; Biggs, *The Sources of Christ III*, p. 15.

80 Cf. the parallel passages from *Christ II*, lines 805–7 and *Judgment Day II*, lines 166–70; Caie, *The Judgment Day Theme in Old English Poetry*, pp. 194–5.

81 Cf. Matthew XXIV.37; Heist, *The Fifteen Signs Before Doomsday*, pp. 27–9.

82 Bethurum, ed., *The Homilies of Wulfstan*, p. 122/7–9; cf. Napier, ed., *Wulfstan*, no. XLIII (*Sunnandæges spell*) 206/14–19 and 207/22–3; no. XLIV (*Sunnandæges spell*), 216/24–217/2.

And witodlice ealswa flod com hwilum ær for synnum, swa cymð eac for synnum fyr ofer mancynn, 7 ðærto hit nealæcð nu swyðe georne.

And truly, just as the Flood came before because of sins, so too because of sins a fire will come over mankind, and now the time is approaching very soon.

The image of apocalyptic cleansing flood and flame in the context of Grendel and his mother is particularly appropriate; they were, after all, of the doomed kin of Cain, whom God had purged in the Flood.[83]

Outside homiletic literature, reference to 'fire and flood' are notably rare; in a land dispute of 968,[84] one party condemns the contentious property *to fyre oððe flode*, rather than that it should pass to the other claimant, while, more intriguingly, Cnut's second law-code (set down not long after the compilation of the *Beowulf*-manuscript) explicitly forbids heathen worship, which it defines as follows (II Cnut V.1):[85]

Hæðenscipe byð, þæt man deofolgyld weorþige hæðene godas 7 sunnan oððe monan, fyr oððe flod, wæterwyllas oððe stanas oððe æniges cynnes wudutreowa.

Heathen practices include the worship of devilish idols, heathen gods, the sun or moon, fire or flood, water-surges or stones or any kind of trees.

The description of Grendel's mere, combining as it does a number of the natural elements (fire, flood, water-surges, stones, and trees) which apparently lent themselves to animistic practice, is a most suitable dwelling for a such a devilish and heathen spirit; as Richard Schrader has suggested: 'the imaginary scene in Beowulf is not hell itself but a place meant to suggest the familiar locale of "devil-worship" '.[86]

In this context the possibility of influence from pagan Latin verse on the *Beowulf*-poet has also been raised with respect to the description of the monster-mere, particularly since almost every aspect of the portrayal can be matched elsewhere. Vergil gives a picture of a deep cave by a dark and turbulent lake in a gloomy grove no bird will fly over at the entrance to the Otherworld (*Aeneid* VI.131–9, 236–42, and 296),[87] and elsewhere compares the fleeing pagan warrior Turnus to a stag pursued by a hound and trapped by a deep-banked river (*Aeneid* XII.749–55).[88] The pagan grove at Massilia is described by Lucan as dark and cold, with gore-spattered and snake-entwined trees where birds would not perch, and into which no wild animals would enter (*Pharsalia* III.399–425 and VI.642–51); Claudian depicts a dark and steaming lake at Aponus (*Carmen* XXVI), in whose

83 See further below, pp. 58–85.

84 Recorded in Sawyer, *Anglo-Saxon Charters*, no. 1447, and Wormald, 'Anglo-Saxon Lawsuits', nos. 38–40.

85 Liebermann, ed., *Die Gesetze*, I, p. 312.

86 Schrader, 'Sacred Groves, Marvellous Waters', p. 81.

87 The similarities between this passage and Hrothgar's description of the mere are discussed by Haber, *A Comparative Study*, pp. 92–6; Renoir, 'The Terror of the Dark Waters', pp. 147–60; Andersson, *Early Epic Scenery*, pp. 145–59; Cornelius, 'Palus Inamabilis', pp. 321–5.

88 Cf. Schrader, 'Sacred Groves, Marvellous Waters', pp. 77–8, who also offers some other, less convincing, parallels.

depths from time to time can be seen 'ancient spears, royal offerings' (*veteres hastae, regia dona*), as well as a thick grove on the slopes of Etna filled with the victory-spoils of the gods, including giants' heads and the bones of huge serpents, where no Cyclops dares graze his sheep (*De raptu Proserpinae* III.332–56).[89] The works of Vergil and Lucan were certainly known and imitated in Anglo-Saxon England from the time of Aldhelm on; less compelling evidence may imply that some of Claudian's work was also available.[90] The direct or indirect influence of these poets on the *Beowulf*-poet may not be entirely out of the question, though the possibility is remote. The vigour of this Latin poetic tradition is perhaps further reflected in the closest analogue to part of the description in *Beowulf* that has been suggested to date: a much later Latin account of a magical lake into which no wild beast will enter, even if pursued by hounds, which is found in Alexander Neckham's *De laudibus divinae sapientiae*.[91]

Within the *Beowulf*-manuscript itself, of course, and ultimately derived from Latin tradition, we have yet another detailed description of a heathen sacred grove, in the *Letter of Alexander to Aristotle* (§ 36), where Alexander visits the sacred trees of the Sun and the Moon, and is told that:

> þær næfre in þæm londum regnes dropa ne cwome ne fugel ne wildeor, ne nænig ætern wyrm þæt her dorste gesecean ða halgan gemæro sunnan 7 monan.
>
> *no drop of rain ever came in that land, nor bird, nor wild beast, nor did any poisonous snake dare to seek out the holy precincts of the Sun and the Moon.*

The *Beowulf*-poet may have had a similarly marvellous grove in mind, although there, of course, there were serpents and dragons in abundance (lines 1425–6). Nor, as we shall see, is this the only aspect in which *Alexander's Letter to Aristotle* can be seen to match certain elements of the description of the monster–mere in *Beowulf*. On the edge of a large river full of undrinkable water in the wilderness, Alexander and his men find a cliff edged with huge and towering trees (§ 12);[92] marching along the river, they come to an island, but when some of Alexander's men attempt to swim across, disaster strikes (§ 15):

> Þa hie ða hæfdon feorðan dæl þære ea geswummen, ða becwom sum ongrislic wise on hie. Þæt wæs þonne nicra mengeo on onsione maran 7 unhyrlicran þonne ða elpendas in ðone grund þære ea 7 betweoh ða yða þæs wæteres þa men besencte 7 mid heora muðe hie sliton 7 blodgodon 7 hie ealle swa fornamon, þæt ure nænig wiste hwær hiora æni cwom. Ða wæs ic swiðe yrre þæm minum ladþeowum, þa us on swylce frecennissa gelæddon. Het hiera ða bescufan in þa ea .L. 7 .C. 7 sona þæs ðe hie inne wæron, swa wæron þa nicoras gearwe tobrudon

89 Schrader, 'Sacred Groves, Marvellous Waters', pp. 78–9.

90 Orchard, *The Poetic Art of Aldhelm*, pp. 130–5, 139–41, and 152–5.

91 Rigg, '*Beowulf* 1368–72: An Analogue', pp. 101–2; Butts, 'The Analogical Mere', p. 118.

92 Particularly striking here is the emphasis in the Old English on the cliff-edge (*On þære ea ofre stod hreod 7 pintreow 7 abies þæt treowcyn ungemetlicre gryto 7 micelnysse þy clyfe weox 7 wridode*), which has no parallel in the Latin. On the alliterative doublet *weox 7 wridode*, which occurs in *Beowulf*, line 1741 in the form *weaxeð ond wrideð*, see Clemoes, 'Style as Criterion', p. 180, and below, pp. 132–3.

hie swa hie þa oðre ær dydon, 7 swa þicce hie in þære ea aweollon swa æmettan ða nicras, 7 swilc unrim heora wæs. Þa het ic blawan mine byman 7 þa fyrd faran.

And when they had swum about a quarter of the river, something terrible happened to them. There appeared a multitude of water-monsters [hippopotami], larger and more terrible in appearance than the elephants, who dragged the men through the watery waves down to the river bottom, and tore them to bloody pieces with their mouths, and snatched them all away so that none of us knew where any of them had gone. Then I was very angry with my guides, who had led us into such danger. I ordered that one hundred and fifty of them be shoved into the river, and as soon as they were in the water-monsters were ready, and dragged them away just as they had done with the others, and the water-monsters seethed up in the river as thick as ants, they were so innumerable. Then I ordered the trumpets to be sounded, and the army to head off.

The sudden appearance of this 'multitude of water-monsters' (*nicra mengeo*), which drag men down to the bottom, is intriguing partly because of the rarity of the term *nicras* in Old English, which, outside *Beowulf* and the *Letter of Alexander to Aristotle* is only found in a prose Life of St Margaret,[93] and in the account of the vision of Saint Paul in Blickling Homily XVI,[94] noted above, but also partly because in Beowulf's accounts of his own exploits, which include killing *nicras* (line 422), 'water-monsters' of the same kind attempt to drag Beowulf himself down to the depths (lines 553–75). Even the trumpets, which Alexander sounds to mark the end of the episode (§ 17), have an echo in the horns blown at the monster-mere in *Beowulf*, which, however, introduce the action there (lines 1423–5 and 1431–2).[95] Eventually, Alexander and his men are directed to a 'large lake' (*mere*), not far from human habitation,[96] thickly overgrown with trees, and infested with serpents and reptiles (§§ 16–18); the general resemblance to the monster mere is again intriguing. Still further parallels link the 'monsters' of *Beowulf* and the *Letter of Alexander*; at one point Alexander and his men are surprised by a fearsome creature attacking suddenly from the fens, which is impervious to any weapon, and which devours two of his companions with its sharp teeth (§ 27):

Ða wæs þæt lond eall swa we geferdon adrugad 7 fen 7 cannon 7 hreod weoxan. Ða cwom þær semninga sum deor of þæm fenne 7 of ðæm fæstene, wæs þæm deore eall se hrycg acæglod swelce snoda hæfde þæt deor seonowealt heafod swelce mona 7 þæt deor hatte *quasi caput luna* 7 him wæron þa breost gelice niccres breastum 7 heardum toðum 7 miclum hit wæs gegyred 7 geteþed. Ond

93 Cockayne, ed., *Narratiunculae anglice conscriptae*, p. 39.

94 Davis, '"Hippopotamus" in Old English', pp. 141–2.

95 In both cases, the effect of the horn-blowing is to make the assembled troop sit down. Whilst such an action is quite natural for Alexander and his men, who promptly begin to eat, the action of the foot-soldiers accompanying Beowulf is decidedly curious, and may indicate that here the *Beowulf*-poet is the borrower. For an alternative explanation of the horns, see Braswell, 'The Horn at Grendel's Mere: *Beowulf* 1417–41', pp. 466–72.

96 Cf. the proximity of the monster-mere in *Beowulf* to Heorot (lines 1361–2): *nis þæt feor heonon / milgemearces þæt se mere standeð.*

hit þa þæt deor ofsloh mine þegnas twegen. Ond we þa þæt deor nowþer ne mid spere gewundigan ne meahte ne mid nænige wæpne, ac we hit uneaþe mid isernum hamerum 7 slecgum gefyldon 7 hit ofbeoton.

Then all the land through which we passed was dried up and marshy, and canes and reeds grew there. Then there came suddenly out of the fen and fastness a beast, and the beast's back was all studded with pegs like a snood, and the beast had a round head like the moon, and the beast was called Quasi caput luna *['moon-head', crocodile], and it had a breast like a sea-monster's breast and it was armed and toothed with hard and large teeth. And that beast slew two of my thegns. And we were unable to wound that beast with spears in any way, nor with any kind of weapon, but with difficulty we beat it and subdued it with iron mallets and sledge-hammers.*

What is particularly striking about this account, which in general terms might apply as well to Grendel, who is equally impervious to weapons (lines 801–4), is the description of the assailant coming 'out of the fen and fastness' (*of þæm fenne 7 of ðæm fæstene*), the more so since Grendel's own domain is described in exactly the same terms (*fen on fæsten*, line 104), in what is the only other example of the alliterative doublet extant in Old English literature. There is, as we have seen, orthographical and morphological evidence that the *Letter of Alexander to Aristotle* and *Beowulf* were both copied from the same exemplar;[97] other parallels of theme may strengthen the case for a still closer connection.[98]

Hrothgar's description of the monster-mere, then, whether drawn from the *Letter of Aristotle to Alexander* or from some vernacular rendering of the *Visio S. Pauli* (or both), may represent a significant blend of imported Latin and native germanic elements, the whole strongly influenced by the Christian homiletic tradition. In keeping with the wisdom and dignity which characterise his appearances throughout the poem, Hrothgar's longest speech to the victorious Beowulf on his return from the same monster-mere, bearing the grisly booty of the giant sword-hilt and Grendel's severed head (lines 1700–84), combines many of the same elements in much the same way. Ettmüller was the first person to describe the speech as a 'sermon',[99] and its very length and position at the heart of the poem have led a number of commentators to stress its importance in the wider structure of the poem; G. V. Smithers considered the passage 'a hinge on which the two halves of the poem are set'.[100] In fact Hrothgar's lengthy speech consists of much more than homiletic advice; Klaeber reckoned the speech 'conspicuous for the blending of heroic and theological motives',[101] and the 'sermon' has been sub-divided in various ways.[102] The opening undoubtedly establishes Hrothgar's authority as an old and experienced

97 See above, pp. 2–3.

98 See further below, pp. 132–9.

99 Ettmüller, ed., *Beowulf*, p. 136; cited by Stanley, *In the Foreground: 'Beowulf'*, p. 240.

100 Smithers, 'The Meaning of *The Seafarer* and *The Wanderer*', p. 8; cf. Goldsmith, *Mode and Meaning in 'Beowulf'*, pp. 183–209.

101 Klaeber, ed., *Beowulf*, p. 190.

102 Cox, *Cruces*, p. 132; Klaeber, ed., *Beowulf*, p.190; Hansen, 'Hrothgar's "*Sermon*" in Beowulf', p. 62.

judge of the deeds of men (lines 1700–9), a theme to which he returns towards the end of his speech, where he muses on the length and success of his own career, before Grendel appeared on the scene (lines 1769–84).[103] But Hrothgar's is but the last of a series of *exempla* which warn of the dangers of complacency and overweening pride. After fulsome praise of Beowulf as a figure at the height of his powers, with considerable promise, Hrothgar posts a warning of the dangers ahead, by citing the case of Heremod, who at one time had seemed equally blessed (lines 1709–24):

Ne wearð Heremod swa
eaforum Ecgwelan, Arscyldingum;
ne geweox he him to willan, ac to wælfealle
ond to deaðcwalum Deniga leodum;
breat bolgenmod beodgeneatas,
eaxlgesteallan, oþþæt he ana hwearf,
mære þeoden mondreamum from,
ðeah þe hine mihtig god mægenes wynnum,
eafeþum stepte, ofer ealle men
forð gefremede. Hwæþere him on ferhþe greow
breosthord blodreow; nallas beagas geaf
Denum æfter dome; dreamleas gebad
þæt he þæs gewinnes weorc þrowade,
leodbealo longsum. Đu þe lær be þon,
gumcyste ongit! Ic þis gid be þe
awræc wintrum frod.

Not so was Heremod to the children of Ecgwela; he did not flourish for the happiness, but for the slaughter and massacre of the Danish people. Swollen with rage he shattered his hearth-companions, his close comrades, until he alone, famous prince, turned from the joys of men, even though mighty God had steeped him with the joys of strength and with powers promoted him beyond all men. Yet in his heart there grew a bloodthirsty spirit; he did not give the Danes rings according to judgment; joyless he endured so that he suffered pain for that struggle, long-lasting grief for his people. Learn from that, and recognise manly virtue. I, experienced in years, have uttered this speech for [or 'about'] you.

Just as the warning example of Heremod is invoked here, after Beowulf's great victory against Grendel's mother, so too his shadow is first raised after the fight with Grendel (lines 901–15). There it is stressed that Heremod had been the equal of Sigemund (as is Beowulf) before his temperament led him to the bad. Heremod's fate, to turn away in lonely exile from the joys of men, recalls that of Grendel himself, the more so since his exile takes place among giants, as Heremod, just like Grendel, passes 'into the power of enemies' (*on feonda geweald*, lines 808 and 903).[104]

103 Müllenhoff, 'Innere Geschichte', pp. 213–14, believed that the two parts of the speech were entirely incompatible, and ascribed the first to his hypothesized interpolater B, as cited by Stanley, *In the Foreground: 'Beowulf'*, p. 241.

104 See further Blake, 'The Heremod Digressions in *Beowulf*', p. 282.

Heremod is but one of a number of figures in Beowulf whose names carry psychological connotations remarkably appropriate to their characters, leading some commentators to see their plight as in some sense allegorical, and Müllenhoff duly recognised in Heremod's activity the kind of zest for conflict suitable to one named 'war-spirit'.[105] Likewise, Kemp Malone demonstrated that the Geatish Queen Hygd ('sense') 'is consistently characterised in terms of her name',[106] while R. E. Kaske and Fred Robinson both contrast her sensibility with the rashness of Hygelac, her husband, whose behaviour they see defined by the sense 'instability of mind'.[107] The same implicit contrast between the physical and psychological worlds runs throughout the remainder of Hrothgar's 'sermon', a pivotal section of the poem, in which homiletic elements are rife, and which requires quotation in full (lines 1724–68):

Wundor is to secganne,
hu mihtig God manna cynne
þurh sidne sefan snyttru bryttað,
eard ond eorlscipe; he ah ealra geweald.
Hwilum he on lufan læteð hworfan
monnes modgeþonc mæran cynnes,
seleð him on eþle eorþan wynne
to healdanne hleoburh wera,
gedeð him swa gewealdene worolde dælas,
side rice, þæt he his selfa ne mæg
his unsnyttrum ende geþencean.
Wunað he on wiste; no hine wiht dweleð
adl ne yldo, ne him inwitsorh
on sefa(n) sweorceð, ne gesacu ohwær
ecghete eoweð, ac him eal worold
wendeð on willan; he þæt wyrse ne con –
oð þæt him on innan oferhygda dæl
weaxeð ond wridað; þonne se weard swefeð,
sawele hyrde; bið se slæp to fæst,
bisgum gebunden, bona swiðe neah,
se þe of flanbogan fyrenum sceoteð.
þonne bið on hreþre under helm drepen
biteran stræle – him bebeorgan ne con –
wom wundorbebodum wergan gastes;
þinceð him to lytel þæt he lange heold,
gytsað gromhydig, nallas on gylp seleð
fætte beagas, ond he þa forðgesceaft
forgyteð ond forgymeð, þæs þe him ær God sealde,
wuldres Waldend, weorðmynda dæl.
Hit on endestæf eft gelimpeð

[105] Müllenhoff, *Beowulf*, p. 51; Klaeber, ed., *Beowulf*, pp. 162–3; Robinson, *The Tomb of Beowulf*, pp. 212–13.

[106] Malone, 'Hygd', p. 358.

[107] Kaske, '"Hygelac" and "Hygd"', pp. 200–6; Robinson, *The Tomb of Beowulf*, pp. 213–17.

þæt se lichoma   læne gedreoseð,
fæge gefealleð;   fehð oþer to,
se þe unmurnlice   madmas dæleþ,
eorles ærgestreon,   egesan ne gymeð.
Bebeorh þe ðone bealonið,   Beowulf leofa,
secg betsta,   ond þe þæt selre geceos,
ece rædas;   oferhyda ne gym,
mære cempa!   Nu is þines mægnes blæd
ane hwile;   eft sona bið
þæt þec adl oððe ecg   eafoþes getwæfeð,
oððe fyres feng,   oððe flodes wylm,
oððe gripe meces,   oððe gares fliht,
oððe atol yldo;   oððe eagena bearhtm
forsiteð ond forsworceð;   semninga bið
þæt ðec, dryhtguma,   deað oferswyðeð.

It is wondrous to tell how mighty God, through his magnanimity deals out to mankind wisdom, land, and rank; he has control of all things. Sometimes he lets a well-born man's thoughts turn to pleasure, grants him in his homeland to possess the joys of the earth, a sheltering stronghold of men, makes subject to him areas of the world, broad kingdoms, so that he himself cannot in his folly perceive any end. He dwells in prosperity; not at all do old age or sickness harm him, nor does grim sorrow darken his spirit, nor does malice cause sword-hatred anywhere, but the whole world moves at his whim; he knows nothing worse until a portion of pride grows and flourishes; when the keeper sleeps, the guardian of the soul; that sleep is too sound, fastened with worries, the slayer very close, who shoots wickedly from his bow. Then under his covering he is struck in the heart with a bitter arrow, with the crooked commands of wonder of the accursed spirit: he cannot defend himself; what he has long held seems to him too little, angry at heart he grows niggardly, not at all honourably dispenses plated rings, but he forgets and neglects the world to come, the portion of glories that God, Ruler of Glory, had granted him. Finally it turns out that the frail body droops and falls doomed, and another succeeds, who doles out treasure recklessly, the ancient heirlooms of the warrior, does not reckon of terror. Guard yourself against that dread horror, my dear Beowulf, best of men, and choose for yourself the better part, eternal rewards; care not for pride, famous warrior! Now the glory of your might lasts for a time; but soon it will turn out that sickness or sword will separate you from your strength, or the fire's embrace or the flood's surge, or the bite of a blade, or the flight of a spear, or dreaded old age, or the brightness of your eyes shall fail and grow dim; finally it shall be that death, noble warrior, shall overpower you.

The implied contrast between worldly success and spiritual decay, between the physical world and the psychological, is explicit in the direct comparison between the 'portion of pride' (*oferhygda dæl*, line 1740) and 'portion of glories' (*weorðmynda dæl*, line 1752) which represent the changing fortunes of mankind, and here, after Beowulf has successfully defeated Grendel's mother, the poet reiterates the message implicit in the contrasting fortunes of Sigemund and Heremod (lines 874–915) or Hygelac and Hama (lines 1197–1214),[108] to which attention is drawn after Beowulf's defeat of Grendel; in each case the moral and didactic approach seems the same, an essentially exegetical technique familiar from vernacular homilies.

The style and content of Hrothgar's speech, moreover, may well owe something to homiletic technique.[109] As Peter Clemoes has pointed out, within the space of a few verses the poet employs no fewer than three alliterative couplings of synonymous or nearly-synonymous finite verbs: *weaxeð ond wridað* (line 1741),[110] *forgyteð ond forgymeð* (line 1751), and *forsiteð ond forsworceð* (line 1767), whereas only seven such pairs are found in the whole of the rest of the poem put together; such alliterative doublets were a frequent adornment of vernacular preaching from the earliest period.[111] Equally significant, perhaps is the reference to the 'soul's keeper' (*sawele hyrde*, line 1742), since the phrase is relatively rare in Old English, being largely confined to homiletic prose, where it is used on several occasions to describe Saint Michael in his role as psychopomp,[112] and no less than three times in the Old English translation of the *Visio S. Pauli*, in each case without warrant in the Latin.[113]

The sleep of such a 'guardian of the soul' is, of course, relatively commonplace within patristic and homiletic tradition; one author, for example, borrowing a motif from a Hiberno-Latin source,[114] notes that 'Almighty God teaches us vigils and prayers; the devil teaches us sleep and slackness' (*God Ælmihtig us lærað wæccan and gebedu, diofol us lærað slæp and slæcnesse*).[115] The 'slayer' (*bona*, line 1743), whose arrows cause such spiritual harm, is presumably to be identified with the devilish 'slayer of the spirit' (*gastbona*, line 177) to whom the poet disapprovingly notes the Danes sacrificing at their heathen shrines. The figure of the arrows of sin is doubtless ultimately indebted to the biblical rhetoric of Ephesians VI.11–16, the influence of which passage on Anglo-Saxon literature is remarkably widespread,[116] but it is still striking that the *Beowulf*-poet, by introducing the figure of the less than reliable

108 Cf. Kaske, 'The Sigemund-Heremod and Hama-Hygelac Passages in *Beowulf*', pp. 491–4.

109 See, for example, Hansen, 'Hrothgar's "sermon" in *Beowulf* as Parental Wisdom', pp. 54–6.

110 Cf. the parallel doublet *weox ⁊ wridode* in the *Letter of Alexander to Aristotle* (§ 12) in the Appendix below, pp. 232–3. See further above, pp. 44–5.

111 Clemoes, 'Style as a Criterion', pp. 180–1; cf. Klaeber, ed., *Beowulf*, p. 192.

112 See, for example, Bazire and Cross, ed., *Eleven Old English Rogationtide Homilies*, III.144–5, p. 53.

113 Healey, ed. *The Old English Vision of St Paul*, lines 91, 104, 131; pp. 67 and 69. Such links further strengthen the possibility that the *Beowulf*-poet was influenced by a vernacular rendering of the *Visio S. Pauli*; cf. Wright, *The Irish Tradition in Old English Literature*, pp. 132–4.

114 Wright, *The Irish Tradition in Old English Literature*, p. 244.

115 Healey, ed. *The Old English Vision of St Paul*, p. 325, lines 79–80; cf. Fadda, ed. *Nuove omelie anglosassoni*, p. 169, lines 72–3, who, however, reads *slæw* for *slæp*. See also Assman, ed. *Angelsächsische Homilien und Heiligleben*, XIV.106–7, p. 168: *deofol us læreð slæpnesse and sent us on slæwðe*, and Wright, '*Docet Deus, docet diabolus*', pp. 451–3.

116 Cf. Hermann, *Allegories of War*, pp. 39–42.

'guardian of the soul' come close to the extended homiletic treatment of the theme most fully explored by the author of Vercelli Homily IV (lines 308-10 and 337–42):[117]

> Þonne hæfð þæt dioful geworht bogan 7 stræla. Se boga bið geworht of ofermettum, 7 þa stræla bioð swa manigra cynna swa swa mannes synna bioð . . . Ælce dæge hæbbað [we] twegen hyrdas: oðer cymð ufan of heofonum, þe us sceall gode bysene onstellan 7 us gode þeawas tæcan, 7 hæfð him on handa þa scyldas þe ic ær nemde 7 þæt sweord, 7 wyle us forstandan æt þam awyrgden diofle, þe of þære stylenan helle cymð mid his scearpum strælum us mid to scotianne.
>
> *Then the devil has made a bow and arrows. The bow is made of pride, and the arrows are of as many kinds as man's sins . . . Each day we have two guardians, and one comes from the heavens above, who is to establish a good example for us and teach us good virtues, and he has in his hand the shields which I mentioned earlier, and the sword, and he wants to defend us against the accursed devil, who comes from steely hell with his sharp arrows, with which to shoot us.*

The 'bow of pride' described here seems remarkably close to the figure depicted in Hrothgar's 'sermon', whilst the notion of a 'guardian of the soul', both here and in the 'sermon', presumably derives ultimately from the biblical *custos animae* of Proverbs XVI.17 and XXII.5,[118] and indeed the extent to which both passages relate to the specific concerns of Hrothgar's 'sermon' is quite striking (Proverbs XVI.16–18 and XXII.4–6):

> posside sapientiam quia auro melior est et adquire prudentiam quia pretiosior est argento. semita iustorum declinat mala custos animae suae servat viam suam. contritionem praecedit superbia et ante ruinam exaltatur spiritum . . . finis modestiae timor Domini divitiae et gloria et vita. arma et gladii in via perversi custos animae suae recedit ab eis.
>
> *Possesse wisdom, because it is better than gold: and gette prudence, because it is more precious than silver. The path of the just avoideth evils: the keper of his soule kepeth his way. Pride goeth before destruction, and before ruine the spirit shal be exalted . . . The end of modestie the feare of our Lord, riches and glorie and life. Armour and swordes in the way of the perverse: but the keper of his owne soule departeth far from them.*

Apart from the general admonition concerning the value of wisdom and the dangers of pride alongside mention of the 'keper of [the] soule' (*custos animae*), the reference here to 'the feare of our Lord' (*timor Domini*) is intriguing in the context of the curious phrase in Hrothgar's 'sermon' in which we are told of a spiritual successor to Heremod who 'does not reckon of terror' (*egesan ne gymeð*, line 1757). Elsewhere

117 Scragg, ed., *The Vercelli Homilies*, pp. 102 and 104; cf. Wright, *The Irish Tradition in Old English Literature*, pp. 260–1.

118 Cf. Klaeber, ed., *Beowulf*, p. 192.

in *Beowulf* the word *egesa* signifies 'terror',[119] but in this one passage may contain a sense approaching 'awe', as Vickrey has argued,[120] and can be compared not only with the phrase *timor Domini* from Proverbs already noted, but also in this context of a call to wisdom by the specific admonition in the Psalms that 'the beginning of Wisdom is the fear of the Lord' (*initium sapientiae timor Domini*, Psalm CX.10). Certainly, precisely such a notion was adopted and underlined in various Old English homiletic texts, for example Vercelli Homily XII (lines 64–7):[121]

> Se egesa us gelædeð fram helwarum, ⁊ he us onfehð to þam uplican rice, ⁊ he drifeð fram us ælce ungleawnesse, ⁊ he us læreð geðeodscype ⁊ snyttro, ⁊ he us cenneð wisdom. He is se egesa.
>
> *Fear leads us from the inhabitants of Hell, and brings us to the kingdom above, and drives from us every folly, and instructs us in learning and understanding, and teaches us wisdom. That is fear.*

By dealing sympathetically with the terror (*egesa*) implicit in the heroic life, the *Beowulf*-poet gently directs us to the benefits of Christian reverence (*egesa*), benefits which even a virtuous pagan, such as Heremod's generous successor, are, as we shall see, emphatically denied.[122]

In this context, of course, of Christian and heroic terminology apparently deliberately manipulated and obscured by the *Beowulf*-poet, the closing words of the poem, in which a eulogy to Beowulf is delivered in the course of what some have seen as a ceremony of pagan apotheosis (lines 3180–2) are particularly striking:[123]

> cwædon þæt he wære   wyruldcyning[a]
> mannum mildust   ond mon[ðw]ærust,
> leodum liðost   ond lofgeornost.
>
> *They said that he was of worldly kings the mildest to men, and*
> *the most gentle, the kindest to his people, and the keenest for fame.*

The allusion to 'worldly kings' (*wyruldcyninga*, line 3180) effectively delimits the extent of Beowulf's endeavours, by its implicit reference to the heavenly king, knowledge of whom is denied to the dead hero, just as earlier in the poem Beowulf has twice been described as 'strongest in might in that day of this life' (*mægene strengest / on þæm dæge þysses lifes*, lines 789–90),[124] in a twin reference which puts Beowulf

119 The simple form *eg(e)sa* occurs in various morphological forms in lines 276, 784, 1827, 2736, and 3154; the compounds *gledegesa* (line 2650), *ligegesa* (line 2780), and *wæteregesa* (line 1260) are also attested, all bearing the same basic sense of 'terror' or 'horror'.

120 See further Vickrey, '*Egesan ne gymeð* and the Crime of Heremod', pp. 295–300.

121 Scragg, ed., *The Vercelli Homilies*, p. 230.

122 See further below, pp. 170–1.

123 Robinson, *The Tomb of Beowulf*, pp. 3–19; the text I have adopted here is that given by Richards, 'A Reexamination of *Beowulf* ll. 3180–3182', p. 165.

124 Cf. lines 196–7 (*mægenes strengest / on þæm dæge þysses lifes*), or the description of the death of Grendel *on ðæm dæge þysses lifes* (line 806).

firmly in his place, as it were: a hero of a bygone and strictly secular age.[125] In contrast to that secular praise, there may well be, as Mary P. Richards has indicated, a strongly religious flavour to the description of Beowulf as 'the mildest to men , and the most gentle' (*mannum mildust ond monðwærust*, line 3181), since the alliterative pair *milde ond monðwære* (or equivalent) is of rather frequent occurrence in Christian contexts, being used to describe, amongst others, Christ, Saint Neot, Bishop Eata, and the Archangel Gabriel.[126] There seems no good reason, however, to doubt that the same words can also be taken in a strictly secular sense, to denote, for example, praise for the prodigality of a generous prince,[127] and it is striking that in *Beowulf* itself Wealhtheow uses very similar terms to praise the Danes (lines 1228–31, my italics):

> Her is æghwylc eorl oþrum getrywe,
> modes *milde*, *man*drihtne hol[d];
> þegnas syndon *geþwære*, þeod ealgearo
> druncne dryhtguman doð swa ic bidde.
>
> *Here is each warrior true to the other, mild of spirit, loyal to their lord. The thegns are united, a people fully prepared, the retainers have drunk [loyally]: they do as I bid.*

That the same words denoting positive Christian virtues should seemingly be attributed to the pagan hero Beowulf only serves to underline the ambiguity of the final word of *Beowulf*, *lofgeornost* ('most eager for praise', line 3182), the dual associations of which were presumably equally apparent to Christian ears in the period when the *Beowulf*-manuscript was being copied.[128] The concept of *lof* ('praise') within *Beowulf* as a positive heroic and secular value to be gained by noble deeds is made clear by gnomic utterance both at the very beginning of the poem, when we are assured that 'it is by deeds of praise that one must prosper in every nation' (*lofdædum sceal / in mægþa gehwære man geþeon*, lines 24–5), and in the middle, during Beowulf's near-fatal conflict with Grendel's mother, when the poet notes that 'so must a man do who intends to gain long-lasting praise in war: he must have no care for his life' (*swa sceal man don, / þonne he æt guðe gegan þenceð / longsumne lof; na ymb his lif cearað*, lines 1534–6). The word *lofgeorn* and its morphological variants, however, are found only twelve times in the extant Old English corpus, of which the example in *Beowulf* represents the sole attestation of the word in verse. In prose, the term is found in three versions of a passage on the seven deadly sins by Ælfric,[129]

125 See further Robinson, *'Beowulf' and the Appositive Style*, p. 54; Frank, 'The *Beowulf* Poet's Sense of History', pp. 54–5.

126 Richards, 'A Reexamination of *Beowulf* ll. 3180–3182', pp. 165–7. Her evidence can be greatly supplemented: I note around twenty collocations of the two words.

127 This is a common meaning for the cognate adjective *mildr* in Old Norse verse; see further Wieland, '*Manna mildost*: Moses and Beowulf', pp. 86–93.

128 Cf. Richards, 'A Reexamination of *Beowulf* ll. 3180–3182', pp. 163–7; Rosier, 'The Two Closings of *Beowulf*', pp. 1–6.

129 Skeat, ed. *Ælfric's Lives of Saints*, I, p. 356, line 302; Morris, ed., *Old English Homilies*, p. 297; Warner, ed., *Early English Homilies*, p. 17, line 19.

once in the sermons of Wulfstan and once more in his *Institutes of Polity*,[130] and six times in the various versions of the Benedictine Rule.[131] In all these cases, the word carries unreservedly negative connotations.[132] By contrast, the word *domgeorn* ('eager for glory'), which occurs only five times, and always in verse, carries a positive sense on all occasions.[133]

The tension between Christian and heroic diction is, of course, fully exploited by a range of Old English poets, and several commentators have focused on a passage from the *Seafarer* which appears to suggest that worldly *lof* can have heavenly benefits (lines 72–80):[134]

> Forþon þæt bið eorla gehwam   æftercweþendra
> lof lifgendra   lastworda betst,
> þæt he gewyrce,   ær he onweg scyle,
> fremum on foldan   wið feonda niþ,
> deorum dædum   deofle togeanes,
> þæt hine ælda bearn   æfter hergen,
> ond his lof siþþan   lifge mid englum
> awa to ealdre,   ecan lifes blæd,
> dream mid dugeþum.
>
> *Therefore it is for all noble men the best memorial and praise of the living who remember him after death, so that before he must go hence, he should merit and achieve on earth by heroic deeds against the enmity of foes, opposing the devil, that the children of men may praise him afterwards, and his praise may live with the angels for ever and ever, the glory of eternal life, joy among the hosts.*

This is but one of a series of passages throughout the *Seafarer* which consciously play on the twin sense of certain terms, both Christian and heroic,[135] most notably *drihten*, which in the space of three lines refers to lords both secular and spiritual.[136] Such passages amply demonstrate the way in which Anglo-Saxon audiences were well-attuned to the dual sense of certain terms, and to the twin values implied. Even while employing words like *milde*, *monðwære*, and *liðe*, which have morally positive

130 Bethurum, ed., *The Homilies of Wulfstan*, *Sermo* 10c, p. 207/128; Jost, ed., *Die 'Institutes of Polity, Civil and Ecclesiastical'*, p. 262.

131 Schröer, ed., *Die angelsächsischen Prosabearbeitungen der Benediktinerregel*, pp. 18/18, 54/9, and 55/3; Schroer, ed., *Die Winteney-Version der Regula S. Benedicti*, pp. 71/22 and 73/9. The word *lofgeorn* also occurs in the appropriate place in the variant texts of the vernacular Rule in Durham, Cathedral library, B. IV. 4 and London, British Library, Cotton Tiberius A. iii; see further Frank and Cameron, ed., *A Plan for the Dictionary of Old English*, no. B.10.3.2, and Venezky and Healey, *A Microfiche Concordance*. On *lofgeorn*, see further below, pp. 56–7.

132 Cf. Stanley, 'Hæthenra Hyht in *Beowulf*', pp. 147–9.

133 Cf. *Andreas*, line 693, 878, 1308; *Elene*, line 1291; *The Wanderer*, line 17.

134 See further Tolkien, 'Beowulf, the Monsters, and the Critics', pp. 280–7; Richards, 'A Reexamination of *Beowulf* ll. 3180–3182', pp. 166–7.

135 Greenfield, 'Attitudes and Values in *The Seafarer*', pp. 18–20.

136 Cf. Gordon, ed., *The Seafarer*, pp. 26–7.

senses in both Christian and heroic terms, it is surely striking that the *Beowulf*-poet uses the superlative form, which might presumably be thought more appropriate in a secular encomiastic context.

As for the superlative form of *lofgeorn*, the positive moral sense of which is far from clear in Christian terms, one might well compare the difficulties perceived by Bede in praising a mighty pagan who was 'most desirous of glory' (*gloriae cupidissimus*):[137]

> His temporibus regno Nordanhymbrorum praefuit rex fortissimus et gloriae cupidissimus Aedilfrid, qui plus omnibus Anglorum primatibus gentem uastauit Brettonum, ita ut Sauli quondam regi Israeliticae gentis comparandus uideretur, excepto dumtaxat hoc, quod diuinae erat religionis ignarus. Nemo enim in tribunis, nemo in regibus plures eorum terras, exterminatis uel subiugatis indigenis, aut tributarias genti Anglorum, aut habitabiles fecit. Cui merito poterat illud, quod benedicens filium patriarcha in personam Saulis dicebat, aptari: 'Beniamin lupus rapax; mane comedet praedam, et uespere diuidet spolia.'
>
> *At this time there was in control of the kingdom of Northumbria a king who was most mighty and most desirous of glory, Æthelfrith, who more than all the leaders of the English devastated the Britons, in such a way that he seemed comparable to Saul, the one-time king of the Israelites, save only that he was ignorant of divine religion. For none of all the ealdormen, none of the kings, made more of their land, once the inhabitants had been annihilated or subdued, either subservient to the English nation or habitable to them. To him might properly be thought fitting that which the patriarch, blessing his son in the person of Saul, once said: 'Benjamin is a ravening wolf, in the morning he shall devour the prey, and in the evening he shall divide the spoil.'*

The comparison with Saul is instructive; for his was no exemplary life, as Eric Stanley has pointed out,[138] citing King Alfred's observations in his translation of Gregory's *Pastoral Care*:[139]

> Swæ swæ Saul Israhela kyning ðurh eaðmodnesse he geearnode ðæt rice, ond for ðæs rices heanesse him weoxon ofermetto. For eaðmodnesse he wæs ahafen ofer oðre menn, ond for ofermettum he wæs aworpen.
>
> *Just as Saul, the king of the Israelites, earned that kingdom through humility, and because of the prestige of that kingdom he grew proud. For his humility he was raised up above other men, and for his pride he was cast down.*

137 Colgrave and Mynors, ed., *Bede's Ecclesiastical History*, p. 116; a footnote suggests that 'the phrase "most eager for glory" reminds one of the OE word "domgeorn" used in such Anglo-Saxon poems as *The Wanderer* and *Judith* [*sic*] to describe the typical heroic warrior. The whole chapter may well be influenced by some lost heroic poem celebrating the deeds of Æthelfrith.'

138 Stanley, 'Hæthenra Hyht in *Beowulf*', p. 148.

139 Sweet, ed., *King Alfred's West-Saxon Version of Gregory's 'Pastoral Care'*, I, p. 112.

Beowulf, like Æthelfrith (and Saul), a heroic king, and equally 'most eager for praise' (*lofgeornost*), is, also, like Æthelfrith, a pagan, and no amount of special pleading can save him: 'to be a heathen is sin enough'.[140] If, as we have seen, there are close parallels to be drawn between the exploits of Beowulf and those of the mighty monster-slaying heroes of the classical past, like Alexander the Great, or (as we shall see) Hercules, then there are also elements clearly drawn from biblical and patristic sources which hint more darkly at the hell-fire and perdition that is the lot of all heathens. It may well be that from a Christian perspective the doubtless heroic Beowulf, in the closing words of the poem which celebrates his mighty deeds, like Alexander and Hercules, would seem damned with feigned praise.

140 Stanley, 'Hæthenra Hyht in *Beowulf*', p. 150.

CHAPTER III

The Kin of Cain

The only biblical events certainly alluded to in *Beowulf* are Cain's killing of Abel and the Flood, which together are described in three separate passages (lines 102–14, 1258–68, and 1688–93).[1] The poet links both biblical themes through the 'race of giants' (*giganta cyn*), who sprang from Cain's exile and curse, rose up against God, and were punished for their presumption by the Flood. Grendel and his mother come from similar stock, being themselves of the kin of Cain, although they are not of precisely the same race of giants; the poet is careful to use the biblical term *gigant* only of those who were drowned in the flood.[2] Presumably the poet has been influenced in this by the flat biblical statement (Isaiah XXVI.14) that 'the giants shall not rise again' (*gigantes non resurgent*), a notion widely repeated in patristic circles by, for example, Augustine (*De civitate Dei* XV.23).[3] On the face of it the poet has assimilated a number of disparate biblical and patristic traditions concerning the origins of giants, the progeny of Cain, the causes of the Flood, and the post-diluvian survival of monsters, as successive commentators have demonstrated.[4] But none of these commentators has been able to agree either on the extent of the poet's background knowledge of traditions apparently widely scattered in the written record, nor on the significance to be attached to such knowledge; it is the very uniqueness of this biblical perspective offered on Grendel and his mother which merits fresh inspection, in order to ascertain more closely both the poet's purpose and the range of Insular attitudes towards the kin of Cain.

The initial allusion to these linked traditions in *Beowulf* follows hard on the first occasion on which Grendel is named, once Hrothgar and the Danes are happily established in their newly-built Heorot (lines 99–114):

1 Klaeber, ed., *Beowulf*, p. xlix.

2 The term *gigant* is only found in one further place in Old English verse, *Genesis A*, line 1268, where *gigantmæcgas* again refers exclusively to the antediluvian race of giants.

3 Cf. Bandy, 'Cain, Grendel, and the Giants of *Beowulf*', p. 240.

4 See particularly Emerson, 'Legends of Cain'; Crawford, 'Grendel's Descent from Cain'; Peltola, 'Grendel's Descent from Cain Reconsidered'; Melinkoff, 'Cain's Monstrous Progeny in *Beowulf*: Part I, Noachic Tradition'; Melinkoff, 'Cain's Monstrous Progeny in *Beowulf*: Part II, Post-Diluvian Survival'; Williams, *Cain and Beowulf*.

Swa ða dryhtguman dreamum lifdon,
eadiglice, oð ðæt an ongan
fyrene fre(m)man feond on helle;
wæs se grimma gæst Grendel haten,
mære mearcstapa, se þe moras heold,
fen ond fæsten; fifelcynnes eard
wonsæli wer weardode hwile,
siþðan him Scyppend forscrifen hæfde
in Caines cynne – þone cwealm gewræc
ece Drihten, þæs þe he Abel slog;
ne gefeah he þære fæhðe, ac he hine feor forwræc,
Metod for þy mane mancynne fram.
Þanon untydras ealle onwocon,
eotenas ond ylfe ond orcneas,
swylce gigantas, þa wið Gode wunnon
lange þrage; he him ðæs lean forgeald.

So those noble men lived in joys, happily, until one began to perform wicked deeds, a fiend in hell; the grim spirit was called Grendel, a well-known wanderer in the borderland wastes, he who inhabited the moors, the fen and the fastness; the unhappy man dwelt for a while in the land of the monster-race, after the Creator had condemned him as one of the kin of Cain: the eternal Lord avenged that killing, because Cain slew Abel; he did not rejoice in that feud, but the Creator cast him far out for that crime, away from mankind. Thence arose all the evil breed: giants and elves and evil monsters, also those gigantic ones who strove against God for a long time; he repaid them for that.

A number of important details are given here. We learn that Grendel is essentially a monstrous exile, a man-shaped creature exciting a degree of pity (*wonsæli wer*),[5] whose dwelling-place is described or implied by a bewildering number of terms (*mearc*, *moras*, *fen*, *fæsten*, and *fifelcynnes eard*) which have as their common feature their remoteness from human habitation.[6] There is perhaps a certain restlessness implied by the number of abodes mentioned, as by the detail that he dwelt in one 'for a time' (*hwile*); elsewhere Hrothgar makes a similar point in his description of Grendel's activities (lines 159–63):

(ac se) æglæca ehtende wæs,
deorc deaþscua, duguþe ond geoguþe,
seomade ond syrede; sinnihte heold
mistige moras; men ne cunnon,
hwyder helrunan hwyrftum scriþað.

5 See further the comments of Baird, 'Grendel the Exile', pp. 378–9; below, pp. 60–4.

6 Emerson, 'Legends of Cain', pp. 865–7, suggests that the passage from *fifelcynnes eard* onwards refers exclusively to Cain, arguing from a number of parallel passages in Middle English; as we shall see, such a suggestion is not incompatible with the identification of Grendel and Cain.

But the awesome one kept on persecuting, the dark death-shadow, lurked and plotted against young and old; held the misty moors in perpetual night; men do not know where such wicked creatures go in their wanderings.

The key phrase here is *hwyrftum scriþað* (line 163), used also by the author of *Christ and Satan* to describe the judgment of the damned (lines 628–32):[7]

Sona æfter þæm wordum werige gastas,
helle hæftas, hwyrftum scriþað
þusendmælum, and þider leadað
in þæt sceaðena scræf, scufað to grunde
in þæt nearwe nið.

Immediately after these words, weary spirits, captives of hell, go in their wanderings in thousands, and there they are despised, in that lair of hostile ones, push on to the depths in that narrow persecution.

The description of the damned here in *Christ and Satan* closely matches what we learn of Grendel elsewhere in *Beowulf*; he too is described as both a 'weary spirit' (*wergan gastes*)[8] and a 'captive of hell' (*helle hæfton*).[9] In the latter case it has been argued that the poet is simply offering a calque on the well-known Latin description of the Devil and each of the damned as a 'captive of hell' (*captivus inferni*), and the phrase has been put forward as but one of a host of examples demonstrating the familiarity of the poet of *Beowulf* with a range of biblical and Christian-Latin texts.[10]

Tom Hill has gone further, plausibly suggesting that the phrase *hwyrftum scriþað* carries the basic sense 'move on in circles' in both *Beowulf* and *Christ and Satan*, and may be traced to the first clause of Psalm XI.9, where it is noted that 'the impious walke round about' (*impii in circuitu ambulant*).[11] As Hill demonstrates, the doctrine was elaborated upon by successive patristic commentators, particularly Augustine,[12] and in Insular sources is found in several Hiberno-Latin saints' Lives, where, as Charles Plummer notes: 'criminals wander fruitlessly round and round, often returning unconsciously to the scenes of their misdeeds'.[13] The same verse, Psalm

7 Cf. the translation by Hill, 'The Return of the Broken Butterfly', p. 275.

8 *Beowulf*, line 133; but see Klaeber, ed., *Beowulf*, p. 133.

9 *Beowulf*, line 788; cf. Whitelock, *The Audience of Beowulf*, pp. 10–11; Klaeber, 'Die christlichen Elemente im Beowulfe', *Anglia* 35 (1911), 254; Bartelinck, 'Les dénominations du diable', pp. 411–12.

10 Klaeber, 'Die christlichen Elemente im Beowulfe', *Anglia* 35 (1911), 111–35, 248–70, 453–82; 36 (1912), 169–99. Cf. Whitelock, *The Audience of Beowulf*, pp. 5–12.

11 Hill, '*Hwyrftum scriþað*'; his reasoning was criticised by Greenfield, 'Old English Words', but Greenfield's observations have themselves been comprehensively rebutted by Hill, 'The Return of the Broken Butterfly'. For the sense of *scriþað*, which is used to describe the movements of Grendel, and the Dragon, and other creatures in *Beowulf*, see now Watanabe, 'Monsters Creep?'.

12 Hill, '*Hwyrftum scriþað*', pp. 380–1.

13 Plummer, ed., *Vitae Sanctorum Hiberniae*, I, p. clxviii; quoted (with incorrect reference) by Hill, 'The Return of the Broken Butterfly', p. 381.

XI.9, is invoked by Gregory the Great in his exegesis on the celebrated response of Satan to God's question as to where he had come from (Job II.3): 'I have gone round about the earth, and walked through it' (*Circuivi terram et perambulavi eam*).[14]

In all this, then, Grendel is a true heir of Cain, who, as the *Beowulf*-poet tells us (lines 109–10), was exiled for his crime 'far from mankind' (*feor . . . mancynne fram*), and both Stanley Greenfield and Joseph Baird have stressed the importance of such exile imagery in the poet's depiction of Grendel.[15] Such a view was fully sanctioned by patristic commentary; according to the Septuagint (Genesis IV.16) Cain was driven from the face of God into the land of Nod (*Naid*), where the Vulgate simply makes him an 'exile' (*profugus*). In his interpretation of the passage Bede addresses both readings, and reconciles them through the traditional Hebrew etymology of *Naid*, enshrined by Jerome, as 'movement or fluctuation' (*motus siue fluctuatio*).[16] Bede goes on to conclude, following Isidore, that 'Cain was to be for ever unstable and wandering, of uncertain abode' (*Cain instabilis semper et fluctuans atque incertarum sedium esset futurus*).[17] In *Beowulf* we are told that Cain went 'guilty' or 'marked' (*fag*) into the wastes, in a passage (lines 1263–7) which, in its similar phraseology, is clearly intended to recall the first allusion to the kin of Cain already noted above:

> he þa fag gewat
> morþre gemearcod mandream fleon,
> westen warode. Þanon woc fela
> geosceaftgæsta; wæs þæra Grendel sum,
> heorowearh hetelic
>
> *He went then stained [or 'guilty'], marked with murder, to flee from the joys of men; he inhabited the wilderness. Thence sprang a multitude of fated spirits, of which Grendel was one, a hateful and savage outcast.*

Grendel too, of course, is *fag*,[18] and is explicitly described as the 'enemy of mankind' (*feond mancynnes*; *mancynnes feond*), shortly after each of the passages on Cain (lines 164 and 1276), so underlining the parallel still further.

Other Anglo-Saxons apart from the *Beowulf*-poet contemplated the fate of Cain, of course, including Bede, who in his exegetical commentary on Genesis IV.11–12 apparently introduces the notion that the exiled Cain could find no rest, giving the following bleak description as but one aspect of God's curse:[19]

14 Cf. Hill, '*Hwyrftum scripað*', pp. 380–1.

15 Baird, 'Grendel the Exile', p. 380; Greenfield, 'The Formulaic Expression of the Theme of "Exile" in Anglo-Saxon Poetry', p. 205; *Hero and Exile*, p. 130.

16 Lagarde, ed., *Liber interpretationis hebraicorum nominum*, p. 69; cf. Jones, ed., *Libri quatuor in principium Genesis*, p. 85, lines 442–3.

17 Ibid., lines 446–7; cf. Isidore, *Quaestiones in uetus testamentum* I.vi.19, PL 83, cols. 226–7.

18 *Beowulf*, lines 978 and 1001; cf. line 811: *he [wæs] fag wið God.*

19 Jones, ed., *Libri quatuor in principium Genesis*, pp. 78–9, lines 216–18; cf. Williams, *Cain and Beowulf*, p. 25.

ut in eadem terra uagus semper esset et profugus, neque ausus uspiam sedes habere quietas.

That he should always be a wanderer and an exile in the same earth, and never dare to have a peaceful abode anywhere.

Bede was successively followed in his interpretation by Alcuin and Hrabanus Maurus, both of whom repeat the notion that Cain was denied a 'peaceful abode' (*sedes quietas*).[20] From a germanic point of view, of course, it is central to the notion of exile that the sufferer is cut off from normal social relations with his lord, and this indeed seems to be the sense behind one of the most puzzling cruces in the poem, describing Grendel's activities in Heorot (*Beowulf*, lines 166–9):[21]

Heorot eardode,
sincfage sel swеartum nihtum; –
no he þone gifstol gretan moste,
maþðum for Metode, ne his myne wisse.

He occupied Heorot, the treasure-adorned hall, through dark nights;
he was not allowed by the Creator to show respect for the gift-throne,
the precious thing, nor did he feel love for it.

Another germanic source, this time the Old Saxon *Genesis* on which the author of the Old English *Genesis B* drew, describes Cain's exile in substantially similar terms (lines 75–8):[22]

Fluhtik scalt thu thoh endi freðig forduuardas nu
libbean an thesum landa, so lango thu thit liaht uuaros.
Forhuatan sculun thi hluttra liudi. thu ni salt io furthur
cuman te thines herron sprako,]
uueslean thar mid uuorðon thinon.

As an exile and a wanderer from now on you shall dwell in this land, as long as you endure the light. Pure folk shall curse you; you shall never again come to the assembly of your lord, exchange words there.

20 Alcuin, *Interrogationes et responsiones in Genesin*, 89, PL 100, col. 525: *Quod est signum Cain, quod posuit Deus, ut non occideretur? Ipsum videlicet signum, quod tremens et profugus semper viveret; nec audere uspiam orbis terrarum sedes habere quietas*; cf. Hrabanus Maurus, *Commentarium in Genesim II*, PL 107, cols. 506–7. Alcuin is here simply combining Bede's words already quoted with a further passage, Jones, ed., *Libri quatuor in principium Genesis*, p. 80, lines 274–6: *ipsum uidelicet signum quod tremens et gemens uagusque et profugus semper uiueret.*

21 My translation here follows the interpretation of Robinson, 'Why is Grendel's Not Greeting the *Gifstol* a *Wræc Micel*?', p. 262. Equally attractive is the suggestion by Bammesberger, 'Five *Beowulf* Notes', pp. 243–8, to interpret the half-line *maþðum for Metode* as *maþðum formetode*, the latter implying a preterite of a verb *formetian* ('despise'). Robinson, 'Why is Grendel's Not Greeting the *Gifstol* a *Wræc Micel*?', p. 261, equally sanctions this view.

22 Doane, ed., *The Saxon Genesis*, pp. 239 and 316; cf. Emerson, 'Legends of Cain', p. 863; Williams, *Cain and Beowulf*, p. 26.

One might also compare the account of Cain's crime and punishment in *Genesis A* (lines 1013–21), which echoes the descriptions of Grendel offered by the poet of *Beowulf*:[23]

þu þæs cwealmes scealt
wite winnan   and on wræc hweorfan,
awyrged to widan aldre.   Ne seleð þe wæstmas eorðe
wlitige to woruldnytte,   ac heo wældreore swealh
halge of handum þinum;   forþon heo þe hroðra oftihð,
glæmes grene folde.   Þu scealt geomor hweorfan,
arleas of earde þinum,   swa þu Abele wurde
to feorhbanan;   forþon þu flema scealt
widlast wrecan,   winemagum lað.

You shall forever for this killing win punishment, and go into exile, accursed for ever. Nor shall the earth grant you fair fruits for your worldly use, but the holy one has swallowed the blood of slaughter from your hands; therefore she shall hold back from you her comforts, the green earth her beauty. Sadly you must go, graceless from your land, since you were Abel's slayer, therefore you must tread the exile's path, a fugitive, hateful to your dear kinsmen.

The image of Cain as a hated fugitive can be matched by a number of the characters in *Beowulf*, including both Grendel and the fallen prince, Heremod, as we have seen; here again it seems possible that the *Beowulf* poet has allowed biblical material to influence his description.[24]

Other aspects of Christian tradition seem to have coloured the poet's depiction of Grendel. So the gruesome description of Grendel's attack concentrates on just those aspects which would cause most offence to a Christian audience (lines 739–45):

Ne þæt se aglæca   yldan þohte,
ac he gefeng hraðe   forman siðe
slæpende rinc,   slat unwearnum,
bat banlocan,   blod edrum dranc,
synsnædum swealh;   sona hæfde
unlyfigendes   eal gefeormod,
fet ond folma.

Nor did the dread one think to delay, but he quickly seized at the first opportunity a sleeping warrior, tore him greedily, bit the joints, drank the blood from the veins, swallowed in sinful gulps [or 'mighty gulps']; he had soon taken full care of the feet and hands of the unliving man.

23 Emerson, 'Legends of Cain', pp. 864–5; cf. *Genesis A*, lines 1049–51: 'Then Cain departed, sad at heart, from God's sight, a friendless exile' (*Him þa Cain / gewat gongan geomormod Gode of gesyhðe, / wineleas wrecca*).

24 See above, pp. 59–60.

The full horror of this cannibalistic feasting is savoured in detail, and to Christian ears must have sounded an unholy offence: there are numerous biblical prohibitions against the drinking of blood, and, as Fred Robinson has pointed out, a great range of Anglo-Saxons, including Bede, Alfred, Ælfric, and Wulfstan, all demonstrate 'an almost obsessive concern with the Old Testament injunction against the drinking of blood'.[25] In the biblical account, it is perhaps significant that after the Flood the eating of many things was permitted (Genesis IX.4), but the consuming of blood alongside flesh was specifically forbidden by God to Noah and his sons (*excepto quod carnem cum sanguine non comedetis*). The poet of *Genesis A* is still more specific at this point in his narrative, making the same link between the consuming of blood and the committing of sin as the *Beowulf*-poet (lines 1518–20):[26]

> Næfre ge mid blode beodgereordu
> unarlice eowre þicgeað,
> besmiten mid synne sawldreore.
>
> *Never impiously, smitten with sin, consume your food with blood, soul-gore.*

Bede, commenting on the same biblical verse, is quick to connect this injunction with the foul practices of the antediluvian giants:[27]

> Ferunt autem quod in hoc maxima fuerit preuaricatio gigantum, quia cum sanguine carnem comederent; ideoque Dominus, illis diluuio exstinctis, carne quidem uesci homines concesserit, sed ne id cum sanguine facerent prohibuerit.
>
> *They say what has been in this matter the greatest sin of the giants, that they consumed flesh with blood; and so the Lord, once he had obliterated them in the Flood, permitted men to eat flesh, but forbade that they eat it with blood.*

The notion that the antediluvian giants ate both flesh and blood can be found echoed in the apocryphal Book of Enoch, more precisely I Enoch, as a number of commentators have pointed out,[28] in a passage which ultimately depends on Genesis VI (I Enoch VII.2–6):[29]

> And [the daughters of men] became pregnant, and bore large giants, and their height was three thousand cubits. These devoured all the toil of men, until men were unable to sustain them. And the giants turned against them in order to devour men. And they began to sin against birds, and against animals, and against reptiles, and against fish, and they devoured one another's flesh and drank the blood from it. Then the earth complained about the lawless ones.

25 Robinson, 'Lexicography and Literary Criticism', pp. 102–3; amongst the more important of the strict biblical injunctions against consuming blood, most of which are noted by Robinson, may be considered the following: Leviticus XVII.10–14; XIX.26; Deuteronomy XII.16 and 23; XV.23.

26 Robinson, 'Lexicography and Literary Criticism', p. 103.

27 Jones, ed., *Libri quatuor in principium Genesis*, p. 132, lines 2138–41; cf. Williams, *Cain and Beowulf*, pp. 14–15; Peltola, 'Grendel's Descent from Cain Reconsidered', p. 289.

28 Kaske, '*Beowulf* and the Book of Enoch', p. 424; Melinkoff, 'Cain's Monstrous Progeny in *Beowulf*: Part I, Noachic Tradition', p. 149.

29 Sparks, ed., *The Apocryphal Old Testament*, p. 190.

Ruth Melinkoff and R. E. Kaske have both argued for the direct influence of traditions from I Enoch and other apocryphal texts, such as the Book of Jubilees, on *Beowulf*.[30] Other indications of the influence of I Enoch in Anglo-Saxon England have been detected in the works of Bede, the Book of Cerne, and the Old English verse *Solomon and Saturn*, and further traces of the work have also been alleged in a Hiberno-Latin setting.[31] A single twenty-five line fragment in British Library, Royal 5. E. xiii, constitutes the only extant manuscript evidence for the text in Anglo-Saxon England.[32]

The consumption of blood is a feature which links not only Grendel and the antediluvian giants, all of whom can in some sense be said to come from the kin of Cain, but is also an essential part of Cain's own story, and is given as a prime reason for God's curse (Genesis IV.11):

> Nunc igitur maledictus eris super terram, quae aperuit os suum et suscepit sanguinem fratris tui de manu tua.
>
> *Now therefore you will be cursed across the earth, who opened her mouth and received your brother's blood from your hand.*

In substantially similar terms, the Anglo-Saxon author of *Genesis A* (lines 1016–17) describes how the holy earth swallowed blood from Cain's hands (*ac heo wældreore swealh/ halge of handum þinum*); both Aldhelm (*Carmen de virginitate*, lines 2725–9) and the author of *Genesis A* (lines 985–95), in what are probably connected passages,[33] saw in Cain's defiling of the earth with blood the roots of spreading malignancy.

A substantially similar notion concerning the origins of worldly strife is found in a curious passage in the Old English poem *Maxims I* (lines 192–200), as Patrizia Lendinara has noted:[34]

> Wearð fæhþo fyra cynne, siþþan furþum swealg
> eorðe Abeles blode. Næs þæt andæge nið,
> of þam wrohtdropan wide gesprungon,
> micel mon ældum, monegum þeodum

30 Cf. n. 28 above.

31 Melinkoff, 'Cain's Monstrous Progeny in *Beowulf*: Part I, Noachic Tradition', p. 160, quoting Kaske, '*Beowulf* and the Book of Enoch', pp. 421–3; Dumville, 'Biblical Apocrypha and the Early Irish', pp. 330–1. See further Biggs, 'I Enoch', in Biggs, Hill, and Szarmach, *Sources of Anglo-Saxon Literary Culture: a Trial Version*, pp. 25–7.

32 Kaske, '*Beowulf* and the Book of Enoch', p. 423. The fragment appears on fols. 79v–80r, and is edited by James, *Apocrypha Anecdota*, pp. 146–50. The manuscript is no. 459 in Gneuss, 'A Preliminary List', where it is described as probably of ninth-century Breton origin, with a Worcester provenance; cf. Dumville, 'Biblical Apocrypha and the Early Irish', p. 331.

33 The connection was first suggested by Charles D. Wright, in a paper, entitled 'The Blood of Abel and the Branches of Sin: *Genesis A*, *Maxims I* and Aldhelm's *De Virginitate*', delivered at the fourth conference of the International Society of Anglo-Saxonists in Stony Brook, but as yet unpublished.

34 Lendinara, 'Un'allusione ai Giganti', p. 87.

bealoblonden nið. Slog his broðor swæsne
Cain, þone cwealm nerede; cuþ wæs wide siþþan
þæt ece nið ældum scod, swa atole waran
drugon wæpna gewin wide geond eorþan,
ahogodan ond ahyrdon heoro sliþendne.

Feud occurred for the kin of men, since the earth first swallowed Abel's blood. That was not the horror of a single day, that sprang far and wide from those drops of strife, a great wickedness for men, for many nations, a dread-mingled menace. Cain slew his beloved brother; killing preserved him. It was widely known afterwards that eternal strife harmed men, as the dread inhabitants experienced the contention of weapons widely throughout the earth, invented and tempered the cruel sword.

One is reminded that in the Book of Enoch it is the fallen Angels of Genesis VI who are specifically credited with teaching metalwork and weapon-smithying to men,[35] just as Genesis IV.22 describes how one of Cain's descendants, Tubal-cain, was a master at the working of brass and iron. It was presumably some such tissue of connections between the art of the weapon-smith and the giants of the Flood that led the *Beowulf*-poet to describe the sword with which Beowulf kills Grendel's mother and decapitates Grendel as a work of just such giants (lines 1557–62):[36]

Geseah ða on searwum sigeeadig bil,
ealdsweord eotenisc, ecgum þyhtig,
wigena weorðmynd; þæt [wæs] wæpna cyst, –
buton hit wæs mare ðonne ænig mon oðer
to beadulace ætberan meahte,
god ond geatolic, giganta geweorc.

He saw then among the war-gear a victory-blessed blade, an ancient giant sword, doughty of edge, glory of battle; that was the best of weapons, except that it was bigger than any other man could carry to the battle-play, fine and noble, the work of giants.

In what has been seen as a further reflection of the Flood, the blade of this giant sword is described as melting in the blood of Grendel and his mother in the same

35 Cf. I Enoch VIII.1: 'And Azazel taught men to make swords, and daggers, and shields and breastplates'. Elsewhere (I Enoch LXIX.6) this 'honour' is ascribed to another of the fallen angels, when the author is cataloguing each of their characteristics: 'And the name of the third is Gadreel: this is the one who showed all the deadly blows to men; and he led astray Eve, and he showed the weapons of death to the children of men, the shield and the breastplate and the sword for slaughter, and all the weapons of death to the sons of men.' Cf. the (at times confused) discussions by Bamberger, *Fallen Angels*, p. 19, and Peltola, 'Grendel's Descent from Cain Reconsidered', p. 290.

36 Cf. the further descriptions of the same sword in *Beowulf* as 'the ancient work of giants' (*enta ærgeweorc*, line 1679) and 'the work of wondrous smiths' (*wundorsmiþa geweorc*, line 1681).

way that ice melts in the spring thaw by the authority of God (lines 1605–11).[37] It is this very hilt which Beowulf brings back, along with Grendel's severed head, as booty from the monster-mere, and which he hands over to Hrothgar for inspection (lines 1687–93):

hylt sceawode,
ealde lafe, on ðæm wæs or writen
fyrngewinnes, syðþan flod ofsloh,
gifen geotende giganta cyn,
frecne geferdon; þæt wæs fremde þeod
ecean Dryhtne; him þæs endelean
þurh wæteres wylm Waldend sealde.

He gazed on the hilt, the ancient heirloom, on which had previously been inscribed the origin of ancient struggle, when the flood, the streaming ocean, slew the race of Giants (they suffered terribly [or 'they dared boldly']); that was a race hostile to the eternal Lord; to them the Ruler gave recompense through the surging of the water.

Malcolm Godden has pointed out the circularity inherent in the invocation of the biblical tale: 'as Grendel is introduced by a reference to the Old Testament legend which described the origin of monsters, so his end is announced by an allusion to the biblical myth of their destruction.'[38] At this point, evidently inspired by the sight of the hilt, with its depiction of overweening ambition laid low, Hrothgar launches into his famous 'sermon' (lines 1700–84), warning Beowulf of the dangers of pride.[39] The poet could not have made the causal connection clearer: Hrothgar's speech is introduced with the customary formula (*Hroðgar maðelode*) at line 1687a, but he does not actually break into words until line 1700, with the description of the hilt, or, more specifically, the description of Hrothgar gazing at the hilt, precisely intervening.

The notion that this sword-hilt, the work of giants, should be inscribed with the details of their demise can again be paralleled in patristic sources; Cassian, for example, describes in detail traditions which tell how the wicked Cham inscribed foul antediluvian secrets on metal and stone, to preserve them from the Flood:[40]

> Quantum itaque traditiones ferunt, Cham filius Noe, qui superstitionibus istis et sacrilegis ac profanis erat artibus institutus, sciens nullum se posse super his memorialem librum in arcam prorsus inferre, in qua erat una cum patre iusto ac sanctis fratribus ingressurus, scelestas artes ac profana commenta diversorum metallorum lamminis, quae scilicet aquarum conrumpi inundatione non

37 Viswanathan, 'On the Melting of the Sword', pp. 361–2; cf. the detailed discussion of this and related passages in both *Beowulf* and the *Liber monstrorum* below, pp. 111–12.

38 Godden, 'Biblical Literature', p. 216.

39 For a detailed analysis of Hrothgar's 'sermon', see above, pp. 47–53; cf. Goldsmith, *Mode and Meaning*, pp. 183–209; Hansen, 'Hrothgar's "Sermon" in *Beowulf*', pp. 53–5.

40 Petschenig, *Iohannis Cassiani Conlationes*, *Conlatio* VIII.xxi.7–8, pp. 239/27–240/10; cf. Williams, *Cain and Beowulf*, p. 35.

possent, et durissimis lapidibus insculpsit. Quae peracto diluuio eadem quae celauerat curiositate perquirens sacrilegiorum ac perpetuae nequitiae seminarium transmisit in posteros.

Various traditions tell that Cham, the son of Noah, who was instructed in those superstitions and sacrileges and profane arts, knowing that he could not bring a book detailing these things into the Ark, in which he was about to go with his righteous father and holy brothers, inscribed these wicked arts and profane commentaries on sheets of various metals and on the hardest rocks, which could not be harmed by the surge of waters. When the Flood was over he sought them out with the same curiosity for sacrilegeous things with which he had hidden them, and transmitted the seeds of perpetual wickedness to later generations.

Similar traditions are reflected elsewhere in Insular sources; James Carney indicates that the medieval Irish 'Poem of Fifty Questions' (*Iarfaigid lib cóecait cest*) specifically addresses the issue of how the history of the kin of Cain survived the flood:[41]

Na da colamain caema
duronsad clanda claena
abrad eolaigh bethad bind
cia dib romair iar ndilind?
.i. na da colamain duronsad clanna Cain guru mardais a sgela iar ndilind 7 frith in colomu [lecda] 7 ní frith in columa aelda.

The two fair columns which unclean races made, let the knowledgeable ones of the fair world say, which of them lasted after the Flood? That is, the descendants of Cain made two columns so that their history would survive after the flood, and one was of stone and the other lime.

A further mid-eighth century Hiberno-Latin work, the *Liber de numeris*, notes a related tradition that Cham wrote letters on lead plates and stones so that they would not be destroyed in the Flood, while the same notion occurs twice in the Irish *Reference Bible*, as James E. Cross has indicated.[42]

The possibility of direct Irish influence on *Beowulf* with respect to traditions concerning the kin of Cain was considered independently by James Carney and Charles Donahue.[43] As is revealed in the first passage in *Beowulf* quoted above, which deals with Grendel and his kin, Cain's progeny were conceived of in quite definite terms (lines 111–14):

Þanon untydras   ealle onwocon,
eotenas ond ylfe   ond orcneas,
swylce gigantas,   þa wið Gode wunnon
lange þrage;   he him ðæs lean forgeald.

41 Carney, *Studies*, pp. 113–14.

42 Cross, 'Old Workings and New Seams', pp. 82 and 88, quoting from a typescript of the unpublished edition by R. E. McNally.

43 Carney, *Studies*, pp. 102–14; Donahue, 'Grendel and the *Clanna Cain*'.

> *Thence arose all the evil breed: giants and elves and evil monsters, also those gigantic ones who strove against God for a long time; he repaid them for that.*

This catalogue of monsters seems curiously particular, and has been widely interpreted by commentators. The word *untydras* is unattested elsewhere, and seems to carry the general sense 'wicked progeny', specified by the tripartite variation of *eotenas ond ylfe ond orcneas*. Of these, 'giants' (*eotenas*) and 'elves' (*ylfe*) presumably refer to man-shaped monsters large and small, while the elsewhere unparalleled *orcneas* is apparently confected from both Latin and Germanic elements, and probably carries a rather unspecific sense of 'hellish creature'.[44] The catalogue concludes with the biblical *gigantas* who strove against God, and were extinguished in the flood, thus preserving a distinction between those biblical and, in Classical terms, Titanic giants, and other *eotenas* which the author seems keen to maintain.[45] A further point that is often made in connection with this catalogue of monsters is that in this and the only later passage which deals specifically with the progeny of monsters, the manuscript shows signs of confusion as to the name of the progenitor: in the first case the scribe has changed *cames* to *caines* (line 107), and in the second case has plainly written *camp* (line 1261).[46] Such apparent confusion between Cain, son of Adam, and Cham (or Ham) son of Noah can be paralleled elsewhere, and Carney, in particular, has seized upon a similarly blurred tradition concerning the progeny of monsters in the Irish *Sex aetates mundi*, a text of no later than the eleventh century.[47] Carney cites two apparently contradictory passages from the text which are found within a few pages of each other in one manuscript, Oxford, Bodleian Library, Rawlinson B. 502,[48] fols. 41v[70]a and 42r[71]b–42v[72]a:[49]

> Ro-forcongar Dia tra for clannaib Seth na ro-chummascdais fri clanna Cain 7 na ro-clannaigdis friu 7 na tucdais mna dib. Tarmi-deochatar dano clanna Seth in forcital sin 7 tucsat ingena clainni Cain ar ba mor a c(h)aemi 7 ro-clannaigset friu dar sargud Dé conid de sin ro-geinset torothuir in domuin .i. fomoraig 7 luchorpain 7 cech n-ecosc torothorda ndodelbda ro-bui for doinib. Otchonnairc Dia immorro tictain doib dar a thimna ro-chinnistar na doíni do huilidilgenn coni[d] de tucad in diliu darsin domun do bad[ud] clainni Cain

44 Cf. Klaeber, 'Die christlichen Elemente im Beowulfe', p. 169.

45 Cf. n. 2 above.

46 In both cases, of course, the confusion is made the more acute since the figure in question is described as the killer of Abel; cf. *þæs þe he Abel slog* (line 108); *ecgbanan angan breþer* (line 1262).

47 Carney, *Studies*, pp. 102–14; cf. Donahue, 'Grendel and the *Clanna Cain*', pp. 168–9.

48 Cf. the facsimile edition by Meyer, ed., *Rawlinson B 502*.

49 Text from Tristram, ed., *Sex Aetates Mundi*, lines 206–12 and 397–412, pp. 215 and 221–2; for the translation, cf. Ó Cróinín, *The Irish Sex Aetates Mundi*, pp. 113 and 119. Cf. Carney, *Studies*, pp. 103–4; as Carney notes, the latter passage 'offers a substantially identical text' to that found in the Lebor na Huidre, which is cited by Melinkoff, 'Cain's Monstrous Progeny in *Beowulf*: Part II, Post-Diluvian Survival', p. 193, quoting the translation of Horgan, *The Irish Nennius*, pp. 7–8. Cf. Best and Bergin, ed., *Lebor na Huidre*, pp. xxvii and (especially) 5.

. . . Do senchus na fomorach 7 na torothur inso sis . . . Conid he Cam de-side cet[d]uine ro-mallachad iar ndilinn. 7 conid he comarba Cain iar ndilinn. Ocus conid huad ro-genatar luchorpain 7 fomoraig 7 goborchinn 7 cech ecosc dodelba archena fil for doinib 7 conid aire tucad dilgenn for Cannanaib 7 tucad a ferann do maccaib Israhel hi comarthu na mallachtan cetna ar ropa do sil Caim do Channanaib. Conid he sin bunad na torothur 7 ni do sil Chain doib amail ad-fiadat Goidil ar ni ro-mair ni dia sil-side iar ndilinn ar rop he fochonn na dilenn do badud clainni Cáin.

God commanded the descendants of Seth not to mingle with the descendants of Cain, and not to make children with them, nor to take wives from among them. But the descendants of Seth violated that advice, and took the maidens of the descent of Cain, for their beauty was great, and they made children with them in defiance of God, so that thence there sprang the monsters of the world, giants and leprechauns, and every monstrous and misbegotten shape folk have had. But when God saw them break his command he decided to destroy folk entirely, so therefore the Flood was sent across the world, to destroy the descendants of Cain. . . . Concerning the history of monsters, that is leprechauns and giants . . . And so Cham is the first person that was cursed after the Flood, and he is the heir of Cain after the Flood, and from him there sprang leprechauns, and giants, and horseheads, and in general every unshapely form that men have. And it is for that reason that the Canaanites were destroyed, and their land was given to the sons of Israel in token of the same curse, because the Canaanites were of the race of Cham. And that is the origin of monsters, and they are not of the seed of Cain, as the Irish say, for none of his line lived after the Flood, for it was the purpose of the Flood to drown the descendants of Cain.

Carney considers both passages to reflect disparate traditions, which he calls 'A' and 'B' respectively, going on to conclude that 'it is immediately obvious that tradition B is a re-statement of tradition A with the substitution of Ham for Cain'.[50] Such a confusion of the roles of Cain and Cham as twin progenitors of evil before and after the Flood is not, however, as unique to *Beowulf* and the *Sex aetates mundi* as Carney suggested; both Bede and Augustine, for example, link intimately the roles and characteristics of the pair.[51] Moreover, parallel confusion is also exhibited in manuscripts of other Anglo-Saxon authors throughout the period, and is found, for example, in the works of both Alcuin and Ælfric.[52]

More telling at first glance are the arguments of both Carney and Donahue concerning the precise description of the offspring of this unnatural biblical union; both maintain a close relationship between the passage from the *Sex aetates mundi* and that found in *Beowulf*, lines 111–14.[53] Combining their observations, we find the following correpondences:

50 Carney, *Studies*, p. 104; cf Donahue, 'Grendel and the *Clanna Cain*', pp. 168–9.

51 Hamilton, 'The Religious Principle in *Beowulf*', p. 320, n. 71; Donahue, 'Grendel and the *Clanna Cain*', p. 168.

52 Alcuin, *Interrogationes et Responsiones in Genesin* XCVI, printed by Migne, PL 100, col. 526; Crawford, ed., *The Old English Version of the Heptateuch*, p. 99. Cf. Williams, *Cain and Beowulf*, p. 31.

53 Carney, *Studies*, p. 105; cf. Donahue, 'Grendel and the *Clanna Cain*', p. 175.

Sex aetates mundi	*Beowulf*
de sin	þanon
ro geinset	onwocon
torothair	untydras
fomoraig	eotenas (gigantas)
luchorpáin	ylfe
goborchind	orcneas

As Carney notes; 'both the Irish word *torothor* and the Anglo-Saxon *untudor* could best be rendered by the German *Missgeburt*: abortion, monstrous birth, monster'.[54] Likewise it seems certain that both *fomoraig* and *eotenas* (and *gigantas*) refer to large monsters, and both *luchorpáin* and *ylfe* to smaller creatures. Striking as such resemblances may appear, there are, as Carney himself implicitly acknowledges, still further parallels for similarly detailed catalogues of monstrous offspring. One such is found in Isidore's *Etymologiae* XI.iii, which Carney argues to have been the ultimate source for the Irish passage,[55] and which also clearly influenced other vernacular descriptions of the kin of Cain, such as the following, from the early twelfth-century Middle High German *Genesis*:[56]

Adam gebot den chinden bi ir libe   sumeliche wurzzen ze
    miden;
dar umbe daz si si niht entarten   an der ir geburte;
sin gebot si werchurn,   ir geburt si verlurn.
Dei chint dei si gebaren   ungelich si waren;
sumelich hieten hobet als ein hunt,   sumelich hieten an den
    brusten munt
an den ahselen ogen,   dei musen sich des hobetes geloben;
sumelich bedahten sich mit den oren,   wundirlich ist ez ze
    horen.
Etlicher het einen fuz   der was michel und groz,
der lief also balde   sam ein tier datzze walde;
Etlichiu gebar ein chint   daz gie an allen vieren sam ein rint.
Sumelich vluren begarwe   [ir vil] schone varwe,
si werden swarz und eislich,   [dem do niht was gelich,
dei ogen schinen in alle stunde,   die zene waren lanch in den
    munde;
[swenne si] die liezzen plechen   so mahten si den tievil
    schrechen.
Alsolich leben liezzen die ver[chornen]   al ir aftirchomen
swie dise [inne] waren [getan]   die geschaft musen dise ozzan
    han.

54 Carney, *Studies*, p. 106.
55 Carney, *Studies*, pp. 106–8.
56 Cf. Emerson, 'Legends of Cain', pp. 883–4.

> *Adam had commanded his children, upon their lives to avoid certain herbs, that they might not thereby degenerate in their nature; his command [the descendants of Cain] disregarded, their nature they lost. The children which they bore were various; some had heads like a dog, some had mouths on their breasts, eyes on their shoulders, and had to live without heads. Some had one foot which was great and large, who straightway ran into the wood like a beast; some brought forth children that walked on all fours like cattle. Some lost altogether their beautiful complexion; they became black and terrible, there was nothing like them; their eyes were gleaming all the time, the teeth in their mouths were long; whenever they showed them they frightened the devil. Such life left the abandoned ones to all those who came after them; whatsoever inner nature the former had, such an outer nature the latter had to have.*

Every single aspect of this multiple description, from the dog-heads on, can be paralleled in Isidore's account (*Etymologiae* XI.iii.15–20), which the German author, like the *Beowulf*-poet and the Irish author of the *Sex aetates mundi*, has connected with the account of the kin of Cain.[57] Indeed, what is interesting in the German text is that the degeneration of the kin of Cain is linked to a prohibition by Adam against the eating of certain herbs, which clearly echoes the prohibition to him against eating the apple, which he too ignored. The notion of the transformation of men into bestial or monstrous forms through the eating of certain herbs, furthermore, appears to derive from Classical descriptions of the magical arts of Circe, who, according to Vergil's *Aeneid* VII.10–20 and Ovid's *Metamorphoses* XIV.245–307, changed the companions of Ulysses in just this way.[58] Her story is alluded to in Isidore's *Etymologiae* XI.iv.1, immediately after the passage in question. Isidore's text circulated widely in Insular circles,[59] and there seems no reason to suppose that the *Beowulf*-poet might not independently have made use of the relevant passage in the same way as his Irish and German counterparts.

But the account of the kin of Cain in the *Sex aetates mundi* is not the only Irish text which provides close parallels to that in *Beowulf.* The Hiberno-Latin *Reference Bible* offers a great number of interesting correspondences, and moreover the influence of this important Irish text in Anglo-Saxon England is not in doubt: extracts from the *Reference Bible* have been found in a late Anglo-Saxon manuscript from Salisbury, Cathedral Library 115, fols. 20–40v,[60] while the influence of the work has been detected on several Old English texts.[61] Two passages of the *Reference Bible* deal in detail with Cain, and have recently been edited by James Cross.[62] The

57 Similar catalogues are, of course also found in the *Wonders of the East* and the *Liber monstrorum*; see further below, pp. 86–7.

58 See further below, pp. 74–5.

59 See, for example, the preliminary survey by Ogilvy, *Books Known to the English*, pp. 166–70.

60 Cf. Wright, 'Hiberno-Latin', p. 90.

61 Cross, 'Old Workings and New Seams', pp. 78–83; Wright, 'Hiberno-Latin', pp. 90–2; Wright, *The Irish Tradition*, pp. 8, 80–1, and 236–7.

62 Cross, 'Old Workings and New Seams', pp. 92–100.

first exhibits a number of the features found in *Beowulf*, as well as commencing with a catalogue of monsters, all of whom are depicted elsewhere, for example in the *Wonders of the East* and the *Liber monstrorum*:[63]

> Sciendum est unde sunt monstra ut homo cum uno oculo in fronte et alii plantis uersis et reliqua. Alii quinquinnis concipiunt. Alii habent cornu in nares. Alii oculos in ceruice. Alii duplicia membra. In oriente homo duplex natus dua capita habens, iiijor oculos, iiijor manus, unus uenter, ii pedes. Agustinus dicit: Haec monstra a Cain nata esse; alii a Cam uel concupuerunt enim filii dei filias hominum inde nati sunt gygantes et [monstruosi] homines id est filii Seth concupuerunt filias Cain inde nati sunt gygantes et monstra ut mulus ex equa et asino, et burdo ex equo et asina. Ita in hominibus quomodo in animantibus filii enim adulterii declinant in aliud genus. Item alii a Cain[64] nati sunt monstra quia ille suas maicas artes et prestrigias antequam intrauisset in arcam scribsit in lapide quia cognouit suum patrem iustum quod non uoluisset illas maicas artes mittere in arcam. Deinde [Cam ueniens] de arca legit omne quod scribsit in lapide et docuit. Deinde per maicam artem uertuntur homines in formam animalium et bestiarum et, legimus, homines in lupos uel asinos uel in aues.
>
> *One might ask whence come monsters like the man with one eye in his forehead and another with his feet turned back, and so on. Some conceive at five years old, others have a horn on their noses, others eyes in their neck, others double limbs. In the East a double man was born with two heads, four eyes, four hands, one stomach, two feet. Augustine says that these monsters are born from Cain, others from Cham, or, if you wish, the sons of God desired the daughters of men, and thence were born giants and monstrous men, that is, the sons of Seth desired the daughters of Cain, and thence were born giants and monsters like a mule from a mare and an ass, and a donkey from a horse and an ass. So amongst men, as amongst animals, the offspring of adultery decline into another species. Again, some are born as monsters from Cain because he inscribed his magic arts and spells on stone before he entered the ark, because he knew that his father was righteous and would not wish to send magic arts into the ark. Then Cham, emerging from the ark, read everything that he had written in stone and taught it. Then through the magic art men are transformed into the shapes of animals and beasts, and, we read, men into wolves or asses or birds.*

In making his edition Cross has used as his base text, the oldest manuscript, Vatican City, Biblioteca Apostolica Vaticana, Reg. lat. 76 (s. viii–ix), emending against two further manuscripts 'only where the meaning may be unclear'.[65] Such a policy is useful in underlining the confusion in the text between Cain and Cham; here Cain is described entering the ark, but Cham leaving it. Not surprisingly, perhaps, one manuscript gives the variant *Cham* for the figure who enters the ark. In this passage, as in *Beowulf*, the *Sex aetates mundi*, and the Middle High German *Genesis* we find a catalogue of monstrous offspring. In this case, however, the source is

63 Cross, 'Old Workings and New Seams', pp. 92–3.

64 One of the three manuscripts reported, Munich, Bayerische Staatsbibliothek, clm 14276 (s. ix in.), gives the variant *Cham*; Cross, 'Old Workings and New Seams', p. 92.

65 Cross, 'Old Workings and New Seams', p. 92.

not Isidore, but Augustine, *De civitate dei* XVI.viii. Another source used by the compiler of the *Reference Bible* is clearly Cassian, *Conlationes* VIII.xxi (quoted above), whose influence on other Irish texts such as the Hiberno-Latin *Liber de numeris* or the vernacular *Iarfaigid lib cóecait cest* has already been noted.[66] If Cassian supplied the detail about the inscription of the black arts on stone to preserve them in the Flood, then the compiler of the *Reference Bible* returned briefly to Augustine, *De civitate dei* XVIII.xvii–xviii, for reference to the use of magic to transform men into animals, thus demonstrating the cut-and-paste nature of his exegetical technique.[67] An identical method is found in the second passage to discuss the progeny of monsters, which occurs more than twenty-five folios further on in the Vatican manuscript:[68]

> Nullus de genere Seth uel Enos mortuus in diluuuio fuit sed tantum de gente Cain qui non sperauerunt in Domino. Hinc illi digni pessima repentina morte deleti sunt. Agustinus: Concupuerunt filii Dei filias hominum. Agustinus dicit et Iohannis Cassianus: Cum esset inter ipsos bonos de gente Seth et illos malos de gente Cain usque nunc utilis ac sancta[69] diuisio. Uidentes post haec filii Seth, qui filii Dei erant, filias hominum, qui de Cain progenie nascebantur, desiderio pulchritudinis earum acensi acceperunt eas uxores. Hinc dicitur: 'Ego dixi, dii estis et filii excelsi omnes. Uos autem sicut homines moriemini, id est in diluuio, et sicut unus de principibus cadetis' [Psalm LXXXI.6–7], id est diabulus. Inde primitus gigantes et magi et omnes artes diabuli de illo adulterio processerunt instinctu diaboli. Hinc Cam[70] doctus filius Noe his artibus ante diluuium sciens diluuium delere totum mundum et recuperare post diluuium, et nouit suum patrem iustum et sanctam noluisset has artes magicas intrare in arcam, scribsit uel sculpsit illas in lapides et post diluuium relegit illas et docuit filiis suis. Inde hucusque magice artes et male cantationes unde homines uertuntur in lupos et in iumenta et assinos et in aues, ut sunt multe fabule. Sicut legimus Circe que socios Ulixis motauit in bestias, et Arcades natantes stagnum conuertuntur in lupos et cum similibus feris per deserta uiuunt. Si uero carne humana non uescuntur iterum post viiii annis eodem stagno renatato reformantur in homines. Si uero hominem edat non reuertit iterum in hominem.[71]
>
> *No-one of the race of Seth or Enos was killed in the Flood, but only of the kin of Cain, who did not believe in the Lord. Hence they were rightly destroyed by a sudden, most terrible, death. Augustine: the sons of God desired the daughters of men. Augustine and John Cassian said: since there was up till now a useful and holy division between the good people of the race of Seth and the bad folk of the kin of*

66 See above, p. 68.

67 Cf. the similar discussion of magical transformation in the Middle High German *Genesis* above, pp. 71–2.

68 Cross, 'Old Workings and New Seams', pp. 99–100.

69 Cross, 'Old Workings and New Seams', p. 99: *sanctam*. This is the reading of all three manuscripts, but simply will not construe.

70 Cross, 'Old Workings and New Seams', p. 99. The base text has *Cain*, but both the other manuscripts read *C[h]am*.

71 Cross, 'Old Workings and New Seams', p. 100. The base text has *homine*, but both the other manuscripts read *hominem*.

> *Cain. After this the sons of Seth, who were the sons of God, seeing the daughters of men, who were born of the kin of Cain, consumed with desire for their beauty, took them as wives. Hence it is said 'I saide: You are goddes, and the sonnes of the highest al. But you shal die as men: and fal as one of the princes', that is, the devil. Then for the first time giants and wizards and all the arts of the devil proceeded from that adultery through the instinct of the devil. Hence Cham, the son of Noah, being learned in these arts, knowing that the whole world was to be destroyed in the Flood, and after the Flood to recover, knowing that his father was righteous and just and would not wish these magic arts to enter the ark, he inscribed or engraved them in stone and after the Flood he read them again and taught them to his sons. Then to this day there are magic arts and incantations whereby men are turned into wolves and into cattle and asses and into birds, and there are many tales. Just as we read of Circe who changed the companions of Ulysses into beasts, and of the Arcades, swimming across a lake, who are turned into wolves and dwell in the wastelands with similar wild animals. If they do not eat human flesh, after they have crossed the same lake nine years later they turn back into men, but if they eat people they do not change back.*

The relationship of this passage to the earlier one is clear, and reflects the same confusion between Cain and Cham, and the latter's role in transmitting the black arts after the Flood. In this case the borrowed passages from Augustine, *De civitate dei* XVIII.xvii–xviii, dealing with the magical transformation of men into beasts, are more fully developed. The same tales are also found in a briefer form in Augustine's own sources, Isidore, *Etymologiae* XI.iv.1 and Pliny, *Naturalis Historia* VII.xxii, and (in the case of Circe) ultimately derive from accounts in Vergil , *Aeneid* VII.10–20 and Ovid, *Metamorphoses* XIV.245–307. The tale of the Arcades given here is particularly interesting in the context of the possible influence of the Irish *Reference Bible* on *Beowulf*, since the story supplies two major themes which, as Cross has noted, are crucial to the description of Grendel and his kin, namely 'cannibalism, and the ogres' home in the wasteland'.[72] One might go further, and note the extent to which the mere-dwelling Grendel and (particularly) his mother are described in lupine terms rather reminiscent of the story of the Arcades: he is a 'savage wolf' (*heorowearh*, line 1267), his mother a 'she-wolf of the depths' (*grundwyrgen*, line 1518) and (twice) a 'sea-wolf' (*brimwylf*, lines 1506 and 1599), and the mere that they both inhabit and share with similar monsters is surrounded by 'wolf-slopes' (*wulfhleoþu*, line 1358). Only the editing and publication of the entire *Reference Bible* will determine how far this idiosyncratic Irish text, the influence of which on other vernacular Old English texts is demonstrable, can be regarded as a direct source for *Beowulf*.

The reliance of the Irish *Reference Bible* on the passage already quoted from Cassian, *Conlationes* VIII.xxi is of particular interest, since elsewhere in the same passage Cassian elaborates further on the kin of Cain in familiar terms:[73]

72 Cross, 'Old Workings and New Seams', p. 82; curiously, Cross only mentions these themes to note their supposed absence in the account found in the *Reference Bible*.

73 Petschenig, *Iohannis Cassiani Conlationes*, *Conlatio* VIII.xxi.8, p. 240/12–16.

> De illis ergo quemadmodum diximus filiis Seth et filiabus Cain nequiores filii procreati sunt, qui fuerunt robustissimi venatores, violentissimi ac truculentissimi viri qui pro inormitate corporum vel crudelitatis atque malitiae gigantes sunt.
>
> *So, just as we have said, from these sons of Seth and daughters of Cain there were more wicked offspring produced, who became the mightiest hunters, most violent and difficult men who from the enormity of their bodies and cruelness and malice are giants.*

Such a reference to the sons of Seth and the daughters of Cain derives from a common exegetical tradition, beginning with Julius Africanus and endorsed by, amongst others, Augustine, explaining the cryptic but crucial passage in Genesis VI.1–2 and 4:[74]

> Cumque coepissent homines multiplicari super terram et filias procreassent, uidentes filii Dei filias eorum quod essent pulchrae, acceperunt sibi uxores ex omnibus quas elegerant . . . Gigantes autem erant super terram in diebus illis. Postquam enim ingressi sunt filii Dei ad filias hominum, illaeque genuerunt. Isti sunt potentes a seculo uiri famosi.
>
> *And after that men began to be multiplied upon the earth, and had procreation of daughters. The sonnes of God seing the daughters of men, that they were faire, tooke to themselves wives out of al, which they had chosen . . . And Giants were upon the earth in those dayes. For after the sonnes of God did companie with the daughters of men, and they brought forth children, these be the mightie of the olde worlde, famous men.*

Two conflicting traditions of exegesis sprang up around these verses, the earliest of which explains the verses as describing the strange mating of mortals and fallen angels, based on the variant reading 'angels' (ἄγγελοι) for 'sons' (*filii*) of the Septuagint, and is witnessed in such texts as the Book of Enoch and the Book of Jubilees, and by such authors as Tertullian, Origen, and Ambrose.[75] This interpretation, vehemently denounced by, amongst others, Jerome,[76] was rapidly superseded by the view, most influentially endorsed by Augustine, *De civitate Dei* XV.23, which identified the 'sons of God' with the offspring of Seth, and the 'daughters of men' with the children of Cain.[77] In Anglo-Saxon England this is the position adopted, as Emerson amply demonstrates,[78] by the author of *Genesis A*, who describes the fruit of such a miscegenation and their antipathy to God in ways which again readily recall the description of Grendel in *Beowulf* (*Genesis A*, lines 1263–9):

> Siððan hundtwelftig geteled rime
> wintra on worulde wræce bisgodon
> fæge þeoda, hwonne Frea wolde

74 Melinkoff, 'Cain's Monstrous Progeny in *Beowulf*: Part I, Noachic Tradition', pp. 146–7; Wickham, 'The Sons of God and the Daughters of Men', pp. 135–47.

75 See further Melinkoff, 'Cain's Monstrous Progeny in *Beowulf*: Part I, Noachic Tradition', p. 146.

76 Melinkoff, 'Cain's Monstrous Progeny in *Beowulf*: Part I, Noachic Tradition', p. 147.

77 Cf. Bamberger, *Fallen Angels*, pp. 78–80.

78 Emerson, 'Legends of Cain', pp. 889–91.

on wærlogan wite settan
and on deað slean dædum scyldige
gigantmæcgas, Gode unleofe,
micle mansceaðan, Metode laðe.

For the next one hundred and twenty years the doomed people were busy with evil, when the Lord wished to inflict punishment on the traitors and put to death those guilty in deed, the race of giants, unloved by God, mighty criminal destroyers, hateful to the Creator.

So, for example, in *Beowulf* Grendel is described as 'doomed' (*fæge*, line 846; cf. *deaðfæge*, line 850), 'guilty' (*scyldig*, line 1683),[79] and a 'criminal destroyer' (*manscaða*, lines 712 and 737),[80] whilst the particular hostility of God towards him is stressed more than once.[81]

What is chiefly of interest, however, in the passage from Cassian quoted above, is not so much his knowledge of a widely-prevalent tradition concerning the offspring of Seth and Cain as his reference to the sons of that union as powerful and overbearing men, the 'mightiest of hunters' (*robustissimi venatores*), since the phrase carries an implicit allusion to Nimrod, grandson of Cham, a great builder of cities, who, according to Genesis X.9, was 'mightie in the earth, and he was a valiaunt hunter before our Lord' (*potens in terra, et erat robustus uenator coram Domino*). Cassian is therefore acknowledging a tradition of post-diluvian giant warriors, derived after the Flood from the kin of Cain through Cham, and chiefly characterised by their overweening pride. Amongst Insular sources, the tradition can be traced in the tenth-century Irish *Saltair na Rann* (lines 2401–4):[82]

Roaintadaigsetar iarcein
sil Seth ocus clann Caein,
corothuismet iartain
trenfir ocus trenchoraid.

After a long time they united, the seed of Seth and the clan of Cain, so that afterwards they begot mighty men and mighty warriors.

More specifically, the same notion is echoed by Bede, in his commentary on the ultimate source-passage, Genesis VI.4:[83]

79 Cf. the further description of Grendel as *ealdres scyldig*, line 1338, where the sense is 'forfeiting his life'.

80 The same word *mansc(e)aða* is used of both Grendel's mother (line 1339), who is of the kin of Cain, and the dragon (line 2514), who is not; cf. the term 'wicked destroyer' (*manfordædla*, line 563), used of the monsters who attack Beowulf during his swimming-match with Breca.

81 So, for example, Grendel is twice described as 'God's enemy' (*Godes andsacan*, lines 786 and 1682), and as one who both 'bore God's anger' (*Godes yrre bær*, line 711) and was 'feuding with God' (*he [wæs] fag wið God*, line 811).

82 Cf. Carney, *Studies*, p. 105.

83 Jones, ed., *Libri quatuor in principium Genesis*, p. 100, lines 983–9.

Gigantes dicit homines inmensis corporibus editos ac potestate nimia preditos, quales etiam post diluuium, id est temporibus Moysi uel David multos fuisse legimus, qui nomen habent Grece ex quod illos iuxta fabulas poetarum terra genuerit. Videntur autem tunc fuisse progeniti, cum posteri Seth de stirpe Cain uxores sibi gratia pulchritudinis contra ius suae dignitatis elegerant . . . Notandum autem quo hoc in loco pro 'gigantibus,' in Hebreo 'cadentes,' id est 'annasilim,' leguntur; facilis atque absolutus est sensus, quia cadentes erant in terram homines in diebus illis, id est terrenis concupiscientiis adherentes, amisso statu Deo deuotae rectitudinis. Gigantes autem illorum lingua proprie 'Raphaim' nominantur.

It calls 'giants' men who were born with huge bodies, endowed with excessive power, such as, even after the Flood, we read that there were many in the times of Moses or David; and they have a Greek name because, according to the fables of the poets, the earth bore them. They seem to have been born when the descendants of Seth, contrary to what was appropriate to their dignity, chose wives from the kin of Cain for the sake of their beauty . . . But it should be noted that in this place for 'giants' it reads in Hebrew 'annasilim', that is, 'the falling ones'; and the sense is simple and absolute, because men were falling into the earth in those days, that is, sticking to earthly delights, having lost the state of proper devotion to God. But in that language giants are properly called 'rephaim'.

Here Bede demonstrates his impressive ability to synthesise disparate sources, preserving at once a Greek etymology, probably drawn from Isidore,[84] which would derive the word 'gigantes' from the Greek words γῆ ('earth') and γένος ('birth'),[85] alongside a Hebrew etymology, probably taken from Jerome, which would derive the word *nephilim*, which replaces Bede's variant form *annasilim* in most texts, from the root *naphal* (נפל, 'to fall').[86] Among the more striking references to giants or *rephaim* to be found in the post-diluvian biblical account are those to Nimrod (Genesis X.8–9), Og of Bashan (Deuteronomy III.11), Goliath (I Samuel XVII.4–5), and Gog of Magog (Ezekiel XXXVIII–XXXIX); all, significantly, are represented as mighty pagan warriors.[87]

It is interesting to note that Alcuin, in the passage already cited, describes the post-diluvian progeny of Sem and Cham in terms similar to that commonly used of Seth and Cain; he is discussing the same (antediluvian) biblical passage Genesis VI, concerning the Sons of God and the Daughters of Men:[88]

Filias hominum, progeniem Cham; et filios Dei sobolem Sem appellare scriptura voluit. Hi avita benedictione religiosi; illae paterna maledictione impudicae: sed

84 Isidore, *Etymologiae* XI.iii.12–14; see further below, pp. 104–5.

85 Cf. the entry in the Corpus Glossary; Hessels, ed., *An Eighth-Century Latin-Anglo-Saxon Glossary*, T93: *Terrigenae gigantes*.

86 Cf. Lagarde, ed., *Liber quaestionum hebraicarum in Genesim* VI.4, p. 10: *Nefilim cadentes*; Lagarde, ed., *Liber interpretationis hebraicorum nominum*, p. 70: *Refaim gigantes*. See further Weissmann, 'Giants and Giantism', pp. 14–15.

87 For the legends surrounding Og of Bashan in particular, see James, *The Lost Apocrypha of the Old Testament*, pp. 40–2.

88 Alcuin, *Interrogationes et Responsiones in Genesin* XCVI, printed by Migne, PL 100, col. 526.

postquam filli Sem concupiscientia victi ex filiabus Cham connubia junxerunt, et tali conjunctione homines immenso corpore, viribus superbi, moribus inconditi, quos scriptura gigantes nominat procreati sunt.

Scripture intends the Daughters of Men to signify the kin of Cham, and the Sons of God the seed of Sem. The latter are pious because of their grandfather's blessing, the former wicked because of their father's curse: but after the sons of Sem were smitten by desire for the daughters of Cham and connected with them in marriage, from such a connection there were produced men with huge bodies, proud in might, rough in manner, whom Scripture calls giants.

Alcuin's account underlines the extent to which the differences in the biblical narrative between Cain, the antediluvian progenitor of evil, and Cham, his post-diluvian counterpart, had become blurred in the patristic tradition, partly to explain the biblical insistence on the continued existence of mighty warriors called giants after the Flood.

Parallel accounts of giant warriors could, of course, be cited from pagan sources themselves; indeed it is notable that Augustine does so, quoting Vergil (*Aeneid* XII.899–900) alongside personal testimony of the great stature of heroes from bygone days (*De civitate Dei* XV.9).[89] Later on in this work (*De civitate Dei* XV.23), Augustine emphasises the point that post-diluvian worldly warriors could be considered giants by quoting from the apocryphal Book of Baruch III.26–8:[90]

Ibi fuerunt gigantes nominati illi, qui ab initio fuerunt statura magna, scientes bellum. Non hos elegit Dominus, neque viam disciplinae invenerunt, propterea perierunt; et quoniam non habuerunt sapientiam, interierunt propter suam insipientiam.

There were those called giants, who were from the beginning of great stature, expert in war. The Lord chose not them, neither did they find the way of knowledge. Therefore did they perish. And because they had not wisdom, they perished through their folly.

In drawing such explicit parallels between biblical giants and proud pagans Augustine is aligning himself with an influential school of patristic thought which sought to explain the origins of much heathen myth in biblical terms.[91] So, for example, Josephus, speaking of the biblical giants of Genesis VI in his *Jewish Antiquities* I.73, says that: 'in fact the deeds that tradition ascribes to them resemble the audacious exploits told by the Greeks of the giants' (ὅμοια γὰρ τοῖς ὑπὸ γιγάντων τετολμῆσθαι λεγομένοις ὑφ' 'Ελλῆνων καὶ οὗτοι δράσαι παραδίδονται).[92]

A still more striking attempt to reconcile biblical giants, human tyrants, and classical monsters is found in another early Insular text, the seventh-century

89 See further below, p. 105.

90 Cf. Peltola, 'Grendel's Descent from Cain Reconsidered', p. 288.

91 Cf. Emerson, 'Legends of Cain', p. 905.

92 Thackeray, ed. and trans., *Josephus, Jewish Antiquities*, pp. 34–5.

Hiberno-Latin poem *Altus prosator*, a hymn concerning the whole sweep of history of the created universe, which combines all these elements in a single stanza:[93]

> Kaduca ac tyrannica
> mundique momentanea
> regum praesentis gloria
> nutu Dei deposita;
> ecce, gigantes gemere
> sub aquis magno ulcere
> comprobantur incendio
> aduri ac supplicio
> Cocytique charybdibus
> strangulati turgentibus,
> scyllis obtecti fluctibus
> eliduntur et scrupibus.
>
> *The transitory and tyrannical momentary glory of the kings of this present world is cast down with the assent of God. Behold, the giants were shown to groan beneath the waters in great pain, to be burnt by fire and torment, choked by the swelling charybdian whirlpools of Cocytus, smothered by scyllian waves, and are crushed by the rocks.*

The explicit link between the giants groaning under the waters, ultimately derived from Job XXVI.5, and the worldly figures of the tyrannical kings is supplied in the ninth-century marginalia in the Milan manuscript of the poem:[94]

> Sicut gigantes sub diluuio gemere propter crudelem fortitudinem quam habuerant, sic reges huius seculi pro iniusticia sua ac superbia et oppressionibus pauperum proicientur in infernum.
>
> *Just as the giants groan beneath the flood because of the cruel strength which they had, so the kings of this world will be cast into hell for their injustice and pride and oppressions of the poor.*

A similar link is made by Gregory in his *Moralia in Job* XXI.30, where, commenting on Job XXVI.5,[95] he draws parallels from Wisdom XIV.6, Proverbs XXVI.16, and Isaiah XXVI.14, and considers 'all these biblical giants as those who are damned through the sin of pride'.[96] A still more likely direct source for the stanza in *Altus prosator* is the exegete Philip the Presbyter (who died in 455 or 456), a disciple of Jerome, and whose *Commentarium in librum Job* can be shown to have exerted a great influence on the poet.[97] Philip comments on Job XXVI.5 as follows:[98]

93 Stevenson, 'Altus Prosator', p. 111; Goldsmith, *Mode and Meaning*, p. 45.

94 Bernard and Atkinson, *The Irish Liber Hymnorum*, I, p. 75; II, p. 161; cited by Goldsmith, *Mode and Meaning*, p. 46.

95 Adriaen, ed., *Gregorii Magni Moralia siue Expositio in Iob*, p. 868; cf. Hamilton, 'The Religious Principle in *Beowulf*', p. 315.

96 Goldsmith, *Mode and Meaning*, p. 46.

97 Stevenson, 'Altus Prosator', pp. 213–16; the *Commentarium in librum Job* is printed by Migne, PL 26, cols. 619–802.

98 *Commentarium in librum Job*, PL 26, col. 688B.

> Gigantes autem appellat scriptura diuina homines superbos, rebelles et contumaces. Diabolus quoque, et sui, propter superbiam translato nomine gigantes nuncupantur.
>
> *Holy Scripture calls men who are proud, rebellious, and stubborn 'giants'. Also the Devil, and his kind, are called 'giants' by another name on account of their pride.*

It is clear that *Altus prosator* was known in Anglo-Saxon England from the earliest period; Aldhelm seems to have been familiar with the work, and it has been suggested that some of its more ornate vocabulary was excerpted in the oldest extant glossaries.[99] Philip the Presbyter was still more influential; he was certainly known to Bede, who cites him twice by name in his *De temporum ratione*,[100] and may have influenced Insular usage of the obscure Latin word *dodrans* ('tidal wave'), as Alan K. Brown has shown.[101] One important Anglo-Saxon manuscript of his *Commentarium in Job* has survived: Oxford, Bodleian Library 426 (s.c. 2327) (s. ix^{med}, Winchester),[102] alongside a further manuscript containing a text of Job with Anglo-Saxon glosses derived from Philip's tract: St Petersburg, Public Library F. v. 1. 3 (s. viii^{2}, Northumbria).[103] The notion that there was a direct link between biblical giants and proud men was therefore clearly current in Insular circles from a very early period, ready to be built on in the ways already discussed.

In a similar way, Alfred, in the Old English version of Boethius (*De consolatione philosophiae*, III, pr. 12),[104] greatly expands what is in the Latin the barest mention of the Classical giants who contended against heaven,[105] bringing together a number of themes discussed above:

> Hwæt, ic wat þæt ðu geherdest oft reccan on ealdum leasum spellum þætte Iob Saturnes sunu sceolde bion se hehsta god ofer ealle oðre godu, ond he sceolde bion þæs heofenes sunu, ond sceolde ricsian on heofenum; ond sceolden gigantes bion eorðan suna, ond ða sceolden ricsian ofer eorþan; ond þa sceolden hi bion swelce hi wæren geswysterna bearn, forðæmþe he sceolde beon heofenes sunu, ond hi eorðan. Ond þa sceolde þæm gigantum ofþincan þæt he hæfde hiera rice; woldon þa tobrecan þone heofen under him; þa sceolde he sendan þunras ond ligeta ond windas, ond toweorpan eall hira geweorc mid, ond hi selfe ofslean.
>
> Ðyllica leasunga hi worhton, ond meahton eaðe seggan soðspell, gif him þa

99 Orchard, *The Poetic Art of Aldhelm*, pp. 54–60; Stevenson, 'Altus Prosator', pp. 67–81.

100 Jones, ed., *De temporum ratione*, §4, p. 185; §29, p. 234; cf. Stevenson, 'Altus Prosator', p. 111.

101 Brown, 'Bede, a Hisperic Etymology, and Early Sea Poetry', pp. 419–32.

102 Gneuss, 'A Preliminary List', no. 576; *CLA* II.234.

103 *CLA* XI.1599; cf. *CLA*: VI.740: Cambrai, Bibliothèque municipale 470 (441) (s.viii^{1}), which Lowe considers to have been written by an Anglo-Saxon in a continental centre. Two further eighth-century continental manuscripts of Philip's *Commentarium in Job* are noted by Lowe, *CLA* V.701 and X.1571.

104 Sedgfield, ed., *King Alfred's Boethius*, pp. 98–9.

105 *Accepisti, inquit, in fabulis lacessentes caelum gigantes; sed illos quoque, uti condignum fuit, benigna fortitudo disposuit* ('You have heard, she said, in tales about the giants attacking heaven; but, as was only fitting, benevolent strength put them down too'); Bieler, ed., *Anicii Manilii Severini Boethii Philosophiae Consolatio*, p. 123.

leasunga næren swetran, ond þeah swiðe gelic ðisum. Hi meahton seggn hwylc dysig Nefrod se gigant worhte . . . Se Nefrod het wyrcan ænne tor on ðæm felda ðe Nensar hatte, ond on ðære þiode ðe Deira hatte, swiðe neah þære byrig þe mon nu hæt Babilonia . . . Ac hit gebyrede, swa hit cynn was, þæt se godcunda wald hi tostencte ær hi hit fullwyrcan mosten, ond towearp ðone tor, ond hiora monigne ofslog.

Now I know that you have heard often told in lying tales that Jove, son of Saturn, was to be the highest god over all the other gods, and to be the son of Heaven, and to rule in Heaven; and the giants were to be the sons of earth, and to rule over the earth; and they were to be as though they were the children of sisters, because he was to be the son of Heaven and they of Earth. And then the giants felt chagrin that he had their kingdom, and they wanted to smash Heaven under him; so he sent thunder-crashes and lightning-blasts, and wind-gusts, to cast down all their work, and kill the giants themselves. They made up lies like this, and might easily have told the truth, if those lies were not sweeter to them, and yet the truth was very like these lies. They could have told what Nimrod the foolish giant did . . . This Nimrod had built a tower on the field called Nensar, among the nation called Deira, very close to the town which people now call Babylon . . . But it turned out, as was natural, that the divine power overthrew them before they could finish it, and destroyed the tower, and slew many of them.

Apart from explicitly calling Nimrod a 'giant' (*Nefrod se gigant*), Alfred is simply following patristic tradition here, as exemplified by Isidore, *Eymologiae* VII.vi.22, who described Nimrod as a tyrant:[106]

Nembroth interpretatur tyrannus. Iste enim prior arripuit insuetam in populo tyrannidem, et ipse adgressus est adversus Deum impietatis aedificare turrem.

Nimrod is interpreted as a tyrant, for he was the first to seize unaccustomed tyranny over a people, and he strove against God in building a tower of impiety.

As Peter J. Frankis has pointed out, in describing the location of the tower as 'among the nation called Deira', Alfred appears to make a twin allusion both to *Dura*, the place where, according to the biblical account, Nebuchadnezzar of Babylon set up an idolatrous image (Daniel III.1), and to *Deira*, 'what had formerly been the southern kingdom of Northumbria, an area rich in the remains of the past, both Roman and Northumbrian, and in Alfred's day an area of pagan Scandinavian settlement'.[107]

Nor was Alfred the only Anglo-Saxon to synthesise Biblical and Classical traditions in this way. Such a blend is implicit in the very title of the series of prose and verse *Solomon and Saturn* dialogues, and the second poetic dialogue in particular has Solomon issue an allusive reminder to Saturn of the dark fate of his proud kin (*Solomon and Saturn II*, lines 318–22):[108]

106 For a detailed survey of medieval attitudes towards Nimrod, see Diane-Myrick, *From the De Excidio Troiae Historia*, pp. 158–85.

107 Frankis, 'The Thematic Significance', p. 264.

108 Menner, ed, *The Poetical Dialogues of Solomon and Saturn*, p. 96; cf. Shippey, ed., *Poems of*

Wa bið ðonne ðissum modgum monnum ðam ðe her nu mid mane lengest
lifiað on ðisse læne gesceafte! Ieo ðæt ðine leode gecyððon;
wunnon hi wið dryhtnes miehtum, forðon hie ðæt worc ne gedegdon.
Ne sceall ic ðe hwæðre, broðor, abelgan; ðu eart swiðe bittres cynnes,
eorre eormenstrynde, ne beyrn ðu in ða inwitgecyndo!

Woe, then shall there be for these proud men who live here longest with wickedness in this transitory creation! Your people made that known of old; they strove against the Lord's might, and so did not bring that work to completion. Yet I shall not enrage you, brother; you are of a very bitter kin, a fierce and mighty race: do not fall in with that wicked instinct!

Here the poet heightens reproach for proud and mighty men by linking them at once with the Titans who tried to overthrow Jove, and by condemning their ilk as a 'very bitter kin, a fierce and mighty race'.[109] In a biblical context (and we must remember that it is Solomon who is speaking) such a reference, albeit oblique, surely calls to mind the similarly damned kin of Cain, and the proud builders of the Tower of Babel. As Menner notes: 'the reference is to the building of the Tower of Babel by Saturn's ancestors, the Chaldeans'.[110] Earlier in the poem a further oblique reference is made by Solomon, linking the Chaldeans, who are again chastised for their pride, with the building of the Tower of Babel (lines 198–201):[111]

Wat ic ðæt wæron Caldeas
guðe ðæs gielpne and ðæs goldwlonce,
mærða ðæs modige, ðæt to ðam moning gelomp
suð ymbe Sanere feld.

I know that the Chaldeans were so boastful in war, so gold-proud, so arrogant in their glories, that a warning came to them, south at the field of Shinar.

The warning in question, is, of course, the destruction of the Tower of Babel at Sennar. Solomon goes on ask a question about the land that no man may tread, and is answered obliquely by Saturn in a passage which has been described as 'the most obscure in the poem' (lines 34–46):[112]

Wisdom and Learning, pp. 92–3; Emerson, 'Legends of Cain', p. 909; Kemble, *Salomon and Saturn*, p. 164.

109 The poet's use of the term *abelgan* in this context is particularly intriguing; in *Beowulf*, as we have seen, the related terms *gebolgen* and *bolgenmod* are used of Beowulf, Grendel, and Heremod. See further above, pp. 35–6.

110 Menner, ed, *The Poetical Dialogues of Solomon and Saturn*, p. 131; cf. Emerson, 'Legends of Cain', p. 909.

111 Menner, ed., *The Poetical Dialogues of Solomon and Saturn*, p. 121; Shippey, *Poems of Wisdom and Learning*, pp. 86–7.

112 Menner, ed., *The Poetical Dialogues of Solomon and Saturn*, p. 121; cf. Shippey, *Poems of Wisdom and Learning*, pp. 86–9.

Se mæra was haten   mereliðende
weallende wulf,   (wer)ðeodum cuð
Filistina,   freond Nebrondes.
He on ðam felda ofslog   fif and twentig
dracena on dægred,   and hine ða deað offeoll.
Forðan ða foldan ne mæg   fira ænig,
ðone mercestede,   mon gesecan,
fugol gefleogan,   ne ðon ma foldan n(ea)t.
Ðanon atercynn   ærest gewurdon
wide onwæcned,   ða ðe nu weallende
ðurh attres oroð   ingang rymað.
Git his sweord scinað   swiðe gescæned,
and ofer ða byrgenna   blicað ða hieltas.

That famous seafarer was called the seething wolf, well-known to the tribes of the Philistines, a friend of Nimrod. He slew on that field twenty-five dragons at daybreak, and then death befell him. Therefore no man can find that land, no person that wasteland, no bird fly there, no more than any beast of the earth. Thence first arose the poison-kin, spread widely, all those who now seething make room for attack through poisonous breath. His sword still shines, highly polished, and its hilt gleams over the burials.

Although the passage has been discussed at length several times,[113] it remains largely opaque. What is striking, however, is the way that the passage appears to allude on the one hand to the various traditions concerning Nimrod and the race of evil associated with the kin of Cain, and on the other to details also found in *Beowulf* itself. Like Beowulf, this *weallende wulf* is a famous sea-farer whose dragon-slaying killed him in the end. Moreover, just as Grendel and his mother, both mighty march-dwellers (*micle mearcstapan*) inhabit a wasteland, like the wolf-shaped Arcades mentioned by Augustine, Isidore, and the compiler of the Irish *Reference Bible*, so too the dragon-slaying here takes part in a desolate marchland (*mercstede*), which, like Grendel's mere, ordinary living creatures shun.[114] And just as the giant-sword in *Beowulf* shone out in the dwelling of Grendel's mother, so too does the dragon-slaying sword of *Solomon and Saturn*.[115]

The ability to synthesise and build imaginatively on a range of traditions concerning antediluvian giants and, after the Flood, mighty human figures of pride, was clearly not restricted to the patristic passages by Augustine, Isidore, and Cassian already quoted; in Insular circles authors as diverse in time and temperament as Bede, Alcuin, Alfred, and a host of anonymous authors, such as the compiler of the Irish *Reference Bible*, or the poets of *Altus prosator* or *Solomon and Saturn II*, were all

113 See particularly Menner, 'Nimrod and the Wolf'; Menner, ed., *The Poetical Dialogues of Solomon and Saturn*, pp. 121–6; Shippey, *Poems of Wisdom and Learning*, pp. 136–7.

114 Cf. the discussion above, pp. 44–7.

115 James, *The Lost Apocrypha of the Old Testament*, p. 41, attempted to connect the account with apocryphal legends concerning the giant Og of Bashan; see further above, pp. 77–9.

engaged in similar activity. It is against such a rich background of imaginative reconstruction on the sparse foundation of the intriguing biblical account of Genesis VI that the efforts of the *Beowulf*-poet need to be judged. If the only direct reference extant from Anglo-Saxon England outside *Beowulf* to the devilish kin of Cain is to be found in the description of the fen-dwelling demons who beset Saint Guthlac as the 'seed of Cain' (*semen Cain*),[116] it is clear that a wide range of Insular sources both allude and contribute to a fertile blend of traditions, biblical, patristic, Classical, and popular, concerning the theme. *Beowulf* combines a similarly rich mixture of traditions, in which proud and mighty pagan heroes jostle strangely with monstrous biblical figures. For a further Insular example of such fusion of Christian and pagan attitudes and characters we may turn to a curious text concerning monsters, which has long been associated with *Beowulf*: the *Liber monstrorum*.

116 In the Latin *Vita S. Guthlaci*; cf. Colgrave, ed. and trans., *The Life of Saint Guthlac*, p. 107; Whitelock, *The Audience of Beowulf*, p. 80.

CHAPTER IV

The *Liber monstrorum*

All or part of the so-called *Liber monstrorum de diversis generibus* ('Book of monsters of various kinds') is extant in no fewer than five manuscripts, all dating from the ninth or tenth cenuries.[1] That the work enjoyed a certain vogue in the period is further evident from two entries in an arguably ninth-century book-list from Bobbio which relate to manuscripts now lost.[2] Amongst the sources freely plundered by the author is Isidore's *Etymologiae*, published shortly after 636, and Michael Lapidge, pointing out that the extensive corruption to be observed in all the extant manuscripts seems to indicate an advanced state of transmission, has suggested that 'the work may therefore be dated with some confidence to the century *c.* 650 x *c.* 750'.[3] Certain details of the orthography of all the manuscripts have long been held to point to their derivation from an Insular exemplar or exemplars, suggesting that the text may have been composed by an Irishman or an Anglo-Saxon.[4] Whether the *Liber monstrorum* was composed by an Insular author on the Continent or was subsequently exported is uncertain, but the clear (and long-recognised) reference early on in the work (I.2) to 'Hygelac, king of the Geats' (*Higlacus, rex Getarum*), as in *Beowulf*, has prompted much speculation in which the possibility of Irish provenance has been all but ignored, and successive scholars (with

1 Wolfenbüttel, Herzog-August Bibliothek, Gudianus lat. 148 (Eastern Francia, s. ix/x, provenance Weissenburg); St Gallen, Stiftsbibliothek, 237 (St Gallen, s. ix1); Leiden, Bibliotheek der Rijks-Universiteit, Voss. lat., Oct. 60 (Fleury, s. ix/x); New York, Pierpoint Morgan Library, 906 (Rheims, s. ix); London, British Library, Royal 15. B. xix (Rheims, s. x). The first printed editions of the *Liber monstrorum* are those by de Xivrey, *Traditions Tératologiques*, pp. 2–330 and Haupt, 'Index lectionum aestivarum 1863', pp. 218–52. The *Liber monstrorum* has recently been re-edited by Bologna, *Liber Monstrorum de diversis generibus* (reviewed by Knock, *Medium Aevum* 48 (1979), 259–62); Butturff, *The Monsters and the Scholar*; Porsia, *Liber Monstrorum*. A further edition and translation is found in the Appendix below, pp. 254–316.

2 Becker, *Catalogi Bibliothecarum Antiqui*, pp. 64–73, at pp. 70 and 73; cf. Lapidge, '*Beowulf*, Aldhelm, the *Liber Monstrorum* and Wessex', p. 164.

3 Lapidge, '*Beowulf*, Aldhelm, the *Liber Monstrorum* and Wessex', pp. 164–5.

4 Porsia, ed., *Liber Monstrorum*, pp. 49–56; Lapidge, '*Beowulf*, Aldhelm, the *Liber Monstrorum* and Wessex', pp. 165–6.

two notable dissenting voices) have been quick to affirm that the *Liber monstrorum* is an Anglo-Latin work.[5]

Notwithstanding the links between the *Liber monstrorum* and *Beowulf*, which, as we shall see, may extend far beyond the simple reference to Hygelac, the work is of crucial importance in understanding a large number of the monsters depicted in the *Beowulf*-manuscript. In the first place, the Latin texts which lie behind the vernacular renderings of *The Wonders of the East* and *Alexander's Letter to Aristotle* were clearly known to the author of the *Liber monstrorum*, and proved to be amongst his most favoured sources.[6] Secondly, as I hope to demonstrate, the *Liber monstrorum*, far from being a casual compendium of the bizarre and outlandish, is in fact the rather subtle and sophisticated work of a learned author who drew on and cunningly manipulated a number of disparate texts to offer a cogent (if uncomforting) view of the monstrous in nature.[7] A catalogue of almost 120 monstrosities is presented, divided up into three books of diminishing length (and, one suspects, dwindling authorial interest) which deal respectively with monstrous men, beasts, and serpents. The celebrated and successively dependent accounts of (mostly human) monsters by Pliny, Augustine, and Isidore all provided useful material for the author of the *Liber monstrorum*,[8] who managed to combine aspects of all their approaches in a text which defies easy categorisation, being neither scientific survey nor well-ordered catalogue nor theological observation.[9]

The effectiveness of the *Liber monstrorum*, I shall argue, stems from the sophisticated and witty way in which the author alludes to and manipulates his sources, both Christian and pagan, an essentially learned and rhetorical technique which is most evident from the extraordinary opening passage, which requires quotation in full:[10]

> De occulto orbis terrarum situ interrogasti et si tanta monstrorum essent genera credenda quanta in abditis mundi partibus per deserta et Oceani insulas et in ultimorum montium latebris nutrita monstrantur, et praecipue de his tribus orbis terrae generibus respondere petebas quae maximum formidinis terrorem humano generi incutiunt, ut de monstruosis hominum partibus describerem et

5 See further Back, 'Sur la date et l'origine', p. 61; Bologna, 'La tradizione manoscritta'; Knock, 'The *Liber Monstrorum*: An Unpublished Manuscript', p. 28; Faral, 'La queue de poisson des sirènes', pp. 441–70; Lapidge, '*Beowulf*, Aldhelm, the *Liber Monstrorum* and Wessex', pp. 165–7; Löfstedt, 'Notizien', p. 117; Porsia, 'Note per una riedizione', pp. 317–19; Thomas, 'Un manuscrit inutilisé', pp. 232–45; Whitbread, '*Beowulf* and the *Liber Monstrorum*', pp. 451–61; Whitelock, *The Audience of Beowulf*, pp. 46–55. With the exception of Knock, all these scholars have settled on an Anglo-Latin origin for the text. Manitius, *Geschichte*, I, pp. 114–18, suggested a Frankish origin.

6 See pp. 317–19 below.

7 Cf. Butturff, 'The Monsters and the Scholar', pp. 11–15; Friedman, *The Monstrous Races*, pp. 149–53.

8 See further the detailed discussion of the so-called 'Plinian Races' by Friedman, *The Monstrous Races*, pp. 4–25.

9 Whitbread, 'The *Liber monstrorum* and *Beowulf*', p. 434; Friedman, *The Monstrous Races*, p. 151.

10 All quotations and translations are taken from the complete edition and translation given below, pp. 254–316.

de ferarum horribilibus innumerosisque bestiarum formis et draconum dirissimis serpentiumque ac uiperarum generibus. Et dum sermo de his per multarum scripturarum auctoritatem uelud excelsi sideris fulgore olim humano generi paene ubique refulsit, mendacia ea nemini iteranda putassem nisi me uentus tuae postulationis a puppi precelsa pauidum inter marina praecipitasset monstra. Ponto namque tenebroso hoc opus aequipero, quod probandi si sint uera an instructa mendacio, nullus patet accessus eaque per orbem terrarum aurato sermone miri rumoris fama dispergebat, quorum maximam partem philosophorum et poetarum scriptura demonstrat, quae semper mendacia nutrit. Quaedam tantum in ipsis mirabilibus uera esse creduntur, et sunt innumerabilia quae si quis ad exploranda pennis uolare potuisset et ita rumoroso sermone tamen ficta probaret, ubi nunc urbs aurea et gemmis aspersa litora dicuntur, ibi lapideam aut nullam urbem et scopulosa cerneret. Et de his primum eloquar quae sunt aliquo modo credenda et sequentem historiam sibi quisque discernat, quod per haec antra monstrorum marinae puellae quandam formulam sirenae depingam, ut sit capite rationis quod tamen diuersorum generum hispidae squamosaeque sequuntur fabulae.

Primoque namque de his ad ortum sermo prorumpit quae leuiore discretu ab humano genere distant, daturus operam de singulis quae terra fouet mortalium nutrix, aut quondam fouisse fertur, quia nunc humano genere multiplicato et terrarum orbe repleto, sub astris minus producuntur monstra, quae ab ipsis per plurimos terrae angulos eradicata funditus et subuersa legimus et nunc reuulsa litoribus prona torquentur ad undas, quaeque turbine poli uertice sub arduo a totius gyri ambitu et omni loco terrarum ad hanc uastam gurgitis se uoraginem uergunt.

You have asked about the secret arrangement [or 'filthiness'] of the lands of the earth, and if as many kinds of monsters are to be credited as are demonstrated in the hidden parts [or 'births'] of the world, raised throughout the deserts and the islands of the Ocean and in the recesses of the farthest mountains, and you were particularly asking me to answer about these three kinds of the world's area which strike the greatest terror of fear in humankind, so that I should record the monstrous parts [or 'births'] of men, and the horrible and innumerable forms of wild beasts, and the most dreadful kinds of dragons, and serpents, and vipers. And whilst discussion of these things once shone almost everywhere for humankind as if with the brightness of a lofty star through the authority of many writings, I should have thought that those lies were unrepeatable to anyone, if the gust of your request had not cast me from the high poop quivering amongst the monsters of the deep. For I compare this task with the dark sea, since there is no clear way of testing whether that rumour which has spread throughout the world with the gilded speech of marvellous report is true or steeped in lies; of which things the writings of the poets and philosophers, which always foster lies, expound the greatest part. Only some things in the marvels themselves are believed to be true, and there are countless things which if anyone could take winged flight to explore, they would prove that, although they should be concocted in speech and rumour, where now there is said to lie a golden city and gem-strewn shores, one would see there rocks and a stony city, if at all. And first I will discuss those things which are in some part to be trusted, and then let each judge for himself the following material, because throughout these monster-filled caverns I shall paint a little picture of a sea-girl or siren, which if it has a head of reason is followed by all kinds of shaggy and scaly tales.

> *For first the discussion takes its beginning with those things which differ by a rather trifling amount from humankind, paying heed to the individuals that the earth, the mother of mortals, spawns, or is said to have once spawned, because now, when humankind has multiplied and the lands of the earth have been filled, fewer monsters are produced under the stars, and we read that in most of the corners of the world they have been utterly eradicated and overthrown by them, and now cast out from the shores they are thrown down to the waves, and that by the churning from the steep summit of the pole they turn from the edge of the entire circle and from every place on earth towards this vast abyss of the flood.*

The author demonstrates considerable command of his material in this dazzling display of rhetorical pyrotechnics. Alliteration is rife, and is particularly noticeable in such phrases as 'uentus tuae *p*ostulationis a *p*uppi *p*recelsa *p*auidum inter *m*arina *p*raecipitasset *m*onstra' or 'ad hanc *u*astam gurgitis se *u*oraginem *u*ergunt'.[11] We also find several conscious examples of wordplay (*paronomasia*), beginning with a pun in the opening sentences (*monstrorum . . . monstrantur . . . demonstrat*);[12] the *Liber monstrorum* is indeed a text in which monsters are demonstrated, and the author may well be alluding to the traditional etymology of *monstrum* attested by, for example, Isidore (*Etymologiae* XI.iii), who stresses the didactic role of monsters in providing at once warning and guidance.[13] The opening sentence also contains a pun on the word *situs*, which can mean both 'region' and 'filth', 'decay'.[14] It is perhaps significant that the word *situs* is used by Vergil in both these senses, since, as we shall see, Vergil's influence on this author is pervasive.[15] The author announces from the outset his attention to deal with matters which are not simply arcane, but positively hostile and dreadful.

Subsequent phrases effectively gloss the double sense of the *occulto orbis terrarum situ*, as the author stresses in turn the innaccessibility of the monsters he is to describe, which are to be found only in the remotest recesses (*in abditis mundi partibus per deserta et Oceani insulas et in ultimorum montium latebris*), and their loathsomeness to man (*quae maximum formidinis terrorem humano generi incutiunt*).[16] A very similar kind of pun, exploiting the double sense of another word like *situs*, is used later in the *Liber monstrorum* to describe the pygmies (I.23), a 'human race' (*genus humanum*) who are said to be both 'unseen' and 'hated' (*inuisum*).[17] In using such a term to describe the pygmies the author of the *Liber monstrorum* has clearly supplemented his source (Augustine, *De civitate Dei* XV.viii), adding his own distinctive gloss. Indeed, the continual sense of conflict and animosity between monsters and men is the hallmark of this author's work, and represents a considerable

11 Cf. Lapidge, '*Beowulf*, Aldhelm, the *Liber Monstrorum* and Wessex', pp. 171–2.

12 These are the only examples of either verb in the whole work.

13 Butturff, 'The Monsters and the Scholar', pp. 11–38.

14 Cf. the apparent pun on *partibus*, with the twin sense 'parts' or 'births'.

15 *Situs* is used by Vergil in the sense of 'filth' or 'decay' in *Georgics* I.72; *Aeneid* VI.462, VII.440, 452; the sense 'region' is required only in *Aeneid* III.451.

16 See further Friedman, 'The Marvels-of-the-East Tradition', pp. 321–34.

17 Cf. Butturf, 'The Monsters and the Scholar', p. 6; Friedman, 'The Monstrous Races', p. 151.

departure from the less antagonistic approaches of such predecessors as Augustine, Isidore, or Pliny. In this opening passage the author outlines his plan to consider in turn monstrous men, beasts, and serpents, but the language is hardly neutral, and the hostile epithets chosen are surely significant (*monstruosis . . . horribilibus . . . dirissimis*).[18] The fall in the number of monsters to be found is directly linked to the increase and spread in mankind (*nunc humano genere multiplicato et terrarum orbe repleto, sub astris minus producuntur monstra*), who are explicitly credited in rather violent language (*eradicata funditus et subuersa . . . et nunc reuulsa*) with their utter annihilation from almost every corner of the globe (*per plurimos terrae angulos*).

But, as in *The Passion of St Christopher* or *Judith* in the *Beowulf*-manuscript, the fundamental opposition between monsters and men is not the only antithesis to be explored and exploited in this opening passage. Contrasts are also established between a monstrous past and a present in which monsters are all but eradicated, and between the glittering of fiction and the harshness of fact.[19] This last contrast, memorably described in terms of the illusory golden city set on gem-strewn shores, which proves to be a rocky cliff-top town, if at all, effectively foreshadows a second major tension which runs impicitly throughout the work, namely that between Christian and pagan lore. For while (as in *Beowulf* itself) there is no explicit allusion to Christ, scripture, or patristic sources anywhere in the text, and while the sole mention of 'gentiles' (*gentiles*) occurs in an interpolated passage found in only one manuscript,[20] the *Liber monstrorum* is shot through with consistent sniping at the very sources, often pagan, on which it depends.[21]

So the description of the Eumenides (I.45), drawn from Vergil, is described as an 'empty tale' (*uana historia*), in contrast with that of the man with crescent-shaped feet (I.25), derived from Augustine, which the author claims to have taken from a 'trustworthy account' (*fideli historia*).[22] In the latter case, of course, the author is indulging in yet another pun; Augustine's tale is faithful precisely because it is full of faith (*fides*). The author is in many instances careful to distance himself from the material he is reporting, largely by the use of a huge variety of phrases such as 'they say', 'we read', 'it is said', which can be found in almost every section of the work.[23]

18 See further Friedman, 'The Monstrous Races', pp. 149–51.

19 Whitbread, 'The *Liber Monstrorum* and *Beowulf*', pp. 440–8.

20 Given below, p. 266, in the critical apparatus to I.12.

21 Butturff, 'The Monsters and the Scholar', pp. 38–57; Whitbread, 'The *Liber Monstrorum* and *Beowulf*', pp. 438–9.

22 Cf. Butturff, 'The Monsters and the Scholar', p. 39.

23 So, for example, we find *adfirmant* (II.23); *adserunt* (I.26); *appellant* (I.15, 17; II.13); *appellauerunt* (I.37); *arbitrantur* (II.14, 23; III.16, 24); *depingitur* (I.5, 46); *depingunt* (II.prol.); *depromit* (I.45); *depromunt* (I.Ep., II.14, 15); *describitur* (I.10, 19,35, 39, 42, 50, 52; II.1, 4, 8, 14, 15, 20, 22; III.3, 9, 13, 16, 21, 23); *describunt* (II.7; III.13); *describuntur* (I.20, 25, 38; II.3; III.7); *descripsit* (II.2, 29); *designabant* (I.13); *dicebantur* (I.11, 38, 49); *dicitur* (I.36); *dicunt* (I.29, 34, 39, 42; II.8, 11, 15, 20; III.24); *dicuntur* (I.Prol.; I.15, 24, 27, 46; III.4, 11, 15); *didicimus* (I.8, 13, 15; II.33); *fertur* (I.Prol.; I.1, 3, 14, 38; II.1, 20, 23, 36; III.1); *ferunt* (I.17, 19, 22, 28, 32, 33, 49, 53, 56; II.8, 12, 15, 16 (twice), 17, 18, 20, 22, 25); *legimus* (I.Prol.; I.4, 9, 26); *legitur* (I.11 (twice), 44); *leguntur* (I.30, 41, 51, 54;

A complementary kind of labelling simply impugns the value of the account offered, and the author employs a similarly wide variety of expressions to signal the falsehood or dissimulation of his sources.[24] That this tension between fact and fiction is a key part of the author's scheme is made clear by his insistence at the very beginning of his work of the difficulty of determining whether the accounts he is about to offer are true or steeped in lies (*uera an instructa mendacio*), an assertion echoed at the end of the third book (and the whole work), where it is stated that among the preceding material can be found things which are true and things lacking any truth (*quaedam uera, quaedam namque omni ueritate carentia*).

In several passages, a number of the contrasts highlighted above are combined, as in the account of the Lernaean Hydra (II.8):[25]

> Ferunt fabulae Graecorum plurima in libris antiquitatum suae philosophiae quondam fuisse quae nunc incredibilia esse uidentur, tam de monstris quam etiam beluis et serpentibus. De quibus partem replicaturi sumus. Inter quae belua Lernae describitur, quam nunc apud inferos esse, tam horrendam stridore quam forma terribilem, Graeci cum quibusdam fingunt Romanis.
>
> *The fables of the Greeks tell of very many things in the books of their philosophy from ancient times which now seem to be incredible, as much about monsters as also beasts and serpents. And we are about to unfold a part of these, amongst which is described the beast of Lerna, which is now in the underworld, and which the Greeks, along with certain Romans, depict as being as horrible in its clamour as dreadful in its form.*

Here we see what is practically a repeated blueprint for the whole work's tripartite structure (*tam de monstris quam etiam beluis et serpentibus*), infused with deliberate chiastic contrast between a fictional past and a sceptical present (*ferunt fabulae . . . plurima . . . quondam fuisse quae nunc incredibilia esse uidentur*). The entire descriptive contents of this section can be traced to four words from Vergil (*Aeneid* VI.287–8), which simply note that the the beast of Lerna screeched horribly (*belua Lernae / horrendum stridens*).

A very similar technique, repeating familiar themes with repeated diction, is found in the opening of Book II:[26]

II.26); *narrantur* (II.9); *narratur* (I.48); *nominauit* (II.6; III.18); *nuncupantur* (III.6, 10); *nuncupati sunt* (I.5); *nuncupatur* (II.24; III.18); *perhibeatur* (I.54); *perhibent* (I.18, 21; III.7, 12, 19); *perhibentur* (I.16; II.2, 9, 30, 31; III.2, 6); *perhibet* (II.10); *perhibetur* (I.14, 23, 35; II.34; III.1, 4, 9 (twice), 14, 21); *putabant* (II.34); *putabatur* (I.1); *putant* (III.13, 24); *reperitur* (II.Prol.); *reperiuntur* (III.25); *scribitur* (I.47); *scribunt* (I.55; II.11, 24, 28, 35; III.18); *testantur* (I.21, 25, 40; II.27); *uocant* (I.23, 24, 53; II.12, 31); *uocatur* (II.31; III.11); *uocauerunt* (II.16).

24 So, for example we find *confingitur* (I.56); *fabulae* (I.Prol.; I.37, 43, 45, 49; II.8, 32; III.1, 23); *fabulantur* (I.34); *fabularum* (I.Epi.); *fabulas* (II.28); *fabulis* (I.45, Epi.); *fabulosis* (I.50);

25 Cf. the comments of Porsia, ed., *Liber Monstrorum*, p. 229.

26 Porsia, ed., *Liber Monstrorum*, p. 219, notes that this passage repeats the elevated style of the Prologue to Book I, but does not point out any of the close (and surely intentional) parallels of diction and imagery.

> De quibus iam tibi nihil scribendum putaui quia et innumerabilia sunt, et eorum cognitio longe ab humano genere, uelut horrendis undarum gurgitis turribus et marino disiungitur muro. Sed tamen ne lucernam uerbi postulantis gurges neglegentiae demergat, de his tibi sermo pauca depromet beluis et horribilibus ignotarum formis bestiarum quae in fluminibus uel stagnis paludibusque, siue in desertis orbis terrarum latebris fuisse quondam, poetae ac philosophi aurato sermone in suis litteraturis inaniter depingunt.
>
> *Concerning these things I have thought nothing worth writing to you, because they are both innumerable, and knowledge of them is far removed from humankind, as if by the terrifying battlements of the sea-waves, and by a wall of sea. But nevertheless, lest the flood of neglect should drown the lamp of the questioning word, a discussion will provide you with a few things concerning these beasts and the horrible forms of unknown beasts which the poets and philosophers emptily depict in the gilded discourse of their writings to have once existed in rivers or lakes and swamps, or in the deserted recesses of the globe.*

Here the author stresses the remoteness of the beasts he is about to describe, highlighting their distance from modern man in time, place, appearance, and truth, the whole account bound by the same kind of marine metaphor that runs through the entire work. Various phrases in the passage deliberately recall others elsewhere in the work; the extraordinary (and apparently biblical) metaphor of the lamp of the questioning word drowned in a flood of neglect (*ne lucernam uerbi postulantis gurges neglegentiae demergat*) neatly turns on its head the repeated images of the winds and waves of questioning which begin and end Book I (*uentus tuae postulationis . . . fluctus tuae postulationis*),[27] while the reference to the poets and philosophers (*poetae ac philosophi*) with their golden speech (*aurato sermone*) taps a further familiar theme easily recognisable from its citation at the beginning of Book I (*aurato sermone . . . philosophorum et poetarum*), and echoed elsewhere.[28]

Much has been made of the range of sources employed in the *Liber monstrorum*, which appear to include such diverse works and authors as the *Historia Alexandri* by Quintus Curtius Rufus, the *Historia adversum paganos* by Orosius, the pseudo-Clementine *Recognitiones*, the *Vita S. Pauli* by Jerome, and the now-lost poem *Orpheus* by Lucan.[29] In fact many of these sources appear to have been drawn on to supply minor and supplementary details for a handful of entries; for the great majority of items the author of the *Liber monstrorum* appears to have relied on a much more restricted range of texts.[30]

27 Manitius, 'Liber monstrorum', p. 114, connects the phrase *lucernam uerbi postulantis* with Psalms CXIX.105: *lucerna pedibus meis verbum tuis*; cf. Whitbread, 'The *Liber Monstrorum* and *Beowulf*', pp. 439–40, who notes a number of other (rather faint) biblical allusions. The Psalm in question includes at the relevant section extravagant praise for God as a teacher, and in using the phrase the author may be signalling a similar relationship between himself and the shadowy figure at whose request he has composed the book.

28 Cf. the use of related phrases in I.5, II.1, II.14, II.19, III.1, and III.23 (twice).

29 Lapidge, '*Beowulf*, Aldhelm, the *Liber Monstrorum* and Wessex', pp. 168–9; Whitbread, 'The *Liber Monstrorum* and *Beowulf*', pp. 440–8.

30 Cf. Whitbread, 'The *Liber Monstrorum* and *Beowulf*', pp. 445–7.

The well-known and successively interdependent accounts of monstrosities by Augustine (*De civitate Dei* XVI.viii) and Isidore (*Etymologiae* X.iii) have been freely plundered, with, generally speaking, Augustine the favoured source throughout Book I, and Isidore throughout Books II and III.[31] Clearly independent knowledge of Pliny, whose *Historia naturalis* was known and used by both Augustine and Isidore, is harder to demonstrate.[32] In addition to these Christian sources, the author had recourse to related pagan texts deriving ultimately from traditions circulating about the person of Alexander the Great. The first of these is the *Letter of Alexander to Aristotle* (*Epistola Alexandri ad Aristotelem*), on which the author draws freely throughout Books II and III.[33] For Book I (and elsewhere) the author of the *Liber monstrorum* draws instead on a version of the related group of texts, a vernacular version of which is found in the Old English *Wonders of the East*.[34] It is perhaps the epistolary framework of these secular Latin texts which leads the author of the *Liber monstrorum* to address his imaginary sponsor.[35] But the single most important source used by the author of the *Liber monstrorum* is Vergil, who is described (III.10) as 'the distinguished poet' (*praecipuus poeta*);[36] nearly one in three of the entries in the work owes something of detail to a wide range of passages from the *Aeneid* or the *Georgics* or both, and Vergilian phraseology pervades the text.[37] It is also clear that the author occasionally supplemented his knowledge of Vergil by referring to some kind of commentary of the sort composed by Servius.[38] In the course of one such commentary, on *Georgics* IV.492, Servius describes Lucan's poem *Orpheus*, and it may be that in his allusions to the work (I.5; II.7; III.3) the author of the *Liber monstrorum* is simply echoing a fuller, now-lost commentary.[39] In a similar way, the passages from the *Liber monstrorum* which scholars have traced to details in Quintus Curtius Rufus and Orosius, both of whom contributed to the traditions concerning Alexander the Great, may simply reflect that the specific versions of the *Letter of*

31 See the list of sources in the Appendix below, pp. 318–20.

32 Cf. Whitbread, 'The *Liber Monstrorum* and *Beowulf*', pp. 443–5.

33 See the list of sources in the Appendix below, pp. 318–20.

34 See the list of sources in the Appendix below, pp. 318–20. Cf. Gibb, 'The Wonders of the East', pp. 4–36; Knock, (in her review of Bologna's edition), pp. 260–1; Knock, 'Wonders of the East', pp. 313–32.

35 The epistolary framework in these texts, deriving ultimately from the letters concerning his Indian campaign attributed to Alexander, and their derivatives, is missing from the Old English *Wonders of the East*, and the Latin versions of the same text extant from Anglo-Saxon England.

36 Similarly positive descriptions of Vergil are quite common in Christian writings from the period; cf., for example, Augustine's description of Vergil as 'the most noble of poets' (*nobilissimus poeta*) in his *De civitate Dei* XV.9, or Aldhelm's designation of him as simply 'that splendid man' (*illustris ille*) in his *De pedum regulis* 202.14.

37 Cf. Whitbread, 'The *Liber Monstrorum* and *Beowulf*', pp. 441–3.

38 Cf. Butturff, 'The Monsters and the Scholar', pp. 196 and 199; Porsia, ed., *Liber Monstrorum,* pp. 143, 145, 147, 158, 159, 191, 193, 205, 209, 227, 251, 277, 279, 283, and 292.

39 Thilo, ed., *Servii Grammatici qui feruntur in Vergilii Bucolica et Georgica Commentarii*, p. 356; cf. Lapidge, '*Beowulf*, Aldhelm, the *Liber Monstrorum* and Wessex', p. 169.

Alexander and the *Wonders of the East* employed by the author had been supplemented from the same tradition.[40]

We can therefore broadly divide the sources employed by the author of the *Liber monstrorum* into three groups:

1. Christian prose sources, notably Augustine and Isidore
2. Pagan prose sources, mostly drawn from material relating to the exploits of Alexander the Great
3. Vergilian material

It is interesting therefore to see that the author of the *Liber monstrorum* arranges these sources with some care.[41] The first few chapters of Book I, for example, rely heavily on material derived from Christian prose sources, particularly Augustine, whilst the Book ends with a string of sections adapted from Vergil. During the middle portion of Book I the author carefully interweaves accounts from Christian and pagan sources, and, for example, throughout the long passage I.17–30 the author alternates seven sections derived from Augustine with seven from the *Wonders*-tradition.[42] In so doing the author is implicitly following his own model, outlined in the Prologue, namely that of the siren:

> Et de his primum eloquar quae sunt aliquo modo credenda et sequentem historiam sibi quisque discernat, quod per haec antra monstrorum marinae puellae quandam formulam sirenae depingam, ut sit capite rationis quod tamen diuersorum generum hispidae squamosaeque sequuntur fabulae.
>
> *And first I will discuss those things which are in some part to be trusted, and then let each judge for himself the following material, because throughout these monster-filled caverns I shall paint a little picture of a sea-girl or siren, which if it has a head of reason is followed by all kinds of shaggy and scaly tales.*

This model of the siren applies not simply to Book I, of course, but to the whole work, which commences by discussing monsters who share human shape and reason (Book I), and finishes by considering in turn tales (and tails!) both shaggy (Book II) and scaly (Book III).

Given the apparent date of composition of the *Liber monstrorum* and the possibility of Insular authorship, there have been numerous efforts to connect the work with known literary activity at the time. Attention has been focused by successive scholars on the prolific and learned Anglo-Saxon author Aldhelm of Malmesbury (who died in 709 or 710),[43] with whose acknowledged work the *Liber monstrorum* shares an intriguing number of similarities in tone, style, and use of sources.[44] There

40 Cf. Butturff, 'The Monsters and the Scholar', p. 198; Porsia, ed., *Liber Monstrorum*, pp. 223, 227, 271, 277, 290, and 291.

41 Cf. Whitbread, 'The *Liber Monstrorum* and *Beowulf*', pp. 442–6.

42 Knock (review of Bologna's edition), p. 262.

43 See further Lapidge and Rosier, *Aldhelm: the Poetic Works*, pp. 5–9.

44 Lapidge, '*Beowulf*, Aldhelm, the *Liber Monstrorum* and Wessex', pp. 168–75; Whitbread, 'The *Liber Monstrorum* and *Beowulf*', pp. 455–61.

is evidence that the *Liber monstrorum* may have circulated under Aldhelm's name in at least one medieval manuscript, and it is certain that the thirteenth-century encyclopedist Thomas of Cantimpré, borrowing freely from both Aldhelm and the *Liber monstrorum*,[45] assigned all such quotations to one 'Adelinus', itself a recognisable variant of Aldhelm's name.[46] Yet despite these links with Aldhelm, there are enough significant differences in syntax and phrasing to suggest that the *Liber monstrorum* was not composed by Aldhelm himself, but perhaps by a colleague, disciple, or imitator working in a similar 'house style';[47] the name of Æthilwald, one of Aldhelm's students, has been suggested by Franco Porsia, although the 'evidence' cited is distinctly thin.[48]

Since Aldhelm's work, which proved highly influential both in England and on the Continent during his own lifetime and for centuries afterwards,[49] bears such close comparison with that of the *Liber monstrorum*, it is instructive to consider the implications of such a link. Just as the author the *Liber monstrorum* deliberately frames his first book, *De monstris*, with a matching pair of nautical images linked by careful verbal reminiscence, so too does Aldhelm in his prose *De virginitate*, a work with which, as Michael Lapidge has argued, the author of the *Liber monstrorum* may have been familiar.[50] The author of the *Liber monstrorum* in the Prologue compares the dangers of his undertaking with being cast adrift in a stormy sea filled with monsters:

> nisi me uentus tuae postulationis a puppi praecelsa pauidum inter marina praecipitasset monstra. Ponto namque tenebroso hoc opus aequipero . . .
>
> *if the gust of your request had not cast me from the high poop quivering amongst the monsters of the deep. For I compare this task with the dark sea . . .*

45 See further Knock, 'The Wonders of the East', pp. 957–95, who isolates no less than thirty-four citations from 'Adelinus' in Thomas of Cantimpré's *Liber de Natura Rerum*. Of these, two represent simple mentions of the name, fifteen sections are drawn from the *Liber monstrorum*, fourteen from Aldhelm's *Enigmata*, and three have elements common to both. One series of nine consecutive sections from Book III of the *Liber de Natura Rerum*, is built on extensive borrowing from nine separate chapters of Book I of the *Liber monstrorum*; Boese, ed., *Thomas of Cantimpré: Liber de Natura Rerum*, p. 100.

46 Lapidge, '*Beowulf*, Aldhelm, the *Liber Monstrorum* and Wessex', pp. 169–71.

47 Lapidge, '*Beowulf*, Aldhelm, the *Liber Monstrorum* and Wessex', p. 176; cf. Orchard, 'Some Aspects', pp. 178–9.

48 Porsia, ed., *Liber Monstrorum*, pp. 102–5. An equally good (which is to say unconvincing) case might be made for authorship by Wihtfrith, another of Aldhelm's students, whose trip to Ireland, contempt for *philosophi*, and knowledge of pagan myth and legend are all described by Aldhelm in his letter to Wihtfrith; Ehwald, ed., *Aldhelmi opera*, pp. 478–80; translated by Lapidge and Herren, *Aldhelm: the Prose Works*, pp. 154–5.

49 See further Lapidge and Orchard, 'Aldhelm'.

50 Lapidge, '*Beowulf*, Aldhelm, the *Liber Monstrorum* and Wessex', p. 176. Elsewhere (p. 169) Lapidge notes that the *Liber monstrorum* (I.3) and Aldhelm's *De virginitate* (Ehwald, ed., *Aldhemi Opera*, p. 252/12–14) share the detail that the Colossus was 107 feet tall, although it may be that, as Porsia, ed., *Liber Monstrorum*, p. 141, has suggested, both authors drew on Jerome's translation of Eusebius' *Chronici canones*, which includes the same detail.

At the end of the first book the author declares himself relieved to reach the shore:

> Haec sunt inmania monstra de quibus me fluctus tuae postulationis tundebat et ea quae de spumosis fabularum gurgitibus ad haec litora congessi.
>
> *These are the huge monsters concerning which the wave of your request buffeted me, and those are the ones which I have gathered to these shores from the foaming torrents of fables.*

The use of the related phrases *uentus tuae postulationis* and *fluctus tuae postulationis*, underpinned by the repetition of the relatively rare noun *postulatio*,[51] effectively binds the passages (and the book) together.[52] In a very similar way Aldhelm uses verbal echoes to connect two extended marine (and monstrous!) images which frame the prose *De virginitate*. Towards the beginning of the work Aldhelm, employing the same rhetorical and alliterative style, compares the spiritual life with that of a sailor on a storm-tossed sea fraught with monsters:[53]

> dum illi periculoso saeculi naufragio grassante dirae tempestatis turbine velut inter Scyllam Siciliae et barathrum voraginis navigantes ad portum coenubialis vitae festinantes, licet aliquantulum quassatis cymbae compagibus, Christo gubernante feliciter pervenerunt.
>
> *While they, as if, with the perilous storm of the world buffeting them in the eddy of a dread tempest, sailing between Sicilian Scylla and the depth of the whirlpool, hasten to the harbour of the monastic life, and with Christ as their helmsman they arrive safely, although the timbers of their craft are somewhat shaken.*

At the end of the book, Aldhelm quite deliberately recalls this passage in comparing his own literary endeavours with the same maritime adventure, using substantially the same language:[54]

> Rimosa namque fragilis ingenii barca dirae tempestatis turbine quassata, licet laborante lacertorum remigio, optatum silentio portum sero attigit; sed tamen nostrae rusticitatis stipulatio superno Christi patrocinio freta fiducaliter confidit, quod nostrarum carbasa antemnarum prosperis ventorum flaminibus sinuata quasi inter Scillam soloecismi et barbarismi barathrum indisruptis rudentibus feliciter transfretaverint, scopulosas quoque labdacismi collisiones et myotacismi voragines incautos quousque sine grammaticorum gubernaculo repertos ad erroris naufragia truciter trudentes minime perhorruerint.
>
> *For the battered bark of my fragile intelligence, shaken by the eddy of a dread tempest although the rowing of arms laboured, reaches at last the port longed-for in silence;*

51 Lapidge, '*Beowulf*, Aldhelm, the *Liber Monstrorum* and Wessex', p. 172.

52 One might equally compare the use of similarly parallel phrases to mark off key sections of the Old English biblical poems *Judith*, *Genesis A*, lines 1–111, and *Daniel*; see further above, pp. 5–6.

53 Ehwald, ed., *Aldhemi Opera*, p. 238/17–21; cf. Lapidge and Herren, *Aldhelm: the Prose Works*, p. 67.

54 Ehwald, ed., *Aldhemi Opera*, pp. 320/20–321/3; cf. Lapidge and Herren, *Aldhelm: the Prose Works*, p. 130.

> *yet however the undertaking of our rusticity, relying on the heavenly support of Christ, has confident faith that the canvas of our sail-yards, swollen by favourable gusts of wind shall with rigging undisturbed have passed safely over (as it were) between the Scylla of solecism and the depth of barbarism, and shall have in no way trembled at the rocky crashings of labdacism [intrusion of l-sounds] and the whirlpools of myotacism [intrusion of m-sounds], forcing those found unprepared without the helmsmanship of grammarians onto the shipwreck of errors.*

This typically expansive account recalls practically every element of the previous passage, and echoes its diction in a manner all but unique in Aldhelm's works. So, for example, Aldhelm repeats the phrase *dirae tempestatis turbine* and the reference to Scylla and Charybdis only in these two places in his whole extant corpus, and clearly expects his audience to identify the 'harbour of the monastic life' to which the virgins of the first passage 'with Christ as their helmsman . . . arrive safely' (*portum coenubialis vitae . . . Christo gubernante feliciter pervenerunt*) with the 'port longed-for' which the virgins of the second passage, having 'passed safely over' the monster-filled sea, finally reach, 'relying on the heavenly support of Christ' (*optatum . . . portum . . . superno Christi patrocinio freta . . . feliciter transfretaverint*).

The use of nautical metaphors is quite commonplace in Latin literature, particularly in verse;[55] Vergil is but one author who speaks in his *Georgics* of setting the sails at the beginning of his work, and furling them at the end, and the theme was echoed by a number of Insular authors.[56] Even Aldhelm's comments about steering the ship of his prose amongst the rocks of grammatical error can be matched by, for example, Ennodius, who at the beginning of his work makes an identical observation.[57] What is significant, apart from a shared interest in alliteration, is that both Aldhelm and the author of the *Liber monstrorum* have here combined this nautical metaphor of literary composition with another marine metaphor much-favoured by Christian authors, which equates the experience of the secular world with a spiritual journey on a storm-tossed sea fraught with dangers.[58] In a substantially similar way another Anglo-Saxon, Alcuin, combines both metaphors towards the end of his lengthy poem on York, *Versus de . . . sanctis Euboricensis ecclesiae*, where he prays that the anchorite Balthere will oversee his undertaking (lines 1322–4):[59]

> et rege nunc nostram pelagi per cerula cymbam
> inter monstra maris, scopulosas inter et undas
> ut possit portum portans attingere tutum.

55 See further Saint-Denis, *Le rôle de la mer* ; Curtius, *European Literature and the Latin Middle Ages*, pp. 128–30.

56 So, for example, one might point to Hiberno Latin authors such as Muirchú, who in the prologue to his *Vita S. Patricii* (composed *c.* 675) likens his literary venture to a perilous voyage in an unseaworthy vessel; cf. Bieler, ed. *The Patrician Texts*, p. 62.

57 Hartel, ed., *Magni Felicis Ennodii Opera Omnia*, I.3: *Sermonum cymbam inter loquelae scopulos frenare.*

58 See further Schmidtke, *Geistliche Schiffahrt.*

59 Cf. Godman, ed., *Alcuin: The Bishops, Kings, and Saints of York*, pp. 132–3 and 165. See further lines 1385–7 and the closing lines 1649–58, where the metaphor is continued.

> *Now steer our boat through the waves of the deep, between the monsters of the deep and the rocky waves, so that it may reach port safely with its load.*

Alcuin was certainly familiar with Aldhelm's work (as he explicitly states in line 1547 of the same poem), and may well have been directly influenced by the relevant passages in the prose *De virginitate*.[60]

Throughout his extant prose, Aldhelm's reference to the sea-monster Scylla is restricted to the two passages just discussed, but in his verse Aldhelm dedicates an entire *Enigma* to this monster. Indeed, the subjects of a number of Aldhelm's *Enigmata* are reflected in the *Liber monstrorum*, as follows:[61]

Topic	*Enigma*	*Liber monstrorum*
Salamander	15	III.14
Minotaur	28	I.50
Lion	39	II.1
Colossus	72	I.3
Scylla	95	I.14, II.20, II.32
Elephant	96	II.3

It is particularly interesting that Aldhelm's *Enigma* 95 ('Scylla') and 96 ('Elephant') are mirrored in the *Liber monstrorum*, since the immediately following *Enigma* 97 ('Night') also finds an intriguing echo in the work. Aldhelm's poem might be quoted in full:

Florida me genuit nigrantem corpore tellus
Et nil fecundum sterili de viscere promo,
Quamvis Eumenidum narrantes carmine vates
Tartaream partu testentur gignere prolem.
Nulla mihi constat certi substantia partus,
Sed modo quadratum complector caerula mundum.
Est inimica mihi, quae cunctis constat amica,
Saecula dum lustrat, lampas Titania Phoebi;
Diri latrones me semper amare solebant,
Quos gremio tectos nitor defendere fusco.
Vergilium constat caram cecinisse sororem:
Ingrediturque solo et caput inter nubila condit
Monstrum horrendum, ingens, cui quot sunt corpore plumae,
Tot vigiles oculi subter, mirabile dictu,
Tot linguae, totidem ora sonant, tot subrigit auris;
Nocte volat caeli medio terraeque per umbras.

60 Cf. Godman, ed., *Alcuin: The Bishops, Kings, and Saints of York*, pp. lxviii–lxix and lxxxii–lxxxiv.

61 Lapidge, '*Beowulf*, Aldhelm, the *Liber Monstrorum* and Wessex', p. 169; Whitbread, 'The *Liber Monstrorum* and *Beowulf*', pp. 455–61, points out a number of other (mostly superficial) similarities between the two works.

> *The fertile earth bore me, black in body, and I bring forth nothing fruitful from my sterile womb, although the poets, telling in song of the Furies, may claim that I spawned in birth the race of Tartarus. No substance of certain birth corresponds to me, but, dusky, now I enfold the four corners of the world. The Titan torch of Phoebus, which is a friend to all while it traverses [or 'illumines']*[62] *the world, is an enemy to me. Cruel robbers used to always love me, and I strive to keep them covered in my dark embrace. Vergil is known to have sung this of my dear sister [Fama]: 'She walks on the ground and hides her head in the clouds, a huge and dreadful monster, on whose body the feathers are matched in number by watchful eyes above, marvellous to tell, and as many tongues and mouths sound forth, as many ears prick up; she flies at night through the shadows, midway between heaven and earth.'*

What is intriguing about this *Enigma* is the extent to which it quotes verbatim from Vergil's description of Fama ('fame', 'reputation', 'rumour'), from *Aeneid* IV.177 and 181–4 (reproduced in the *Enigma* as lines 12–16), inextricably linking this fabulous creature with the concept of 'night', since the author of the *Liber monstrorum* makes the same connection in his description of a 'nocturnal monster':[63]

> Et dicunt, quod dici nefandum est, monstrum quoddam nocturnum fuisse, quod semper noctu per umbram caeli et terrae volabat, homines in urbibus horribili stridore territans, et quot plumas in corpore habuit, tot oculos, totidem aures et ora. Semper quoque sine requie et somno fuisse describitur.
>
> *And they say what is impious to say, that there is a certain monster of the night, which always used to fly by night through the shade of the sky and the earth, terrifying people in cities with its dreadful cry, and it had as many eyes and ears and mouths, as it had feathers. And it is always said to have been without rest or sleep.*

While the two descriptions overlap substantially in their dependence on Vergil, the author of the *Liber monstrorum*, unlike Aldhelm, has ignored the earlier verse (*ingrediturque solo et caput inter nubila condit*) in favour of that which immediately follows the common description (*Aeneid* IV.185), and describes Fama as screaming and being without sleep (*stridens, nec dulci declinat lumina somno*).

The key question here is why the author of the *Liber monstrorum* saw fit to include this *nocturnum monstrum* at all, and why he specifically chose to place it in his first book, concerning man-shaped monsters. Vergil explicitly says that Fama is born of Earth (*Aeneid* IV.178–9),[64] and Aldhelm, by stating in his *Enigma* that Fama is the

62 The same pun, which is not unlike those in the *Liber monstrorum* pointed out above, pp. 89–90, is apparently popular with other Anglo-Latin authors familiar with Aldhelm's work, as witness its employment by Boniface, in a letter to Eadburg dated 735/6; see further Tangl, ed., *S. Bonifacii et Lulli Epistolae*, p. 54.

63 Cf. Porsia, ed., *Liber Monstrorum*, p. 197; Whitbread, 'The *Liber Monstrorum* and *Beowulf*', pp. 458–9.

64 The traditional etymology for the word 'gigant'; cf. further above, pp. 78–9, and below, pp. 104–5.

sister of Earth-born Night, implies as much. Specifically, Vergil states that Fama was spawned alongside the giants Coeus and Enceladus, two of the Titans who fought against the gods.[65] As such, Fama takes her rightful place towards the end of the first book of the *Liber monstrorum* (I.42) alongside those whom Vergil depicts as either born of Earth or in conflict against the gods (or both), such as Tityos (I.47; cf. *Aeneid* VI.595–7), Aegeon (I.48; cf. *Aeneid* X.565–8), and the Aloidae (I.55; cf. *Aeneid* VI.582–4).[66] Indeed the first book closes by condemning 'what they say in highly disgraceful fables about hellish people, such as . . . Coeus, Iapetus, Typhoeus, and certain others' (*quod de inferis hominibus . . . Coeo, Iapeto, Typhoeo, et ceteris quibusque turpissimis depromunt fabulis*), a phrase which appears to be a clear allusion to *Georgics* I.278–80, where Vergil speaks of those Earth-born giants who warred against the gods:[67]

tum partu Terra nefando
Coeumque Iapetumque creat saevumque Typhoea
et coniuratos caelum rescindere fratres.

Then by an unspeakable birth the Earth created Coeus, Iapetus, and savage Typhoeus, and the brothers who had sworn to break down heaven.

The exploits of these unnamed brothers (*fratres*) in the succeeding passage have apparently been conflated by Vergil, and, interestingly, the author of the *Liber monstrorum*, with those of the Aloidae (I.55).[68] Evidently the link is made because of the repeated phrases *caelum rescindere* (*Georgics* I.280) and *rescindere caelum* (*Aeneid* VI.583); at all events the author of the *Liber monstrorum* goes beyond his immediate source in making explicit the motive of the assault of the Aloidae (I.55): a 'burning desire to rule' (*pro flammea regnandi cupidine*). One might well compare what other Insular commentators made of the Classical episode of Titans, who saw in their tale a parallel to the efforts of the fallen angels against God; both sets of aggressors are, as we have seen, universally condemned for their overweening pride.[69] Aldhelm voices typically forthright condemnation for the vice, which he intimately connects with satanic rebellion:[70]

> Nam in conflictu octo principalium vitiorum, licet ultima ponatur, tamen quasi atrox regina tyrannicae potestatis imperium et dominandi monarchiam prae ceteris sibi usurpare dinoscitur, quia sine ancipiti ambiguitatis scrupulo veraciter

65 On the giants who fought against the gods, cf. above, pp. 78–80.
66 Cf. Porsia, ed., *Liber Monstrorum*, pp. 203 and 211.
67 Cf. Porsia, ed., *Liber Monstrorum*, p. 213.
68 The author of the *Liber monstrorum* states that the Aloidae tried three times (*ter*) to assail heaven, while no such specific mention is made in what is evidently the main source-passage, *Aeneid* VI.582–4; such an assertion is, however, made in the companion-passage (*Georgics* I.281).
69 Cf., for example, the passages by Bede and Alfred quoted above, pp. 81–2.
70 Ehwald, ed., *Aldhelmi Opera*, p. 239/7–12; cf. Lapidge and Herren, *Aldhelm: the Prose Works*, p. 67.

> credendum est, quod . . . Lucifer parasitorum sodalibus vallatus et apostatarum satellitibus glomeratus in profundum superbiae barathrum et tetrum elationis tumidae tartarum cassabundus corruisset.
>
> *For in the battle of the eight chief vices, although [Pride] is placed last, like a fierce queen she is recognised to usurp for herself above all others the rule of tyrannical power and the monarchy of dominance, because it is truly to be believed without any wavering shadow of a doubt, that Lucifer, surrounded by his parasitical comrades, and hemmed in with his apostate colleagues dashed headlong into the deep pit of pride and the dread hell of swollen arrogance.*

Both Fama and the Titans, the author of *Liber monstrorum* seems to be saying, come from like stock.

It is interesting to consider the way in which Aldhelm demonstrates his own detailed knowledge of Vergil in his *Enigma* on Night; the 'poets' (*vates*) on whose account of the parentage of the Eumenides Aldhelm depends turn out to be Vergil (*Aeneid* XII.845–8).[71] An equally encyclopedic knowledge of Vergil's works is evident in the *Liber monstrorum*, who likewise masks his borrowings from Vergil by vague references to 'poets' (*poetae*),[72] and whose own account of (for example) the Eumenides is similarly dependent on disparate passages from both the *Aeneid* and the *Georgics*. The blending of these Vergilian passages is instructive of the method of the author of the *Liber monstrorum*, whose description of the Eumenides runs as follows (I.45):

> Eumenides quoque quasdam mulieres uana historia depromit, quae uipereum crinem habuerunt, sanguineis uittis innexum, quo caerulei angues per uesanam discordiam scatebant. Quarum ferrei thalami apud inferos incredibilibus figuntur fabulis.
>
> *A false tale also promotes certain women, the Eumenides, who had viperous hair tied back with bloody headbands, in which azure snakes were thrashing in mad anger. And their iron bed-chambers are imagined in incredible fables to be in Hell.*

The two source-passages from Vergil read as follows:

> ferreique Euemenidum thalami et Discordia demens
> vipereum crinem vittis innexa cruentis
>
> *Aeneid* VI.280–1
>
> caeruleosque implexae crinibus anguis
> Eumenides
>
> *Georgics* IV.482–3

It is clear that the author of the *Liber monstrorum* has done little more than combine these two widely-separated descriptions, and it is equally evident that the author has

71 On Aldhelm's knowledge of Vergil, see further Orchard, *The Poetic Art of Aldhelm*, pp. 130–5.

72 For example in the description of the 'sea-dogs' (II.19), which is clearly dependent on *Aeneid* III.432.

(perhaps intentionally) misconstrued the subject of the first passage, *Discordia demens*, who appears in his account in quite a dfferent guise (*per uesanam discordiam*). This is but one of a number of places where the author of the *Liber monstrorum* gives a somewhat blurred or inaccurate representation of his Vergilian source.[73] Occasionally the misrepresentation borders on the farcical; where Virgil lends exotic solemnity to his account of the death of Cleopatra (*Aeneid* VIII.696–700) by reference to the dog-faced Egyptian god Anubis (*latrator Anubis*),[74] the author of the *Liber monstrorum* (III.23) reduces the scene to comedy by mention of 'barking clouds' (*nubes latrantes*)![75] But it is clear that the author of the *Liber monstrorum* is a keen Latinist, steeped in Vergil, and, particularly in the Prologue, exhibiting rhetorical pretensions; I should prefer, with Michael Lapidge, to see this and other such misrepresentations of his source as calculated and deliberate, 'mischievous witticism directed at readers who knew their Vergil'.[76]

Both Vergil and Aldhelm stress that Fama (and Night) treads the earth with her feet but that her head is hidden in the clouds (*ingrediturque solo et caput inter nubila condit*), a detail which the author of the *Liber monstrorum* does not explicitly mention. However, Vergil repeats the same verse verbatim in his description of Orion (*Aeneid* X.763), and it may be that this Vergilian association between Fama and Orion led the author of the *Liber monstrorum* to include the giant hunter as the last in his catalogue of man-shaped monsters (I.56):[77]

> Orion autem talis fuisse confingitur ut omnia maria transire potuisset et profundissimi quamuis gurgitis undas superare humeris et sicut ornos aut ingentia robora de montibus euulsa radicitus traxit. Ferunt eum iuga peragrasse montium et capite sublimia caeli nebula pulsasse.
>
> *But Orion is imagined to have been such that he could cross all seas and overtop with his shoulders the waves of even the deepest flood. And thus he dragged mountain ashes and huge oaks torn up by their roots from the mountains. They say he crossed the peaks of mountains, and knocked the high clouds of the sky with his head.*

One is reminded that just as the Titans and their struggle against the gods were considered by Christian authors to mirror the conflict against God of the fallen angels and Satan, so Orion, the mighty hunter, finds a biblical echo in Nimrod, the spiritual descendant of the kin of Cain after the Flood,[78] whom patristic sources, as we have seen, again associate with the sin of Pride.[79]

What links the giant Orion and Fama further, of course, is fame or reputation; to the Christian author of the *Liber monstrorum* the Vergilian notion that fame (*fama*)

73 See further Whitbread, 'The *Liber Monstrorum* and *Beowulf*', pp. 459–60.

74 Anubis is sometimes depicted alongside the *cynocephali* in patristic accounts, for obvious reasons, and may have helped to identify them with the forces of paganism; see further above, pp. 17–18.

75 Cf. Porsia, ed., *Liber Monstrorum*, p. 285.

76 Lapidge, '*Beowulf*, Aldhelm, the *Liber Monstrorum* and Wessex', p. 168.

77 Cf. Porsia, ed., *Liber Monstrorum*, p. 213.

78 See above, pp. 77–8.

79 Cf. further above, pp. 81–2.

was born of Earth would have seemed particularly appropriate. It is intriguing to note, therefore, that Aldhelm, who, as we have seen, was well aware that Fama (like Orion) treads the earth and hides its head in the clouds, ascribed precisely the same characteristic (drawing on the same Vergilian verse) to Pride (*Superbia*), a familar partner in human heroic endeavour, described here leading the Vices into battle with the Virtues in Aldhelm's *Carmen de virginitate* (lines 2702–9):[80]

> Octavam cumulat truculenta Superbia turmam
> Militibus Christi torquentem pila piacli;
> Quae glomerare studet ventosa fraude maniplos
> Et graditur semper fastu comitata maligno,
> Dumque pedes pergit per mundi crimina fallax,
> Sed cristata caput quassat sub nubibus atris;
> Nam plerumque probos propriis prosternere telis
> Nititur et strages alienis factitat armis.
>
> *Fierce Pride assembles an eighth warrior-band, launching missiles of sin at the soldiers of Christ; with windy fraud she seeks to gather her troops, and always strides with wicked arrogance at her side. Deceptive, while she moves her feet through the crimes of the world, yet her crested head knocks against the dark clouds; for frequently she strives to lay low the virtuous with her own shafts, and causes slaughter with another's arms.*

The description of Pride launching missiles of sin against the soldiers of Christ vividly recalls the homiletic imagery of Hrothgar's 'sermon' in *Beowulf* (lines 1741–4).[81] Aldhelm, like Hrothgar, clearly links Pride with both martial and heroic ideas, apparently merging Virgil's description of Fama (*ingrediturque solo et caput inter nubila condit, Aeneid* IV.177) with that of the giant Atlas, whose pine-wreathed head is battered by dark clouds, and wind, and rain (*cui nubibus atris / piniferum caput et vento pulsatur et imbri, Aeneid* IV.248–9); it seems possible that in his depiction of the windy fraud (*ventosa fraude*) with which Pride summons her minions Aldhelm may be thinking of the formal boast or vaunting (*beot*) of the Germanic warrior.[82] Certainly Aldhelm goes on in the *Carmen de virginitate* to link Pride both with the crime of Cain and the blossoming of sin (lines 2721–9),[83] and with the Fall of Lucifer (lines 2732–51).[84] The Anglo-Saxon Boniface, apparently borrowing independently

80 The passage has no counterpart in the prose *De virginitate*; cf. Lapidge and Rosier, *Aldhelm: the Poetic Works*, p. 162.

81 See above, pp. 50–1. The description of Pride shooting missiles of sin equally recalls the passage from Vercelli Homily IV quoted above, together with a range of related passages in the vernacular.

82 Aldhelm seems to have regarded the adjective *ventosus* ('windy') as particularly appropriate for Pride; he makes use of the term only three further times in his works, each time in the *Carmen de virginitate*, and with this special connotation: cf. *ventoso fastu* (*CdV* 620); *ventoso pectore* (*CdV* 2717), and *ventosa superbia* (*CdV* 2757).

83 See above, pp. 65–6.

84 Pride is equally blamed for Lucifer's Fall in the passage from the prose *De virginitate* quoted above, pp. 100–1.

from Vergil's description of Fama and Orion in his *Enigmata*, ascribes the same capacity to Pride (*Superbia*), who boasts of walking the earth, and scraping the clouds with her head (*in terris gradio, sed nubila vertice tango*);[85] Boniface too stresses that Pride was the cause of Lucifer's desire to overthrow God.

The hostility of Lucifer towards God, motivated by overweening pride, neatly parallels the hostility towards the pagan gods of Earth-born giants like the Aloidae; their very size, whereby, like Earth-born Fama and Superbia, they walked the earth with their heads grazing heaven, could be interpreted as a manifestation of their ambitions.[86] It was left to Isidore to make the connection, albeit negatively, between sacred and profane history, and between the monstrous and human races, in the course of explaining the traditional etymology of Giants (*Gigantes*) in his *Etymologiae* (XI.iii.12–14):

> Sicut autem in singulis gentibus quaedam monstra sunt hominum, ita in universo genere humano quaedam monstra sunt gentium, ut Gigantes, Cynocephali, Cyclopes, et cetera. Gigantes dictos iuxta Graeci sermonis etymologiam, qui eos γηγένεις existimant, id est terrigenas, eo quod fabulose parens terra inmensa mole et similes sibi genuerit. Γῆ enim terra appellatur: γένος genus; licet et terrae filios vulgus vocat: quorum genus incertum est. Falso autem opinatur quidam inperiti de Scripturis sanctis praevaricatores angelos cum filiabus hominum ante diluvium concubuisse, et exinde natos Gigantes, id est nimium grandes et fortes viros, de quibus terra conpleta est.
>
> *But just as in individual races there are certain monstrous men, so in the entire human species there are certain monstrous races, like Gigantes, Cynocephali, Cyclops, and others. Gigantes are so-called according to the etymology of Greek speech, and they reckon them* γηγένεις, *that is 'earth-born', because according to fable the earth their mother gave birth to them with vast bulk and similar to herself. For* γῆ *means 'earth',* γένος *'breed', although they are also commonly called 'sons of earth', and their race is uncertain. However those inexperienced in Holy Scripture falsely reckon that colluding angels slept with the daughters of men before the flood, and that from them were born Gigantes, that is excessively large and strong men, with whom the earth was filled.*

Amongst Insular authors Bede certainly makes use of this passage, and incorporates it into his own exegesis on Genesis VI, as we have seen.[87]

In a work which leans so heavily on Isidore, it is hardly surpising that the author of the *Liber monstrorum* has included in his opening book separate sections on all three of the monstrous races here specified: Gigantes (I.54), Cynocephali (I.16), and Cyclops (I.11). The section on Gigantes, which again comes towards the end of Book I of the *Liber monstrorum*, however, appears to owe little to Isidore, and offers instead an idiosyncratic vision (I.54):

85 Glorie, ed., *Enigmata Bonifatii*, p. 301.

86 See further above, pp. 100–3.

87 The passage in question is quoted above, pp. 77–8.

> Gigantes enim ipsos tam enormis alebat magnitudo ut eis omnia maria pedum gressibus transmeabilia fuisse perhibeatur. Quorum ossa in litoribus et in terrarum latebris, ad indicium vastae quantitatis eorum, saepe conperta leguntur.
>
> *Indeed giants used to grow to such an enormous size that it is said that all the sea were passable to them on foot. And their bones are often found, according to books, on the shores and in the recesses of the world, as an indication of their vast size.*

The notion that giant bones should be found on the sea-shore naturally invites the speculation that they may have been washed up there by the tide, and appears to confirm the ultimately biblical speculation, voiced elsewhere in the *Liber* monstrorum, that monsters and giants were eradicated in the Flood.[88] No direct source for this passage has been found, although there are a number of parallels amongst the acknowledged range of the author's reading. Augustine notes the great stature of men before the Flood (*De civitate Dei* XV.9); he claims to have seen for humself a huge tooth found on the sea-shore at Utica. Similar tales are recorded by Tertullian and Rufinus, as Franco Porsia has noted.[89] But Augustine goes further, and cites Pliny, Homer, and (in particular) Vergil as evidence of the vast stature of men from bygone days (*De civitate Dei* XV.9):

> Unde et nobilissimus eorum poeta Vergilius de ingenti lapide, quem in agrorum limite infixum vir fortis illorum temporum pugnans et rapuit et cucurrit et intorsit et misit:
>
> Vix illum (inquit) lecti bis sex cervice subirent,
> Qualia nunc hominum producit corpora tellus,
>
> significans maiora tunc corpora producere solere tellurem. Quanto magis igitur temporibus recentioribus mundi ante illud nobile diffamatum diluvium!
>
> *Whence [the pagans'] most distinguished poet, Vergil, [says something] about a huge stone, which has been set up on the edge of some fields. A mighty warrior from those days snatched it up, ran, swung it round, and hurled it. As [Vergil] says:*
>
> *Scarcely could a dozen men lift that [stone] on their neck,*
> *With men's bodies such as the earth now produces*
>
> *He is indicating that the earth normally produced larger bodies then. How much more, then, in the days when the world was newer, before that renowned and notorious Flood!*

What is of interest here is Augustine's explicit association of pagan warriors with the antediluvian giants,[90] an association incidentally strengthened by the reference here to the notion that the bodies of such warriors are produced by the Earth, an image which concurs with the traditional Isidoran etymology of Gigantes, noted

88 One might compare, for example, the statements which close the Prologue, quoted above, pp. 88–9.

89 Porsia, ed., *Liber Monstrorum*, p. 211; Tertullian, *De resurrectione carnis*, PL 2, cols. 854–5; Rufinus, *Recognitiones S. Clementis*, PG 1, col. 1223.

90 Similar notions are found in Insular sources also; cf. above, pp. 77–9.

above. The theme of the extraordinary stature of the pagan warriors of old appears elsewhere in Vergil's work, for example in his famous description of future farmers digging up the bones of those who fought at Philippi, and marvelling at their size (*Georgics* I.493–7):

> Scilicet et tempus veniet, cum finibus illis
> agricola incurvo terram molitus aratro
> exesa inveniet scabra robigine pila,
> aut gravibus rastris galeas pulsabit inanis,
> grandiaque effossis mirabitur ossa sepulcris.
>
> *Yes, and a time will come when in that land a farmer working the soil with curved plough will find spears eaten up with mouldy rust, or will strike with his heavy hoe on empty helms, and will wonder at the huge bones from upturned graves.*

Presumably it was at least partly thanks to Vergilian passages like this that the author of the *Liber monstrorum* includes amongst the wondrous creatures of Book I the warrior Eryx, whose appearance in the funeral-games of *Aeneid* V.401–5 wearing boxing-gloves made from the hides of seven oxen is transmuted in the *Liber monstrorum* (I.51), in keeping with his martial status: now he carries a mighty shield made of seven ox-hides.[91] The author's comment that Eryx was no monster, but a man of monstrous size (*non tamen monstrum, sed homo monstruosa magnitudine fuit*), seems in context somewhat disingenuous.

One might also note that in his careful depiction of the Gigantes the author of the *Liber monstrorum* implicitly links this section of his work with others; the comment that the Gigantes were so large that all seas were passable on foot to them (*tam enormis alebat magnitudo ut eis omnia maria pedum gressibus transmeabilia fuisse perhibeatur*) is surely echoed deliberately in the account of the giant hunter Orion, described as so large that he could cross all seas (*talis fuisse confingitur ut omnia maria transire potuisset*), which follows almost immediately (I.56). The link is all the clearer in that the phrase in question owes nothing directly to Vergil's description of Orion (*Aeneid* X.763–7), which was certainly the main source.[92]

The second element in the depiction of Gigantes is the claim by the author of the *Liber monstrorum* that their huge bones are said to be found on the shores and in the hidden places of the earth (*quorum ossa in litoribus et in terrarum latebris, ad indicium vastae quantitatis eorum, saepe conperta leguntur*). Once again the author appears to be drawing a parallel with material elsewhere in his work; at the beginning of the *Liber monstrorum* the author has drawn attention to the giant bones of Hygelac, king of the Geats, by the shores of the Rhine (I.2), and elsewhere he speaks of the body of a giant girl washed up on the shores of western Europe (I.13). No Latin source has been discovered for either of these passages, but both have interesting Insular (and vernacular) connections.

91 Cf. Porsia, ed., *Liber Monstrorum*, p. 207.
92 Cf. Porsia, ed., *Liber Monstrorum*, p. 213.

Hygelac's appearance both in the *Liber monstrorum* and in *Beowulf* is but one of a number of possible links between the two works, as we shall see, while the passage concerning the giant girl also appears in a late Irish manuscript, in a rendering extremely close to that in the *Liber monstrorum*, of which it is presumably a direct translation:[93]

> Bean dorala gan ḟās a cīch a trāigh mara a nEoruip. Cōeca troigh ina hairdi, [e]adhōn ō dā slinnēn co troighidh, secht troighi a lethead a hochta. Brat corcra uimpi, a lāmha a ceangal for a druim anīar 7 sī ar mbein a cind dí 7 as amlaidh sin rolāidh an tonn a tīr hī. Finit.
>
> *A woman, whose breasts had not grown, was cast up on a sea shore in Europe. She was fifty feet tall, that is from her shoulders to her feet, and her chest was seven feet across. There was a purple cloak on her. Her hands were tied behind her back, and her head had been cut off; and it was in this way that the wave cast her up on land. Finit.*[94]

The account in the *Liber monstrorum* hardly differs at all (I.13):

> Et quandam puellam in occiduis Europae litoribus, necdum turgentibus mammis, repertam didicimus, quae undae gurgitum ab Oceano terris aduexerunt; cuius magnitudinem lapidibus designabant. Erat enim ipsius corporis longitudo .L. pedum, et inter humeros .VII. latitudinis habuit. Purpureo induta pallio, uirgis alligata et in caput occisa peruenerat.
>
> *And we have heard tell of a certain girl, not yet with swelling breasts, discovered on the western shores of Europe, whom the waves of the sea brought to land from the Ocean; they marked her size with stones. Indeed fifty feet was the length of her body, and she was seven feet wide between the shoulders. She had come dressed in a purple cloak, bound with saplings, and fatally wounded in the head.*

The differences between the two versions, although slight, are not without interest. The Irish version states that the girl had her hands tied behind her back,[95] and that (a typically Celtic touch?) her head had been cut off; the *Liber monstrorum* appears to allude to binding with saplings, and an indeterminate head-wound. More intriguing is the insistence in the *Liber monstrorum* that the girl was dicovered on the western shores of Europe, which is absent in the Irish version, perhaps because the Irish themselves inhabited those very shores, and felt no need for such specification. Both versions mention the wearing of a purple cloak, perhaps intended as a sign of royalty; one is reminded of yet another of Vergil's descriptions of the mighty heroes of bygone days, namely that of the huge headless corpse of Priam, 'proud ruler of Asia' (*superbum regnatorem Asiae*), on the sea-shore (*Aeneid* II. 557–8):

93 Transcription by Kuno Meyer from Edinburgh, National Library of Scotland, MS Adv. 72.1.26 (Gaelic XXVI), printed in Bergin *et al.*, ed., *Anecdota*, III, p. 10.

94 Translated by Jackson, *A Celtic Miscellany*, p. 166.

95 An expansion on the curious Latin *uirgis alligata*, for which no direct source or analogue has so far been suggested.

iacet ingens litore truncus
avolsumque umeris caput et sine nomine corpus.
His huge trunk lies on the shore, the head struck from the shoulders,
a corpse without a name.

The Irish description of the giant girl is followed in the same manuscript by a companion-piece, ostensibly depicting a similar wonder:

> Bean ele dono rorala a mhuir a nAlbuin ⁊ dā troigh dēc ar nāi cēd a fad fēin. Secht troighti dēc etar a dā cīch ⁊ a sē dēc a fad a trillsi ocus a secht a fad meōir a lāmha. Secht troighti a fad a srōna, dā troigh iter a dā malaig. Gilithear gēis nō ūan tuin[n]e gach mball dí ⁊ rl. ⁊ rl.
>
> *Another woman was cast up from the sea in Scotland, and she was a hundred and ninety-two feet long; there were seventeen feet between her breasts, and sixteen was the length of her hair, and seven the length of the finger of her hand. Her nose was seven feet long, and there were two feet between her eyebrows. Every limb of her was as white as the swan or the foam of the wave, etc. etc.*

The interest of this version lies precisely in the fact that it can itself be closely matched by much earlier vernacular accounts in the Book of Lismore,[96] as well as in a number of closely-related annals such as the *Chronicon Scotorum* (*s.a.* 900), the Annals of Ulster (*s.a.* 891), the Annals of the Four Masters (*s.a.* 891), and the Annals of Inisfallen (*s.a.* 906).[97] In each case the woman is described by the same features (overall size, and length of hair, fingers, and nose), with little variation.[98] The *Chronicon Scotorum* adds, as in the text discussed here, that there were six feet between her breasts, and all versions describe the whiteness of her skin. Such creatures clearly caught the Irish imagination; according to a vernacular *Life*, St Brendan was walking by the sea-shore when he came upon a recognisably similar figure:[99]

> Ni fada dochuattar assin, an tan fuaratar inghen min maccdacta mong-bhuidhe, gilither snechta no úan tuinne hí, ⁊ sí marbh iar ttabairt buille do ghae dhi tréna formna, co ndechaid eter a da cích. Ba dermair immorro mét na hingine sin; ced traigidh ina hairde, ⁊ noi ttroigthi eter a da cích, ceithre troighthi i ffod a srona, ⁊ secht troighti hí ffod a méoir medhoin.
>
> *They had not gone far from there when they found a fair young maiden, with golden tresses, as white as the snow or the foam of the wave, lying dead from the thrust of a spear which had entered between her shoulders and come out between her breasts; her nose was four feet long, and her middle finger seven feet long.*

96 See Stokes, *Lives of Saints*, pp. xlii–xliii.

97 Hennessy, ed., *Chronicon Scotorum*, pp. 176–7; Mac Airt and Mac Niocaill, ed., *The Annals of Ulster*, pp. 346–7, O'Donovan, ed., *Annála Ríoghachta Éireann*, pp. 346–7; Mac Airt, ed., *The Annals of Innisfallen*, pp. 142–3.

98 Her length is given as either 195 feet (*Chronicon Scotorum* and Annals of Ulster) or 192 (Annals of Inisfallen); her hair is fifteen feet long (*Chronicon Scotorum*), or seventeen (Annals of Ulster), or sixteen (Annals of Inisfallen); her fingers six feet long (*Chronicon Scotorum* and Annals of Inisfallen) or seven (Annals of Ulster); her nose seven feet long (*Chronicon Scotorum* and Annals of Ulster) or six (Annals of Inisfallen).

99 *Betha Brenainn Clúana Ferta*, § 87; Plummer, ed., *Bethada Náem nÉrenn*, I, p. 62; II, p. 61.

The saint revives the giant woman, and, without further ado, baptises her. He asks her about her kin, and she says that she is one of the people of the sea. After expressing a wish to go to heaven, she is given the eucharist by the saint, and promptly expires. Nor is this an isolated incident in the Irish Saints' Lives.[100]

The ubiquity of such sea-bourne heathen giantesses in (admittedly much later) Irish texts raises acute questions as to whether all can be traced ultimately to the *Liber monstrorum*, in the absence of any clear Latin source. It is, however, intriguing to note that the *Liber monstrorum* itself contains another account of a young woman, fatally wounded in the head, who met her end at the water's edge (III.3):

> Hydra anguis armatus fuisse describitur, quae Euridicen, coniugem Orphei, in ripa fluminis capite truncauit et demersit in gurgitem; et sicut Scylla monstris, ita et haec serpentibus praecincta fuisse fingitur. Cuius tale signum Hercules in suo clipeo cum aliis .C. gerebat anguibus.
>
> *The Hydra is described as having been an armed snake which struck Eurydice, the wife of Orpheus, in the head, on a river-bank [or perhaps 'on a river-bank at the head of a river'], and drowned her in the flood; and just as Scylla was girt about with monsters, so too this is imagined to have been girt about with serpents. Hercules used to wear such a sign on his shield, along with a hundred other snakes.*

One presumes that the source for the latter account is Lucan's now-lost poem *Orpheus*, which is alluded to on two earlier occasions in the *Liber monstrorum* (I.5 and II.7),[101] especially since the details given here cannot be matched precisely in any other Classical account of Eurydice's demise.[102] In that case, it would appear that the author of the *Liber monstrorum* has made Eurydice a giantess, alongside other Classical figures such as Eryx, and that the depiction of her sea-shore corpse might suit a wider rhetorical purpose, as we shall see.

But if the dead giantess washed-up on the shore has Irish vernacular analogues, then another huge sea-shore corpse has often called to mind the world of germanic heroic poetry. Interest in the *Liber monstrorum* has tended to focus on the relationship of the work to *Beowulf*, fostered by the clear reference to Hygelac, who appears to be the only germanic figure mentioned in the *Liber monstrorum* at all (I.2):[103]

> Et fiunt monstra mirae magnitudinis, ut rex Higlacus, qui imperauit Getis et a Francis occisus est, quem equus a duodecimo aetatis anno portare non potuit. Cuius ossa in Rheni fluminis insula, ubi in Oceanum prorumpit, reseruata sunt, et de longinquo uenientibus pro miraculo ostenduntur.
>
> *And there are monsters of an amazing size, like King Hygelac, who ruled the Geats and was killed by the Franks, whom no horse could carry from the age of twelve. His*

100 Cf. Plummer, ed., *Bethada Náem nÉrenn*, II, p. 332.

101 See further above, p. 92.

102 In particular the curious phrase *capite truncauit* is without obvious parallel (although one might compare the equally unusual *in caput occisa* of *Liber monstrorum* I.13). See further Porsia, ed., *Liber Monstrorum*, p. 265.

103 See particularly Whitbread, 'The *Liber Monstrorum* and *Beowulf*', pp. 461–5 and Lapidge, '*Beowulf*, Aldhelm, the *Liber Monstrorum* and Wessex', pp. 162–7 and 176–8, together with the references there cited.

bones are preserved on an island in the river Rhine, where it breaks into the Ocean, and they are shown as a wonder to travellers from afar.

The passage has been taken equally as evidence that the author of the *Liber monstrorum* was familiar with *Beowulf*, and vice versa, while others have doubted that there is any sign that the either author knew the other's work.[104] Perhaps the most telling objection to the notion that the author of the *Liber monstrorum* knew the oral tradition behind *Beowulf*, if not the poem itself, is voiced by Ann Knock: 'Not only is there no evidence that the *Beowulf* poet envisaged Hygelac as being of abnormal size, but it is surely inconceivable, if the compiler of the *Liber monstrorum* knew the Beowulf tradition, that he should have selected Hygelac from it by name, neglecting Grendel and his mother, gold-hoarding dragons and even Beowulf himself'.[105] Whilst one might plausibly counter that, to judge by the other 'monsters' and 'giants' detailed in his first book, any pagan warrior whose bones are described on the sea-shore in the *Liber monstrorum* is likely to be depicted as monstrously huge, and that in any case there are several medieval traditions which specifically deal with the mighty stature of the Geats,[106] the second part of Knock's observation highlights the efforts of those keen to make further links between the two works. Both Dorothy Whitelock and Margaret Goldsmith consider that the absence of, for example, Grendel and the dragon from the *Liber monstrorum* can be ascribed to their 'popular, and not learned, origin,'[107] whilst Leslie Whitbread has gone the furthest, in attempting to associate in rather general terms the descriptions of the monsters in *Beowulf* with those found in the *Liber monstrorum*.[108] But his approach, which focuses on a handful of creatures from the *Liber monstrorum* such as swamp-monsters with human heads (I.34), nocturnal flying monsters (I.42), nocturnal shape-changers (II.20), and shore-dwelling predators (I.32), is perhaps insufficiently specific to prove conclusive. One might as well point to the description of the crocodile (II.25), murderous when roused from its slumber at the water's edge, as an analogue for the vengeful activities of the dragon in *Beowulf*.

Of more immediate relevance to the depiction of the monsters in *Beowulf* is the very structure of the *Liber monstrorum*, with its three main sections dealing in turn with monstrous men, monstrous beasts, and finally monstrous serpents, since it has been argued by Nora Chadwick that a series of conflicts with just such a combination of creatures provides the paradigm for Beowulf's endeavours, a suggestion which seems to be borne out in several Norse parallels.[109] Likewise a general similarity of approach may be discerned in the fact that while each work is clearly infused with Christian thought and imagery, neither *Beowulf* nor the *Liber monstrorum* makes its

104 Goldsmith, *Mode and Meaning*, pp. 98–9; cf. Whitelock, *The Audience of Beowulf*, p. 53; Sisam, *The Structure of Beowulf*, p. 6.

105 Knock (review of Bologna's edition), p. 261.

106 See particularly Leake, *The Geatas of 'Beowulf'*, pp. 12–42; cf. *Liber Monstrorum* I.3 (Colossus).

107 Whitelock, *The Audience of Beowulf*, p. 53; cf. Goldsmith, *Mode and Meaning*, p. 99.

108 Whitbread, 'The *Liber Monstrorum* and *Beowulf*', 465–9.

109 See in particular Chadwick, 'The Monsters and Beowulf', pp. 172–93, and Opland, 'A Beowulf Analogue', pp. 54–8.

religious allegiance explicit.[110] Finally, one might point to the first, most obvious, and, in the context of its known sources, most original aspect of the *Liber monstrorum*, namely its depiction of monsters as fundamentally hostile to the human race, and essentially remote, to be found only 'in the hidden parts of the world, throughout the deserts and island of the Ocean, and in the recesses of the farthest mountains' (*in abditis mundi partibus per deserta et Oceani insulas et in ultimorum montium latebris*). After Hrothgar has described the watery lair of Grendel's mother, which certainly qualifies as remote, Beowulf himself makes the formulaic boast to pursue his foe, wherever he goes (*Beowulf*, lines 1392–4):

> Ic hit þe gehate: no he on helm losaþ,
> ne on foldan fæþm,   ne on fyrgenholt,
> ne on gyfenes grund,   ga þær he wille!
>
> *I promise you this, he shall not escape under cover, nor into the bosom of the earth, nor into the mountain-forest, nor to the depth of the ocean, let him go where he will!*

The parallel is not exact, but Beowulf's boast provides but one further example of how the *Liber monstrorum* and *Beowulf*, however one determines their precise literary relationship, share a number of mutually illuminating attitudes and themes.

It is perhaps more fruitful to examine specific details, such as Grendel's eyes, which are described as shining with an 'unlovely light, most like a flame' (*Beowulf*, lines 725–6). Analogues have been widely sought from many sources, including Saints' Lives, but a clear parallel is to be found in the description of the monstrous men in the *Liber monstrorum* (I.36), who lived on an island in the East, and were like other men except that their eyes shine like torches (*eorum oculi sicut lucerna lucent*); such flaming eyes can be matched several times in the *Liber monstrorum*.[111] One of the few passages in the *Liber monstrorum* which remains as yet unsourced, moreover, speaks of a breed of beast, the fiercest of all, whose venom is of extraordinary corrosive power, and can melt metal (II.23):

> Bestia autem illa inter omnes beluas dirissima fertur, in qua tantam ueneni copiam adfirmant ut eam sibi leones quamuis inualidioris feram corporis, timeant, et tantam uim eius uenenum habere arbitrantur, ut eo licet ferri acies intincta liquescat.
>
> *But that beast is said to be amongst the fiercest of all brutes, in which they assert that there is such a quantity of venom that lions fear it although it is an animal of weaker body, and they reckon that its poison has such strength, that the cutting-edge even of iron, dipped in it, melts.*

Notably similar properties are exhibited by the poisonous blood of Grendel and his mother, which melts the giant-sword in a manner which evidently fascinated the poet (*Beowulf*, lines 1605–17):

110 See further above, pp. 90–2.

111 Cf. I.28; III.2; III.5; III.7; III.10; indeed this passage from the *Liber monstrorum* (along with several of the others noted) can be traced to the *Wonders of the East* § 23.

Þa þæt sweord ongan
æfter heoþoswate   hildegicelum,
wigbil wanian;   þæt wæs wundra sum,
þæt hit eal gemealt   ise gelicost,
ðonne forstes bend   Fæder onlæteð,
onwindeð wælrapas,   se geweald hafað
sæla ond mæla;   þat is soð Metod.
Ne nom he in þæm wicum,   Weder-Geata leod,
maðmæhta ma,   þeh he þær monige geseah,
buton þone hafelan   ond þa hilt somod
since fage;   sweord ær gemealt,
forbarn brodenmæl;   wæs þæt blod to þæs hat
ættren ellorgæst,   se þær inne swealt.

Then that sword began, because of the struggle-gore, that war-blade to melt in battle-icicles; it was a marvel that it all melted most like ice, when the Father loosens the bonds of frost, unwinds the water-fetters, he who has command of times and seasons; he is the true God. The prince of the Weder-Geats did not remove from that dwelling any more precious treasures, although he saw many there, but that head and the hilt too, inlaid with treasure; the sword had melted, the patterned-blade entirely burned; the blood was too hot, the poisonous alien spirit, who died therein.

Beowulf's own account of the melting blade (*Beowulf*, lines 1666–8) contains several deliberate verbal echoes (indicated by italics), and testifies further to the poet's fascination with the theme:

Þa þæt hilde*bil*
forbarn brogdenmæl,   swa þæt *blod* gesprang,
hatost heaþoswata.

Then that war-blade, the patterned weapon, entirely burned up, as the blood gushed out, the hottest of battle-gore.

It may be that Sigemund's dragon had corrosive properties not dissimilar; all we hear of that dead monster's fate is that 'heat melted the worm' or 'the hot worm melted' (*wyrm hat gemealt*, line 897).[112] No credible source for this melting blade in *Beowulf* has been found; Martin Puhvel has offered a number of Celtic parallels, themselves of uncertain origin and date, and an example from a nineteenth-century Icelandic folktale; all seem rather fanciful.[113] The blade that melts in the blood of the race of Cain in *Beowulf* provides an apt metaphor for the very theme engraved upon its hilt, namely the flood that destroyed the race of giants.[114]

112 Cf. the comment that Beowulf's fire-dragon was consumed in flames (*Beowulf*, lines 3040–1).

113 Puhvel, 'The Melting of the Giant-Wrought Sword', pp. 39–44; see further above, pp. 66–7.

114 Cf. Viswanathan, 'On the Melting of the Sword', pp. 360–3.

It is left to the aged Hrothgar to examine what is depicted on the monstrous weapon (*Beowulf*, lines 1687–93). At this point, evidently inspired by the sight of the hilt, with its depiction of overweening ambition laid low, Hrothgar launches into his famous 'sermon' (*Beowulf* 1700–84), warning Beowulf of the dangers of pride.[115] It is the sight of the dreadful fate of the overweening giants, destroyed in the Flood, which spurs Hrothgar to deliver his 'sermon'; a parallel doom, we are told, has been meted out to the monsters of the *Liber monstrorum*, which explains why they are so seldom seen (I.Prol.):

> nunc humano genere multiplicato et terrarum orbe repleto, sub astris minus producuntur monstra, quae ab ipsis per plurimos terrae angulos eradicata funditus et subuersa legimus et nunc reuulsa litoribus prona torquentur ad undas, quaeque turbine poli uertice sub arduo a totius gyri ambitu et omni loco terrarum ad hanc uastam gurgitis se uoraginem uergunt.
>
> *Now, when humankind has multiplied and the lands of the earth have been filled, fewer monsters are produced under the stars, and we read that in most of the corners of the world they have been utterly eradicated and overthrown by them, and now cast out from the shores they are thrown down to the waves, and that by the churning from the steep summit of the pole they turn from the edge of the entire circle and from every place on earth towards this vast abyss of the flood.*

This passage in the *Liber monstrorum* has been independently ascribed by Whitbread to the direct influence of 'the biblical notion of the giants drowned in the flood (Genesis VI.4–7; Wisdom XIV.6) or groaning beneath the waters (Job XXVI.5)'.[116] As we have already seen, the *Beowulf*-poet and the author of the *Liber monstrorum* share the link between the giants drowned in the flood, and the annihilation of monsters, and the dangers of pride with other Insular authors also, such as Bede or the anonymous author of *Altus prosator*, which, as its influence on both Aldhelm and the compilers of various glossaries demonstrates, was known in Anglo-Saxon England from an early period.[117]

One might return to the fact that the author of the *Liber monstrorum* considers the pagan germanic hero Hygelac so early on in his narrative, alongside what he apparently considers factual accounts. The important question, surely, is not why Grendel or the dragon (or Beowulf) are not included in the *Liber monstrorum*, but why Hygelac is. His gigantic size, as depicted in the *Liber monstrorum*, passes unmentioned in *Beowulf* and the Frankish chronicles which describe his exploits,[118] all of which, however, focus on the final foray into Frankish territory in which he lost his life. This hapless venture, alluded to on no fewer than four separate occasions

115 See further above, pp. 47–53.

116 Whitbread, '*Beowulf* and the *Liber Monstrorum*', pp. 439–40. As Whitbread concludes of this passage from the *Liber monstrorum*: 'This, in more prosaic terms, is the fate of the dragon in *Beowulf* 3131–33' (p. 440).

117 See further above, pp. 80–4.

118 The only possible reference to Hygelac's size in *Beowulf*, line 1926 (*heah*), is problematic, since the adjective might equally apply to his hall; cf. Goldsmith, *Mode and Meaning*, p. 99.

in *Beowulf* (lines 1202–14; 2354–79; 2501–9; 2910–21), appears to have been a singularly ill-judged affair;[119] as Klaeber characterises the venture: 'not content with his success in the North, Hygelac even undertook a ravaging expedition into the Frankish lands'.[120] Kemp Malone is still blunter: 'Hygelac's expedition had no high moral purpose. The king and his men were out for booty'.[121] In his opening allusion to the incident, the *Beowulf*-poet is explicit concerning the motive for the expedition: Hygelac attacked the Franks because of pride (*for wlenco*).[122] Was that the reason why Hygelac was to languish amongst monsters in the *Liber monstrorum*?

The monstrosity of such human heroes, 'the mightie of the olde worlde, famous men' (*potentes a seculo uiri famosi*), of Genesis VI.4, castigated in patristic commentary, is further implicit throughout the *Liber monstrorum* in its author's insistence on including such figures alongside other man-shaped monsters.[123] Chief amongst these 'mightie of the olde worlde' is surely Hercules, who appears in each of the three main sections of the *Liber monstrorum*, both as monster and monster-slayer (I.12; II.1, 6, 14; III.1, 3, 20),[124] and whose initial appearance is distinctly ambiguous:

> Quis Herculis fortitudinem et arma non miretur, qui in occiduis Tyrrheni maris faucibus columnas mirae magnitudinis ad humani generis spectaculum erexit, quique bellorum suorum tropaea in Oriente iuxta Oceanum Indicum ad posteritatis memoriam construxit, et postquam paene totum orbem cum bellis peragrasset et terram tanto sanguine maculauisset, sese moriturum flammis ad deuorandum inuoluit?
>
> *Who does not admire [or 'wonder at'] the courage and weaponry of Hercules, who, at the western entrance to the Mediterranean, erected pillars of an amazing size as a spectacle for the human race, and who constructed trophies of his wars in the East by the Indian Ocean, as a memorial for posterity, and afterwards travelled in battles through almost the entire world, and spattered the earth with so much blood, and at the point of death wrapped himself in flames to be consumed?*

This, the only direct question in the entire work, addresses the crucial dilemma for Christians assessing their pagan heroic past: were such figures to be admired or simply wondered at?[125] The nicely ambiguous Latin (*quis . . . non miretur*) covers both

119 See further above, pp. 106–7.

120 Klaeber, ed., *Beowulf*, p. xxxix.

121 Malone, 'Beowulf', p. 166.

122 *Beowulf*, line 1206; cf. Bandy, 'Cain, Grendel, and the Giants of *Beowulf*', pp. 244–6. One might note that the same motive is ascribed to Beowulf for his own trip to Denmark by both the watchman (line 338) and Unferth (line 508).

123 Cf. Lapidge, '*Beowulf*, Aldhelm, the *Liber Monstrorum* and Wessex', p. 168.

124 One might also note the mention of Hercules in the interpolated passage printed below, p. 278, in the critical apparatus to I.36. Hercules is also listed as a monster by Thomas of Cantimpré, in a passage directly borrowed from the quoted chapter of the *Liber monstrorum*; Boese, ed., *Thomas of Cantimpré: Liber de Natura Rerum*, p. 100.

125 On the dilemma posed by pagan heroic verse to Christians throughout the medieval period, see, for example, Kratz, *Mocking Epic*, pp. 12–23.

possibilities. The great sea-side monuments in East and West can only be interpreted in Christian eyes as sand-castles to pride,[126] the more so, perhaps, since later pagan heroes (like Beowulf) saw fit to celebrate their own deeds in similar ways.[127] The blood and battle that are the essential backdrop for heroic endeavour are here impugned, and the author of the *Liber monstrorum* leaves open the precise sense of his closing remarks: according to heroic legend Hercules, burning in the hot blood of the centaur Nessus, whom he had slain, was indeed assigned to the funeral pyre, but a Christian might well consider that his ultimate reward would be to be devoured by other, hotter, flames. This is certainly the sense of Ælfric's remarks on Hercules, written at around the time the *Beowulf*-manuscript was being compiled. In his account of the Passion of Chrysanthus and Daria, in which, incidentally, he adopts a tripartite division of men, beasts, and serpents similar to that used in the *Liber monstrorum* itself to denote the unfortunate victims of Hercules' wrath, Ælfric grimly asks:[128]

> Hwylc halignyss wæs on þam hetelan Ercule
> þam ormætan ente þe ealle acwealde
> his nehgeburas and forbærnde hine sylfne
> swa cucenne on fyre siððan he acweald hæfde
> men and þa leon and þa micclan næddran?
>
> *What holiness was in that hateful Hercules, the huge [or 'excessive'] giant, who slaughtered all his neighbours, and burned himself alive in the fire, after he had killed men, and the lion, and the great serpent?*

The key role of Hercules, 'the huge giant',[129] a monstrous slayer of monsters, in the *Liber monstrorum*, as well as his depiction here by Ælfric, is instructive in introducing a further heroic monster-slayer from pagan days, who consciously looked to surpass the deeds of Hercules, and whose pervasive depiction both in the *Liber monstrorum* and in the *Beowulf*-manuscript is equally ambiguous: Alexander the Great.[130]

126 See further below, pp. 138–9.

127 See now Robinson, *The Tomb of Beowulf*, pp. 3–19.

128 Skeat, ed., *Ælfric's Lives of Saints*, II, p. 384/112–16.

129 See further below, pp. 124–5.

130 Patrizia Lendinara, 'Il *Liber Monstrorum* e i glossari anglosassoni', in *L'immaginario nelle letterature germaniche del medioevo*, ed. Adele Cippolla (Milan, 1995), pp. 203–25, has recently argued for intimate knowledge of the *Liber monstrorum* in Anglo-Saxon England, but her article, which she kindly sent me, came too late for its arguments to be incorporated here.

CHAPTER V

The Alexander-Legend in Anglo-Saxon England

The Old English *Letter of Alexander to Aristotle* has excited little attention over the years: the standard edition is old and rather unreadable, and the text problematic.[1] Accordingly, any critical interest has always tended to focus on linguistic and editorial matters rather than on any perceived literary interest.[2] Recent work in other fields, however, has greatly enhanced understanding of the reception and transmission of the Latin *Epistola Alexandri ad Aristotelem* upon which the Old English version is based, and such studies throw the comparative neglect of the *Letter* into still greater relief.[3] The *Letter* raises several important questions about the

1 The *Letter* has been edited most recently by Rypins, *Three Old English Prose Texts*, pp. 1–50. Rypins declares his aim 'to reproduce the MS. as nearly in facsimile as possible (p. xlix), and he follows the manuscript line for line and page for page throughout, with few emendations, even where clearly required. A far more readable text, though less accurate, is provided by Baskervill, 'The Anglo-Saxon Version of the *Epistola Alexandri ad Aristotelem*'. The only translation of the Old English text previously available is by Davidson and Campbell, 'The Letter of Alexander the Great'. Here I have followed the text and translation given in the Appendix below, pp. 224–53; the division into sections is mine, and is provided simply to facilitate comparison between Latin and Old English versions, and with the translation.

2 See, for example, Holder, 'Collationen zu angelsächsischen Werken II. *Epistola Alexandri ad* Aristotelem'; Klaeber, 'Notes on Old English Prose Texts'; Braun, *Lautlehre der angelsächsischen Version der 'Epistola Alexandri ad Aristotelem'*; Rypins, Notes on *Epistola Alexandri ad Aristotelem*'; Bradley and Sisam, 'Textual Notes on the Old English *Epistola Alexandri* '; Rypins, 'The Old English *Epistola Alexandri ad Aristotelem*'; Swaen, 'Is *seo hiow* = "Fortune" a Ghost-Word?'; Davis, ' "Hippopotamus" in Old English'; Malone, 'Readings from Folios 94 to 131, Cotton Vitellius A xv'; Berg, 'Tales of Alexander and the East'; Pickles, 'Studies in the Prose Texts of the *Beowulf* Manuscript', pp. 88–119; Bridges, 'Empowering the Hero'.

3 See particularly, for example, the exemplary edition of Boer, ed., *Epistola Alexandri ad Aristotelem*, as well as a number of other important studies such as Cizek, 'Ungeheuer und magische Lebewesen in der *Epistola Alexandri ad magistrum suum de situ Indiae*'; Pfister, *Kleine Schriften zum Alexanderroman*; Pfister, *Der Alexanderroman mit einer Auswahl aus den verwandten Texten*; Gunderson, *Alexander's Letter to Aristotle about India*; Lecouteux, *Kleine Texte zur Alexanderssage*, especially pp. 22–45; Haycock, ' "Some Talk of Alexander and Some of Hercules" '; Tristram, 'Der insulare Alexander'; Tristram, 'More Talk of Alexander'. See now Gillies, 'Ffigur Alexander: tystiolaeth o brydyddiaeth farddol Aeleg'; I am grateful to Patrick Sims-Williams for drawing the last of these items to my attention.

interpretation of the popular Alexander-legend in Anglo-Saxon England, as well as casting light on a number of closely-related texts such as the *Liber monstrorum*, the *Wonders of the East*, and, of course, *Beowulf*, which immediately follows the *Letter* in the *Beowulf*-manuscript.[4] Here I hope to set the *Letter* in context by first considering the potency, popularity, and bias of legends attached to Alexander the Great in Anglo-Saxon England, before assessing the textual relations of the *Letter* together with its style and purpose. Finally I wish to suggest in the light of these indications how the *Letter* was received in Anglo-Saxon England, and how such a reception may have important implications for the contemporary Anglo-Saxon reception of *Beowulf* itself.

There are two quite distinct prevailing views of Alexander throughout the medieval period, the essence of both of which can be traced back to the earliest (and ultimately historical) sources.[5] The first viewpoint considers Alexander in an overwhelmingly positive light as an explorer, inventor, and discoverer of many of the world's marvels. Indeed, in such sources the terrestrial world is seldom enough: Alexander traverses the sky in the company of griffins,[6] and plumbs the ocean in a proto-submarine.[7] Numerous tales of monsters and marvels stem from the travel literature of Alexander's historical Indian campaign.[8] Behind the wondrous facade, it even appears that distorted elements of genuine accounts may have filtered down. The Old English *Wonders of the East* firmly maintains in the course of a rather garbled account (§ 12) that creatures which the sources make clear were hippopotami sweat blood, while modern research has shown that the 'skin [of the hippopotamus] exudes red droplets which protect from sunburn (and possibly infection)'.[9] The second view of Alexander is overwhelmingly hostile, as implacably negative as the first is positive. Alexander is portrayed as a megalomaniac, a tyrannical mass-murderer, a figure of extreme Pride.[10] This attitude can also be traced to 'historical' accounts, by Arrian, and Quintus Curtius Rufus, and is based on a number of the more reprehensible incidents in Alexander's historical career such as the sack of Thebes, the burning of Persepolis, and (in particular) the murder of Cleitus.[11] This view, mediated in Latin by Seneca and Cicero, and in the opening verses of the biblical First Book of Maccabees, was inevitably the one seized upon by the Church Fathers, and given

4 See further Rypins, *Three Old English Prose Texts*, pp. vii–xlvii.

5 Cf. Holländer, 'Alexander: *Hybris* und *Curiositas*'; Tristram, 'More Talk of Alexander', p. 660.

6 Cf. Cary, *The Medieval Alexander*, pp. 340–1; Michael, *Alexander's Flying Machine*; Settis-Frugoni, *Historia Alexandri elevati*.

7 Cf. Cary, *The Medieval Alexander*, pp. 134–5 and 340–1; Ross, *Alexander and the Faithless Lady*.

8 Cary, *The Medieval Alexander*, pp. 9–18.

9 Crystal, ed., *The Cambridge Encyclopedia*, p. 569.

10 Cary, *The Medieval Alexander*, pp. 101–2 and 121–30.

11 See, for example, Lane Fox, *Alexander the Great*, pp. 309–14; Green, *Alexander of Maecedon*, pp. 361–6. Most recently O'Brien has ascribed many of Alexander's more morally questionable activities to an acute case of alcoholism; see, for example, O'Brien, *Alexander the Great: the Invisible Enemy*, pp. 133–40.

fresh impetus by Jerome and (particularly) Orosius.[12] As George Cary notes: 'Orosius did not spare Alexander, rather he carried the Stoic abuse of him to its last extreme for the benefit of his Christian readers. For him, Alexander was a ruthless, bloodthirsty conqueror fired by his insane love of glory in battle.'[13]

Most of the broad spectrum of texts which deal with Alexander can quickly be assigned to one of these two categories, according to the aspect highlighted, what I have termed 'pride' and 'prodigies', and others, with specific reference to Alexander, *hybris* and *curiositas*.[14] So, for example (to cite only texts of which Latin manuscripts were available in England before the twelfth century), the account provided by Orosius is one of unmitigated hubris and tyranny, while the Latin *Letter of Alexander* is a breathless tale of undiluted wonder.[15] As the body of legendary material grew, a few texts appeared which attempted to reconcile the two opposing views. One such (again, found in Latin in an English manuscript of late eleventh- or perhaps early twelfth-century date) is the so-called *Collatio Alexandri cum Dindimo rege Bragmanorum*, in which Alexander corresponds with the philosophers of India and is educated in their ways, but through wilful arrogance refuses to accept the value of their philosophical and pacific virtues against his life of war; his is the pride, and they are the prodigies.[16]

In time this easy distinction between the twin aspects of pride and prodigies breaks down further, as both views become current, and texts contaminated. So the tenth-century Irish macroform *Imthúsa Alexandair* simply combines Orosius, the *Letter to Aristotle*, and the *Collatio*, but, as Hildegard Tristram has indicated, studiously ignores all the moral condemnation of Orosius to produce a purely heroic and pseudo-historical tale of wonder.[17] The Irish view of Alexander is not entirely rose-tinted, however; Kuno Meyer pointed out long ago that in Irish verse Alexander's stock epithet is 'proud' (*úaibrech*).[18] In the same way, three Welsh poems, two on Alexander, one on Hercules, often depicted as the *figura* of Alexander, preserved in the Book of Taliesin, but dated by Marged Haycock earlier than the twelfth century, clearly draw on Orosius, but are pervaded with a positive admiration of Alexander's wondrous exploits, including both his submarine adventures and his celestial flight.[19] A single line commenting on Alexander's death: 'better if it had happened sooner' (*kyn no hyn bei gwell digonet*) hints at the darker alternative tradition.[20] Other medieval authors were equally keen to elaborate particular aspects of their source: Walter of Châtillon's late twelfth-century *Alexandreis* plays on the Orosian notion

12 Cf. Tristram, 'More Talk of Alexander', p. 660.

13 Cary, *The Medieval Alexander*, p. 113.

14 Holländer, 'Alexander: *Hybris* und *Curiositas*'.

15 Cary, *The Medieval Alexander*, pp. 14–16 and 60–2.

16 Cary, *The Medieval Alexander*, pp. 13–14.

17 Tristram, 'Der insulare Alexander', pp. 133–40

18 Meyer, 'Die Geschichte von Phillip und Alexander', p. 5; cf. Tristram, 'More Talk of Alexander', p. 661.

19 Haycock, ' "Some Talk of Alexander and Some of Hercules" '.

20 Cf. Tristram, 'More Talk of Alexander', p. 659.

of Alexander's excessive pride,[21] but it took an Icelander, Bishop Brandr Jónsson of Hólar (who died in 1264), in his rendering of Walter's work, *Alexanders saga*, to highlight the hubris of his eponymous 'hero'.[22] At one point the bishop puts into the mouth of Alexander the following anachronistic words:[23]

> Ef ek skyldi annars hvárs, þá vildi ek himinríkis heldr missa en frægðarinnar
>
> *If I had to lose one of these two, then rather the kingdom of heaven than my fame.*

Such sentiments are all too frequent in the Icelandic text, a wonderfully overblown and vivid account, which often surpasses its source in its highly ornate rhetoric.[24]

As in medieval Ireland, Wales, and Iceland, Anglo-Saxon England was witness to a diversity of traditions concerning Alexander.[25] Vernacular references to Alexander the Great in Anglo-Saxon literature are scarce, but widely spread; such evidence suggests a persistent tradition deriving from several sources.[26] Apart from the *Letter*, Alexander features in two other Old English translations, namely those of the *Historiarum adversum paganos libri vii* of Orosius and the *Wonders of the East* in the *Beowulf*-manuscript.[27] A further reference to one *Alexandreas* as 'the most powerful of all the race of men' (*Widsith*, line 15–16) might be mentioned, although, as Joyce Hill has indicated 'the garbled form of the name, which contaminates Alexander (the Great) with Andreas (the Saint), suggests ignorance rather than knowledge'.[28] Pickles' list can be supplemented by a single reference at the beginning of Ælfric's homily on the Maccabees to *Alexander se egefulla cyning* which clearly derives from his biblical source, the uncomplimentary I Maccabees I.1.[29] A further reference to the borders of the Indian king Porus in a lengthy geographic list in the verse *Solomon and Saturn II* (line 189) points to more independent knowledge.[30] Certainly, however, the Old English Orosius and *Wonders of the East* are alone sufficient to demonstrate that the two prevailing medieval views of Alexander, as explorer and seeker of marvels on the one hand and moral *exemplum* of pride on the other, were

21 Cary, *The Medieval Alexander*, pp. 63–6; Colker, ed., *Galteri de Castellione Alexandreis*, pp. 3–274; Harich, *Alexander epicus*, pp. 15–96; Kratz, *Mocking Epic*, pp. 61–155; Pritchard, *The Alexandreis*, pp. 32–233.

22 Unger, ed., *Alexanders saga*; Jónsson, ed. *Alexanders saga*; Lönnroth, 'Hetjunar líta bleika akra'; Lönnroth, *Njáls saga. A Critical Introduction*, pp. 107–10 and 153–7.

23 Jónsson, ed., *Alexanders saga*, p. 16; cf. Lönnroth, *Njáls saga. A Critical Introduction*, p. 154. The Latin original is not similarly anachronistic; line 502 has Alexander say that 'I would wish to prefer this alone [i.e. fame] to the Elysian fields' (*Elysiisque velim hanc solam praeponere campis*).

24 Cf. Kristjánsson, *Eddas and Sagas*, pp. 333–4.

25 Pfister, 'Auf den Spuren Alexanders des Grossen in der älteren englischen Literatur'; Tristram, 'Der insulare Alexander', pp. 140–4.

26 Pickles, 'Studies in the Prose Texts of the *Beowulf* Manuscript', pp. 112–13.

27 Bately, ed., *The Old English Orosius*, especially III.viiii (pp. 67–74); for *The Wonders of the East*, see further below, pp. 131–2.

28 Hill, ed., *Old English Minor Heroic Poems*, p. 78.

29 Skeat, ed., *Ælfric's Lives of the Saints*, II, p. 66.

30 Cf. O'Keeffe, 'The Geographic List of *Solomon and Saturn II*', p. 138.

both represented in Anglo-Saxon England.[31] The Anglo-Latin evidence, largely neglected by Pickles in his survey, sustains this notion, but requires careful analysis and consideration.

Pride of place on any such list must go to the *Liber monstrorum*.[32] Apart from seven explicit references to Alexander (II.3, 7, 17, 23, and 29; III.4 and 11), the *Liber monstrorum* borrows extensively from the Latin sources of both the Old English *Letter of Alexander to Aristotle* and the *Wonders of the East*.[33] Alcuin, furthermore, in a characteristically unsubtle display of egocentricity, appears to have sent Charlemagne a copy of the *Collatio Alexandri cum Dindimo*, with its implicitly unfavourable contrast between secular and spiritual power;[34] Ludwig Traube, moreover, thought he could detect Insular traces in the later Continental manuscript tradition of that text.[35] The *Collatio* was possibly available in very late Anglo-Saxon England too; a single manuscript, London, British Library, Royal 13. A. i, contains a number of Alexander-texts, including an *Epitome* of the fourth-century Latin translation by Julius Valerius Alexander Polemius from the Greek Romance of Alexander the Great (fols. 2–51v), the *Epistola Alexandri ad Aristotelem* (a version of the text on which the Old English *Letter* depends, fols. 51v–78),[36] a short verse *Epitaphium Alexandri* (fol. 78), and the *Collatio* itself (fols. 78v–94v).[37] There follows in this manuscript an incomplete version of an idiosyncratic compilation entitled *Parua recapitulatio de eodem Alexandro et de suis* (fols. 94v–98v), which exists elsewhere in five later manuscripts, all English, and has been thought on that basis an Anglo-Latin work.[38] In the same context one might indicate reference to a *Commonitorium Palladii de Bragmanis* in the list of books donated by Sæwold, the Anglo-Saxon abbot of Bath, to the church of Saint-Vaast in Arras *c.* 1070.[39] The very manuscript in question survives, a tenth-century collection of Ambrosian material, Arras, Bibliothèque Municipale 1068, with the *Commonitorium* itself on fols. 34r–53v, and the text includes a description of a series of conversations on the active and ascetic life, contrasting the physical and the psychological or spiritual, between Alexander and the Brahman Dindymus.[40] Clearly there was no shortage of materials relating to Alexander the Great in Anglo-Saxon England, reflecting a range of traditions.

Orosius is unequivocally hostile towards Alexander, whom he viewed as a dangerous

31 See further, for example, Holländer, 'Alexander: *Hybris* und *Curiositas*'.

32 See further above, pp. 86–115.

33 See further below, pp. 317–19.

34 Alcuin, *Carmen* LXXXI; Dümmler, ed., MGH PLAC I, p. 300. Cf. Kübler, ed., *Julii Valerii Alexandri Polemi Res Gestae Alexandri Macedonis*, p. xxvii.

35 Traube, *Vorlesungen und Abhandlungen*, III, p. 113; Pickles, 'Studies in the Prose Texts of the *Beowulf* Manuscript', p. 113. See further Cary, 'A Note on the Medieval History of the *Collatio Alexandri cum Dindimo*'.

36 See further the edition and translation in the Appendix below, pp. 204–23.

37 See Gneuss, 'A Preliminary List', p. 31 (no. 481), who dates the manuscript 's. xi ex.'; David Dumville has suggested to me that s. xi/xii might be more realistic.

38 The text is edited and discussed by Ross, '*Parua recapitulatio*: An English Collection'.

39 See Lapidge, 'Surviving Booklists', pp. 59–61.

40 Cary, *The Medieval Alexander*, pp. 12–13; Jackson, 'Palladius Helenopolitanus'.

pagan tyrant brought low by his own pride.[41] The Old English version does nothing to alleviate this impression, and this *sensus moralis* seems indeed to have been accentuated.[42] In a number of additions and amendments to his Latin source, the Old English translator clearly undermines Alexander, and seeks to stress his cruelty and pride beyond even the grim depiction of Orosius. Many of the changes made are quite minor, but the cumulative effect is convincing. So, for example, in his description of the Battle of Granicus, Orosius praises the generalship of Alexander, and the valour of his Macedonian troops:[43]

> Primo eius cum Dario rege congressu, sescenta milia Persarum in acie fuere, quae non minus arte Alexandri superata, quam uirtute Macedonum, terga uerterunt.
>
> *At his first encounter with King Darius, there were six hundred thousand Persians in the battle-line, who fled, defeated no less by the skill of Alexander than by the force of the Macedonians.*

The Old English translator, on the other hand, appears to attribute Alexander's success to base cunning rather than valour, and omits all mention of his troops:[44]

> On þæm ærestean gefeohte þe Alex[an]der gefeaht wið Darius an Perseum, Darius hæfde siex hund .M. folces. He wearþ þeh swiþor beswicen for Alexandres searewe þonne for his gefeohte.
>
> *In the first battle which Alexander fought against Darius and the Persians, Darius had six hundred thousand men. But he was rather tricked by Alexander's cunning than by his fighting.*

A parallel zeal to make Alexander's battlefield success seem a personal crusade of questionable merit is evident in the Old English translator's tinkering with the rather neutral Latin description of a later hard-fought Macedonian victory, to make it appear that Alexander had scraped an underhand success. The Latin text provides a terse account:[45]

> Commissoque praelio, diu anceps et cruenta pugna tandem tristem paene victoriam Macedonibus dedit.
>
> *After battle had been joined, a fierce and for a long time indecisive struggle gave at last a grim close-run victory to the Macedonians.*

The Old English translator puts the spotlight firmly on the actions of Alexander himself, and claims that the victory won by him was 'unworthy':[46]

41 Cary, *The Medieval Alexander*, p. 119.

42 Tristram, 'Der insulare Alexander', pp. 144–5; Tristram, 'More Talk', p. 658. The *Historiarum aduersum paganos libri vii* of Paulus Orosius is edited by Zangemeister; the Old English version is edited by Bately, *The Old English Orosius*.

43 Zangemeister, ed., *Historiarum aduersum paganos libri vii*, p. 172/9–11.

44 Bately, ed., *The Old English Orosius*, p. 68/13–5.

45 Zangemeister, ed., *Historiarum aduersum paganos libri vii*, p. 181/7–9.

46 Bately, ed., *The Old English Orosius*, p. 73/4–6.

> 7 hie lange wæron þæt dreogende ær heora aðer mehte on oþrum sige geræcan, ær Alexander late unweorðlicne sige geræhte.
>
> *And they were enduring that for a long time before either of them could gain a victory over the other, before Alexander finally won an unworthy victory.*

In much the same way, the Old English translator expands the scarcely positive description of Alexander's treatment of the dead Darius and his family to make his actions still more monstrous. The Latin states baldly that:[47]

> Hunc mortuum inani misericordia referri in sepulchra maiorum sepelirique praecepit: cuius non dicam matrem vel uxorem, sed etiam parvulas filias crudeli captivitate retinebat.
>
> *When [Darius] was dead, [Alexander], with empty pity ordered that he be brought to the tombs of his ancestors and buried; and I shall not describe how he held in cruel captivity not only mother and wife, but even his little daughters.*

The Old English is far more emotive:[48]

> He þa Alexander him anum deadum lytle mildheortnesse gedyde, þæt he hiene hett bebyrgean an his ieldrena byrg, þe he siþþan nanum ende his cynne gedon nolde ne his wif[e], ne his meder, ne his bearnum, ne þætte ealra læst wæs, his gingran dohtor he nolde buton hæftniede habban, seo wæs lytel cild.
>
> *Then Alexander granted a little pity to Darius alone, once dead, in that he had him buried in the tombs of his ancestors, but he would not grant that afterwards at their end to any of his family, neither to his wife, nor his mother, nor to his children, nor even, which was least of all, would he take his youngest daughter, but in bondage; and she was a little child.*

At every point, Alexander is depicted in the vernacular translation as much more bloodthirsty and unreasonable than in the Latin original, itself scarcely squeamish; this bias is particularly apparent, for example, in the Old English version of Alexander's single combat with Porus, or his grim despatch of the faithful and aged Cleitus.[49] Those aspects of Alexander's activities which could be guaranteed to produce the maximum distaste in Christian audiences are dwelt upon; as the Old English translator notes:[50]

> He Alexander toecan þæm þe he hienende wæs ægþer ge his [agen] folc ge oðerra cyninga, he wæs sin[þyrst]ende monnes blodes.

47 Zangemeister, ed., *Historiarum aduersum paganos libri vii*, p. 176/11–14.

48 Bately, ed., *The Old English Orosius*, p. 70/11–5.

49 Bately, ed., *The Old English Orosius*, p. 72/13–23 and 71/13–25.

50 Bately, ed., *The Old English Orosius*, p. 71/23–5. Cf. the description of Alexander on his return to Babylon, still thirsting for men's blood (*þagiet þa Alexander ham com to Babylonia, þagiet wæs on him se mæsta þurst monnes blodes*): Bately, ed., *The Old English Orosius*, p. 74/7–8. The Latin text is equally explicit: *sed Alexander humani sanguinis insaturabilis, sive hostium sive etiam sociorum, recentem tamen semper sitiebat cruorem* (Zangemeister, ed., *Historiarum aduersum paganos libri vii*, p. 179/7–8).

But Alexander, as well as destroying both his own people and those of other kings, was continually thirsting for man's blood.

Such an explicit expansion of the Latin source must have greatly deepened revulsion at Alexander's acts in an Anglo-Saxon England which, as we have seen, was particularly influenced by biblical injunctions against the drinking of any blood, whether metaphorical or not.[51]

Alexander's unique concern for personal glory is a further characteristic undoubtedly present in Orosius' Latin, and greatly expanded upon in the Old English, as in the description of Alexander's personal role in the storming of one particular city, where he was wounded. The Latin simply states that:[52]

In eo proelio sagitta sub mamma traiectus, fixo genu eatenus pugnavit, donec eum, a quo vulneratus esset, occideret.

In that battle, when he was struck by an arrow under the nipple, he dropped to his knee and kept on fighting until he had killed the man who had wounded him.

The Old English expands considerably, apparently from sheer martial pleasure:[53]

Ðær wearð Alexander þurhscoten mid anre flan underneoðan oþer breost. Nyte we nu hwæðer sie swiþor to wundrianne, þe þæt, hu he ana wið ealle þa burgware hiene awerede, þe eft þa him fultum com, hu he þurh þæt folc geþrang þæt he ðone ilcan ofslog þe hiene ær þurhsceat, þe eft þara þegna angin þa hie ungetweogend[lice] wendon þæt heora hlaford wære on heora feonda gewealde, oððe cuca oððe dead, þæt hie swaþeah noldon þæs weallgebreces geswican, þæt hie heora hlaford ne gewræcen, þeh þe hie hiene meðigne on cneowum sittende metten.

Then Alexander was wounded with an arrow under one breast. We know not now which is the cause for greater wonder; how he defended himself alone against all the city-dwellers, or again, when help came to him, how he so forced a way through the crowd, that he killed the same man, that had shot him, or the activity of his thegns, who knew full well that their lord was in the power of enemies, either alive or dead, and yet they would not refrain from storming the breach in the wall, to avenge their lord, though they found him weary on his knees.

Perhaps most extraordinary in this account is the apparent need felt to stress the loyalty of Alexander's men, itself a reflection on the quality of their leader, whose ability to inspire them to customary allegiance may be in question.[54]

A further way in which the Old English version elaborates on Orosius' theme is in its depiction of pride and Alexander's concern for personal glory. For Orosius, Alexander's murder of Cleitus was tyrannical: Cleitus had simply defended the memory of his former king, and suffered unjustly for daring to stand up to a son in his cups:[55]

51 Cf. the detailed discussion above, pp. 63–5.

52 Zangemeister, ed., *Historiarum aduersum paganos libri vii,* pp. 181/16–182/1.

53 Bately, ed., *The Old English Orosius,* p. 73/18–27.

54 Cf. Bately, ed., *The Old English Orosius,* p. 262.

55 Zangemeister, ed., *Historiarum aduersum paganos libri vii,* p. 179/3–7.

> Clitus quoque annis gravis, amicitia uetus nefarie interfectus: qui cum in conuiuio aduersus regem, sua opera patri Philippo praeponentem, memoriam patris tueretur, ab offenso frustra rege uenabulo transfossus, commune conuiuium moriens cruentauit.
>
> *Cleitus too, heavy with years, an old friend, was disgracefully slain: for he, when at a banquet he defended the memory of Phillip against the king, who was putting his own deeds ahead of those of his father, was skewered by a hunting-spear thrown needlessly by the king and as he died he spattered with blood the common banquet.*

In the Old English, by contrast, Cleitus offers Alexander a much more direct affront to his pride by not simply defending Philip, but preferring him:[56]

> 7 Clitus, se wæs ægðer ge his þegn ge ær Philippuses his fæder, þa hie sume siþe druncne æt heora symble sætan, þa angunnon hi trea[h]tigean hwæðer ma mærlecra dæda gefremed hæfde, þe Philippus þe Alexander. Þa sægde se Clitus for ealdre hyldo þæt Philippus mare hæfde gedon þonne he. He þa Alexander ahleop 7 hiene for þære sægene ofslog.
>
> *And Cleitus, who was a thegn of both [Alexander] and Phillip, his father, when they were on a certain occasion sitting drunk at their banquet, they began to discuss which of them had accomplished the worthier deeds, Phillip or Alexander. From ancient loyalty Cleitus said that Phillip had done greater deeds than [Alexander]. Then Alexander jumped up and killed him for saying so.*

A similar concern for personal glory at any cost motivates Alexander in his attack on the one Indian city to elude him; Orosius indicates that Alexander was driven by pride and a desire to emulate the mighty heroes of old:[57]

> Peragrata perdomitaque Alexander India cum ad saxum mirae asperitatis et altitudinis, in quod multi populi confugerant, peruenisset, cognoscit Herculem ab expugnatione eiusdem saxi terrae motu prohibitum. Aemulatione permotus, ut Herculis acta superaret, cum summo labore ac periculo saxo potitus omnes loci eius gentes in deditionem accepit.
>
> *After he had travelled and subjugated India, Alexander came to a rock of wondrous size and harshness, to which many people had fled, and he knew that Hercules had been prevented from storming the same rock by an earthquake. Inspired by rivalry and the desire to surpass the deeds of Hercules, he took control of the rock after the greatest effort and danger, and accepted the surrender of all the people of that place.*

The Old English translator consciously elaborates and develops the same motif:[58]

> Æfter þæm þe Alexander hæfde ealle Indie him to gewildon gedon, buton anre byrg, seo wæs ungemettan fæste mid cludum ymbweaxen, þa geascade he þæt Ercol se ent þær wæs to gefaren on ærdagum, to ðon þæt he hie abrecan þohte; ac he hit for þæm ne angan þe þær wæs eorþbeofung on þære tide. He þa

56 Bately, ed., *The Old English Orosius*, p. 71/17–23.

57 Zangemeister, ed., *Historiarum aduersum paganos libri vii*, p. 179/17–180/5.

58 Bately, ed., *The Old English Orosius*, p. 72/5–12.

> Alexander hit swiþost for þæm angann þe he wolde þæt his mærþa wæren maran þonne Ercoles, þeh ðe he hie mid micle forlore þæs folces begeate.
>
> *After Alexander had subjugated all India except for one town which was remarkably secure and surrounded by crags, he discovered that Hercules the Giant had gone there in days gone by, because he wished to conquer it, but he was unsuccessful due to an earthquake at that time. Then Alexander wanted to take the place, most of all because he wanted his glorious deeds to surpass those of Hercules, even though he captured [the place] with a great loss of his own men.*

In referring to the heavy losses sustained, the Old English translator may simply be underlining Alexander's ruthlessness, rather than necessarily supplementing Orosius from another source (Janet Bately suggests Quintus Curtius);[59] we can be sure, however, that the Old English translator did have access to further traditions concerning Alexander, the most obvious of which is that concerning the allegations that he was fathered by the priest and prophet Nectanebus, whom Orosius does not mention at all, but who features in a lengthy digression in the Old English version.[60] Bately mentions the possibility that the translator was expanding on material available to him through such authors as Julius Valerius or Fulgentius (evidence of whose further influence on the text is conspicuously lacking), or perhaps a manuscript gloss.[61] Both Nectanebus and the tales about him, however, are mentioned in the so-called *Parua recapitulatio*, the possible English provenance of which has already been noted, which discusses the alleged intrigue of Olympias and Nectanebus in a dozen lines or so with the explicit purpose of supplementing the accounts of the 'hystoriographi', doubtless including Orosius, from whose work the author later quotes.[62] Still more significant, perhaps, is the almost unconsciously expanded description of Hercules here as 'Hercules the Giant' (*Ercol se ent*), a designation which occurs twice in the Old English version, but which has no warrant whatsoever in the Latin text.[63] Nor is this the only time that Hercules is represented in Old English tradition as being a (rather disreputable) giant;[64] and, as we have seen, the *Liber monstrorum* depicts Hercules not merely as monster-slayer, but as monster.[65]

The *Liber monstrorum* relies for its traditions of Alexander exclusively on the *Epistola Alexandri ad Aristotelem*, from which much of its teratological information is derived.[66] The extent of borrowing is impressive: I count around twenty passages in the *Liber monstrorum* clearly copied from the *Epistola*, and the weight of evidence

59 Bately, ed., *The Old English Orosius*, p. 261.

60 Bately, ed., *The Old English Orosius*, p. 69/20–31.

61 Bately, ed., *The Old English Orosius*, pp. 258–9.

62 Ross, '*Parua recapitulatio*: An English Collection', pp. 158 and 164.

63 Bately, ed., *The Old English Orosius*, pp. 30/15 and 72/7

64 There are two further instances in Old English of Hercules being depicted as a giant: Napier, ed., *Wulfstan*, no. XLII (*De falsis deis*), p. 197/18; Skeat, ed., *Ælfric's Lives of Saints*, II, p. 384/113.

65 See further above, pp. 114–15.

66 See, for example, Butturff, *The Monsters and the Scholar*, p. 7; Whitbread, 'The *Liber Monstrorum* and *Beowulf*', pp. 445–6; Porsia, ed., *Liber Monstrorum*, p. 70; Lapidge, '*Beowulf*, Aldhelm, the *Liber Monstrorum* and Wessex', p. 167.

is sufficient to determine not simply the fact and direction of borrowing, but even the specific underlying manuscript tradition.[67] Indeed it is somewhat surprising that no previous scholar has attempted to isolate such a tradition, given the general availability of Walther Boer's excellent critical edition of the *Epistola*, and the number of subsequent studies of the *Liber monstrorum*.[68] Boer's text is based on twenty-eight representative manuscripts out of sixty-seven noted, divided into four clearly separate groupings.[69] The compiler of the *Liber monstrorum*, can be shown to have had access to a text which was closely affiliated to Boer's group II of manuscripts, and which, within that collection, shares a number of idiosyncratic readings with a group of four English manuscripts including (and especially) the earliest, London, British Library, Royal 13. A. i.[70] The following five examples will illustrate the common tradition; I print parallel passages from the *Liber monstrorum* and Boer's text of the *Epistola Alexandri* (italicising significant variants), with brief commentary.

(a) The 'Dentestyrannus':[71]

Fuit praeterea quaedam in Indorum finibus bestia maior, ut ferunt, elefanto, colore nigro, quam Indi dentem tyrannum uocauerunt. Quae in medio toruae frontis tria cornua gessit, et tantae animositatis erat, ut sibi conspectis hominibus, non tela neque ignes, nec ulla uitaret pericula. Quam ferunt Alexandrum, mortuis .XXVI. militibus, tandem confixam occidisse uenabulis.

Moreover there was a beast on the borders of India, so they say, larger than an elephant and black in colour, which the Indians call 'Tyrant's tooth' [rhinoceros]. It bore three horns in the middle of its cruel forehead, and it was of such savagery that when it caught sight of humans, it would shun no weapons or fires or any dangers. They say that Alexander at last pierced it with hunting-spears, after twenty-six of his soldiers had died, and slew it.

Una praeterea novi generis bestia maior elephanto affuit, tribus armata in fronte cornibus, quam Indi appellare *dentityrannum*[72] soliti sunt, equo simile caput gerens atri coloris. Haec potata aqua intuens castra in nos subito impetum dedit nec ignium tardatur compositis ardoribus. Ad quam sustinendam cum opposuissem Macedonum manum, *triginta sex*[73] occidit, duos et quinquagenta calcatos inutiles fecit vixque ipsis defixa est venabulis.

67 Porsia has proved the most avid collector of parallels, including a small number which are rather faint; see his edition of the *Liber monstrorum*, pp. 129, 135, 157, 165, 167, 169, 221, 223, 227, 231, 233, 239, 245, 249, 251, 253, 259, 265, 269, 273, and 283; cf. Butturff, *The* Monsters and the Scholar, pp. 195, and 197–200. See further the Appendix below, pp. 317–19.

68 See further above, pp. 86–7.

69 Boer, ed., *Epistola Alexandri*, pp. iii–xxxiv.

70 This manuscript forms the basis for the Latin edition of the *Epistola Alexandri* given in the Appendix below, pp. 204–23. The three other Latin texts of the *Epistola Alexandri* in this related English group, all found in manuscripts of the twelfth century, are: Cambridge, University Library, Mm.V.29, fols. 143v–149v; London, British Library, Royal 15. C. vi, fols. 116–124; London, British Library, Royal 12. C. iv, fols. 160v–170v. See Boer, ed., *Epistola Alexandri*, pp. x, xiii–xiv, and xxiv–xxvi.

71 *Liber monstrorum* II.16; Boer, ed., *Epistola Alexandri*, pp. 20/6–21/2 (my § 20).

72 Group II: *dentemtyrannum*.

73 Group II: *.XXVI.*

Moreover there was a beast of a new kind, bigger than an elephant, armed in the forehead with three horns, which the Indians are accustomed to call Tyrant's tooth, having a head of black colour like a horse. Once it had drunk some water it saw our camp and immediately attacked it, nor was it deterred by the heat of our fires. When I had positioned a band of Macedonians to face the beast, it killed thirty-six, trampled fifty-two and made them useless, and was only with difficulty pierced with hunting-spears.

Neither of the significant readings *dentemtyrannum* and *XXVI* is unique to Boer's group II, but the combination is; the compiler of the *Liber monstrorum* shows himself here, as elsewhere, to be a diligent, if not slavish, copyist.

(b) The Two-Headed Beast:[74]

Ferunt et in India beluam fuisse quae habuit bina capita, alterum lunae bicornis ut puta imaginem, alterum corcodrilli gerebat. Et tergo serrato et saeuis armata dentibus quondam in Alexandri milites prosiliens duos occidisse describitur.

And they say that in India there is a beast which had two heads; it bore one (imagine!) the image of a two-horned moon, the other of a crocodile. And with its serrated back and armed with savage teeth it is described once as having leapt out on Alexander's soldiers and killed two.

Palus erat sicca et coeno abundans. Per quam cum transire temptaremus, belua novi generis prosilivit serrato tergo, hippotami pectore, duo capita *habens*[75], unum *leaenae*[76] simile, *corcodrillo*[77] gerens alterum simillimum duris munitum dentibus, quod caput duos milites repentino occidit ictu.

There was a dry swamp, thick with reeds, through which we tried to pass. But a beast of a new kind leapt out, with a serrated back, the belly of a hippopotamus, having two heads, one like a lioness, the other most like a crocodile, armed with hard teeth, which by its sudden attack killed two soldiers.

The fact that several manuscripts of the *Epistola* omit to mention that the beast in question has two heads (including Boer's group III) clearly discounts the possibility that the compiler of the *Liber monstrorum* had such texts before him, an important consideration given that many of the same manuscripts (including group III) have the further significant variant *lunae* for *leaenae*. Only group II has both required readings, and within group II, only London, British Library, Royal 13. A. i and another, closely related, later English manuscript Cambridge, University Library, Mm. V. 29 have the variant *corcodrilli* for *corcodrillo*, which may explain the preference in the *Liber monstrorum* for two parallel genitive forms (*lunae* and *corcodrilli*) in place of the parallel dative forms of the *Epistola* (*leaenae* and *corcodrillo*).

74 *Liber monstrorum* II.22; Boer, ed., *Epistola Alexandri*, p. 29/1–5 (my § 27).

75 Several manuscripts, including all of Boer's group III, and most of his group IV, omit *duo capita habens*.

76 Group II: *lunae*.

77 London, British Library, Royal 13. A. i: *corcodrilli*.

(c) The Giant Bats:[78]

Alexander Macedo se in India mures uulpium statura uidisse ad Aristotelem descripsit, qui morsibus pestiferis homines et iumenta lacerabant.

Alexander of Macedon described to Aristotle that he had seen mice in India the size of foxes, and they used to tear men and pack-animals with their destructive biting.

Ante lucanum deinde tempus *caelo*[79] pestes venere candido versicolores in modum *ranarum*,[80] cum quibus mures Indici in castra pergebant vulpibus similes, quorum morsu vulnerata quadrupedia statim exspirabant; hominibus idem non usque ad interitum nocebant.

Then at the time before dawn, under a clear sky there came some pests multi-coloured like frogs, along with whom Indian mice like foxes came into the camp, and wounded by their bite the pack-animals immediately perished; but they were not completely fatal to men.

The *Epistola* clearly describes the attack of shiny mouse-like creatures as big as foxes; one assumes that large bats are intended. Only the four related English manuscripts from Boer's group II, including London, British Library, Royal 13. A. i, omit the significant word *caelo*, without which all suggestion of an airborne threat is entirely lost, as in the *Liber monstrorum*. All texts from group II, moreover, include the extraordinary variant *zonarum* ('girdles') for *ranarum* ('frogs'), which seems to have perplexed even the ingenious compiler of the *Liber monstrorum*, who passes over it in uncharacteristic silence.

(d) The 'Eternal' Beast:[81]

Et sunt quoque, ut ferunt, in India beluae, quas aeternas, ob uiuidam uirtutem, uocant. Quae in suis uerticibus ossa serrata uelut gladios gestant, quibus arietino, dum aduersus incurrunt, impetu, obpositi transuerberantur clipei.

And there are also, so they say, beasts in India [crocodiles], which they call eternal on account of their lively strength. And they bear serrated bones like swords on their heads, by which, when they attack shields, charging like a ram, the opposing shields are split apart.

Inde profecti et flatum Euri venti secuti incidimus *externas*[82] feras, de quarum capitibus velut gladii a vertice serrata eminebant ossa, quae more *taurorum*[83] in adversos incurrunt homines; et invictae ferae plurimorum militum clipeos cornu suo transverberabant.

Then setting out, following the East wind, we came upon some foreign beasts, from the tip of whose head serrated bones stood out like swords, which they charge men like bulls. And the invincible wild beasts split the shields of very many soldiers with their horns.

78 *Liber monstrorum* II.29; Boer, ed., *Epistola Alexandri*, p. 21/3–7 (my § 21).

79 London, British Library, Royal 13. A. i omits *caelo*.

80 Group II: *zonarum* (!).

81 *Liber monstrorum* II.12; Boer, ed., *Epistola Alexandri*, p. 58/6–10 (my § 41).

82 London, British Library, Royal 13. A. i: *in (a)eternas*.

83 London, British Library, Royal 13. A. i: *arietino*.

The significant variant *arietino* for *taurorum* is found predominantly in Boer's groups III and IV; amongst group II texts the reading is restricted to the related goup of four English manuscripts discussed, including Royal 13. A. i. The crucial further variant *in (a)eternas* for *externas* is, however, found in only one of the four manuscripts in this English group, namely Royal 13. A. i.

(e) The Serpents of Iordia:[84]

> Dicuntur et in India serpentes gigni in ualle que uocatur Iordia, per eorum colla lapides pretiosi ualde nascuntur, nitores quorum zmaragdi nuncupantur; lasere quoque et albo pipere pascuntur. Quorum Alexander Macedo paucos de ualle pyramidibus quingentorum et quinque pedum habentibus longitudinem clausa lapidum extulit.
>
> *Serpents are also said to be born in India in a valley which is called Iordia, in whose necks are found very precious stones, and their glitterings are called emeralds. They are fed on laser and white pepper. Alexander of Macedon carried off a few of the stones from the valley, closed off by pyramids with a length of five hundred and five feet.*
>
> Pervenimus deinde in vallem *Diardinis*[85], in qua serpentes habitabant, habentes *in*[86] *collo*[87] lapides qui smaragdi apellantur. Hi serpentes lasere et albo pascuntur pipere; hi lumen in oculis profusum accipiunt. Hi vallem nulli adeundam incolunt: nam super hanc vallem sunt piramides institutae pedum *tricenum*[88] quinum, ab antiquis Indorum ob hanc causam aedificatae. Sed hi serpentes, quos paulo ante descripsimus, inter se quotannis vere primo depugnant multique morsibus depereunt. Inde nos paucos extulimus ingentis formae smaragdos.
>
> *Then we came into the valley of Diarden, in which there dwelt serpents, having stones called emeralds in their necks. These serpents feed on laser and white pepper; they have bright light in their eyes. No-one dwells in the approach to the valley, for above this valley pyramids are set up, thirty-five feet high, built by the ancestors of the Indians for that reason. But these serpents, which we have described a little earlier, fight amongst themselves every year at the beginning of spring, and many perish from the bites. Then we took a few emeralds of a huge size.*

Variant forms of the name of the valley are found, of which *Iordeam* (group II) and more particularly *Iordiam* (group III) may be mentioned. Further minor variants within group II, and especially in Royal 13. A. i, may explain aspects of the phrasing in the *Liber monstrorum*. It is, perhaps, easiest to explain the *Liber monstrorum*'s insistence on the enlarged size of the pyramids (here transferred to the valley itself) as the last in a chain of misreadings. At all events, it is clear that the closest text to that borrowed by the compiler of the *Liber monstrorum* is that found in Royal 13. A. i.

84 *Liber monstrorum* III.11; Boer, ed., *Epistola Alexandri*, pp. 53/6–54/4 (my § 41).

85 Group II: *Iordeam.*

86 Group II omits *in.*

87 London, British Library, Royal 13. A. i: *colla.*

88 London, British Library, Royal 13. A. i: *vigenum.*

The notion that the compiler of the *Liber monstrorum* had access to an idiosyncratic text of the *Epistola* closely related to that found in a distinctive English group of manuscripts, and in particular to the version preserved in the earliest English manuscript is of some interest in establishing the possibility of a specifically English tradition of the text, especially since Thomas Hahn has demonstrated conclusively that the fifteenth-century Middle English *Letter of Alexander to Aristotle* also drew on a Latin original sharing a number of idiosyncratic readings with that tradition.[89] That this idiosyncratically English tradition was not, however, the only one available in Anglo-Saxon England is also clear: the Old English *Letter of Alexander to Aristotle* draws on a quite distinct and separate text, as we shall see.[90] It is, however, clear that there were further elements of an Alexander tradition available to the author of the *Liber monstrorum* which do not seem to derive from the *Epistola.* One such is the naming of the inhabited rock Aornis (*Liber monstrorum* II.6) which an earthquake deterred Hercules from capturing, and which Alexander stormed to surpass his predecessor; the rock is named by Quintus Curtius Rufus (*Historia Alexandri Magni* VIII.11 22), but is omitted from other sources, such as Orosius.[91]

What is striking, however, is the way in which the author of the *Liber monstrorum*, by careful selection of particular episodes from the *Epistola Alexandri*, presents a picture of Alexander predominantly in opposition to the monstrous creatures he encounters. In the *Liber monstrorum* Alexander's role is wholly antagonistic; on five of the seven occasions when his name is mentioned the author stresses either how the monstrous beast or serpent in question terrorised Alexander and his men or how Alexander destroyed the threat.[92] Alexander neither ignores nor appeases monsters; as the author of the *Liber monstrorum* has it: 'Alexander is held to have waged war [against them]' (*bellum contulisse perhibetur*).[93] Such a hostile view of monsters characterises the whole of the *Liber monstrorum*, as we have seen.[94]

89 Hahn, ed., 'The Middle English *Letter of Alexander to Aristotle*', p. 115. Comparison of the Middle English text for the five passages discussed is instructive; in each case the distinctive variants occur. So the Middle English translator, who is far more of a literalist than the compiler of the *Liber monstrorum*, renders passage (c) above as: 'Therof and from that, bifore lucan a litel tyme, with white lecherous beestis havyng dyvers colour in maner of girdelis, with whiche myse, to sight and shewyng like vnto foxes, wenten in to the castels. Of whos bityng .iiii. footed beestis wern wounded and anon deiden. Men with the same bityng gretely noied, But nat vnto the deth' (lines 241–5), so both omitting *caelo* and translating the variant *zonarum* ('girdelis') for *ranarum*. Most significantly, the Middle English author renders the *externas feras* of passage (e) as 'most wielde bestis' (ll. 559–60), clearly translating the variant reading *in ferocissimas feras* unique to the three later English manuscripts listed in n. 70 above.

90 See further below, pp. 135–9.

91 See the comments of Porsia, *Liber Monstrorum*, p. 227; Butturff, *The Monsters and the Scholar*, p. 198. The passage in question is quoted above, pp. 124–5.

92 *Liber monstrorum* II.2, 6, 16, 22, and 29; III.4, and 11. In every case but *Liber monstrorum* II.2 and III.11 Alexander and his men are fighting the monsters, and on these two occasions the antagonism can be implied.

93 *Liber monstrorum* III.4.

94 See above, pp. 89–90.

A similarly antagonistic approach characterises Alexander's appearences in the Old English *Wonders of the East* and its related Latin sources.[95] Alexander is named early in the text (§ 2), in a casual reference to his act, again following Hercules, of setting up mighty monuments in distant lands to commemorate his deeds:[96]

> Þær syndan þa mycclan mærða þæt syndan ða geweorc þe se miccla macedonisca Alexander het gewyrcean.
>
> *There are the great monuments there, which are the works which the mighty Alexander of Macedon had made.*

These same monuments are mentioned by Orosius, and recur both in the *Liber monstrorum* as an indication of the excessive pride of both Alexander and Hercules,[97] and right at the end of the *Letter of Alexander to Aristotle* (§ 41), as we shall see. Alexander is named only twice more in the *Wonders of the East* (§§ 27 and 30); both sections concerned deal with his role as a slayer of monsters, and indeed constitute the only allusions to such an act in the whole text. The first of these describes an encounter with some monstrous women:

> Ðonne sindon oðre wif ða habbað eoferes tucxas 7 feax oð helan side, 7 on lendenum oxan tægl. Þa wif syndon ðreotyne fota lange 7 heora lic bið on marmorstanes hwitnysse. 7 hi habbað olfenda fet 7 eoferes teð. For heora micelnesse hie gefelde wurdon fram ðam mycclan macedoniscan Alexandre. Þa he hi lifiende gefon ne mihte, þa acwealde he hi for ðam hi syndon æwisce on lichoman 7 unweorðe.
>
> *Then there are other women who have boar's tusks and hair down to their heels and ox-tails on their loins. Those women are thirteen feet tall and their bodies are of the whiteness of marble. And they have camel's feet and boar's teeth. Because of their size they were killed by Alexander the Great of Macedon. He killed them because he could not capture them alive, because they have offensive and disgusting bodies.*

As Sisam notes, the Latin original states that the women were killed because of their filth (*pro sua obscoenitate*), which would naturally be translated by *of hyra unclenesse*;[98] scribal error has produced *for heora micelnesse* ('because of their size'), but size alone, as in the *Liber monstrorum*,[99] seems to have been felt enough to justify hostility. More puzzling is the second reference, to a race of less offensive people:

> Ðis mannkynn lifað fela geara, 7 hi syndon fremfulle menn. 7 gyf hwylc mann to him cymeð þonne gyfað hi him wif ær hi hine onweg lætan. Se macedonisca Alexander, þa ða he him to com, þa wæs he wundriende hyra menniscnysse, ne wolde he hi cwellan ne him nawiht laðes don.

95 Cf. Friedman, 'The Marvels-of-the-East Tradition', pp. 321–34.

96 See further above, pp. 124–5.

97 On the monuments of Hercules so scorned in the *Liber monstrorum*, see further above, pp. 114–15.

98 Sisam, *Studies*, p. 69.

99 See further above, pp. 104–6.

> *This race of people live for many years, and they are generous people. If anyone visits them they give him a woman before they let him go. When Alexander of Macedon visited them, he was amazed at their humanity, and would not kill them or cause them any harm.*

The author's comment that Alexander would not kill these people is something of a *non sequitur*, unless we assume that it was Alexander's normal reaction to slay monsters.[100] Such an assumption is indeed borne out by other texts, such as the *Liber monstrorum*, as we have seen. Elsewhere in the *Wonders of the East*, the fierce hostility between the worlds of monsters and men is a constant theme: the marvellous creatures encountered either prudently flee from the sight of men, or devour them.[101] Clearly Alexander is no ordinary man, and his extraordinary nature becomes still further stressed by the text that follows the *Wonders of the East* in the *Beowulf*-manuscript, the *Letter of Alexander to Aristotle*.

Critical opinion of the literary merits of the Old English *Letter of Alexander to Aristotle* has varied according to the perceived quality of the translation. Richard Wülcker thought the work 'eine recht getreue Übersetzung', whilst Kenneth Sisam dismissed the *Letter* as 'a free rendering, at times an adaptation, with patches of literalness';[102] Stopford Brooke's rather generous assessment of the translation as 'accurate . . . and done in excellent English' so incensed John Pickles as to doubt whether Brooke had read the work.[103] It is fair to say that few have managed to muster much enthusiasm for the style and quality of the piece, and more recent criticism remains as tepid (and consistent) as ever.[104] As pure translation, the *Letter* is clearly flawed in its frequent departures of style and substance from the original text. The effect of these alterations, however, requires close consideration to determine whether the anonymous translator was working with some clear purpose in mind, or (as previous scholars have been all too quick to assume) was simply unskilled.[105]

The most evident stylistic feature of the Old English translation is its persistent use of repetitive word pairs, or doublets (I count almost two hundred examples), often rendering a single Latin term in a manner characteristic of many other Old English translations.[106] So, for example, we find the following: *gleawnis 7 snyttro* (for *prudentia*); *geseoð 7 sceawigað* (for *intueri*); *gehyhte 7 gelyfe* (for *spero*); *gewinnes 7*

100 Cf. Cary, *The Medieval Alexander*, pp. 35–6.

101 See further above, pp. 26–7.

102 Wülcker, *Grundriss zur Geschichte der angelsächsischen Litteratur*, p. 505; Sisam, *Studies*, p. 84.

103 Brooke, *English Literature . . . to the Norman Conquest*, p. 293.

104 Cf. Greenfield and Calder, *A New Critical History of Old English Literature*, p. 99, who describe the *Letter* as 'heavy and ponderous in its somewhat shaky translation and in its excessive use of doublets for single Latin words', with those of Davis, in his revised 9th edition of *Sweet's Anglo-Saxon Primer*, p. 104, who says of the *Letter* that 'its style is flat and ungraceful, disfigured especially by the frequent use of pairs of near-synonyms to render a single Latin word'.

105 Cf. Butturff, 'Style as a Clue to Meaning', pp. 81–2.

106 The fullest study of this phenomenon is that of Koskenniemi, *Repetitive Word Pairs*; see especially pp. 12–43. Whilst useful, this survey is regrettably incomplete, and does not, for example, include any significant discussion of the *Letter*.

compes (for *militiae*); *aberan 7 alædan* (for *ferre*); *for 7 siðfæt* (for *iter*); *ungleawe 7 unwise* (for *imprudentes*); *in þære sweartan niht 7 in þære þystran* (for *caeca nocte*); *leges 7 fyres* (for *ignium*); *fremsumlice 7 luflice* (for *benigne*).[107] It is clear, however, that this stylistic feature is not simply the result of an over-zealous translation-technique:[108] a large number of similar phrases are found which have no Latin equivalent at all, as can be seen in the brief Old English introduction to the *Letter*, which has no real warrant in the source. The Latin original is sparse, simply introducing the piece (§ 1):[109]

> Epistola Alexandri Macedonis ad Aristotelen magistrum suum de itinere suo et de situ Indiae.
>
> *[Here begins] the letter of Alexander the Macedonian to Aristotle his teacher, concerning his travels and the situation of India.*

The Old English version is much more elaborate, and includes a number of doublets and other purely stylistic expansions:

> Her is seo gesetenis Alexandres epistoles þæs miclan kyninges 7 þæs mæran macedoniscan þone he wrat 7 sende to Aristotile his magistre be gesetenisse Indie þære miclan þeode, 7 be þære widgalnisse his siðfato 7 his fora, þe he geond middangeard ferde.
>
> *Here is the text of the letter of Alexander, the great king and the famous Macedonian, which he wrote and sent to Aristotle, his teacher, concerning the situation of the great nation of India, and the extent of his expeditions and his travels, which he made throughout the world.*

To some extent, moreover, the richness of diction witnessed by this persistent use of doublets has a basis in the exuberant Latinity with which the more exotic of Alexander's experiences and activities are described; repetitive word pairs are a frequent feature of the original also. So we find, for example: *þurh monifeald gewin 7 þurh micle frecennisse* (for *per summos labores et pericula*); *gelpan 7 secgan* (for *captantem iactantemque*); *mærlices 7 micellices* (for *tam illustre et tam magnifice*); *wop 7 tearas* (for *fletum et ululatum*).[110] At times the apparent exuberance of the Old English is found to match rather closely the similar rhetorical richness of the Latin, as in the following passage hinting at the abundant wildlife of India (§ 9):

> Praedixerant nobis incolae regionis eius, ne serpentes et rabida ferarum genera incideremus quae plurima in his uallibus et campis siluisque ac montibus habitabant, nemorum saxorumque latebris occulta.
>
> *The inhabitants of that region warned us, in case we met serpents and fierce kinds of wild beasts, of which very many dwelt in these valleys and fields and woods and mountains, hidden by the shelter of rocks and groves.*

107 §§ 2, 3, 4 (twice), 11, 14 (twice), 19, 20, and 23.
108 Cf. Bately, 'Old English Prose Before and During the Reign of Alfred, pp. 123–5.
109 Text from Boer, ed., *Epistola Alexandri*, p. 1; for a variant version, cf. the text given in the Appendix below, p. 204.
110 §§ 2, 4, 32, and 40.

The Old English translator manages to provide a still richer rendering:

> Þa sægdon us ða bigengean þæs londes þæt we us warnigan scoldon wið þa missenlican cynd nædrena 7 hrifra wildeora þy læs we on ða becwomon. Þæra mænego in ðissum dunum 7 denum 7 on wudum, 7 on feldum eardigeað 7 in stanholum hie selfe digliað.
>
> *Then the inhabitants of the land told us that we should beware the various kinds of serpents and savage wild beasts, in case we came upon them. A multitude of them dwell in these hills and valleys, and in woods, and in open country, and they hide themselves in stony hollows.*

The same stress on the inaccessibility of monstrous beasts that is to be observed in the *Liber monstrorum* is expressed here.[111] Again, the Old English sometimes surpasses the original in style and effect; in Latin (§ 10) we read how Alexander was forced to march 'through sands burning with sun and places lacking moisture' (*per feruentes sole harenas et egentia humoris loca*), whilst the Old English paints a picture altogether richer in diction (and alliteration):

> þurh þa weallandan sond, 7 þurh þa wædlan stowe wætres 7 ælcere wætan.
>
> *through the boiling sands, and through places devoid of water or any moisture.*

If the sense remains broadly the same, there is a clear difference in stylistic adornment. The same rhetorical and alliterative pretensions, together with the same key phrases, are evident in the Old English rendering of a subsequent passage (§ 33):

> Ða foran we 7 usic þa ladteowas læddon þurh þa wædlan stowe wætres 7 þurh þa unarefndon lond wildeora 7 wyrma þa wæron wunderlicum nomum on Indisc geceged.
>
> *Then we set out and the guides led us through a place bereft of water and through lands unbearable with wild beasts and serpents called by marvellous Indian names.*

In this case the Latin source is much more prosaic:[112]

> Qui nos, ut diximus, per immania et egentia plerumque aquarum plenaque serpentium ferarumque loca deduxerunt in proximam oraculi sedem. De quibus feris et serpentibus, quia innumerae et Indica lingua erant uocitatae, scribendum tibi non putaui.
>
> *And [the guides] led us, as we have said, through immense places lacking much water, and full of serpents and wild beasts, and brought us near to the place of the oracle. But I have not thought it worth writing to you about these wild beasts and serpents, since they were many and called by Indian names.*

111 See further above, pp. 87–90. Cf. the account given in § 26: 'But as we travelled we saw nothing but desolate expanses and woods and hills by the ocean, which were impassable for men because of wild beasts and serpents' (*ac þa ne gesawon we swa swa we þa geferdon noht elles buton þa westan feldas 7 wudu 7 duna be þæm garsecge, ða wæron monnum ungeferde for wildeorum 7 wyrmum*).

112 Boer, ed., *Epistola Alexandri*, pp. 40/9–41/3; for a variant version of the text, see below, p. 218.

In abbreviating his source, and introducing heightened stylistic effects such as alliteration, the translator of the Old English text brings an immediacy to his narrative that is occasionally lacking in the Latin.

The Old English translator has altered his source in other ways. The descriptions of Alexander's martial activities are considerably expanded, so much so that Sisam remarks that the Old English author's 'interest is mainly in the campaign and the general'.[113] This is clear particularly in the account of Alexander's dealings with Porus, where a description of Alexander's trip into the enemy camp in disguise is told in far more detail than in the Latin (§ 24),[114] while the text of Porus's letter to Alexander is entirely omitted, as in a number of Latin versions.[115] More significant is the fact that the Old English text is brought to an abrupt conclusion shortly after Alexander learns from the talking trees of the Sun and the Moon the prophecy of his own impending death. The final section of the Latin (§ 41), with its continued description of wonders and marvels, has been dramatically abbreviated, in a way which cannot be paralleled precisely in any of the extant manuscripts,[116] nor indeed in any of the many extant vernacular versions.[117] The effect of this is to focus attention firmly on the character of the king himself. As Douglas Butturff concludes: 'the translator intended to provide by his work an exemplum on the superbia of earthly rulers; and . . . he did so by consistently exposing the egotism of the Macedonian potentate who was humbled by the inevitable fate of all mortals.'[118]

In altering his source in order to stress the self-absorption of Alexander, the Old English author is occasionally led to (intentional?) solecism, as in the following passage, where an already sumptuous description of the splendour of Alexander's army is changed by the free addition of possessive pronouns into a self-indulgent celebration of personal glory; the Latin (with first-person references italicised) reads as follows (§ 11):[119]

> Et sane miles ita locupletatus erat, ut uix ferre pondus auri posset. Accedebat quoque armorum non parua gravitas, quia omnia *ego* incluseram laminis. Ita totum agmen *me* ueluti sidere aut fulgore clarum radiantibus auro insignibusque sequebatur cum signis et uexillis. Eratque inter uarietates spectaculum in

113 Sisam, *Studies*, p. 88; cf. Greenfield and Calder, *A Critical History of Old English Literature*, p. 65; Butturff, 'Style as a Clue to Meaning', p. 81.

114 The close parallel between this episode and that told by William of Malmesbury about King Alfred has not passed unnoticed; cf. Sisam, *Studies in the History of Old English Literature*, p. 90. Subsequently, similar tales are recorded about a number of English and Anglo-Norman heroes, such as Horn and Havelock; I am grateful to Morgan Dickson for sharing with me details of her research on the theme.

115 In fact most of the extant manuscripts contain a similar omission; cf. Boer, ed., *Epistola Alexandri*, p. 26.

116 All the manuscripts of Boer's group II, including Royal 13. A. i, the reading of which is given in the Appendix below, pp. 204–23, exhibit considerable abbreviation of § 41, although none has quite such extensive abridgement as implied in the Old English rendering.

117 Butturff, 'Style as a Clue to Meaning', p. 85; Tristram, 'More Talk of Alexander', p. 658.

118 Butturff, 'Style as a Clue to Meaning', p. 82.

119 Boer, ed., *Epistola Alexandri*, p. 8/3–10; for a variant version of the text, see below, p. 207.

conspiciendo talem exercitum, quia ornatu pariter et inter gentes ceteras eminebat. *Ego* certe respiciens felicitatem *meam* insigni numero iuuentutis immenso afficiebar gaudio.

And indeed each soldier was so wealthy that he could scarcely carry the mass of gold. In addition there was no small weight of armour, because I had encased everything in metal plates. So the whole army was following me, bright like a star or a bolt of lightning, shining with gold and resplendent, with banners and pennants. And it was a sight to see such an army in its different array, since in ornament it was outstanding equally even among other nations. And I, indeed, gazing on my good fortune in the splendid number of young men was touched by great joy.

The Old English is altogether more egocentric (§ 11):[120]

Ond efne swiðe þa *mine* þegnas 7 eal *min* weorod wæs gewelgod þæt hie uneðe ealle þa byrðene þæs goldes mid him aberan 7 alædan meahton. Swelce eac heora wæpena noht lytel byrðen wæs for þon eal heora wæpenu þæra *minra* þegna 7 ealles *mines* weoredes 7 heriges *ic* het hie mid gyldenum þelum bewyrcean. Ond eall *min* weorod wæs on þa gelicnesse tungles oððe ligite for þære micelnisse þæs goldes. Hit scan 7 berhte, foran swa ymb *me* uton mid þrymme 7 herebeacen 7 segnas beforan *me* læddon. Ond swa micel wundor 7 wæfersien wæs þæs *mines* weoredes on fægernisse ofer ealle oþre þeodkyningas þe in middangearde wæron. Ða sceawede *ic* seolfa 7 geseah *mine* gesælinesse 7 *min* wuldor 7 þa fromnisse *minre* iuguðe 7 gesælignisse *mines* lifes, þa wæs *ic* hwæthwugo in gefean in *minum* mode ahafen.

And indeed my thegns and all my troop had gained so much wealth that they could only with difficulty bring and carry with them the burden of all that gold. Also their weapons were no little burden because I had commanded that all the weapons of my thegns and all my troop and army be covered with gold plate. And all my troop looked like stars or lightning because of the amount of the gold. It shone and glittered before me and around me in glory, and they led before me war-banners and standards. And so great was the sight and spectacle of that troop of mine in splendour beyond all the other mighty kings there have been in the world. When I myself gazed and saw my prosperity and my glory and the success of my youth and the prosperity of my life, I was somewhat uplifted with joy in my heart.

Alexander exudes what in the Latin is a touching pride in the appearance of his men, and in the Old English is a disturbing arrogance in his own esteem. There are in the Latin only four first-person references, while the Old English has sixteen.[121] Alexander's pride, moreover, exceeds his grammar; the Latin has the Macedonian army pre-eminent above that of other nations (*gentes*), while in the Old English Alexander thinks more selfishly of mighty kings (*þeodkyningas*).[122] The diction of

120 Cf. Butturff, 'Style as a Clue to Meaning', p. 83.

121 In the whole text, there are 153 first-person references in the Latin, and 481 in the Old English.

122 The use of the term *þeodkyningas* calls to mind the prominent occurence of the same compound in the second line of *Beowulf.* The author of the *Letter of Alexander* has a

this passage, with its frequent use of doublets (*scan 7 berhte*; *wundor 7 wæfersien*; *sceawede 7 geseah*) is characteristically rich and over-wrought; one might cite in particular the translation of *felicitatem meam insigni numero iuuentutis* by *mine gesælinesse 7 min wuldor 7 þa fromnisse minre iuguðe 7 gesælignisse mines lifes*. In rendering the Latin, the Old English author has given Alexander a diction the decadence of which appears to match his morals.

Two further examples of the way that the Old English translator has manipulated his source can be treated briefly together.[123] In both the Latin stresses Alexander's selflessness in giving priority to the needs of his men, as commonly described elsewhere;[124] in the Old English Alexander is more pragmatic. The first describes Alexander's reaction to the lack of water in his desert-march, and the Latin makes it clear that for Alexander his men come first (§ 14):[125]

> Quae res me dupliciter torsit. Primo de statu exercitus magis quam de proprio meo sollicitus fui periculo.
>
> *And the situation troubled me in two ways; I was concerned about the danger first to the army rather than my own peril.*

The Old English version reverses the priorities precisely:

> Seo wise wæs þa in me on twa healfa uneþe ærest be minre seolfre nedþearfe, 7 mines weorodes.
>
> *Things had then become difficult for me for two reasons: first with regard to my own necessity, and that of my troops.*

In an identical way, a later passage describes Alexander's reactions on finding precious water (§ 16):[126]

> Cum ergo dulci aqua potata gaudio alacer pecora et impedimenta cum exercitu pariter et lassa quadrupedia militum refecissem, castra in longum stadia uiginti duo totidemque in latum collocari iussi.
>
> *So when I had swiftly refreshed the cattle and the pack-animals with sweet water joyfully consumed, along with the army and the tired beasts of the soldiers, I ordered a camp to be set up twenty-two* stadia *broad and the same number long.*

Once again the Old English version depicts Alexander in more selfish terms:

> Ða wæs ic gefeonde þæs sweran wætres 7 þæs ferscan 7 þa sona minne þurst ærest gelehte 7 þa eal min weored, ða het ic wætrian sona ure hors 7 ure nieteno eall wæron hie swiðe mid þurste fornumene ða het ic sioððan sona þa fyrd wician. Wæs seo wicstow ða on lengo .XX.es furlonga long, 7 swa eac in brædo.

penchant for such compounds, including several with a poetic and heroic flavour, as noted by Bately, 'Old English Prose Before and During the Reign of Alfred', p. 113.

123 Cf. Butturff, 'Style as a Clue to Meaning', p. 82.

124 Cf. Cary, *The Medieval Alexander*, p. 160.

125 Boer, ed., *Epistola Alexandri*, p. 11/6–7; for a variant version of the text, see below, p. 208.

126 Boer, ed., *Epistola Alexandri*, p. 15/9–11; for a variant version of the text, see below, p. 209.

I was delighted in this clean fresh water, and immediately slaked my thirst and then that of all my troop, and immediately ordered all our horses and our animals to be watered, since they were all greatly suffering with thirst. After that I immediately ordered the army to pitch camp. The campsite was twenty furlongs in length, and the same in width.

Again, one should stress that no other extant version of the *Letter*, whether Latin or vernacular, manipulates the text in quite this way.

In this characteristically Anglo-Saxon context, in which at every turn Alexander is presented as at once prouder and more violent than in the Latin source, the closing words of the Old English *Letter*, which have little warrant in the Latin, must have had for Christian ears a distinctly chilling ring. The Latin tells of the building of monuments to Alexander to surpass those of Bacchus and Hercules, and the need to leave a physical mark (*indicium*) or monument of glory to future generations (§ 41):[127]

Atque in ultima India ultra Liberi et Herculis trophea, quae centum erant, ego quinque mea aurea altiora denis pedibus statui imperaui, quae miraculo futura sunt, carissime praeceptor, posteris saeculis non paruo. Nouum perpetuumque statuimus uirtutibus monimentum inuidendum, ut immortalitas esset perpetua et nobis opinio et animi industriae, optime Aristoteles, indicium.

And in the farthest reaches of India, beyond the monuments of Bacchus and Hercules, which were a hundred [feet tall], I ordered my five golden trophies to be set up, ten feet taller, to be no small wonder, dearest teacher, to coming generations. We have set up to be gazed upon [or 'envied'] a new and permanent monument to courage, so that there might be for us immortality and esteem forever, and a sign, finest Aristotle, of the exertion of the spirit.

After an initial statement of personal authority (*ego . . . mea*), it is surely telling (and characteristic) that in the Latin Alexander switches to the first person plural (*nobis*); his monument is to the shared glory of himself and his teacher and his men. In the Old English *Letter* Alexander (equally characteristically) is more blunt and egocentric, and the heroic diction sounds curiously empty and hollow:[128]

Ond me næs se hrædlica ende mines lifes swa miclum weorce swa me wæs þæt ic læs mærðo gefremed hæfde þonne min willa wære. Ðas þing ic write to þon min se leofa magister þæt þu ærest gefeo in þæm fromscipe mines lifes 7 eac blissige in þæm weorðmyndum. Ond eac swelce ecelice min gemynd stonde 7 hleouige oðrum eorðcyningum to bysne, ðæt hie witen þy gearwor þrym 7 min weorðmynd maran wæron, þonne ealra oþra kyninga þe in middnagearde æfre wæron.

And to me the swift ending of my life was not so much pain as the fact that I had achieved less glory than I would have wished. I write these things to you, my beloved teacher, that you first can rejoice in the success of my life, and exult in the honours.

127 Boer, ed., *Epistola Alexandri*, pp. 59/6–60/4; for a variant version of the text, see below, pp. 222–3. On the significance of these monuments, see further above, pp. 114–15.

128 One might also note that the Old English version is far less concerned with the physical structure of any monument, than with its significance.

> *And also my memory shall forever stand and tower as an example for other earthly kings, so that they know the more readily that my power and my honour were greater than those of all the other kings who have ever lived in the world.*

In concluding his text this way, the author of the Old English *Letter* appears here, as elsewhere, to have given an Orosian perspective to the Latin wonder-tale. The text still deals with a mighty hero, the mightiest indeed of mortal men, who travelled to distant lands in his youth in quest of glory, a monster-slayer and a treasure-laden king who was to die before his time and leave monuments and memories to his people, whose own fate would decline. But in the Christian perspective, Alexander is truly an example to 'earthly kings' *(eorðcyningum)* of how their powers and glory must ultimately perish. On the following page of the manuscript,[129] and in familiar heroic language,[130] another tale of men and monsters, with much the same heroic theme, begins (*Beowulf*, lines 1–3):

> Hwæt we Gar-Denum   in geardagum
> þeodcyninga   þrym gefrunon
> hu þa æðelingas   ellen fremedon!
>
> *Lo, we have heard of the power of mighty kings in days gone by, how those princes performed deeds of valour.*

The way that Alexander, like Hercules in the *Liber monstrorum*, can be depicted as a monstrous figure of pride, a monster-slayer who, in Christian eyes, is every bit as outlandish and inhuman as the creatures he fights, is surely instructive in considering *Beowulf* in the context of the manuscript which contains it. That other medieval authors, albeit much later in the period, recognised similar literary potential for merging the physical and psychological worlds of men and monsters, and of pride and prodigies, in their own texts can be demonstrated still further, by assessing the way in which the tale of a later Germanic monster-slayer is told, several centuries after the events it purports to depict, in a text which has been much discussed for the close analogues it offers to the monster-battles in *Beowulf*: the Icelandic *Grettis saga*.

129 For the layout of the manuscript, cf. Malone, ed., *Nowell Codex*, pp. xxv–xxvii.

130 See further Bately, 'Old English Prose Before and During the Reign of Alfred', p. 113, where she speaks of 'a fondness for compounding of a type typical of poetry' in the *Letter*.

CHAPTER VI

Grettir and Grendel Again

Grettis saga Ásmundarsonar is amongst the best-loved tales of medieval Iceland, and has been described as 'the last of the great Icelandic sagas'.[1] The author of *Grettis saga* borrowed freely from a great number of written sources, including a now-lost biography of Grettir composed *c.* 1280 by Sturla Þórðarson.[2] Mention is made of five other sagas in the course of the narrative, of which three still survive, and the unacknowledged use of eleven further vernacular Icelandic sources has been detected.[3] It is also clear, however, that in the final part of the saga now known as *Spésarþáttr* the author has made considerable use of some version of the Tristram legend,[4] and Hermann Pálsson has demonstrated that this is not the only 'learned' or latinate element in *Grettis saga*.[5] In addition to all these written sources, Guðni Jónsson has further stressed the importance of oral sources in the composition of those parts of the saga which have always been recognised as having a fabulous or folktale element.[6] *Grettis saga* therefore provides a useful index of the broad range of both written and oral sources upon which saga-authors might draw in composition, and, moreover, its structure, contents, and style have been closely examined in a wide range of studies over the past twenty-five years.[7]

The interest of scholars of *Beowulf* in *Grettis saga* dates from almost a century ago, when the Icelander Guðbrandur Vígfússon first read *Beowulf* and noted a number of similarities between the ways in which Beowulf and Grettir each dispose of their monstrous enemies; in particular he indicated that: 'Where everything else

1 Fox and Pálsson, *Grettir's saga*, p. vii.

2 Nordal, *Sturla Þórðarson og Grettis Saga*, pp. 17–24.

3 Jónsson, ed., *Grettis saga*, pp. xvii–xxxi; cf. Fox and Pálsson, *Grettir's Saga*, p. vii.

4 Schach, 'Tristan in Iceland', pp. 156–60; Schach, 'Some Observations', pp. 111–21.

5 Pálsson, '*Sermo datur cunctis*', suggests that the author may have been familiar with the *Disticha Catonis*.

6 Jónsson, ed., *Grettis saga*, pp. xlii–lx.

7 See especially Arent, 'The Heroic Pattern'; Ciklamini, 'Grettir and Ketill Hœngr'; Pálsson, 'Drög að siðfræði Grettis sögu'; Glendinning, '*Grettis saga* and European Literature'; Motz, 'Withdrawal and Return'; Hume, 'The Thematic Design of *Grettis saga*'; Halldórsson, 'Goðsögnin um Gretti'; Motz, 'The Hero and his Tale'; Pálsson, '*Sermo datur cunctis*'; Halldórsson, 'Tröllasaga Bárðdæla og Grettluhöfundur'; Cook, 'The Reader in *Grettis saga*'; Hastrup, 'Tracing Tradition'; Zimmermann, 'Vorbildisches Verhalten? Zum Thema der *Grettis saga*'; Cook, 'Reading for Character in *Grettis saga*'; Thorsson, 'Grettla'.

is transformed, one word still remains as a memorial of its origin, viz. in the English epic *hæftmece* and in the Icelandic saga *heptisax*, both occurring in the same place of the legend, and both hapax legomena in their respective literatures'.[8] Within a few years there was a flurry of activity by scholars keen to build on such promising links.[9] Guðbrandur Vígfússon subsequently refined his own views in two collaborative publications with Frederick York Powell,[10] concluding that 'the story in . . . [*Grettis saga*] we take to be an echo, not of the present diluted epic [*Beowulf*], but of the lays from which the epic was later made up'.[11] The earliest efforts, developed in detail by later scholars,[12] focused on perceived similarities between the monster-battles in *Beowulf* and in two episodes from *Grettis saga* in which Grettir is called upon to deal with supernatural enemies in the shape of the *draugr* ('walking dead') Glámr at Forsæludalr (chapters 31–5),[13] and the various monsters associated with the hauntings at Sandhaugar (chapters 64–6).[14]

But more recent scholarship has indicated a number of other episodes in *Grettis saga* which also share the same elements from *Beowulf*.[15] One can therefore examine in detail the ways in which the author of *Grettis saga* played on these shared themes consciously and with great skill, incorporating them carefully into the structure of his story.

Current scholarship indicates five principal episodes which are built around a series of narrative details shared with *Beowulf*. Each can be characterised as follows:

[1] Grettir battles against the *draugr* Kárr inn gamli (chapter 18)[16]
[2] Grettir battles against a Norwegian bear (chapter 21)[17]
[3] Grettir battles against the *draugr* Glámr at Forsæludalr (chapters 31–5)[18]
[4] Grettir battles against two monsters at Sandhaugar (chapters 64–6)[19]
[5] Þorbjǫrn battles against Grettir on Drangey (chapters 81–2)[20]

8 Vígfússon, ed., *Sturlunga Saga* I, p. xlix, n. 1; cf. Liberman, 'Beowulf-Grettir', p. 354.
9 See, for example, Gering, 'Der *Beowulf* und der islaëndische *Grettissaga*' (and the review by J. M. Garnett, *American Journal of Philology* 1 (1880), 491–7); Smith, 'Beowulf-Gretti'.
10 Vígfússon and Powell, *An Icelandic Prose Reader*, p. 405; Vígfússon and Powell, *Corpus Poeticum Boreale* II, pp. 501–3; cf. Liberman, 'Beowulf-Grettir', pp. 353–91.
11 Vígfússon and Powell, *Corpus Poeticum Boreale* II, p. 502.
12 See in particular Lawrence, 'The Haunted Mere in *Beowulf*'; Lawrence, 'Grendel's Lair'; Chambers, *Beowulf: an Introduction*, pp. 146–82.
13 Jónsson, ed., *Grettis saga*, pp. 104–23.
14 Jónsson, ed., *Grettis saga*, pp. 209–17.
15 See in particular Stedman, 'Some Points of Resemblance'; Danielli, 'Initiation Ceremonial'; Taylor, 'Two Notes on *Beowulf*'; Harris, 'The Deaths of Grettir and Grendel'; Jorgensen, 'Grendel, Grettir, and Two Skaldic Stanzas'; Turville-Petre, '*Beowulf* and *Grettis saga*'; Jorgensen, 'Beowulf's Swimming-Contest with Breca'; McConchie, 'Grettir Ásmundarson's fight with Kárr the Old'; Wachsler, 'Grettir's Fight with a Bear'.
16 Jónsson, ed., *Grettis saga*, pp. 56–61.
17 Jónsson, ed., *Grettis saga*, pp. 73–8.
18 Jónsson, ed., *Grettis saga*, pp. 104–23.
19 Jónsson, ed., *Grettis saga*, pp. 209–17.
20 Jónsson, ed., *Grettis saga*, pp. 256–64.

These five episodes in *Grettis saga*, based, as we shall see, on the same narrative paradigm as that of the first two monster-battles in *Beowulf*, are, as I hope to demonstrate, central to the construction of the whole saga. This common paradigm therefore informs the entire structure of *Grettis saga*, and the similarity between certain episodes in the saga and *Beowulf* is not simply what Chambers has called 'an interesting literary curiosity',[21] but offers fundamental clues to the understanding of both the Icelandic author's art, and the way in which the monster-battles in *Beowulf* might be interpreted for artistic ends.

It may be helpful if I anticipate my own conclusions concerning the structure of *Grettis saga*, which I would interpret as a five-act tragedy, in which the hero begins by battling ravaging monsters (episodes [1] and [2]), is cursed (episode [3]), and ends up transformed into a 'monster' himself, killed, Harris has noted,[22] as only monsters can be (episode [5]). Other commentators have considered *Grettis saga* to fall naturally into five sections also, although none has interpreted the structure of the saga in quite this manner.[23] Richard Harris considered the five episodes to be considered here as 'a set of fugue-like variations on a single theme',[24] yet saw no fundamental structural principal of the sort I suggest. But clearly, as R. N. Coffin indicates: 'In the process of time Grettir is forced to become what he fights'.[25]

The basic narrative paradigm upon which I shall draw for comparison is derived directly from the first two of Beowulf's monster-battles; the episodes of Grendel and Grendel's mother, comprising roughly *Beowulf*, lines 1–2199, can broadly be summed up as follows:

1. Grendel inhabits a remote and inaccessible waterbound home.
2. He is incensed by the noise of carousal at Heorot.
3. He ravages the inhabitants.
4. Beowulf hears of Grendel's depredations.
5. He resolves against advice to help.[26]
6. Beowulf makes a sea-voyage to Heorot to visit King Hrothgar.
7. He is snubbed by Unferð, an important retainer of the king.
8. He berates Unferð for his failure to kill Grendel.

21 Chambers, ed., *Beowulf: an Introduction*, p. 50.

22 Harris, 'The Deaths of Grettir and Grendel', p. 38.

23 Cf. Arent, 'The Heroic Pattern', pp. 184–98; Fox and Pálsson, *Grettir's Saga*, pp. x–xiii; Thorsson, 'Grettla', pp. 103–6.

24 Harris, 'The Deaths of Grettir and Grendel', p. 52.

25 Coffin, '*Beowulf* and its Relationship to Norse and Finno-Uguric Beliefs and Narratives', p. 73. Similar comments have been made with regard to some of the characters in the *Beowulf*-manuscript itself, most notably Alexander, of whom Weissmann, 'Giants and Giantism', p. 76, notes: 'There seems to be an inverted image in the story of how the great conqueror Alexander goes out looking for monsters, and, in the end, becomes a spiritual monster himself'.

26 The advice is that of Hygelac, mentioned in lines 1994–7, and appears to be flatly contradicted by Beowulf himself in lines 202–4 and 415–17. On Hygelac's dubious moral character, see above, pp. 113–14.

9. He hears from Hrothgar about the horror of Grendel.
10. He resolves to fight him single-handed.
11. Grendel appears at evening, carrying his *glof*.[27]
12. They fight; the place is wrecked.
13. Beowulf rips off Grendel's arm.
14. Grendel escapes towards his underwater home.
15. An expedition is undertaken to the inaccessible monster lair.
16. Beowulf hears of the depredations of Grendel's mother.
17. He resolves to fight her single-handed.
18. An expedition is undertaken to the mere; Beowulf goes on alone.
19. He dives into mere, and arrives at a dry cave at evening.
20. He sees a mysterious light in the cave.
21. He grapples with Grendel's mother.
22. She wields a *seax*, he a *hæftmece*.
23. He kills her with a giant sword from the cave.
24. He decapitates Grendel.
25. The sword-blade melts; the engraved hilt remains.
26. The Danes see blood in the water, fear the worst, and flee.
27. Beowulf leaves the cave with booty (the hilt and the head).
28. He returns to Hrothgar and recounts his adventures.
29. He is rewarded by Hrothgar with horses and equipment.
30. He is given a lecture on the dangers of pride.

A number of elements in the part of the story dealing with Grendel's mother (elements 16–30) simply repeat or echo those that are found earlier in the Grendel episode (elements 1–15); so in this list features 4 and 16, 10 and 17, and 15 and 18 can be considered partly or wholly parallel. In the same way, several of the incidents in this list find parallels in the later account of Beowulf's fight with the dragon; features 1, 3, 4, 17, 18, 19, 20, 26, and 27 correspond in part or in whole. Such a crude list of basic incidents in these two earlier monster-battles naturally glosses over a great amount of important subsidiary detail, but provides a useful basis for simple comparison with similar narrative paradigms underlying each of the five episodes from *Grettis saga* considered here.

Episode [1]: *Grettir battles against the draugr Kárr inn gamli*

The principal details of this episode (chapter 18)[28] can be represented as follows, where the numbers on the extreme right-hand side of the page refer to parallel incidents from the numerical scheme already given for *Beowulf*:

27 The *glof* is only mentioned in line 2085, but is a common feature of many analogous accounts. Cf. Klaeber, ed. *Beowulf*, p. 205; Anderson, 'Grendel's *glof*', pp. 1–8.

28 Jónsson, ed., *Grettis saga*, pp. 56–61.

A. Grettir makes a sea-voyage to Háramarsey. (6)
B. He is snubbed by Þorfinnr. (7)
C. He sees a mysterious light on the headland. (20)
D. A monster inhabits a barrow by the sea. (1)
E. He hears of Kárr the *draugr*, and his depredations. (4)
F. He decides against advice to break into his lair. (5)
G. He resolves to meet Kárr alone. (10)
H. An expedition is undertaken to the barrow along with Auðunn. (15)
I. They dig all day, and reach the barrow-chamber at evening. (19)
J. Grettir goes on alone; Auðunn guards the rope. (18)
K. Grettir fights Kárr; the place is wrecked. (12)
L. Auðunn fears the worst, and flees. (26)
M. Grettir decapitates Kárr with the sword Jǫkulsnautr. (24)
N. He removes booty; special mention is made of a *sax* (Kársnautr). (27)

The relationship of this episode to *Beowulf* was first discussed in detail by Taylor and later, apparently independently, by McConchie;[29] it is referred to in passing by Klaeber,[30] but does not merit mention in the collection of Beowulfian parallels and analogues published by Garmonsway and Simpson.[31]

Grettir's expedition is primarily undertaken to gain treasure, and the secondary motive, that of freeing the local populace from a troublesome menace, is rather underplayed in this episode. A number of Old English and Norse sources focus on the treasure to be had from the barrows of the dead,[32] and it is important to note that Grettir's immediate motivation for confronting the supernatural is greed for gain. That Grettir's first monstrous foe should be a revenant, the undead *draugr* Kárr, is of some interest, since a number of scholars of *Beowulf* have identified Grendel with similar monsters, well-documented from Scandinavian sources.[33]

In *Grettis saga* the conflict with Kárr is integrated into the larger structure of the saga by the fact that Grettir gains from it the short sword (*sax*) which he is to carry for the rest of his life, and with which he is to accomplish many of his later feats. The importance of this *sax* is first made clear in the episode when Grettir returns to Þorfinnr's hall, and spreads out on the table all the treasure he has taken from the barrow:[34]

29 Taylor, 'Two Notes on Beowulf'; McConchie, 'Grettir Ásmundarson's fight with Kárr the Old'.

30 *Beowulf*, ed. Klaeber, p. xvi, n. 1.

31 Garmonsway and Simpson, *'Beowulf' and its Analogues*.

32 Cf. Davidson, 'The Hill of the Dragon'; Grinsell, 'Barrow Treasure'.

33 See, for example, Chadwick, 'Norse Ghosts'; Coffin, '*Beowulf* and its Relationship to Norse and Finno-Uguric Beliefs and Narratives', pp. 117–42; Hume, 'From Saga to Romance'; Lecouteux, *Fantômes et revenants au moyen âge*, pp. 203–9; Niles, *Beowulf: the Poem and its Tradition*, pp. 10–11; Lapidge, '*Beowulf* and the Psychology of Terror', pp. 375–7.

34 Jónsson, ed., *Grettis saga*, p. 59/9–11.

> Einn gripr var sá, er Gretti stóðu mest augu til; þat var eitt sax, svá gott vápn, at aldri kvazk hann sét hafa betra; þat lét hann síðast fram.
>
> *There was one treasure to which Grettir's gaze strayed most: it was a* sax, *so fine a weapon that he said he had never seen a better. That was the last thing he gave up.*

Further stress is laid on the *sax* when Þorfinnr asks Grettir about the source of the treasure, specifically prompted by the sight of this weapon, and is answered in a verse.[35] Þorfinnr repeats his question, but this time asks explicitly about the *sax*, and is answered in a second verse, which deals exclusively with the weapon.[36] The verse is worth quoting in full:

> Fekk í firna dǫkkum,
> fell draugr, tekit haugi
> sax, þats seggja vexir
> sǫ́r, hyrlestir bǫ́ru;
> ok skyldi mér aldri
> jalms dýrlogi hjalma
> ýtum hættr, ef ættak,
> angrs hendi firr ganga.
>
> *I won in a fearfully dark barrow that* sax *which increases men's wounds, o gold-giver. The* draugr *fell. The precious flame of the clash of the grief of helmets, dangerous to men, would never pass from my hand, if it was in my possession.*

Þorfinnr's insistence that Grettir perform some further feat of valour before he is given the *sax* is met when he uses the weapon to defeat a band of visiting berserks, and again the *sax* is given some prominence; Þorfinnr thanks Grettir profusely, and offers him money and hospitality, which Grettir accepts.[37] But the saga goes on:[38]

> Þá gaf hann Gretti saxit góða; þat bar Grettir, meðan hann lifði, ok var in mesta gersemi.
>
> *Then [Þorfinnr] gave Grettir the fine* sax: *he carried it as long as he lived, and it was a great treasure.*

This same *sax*, the importance of which is therefore stressed several times in this episode, recurs throughout the rest of the saga, and is the weapon with which Grettir fights every monster, but it is not specifically named as a treasure won from the *draugr* Kárr until Grettir's final battle,[39] in which he himself falls, and where, as indicated, the *sax* is indeed the last thing to leave his hands, in rather grisly circumstances, as we shall see.

35 Jónsson, ed., *Grettis saga*, p. 59/11–22.
36 Jónsson, ed., *Grettis saga*, p. 60/1–14.
37 Jónsson, ed., *Grettis saga*, pp. 60–73.
38 Jónsson, ed., *Grettis saga*, p. 73/7–9.
39 Jónsson, ed., *Grettis saga*, p. 260.

The notion that a hero might obtain his weapon from the otherworld or the land of the dead seems to have been a common motif in Norse saga; Inger Boberg notes ten instances where swords and other weapons are specifically taken from barrows.[40] The closest parallel to this episode in *Grettis saga* is found in the plundering of the barrow of the *draugr* Sóti by Hǫrðr, the eponymous hero of *Harðar saga ok hólmverja*, and it is worth noting that the same incident has been independently adduced by Chadwick as an analogue for the monster-fights in *Beowulf*.[41] Hǫrðr is aided in his expedition by a mysterious hooded helper-figure who calls himself Bjǫrn ('bear') and lends a sword which is used to gain entry to the barrow, but proves ineffective in Hǫrðr's battle with Sóti, which is a strictly hand-to-hand grapple.

In *Harðar saga*, however, Sóti's treasure (including his sword) brings with it a curse, as does the dragon's treasure in *Beowulf* and a number of other hoards in Northern legend.[42] One might note in particular that the sword which Þorvaldr Þiðrandason takes from the waterbound cave of the troll Geitir one evening (in an incident in *Fljótsdæla saga* with numerous parallels with the episodes from *Beowulf* and *Grettis saga* discussed here) is specifically cursed, a fact which overshadows much of the later narrative.[43] In view of the fact that the *sax* Kársnautr is used to decapitate Grettir himself towards the end of *Grettis saga*, and that the malign influence of the weapon does not appear to diminish even after Grettir's death (it also proves to be the bane of Grettir's own slayer, Þorbjǫrn), it is important to ask whether an Icelandic audience might have assumed that in *Grettis saga* also the *sax* from the monster's lair is cursed, since certainly such a curse *is* found on the sword Tyrfingr which is taken (again in parallel circumstances) from her father's barrow by Hervǫr in *Hervarar saga*.[44] This *sax* snatched from the barrow of the dead has in any case an important role in linking each of the four remaining episodes from *Grettis saga* examined here, and even at the moments of Grettir's greatest triumphs provides a grim reminder of Grettir's doom.

Episode [2]: *Grettir battles against a Norwegian bear*

The next episode in the saga (chapter 21),[45] in which Grettir disposes of a bear and quarrels with an unfriendly kinsman of Þorkell, his host, follows on immediately after Grettir has left Þorfinnr's house, and has likewise been noted as sharing certain narrative details with *Beowulf*.[46] The main features of this episode which find parallels in *Beowulf* can be represented as follows:

40 Boberg, *Motif-Index*, p. 62, no. D838.5; cf. Turville-Petre, '*Beowulf* and *Grettis saga*', pp. 354 and 357, n. 23; Hume, 'From Saga to Romance', p. 4.

41 'The Monsters and Beowulf', p. 181

42 Cf. Boberg, *Motif-Index*, pp. 198 and 203, nos. M472 and N591; Chadwick, 'Norse Ghosts', p. 107.

43 Jóhannesson, ed., *Fljótsdæla saga*, pp. 224–30.

44 Cf. Boberg, *Motif-Index*, p. 111, no. F451.5.2.13; Tolkien, *The Saga of Heidrek the Wise*, pp. ix–xi.

45 Jónsson, ed., *Grettis saga*, pp. 73–8.

46 Danielli, 'Initiation Ceremonial', pp. 229–45; Taylor, 'Two Notes on *Beowulf*', pp. 13–6; Klaeber, ed., *Beowulf*, p. xiv, n. 3; Wachsler, 'Grettir's Fight with a Bear'.

A.	Grettir makes a sea-voyage to Sálpti to visit Þorkell.	(6)
B.	He is snubbed by Bjǫrn, an important retainer.	(7)
C.	A great bear is incensed by the noise of carousel.	(2)
D.	He ravages men and cattle.	(3)
E.	An expedition is undertaken to the bear's inaccessible lair.	(15)
F.	Grettir berates Bjǫrn for his failure to kill the bear.	(8)
G.	An expedition is undertaken to the lair; Grettir goes on alone.	(18)
H.	He reaches the lair at evening.	(19)
I.	He cuts off the bear's paw with the sword Jǫkulsnautr.	(13)
J.	He stabs the bear to death with the *sax* Kársnautr.	(23)
K.	He leaves the lair with booty (the paw and the cloak).	(27)

Again, the authors of both *Grettis saga* and *Beowulf* seem to be drawing on the same basic narrative paradigm.

It is important to highlight the fact that Þorkell's kinsman, Bjǫrn ('bear'), who is a figure unattested elsewhere, is both indirectly responsible for the bear's ravages (since it is the noise of his carousal which first rouses the beast), and shares with his namesake a certain narrative function (both becoming Grettir's foes).[47] By contrast one might recall the shadowy helper-figure named Bjǫrn who appears in *Harðar saga* and lends Hǫrðr a sword.[48] The shadow of the bear hangs also over *Beowulf*; one might compare Walter Skeat's notorious suggestion that in the Old English epic Beowulf ('Bee-wolf') is himself simply a bear,[49] which foreshadowed Friedrich Panzer's magisterial survey of the so-called 'Bear's Son' folk-tale and its relevance to the plot of the poem,[50] or, more recently, R. N. Coffin's arguments concerning alleged traces of a bear-cult in *Beowulf*.[51] Likewise a number of scholars have compared Bjǫrn's recalcitrant and grudging behaviour towards Grettir with that of Unferð towards Beowulf, and A. R. Taylor believes that the discourtesy towards strangers exhibited by both Bjǫrn and Unferð was a characteristic of their shared prototype.[52] And Unferð's lending of the sword Hrunting to Beowulf, a weapon which proves useless in combat against Grendel's mother, can be matched by Bjǫrn's loan of a sword to Hǫrðr simply to gain entry to the barrow of the *draugr* Sóti in *Harðar saga*, a sword which is pointedly *not* used in the subsequent battle, in which weapons are largely eschewed. Such parallels support the notion that the role of Unferð in *Beowulf*, which has long troubled scholars, is an original feature of the

47 Jónsson, ed., *Grettis saga*, p. 75/1.

48 Vilmundarson and Vilhjálmsson, ed., *Harðar saga*, pp. 39–41.

49 Skeat, 'On the Signification of the Monster Grendel'.

50 Panzer, *Studien zur germanischen Sagengeschichte*, pp. 254–75; cf. Klaeber, ed., *Beowulf*, pp. xii.xiv.

51 Coffin, '*Beowulf* and its Relationship to Norse and Finno-Uguric Beliefs and Narratives', pp. 143–68.

52 Taylor, 'Two Notes on *Beowulf*', pp. 16–17; cf. Jorgensen, 'The Gift of the Useless Weapon', p. 87.

tale, and that Unferð, who is actually called Bjǫrn in some Norse analogues, can be considered as a type of antihero to the bear-named Beowulf.[53]

In *Beowulf*, Unferð performs a further function in the structure of the poem, undermining the hero's credibility by giving a partial version of Beowulf's contest with Breca, and it is striking that whilst no parallel for Beowulf's swimming-match with Breca is found in this episode of *Grettis saga*, there *is* a close analogue for such a test of swimming-prowess elsewhere in the saga, and there too Grettir's rival has the bear-name Bjǫrn.[54] In the case of Grettir's swimming-match with the heroic outlaw Bjǫrn Hítdœlakappi along the length of the Hítará, there is further mention of such a contest in *Bjarnar saga* itself, where, however, it is no more plausible than in *Grettis saga*.[55] Philip Jorgensen has collected a large number of Norse parallels for Beowulf's swimming contest with Breca, and notes two further instances in *Grettis* saga where Grettir's prodigious swimming-powers are mentioned.[56] The distance alleged to have been swum by Bjǫrn and Grettir is not excessive (about 29km, with a descent of about 150m), but a number of other obstacles (fast-flowing, boulder-strewn water, and in particular the two large waterfalls now called Brúarfoss and Kattarfoss) render the feat surely no less marvellous than that of Beowulf and Breca.[57] One is reminded of the three improbably large boulders, each named Grettishaf, which Grettir lifts in the course of the saga simply to pass the time;[58] Guðmundur Andri Thorsson's wry observation on later Icelandic place-names is equally apposite:[59]

> Sé gljúfur ófært, tindur ókleifur, steinn svo mikill að enginn lyftir virðist alþýða manna umsvifalaust hafa tengt nafn Grettis þar við, því hann stökk yfir gilin, kleif tindana og hóf upp björgin sem enginn annarr.
>
> *If there is an uncrossable gorge, an unscaleable peak, or a boulder so large that no ordinary man could lift it, Grettir's name has been promptly attached to it, on the grounds that he leapt over chasms, climbed peaks, and heaved up rocks like no one else.*

53 Cf. Klaeber, ed., *Beowulf*, pp. 148–9; Bonjour, *The Digressions in Beowulf*, p. 18; Niles, *Beowulf: the Poem and its Tradition*, p. 21.

54 Jónsson, ed., *Grettis saga*, pp. 187/14–188/2.

55 Nordal and Jónson, ed., *Bjarnar saga*, p. 163/1–2.

56 Jorgensen, 'Beowulf's Swimming-Contest with Breca', pp. 55–6.

57 In the summer of 1993 I undertook a solo walking-trip the length of the Hítará, circumnavigating Hítarvatn, and tracing the river down to the sea. The lake can be swum; the river, at times dangerous to ford on foot, is quite beyond swimming, notwithstanding the waterfalls. Several places en route are still associated with the marvellous outlaw Grettir (for example Grettisbæli, Grettisoddi, and Grettisstillur), all equally improbable (and, as refuges, uncomfortable). I should like to thank the managers of the Scandinavian Studies Fund in Cambridge for partly financing this trip, and to take the opportunity to thank Dick Phillips, the Stevens family, and everyone at Fljótsdal for eight splendid summers of hospitality in Icelandic mountains.

58 Jónsson, ed., *Grettis saga*, pp. 48, 102, and 192; cf. Cook, 'The Reader in *Grettis saga*', p. 147.

59 Thorsson, 'Grettla', p. 100.

In the context of a discussion of their alleged swimming-match, it is important to note that a number of other parallels have been adduced between the sagas of the two outlaws Bjorn and Grettir,[60] not least of which is the fact that both are decapitated, and have their heads offered to their respective mothers.[61]

Grettir's marvellous swimming ability, moreover, surely matches that of Beowulf himself, and may again suggest that this is an original characteristic of their common prototype; in this context recent attempts to rationalise the superhuman swimming-feats of Beowulf,[62] may need to be reassessed, as indeed later critics have done.[63]

But it is Grettir's battle with the bear itself in this chapter which offers most parallels to the monster-fights in *Beowulf.* In this episode there is the curious narrative detail that Grettir employs two weapons in his battle, the sword Jǫkulsnautr with which he slices off the bear's paw, and the *sax* Kársnautr, with which he deals the death-blow.[64] A number of intriguing parallels in both Old English and Norse are indicated. In *Gunnlaugs saga ormstungu* Gunnlaugr uses two swords in his battle against the berserk Þórormr, since the first one is apparently bewitched, and will not bite,[65] whilst in *Egils saga Skallagrímssonar* there are three episodes in which, as Peter Foote has noted,[66] Egill employs two weapons to dispose of his berserk foes.[67] The first of these episodes in *Egils saga*, in which Egill disposes of his arch-enemy Berg-Ǫnundr, moreover, shares with *Grettis saga* a number of narrative details drawn from the same common paradigm as *Beowulf.* Egill arrives by sea at evening at an island where his enemies are gathered and, leaving his companions behind, goes on alone armed with two weapons.[68] He meets some locals, who tell him of a ravaging bear loose on the island, and lures his enemies out to hunt by pretending to be that same bear. When Berg-Ǫnundr, who has separated from his companions and is also wielding two identical weapons, attempts to slay this 'bear', Egill kills him, and almost decapitates him with his sword.[69] The second and third episodes in *Egils saga* in which Egill employs two weapons against his foes are similarly intriguing in this

60 Cf. Laxness, 'Lítil samantekt um útilegumenn', pp. 86–130; Harris, 'The Deaths of Grettir and Grendel', p. 47.

61 Jónsson, ed., *Grettis saga*, pp. 263–4, n. 4.

62 See, for example, Wentersdorf, 'Beowulf's Withdrawal from Frisia'; Robinson, 'Elements of the Marvellous'; Earl, 'Beowulf's Rowing-Match'; Robinson, *The Tomb of Beowulf*, pp. 20–35.

63 See, for example, Anderson, 'Beowulf's Retreat from Frisia'; Greenfield, 'A Touch of the Monstrous in the Hero'; Niles, *Beowulf: the Poem and its Tradition*', pp. 4–5.

64 For such a weapon-combination in art, one might compare a number of representations of a warrior combating monstrous beasts with both sword and *sax*, for example the celebrated Torslunda bronze matrix for making helmet designs, discussed by Arent, 'The Heroic Pattern', pp. 133–8, especially plate 2. The relevant illustration from the Torslunda die has been reproduced on the title page of this book, from a drawing of the die which appears in Newton, *The Origins of 'Beowulf'*, p. 107, fig. 7; I am grateful to Sam Newton for permission to reproduce the illustration here.

65 Nordal and Jónsson, ed., *Gunnlaugs saga*, p. 73/3–18.

66 Foote and Quirk, *The Saga of Gunnlaug Serpent-Tongue*, pp. xviii and 16.

67 Chapters 57, 64, and 65: Nordal, ed., *Egils saga*, pp. 163–73, 199–206, and 207–11.

68 Nordal, ed., *Egils saga*, pp. 166/28–167/10.

69 Nordal, ed., *Egils saga*, p. 168/3–24.

respect, since, as Karen Grimstad has pointed out in another context, these are the only occasions in the saga in which Egill is pitted against 'superhuman opponents'.[70] These enemies, Ljótr and Atli, are both mighty berserks and, since the battles take place under the formal rules of the *hólmgang*, both are fought on islands; in the second case Egill is frustrated when his sword, apparently bewitched, will not bite, and simply tears the throat from his opponent with his teeth.[71]

It is interesting to note that in these Icelandic sources Gunnlaugr slays Þórormr in the Anglo-Saxon England of Æthelred the Unready, whilst Egill kills Berg-Ǫnundr soon after leaving the Anglo-Saxon court of Æthelstan, and Ljótr and Atli soon after leaving the court of Eiríkr blóðǫx at York, since in the Anglo-Saxon poem *Beowulf* the eponymous hero also employs two weapons, one of which will not bite, against both Grendel's mother and the dragon.[72] It is stressed, moreover, that Grendel, like the berserk opponents of Gunnlaugr and Egill, has the power to bewitch swords so that they will not bite (*Beowulf*, lines 801–5). Furthermore in the case of Beowulf's battle with the dragon, after the sword Nægling has snapped, Beowulf deals the dragon his death-blow with a hitherto unmentioned *wælseax* (*Beowulf*, line 2703); it may be significant that the word *seax* occurs in *Beowulf* only here and, again, in the battle against Grendel's mother, where, however, it is wielded by the monster (line 1545).[73] Likewise in *Grettis saga*, whilst the sword given Grettir by his mother, Jǫkulsnautr, proved decisive in the battle against Kárr, it is the *sax* won in that adventure which is the bear's bane in this episode. Jǫkulsnautr passes out of Grettir's keeping; he gives it to his ill-fated brother Atli,[74] and in the battles to come Grettir relies exclusively on his brute strength and his *sax*, both weapons associated more with monsters than with men.[75]

In this episode in *Grettis saga*, moreover, we are told that the *sax* is attached to Grettir's wrist by a cord fastened to its handle, here described as a *meðalkafli*.[76] H. Falk has pointed out that the term *meðalkafli* is usually applied only to the grip of a sword, and that its application to the handle of the *sax* Kársnautr, repeated twice in the final episode after Grettir's death,[77] marks out the weapon as remarkable.[78] In the parallel episodes in *Gunnlaugs saga* and *Egils saga* noted it is striking that there too Gunnlaugr and Egill have their second weapon tied to their wrist,[79] but that in each case it is a sword (*sverð*). To underline the closeness of the parallel, in *Gunnlaugs saga* the author stresses that Gunnlaugr's wrist is connected to the *meðalkafli* on the sword.

70 Grimstad, 'The Giant as Heroic Model', p. 298, n. 34.

71 Nordal, ed., *Egils saga*, p. 210/1–5.

72 Cf. Culbert, 'The Narrative Function of Beowulf's Swords', pp. 16–19.

73 One might add further the intriguing lines describing the dead dragon at the dying Beowulf's side: '*him on efn ligeð ealdorgewinna / siexbennum seoc; sweorde ne meahte / on þam aglæcean ænige þinga / wunde gewyrcean*' (*Beowulf*, lines 2903–6), which appears to make some distinction between the efficacy of the sword and the *seax* in dealing with the *aglæca*.

74 Jónsson, ed., *Grettis saga*, p. 140/15–16.

75 Cf. Boberg, *Motif-Index*, p. 118, nos. F531.4.5.1, F531.4.5.2, F531.4.5.3.

76 Jónsson, ed., *Grettis saga*, p. 76/14–18.

77 Jónsson, ed., *Grettis saga*, p. 261/20 and 26.

78 Falk, *Altnordische Waffenkunde*, p. 10; cf. Taylor, 'Two Notes on Beowulf', p. 16.

79 Nordal, ed., *Egils saga*, p. 209/6–7; Nordal and Jónsson, ed., *Gunnlaugs saga*, p. 73/10–11.

Joan Turville-Petre has pointed out that the 'ancient giant sword' (*ealdsweord eotenisc*) which Beowulf discovers in the dwelling of Grendel's mother is likewise described by the unique term *fetelhilt* (*Beowulf*, line 1563),[80] which appears to signify a weapon designed for similar attachment (being derived from the root of the verb *fetlian* 'attach, connect'), and she suggests that the important word *hæftmece* (*Beowulf*, line 1457), which formed the initial basis for a comparison of *Beowulf* and *Grettis saga*, may, together with its Icelandic cognate *heptisax*, refer to the same kind of attached weapon (compare the verb *hæftan* 'bind, hold captive').[81]

It is particularly striking that in the conflict with the bear in *Grettis saga*, as in the parallel examples from *Gunnlaugs saga*, *Egils saga*, and *Beowulf*, it is the 'hero' who wields this connected weapon, but that in the later episode in *Grettis saga* it is the giant who holds the *heptisax*. This evidence flatly contradicts the suggestion of Liberman that the *heptisax* was 'originally' the monster's sword.[82] I shall argue further below that in this later episode, which occurs after Grettir has been cursed by Glámr, Grettir himself, who is clearly the sudden and unexpected assailant, is fulfilling the role of the 'monster'.

After Grettir returns to Iceland his exultation in his own excessive strength is stressed many times, together with an ominous sense of his growing pride. As soon as he comes home to Bjarg, the saga-author laconically notes:[83]

> Þá gerðisk ofsi Grettis svá mikill, at honum þótti sér ekki ófœrt.
>
> *By this time Grettir's pride had grown so great that nothing seemed to him beyond his powers.*

Grettir immediately causes great disturbances in his area, but is frustrated in his attempts to provoke battles amongst merely human enemies. One such, Barði Guðmundarson, controls his temper in the face of Grettir's grievous insults, and the pair part with a frosty exchange:[84]

> 'Bleyðask þykki mér þú, Barði', sagði Grettir, 'ef þú þorir eigi at berjask við mik.' 'Kalla þú þat sem þú vill,' segir Barði, 'en í ǫðrum stað vilda ek, at þú kœmir fram ójafnaði þínum en við mik; er þat eigi ólíkligt, því at nú gengr ór hófi offors þitt.
>
> *'It seems to me that you are a coward, Barði, if you don't dare to battle with me', said Grettir. 'Call it what you like', says Barði, 'but I'd be happy if you exercise your arrogance in some other place than against me; and that's not unlikely, since your overbearing is quite out of control'.*

80 Turville-Petre, '*Beowulf* and *Grettis saga*', pp. 352–3.

81 Cf. Davidson, *The Sword in Anglo-Saxon England*, pp. 129–35; Brady, 'Weapons in Beowulf', pp. 101–2

82 Liberman, 'Beowulf-Grettir', p. 374.

83 Jónsson, ed., *Grettis saga*, p. 95/3–4.

84 Jónsson, ed., *Grettis saga*, p. 106/15–20.

Barði's words are explicitly given the force of prophecy (*spá*) by the saga-author,[85] and the episode (and the chapter) ends on a highly ominous note:[86]

> Eptir skilnað þeira Barða fór Grettir aptr til Bjargs. Þá þótti Gretti mikit mein, er hann mátti hvergi reyna afl sitt, ok fréttisk fyrir, ef nǫkkut væri þat, er hann mætti við fásk.
>
> *After his parting from Barði, Grettir returned to Bjarg. It seemed a big problem to Grettir that he could not try his strength anywhere, and he asked around, to see if there were something he could tackle.*

The single word *nǫkkut* ('something') is a good example of this storyteller's understated art. A solution to Grettir's problem is immediately found in the very next chapter, which begins in beguilingly conventional style:[87]

> Þórhallr hét maðr, er bjó á Þórhallsstǫðum í Forsœludal
>
> *There was a man named Þórhallr, who lived at Þórhallsstaðir in Forsæludalr.*

Hindsight of the happenings in this 'Shadow-valley' (*Forsæludalr*), examined in detail in the next episode considered here, lends these words a distinct chill.

Episode [3]: *Grettir battles against the draugr Glámr in Forsæludalr*

The episode in *Grettis saga* in which Grettir battles against the *draugr* Glámr (chapters 31–5) has been studied by a great number of scholars over the years.[88] As with the two episodes from *Grettis saga* already discussed, the basic narrative features of this part of the saga can be represented as follows:

A. Grettir hears of the depredations of the *draugr* Glámr. (4)
B. He resolves against advice to help. (5)
C. He travels to visit Þórhallr at Forsæludalr. (6)
D. He hears from Þórhallr about the horror of Glámr. (9)
E. He resolves to fight him single-handed. (10)
F. Glámr appears in the evening. (11)
G. They fight; the place is wrecked. (12)
H. Grettir wins but is cursed by the dying Glámr.
I. He is rewarded by Þórhallr with a horse and equipment. (29)
J. He visits Þorvaldr and recounts his adventure. (28)
K. He is given a lecture on the dangers of pride. (30)

Once again it seems clear that here the author of *Grettis saga* is drawing on a narrative paradigm common to *Beowulf*. But it is important to stress that Grettir's battle

85 Jónsson, ed., *Grettis saga*, p. 106/20.
86 Jónsson, ed., *Grettis saga*, p. 107/14–17.
87 Jónsson, ed., *Grettis saga*, p. 107/18–19.
88 Jónsson, ed., *Grettis saga*, pp. 104–23.

against Glámr is itself but the third in a series of monster-fights at Forsæludalr. Glámr himself begins as a human monster-slayer, contending against the unspecified evil being (*meinvættr nǫkkur*)[89] that haunts the farm. Indeed Glámr comes to Forsæludalr to work as a shepherd with a reputation and bearing not unlike Grettir's own; Skapti Þoroddsson, whose keen judgment is praised in the saga, describes Glámr as big and powerful, but not to everyone's taste (*mikill ok sterkr ok ekki mjǫk við alþýðuskap*).[90] The first description of Glámr conveys something of his otherness:[91]

> Þessi maðr var mikill vexti ok undarligr í yfirbragði, gráeygr ok opineygr, ulfgrár á hárslit.
>
> *The man was huge in stature and remarkable in appearance, with staring grey eyes and a shock of wolf-grey hair.*

He is an outsider of alarming appearance who is harsh and uncompromising to his host Þórhallr and his family, and the author stresses that his unchristian manner accurately reflects his lack of faith:[92]

> Kirkja var á Þórhallsstǫðum; ekki vildi Glámr til hennar koma; hann var ósǫngvinn ok trúlauss, stirfinn ok viðskotaillr; ǫllum var hann hvimleiðr.
>
> *There was a church at Þórhallsstaðir, but Glámr wouldn't go there, for he hated the singing and had no faith. He was harsh and difficult, and universally loathed.*

Glámr's alleged aversion to church-music (*ósǫngvinn*) seems to spring from a literary motif, and recalls both the incensing of the Norwegian bear earlier in the saga and, more pointedly, the provocation of Grendel in *Beowulf* by the sounds of carousal (and more specifically by the song of creation) in Heorot.[93] There is a further interesting analogue in *Þorsteins þáttr skelks* in *Flateyjarbók*, in which a rather comic *draugr* is unable to bear the noise of churchbells.[94] As John Lindow has pointed out with regard to *Þorsteins þáttr*, 'the churchbells . . . belong to legend'.[95] In *Grettis saga* it seems to be the church itself which belongs to legend, invented to point up the Christian motif which runs through this and parallel episodes; it is highly unlikely that there was in fact a church at Þórhallsstaðir at this period, as Guðni Jónsson has noted.[96] Again, it seems significant that Glámr's battle with the unseen monster occurs at Christmas, just as did Grettir's battle with the bear, and as do both his later contests at Forsæludalr and Sandhaugar. That battles against monsters and berserks often occur around the time of the Yule-tide festival is particularly stressed by Mary

89 Jónsson, ed., *Grettis saga*, p. 109/3.
90 Jónsson, ed., *Grettis saga*, p. 109/7–8.
91 Jónsson, ed., *Grettis saga*, p. 110/2–4.
92 Jónsson, ed., *Grettis saga*, pp. 110/28–111/3.
93 Emerson, 'Grendel's Motive in Attacking Heorot', p. 117.
94 Nordal, ed., *Flateyjarbók* I, pp. 462–4; cf. Coffin, 'Beowulf and its Relationship to Norse and Finno-Uguric Narratives', p. 203.
95 Lindow, '*Þorsteins þáttr skelks*', p. 271; cf. Lindow, *Swedish Legends and Folk-Tales*, pp. 82–4.
96 Jónsson, ed., *Grettis saga*, pp. 110, n. 5.

Danielli and R. N. Coffin.[97] Glámr, moreover, is explicitly heathen, and he tells his host's wife how much he preferred it in pagan days (*þótti mér þá betri siðr, er menn váru heiðnir kallaðir*).[98] Glámr's antipathy to Christianity is made still clearer after his battle with the monster, in which he is himself killed, but is presumed to have dealt his enemy a mortal blow: attempts to bring his body to church for Christian burial have to be abandoned, and his mortal remains are left under a cairn on unconsecrated ground. For a closely parallel incident, including verbal similarities, one might compare the accounts of the hauntings of the pagan *draugr* Þórólfr bægifót in *Eyrbyggja saga*;[99] Þórólfr's activities are only curtailed by his subsequent reburial and, eventually, cremation by Christians.[100]

Grettir's own relationship with Christ is less clear-cut. When he passes the winter on the Geitland-glacier with Þórir, who is described as both a 'giant and a half-troll' (*blendingr, þurs einn*),[101] Grettir observes the seasonal fast by eating only suet and liver, but allows himself to be provoked into anger at the church where he is to undergo ordeal over the burning of the sons of Þórir, thus forfeiting his right to the ordeal.[102] This latter incident shows Grettir in a peculiarly ambiguous light; his vindictive striking of the boy who taunts him is decidedly unchristian, and yet it may be, as Robert Cook suggests,[103] that the saga-author describes the boy as an 'unclean spirit' (*óhreinn andi*) in deliberate recollection of the *spiritus immundus* who cries out against Jesus in the Synagogue at Capernaum (Mark I.23–6). Many characters in the saga, however, share no such opinions of Grettir's relationship with Christ; when Þorbjǫrn ǫngull comes to Drangey to kill Grettir he is asked who showed him the way, and immediately replies that he has been led there by Christ (*Kristr vísaði oss leið*).[104] Grettir here, as often towards the end of his life, is clearly portrayed as a type of Antichrist. When he first comes to Drangey, Grettir is described by the local populace as a 'wolf' or 'outlaw' (*vargr*),[105] and it is interesting to note that the Old English cognate of this term occurs only once in *Beowulf*, where it appears in the unique compound *heorowearh* (*Beowulf*, line 1267) applied to Grendel.[106] Grendel, moreover, seems particularly well-suited to the term 'son of a sea-ogress' (*margýgjusonr*),[107] unique in Norse, and yet it is this very term of abuse which in *Grettis saga* leads directly to Grettir striking the boy taunting him as he attempts to undergo ordeal for the killing of the sons of Þórir, and indirectly to Grettir's subsequent outlawry in Iceland.

97 Danielli, 'Initiation Ceremonial', pp. 229–40; Coffin, 'Beowulf and its Relationship to Norse and Finno-Uguric Narratives', pp. 143–68.

98 Jónsson, ed., *Grettis saga*, p. 111/11–12.

99 Sveinsson and Þórðarson, ed., *Eyrbyggja saga*, pp. 93–95, 115, and 169.

100 Cf. McCreesh, 'Structural Patterns', pp. 273–5.

101 Jónsson, ed., *Grettis saga*, p. 200/17.

102 Jónsson, ed., *Grettis saga*, p. 200, n. 4.

103 Cook, 'The Reader in *Grettis saga*', p. 151.

104 Jónsson, ed., *Grettis saga*, p. 260/24–5.

105 Jónsson, ed., *Grettis saga*, p. 229/4.

106 For the lupine associations of the term, see further above, pp. 75 and 84.

107 Jónsson, ed., *Grettis saga*, p. 133/15.

From being a monster-slayer, Glámr becomes a monster, a *draugr*: like Kárr, one of the walking dead.[108] Another outsider, named Þorgautr, is brought to Forsæludalr by Þórhallr and offered employment. This rather surly figure, like Glámr before him and Grettir afterwards, professes nonchalance in the face of Þórhallr's monstrous visitant, and, whilst clearly cast from a smaller mould, shares a number of other features with this pair:[109]

> Hann var útlendr at kyni, mikill ok sterkr, hann hafði tveggja manna afl; hann var lauss ok einn fyrir sér.
>
> *He was a foreigner by birth, big and powerful, with the strength of two men; he was footloose and independent.*

Þorgautr's brush with the new monster in the shape of Glámr, again at Christmas, proves fatal, but *his* corpse does not walk; the difference between his burial and that of Glámr himself is underlined in the saga:[110]

> Síðan fœrðu þeir hann til kirkju, ok varð engum manni mein at Þorgauti síðan.
>
> *Afterwards they brought him to the church, and no man suffered any harm from Þorgautr after that.*

After a description of the renewed violence of the triumphant Glámr, Grettir is reintroduced into the saga, hears about the depredations of Glámr, and resolves to go to Þórhallsstaðir.

At this precise point in the narrative the author inserts a brief episode in which Grettir discusses his decision with his maternal uncle Jǫkull Bárðarson, who strongly advises his nephew not to tangle with Glámr. This is the only occasion in which Jǫkull appears in *Grettis saga*, and it is clearly important to the structure of the story that at this one point Grettir ignores the advice not of a casual acquaintance, as elsewhere in the saga, but of one to whom as his mother's brother he owes the greatest respect.[111] The exchange between uncle and nephew is therefore particularly revealing, for as Jǫkull says:[112]

> 'Er . . . miklu betra at fásk við mennska menn en við óvættir slíkar.' Grettir kvað sér hug á at koma á Þórhallsstaði ok sjá, hversu þar væri um gengit. Jǫkull mælti: 'Sé ek nu, at eigi tjáir at letja þik, en satt er þat, sem mælt er, at sitt er hvárt, gæfa eða gørvigleikr.'
>
> *'It . . . is much better to contend with human beings than with such monsters.' Grettir said that he still intended to go to Þórhallsstaðir and see how things had gone. Jǫkull said: 'I see now that it's no good discouraging you, but it is true, what is said that good luck and great ability are quite different things.'*

108 Cf. Chadwick, 'Norse Ghosts', pp. 50–1.
109 Jónsson, ed., *Grettis saga*, p. 113/16–7.
110 Jónsson, ed., *Grettis saga*, pp. 114/28–115/1.
111 Cf. the comments of Scragg, ed. *The Battle of Maldon*, p. 75.
112 Jónsson, ed., *Grettis saga*, p. 117/14–19.

Whilst, as Robert Cook has noted,[113] the grim and unmanageable picture of Jokull which the saga-author paints greatly undermines the force of his warning, the very fact that such advice is offered foreshadows the encounter with Glámr as the major turning point in the narrative, as both Marlene Ciklamini and Kathryn Hume have stressed.[114]

The battle with Glámr is a justly celebrated masterpiece of the Norse descriptive art, and many parallels with the monster-fights in *Beowulf* have been highlighted by numerous previous scholars. Particular stress is often laid on the terrifying effect of Glámr's gaze on Grettir as he glances up at the moon, since attention has already been drawn to Glámr's staring grey eyes even before his transformation into a *draugr*;[115] his strange gaze has been thought to provide a parallel to the fiery and frightening glance of Grendel in *Beowulf* (lines 727–8).[116] A further parallel may be found in the description of a giant with eyes like gleaming mill-stones in *Partalopa saga*,[117] whilst Fred Robinson has recently indicated that in the Old English Life of St Margaret a devil with eyes like flames assails the saint in the form of a dragon; numerous other parallels from the *Liber monstrorum* and the *Wonders of the East* have already been noted.[118] Here I should rather focus on Glámr's curse, which has no clear parallel in *Beowulf*, but which is central to the structure of *Grettis saga*:[119]

> 'Mikit kapp hefir þú á lagit, Grettir,' sagði hann, 'at finna mik, en þat mun eigi undarligt þykkja, þó at þú hljótir ekki mikit happ af mér. En þat má ek segja þér, at þú hefir nu fengit helming afls þess ok þroska, er þér var ætlaðr, ef þú hefðir mik ekki fundit; nú fæ ek þat afl eigi af þér tekit, er þú hefir aðr hreppt, en því má ek ráða, at þú verðr aldri sterkari en nú ertu, ok ertu þó nógu sterkr, ok at því mun mǫrgum verða. Þú hefir frægr orðit hér til af verkum þínum, en heðan af munu falla til þín sekðir ok vígaferli, en flest ǫll verk þín snúask þér til ógæfu ok hamingjuleysis. Þú munt verða útlægr gǫrr ok hljóta jafnan úti at búa einn samt. Þá legg ek þat á við þik, at þessi augu sé þér jafnan fyrir sjónum, sem ek ber eptir, ok mun þér þá erfitt þykkja einum at vera, ok þat mun þér til dauða draga.'
>
> *'You have used great pluck to meet me, Grettir,' he said, 'but it won't seem remarkable if you get no great luck from me. I can tell you, you have now acquired only half the strength and vigour which were allotted to you, if you hadn't met me. I cannot take away from you that strength which you have already got, but I can see to it that you never become stronger than you are now; and you are strong enough, as it will seem to many. Up to now you have become famous through your deeds, but from now on outlawry and slaughter will come your way, almost every deed will bring you to ill luck and misfortune. You will be made an outlaw, and destined always to sleep rough and alone. I also lay this on you, that these eyes of mine be always in your sight, and they will make it hard for you to be alone, and that will drag you to your death.'*

113 Cook, 'The Reader in *Grettis saga*', p. 1[illegible]9.

114 Ciklamini, 'Grettir and Ketill Hœngr', p. 139; Hume, 'The Thematic Design of *Grettis saga*', pp. 473–4.

115 Jónsson, ed., *Grettis saga*, p. 109/8.

116 Cf. Chadwick, 'Norse Ghosts', p. 106.

117 Boberg, *Motif-Index*, p. 115, no. F531.1.1.2.

118 Robinson, *'Beowulf' and the Appositive Style*, p. 32; see further above, pp. 111–12.

119 Jónsson, ed., *Grettis saga*, p. 121/14–29.

The beginning of this curse, with its careful rhyming contrast between 'great pluck and great luck' (*mikit kapp . . . mikit happ*) consciously echoes the alliterative contrast between 'good luck and great ability' (*gæfa eða gørvigleikr*) indicated by Grettir's maternal uncle Jǫkull in his final and fatally-ignored warning. Grettir has overstepped the mark here, and beheads Glámr with the *sax* Kársnautr in a clear echo of his earlier treatment of the *draugr* Kárr.[120] As Coffin notes of these and parallel incidents: 'The only possible method of quieting the *draugr* is decapitation';[121] Boberg quotes six further examples.[122] One might cite further in this context the later decapitation in *Grettis saga* of Grettir himself, or the similar beheading in *Beowulf* of Grendel, or even that of Holofernes by Judith.[123] Equally importantly, in view of the perceived parallels between this episode in the saga and the monster-fights in *Beowulf*, Grettir now visits his old family friend Þorvaldr Ásgeirsson and recounts his exploit in detail, only to receive some advice which, though well-intentioned, seems too little, and too late:[124]

> Þorvaldr bað hann hafa sik spakan, – 'ok mun þá vel duga, en ella mun þér slysgjarnt verða'.
>
> *Þorvaldr told him to keep himself under control, – 'and then things will turn out fine, but otherwise you will become ill-fated.'*

The call for moderation and circumspection has a close parallel in the substance of Hrothgar's so-called 'sermon' (*Beowulf*, lines 1700–84), although here the message is rather more concisely phrased.[125]

After his battle with Glámr, it is noticeable that Grettir becomes increasingly aligned with trolls and giants and other curious creatures. Soon after his victory at Þórhallsstaðir Grettir makes a return trip to Norway, scene of his earlier monster-slaying triumphs, but on this occasion becomes identified with the rampaging creatures he once defeated. Grettir allows himself to be taunted by his ship-mates into swimming across a channel in bad weather to get fire, with appalling consequences.[126] The scene again has subtle parallels with *Beowulf*; in *Grettis saga* the unsuspecting sons of the Icelander Þórir of Garðr and their companions, a band of twelve all told, are carousing in an unnamed hall by their blazing fire when Grettir, who has heard their clamour, appears from the darkness rather like Grendel bursting into Heorot in *Beowulf*:[127]

> Grettir ræðr nú inn í húsit ok vissi eigi, hverir fyrir váru. Kuflinn var sýldr allr, þegar hann kom á land, ok var hann furðu mikill tilsýndar, sem troll væri. Þeim, sem fyrir váru, brá mjǫk við þetta, ok hugðu, at óvættr myndi vera; bǫrðu þeir hann með ǫllu því, er þeir fengu til, ok varð nú brak mikit um þá, en Grettir hratt þeim fast af handleggjum.

120 Cf. Jónsson, ed., *Grettis saga*, pp. 50/17–18 and 122/2–3.
121 Coffin, '*Beowulf* and its Relationship to Norse and Finno-Uguric Narratives', p. 129.
122 Boberg, *Motif-Index*, p. 98, no. E431.7.2; cf. Chadwick, 'Norse Ghosts', p. 55.
123 See above, pp. 9–10.
124 Jónsson, ed., *Grettis saga*, p. 122/25–6.
125 For an analysis of the so-called 'sermon', see further above, pp. 47–63.
126 Jónsson, ed., *Grettis saga*, pp. 130–1.
127 Jónsson, ed., *Grettis saga*, p. 130/21–8.

> *Now Grettir bursts into the house and did not know who was there. His cloak was completely frozen, as soon as he came to land, and he was a mighty sight, as though he were a troll. Those inside were greatly startled, and thought he must be a monster; they set about him with everything they could lay their hands on, and there was a huge disturbance, but Grettir warded them off firmly with his arms.*

The author stresses that Grettir is attracted to this hall by his glimpse of firelight, just as he had been drawn to the barrow of the *draugr* Kárr by the mysterious light emanating from it; Coffin has considered a number of parallel episodes, including several from *Beowulf*, where a waterbound monster's den gives off an uncanny light.[128] In this instance the motif has been subverted: the 'monster' Grettir is approaching the halls of men, but here Grettir, like Grendel and his mother, meets rather stiffer resistance than anticipated. Like Grendel and his mother, Grettir escapes, but the hall and all inside are burned.[129] This incident in *Grettis saga* is pivotal in the narrative structure, since it is as a direct result of the accidental burning of this hall in Norway that Grettir is outlawed in Iceland, as Marlene Ciklamini has stressed.[130] Whilst still in Norway Grettir offers to undergo ordeal in church to clear his name of the guilt of the burning, but, as already mentioned, allows himself to be provoked by a mysterious young lad who, presumably alluding to Grettir's night-time swimming-feat, calls him the son of a sea-ogress (*margýgjusonr*).[131]

The next phase in the saga concentrates on the period of Grettir's outlawry, and contains many of the more monstrous and mysterious elements in the tale.[132] Grettir associates with a number of fantastic beings, including the shadowy Loptr, who outmatches even Grettir for strength, and lives at the glacier Balljǫkull.[133] When Grettir is assailed by Þórir of Garðr he is unwittingly helped by the same Loptr, who now calls himself Hallmundr, and who slays twice as many enemies as Grettir. Þórir, equally ignorant of Hallmundr's help, cannot understand how so many men are being killed:[134]

> 'Þat hefi ek spurt,' sagði hann, 'at Grettir væri afbragðsmaðr fyrir hreysti sakar ok hugar, en þat vissa ek aldri, at hann væri svá fjǫlkunnigr, sem nú sé ek, því at þar falla hálfu fleiri, sem hann horfir bakinu við; nú sé ek at hér er við troll at eiga, en ekki við menn.'
>
> *'I have heard', he said, 'that Grettir was an outstanding man in vigour and courage, but I never knew that he was such a sorcerer, as I now see, since twice as many are falling behind his back; I now see that we are dealing with trolls, and not with any men.'*

128 Cf. Coffin, '*Beowulf* and its Relationship to Norse and Finno-Ugric Narratives', pp. 105–[illegible].

129 One notes that a similar fate by fire is hinted at for Heorot in *Beowulf*, lines 82–5, immediately after the description of its construction; cf. Klaeber, ed. *Beowulf*, pp. 129–30.

130 Ciklamini, 'Grettir and Ketill Hœngr', p. 140.

131 Jónsson, ed., *Grettis saga*, p. 133/15.

132 Ciklamini, 'Grettir and Ketill Hœngr', pp. 146–9

133 Jónsson, ed., *Grettis saga*, pp. 175–8.

134 Jónsson, ed., *Grettis saga*, p. 184/2–7.

Here the author uses Þórir as his mouthpiece, and employs the term *troll* as a cunningly ambiguous term which Þórir applies to Grettir, but which the audience are free to interpret as fitting for both Grettir and Hallmundr, who has come to his aid.

Although Hallmundr is not elsewhere explicitly described as a troll, his *modus vivendi* is suggestive.[135] Hallmundr lives in a large cave behind the glacier with his strapping daughter, and is later able to direct Grettir to stay at another glacier, Geitlandsjǫkull, ruled over by the giantish half-troll Þórir, who also shares his dwelling with a number of daughters, to Grettir's great delight.[136] This phase of the saga is discussed in detail by Mary Sandbach;[137] Inger Boberg cites about thirty parallels of giants and trolls living in very similar circumstances elsewhere in Norse.[138] In *Beowulf* there is an obvious parallel for supernatural family-groups in remote (often waterbound) lairs in Grendel and his mother.[139] In *Grettis saga* it is interesting to note that Hallmundr, like Glámr, and like Grettir himself, had been a noted battler with monsters in his youth; before he dies he recites a lengthy poem detailing his life's exploits to his daughter, in which he boasts of fighting and slaying giants and their kin, as well as rock-dwellers, evil spirits, half-trolls, elves and monsters.[140] This long poem, the *Hallmundarkviða*, clearly belongs to the genre of the autobiographical poem spoken at the point of death in a cave or barrow (*ævikviða*), which Nora Chadwick has persuasively connected with the supernatural figures of the *draugr* and the *haugbúi*.[141] There is, therefore, a case to be made that Hallmundr, like Glámr, and Grettir himself, becomes what he fights.[142]

It is, moreover, intriguing to note that before death Hallmundr has his *aevikviða* engraved in runes on a rod (*kefli*), since just such an runic rod (*rúnakefli*)[143] inscribed with verses is carved by Grettir himself in the monster-cave after his second battle at Sandhaugar discussed below, and very similar booty is brought back from the monster-mere by Beowulf in the shape of the engraved sword-hilt.[144] One might note further that in *Egils saga* Egill utters the poem *Sonatorrek* whilst in the process of starving himself to death, and his daughter Þorgerðr duly carves the poem in runes on a stick (*kefli*),[145] especially since Grimstad has highlighted the giant-like streak which manifests itself in several members of Egill's family.[146]

135 Finnbogason, 'Hallmundarkviða'; Ciklamini, 'Grettir and Ketill Hœngr', p. 148.
136 Jónsson, ed., *Grettis saga*, pp. 199–200.
137 Sandbach, 'Grettir in Thorisdal'.
138 Boberg, *Motif-Index*, p. 119, no. F531.6.2.1.
139 Chadwick, 'The Monsters and Beowulf', pp. 181–9.
140 Jónsson, ed., *Grettis saga*, p. 204/15–26.
141 Chadwick, 'Norse Ghosts', pp. 106–16.
142 Cf. Ciklamini, 'Grettir and Ketill Hœngr', pp. 140–9.
143 Jónsson, ed., *Grettis saga*, p. 216/19.
144 Cf. Taylor, 'Two Notes on *Beowulf*', p. 16. It may be significant to note in this context that the word *meðalkafli* is twice used of the handle of Grettir's *sax*, and that the second element of this term (*kafli*) is itself related to the word *kefli* used of both runically-inscribed rods in *Grettis saga*.
145 Nordal, ed., *Egils saga*, p. 245/18
146 Grimstad, 'The Giant as Heroic Model', p. 285.

Grettir himself has often been compared with Egill in temper and attitude, and is certainly descended from like kin. Both can trace their ancestry back to the fiercely-named Ulfr inn óargi ('Wolf the Fearless'), who, like Hallmundr, is said to have composed a lengthy poem celebrating his glorious deeds on the night that he died.[147] Ulfr gave his children bear-names: the daughter Hallbera ('Half-she-Bear') and the son Hallbjǫrn ('Half-he-Bear'), nicknamed 'half-troll'. Egill Skallagrímsson is descended directly from Hallbera, and Grettir's mother claims kinship from Hallbjǫrn hálftroll through his son Ketill hængr ('male salmon'), himself a celebrated monster-slayer.[148] Marlene Ciklamini has demonstrated that Grettir too shares many giant-like and monstrous features with Ketill, particularly after Glámr's curse.[149]

Throughout this same phase in *Grettis saga* there are a number of attempts to kill Grettir, often in ways more suitable to the slaying of a monster. The two most serious attempts are sandwiched between Grettir's first meeting with Loptr/Hallmundr and his brief sojourn at Balljǫkull; each centres on efforts to kill Grettir with his own weapon, the *sax* Kársnautr. In the first case an outlaw named Grímr has been bribed to kill Grettir, and seizes his moment when he thinks his host is asleep, reaching up for the *sax* on the wall, where it hangs above Grettir's bed.[150] Richard Harris has noted that: 'killing, or attempting to kill, a sleeping man is a common enough event in the sagas, but using the victim's own sword is a device usually reserved for cases where an unnatural being is being dealt with'.[151] One might note that in *Beowulf* it is with the *hæftmece* hanging on the wall of her home that Beowulf dispatches Grendel's mother, and that later in *Grettis saga* the hapless giant under the waterfall makes an abortive attempt to reach for a sword on his own wall to fend off his assailant Grettir. No fewer than eleven instances are recorded from medieval Icelandic literature where a giant or troll or ogre can only be killed by their own sword.[152] In the following chapter of *Grettis saga* another outlaw named Þórir rauðskeggr sends Grettir off to perform a feat of swimming, and attempts to kill him with his own *sax* as he emerges from the water. Grettir, rather miraculously, is able to dodge the blow, and by a further prodigious feat of underwater swimming emerges behind his unwitting assailant, grapples with him, and eventually decapitates him with the same *sax*.[153] Clearly, however, Grettir has at this point come to be viewed as troublesome, if not downright monstrous, and this is the side of his character which comes to the fore in the last two episodes analysed.

147 Nordal, ed., *Egils saga*, p. 3, n. 2; cf. Grimstad, 'The Giant as Heroic Model', p. 285.

148 Ketill's nickname derives from his modest assertion to his father that he had killed a salmon when in fact he had just slain a dragon; cf. Jónsson, ed., *Ketils saga hængs*, p. 153.

149 Ciklamini, 'Grettir and Ketill Hœngr', p. 139.

150 Jónsson, ed., *Grettis saga*, pp. 178–80.

151 Harris, 'The Deaths of Grettir and Grendel', p. 38.

152 Boberg, *Motif-Index*, p. 267, no. Z312.2; cf. Schück, *Studier i Beowulfsagen*, p. 18; Lehmann, 'Atertanum fah' p. 232, n. 4; Harris, 'The Deaths of Grettir and Grendel', p. 38.

153 Jónsson, ed., *Grettis saga*, pp. 180–3.

Episode [4]: *Grettir battles against two monsters at Sandhaugar*

As with the earlier episodes examined, the monster-battles at Sandhaugar (chapters 64–6)[154] may be repesented schematically as follows:

A. Grettir hears of supernatural depredations. (4)
B. He resolves against advice to help. (5)
C. He travels to visit Þorsteinn's widow at Sandhaugar. (6)
D. A troll-wife appears in the evening carrying a trough and a cleaver. (11)
E. They fight; the place is wrecked. (12)
F. He cuts off her right arm with his *sax*. (13)
G. She escapes towards her waterfall-home. (14)
H. An expedition is undertaken to the waterfall; Grettir goes on alone. (18)
I. He dives under the waterfall, and arrives at a dry cave at evening. (19)
J. He sees a mysterious light in the cave. (20)
K. He fights a giant. (21)
L. The giant wields a *heptisax*, Grettir a *sax*. (22)
M. The giant reaches for a sword hanging on the wall of the cave. (23)
N. Grettir stabs and kills him with his *sax*. (23)
O. The priest sees blood in the water, fears the worst, and flees. (26)
P. Grettir leaves the cave with booty (including a rune-stave). (27)

The extent to which the author of *Grettis saga* is indebted here to the same narrative paradigm as the poet of *Beowulf* is abundantly clear.

The hauntings at Sandhaugar are described as taking place over two consecutive Christmas festivals. In the third year, news of the hauntings had spread far and wide in the district:[155]

> Grettir hafði spurn af þessu, ok með því at honum var mjǫk lagit at koma af reimleikum eða aptrgǫngum, þá gerði hann ferð sína til Bárðardals ok kom atfangadag jóla til Sandhauga. Hann dulðisk ok nefndisk Gestr. Húsfreyja sá, at hann var furðu mikill vexti, en heimafólk var furðu hrætt við hann; hann beiddisk þar gistingar.
>
> *Grettir got wind of this, and since he was greatly disposed towards putting an end to hauntings and ghosts, he set off for Bárðardalr, and arrived at Sandhaugar on the day before Christmas. He concealed his name, and called himself Gestr. The housewife saw that he was an extremely big man, but the rest of the household were extremely frightened of him; he asked for lodging.*

Quite apart from the obvious parallel to the monster-battles at Forsæludalr over three consecutive Christmas festivals, the initial comment here that Grettir has become

[154] Jónsson, ed., *Grettis saga*, pp. 209–17.
[155] Jónsson, ed., *Grettis saga*, p. 210/16–22.

regarded as now expert in the disposal of monstrous beings is clearly important to the structure of the saga, and is indeed repeated almost verbatim in Grettir's epitaph.[156] Such an observation again underlines Grettir's alienation from the world of men, and his increasing identification with the creatures that he fights.

Here in Bárðardalr Grettir aids the housewife across the swollen river to get to church on Christmas eve in a typical show of strength, but it is notable that he does not attend the service himself, but instead turns back to battle with his monstrous foes.[157] At this point in the narrative there is yet another indication of Grettir's ambiguous nature:[158]

> Húsfreyja kóm til Eyjardalsár til tiða, ok undruðu menn um ferðir hennar yfir ána. Hon sagðisk eigi vita, hvárt hana hefði yfir flutt maðr eða troll.
>
> *The housewife arrived at Eyjardalsá for mass, and people were amazed at her journey across the river. She said she didn't know whether it was a man or a troll that had carried her across.*

Back at Sandhaugar, Grettir comes face to face with a huge troll-woman carrying a trough and a cleaver, who attacks him where he is lying. Despite both participants being armed, they grapple first hand-to-hand, smashing up the hall before the ogress drags Grettir off towards her waterbound lair.[159] Finally Grettir slices off her right arm with his *sax*, and she escapes to her home behind a waterfall, while Grettir returns home to be nursed by the housewife.

In his later adventures in the monster-lair, it is important to stress that throughout the episode Grettir plays the role of assailant; the troll-woman who had attacked him earlier is nowhere mentioned, and the (male) giant that Grettir surprises in the cave can be seen (like Grendel's mother) as an unwitting victim. As in the incident where Grettir swam to get fire from the hall occupied by Þórir's sons, Grettir's entrance into the cave is preceded by a swimming-feat, and his sudden evening appearance in the firelit cave prompts from the surprised resident an entirely parallel response.[160] In the earlier episode, as we have seen, the author is at pains to demonstrate that Grettir is perceived as a ravaging troll by the sons of Þórir; here his technique is rather more subtle, but no less clear to an audience who appear to have been expected to recognise the narrative paradigm upon which the author draws. In the parallel incident in *Beowulf*, which takes place in the hall of Grendel's mother, it is Beowulf who wields the *hæftmece*; Grendel's mother has a *seax*. In *Grettis saga*, by contrast, it is the giant who holds the *heptisax*, whilst Grettir uses his *sax*. Again, in *Beowulf* it is the hero who reaches for the sword on the wall to kill his monstrous assailant, but in *Grettis saga* it is the hapless giant who makes an abortive attempt to get hold of a sword on the cave-wall.

Despite Grettir's dual role at this point in the saga, where he appears a rather

156 Jónsson, ed., *Grettis saga*, pp. 289/29–290/1.
157 Jónsson, ed., *Grettis saga*, pp. 210/24–211/17.
158 Jónsson, ed., *Grettis saga*, p. 211/27–30.
159 Jónsson, ed., *Grettis saga*, pp. 212/4–213/2.
160 Jónsson, ed., *Grettis saga*, p. 215/13–22.

unsettling and grim figure battling at the margins of the worlds of monsters and men, the outlaw gains greatly in reputation, but not in material reward,[161] from his slaying of both the troll-woman and the giant:[162]

> Þóttusk menn þat vita, at þessar óvættir myndi valdit hafa mannahvǫrfum þar í dalnum; varð ok aldri mein af aptrgǫngum eða reimleikum þar í dalnum síðan; þótti Grettir þar gǫrt hafa mikla landhreinsun.
>
> *People realized that these monsters must have been responsible for the disappearance of folk in the valley; and there was never any problem from ghosts or monsters afterwards in the valley; Grettir seemed to have cleansed the land greatly.*

The word *landhreinsun* ('land-cleansing') here calls to mind the repeated use in *Beowulf* of the word *fælsian* ('cleanse' – *Beowulf*, lines 432, 825, 1176, 1620, and 2352), always with reference to Beowulf's battles with Grendel or his mother.[163]

The Sandhaugar incident plays an important structural role in the saga: immediately after Grettir leaves Barðardal he escapes west, seeking sanctuary, but is turned away:[164]

> En er hann kom á Mǫðruvǫllu til Guðmundar ins ríka, beiddi hann þá Guðmund ásjá, en hann kvað sér ekki hent við honum at taka, – 'en sá einn er þér,' sagði Guðmundr, 'at koma þér þar niðr, sem þú mættir vera óhræddr um líf þitt.' Grettir kvazk eigi vita, hvar þat væri. Guðmundr mælti: 'Ey sú liggr á Skagafirði, er heitir Drangey; hon er svá gott vígi, at hvergi má komask upp á hana, nema stigar sé við látnir. Gætir þú þangat komizk, þá veit ek eigi þess manns ván, er þik sœki þangat með vápnum eða vélum, ef ðú gætir vel stigans.'
>
> *But when he came to Mǫðruvellir to Guðmundr inn ríki, he asked Guðmundr for shelter, but he said it would prove difficult for him to take him in. 'The best thing for you', he said, 'is to find yourself somewhere you don't have to live in fear of your life'. Grettir said he did not know where that might be. Guðmundr said: 'there is an island in Skagafjǫrðr called Drangey; it is a great stronghold, since no one can get up on it unless they use ladders. If you were able to get there, I think it would be beyond anyone to attack you there with weapons or strategems, so long as you took good care of the ladder'.*

This is the first time that the island Drangey is mentioned in the saga, the place to which Grettir retreats to spend his final years, and where he is finally killed. Guðni Jónsson has pointed out that this episode, which serves no other purpose than to introduce Drangey into the story, is entirely at variance with the internal chronology of the saga; Guðmundr had died at least three years before Grettir's retreat to the island.[165] If Guðmundr was indeed held responsible for suggesting Drangey as a

161 Ciklamini, 'Grettir and Ketill Hœngr', p. 151.

162 Jónsson, ed., *Grettis saga*, pp. 217/19–218/4.

163 Cf. Klaeber, ed., *Beowulf*, p. 143, where he notes that Hercules, whose role as a monstrous monster-slayer is considered above, pp. 114–15, says something similar when Sophocles, in his *Trachiniae*, has him boastfully proclaim 'I have come to cleanse the land' (γαῖαν καθαίρων ἱκόμην, line 1061; Lloyd-Jones and Wilson, ed., *Sophoclis Fabulae*, p. 284).

164 Jónsson, ed., *Grettis saga*, p. 218/10–20.

165 Jónsson, ed., *Grettis saga*, p. 218, n. 2.

possible refuge to Grettir, then it is clear that the author of the saga has deliberately placed the incident out of chronological sequence in order to highlight Grettir's decision to hide away on Drangey immediately after what was to prove his final monster-fight. There have, moreover, been a number of exploratory excavations on Drangey, in attempts to verify this part of the saga. None has proved at all conclusive;[166] as Harris notes: 'the location of Grettir's hut on Drangey is, in its way, as elusive as that of Grendel's cave in relation to the mere'.[167] At his remote and waterbound lair on Drangey Grettir's activity becomes still more intolerable to human society, and in the final episode examined here it becomes clear that in his island refuge the celebrated monster-slayer is himself slain after the fashion of a monster.

Episode [5]: *Þorbjǫrn battles against Grettir on Drangey*

Richard Harris has demonstrated that alongside the four episodes discussed above, in which Grettir battles against a series of monsters, the death of Grettir himself at the hands of Þorbjǫrn ǫngull (chapters 81–2)[168] should be considered a further analogue for the monster-fights in *Beowulf*; in particular Harris encourages 'the recognition of Grettir's death as a parallel to the fate of Grendel'.[169] The episode of Grettir's death can be represented as follows:

A.	Grettir inhabits the remote and inaccessible island of Drangey.	(1)
B.	He ravages neighbouring farms.	(3)
C.	Þorbjǫrn hears of Grettir's depredations.	(4)
D.	An expedition is undertaken to Drangey.	(15)
E.	Þorbjǫrn arrives in the evening after a sea-voyage.	(19)
F.	They fight, Grettir dies.	(12)
G.	Þorbjǫrn cuts off Grettir's hand.	(13)
H.	He decapitates Grettir with his own *sax*, Kársnautr.	(24)
I.	The *sax* is damaged.	(25)
J.	Þorbjǫrn leaves Drangey with booty (the *sax* and the head).	(27)

Again, the shared narrative paradigm which underlies both *Grettis saga* and *Beowulf* is clear. Moreover Harris's suggestion that Grettir and Grendel are somehow parallel characters is not new; Nora Chadwick had urged such an identification many years before,[170] and her views were subsequently elaborated by others.[171] Douglas Stedman,

166 Cf. Kålund, *Bidrag til en historisk-topografisk beskrivelse af Island*, II, pp. 58–61; Jónsson, 'Tvö Grettisbæli'; Jónsson, 'Drangey'.

167 Harris, 'The Deaths of Grettir and Grendel', p. 42.

168 Jónsson, ed., *Grettis saga*, pp. 256–64.

169 Harris, 'The Deaths of Grettir and Grendel', p. 25.

170 Chadwick, 'Norse Ghosts', p. 51; Chadwick, 'The Monsters and Beowulf', p. 193.

171 See, for example, Hume, 'The Thematic Design of *Grettissaga*', pp. 475–6; Liberman, 'Beowulf-Grettir', pp. 387–90.

however, had earlier pointed out that in his final conflict, bereft of all companions but his brother Illugi, Grettir resembled not Grendel but Beowulf himself, fighting his final battle with only Wiglaf at his side.[172] That at the end of his life Grettir has been independently identified with both Beowulf the hero and Grendel the monster underlines the ambiguous aspects of his nature which has become more apparent as the saga has progressed.

Grettir falls clutching the *sax* Kársnautr which he had won from the barrow of the *draugr*, and which he has used in all his subsequent battles. There have already been two attempts on his life with this *sax*, and he releases it only when Þorbjǫrn cuts off his hand. One might recall with a shudder the author's words at the very beginning of Grettir's monster-fighting career, when he brings back treasure from the barrow of the undead Kárr, words now fulfilled in grisly glory:[173]

> Einn gripr var sá, er Gretti stóðu mest augu til; þat var eitt sax, sva gott vápn, at aldri kvazk hann sét hafa betra; þat lét hann síðast fram.
>
> *There was one treasure to which Grettir's gaze strayed most: it was a sax, so fine a weapon that he said he had never seen a better. That was the last thing he gave up.*

It is this same *sax* which is used to decapitate Grettir, just as it had once been used to decapitate Kárr, Glámr, and a host of berserks. The *sax* is specifically excluded from the general share-out of the plunder, passing into the personal possession of Grettir's killer, Þorbjǫrn.

Þorbjǫrn himself, in common with a number of Grettir's earlier foes, notably the recalcitrant Bjǫrn of episode [2] above, has a bear-name.[174] That the same may be true of Beowulf, a heroic figure of whom no historical sources speak, may be relevant here, since Richard Harris notes that the figure of Þorbjǫrn ǫngull has left no traces in Icelandic history or literature outside this single saga:[175]

> External sources are . . . silent about the existence of Grettir's slayer – a man who, one might have thought, would have earned a place in Icelandic history for having laid to rest one of the country's greatest outlaws. But, as Guðni Jónsson points out, neither Þorbjǫrn Þórðarson, nor his brother Hjalti, nor his sister Þórdís are mentioned anywhere except in *Grettis saga*. Nor is Bjǫrn at Haganes, who loans a boat to the men, found elsewhere. Þorbjǫrn himself, then, and several principal figures in the project (to kill Grettir), exist only in the saga, which, if not in itself conclusive evidence of pure fabrication, is nevertheless a thin thread for the slayer of so great a man as Grettir Ásmundarson to hang by.

One notes in particular the fact that Þorbjǫrn, like Hǫrðr in *Harðar saga* in what has been suggested above as a parallel incident, relies on a shadowy helper-figure with the bear-name Bjǫrn to reach the lair of his foe. The author of the saga seems

172 Stedman, 'Some Points of Resemblance', pp. 26–8.
173 Jónsson, ed., *Grettis saga*, p. 59/9–11.
174 See further above, pp. 147–8.
175 Harris, 'The Deaths of Grettir and Grendel', p. 49; cf. Jónsson, ed., *Grettis saga*, p. 226, n. 3 and p. 227, n. 4.

to have taken further steps to align Þorbjǫrn with the heroic type commonly known as the Bear's Son,[176] and exemplified by Grettir himself, by providing him with a recalcitrant and surly youth to match Grettir's own,[177] as Harris has noted.[178] Both Þorbjǫrn and Grettir are therefore seen to share a rather sluggish and unpromising childhood not unlike that attributed to Beowulf (*Beowulf*, lines 2183–8).[179] Moreover just as Grettir's monster-slaying activities are rewarded by outlawry and a sorry end, so too Þorbjǫrn gains no thanks for ridding the local populace of Grettir's ravages, but is instead exiled and killed abroad by Grettir's avenging brother, Þorsteinn drómundr. And just as the doom-laden *sax* Kársnautr was used to decapitate Kárr and later Grettir, so it is this same weapon, now called Grettisnautr, which gives its third unlucky owner a fatal head-wound:[180]

> Tók Drómundr nu við saxinu, ok jafnskjótt reiddi hann þat upp ok hjó til Ǫnguls. Kom þat hǫgg í hǫfuðit ok varð svá mikit, at í jǫxlum nam staðar; fell Þorbjǫrn ǫngull dauðr til jarðar.
>
> *Drómundr now took the* sax, *and swiftly raised it up and struck at [Þorbjǫrn] ǫngull. The blow hit him in the head, and was so mighty that it stopped at his molars; Þorbjǫrn ǫngull fell down dead to the ground.*

After this killing the *sax* disappears from the saga.

In commenting on the perceived similarities between *Grettis saga* and *Beowulf* Guðbrandur Vígfússon quoted the now-celebrated observation of Arni Magnússon that:[181]

> Grettis saga gengur nær fabulae en historiae; er full með fabulas, parachronismos; er interpoleruð úr einhverju opere Sturlu, og hans ætla eg vísurnar sé. Grettis saga sú, er vér höfum, er interpoleruð úr þeirri, er Sturla Þórðarson hefir ritað, og það kannske seint á tímum. Interpolator mun hafa sett fabulas þar in. Eg minnst mig að hafa séð gamalt fragment úr þessarri Grettis sögu. Annars er eigi óvíst, að Grettis saga Sturlu hafi og fabulosa verið, ok líkara þykir miér, að Sturla hafi komið við vísurnar, er standa í þeirri, sem vér nú höfum. Þessi saga er fabulis plena.
>
> Grettis saga *approaches fable more closely than history; it is full of fables and anachronisms; it is interpolated from a certain work of Sturla [Þórðarson], and I reckon that the verses are his. The* Grettis saga *that we have, is interpolated, perhaps quite late, from the one that Sturla Þórðarson wrote. The interpolator must have put the fables in. I remember having seen an ancient fragment of this* Grettis saga. *For the rest, it is not uncertain that Sturla's* Grettis saga *was also fabulous, and it seems quite likely that Sturla has contributed the verses which stand in the version which we now have. This saga is full of fables.*

176 See further above, p. 147.

177 Jónsson, ed., *Grettis saga*, pp. 226–7.

178 Harris, 'The Deaths of Grettir and Grendel', pp. 49–50.

179 Cf. Klaeber, ed., *Beowulf*, p. xiv, n. 3 and p. xxvii, n. 6; Eliason, 'Beowulf's Inglorious Youth'; Tripp, 'Did Beowulf Have an "Inglorious Youth"?'.

180 Jónsson, ed., *Grettis saga*, p. 273/7–11.

181 Vígfússon, *Sturlunga Saga* I, p. 1, n. 1.

In the light of the evidence indicated since Guðbrandur Vígfússon first made his discovery, one is tempted to return to the views of some earlier scholars,[182] and suggest that for *Grettis saga* the *fabula* in question was *Beowulf*. It is certainly striking that amongst the earliest settlers of Iceland listed in *Landnámabók* is one Bjólfr,[183] whose name appears to be a cognate form of Beowulf, and who together with a single entry in the Lindisfarne *Liber vitae* provides the only evidence that others shared the Geatish hero's name.[184] That Stefán Einarsson found on a pre-war map a mountain called Grendill in East Iceland, in the territory claimed by the settler, excited speculation for a time, but proved a red herring.[185] Whilst R. K. Chambers has pointed out the great difficulties in assuming that some written version of *Beowulf* might have travelled to Iceland,[186] others have argued that the tales from *Beowulf* might have been brought to Iceland orally by any number of travellers, although few have gone so far as Eiríkur Magnússon, who believed that the settler Auðunn skǫkull was individually responsible.[187] It seems clear, however, that the author of *Grettis saga* assumed in his audience a detailed knowledge of a narrative paradigm also found in *Beowulf*, and which he was to use and adapt five times in key episodes of his saga.

If the notion that some version of *Beowulf* reached Iceland is rejected, one may assume the existence of an independent oral source common to both *Beowulf* and *Grettis saga*. This is the view which Guðbrandur Vígfússon himself favoured, one shared by the great majority of modern scholars, and which Anatoly Liberman, after a comprehensive review of previous scholarship, sums up as follows:[188]

> The 'common source', that is, the ancient tale about a hero killing monsters, originally had nothing to do with Beowulf or Grettir; it is used in an Old English heroic poem and later in an Icelandic saga, because both Beowulf and Grettir were expurgators, and the plot fitted their characters.

This notion of a common source, which appears to have been adapted by other Icelandic authors also, presumably carries with it the implication that just as one might interpret the structure of *Grettis saga* with regard to *Beowulf*, so elements in the Icelandic saga might well cast light on certain aspects of the older epic. Here one might simply observe that in *Beowulf*, as in *Grettis saga*, the initial distinction between the worlds of monsters and men becomes increasingly blurred. We have already seen how human are the qualities assigned to the monsters in *Beowulf*, and how monstrous are some of the men.[189] So R. E. Kaske examines in detail what he initially describes as 'the ten possible occurrences of *eoten* 'giant' and its declensional forms in *Beowulf*', and concludes that:[190]

182 Cf. Boer, ed., *Grettis saga Ásmundarsonar*, pp. 149–71; Heusler, *Die altgermanische Dichtung*, p. 53.
183 Benediktsson, ed., *Landnámabók*, II, p. 306/4–8.
184 Turville-Petre, '*Beowulf* and *Grettis saga*', p. 356.
185 Einarsson, 'Bjólfur and Grendill'; Einarsson, 'Beowulfian Place-Names'.
186 Chambers, *Beowulf: an Introduction*, pp. 461–72.
187 Cf. Liberman, 'Beowulf-Grettir', p. 356.
188 Liberman, 'Beowulf-Grettir', p. 390.
189 See further above, pp. 29–33.
190 Kaske, 'The *Eotenas* in *Beowulf*', p. 301.

> Considered in themselves, however, our series of references to *eotenas* seem to follow a fairly regular progression from monsters to men – beginning with 'giants' who from their description seem less human than monstrous (112, 421) and proceeding in turn to the anthropomorphic giant Grendel (668, 761), the unidentified giants of Sigemund (883), the 'giants' of Heremod who represent unidentified human foes (902), and finally those of the Finn episode who represent human foes identified also as Frisians.

Beowulf himself, by contrast, begins very much as a member of the courtly world of men, but as the moral imperative diminishes in his three chief battles with monsters, with a corresponding increase in the amount of weaponry he brings to bear,[191] he gradually becomes identified with the figures he fights, described, like them, as an *aglæca* (*Beowulf*, line 2592), and ends up buried with the cursed treasure of a dragon in a barrow by the sea. A very similar funeral marks the beginning of the depredations of the *draugr* Kárr inn gamli, Grettir's first foe.

Perhaps the real value of the recognition of the common narrative paradigm which performs such an important structural function in both *Beowulf* and *Grettis saga* is that it concentrates attention on the overlapping of the worlds of monsters and men which is found in each. Thorsson notes of *Grettis saga* that:[192] *Heimur manna og heimur trölla skarast ekki. Grettir ráfar þar á milli* ('the world of monsters and the world of men are not separate; Grettir wanders in between'). The same could be said of Beowulf himself. Both Beowulf and Grettir are, like Hervǫr seeking a sword in her dead father's barrow, 'between worlds' (*heima í millim*); each is a superhuman figure that the mundane world of men cannot quite constrain. This is the shared tragedy of such essentially heathen heroes whose tales are retold in a Christian world, who must begin with proud hope and bravado, and end haunted with melancholy, defeated but not diminished. Perhaps the best epitaph for both Beowulf and Grettir is offered by the warning words of Friedrich Nietzsche, writing just a few years after Guðbrandur Vígfússon first stressed the close narrative links between *Beowulf* and *Grettis saga*, and himself dogged by the search for another kind of Superman:[193]

> Wer mit Ungeheuern kämpft, mag zusehn, dass er nicht dabei zum Ungeheuer wird. Und wenn du lange in einen Abgrund blickst, blickt der Abgrund auch in dich hinein.
>
> *The man who battles with monsters might take care, lest he thereby becomes a monster. And if you gaze for long into an abyss, the abyss gazes also into you.*

It is surely contemplation of just such an abyss which leads both Beowulf and Grettir (and, according to the Old English version of his *Letter*, Alexander) to go to their deaths in uncharacteristically melancholy mood; for as Eric Stanley has noted, being heathens, 'they have no hope'.[194]

191 Rogers, 'Beowulf's Three Great Fights'; Sisam, 'Beowulf's Fight with the Dragon', p. 136; see above, pp. 28–9.

192 Thorsson, 'Grettla', p. 101.

193 Nietzsche, *Jenseits von Gut und Böse*, p. 98, no. 146.

194 Stanley, 'Hæthenra Hyht in *Beowulf*', p. 151.

Postscript

The texts of the *Beowulf*-manuscript, then, together with the *Liber monstrorum* and *Grettis saga*, share more than a twin interest in the dangers of human pride and in battles against outlandish monsters; all are concerned with the relationship between pagan past and Christian present, and with the tension between an age which extolled heroic glory and an age in which vainglory was condemned. Such a tension is evident in the very language of the texts, in which words and themes from the heroic pagan past are transformed in Christian usage. The heathen warriors and monster-slayers, such as Hercules, Alexander, Beowulf, and Grettir, have themselves become monsters in Christian eyes. Such a transformation is, as we have seen, illustrated not simply by the way that old tales are reinterpreted, but by the very diction of those tales. The Norse word *draugr* is a case in point, applied to the undead Glámr in *Grettis saga*, whilst in *Beowulf* Grendel himself is often held to be a revenant of a similar stamp.[1] One might suppose, therefore, that the word denoted solely something monstrous and uncanny. But the homograph *draugr* is also widely attested in Norse skaldic verse, including some of the earliest extant, in the plain sense '(heathen) warrior'.[2] There seems little overlap between the terms so far as chronology (or even etymology) is concerned, since the sense 'warrior' apparently 'fell from use at an early date',[3] whilst the sense 'zombie', 'walking dead', is attested in Iceland to this day. It seems possible that the word represents a demonization of pagan warriors, who begin as positive heroic figures, and end up as the bogey-men of folklore. The physical existence into Christian times of pagan burial-mounds, often (as in *Grettis saga* or *Beowulf*) situated by flowing water, can only have aided the identification. In the same way, one might point out that not only does Grettir have a monstrous ancestry, and commit monstrous deeds, but he even has a monstrous name: the common noun *grettir* is attested as a poetic term (*heiti*) for 'worm' or 'dragon' (*ormr*) even in *Grettis saga* itself.[4]

1 See further above, pp. 140–7.
2 Neckel, 'Altnordisch *draugr* in Mannkenningar', pp. 189–200; Lindow, *Comitatus, Individual and Honor*, pp. 84–96.
3 Lindow, *Comitatus, Individual and Honor*, p. 93.
4 Cf. Arent, 'The Heroic Pattern', pp. 184–6. One might compare the suggestion, most extensively considered by Tripp, *More about the Fight with the Dragon*, especially pp. 13–17, that the dragon in *Beowulf* was originally a man, transformed through greed into dragon-shape.

But if the old heroes were becoming slowly demonised, then new biblical and Christian heroes, like Judith and Christopher in the *Beowulf*-manuscript, were emerging to fight their own demons, and to be fêted in the traditional heroic diction and manner of the past. The Anglo-Saxon literary tradition is one in which Christian virtues and pagan heroic diction become gradually intertwined, and the past is constantly reassessed and reinterpreted in the light of the new learning. In such an atmosphere old heroes find new audiences, whether those heroes come from a germanic past, like Beowulf (or, in Iceland, Grettir), or from a Classical tradition, like Hercules or Alexander, inherited alongside the new Latin learning. Alfred, introducing that new learning into the vernacular, and writing his translation of Boethius in perhaps the same period in which the *Letter of Alexander* was itself translated, is a lone voice suggesting that the examples of old heroes were not necessarily to be scorned:[5]

> Wella, wisan men, wel; gað ealle on þone weg ðe eow lærað þa foremæran bisna þara godena gumena 7 þara weorðgeornena wera þe ær eow wæron. Eala, ge eargan 7 idelgeornan; hwy ge swa unnytte sien 7 swa aswundne? Hwy ge nyllen ascian æfter þæm wisum monnum 7 æfter þæm weorðgeornum, hwylce hi wæron þa þe ær eow wæron? 7 hwy ge þonne nyllen, siððan ge hiora þeawas geascod hæbben, him onhirian, swa ge swiðost mægen? forðæm hi wunnon æfter weorðscipe on þisse worulde, 7 tiolodon goodes hlisan mid goodum weorcum, 7 worhton goode bisne þæm þe æfter him wæron. Forðæm hi wuniað nu ofer ðæm tunglum on ecre eadignesse for hiora godum weorcum.
>
> *Ah, you wise men, you all walk in the paths shown you by the famous examples of the good men who came before, and of those who were eager for honour. Alas, you wretches and vainglorious men, why are you so useless and so idle? Why won't you inquire after those wise men and after those who were eager for honour, to find out what sort of men they were, who came before you? And why, once you have found out their virtues, won't you emulate them, as much as you can? Because they strove after honour in this world, and obtained great glory by their good deeds, and provided a good example for those who came after them, they now dwell above the stars in eternal bliss, because of their good deeds.*

But it is interesting that Alfred names no names, and directs his praise to the ancient figures who were 'eager for honour' (*weorðgeorn*) and did 'good deeds', specifically excluding the 'vainglorious' (*idelgeorn*). But we have seen how towards the end of the Anglo-Saxon period a much more negative view of pagan heroes such as Hercules or Alexander prevails amongst authors like Ælfric,[6] writing at the time when the *Beowulf*-manuscript was itself being compiled, in which a much harsher judgment on the heroic values of vaunting and pride is offered:[7]

5 Sedgfield, ed., *King Alfred's Boethius*, p. 139/5–17. Cf. the comments of Frank, 'The *Beowulf* Poet's Sense of History', p. 59.

6 See above, pp. 114–15.

7 Skeat, ed., *Ælfric's Lives of Saints*, I, pp. 356–8, lines 300–11; cf. Morris, ed., *Old English Homilies*, p. 297; Warner, ed., *Early English Homilies*, p. 17.

Se seofeða leahter is iactantia gecweden
þæt is ydel gylp on ængliscre spræce
þæt is ðonne se man bið lofgeorn and mid licetunge færð
and deð for gylpe gif he hwæt dælan wile
and bið þonne se hlisa his edlean ðære dæde
and his wite andbidað on ðære toweardan worulde.
Seo eahtoðe leahter is superbia gehaten
þæt is on ænglisc modignyss gecweden
seo is ord and ende ælcere synne
seo geworhte englas to atelicum deoflum
and þone man macað eac gif he modigað to swyðe
þæs deofles geferan ðe feol ær ðurh hi.

The seventh sin is called iactantia, *that is 'boastfulness' in the English tongue, that is, when a man is eager for glory [*lofgeorn*] and passes with hypocrisy, and, if he gives anything away, he does it for show, and then glory is his reward for the deed, and his punishment lies waiting in the world to come. The eighth sin is named* superbia, *which is called in English 'pride', and it is the beginning and end of every sin; it made angels into dread devils, and, if a man is too proud, it will make him the companion of the devil, who first fell thereby.*

If such was the lot of the man who was 'eager for glory' (*lofgeorn*), how much more so for the man who was, like Beowulf, 'most eager for glory' (*lofgeornost*)? And, of course, the Greeks had a word for it: in an epitaph for Alexander which, in its description of his superlative personal beauty, consideration, daring, and generosity bears comparison with the eulogy for Beowulf, Arrian describes Alexander as φιλοτιμότατος ('most eager for fame').[8]

Just as Alexander's famous exploits lived on, and found new settings in, for example, the *Wonders of the East* and the *Liber monstrorum,* so too the monster-slaying deeds of Hercules and Grettir survived to offer entertainment and a warning, for those with ears to hear. The exploits of Beowulf can be seen in the same context. It is surely no mistake that the *Beowulf*-manuscript should combine texts of a biblical, patristic, secular Latin, and popular germanic nature in one mixed codex combining and contrasting in prose and verse themes Christian and heroic, and worlds psychological and physical, showing unforgettably how prodigious pride can make monsters of men, and providing an emphatic answer, after all, to Alcuin's ungenerous question: *sic Hinieldus cum Christo* ('this is what Ingeld has to do with Christ').

8 Robson, ed., *Arrian: Anabasis Alexandri,* VII.xxviii.1, p. 296.

APPENDICES

Texts, Translations, and Sources

The texts and translations provided here are intended to facilitate reference in the discussion above, as well as to invite direct comparison both between texts and between vernacular and Latin versions; the priority has therefore been to provide serviceable editions and translations of texts which are not currently available in translation, or which cannot be easily found in an edited version convenient for close comparison of the sort envisaged here. Earlier editions and translations of the texts given here have been noted in the discussion above and freely consulted here, as indicated by the various sigla cited.

The translations offered are deliberately conservative and functional, intended mainly as aids to the further study of the original, and therefore in the cases of the *Wonders of the East* and the *Letter of Alexander*, where the Old English renderings are themselves closely dependent on Latin sources, I have provided translations of the Old English alone. For convenience of reference I have subdivided the various versions of the *Letter of Alexander* into forty-one sections, both for ease of comparison between the Old English rendering and a version of the Latin source, and to facilitate comparison of parallel episodes and marvels recorded in various subsections in the other texts. Appendix IIIc, which provides a bare list of sources of the *Liber monstrorum*, provides a preliminary index for just such a comparison.

In the presentation of Latin texts, I have levelled manuscript *e*, *ę* (*e-caudata*), *æ*, and *ae* to *ae*, in cases where that is the recognised classical norm, and similarly levelled manuscript *v* and *u* to *u* for the lower case form. I have ignored some other minor spelling-variants (such as *oe* for *e* in words like *femina*) in the critical apparatus, except in the case of the St Gallen manuscript of the *Liber monstrorum*, which has not previously been collated, and which is therefore reported in full. Even minor orthographical variants have been recorded for the Old English texts of the *Letter of Alexander to Aristotle* and the *Wonders of the East*, where only one or two manuscripts are at issue. With respect to the *Wonders of the East*, this includes recording in the critical apparatus a handful of examples of a rather eccentric form of *k*, closely resembling *pc*, which the scribe of the Tiberius-manuscript occasionally uses alongside a more standard variant. In most cases of emendation apart from my own I record only the name of the first proposer, although where such a variant significantly distinguishes previous editions I have also recorded the adoption of the variant by subsequent editors. In this way I hope to encourage reference to earlier editions, particularly where, as in the case of the *Wonders of the East*, considerable further annotation is available. I have consciously relegated to the critical apparatus the chapter-headings of the *Liber monstrorum*, which are found in some manuscripts, but which do not seem to me to be an original feature of the text. I have, however, faithfully recorded all variants, alongside the usage of the three most recent editors, to illustrate both the degree of corruption to be observed in the manuscripts, where (as I believe) scribes simply excerpted parts of the text and prefaced their quotation with the word *de*, often forgetting to change the relevant word-ending, as well as the temptation provided to every editor to further hybridise the text. Where the text has proved readable, I have retained it; and this has been my practice throughout the following Appendices.

APPENDIX Ia

The Wonders of the East

Latin text

SIGLA
T London, British Library, Cotton Tiberius B. v, fols. 78v–87r
B Oxford, Bodleian Library 614, fols. 36r–48r
G Gibb, 'Wonders of the East', pp. 112–24
K Knappe, *Die Wunder des Ostens*, pp. 43–64
C Cockayne, *Narratiunculae anglice conscriptae*, pp. 62–7
P Pickles, 'Studies in the Prose Texts of the *Beowulf* Manuscript', pp. 41–7
R Rypins, *Three Old English Prose Texts*, pp. 101–7
L Lecouteux, *De rebus in Oriente mirabilibus*, pp. 5–55
O Knock, 'Wonders of the East', pp. 885–96

§ 1. Colonia[a] est initium ab Antimolima quae[b] habet stadia numero[c] quingenta, quae faciunt leuuas[d] trecenta sexaginta octo; quae insula habet multitudinem ouium et inde ad Babiloniam stadia sunt centum sexaginta octo numero, quae [e]faciunt leuuas[e] [f].C. et .XV.[f].

§ 2. Haec colonia est maxime negotiatorum, ubi nascuntur[a] berbices magnitudine boum habitantes usque ad Medorum ciuitatem cui nomen est Archemedon, quae maxima est [b]ad Babiloniam[b]. Inde sunt stadia ad Babiloniam numero .CCC. quae faciunt leuuas[c] .CC. ab Archemedone; ibi sunt illa magna insignia quae magnus Alexander operari iusserat, quae terra habet in longitudine et latitudine stadia numero .CC., quae faciunt [d]leuuas .CXXXIII.[d] et dimidium miliarium.

§ 1
a Colonia] colononia *B*
b quae] quia *TB* quae *K* quid *L*
c numero] *om. B*
d leuuas] leugas *B*
e...e faciunt leuuas] fatiunt leugas *B*
f...f .C. et .XV.] *om. T*

§ 2
a nascuntur] nascitur *B*
b...b ad Babiloniam] *gloss.* .i. excepto babilonia *TB*
c leuuas] leugas *B*
d...d leuuas .CXXXIII.] leugas .CXXIII. *B*

§ 3. Est locus euntibus ad Mare Rubrum qui dicitur Lentibelsinea, in quibus gallinae nascuntur quales apud nos rubicundo colore. Has cum aliquis adprehendere[a] uoluerit, [b]manu suaque tetigerit, totum[b] corpus conburit[c].

§ 4. Praeterea ibi bestiae[a] nascuntur. Hae cum sonum audierint hominum statim[b] fugiunt; pedes habent octenos, oculos habent[c] gorgoneos, bina capita habent. Si quis eas[d] uoluerit adprehendere[e], corpora sua inarmant.

§ 5. Hascellentia[a] Babiloniam proficiscentibus habet[b] stadia .IX. quae subiacet regionibus Medorum omnibus bonis plena. Hic locus serpentes habet capita bina habentes, quorum oculi nocte sicut lucernae lucent.

§ 6. Nascuntur et ibi onagri cornua boum habentes forma maxima. Hi in dextera[a] parte a Babilonia ducunt se in occulto ad Mare Rubrum propter serpentes qui in illis locis nascuntur, qui uocantur Corsias, habentes cornua similia arietibus: hii quem percusserint[b] moritur; ubi nascitur abundantia piperis quod serpentes seruant sua industria. Homines[c] hoc piper sic tollunt: incendunt ea loca et serpentes sub terram fugiunt; [d]ideo nigrum[d] est piper. A Babilonia usque Persiam ciuitatem ubi nascitur piper stadia sunt .DCCC. quae faciunt [e]leuuas .DCXXIII.[e] et dimidium miliarium; loca illa sterilia sunt propter multitudinem serpentium.

§ 7. Similiter ibi nascuntur Cenocephali, quos nos Conopoenas appellamus, habentes iubas equorum, aprorum[a] dentes, canina capita, ignem et flammam flantes; hic est ciuitas uicina, diues omnibus bonis plena: dexteriore parte ducitur illa terra ab Aegypto[b].

§ 8. In [a]aliqua regione[a] nascuntur homines statura pedum .VI. barbas habentes usque ad genua, comas usque ad talos, qui Homodubii appellantur et pisces crudos manducant.

§ 3

a adprehendere] apprehendere *B*

b...b manu . . . totum] manum suam quam tetigerit totumque *TB* manu suaque tetigerit totum *G*

c conburit] *add.* quae ueneficia sunt *G*

§ 4

a bestiae] bestiole *B*

b statim] longe *G*

c habent] autem *B*

d eas] eos *TB* eas *K*

e adprehendere] apprehendere *B*

§ 5

a Hascellentia] Hascellentia regio que subiacet regionibus medorum omnibus bonis plena. babiloniam proficcicentibus habent stadia .IX. *B*

b habet] habent *B*

§ 6

a dextera] dextra *B*

b percusserint] percusserunt *TO* percusserint *BP* percusserint cito *G*

c homines] *suppl.* *G*

d...d ideo nigrum] ideoque niger *B*

e...e leuuas .DCXXIII.] leugas .DCXX. *B*

§ 7

a aprorum] aprum *B*

b Aegypto] egipto

§ 8

a...a aliqua regione] aliqua *T* alia regione *G*

§ 9. Capi uocatur[a] fluuius in eodem loco [b]qui apellatur[b] Gorgoneus; ibi nascuntur formicae statura canum, habentes pedes quasi locustae rubro colore nigroque, fodientes aurum: et quod per noctem fodiunt sub terra profertur foras usque diei horam quintam. Homines autem qui audaces sunt illud tollere sic [c]tollunt: ducunt aput se[c] camelos masculos et feminas illas quae habent [d]foetus. Foetus autem[d] trans flumen Gargulum[e] alligatos relinquunt et [f]camelis foeminis aurum inponunt[f]. Illae[g] autem pietate ad suos pullos festinantes[h], ibi masculi remanent, et illae formicae sequentes inueniunt eos masculos[i] et comedunt eos[j]; dum [k]circa autem[k] eos occupatae sunt, feminae transeunt flumen cum hominibus[l]; sunt autem tam ueloces ut putes eos uolare.

§ 10. Inter duas has amnes colonia[a] est Locothea quae inter Nilum et Brixontem posita est; nam Nilus est capud[b] fluuiorum et per Aegiptum fluit, quam Aegipti Archoboleta uocant, quae est 'aqua magna'. In his locis nascitur multitudo magna elephantorum.

§ 11. Nascuntur et ibi homines habentes staturam[a] pedum .XV., corpus habentes candidum, duas in uno[b] habentes capite facies, [c]rubra genua[c], naso longo, capillis nigris; cum tempus gignendi fuerit, suis nauibus[d] transferuntur in Indiam et ibi prolem reddunt.

§ 12. Item Ciconia[a] in Gallia nascuntur homines tripertito colore, quorum capita capita leonum, longi[b] pedibus .XX., ore amplissimo sicut uannum; hominem cum cognouerint[c], aut si quis persequatur, longe fugiunt et [d]sanguinem sudant[d]: hi[e] putantur homines fuisse.

§ 13. Trans[a] Brixontem flumen ad orientem nascuntur homines longi et magni, habentes femora et surras .XII. pedum latera cum pectore .VII. pedum, colore nigro, quos Hostes rite appellamus, nam quoscumque capiunt comedunt[b].

§ 9

a uocatur] *om. T* appellatur *G*

b...b qui apellatur] apellatur *T* qui appellatur *B*

c...c tollunt ducunt aput se] tollent aput *T* tollunt accipiunt *B* tollunt ducunt aput se *G*

d...d foetus foetus autem] foetas foetas autem *T* fetus qui ad flumen predictum pervenientes fetus *B*

e Gargulum] *om. B*

f...f camelis foeminis aurum inponunt] et ipsi cum camelis fluuium transeunt et auro collecto camelis feminis illud inponunt *B*

g Illae] illis *B*

h festinantes] festinantibus *B*

i masculos] *om. B*

j eos] *om. B*

k...k circa autem] autem circa *B*

l hominibus] auro et hominibus *B*

§ 10

a colonia] *gloss.* .i. habitatio *T*

b capud] caput *B*

§ 11

a staturam] statura *T* staturam *BC*

b uno] una *TB* uno *C*

c...c rubra genua] rubros pedes et genua *G*

d nauibus] manibus *TB* nauibus *K*

§ 12

a Ciconia] liconia *TB* Ciconia *G*

b longi] *om. T*

c cognouerint] cognouerunt *T*

d...d sanguinem sudant] sanguine sudent *TB* sanguinem sudant *K*

e hi] hii *B*

§ 13

a Trans] tras *T*

b comedunt] cito comedunt *B*

§ 14. Sunt et aliae bestiolae in Brixonte quae Lertices apellantur[a], auribus asininis, uellere ouino, pedibus auium[b].

§ 15. Est et alia insula in Brixonte ad meridiem in qua nascuntur homines sine capitibus qui in pectore habent oculos et os; alti sunt pedum .VIII. et lati [a]simili modo[a] pedum .VIII.

§ 16. Nascuntur et ibi dracones longitudinem habentes .CL. pedum, uastitudine columnarum: propter [a]multitudinem draconum[a] nemo facile adire potest trans flumen.

§ 17. Post hunc locum alia est regio, [a]in dexteriore parte oceani[a], habens[b] stadia .CCCXXIII., quae faciunt [c]leuuas .CCL.VI.[c] et miliarium unum, ubi nascuntur Homodubii qui usque ad umbilicum hominis speciem habent, reliquo corpore onagro similes, [d]longis cruribus[d] ut aues, lena uoce: sed hominem[e] cum uiderint longe fugiunt.

§ 18. Est et alius locus hominum barbarorum habens sub se reges numero .CX.; quod[a] genus pessimum et barbarorum[b] est. Sunt et alibi laci[c] duo, unus[d] solis et alius lunae: qui solis est die calidus nocte frigidus, qui lunae est nocte calidus die frigidus. Longitudo[e] eorum .CC. stadia sunt, quae[f] faciunt leuuas[g] .CXXXIII. et dimidium miliarium.

§ 19. Hoc loco arbores nascuntur similes[a] lauro et oliuae, in quibus arboribus balsamum[b] nascitur, et inde proficiscentibus[c] locus est qui habet stadia .CLI. quae faciunt leuuas[d] .L. et .I. miliarium.

§ 14
a apellantur] apellatur *T* appellatur *B* apellantur *K*
b auium] ouum *T*

§ 15
a...a simili modo] similiter *B*

§ 16
a...a multitudinem draconum] multitudinem uero draconum illorum *B*

§ 17
a...a in dexteriore . . . oceani] oceano dexteriore parte *T*
b habens] *om. T*
c...c leuuas .CCLVI.] leuuas .CCLVI. *TL* leugas .CCLIII. *B*
d...d longis cruribus] longis pedibus *T* cruribus *B*
e homines] hominem *T*

§ 18
a quod] *om. T*
b barbarorum] barbarum *B* barbarissimum *G*
c laci] loci *T* loca *B* lacus *C*
d unus] unis *T*
e Longitudo] lungitudo *B*
f quae] qui *TB* quae *K*
g leuuas] leugas *B*

§ 19
a similes] silniles *B*
b balsamum] basamum *T*
c proficiscentibus] prorofiscicentibus *B*
d leuuas] leugas *B*

§ 20. Itaque insula est in Rubro Mari in qua hominum genus est quod apud nos appellatur Donestre, quasi diuini[a] a capite usque ad umbilicum, [b]quasi homines reliquo corpore similitudine humana, nationum[b] omnium[c] linguis loquentes[d]; cum alieni generis hominem uiderint, ipsius[e] lingua appellabunt eum et parentum eius[f] et cognatorum nomina[g], blandientes sermone ut decipiant eos et perdant; cumque conprehenderint[h] eos, perdunt eos et comedunt, et postea [i]conprehendunt caput ipsius[i] hominis quem comederunt[j] et super ipsum plorant.

§ 21. Ultra hoc ad orientem nascuntur homines longi pedum .XV., lati pedum .X., caput[a] magnum et aures habentes tamquam[b] uannum: unam[c] sibi nocte substernunt, de alia[d] se cooperiunt et tegunt se his auribus, leui[e] et candido corpore sunt quasi lacteo. Homines cum uiderint tollunt sibi aures et longe[f] fugiunt quasi putes eos uolare.

§ 22. Est et alia insula in qua nascuntur homines quorum oculi sicut lucernae[a] lucent.

§ 23. Est et alia insula stadia habens longitudine et latitudine .CCC.LX., quae faciunt leuuas[a] .CX., ubi est Belis templum in diebus regis et Iobis aereo et ferreo opere constructum quod etiam Beliobiles dicitur; et inde est aedis solis ad orientem ubi est sacerdos quietus qui illa oppida maritima obseruat.

§ 24. Est et uinea aurea in oriente ad solis ortum quae habet uuas pedum .CL. de qua nascentes[a] pendent margaritae.

§ 25. Est et altera regio in terra Babiloniae, et mons ibi est maximus inter Mediam et Armeniam, mons maximus et altissimus. Sunt ibi homines honesti: hi[a] retinent Mare Rubrum imperio ubi nascuntur margaretae[b] pretiosissimae.

§ 20

a diuini] diuine *T* diuinum *B* diuini *G*

b...b quasi . . . nationum] deformatum ab hominum specie reliquo corpore similitudine existens humana nascionumque diuersarum *B*

c omnium] *suppl. G*

d loquentes] loquuntur qui *B*

e ipsius] ipsus *B*

f eius] eis *B*

g nomina] nomina inquirunt *B*

h conprehenderint] comprehenderint *B*

i...i conprehendunt caput ipsius] comprehendunt capud ipsis *B*

j comederunt] commederunt *T* comederint *B*

§ 21

a caput] capud *B*

b tamquam] tanquam *B*

c unam] quarum unam *B*

d alia] alia uero *B*

e leui] leue *T* leui autem *B*

f longe] cito *B*

§ 22

a lucernae] lucerna *T*

§ 23

a leuuas] leugas *B*

§ 24

a nascentes] nascenter *B*

§ 25

a hi] hii *B*

b margaretae] margarite *B*

§ 26. Circa hunc locum nascuntur mulieres barbas habentes usque ad mamillas, pelliculas equorum ad uestimentum[a] habentes, et hae uenatrices maxime sunt[b]: pro canibus tigres et leopardos nutriunt, et omnia genera bestiarum quae in eodem monte nascuntur cum illis uenantur.

§ 27. Et aliae sunt mulieres ibi, dentes aprorum[a] habentes, capillos usque ad talos, in lumbis caudas boum, quae sunt altae pedum .XIII., specioso[b] corpore quasi marmore candido, pedes habentes cameli, [c]dentes asininos[c], quarum multae ex ipsis ceciderunt pro sua obscenitate a magno nostro Macedone Alexandro [d]quia illas[d] uiuas adprehendere[e] non potuit, occidit, ideo quia sunt publicato corpore et inhonesto.

§ 28. Secus oceanum sunt genera bestiarum quae Catini nuncupantur: isti formosi sunt [a]et ibi sunt[a] homines cruda carne et melle uescentes.

§ 29. In sinistra parte [a]regio est Catinorum, et ibi[a] reges sunt hospitales, sub se multos habentes tyrannos confines; secus oceanum[b] a sinistra[c] parte sunt reges conplures.

§ 30. Hoc genus hominum multos uiuit annos; homines sunt benigni, et si qui ad eos uenerint[a], cum mulieribus eos[b] remittunt. Alexander autem Macedo[c] cum ad eos uenisset miratus est eorum humanitatem nec uoluit eis nocere nec ultra uoluit occidere.

§ 31. Sunt arbores in quibus lapides pretiosi nascuntur et ibi germinantur[a].

§ 32. Aliud genus est hominum ualde nigrum qui Ethiopes uocantur.

§ 33. Est et uineola ubi est[a] lectus eburneus longitudine .CCC.VI. pedum.

§ 26

a uestimentum] uettimentum *B*

b sunt] *suppl. G*

§ 27

a aprorum] aprum *B*

b specioso] spetioso *B*

c...c dentes asininos] aprinos *T om. B* dentes asininos *G*

d...d quia illas] quos quia *B*

e adprehendere] apprehendere *B*

§ 28

a...a et ibi sunt] et ubi sunt *T* sunt autem et ibi *B*

§ 29

a...a regio . . . ibi] catinorum regio est in qua *B* regio est Catinorum et ubi *G*

b oceanum] occeanum *B*

c sinistra] sinistra uero *B*

§ 30

a uenerint] uenerunt *T*

b eos] *om. B*

c Macedo] macedis *T*

§ 31

a germinantur] germinabuntur *T*

§ 33

a est] *om. B*

§ 34. Est et mons Adamans ubi est[a] Griphus auis quae .IIII.or pedes habet, caput aquilinum et caudam bouis[b].

§ 35. [a]In eo etiam monte est auis Foenix quae habet cristas[b] quasi orbes pauonis, nidum habet de cinnamomo: ipsa in sinu suo post mille annos ignem incendit et noua de fauilla[c] exurgit[d][a].

§ 36. Est et alius[a] mons ubi sunt homines nigri ad quos nemo accedere potest quia ipse mons ardet.

§ 37. Aperuit[a] Mambres libros magicos fratris[b] sui Iamnis, et fecit nicromantiam, et eduxit ab inferis idolum fratris[c] sui. Respondit[d] ei anima Iamnis[e] dicens: 'Ego frater tuus[f] non iniuste mortuus sum, sed uere iuste, [g]et ibit[g] aduersum me iudicium Dei[h], quoniam sapientior[i] eram omnium sapientium magorum, et astiti[j] duobus fratribus Moysi et Aaron, qui fecerunt signa et prodigia magna. Propter hoc[k] mortuus sum et deductus sum de medio ad inferos, ubi est combustio magna et lacus perditionis unde non est ascensus. Et nunc, frater mihi Mambre, adtende tibi in uita tua ut benefacias filiis[l] tuis et amicis: apud inferos enim nihil est boni nisi tristitia et tenebrae, et postquam mortuus fueris et ueneris ad inferos, inter mortuos [m]fuerit abitatio[m] tua in terra, lata cubitis duobus[n] et longa cubitis quattuor[o].'

§ 34

a est] *om. B*

b bouis] bonis *T*

§ 35

a...a In . . . exurgit] in predicto etiam monte est auis fenix dicta quod colorem feniceum habet uel quod sit in toto orbe singularis et unica que habet cristas quasi orbes pauonis. Hec quingentis annis ultra uiuens dum se uiderit senuisse collectis aromatum uirgulis rogum sibi instruit et conuersa ad radium solis alarum plausu uoluntarium sibi incendium nutrit et moritur. De cuius humore carnis uermis exurgit paulatimque adolescit induitque alarum remigia atque in superioris auis spetiem formamque reparatur *B*

b cristas] xpas *T*

c fauilla] fafilla *T* fauilla *K*

d exurgit] exurget *T* exurgit *G*

§ 36

a alius] altus *B*

§ 37

a Aperuit] refertur quod post mortem Iamnes magi frater illius *B*

b fratris] fratres *T*

c fratris] fratres *T*

d Respondit] quo facto respondit *B*

e Iamnis] Iamnes *TB* Iamnis *G*

f tuus] mihi *B*

g...g et ibit] est enim *B*

h Dei] *om. T*

i sapientior] sapientor *G*

j astiti] restiti *B*

k hoc] hoc igitur *B*

l filiis] filius *G*

m...m fuerit abitatio] erit habitatio *B*

n duobus] *om. T*

o quattuor] quatuor *B*

APPENDIX Ib

The Wonders of the East

Old English text

SIGLA

T London, British Library, Cotton Tiberius B. v, fols. 78v–87r
V London, British Library, Cotton Vitellius A. xv, fols. 98v–106v
G Gibb, 'Wonders of the East', pp. 84–99
N Gordon, 'Old English Studies', pp. 66–72
K Knappe, *Die Wunder des Ostens*, pp. 43–64
C Cockayne, *Narratiunculae anglice conscriptae*, pp. 33–9
P Pickles, 'Studies in the Prose Texts of the *Beowulf* Manuscript', pp. 57–87
R Rypins, *Three Old English Prose Texts*, pp. 51–67
S Sisam, *Studies in the History of Old English Literature*, pp. 80–2
A Garrad, 'Wonders of the East', pp. 1–19
O Knock, 'Wonders of the East', pp. 875–84

§ 1. Seo landbunes[a] is[b] on fruman from Antimolima[c] þam[d] lande[e]; ðæt[f] land[g] is on rime[h] þæs læssan milgetæles [i]ðe stadia[i] hatte fif hund, 7 þæs [j]micclan milgetæles[j] þe leuua[k] hatte ðreo[l] hund 7 eahta 7 syxtig[m]. On ðam[n] ealande byð[o] micel menigeo[p] sceapa. 7 þanon is to Babilonia[q] þæs læssan milgetæles stadia[r] hundteontig 7 eahta 7 syxtig[s], 7 [t]ðæs micclan[t] þe leuua[u] hatte fiftyne 7 hundteontig.

§ 2. Seo landbunes[a] is [b]swiðost cypemonnum[b] geseted. Þær beoð [c]weðeras acennede[c] on oxna micelnesse; þa buað oð Meda burh. Þære [d]burhge noma[d] is Archemedon. Seo[e] is mæst to Babilonia byrig[f]. [g]Þanon is to Babiloniam[g] þæs[h] læssan milgetæles stadia[i] .CCC. 7 þæs maran þe leuua[j] hatte .CC. from Archemedon. Þær syndan[k] þa mycclan[l] mærða þæt [m]syndan ða geweorc[m] þe se miccla[n] macedonisca Alexander[o] het gewyrcean[p]. [q]Ðæt lond[q] is on lenge 7 on [r]bræde ðæs[r] læssan milgetæles [s]ðe stadia hatte .CC.[s] 7 þæs [t]micclan ðe leuua[t] hatte [u].C.XXXIII. 7 an half[u] mil.

§ 1

a landbunes] londbuend *T* landbuend *V*
b is] *om. TV suppl. G*
c Antimolima] Antimolime *V*
d þam] þæm *V*
e lande] landum *T*
f ðæt] ðæs *T* þæs *V* ðæt *G*
g land] landes *TV* land *G*
h rime] gerime *V*
i...i ðe stadia] þe stadio *V*
j...j micclan milgetæles] miclan *V*
k leuua] leones *V*
l ðreo] þreo *V*
m syxtig] .LX. *V*
n ðam] þæm *V*
o byð] bið *V*
p menigeo] mænegeo *V*
q Babilonia] babilonian *V*
r stadia] stadio *V*
s syxtig] .LX. *V*
t...t ðæs micclan] þæs miclan milgetæles *V*
u leuua] leones *V*

§ 2

a landbunes] londbunis *V*
b...b swiðost cypemonnum] swyðust cepemonnum *V*
c...c weðeras acennede] weðras acenned *V*
d...d burhge noma] burge nama *V*
e Seo] sio *V*
f byrig] burh *V*
g...g Þanon is to Babiloniam] þanon is to Babilonia *T* þonon syndon *V* Þanon is to Babiloniam *KC*
h þæs] in þæs *T*
i stadia] stadi *V*
j leuua] leon *V*
k syndan] syndon *V*
l mycclan] miclan *V*
m...m syndan ða geweorc] syndon þa weorc *V*
n miccla] micla *V*
o Alexander] alexsander *V*
p gewyrcean] gewyrcan *V*
q...q Ðæt lond] þæt land *V*
r...r bræde ðæs] bræde .CC. þæs *V*
s...s ðe . . . .CC.] stadi *V*
t...t micclan ðe leuua] miclan þe leo *V*
u...u .C.XXXIII. 7 an half] .C.XXX. 7 healf *V*

APPENDIX Ic

The Wonders of the East

A translation of the Old English text

§ 1. The colony is at the beginning of the land Antimolima, which land is 500 in the tally of the lesser measurement, which are called *stadia*, and 368 of the greater, which are called *leuuae* ['leagues']. On that island there is a great multitude of sheep, and from there to Babylon it is 168 of the lesser measurement called *stadia*, and 115 in the greater measurement called *leuuae*.

§ 2. The colony is mostly populated with merchants; there are rams born there as big as oxen, living right up to the city of the Medes. The name of that city is Archemedon. It is the biggest city after Babylon. To there from Archemedon is 300 of the lesser measurement, *stadia*, and 200 of the greater, called *leuuae*. There are great monuments there, which are the works which the mighty Alexander of Macedon had made. The land is in length and breadth 200 of the lesser measurement, *stadia*, and 133 and a half of the greater, called *leuuae*.

§ 3. Sum stow is ðonne[a] mon færð[b] to ðare[c] Readan Sæ, seo is gehaten[d] Lentibelsinea. [e]On ðan[e] beoð henna [f]akende gelice ðam[f] þe mid us beoð reades hiwes[g]. [h]7 gyf[h] hi hwylc[i] [j]mon niman wile oððe hyra æthrineð ðonne forbærnað hi[j] sona eall[k] his lic. Þæt syndon ungefregelicu[l] lyblac[m].

§ 4. Eac [a]swa ðær[a] beoð [b]wildor kennede[b]. Þa deor þonne [c]hi monnes[c] stefne gehyrað, þonne [d]raðe hi fleoð[d]. Þa deor habbað eahta fet, 7 wælkyrian[e] eagan, 7 twa heafda[f]. [g]Gyf hi hwylc mann gefon wile[g], þonne [h]hiera lichoman þæt hy onælað[h]. [i]Þæt syndon[i] ungefregelicu[j] deor.

§ 5. [a]Hascellentia hatte þæt land, þonne mon to Babilonia færð, þæt is þonne ðæs læssan milgetæles þe stadia hatte .IX. mila lang 7 brad. Þæt [b]bugeð to[b] Meda rice. Þæt land is eallum godum gefylled[a]. [c]Ðeos steow næddran hafað[c]. Þa næddran[d] habbað twa heafda[e], ðæra[f] eagan scinað nihtes swa leohte swa blacern[g].

§ 6. On sumon lande [a]assan beoð akende[a] þa habbað swa micle hornas swa oxan. Þa syndon on ðam[b] mæstan westene[c] þæt is on ða[d] suð healfe [e]fram Babilonia[e]. Þa bugað[f] to þære[g] Readan Sæ, for [h]ðæra næddrena mænigeo[h] þe in ðam[i] stowum beoð þa hattan[j] Corsias. Ða[k] habbað swa micle hornas swa weðeras. [l]Gyf hi hwylcne

§ 3

a ðonne] *om. TV suppl. N*
b færð] fereð *V*
c ðare] ðære *V*
d gehaten] haten *V*
e...e On ðan] þæm *V*
f...f akende gelice ðam] acenned onlice þonne *V*
g hiwes] heowes *V*
h...h 7 gyf] gif *V*
i hwylc] hlyc *T*
j...j mon . . . forbærnað hi] man niman wile oþþe him o æthrineð þonne forbærnað hy *V*
k eall] eal *V*
l ungefregelicu] ungefrelicu *T* ungefrælicu *V* ungefregelicu *G*
m lyblac] liblac *V*

§ 4

a...a swa ðær] þonne þær *V*
b...b wildor kennede] wildeor acenned *V*
c...c hi monnes] hy mannes *V*
d...d raðe hi fleoð] fleoð hy feor *V*
e wælkyrian] wælcyrian *V*
f heafda] heafdu *V*
g...g Gyf . . . wile] gif him hwylc mon onfon wille *V*
h...h hiera lichoman þæt hy onælað] gewræðað hy sona grimlice ongen *T*
i...i Þæt syndon] *om. T*
j ungefregelicu] þa ungfrægelicu *V*

§ 5

a...a Hascellentia . . . gefylled] *om. V*
b...b bugeð to] bueð oð *T om. V* bugeð to *N*
c...c Ðeos . . . hafað] ..os stow hafað nædran *V*
d næddran] nædran *V*
e heafda] heafdu *V*
f ðæra] þara *V*
g blacern] blæcern *V*

§ 6

a...a assan beoð akende] eoselas byð acende *V*
b ðam] ðære *V*
c westene] wæstme *V*
d ða] þa *V*
e...e fram Babilonia] from babiloniam *V*
f bugað] buað *TV* bugað *N*
g þære] þæm *V*
h...h ðæra . . . mænigeo] þara nædrena mænego *V*
i ðam] þæm *V*
j hattan] hatton *V*
k Ða] þa *V*
l...l Gyf hi hwylcne monn] gif hy hwilcne man *V*

§ 3. As you go towards the Red Sea there is a place called Lentibelsinea, where there are hens born like ours, red in colour. If any one tries to take or touch them, they immediately burn up all his body. That is extraordinary magic.

§ 4. Wild beasts are also born there. When these wild beasts hear a human voice, they run quickly. The beasts have eight feet, and valkyrie-eyes, and two heads. If anyone tries to touch them, they set their bodies aflame. They are extraordinary beasts.

§ 5. Hascellentia is the name of the land on the way to Babylon, that is in length and breadth nine of the lesser measurements called *stadia*. It is subject to the kingdom of the Medes, and that land is filled with all good things. This place contains serpents. The serpents have two heads, whose eyes shine at night as brightly as lanterns.

§ 6. In one land there are born donkeys which have horns as big as oxen. They are in that very great wasteland which is in the southern part of Babylonia. They retreat to the Red Sea, because of the multitude of snakes called Corsiae which are in those places. They have horns as big as rams. If they strike or touch anyone, he immediately

monn[l] sleað [m]oððe æthrinað[m] þonne swylt[n] he sona. On [o]ðam londum byð piperes genihtsumnys[o]. Þone pipor [p]þa næddran healdað[p] on [q]hyra geornfulnysse[q]. Đone[r] pipor mon swa nimeð þæt mon þa stowe mid fyre onæleð 7 [s]þonne ða næddran[s] of dune on eorðan[t] þæt hi[u] fleoð; forðan[v] se pipor byð[w] sweart. [x]Fram Babilonia[x] oð Persiam þa burh ðær[y] se pipor weaxet[z] is þæs læssan milgetæles[a] þe stadia hatte eahta hund mila. Of þam is geteald þæs miclan milgetæles þe leuua[b] hatte syx[c] hund 7 [d].III. 7 .XX. 7 .I.[d] healf mil. Seo stow is unwæstmberendlicu[e] for [f]þæra næddrena menigeo[f].

§ 7. Eac swylce þær beoð cende Healfhundingas ða[a] syndon hatene Conopoenas[b]. Hi[c] habbað horses manan[d] 7 eoferes tucxas[e] 7 hunda heafda[f], 7 heora [g]oruð byð[g] swylce fyres lig[h]. Þas land beoð neah ðam[i] burgum þe beoð eallum woruldwelum[j] gefylled, þæt is [k]on þa[k] suð healfe Aegiptna[l] landes.

§ 8. On sumon lande beoð [a]menn akende ða beoþ[a] on lenge six[b] fotmæla lange[c]. Hi habbað beardas oþ[d] cneow side 7 feax oð helan. Homodubii [e]hi sindon[e] hatene, þæt [f]bioð twylice[f], 7 be [g]hreawan fisceon hi libbað[g] 7 þa etað[h].

m...m oððe æthrinað] oþþe a æthrineð *V*
n swylt] swylteð *V*
o...o ðam . . . genihtsumnys] þam landum bið pipores genihtsumnis *V*
p...p þa næddran healdað] healdaþ þa næddran *V*
q...q hyra geornfulnysse] heora geneornesse *V* heora geornnesse *KPR* heora gecneor(d)nesse *S*
r Đone] þone *V*
s...s þonne ða næddran] þa nædran þonne *V*
t eorðan] þa eorþan *V*
u hi] *om. V*
v forðan] forþon *V*
w byð] bið *V*
x...x Fram Babilonia] from babiloniam *V*
y ðær] þar *V*
z weaxet] weaxeð *V*
a milgetæles] milgeteles *V*
b leuua] leones *V*
c syx] .VI. *V*
d...d .III. 7 .XX. 7 .I.] .XXIII. 7 an *V*
e unwæstmberendlicu] unwæstmberenlicu *V*
f...f þæra næddrena menigeo] þara nædrena mænegeo *V*

§ 7
a ða] þa *V*
b Conopoenas] conopenas *V*
c Hi] hy *V*
d manan] mana *V*
e tucxas] tuxas *V*
f heafda] heafdu *V*
g...g oruð byð] oroð bið *V*
h lig] leg *V*
i ðam] þæm *V*
j woruldwelum] worldwelum *V*
k...k on þa] *om. T*
l Aegiptna] egyptana *V*

§ 8
a...a menn . . . beoþ] menn aþcende ða beoþ *T* men acende þa beoð *V*
b six] syx *V*
c lange] *om. V*
d oþ] of *T*
e...e hi sindon] hy syndon *V*
f...f bioð twylice] beoð twimen *V*
g...g hreawan . . . libbað] hreawum fixum hy lifiað *V*
h etað] etaþ *V*

dies. In those lands there is an abundance of pepper. The snakes keep the pepper in their eagerness. In order to take the pepper people set fire to the place and then the snakes flee down into the earth; because of this the pepper is black. From Babylon to the city of Persia where the pepper grows is in the lesser measure which is called *stadia* 800 units. It is reckoned in the greater measure that is called *leuuae* six hundred and twenty-three and a half units. The place is barren because of the multitude of the snakes.

§ 7. Also there are born there half-dogs who are called Conopenae. They have horses' manes and boars' tusks and dogs' heads and their breath is like a fiery flame. These lands are near the cities which are filled with all the worldly wealth: that is, in the south of Egypt.

§ 8. In one land people are born who are six feet tall. They have beards to their knees, and hair to their heels. They are called Homodubii, that is 'doubtful ones', and they eat raw fish and live on them.

§ 9. Capi hatte seo ea in [a]ðære ylcan[a] stowe þe is haten Gorgoneus, þæt is Wælcyrginc[b]. Þær beoð [c]akende æmættan[c] swa micle swa hundas. [d]Hi habbað fet swylce[d] græshoppan, hi syndon[e] reades hiwes[f] 7 blaces[g]. Þa æmettan delfað gold up of [h]eorðan fram[h] foran nihte oð ða fiftan tid dæges. [i]Ða menn ðe[i] to ðam[j] dyrstige beoð þæt hi þæt gold nimen, þonne lædað[k] hi[l] mid him [m]olfenda myran[m] mid hyra folan 7 stedan. Þa folan [n]hi getigað[n] ær hi[o] ofer þa ea faran[p]. Þæt gold hi[q] gefætað on [r]ða myran[r] 7 hi[s] sylfe onsittað 7 þa stedan[t] þær forlætað. [u]Ðonne ða[u] æmettan hi[v] onfindað, 7 þa hwile ðe[w] þa æmettan [x]ymbe ða[x] stedan abiscode[y] beoð, þonne ða[z] men mid þam myran[a] 7 þam[b] golde ofer ða[c] ea farað[d]. Hi[e] beoð [f]to þam swifte[f] þæt [g]ða men[g] wenað þæt [h]hi fleogende syn[h].

§ 10. [a]Betwyn þyssum[a] twam ean is londbunes[b] Locotheo hatte, þæt is betwyh[c] Nile 7 Brixonte[d] geseted. Seo[e] Nil is ealdor fullicra[f] ea, 7 heo floweð[g] of Ægiptna[h] lande. 7 hi [i]næmnað ða[i] ea Archoboleta, þæt is haten þæt miccle[j] wæter. On þyssum stowum[k] beoð akende[l] þa miclan [m]menigeo ylpenda[m].

§ 11. Ðær beoð akende[a] men, ða[b] beoð fiftyne fota lange 7 hi[c] habbað hwit lic 7 tu[d] neb on anum heafde, [e]fet 7[e] cneowu[f] [g]swiðe read[g], 7 lange nosu[h] 7 sweart feax.

§ 9
a...a ðære ylcan] þære ilcan *V*
b Wælcyrginc] wælkyrging *V*
c...c akende æmættan] aþcende æmættan *T* cende æmetan *V*
d...d Hi habbað fet swylce] hy habbaþ swelce swa *V*
e syndon] syndan *V*
f hiwes] heowes *V*
g blaces] blaces heowes *V*
h...h eorðan fram] eorþan from *V*
i...i Ða menn ðe] þa men þe *V*
j ðam] þon *V*
k lædað] nimað *T*
l hi] hy *V*
m...m olfenda myran] olfendan meran *V*
n...n hi getigað] hy gesælað *V*
o hi] hy *V*
p faran] faren *V*
q hi] hio *V*
r...r ða myran] þa meran *V*
s hi] hy *V*
t stedan] steðan *V*
u...u Ðonne ða] þonne þa *V*
v hi] hy *V*
w ðe] þe *V*
x...x ymbe ða] embe þone *V*
y abiscode] abysgode *V*
z ða] þa *V*
a myran] meran *V*
b þam] mid þam *V*
c ða] þa *V*
d farað] fareð *V*
e Hi] hy *V*
f...f to þam swifte] swa hrædlice ofer þære ea *V*
g...g ða men] men *V*
h...h hi fleogende syn] hy fleogan *V*

§ 10
a...a Betwyn þyssum] Betwih þysson *V*
b londbunes] londbunis *V*
c betwyh] betwih *V*
d Brixonte] bryxonte *V*
e Seo] *om. V*
f fullicra] fallicra *V* eallicra *S*
g floweð] faweð *T*
h Ægiptna] egypta *V*
i...i næmnað ða] nemnað þa *V*
j miccle] micle *V*
k stowum] *om. V*
l akende] acende *V*
m...m menigeo ylpenda] mænego olfenda *V*

§ 11
a akende] cende *V*
b ða] hy *V*
c hi] hy *V*
d tu] twa *V*
e...e fet 7] *om. T*
f cneowu] bið þæt cneo *T*
g...g swiðe read] swyðe reade *V*
h nosu] nosa *V*

§ 9. The river is named Capi in the same place, which is called Gorgoneus, that is 'valkyrie-like'. Ants are born there as big as dogs, which have feet like grasshoppers, and are of red and black colour. The ants dig up gold from the ground from before night to the fifth hour of the day. People who are bold enough to take the gold bring with them male camels, and females with their young. They tie up the young before they cross the river. They load the gold onto the females, and mount them themselves, and leave the males there. Then the ants detect the males, and while the ants are occupied with the males, the men cross over the river with the females and the gold. They are so swift that one would think that they were flying.

§ 10. Between these two rivers is a colony called Locotheo, which is situated between the Nile and the Brixontes. The Nile is the prince of great rivers, and flows through Egypt. And they call the river Archoboleta, which means 'great water'. In these regions are born great multitudes of elephants.

§ 11. There are people born there, who are fifteen feet tall and have white bodies and two faces on a single head, feet and knees very red, and long noses and black hair.

Þonne [i]hi kennan[i] willað, þonne farað hi[j] [k]on scipum[k] to Indeum, 7 þær[l] hyra [m]gecynd on weorold bringað[m].

§ 12. Ciconia[a] in Gallia hatte þæt land þær beoð men [b]acenned þreosellices hiwes[b], þara heafda[c] beoð gemona[d] swa leona heafdo[e], 7 hi beoð twentiges[f] fota lange 7 hi[g] habbað micelne muð [h]swa fann. Gif hi[h] hwylcne man[i] on ðam[j] landum ongitað [k]oððe geseoþ[k] oððe him [l]hwylc folligende[l] bið, þonne [m]feorriað hi 7 fleoð[m], 7 blode [n]þæt hi[n] swætað. Þas beoð [o]menn gewenede[o].

§ 13. Begeondan Brixonte ðære[a] ea, east ðanon[b], beoð men acende lange 7 micle, þa habbað fet 7 [c]sceancan twelf[c] fota lange, sidan mid breostum seofan[d] fota lange. [e]Hi beoð sweartes hiwes 7[e] [f]hi syndan Hostes nemde[f]. Cuðlice swa hwylcne mann[g] swa [h]hi gefoð[h], þonne fretað hi hine[i].

§ 14. Ðonne syndon[a] [b]on Brixonte[b] wildeor þa hattan[c] Lertices. Hi[d] habbað eoseles earan 7 sceapes wulle 7 fugles[e] fet.

§ 15. [a]Ðonne is oðer[a] ealand[b] suð fram[c] Brixonte on þam[d] beoð [e]menn akende[e] butan[f] heafdum, þa habbaþ[g] on heora[h] breostum heora eagan 7 muð. [i]Hi syndan[i] eahta fota lange 7 eahta fota brade.

i...i hi kennan] hy cennan *V*
j hi] hy *V*
k...k on scipum] *om. T*
l þær] *om. T*
m...m gecynd . . . bringað] gecynda in world bringaþ *V*

§ 12
a Ciconia] Liconia *T*
b...b acenned . . . hiwes] acende on drys heowes *V* ondrysnlices heowes *KA* on þrym heowum *RS* on ðrys heowes *PD*
c heafda] heafdu *V*
d gemona] gemonu *V*
e heafdo] heafdu *V*
f twentiges] .XX. *V*
g hi] hy *V*
h...h swa . . .hi] swæfon gyf *V*
i man] monnan *V*
j ðam] þæm *V*
k...k oððe geseoþ] *om. T*
l...l hwylc folligende] hwilc man folgiende *V*
m...m feorriað hi 7 fleoð] feor þæt hi fleoð *V*
n...n þæt hi] hy *V*
o...o menn gewenede] men gewende *V*

§ 13
a ðære] þære *V*
b ðanon] þonon *V*
c...c sceancan twelf] sconcan .XII. *V*
d seofan] seofon *V*
e...e Hi . . . 7] *om. V*
f...f hi . . . nemde] hostes hy synd nemned *V*
g mann] man *V*
h...h hi gefoð] hy gelæccað *V*
i hine] hyne *V*

§ 14
a syndon] seondon *V*
b...b on Brixonte] *om. V*
c hattan] hatton *V*
d Hi] hy *V*
e fugles] fugeles *V*

§ 15
a...a Ðonne is oðer] þonne syndon oþere *V*
b ealand] ealond *V*
c fram] from *V*
d þam] þon *V*
e...e menn akende] *om. V*
f butan] buton
g habbaþ] habbað *V*
h heora] *om. T* hyra *V*
i...i Hi syndan] hy seondon *V*

When they want to give birth, they travel in ships to India, and bring their young into the world there.

§ 12. There is a land called Ciconia in Gallia, where people are born of threefold colour, whose heads have manes like lions' heads, and they are twenty feet tall, and have mouths as big as fans. If they see or perceive anyone in those lands, or if anyone is following them, then they take flight and flee, and sweat blood. They are thought to be men.

§ 13. Beyond the River Brixontes, east from there, there are people born big and tall, who have feet and shanks twelve feet long, flanks with chests seven feet long. They are of a black colour, and are called Hostes. As certainly as they catch a person they devour him.

§ 14. Then there are on the Brixontes wild animals which are called Lertices. They have donkey's ears and sheep's wool and bird's feet.

§ 15. Then there is another island, south of the Brixontes, on which there are born men without heads who have their eyes and mouth in their chests. They are eight feet tall and eight feet wide.

§ 16. Ðær[a] beoð dracan[b] kende[c], ða[d] beoð on lenge hundteontiges[e] fotmæla [f]and fiftiges lange[f], 7[g] beoð greate swa stænene sweras micle. For ðara[h] dracena [i]micelnysse nænig mann naht eaðelice[i] on þæt land gefaran mæg[j].

§ 17. Fram[a] þisse stowe is oðer rice on ða[b] suð halfe[c] þæs[d] garsecges, þæt is geteald þæs læssan milgetæles[e] stadia[f] .CCC. 7 [g]þreo 7 twentig[g], 7 þæs miclan [h]ðe leuua[h] hatte [i].CC.L.V.[i] 7 an mil. 7[j] þær beoð kende[k] Homodubii þæt byð[l] twylice[m]. [n]Hi beoþ oð ðene nafelan[n] on menniscum gescape[o] 7 syððan[p] on eoseles gescape[q]; hi[r] habbað [s]long sceancan[s] swa fugelas 7 liðelice[t] stefne. [u]Gyf hi hwylcne mon[u] on ðam[v] landum ongitað[w] oððe geseoð þonne [x]feorriað hi 7 fleoð[x].

§ 18. Ðonne is oðer[a] stow ellreorde[b] men beoð on, 7 þa habbað kyningas[c] under him[d] ðæra[e] is [f]getald .CX.[f] Þæt syndon ða[g] wyrstan men 7 þa ellreordigestan[h]. [i]Þær syndan .II. seaðas, oðer sunnan 7 oðer monan[i]. Se ðe[j] sunnan is[k] se byð[l] dæges hat 7 nihtes ceald, 7 se ðe[m] monan is[n] se bið neahtes[o] hat 7 dæges cald[p]. Heora widnes[q] is .CC. mila[r] [s]ðæs læssan getales þe stadia hatte[s] 7 ðæs[t] maran [u]ðe leuua[u] hatte .CXXXIII. 7 an healf mil.

§ 16

a Ðær] þar *V*
b dracan] *om. V*
c kende] cende *V*
d ða] þa *V*
e hundteontiges] hundteontige *V*
f...f 7 fiftiges lange] lange 7 fiftiges *V*
g 7] hy *V*
h ðara] þara *V*
i...i micelnysse . . . eaðelice] micelnesse ne mæg nan man nayþelice *V*
j mæg] *om. V*

§ 17

a Fram] from *V*
b ða] þa *V*
c halfe] healfe *V*
d þæs] *om. V*
e milgetæles] milgeteles *V*
f stadia] þe stadia hatte *V*
g...g þreo 7 twentig] .XXXIII. *V*
h...h ðe leuua] þe leones *V*
i .CC.L.V.] .CC.LIII. *V*
j 7] *om. V*
k kende] cende *V*
l byð] beoð *V*
m twylice] *om. V*
n...n Hi beoþ oð ðene nafelan] hy habbað oð ðone nafolan *V*
o gescape] gesceape *V*
p syððan] syþþan *V*
q gescape] gelicnesse *V*
r hi] 7 hy *V*
s...s long sceancan] longe sconcan *V*
t liðelice] liþelice *V*
u...u Gyf . . . mon] gif hy hwilcne man *V*
v ðam] þæm *V*
w ongitað] ongytað *V*
x...x feorriað . . . fleoð] fleoð hy feor *V*

§ 18

a oðer] oþer *V*
b ellreorde] elreordge *V*
c kyningas] cynigas *V*
d him] *om. V*
e ðæra] þara *V*
f...f getald .CX.] geteald .C. *V*
g ða] þa *V*
h ellreordigestan] elreordegestan *V*
i...i Þær . . . monan] 7 þar syndon twegen seaþas oþer is sunnan oþer monan *V*
j ðe] *om. V*
k is] seað *V*
l byð] bið *V*
m ðe] *om. V*
n is] seað *V*
o neahtes] nihtes *V*
p cald] ceald *V*
q widnes] wide *T*
r mila] *om. V*
s...s ðæs . . . hatte] þæs læssa milgeteles stadia *V*
t ðæs] þæs *V*
u...u ðe leuua] þe leones *V*

§ 16. Dragons are born there, who are one hundred and fifty feet long, and are as thick as great stone pillars. Because of the abundance of the dragons, no one can travel easily in that land.

§ 17. From this place there is another country on the south side of the ocean, which is reckoned in the lesser measurement known as *stadia* 323, and in the greater which is called *leuuae* 255. There are born there *Homodubii*, that is 'doubtful ones'. They have a human shape to the navel and below that the shape of a donkey, and they have long legs like birds, and a soft voice. If they see or perceive anyone in those lands, they run far off and flee.

§ 18. Then there is another place with barbarous people, and they have kings under them to the number of 110. They are the worst and most barbarous people, and there are two lakes there, one of the sun and the other of the moon. The sun's lake is hot in the day and cold at night, and the moon's lake is hot at night and cold in the day. Their width is in the lesser measurement which is called *stadia* 200 units and in the greater called *leuuae* one hundred and thirty-three and a half.

§ 19. On þysse[a] stowe beoð treowcynn[b] þa beoð laurbeame[c] 7 eletreowum gelice[d]. Of ðam[e] treowum balsamum[f] se deorweorðesta ele bið [g]eall kenned[g]. Seo stow is þæs læssan [h]milgetæles ðe[h] stadia hatte .CLI.[i] 7 þæs maran[j] þe [k]leuua hatte .LI.[k].

§ 20. Ðonne is sum [a]ealand on ðære[a] Readan Sæ, þær is moncynn[b] þæt is mid us Donestre genemned, þa syndon geweaxene swa frihteras[c] fram ðan[d] heafde oð ðone nafelan[e], 7 se oðer dæl [f]byð mannes lice gelic[f]. 7 hi[g] cunnon eall[h] mennisc[i] gereord. Þonne hi[j] fremdes [k]kynnes mann[k] geseoð, [l]ðonne næmnað hi hine[l] 7 his magas cuðra[m] manna naman, 7 mid leaslicum wordum hine[n] beswicað, 7 [o]him onfoð[o], 7 þænne[p] æfter þan hi[q] hine fretað ealne [r]butan his[r] heafde 7 þonne sittað 7 wepað ofer ðam[s] heafde.

§ 21. Ðanan[a] is east ðær[b] beoð men akenned[c] þa beoð awæstme[d] fiftyne fota lange 7 [e]on bræde tyn[e] fotmæla[f]. Hi[g] habbað [h]micle heafda[h] 7 earan [i]swa fann[i]. Oþer eare hi[j] him on niht underbredað[k], 7 mid oðran[l] hy wreoð him. Beoð þa earan swiðe leohte 7 hi[m] beoð an[n] lichoman swa hwite swa meolc. 7[o] [p]gif hi hwylcne mann[p] on [q]ðam landum[q] geseoð [r]oðþe ongytað[r], þonne [s]nimað hi heora[s] earan on[t] hand 7 [u]feorriað hi 7 fleoð[u], swa hrædlice swa is wen [v]þætte hi[v] fleogen.

§ 19
a þysse] þisse *V*
b treowcynn] treowcyn *V*
c laurbeame] lawern beabe *V*
d gelice] onlice *V*
e ðam] þæm *V*
f balsamum] balzamum *V*
g...g eall kenned] acenned *V*
h...h milgetæles ðe] milgeteles þe *V*
i .CLI.] .C.LI. *V*
j maran] miclan *V*
k...k leuua hatte .LI.] leon .LII. *V*

§ 20
a...a ealand on ðære] ealond in þære *V*
b moncynn] mancyn *V*
c frihteras] frifteras *V*
d ðan] þam *V*
e nafelan] nafolan *V*
f...f byð . . . gelic] bið mennisce onlic *V*
g hi] hy *V*
h eall] *om. V*
i mennisc] mennisce *V*
j hi] hy *V*
k...k kynnes mann] cynnes mannan *V*
l...l ðonne næmnað hi hine] þonne nemnað hy hyne *V*
m cuðra] cuþra *V*
n hine] hy hine *V*
o...o him onfoð] hine gefoð *V*
p þænne] *om. V*
q hi] hy *V*
r...r butan his] buton þon *V*
s ðam] þam *V*

§ 21
a Ðanan] Ðonne *V*
b ðær] þær *V*
c akenned] aþcenned *T* acende *V*
d awæstme] on wæstme *V*
e...e on bræde tyn] .X. brade *V*
f fotmæla] *om. V*
g Hi] hy *V*
h...h micle heafda] micel heafod *V*
i...i swa fann] swæfon *V*
j hi] hy *V*
k underbredað] underbreðað
l oðran] oþran *V*
m hi] hy *V*
n an] swa on *V*
o 7] *om. V*
p...p gif . . . mann] gyf hy hwilcne mannan *V*
q...q ðam landum] þæm lande *V*
r...r oðþe ongytað] *om. T*
s...s nimað hi heora] nymað hy hyra *V*
t on] him on *V*
u...u feorriað . . . fleoð] feor þætte hi fleoð *T* fleoð swyðe *V*
v...v þætte hi] þæt hy *V*

§ 19. In this place there are kinds of trees which are like laurel and olive. From these trees the most expensive oil, balsam, is wholly produced. The place is in the lesser measurement that is called *stadia* 151 and in the greater which is called *leuuae* fifty-one.

§ 20. Then there is an island in the Red Sea where there is a race of people we call Donestre, who have grown like soothsayers from the head to the navel, and the other part is human. And they know all human speech. When they see someone from a foreign country, they name him and his kinsmen with the names of acquaintances, and with lying words they beguile him and capture him, and after that eat him all up except for the head, and then sit and weep over the head.

§ 21. Going east from there is a place where people are born who are in size fifteen feet tall and ten broad. They have large heads and ears like fans. They spread one ear beneath them at night, and they wrap themselves with the other. Their ears are very light and their bodies are as white as milk. And if they see or perceive anyone in those lands, they take their ears in their hands and go far and flee, so swiftly one might think that they flew.

§ 22. Đonne is sum [a]ealand in ðam[a] beoð men akend[b] þara eagan scinað[c] swa leohte swa man[d] micel blacern onæle on[e] þystre[f] nihte.

§ 23. Đonne is sum ealand[a] þæt is ðæs læssan milgetæles[b] ðe stadia hatte on lenge 7 on bræde .CCC. 7 .LX., 7 þæs miclan [c]ðe leuua[c] hatte .XC.[d] Þær wæs timbred[e] on Beles dagum [f]þæs cinges 7[f] Iobes templ[g] of isernum geweorcum[h] 7 of [i]ærenum geworht[i]. 7 on [j]ðære ylcan[j] stowe is [k]east ðanon eac oþer templ sunnan halig to þam is sum geþungen 7 gedefe sacerd to gesett, 7 he ða hofa gehealdeð 7 begymeþ[k].

§ 24. Đonne is gylde[a] wingeard æt sunnan upgange[b] se hafað berian[c] hundteontiges fotmæla lange[d] 7 fiftiges. [e]On ðam[e] bergean beoð cende [f]swylce meregrota oððe gymmas[f].

§ 25. Đonne is oðer[a] rice on Babilonia landum þær is seo mæste dun betweoh[b] Media dune 7 Armenia[c]. Seo is ealra duna mæst 7 higest[d]. [e]Þær syndon gedefelice menn þa habbað him[e] [f]to kynedome 7 to anwealde þa Readan Sæ[f]. Þær beoð [g]kende þa deorworðan gimmas[g].

§ 26. Ymb þa[a] stowe beoð wif akenned[b], ða[c] habbað beardas swa side oð heora[d] breost, 7 horses hyda hi habbað him to hrægle gedon. [e]Þa syndan huntigystran swiðe genemde[e], 7 fore[f] hundum tigras 7 leopardos[g] þæt hi[h] fedað þæt syndan[i] þa kenestan[j] deor. 7 ealra ðæra[k] wildeora kynn[l], þæra[m] þe on ðære dune akende[n] beoð, [o]þæt hi gehuntigaþ[o].

§ 22
[a...a] ealand in ðam] ealond on þam *V*
[b] akend] acende *V*
[c] scinað] scinaþ *V*
[d] man] ma *T*
[e] on] *om.* V
[f] þystre] þeostre *V*

§ 23
[a] ealand] ealond *V*
[b] milgetæles] milgeteles *V*
[c...c] ðe leuua] þe leones *V*
[d] .XC.] .CX. *V*
[e] timbred] getymbro *V*
[f...f] þæs cinges 7] *om.* *V*
[g] templ] temple *V*
[h] geweorcum] geworcum *V*
[i...i] ærenum geworht] glæs gegotum *V*
[j...j] ðære ylcan] þære ilcan *V*
[k...k] east . . . begymeþ] æt sunnan upgange setl quietus þæs stillestan bisceopes se nænine oþerne mete ne þige buton sæostrum 7 be þam he lifede *V*

§ 24
[a] gylde] gylden *V*
[b] upgange] upgonge *V*
[c] berian] bergean *V*
[d] lange] *om.* *V*
[e...e] On ðam] of þæm *V*
[f...f] swylce . . . gymmas] saragimmas *V*

§ 25
[a] oðer] oþer *V*
[b] betweoh] betwih *V*
[c] Armenia] armoenia *V*
[d] higest] hyhst *V*
[e...e] Þær . . . him] *om.* *V*
[f...f] to kynedome . . . Sæ] to cynedome þone readan sæ 7 to anwalde *V*
[g...g] kende . . . gimmas] cende sarogimmas *V*

§ 26
[a] þa] þas *V*
[b] akenned] *om.* T acenned *V*
[c] ða] þa *V*
[d] heora] hyra *V*
[e...e] Þa . . . genemde] hundicgean swiðast nemde *V*
[f] fore] from *V*
[g] leopardos] leon 7 loxas *V*
[h] hi] hy *V*
[i] syndan] syndon *V*
[j] kenestan] cenestan *V*
[k] ðæra] þara *V*
[l] kynn] cyn *V*
[m] þæra] *om.* *V*
[n] akende] acende *V*
[o...o] þæt hi gehuntigaþ] mid heora scine þæt hy to gehuntiaþ *V*

§ 22. Then there is an island on which people are born whose eyes shine as brightly as if one had lit a great lantern on a dark night.

§ 23. Then there is an island, which is in length and breadth in the lesser measurement that is called *stadia* 360, and in the greater called *leuuae* 90. There was built in the days of Belus the king and Jove a temple made from wrought iron and brass. And in the same place there is east from there another temple, sacred to the sun, in which is ordained a fine and gentle priest, and he governs the halls and looks after them.

§ 24. Then there is a golden vineyard near the rising of the sun which has berries of 150 feet. On them, berries are produced like pearls or jewels.

§ 25. There is another kingdom in the lands of Babylon where there is found the biggest mountain between the mountain of Media and of Armenia. It is the biggest and highest of all mountains. There are decent people there who have power and dominion over the Red Sea. Precious jewels are produced there.

§ 26. Around those places there are born women, who have beards down to their breasts, and have made clothes out of horse's hide. They are called great huntresses, and instead of dogs they breed tigers and leopards, that are the fiercest beasts. And they hunt for all the kinds of wild beasts which are born on the mountain.

§ 27. Đonne [a]sindon oðre[a] wif ða[b] habbað eoferes tucxas[c] 7 feax oð helan side, 7 [d]on lendenum oxan tægl[d]. Þa wif syndon ðreotyne[e] fota lange 7 heora[f] lic bið on marmorstanes hwitnysse[g]. 7 hi[h] habbað olfenda[i] fet 7 eoferes[j] teð. [k]For heora[k] unclennesse[l] [m]hie gefelde wurdon fram ðam mycclan[m] macedoniscan Alexandre. Þa [n]he hi lifiende gefon ne mihte, þa acwealde he hi for ðam hi[n] syndon æwisce on lichoman 7 unweorðe[o].

§ 28. Be þam[a] garsecge is[b] wildeora cynn[c] þa [d]hattan Catini þa[d] syndon freawlitige[e] deor. 7 þær syndon [f]menn ða[f] be hreawan[g] flæsce 7 be [h]hunige lifigeað[h].

§ 29. On þam[a] wynstran dæle [b]þæt rice is[b] þe ða deor on beoþ[c] Catinos, 7 þær beoð gæstliþende[d] menn[e], cyningas þa habbað[f] under him[g] mænigfealde[h] leodhatan. Heora landgemære beoð[i] neah þam[j] garsecge, 7[k] [l]þanan fram þam[l] wynstran dæle [m]syndan manege cyningas[m].

§ 30. Đis [a]mannkynn lifað[a] fela geara, 7 hi[b] syndon fremfulle[c] menn[d]. 7[e] [f]gyf hwylc mann to him cymeð[f] þonne gyfað[g] hi[h] him wif ær hi[i] hine onweg lætan[j]. Se

§ 27

a...a sindon oðre] syndan oþere *V*

b ða] þa *V*

c tucxas] tuxas *V*

d...d on lendenum . . . tægl] oxan tægl on lendunum *V*

e ðreotyne] þryttyne *V*

f heora] hyra *V*

g hwitnysse] hiwnesse *V*

h hi] hy *V*

i olfenda] olfendan *V*

j eoferes] eoseles *V*

k...k For heora] of hyra *V*

l unclennesse] mycelnysse *T* micelnesse *V* unclennesse *N*

m...m hie . . . mycclan] hy gefylde wæron from þæm miclan *V*

n...n he . . . for ðam hi] cwealde he hy þa he hy lifiende oferfon ne mehte for þon hy *V*

o unweorðe] unweorþe *V*

§ 28

a þam] þæm *V*

b is] *om.* *V*

c cynn] cyn *V*

d...d hattan Catini þa] hatton catinos þær *V*

e freawlitige] freawliti *V*

f...f menn ða] men þe *V*

g hreawan] hreawum *V*

h...h hunige lifigeað] hunie lifiað *V*

§ 29

a þam] þæm *V*

b...b þæt ... is] þær rices *T* þæs rices *V* þæt rice is *G*

c beoþ] buaþ *V*

d gæstliþende] eastliðende *T*

e menn] men *V*

f habbað] habbaþ *V*

g him] om. *V*

h mænigfealde] monigfealde *V*

i beoð] buað *T* buaþ *V* beoð *G*

j þam] þæm *V*

k 7] om. *V*

l...l þanan . . . þam] þanon fræm þæm *V*

m...m syndan manege cyningas] syndon fela cyninga *V*

§ 30

a...a mannkynn lifað] mannþcynn lifað *T* mancyn lyfað *V*

b hi] hy *V*

c fremfulle] fremfulfe *T*

d menn] men *V*

e 7] *om.* *V*

f...f gyf . . . cymeð] gif hwilc mon him to cymð *V*

g gyfað] gyfad *T* gifað *V* gyfað *G*

h hi] hy *V*

i hi] hy *V*

j lætan] læten *V*

§ 27. Then there are other women who have boar's tusks and hair down to their heels and ox-tails on their loins. Those women are thirteen feet tall and their bodies are of the whiteness of marble. And they have camel's feet and boar's teeth. Because of their uncleanness they were killed by Alexander the Great of Macedon. He killed them because he could not capture them alive, because they have offensive and disgusting bodies.

§ 28. By the ocean is a breed of wild animals that is called Catini, and they are very beautiful animals. And there are people there who live on raw meat and honey.

§ 29. On the left-hand side is the kingdom in which there are wild animals called Catini, and there are hospitable people there, kings who have subdued many tyrants. Their boundaries border on the Ocean, and from there, from the left-hand section, there are many kings.

§ 30. This race of people live for many years, and they are generous people. If anyone visits them they give him a woman before they let him go. When Alexander

macedonisca Alexander, þa ða[k] he him to com, þa wæs he wundriende[l] hyra menniscnysse[m], ne wolde he hi cwellan ne him [n]nawiht laðes don[n].

§ 31. Ðonne syndon [a]treowcynn of ðam ða[a] deorweorstan[b] stanas beoð[c] acende, 7 þanon þætte[d] hi[e] growað.

§ 32. Ðær mannkynn[a] is þæt[b] syndan[c] sweartes hiwes[d] on ansyne[e], þa man[f] hateð silhearwan[g].

§ 33. Ðonne is sum land wingeardas weaxat on swiðast, þær bið rest of elpenda bane geworht. Seo is on lenge þreo hund fotmæla lang 7 syxa.

§ 34. Ðonne is sum dun Aðamans[a] hatte. On ðære dune bið þæt fugelcynn þe Grifus hatte. Þa fugelas habbað feower fet 7 hryðeres tægl 7 earnes heafod.

§ 35. On þære ylcan stowe byð oðer fugelcynn Fenix hatte. Þa habbað cambas on heafde swa pawan, 7 hyra nest þætte hi wyrcaþ of ðam deorweorðestan wyrtgemangum þe man cinnamomum hateð. 7 of his æðme[a] æfter þusend gearum he fyr onæleð 7 þonne geong upp of þam yselum eft ariseþ.

§ 36. Ðonne is oðer dun þær syndon swearte menn, 7 nænig oðer man to ðam mannum geferan mag for ðam þe seo dun byð eall byrnende.

§ 37. Her segð hu Mambres ontynde ða drylican bec his broðer[a] Iamnes, 7 him geopenude þa heagorune ðæs deofelgildes his broður. Andswarode him Iamnes saul þyssum wordum: 'Þu, broðor, ic naht unrihtlice eom dead, ac soðlice 7 rihtlice ic eom dead 7 Godes dom wið me standeð for þam ðe ic wæs ana wisera þonne ealle oðre dryas 7 ic wiðstod twam gebroðrum Moyses hatte 7 Aaron, þa worhtan þa micclan tacna 7 forebeacnu. For þan ic eom dead 7 for þam ic eom gelædd on helwara rice mid, þær is seo miccle hatnys þæs ecan wites, 7 þær is se seað þæs singales susles þanon ne byð ænig upp adon. Nu, min broðer Mambre, beheald þe on þinum life þæt ðu do wel þinum bearnum 7 þinum freondum, for þan þe on helle ne byð nawiht godes nemðe unrotnys 7 þystru. 7 æfter þam þe ðu dead bist, þonne cymst þu to helle 7 betwix deadum mannum bið þin eardungstow, niðer on eorðan, 7 þin seað bið twegea cubita wid 7 feowra lang.'

k ða] se *V*
l wundriende] wundrende *V*
m menniscnysse] menniscnesse *V*
n...n nawiht ... don] nan lað on *V* man lað don *A*

§ 31
a...a treowcynn ... ða] treowcyn on þæm þa *V*
b deorweorstan] deorwyrþystan *V*
c beoð] synd of *V*
d þætte] *om. V*
e hi] hy *V*

§ 32
a mannkynn] moncyn *V*
b þæt] *suppl. G*
c syndan] seondon *V*
d hiwes] hyiwes *V*
e ansyne] onsyne *V*
f man] mon *V*
g silhearwan] sigelwara *gloss.* wurhasa *V*

§ 33-37 *om. V*

§ 34
a Aðamans] Adamans *G*

§ 35
a æðme] fæðme *KA*

§ 37
a broðer] breðer *T*

of Macedon visited them, he was amazed at their humanity, and would not kill them or cause them any harm.

§ 31. Then there are kinds of tree from which the most precious stones are produced, and upon which they grow.

§ 32. There is another race of people there of black colour to look at, who are called Ethiopians (*sigelwara*).

§ 33. Then there is land in which very many vineyards grow, where there is a couch of ivory. It is 306 feet long.

§ 34. Then there is a mountain called Adamans. On that mountain is the kind of bird which is called a Gryphon. Those birds have four feet and the tail of a cow and the head of an eagle.

§ 35. In the same place is another kind of bird called Phoenix. They have crests on their heads like peacocks, and they build their nests from the most precious spices, which are called cinnamon; and from its breath, after a thousand years, it kindles a flame, and then rises up young again from the ashes.

§ 36. Then there is another mountain where there are black people, and no one else can approach those people because the mountain is all aflame.

§ 37. Here it says how Mambres opened the magical books of his brother Iamnes, and to him were revealed the deep mysteries of his brother's idolatry. The soul of Iamnes answered him with these words: 'Brother, I am dead not unjustly, but rightly and justly am I dead, and God's judgment stands against me because I alone was wiser than all the other sorcerers, and I withstood the two brothers called Moses and Aaron, who performed those great portents and signs. For that reason am I dead, and for this am I brought to the midst of the kingdom of hell, where there is the great heat of eternal punishment, and where there is the pit of perpetual torment from which no one ever ascends. Now, my brother Mambres, take care that you do well to your children and your friends, because in hell there is nothing good, only misery and darkness; and after you are dead, then you will come to hell, and your dwelling-place will be among the dead, down in the ground, and your pit will be two cubits wide and four cubits long.'

APPENDIX IIa

The Letter of Alexander to Aristotle

Latin text

SIGLA

R London, British Library, Royal 13. A. i, fols. 51v–78r

B Boer, ed., *Epistola Alexandri ad Aristotelem*, pp. 1–60

§ 1. [51v] [a]INCIPIT EPISTOLA [52r] ALEXANDRI REGIS MAGNI MACEDONIS AD MAGISTRUM SUUM ARISTOTELEM[a].

§ 2. Semper memor tui, etiam inter dubia bellorumque nostrorum pericula, carissime praeceptor ac secundum matrem meam sororesque meas acceptissime, et quoniam te deditum philosophiae noueram, scribendum tibi [52v] de regionibus Indiae ac statu[a] caeli innumerisque serpentium et hominum ferarumque generibus existimaui, ut aliquid per nouam[b] rerum cognitionem studio et ingenio possit accedere. Quamquam in te consummata prudentia nullumque adiutorium expostulet ratio doctrinae quae a te et tuo seculo ac futuris temporibus conueniat, tamen, ut mea gesta cognosceres que diligis et ne quid inusitatum haberes, ea quae in India coaceruata[c] per summos labores ac pericula Macedonum scribendum[d] tibi putaui.

§ 3. Etenim sunt digna memoriae singula ac multis modis coaceruata, quem ad modum inspexi: non crediderim cuiquam esse tot prodigia, [53r] nisi subicta[a] meis oculis prius[b] cuncta ponderauissem. Mirandum est terra mater[c] quantum aut bonarum rerum pariat aut malarum, [d]contemplaris existat et pariens[d] publica ferarum ac fructuum metallorumque animalium[e]. Quae si omnia liceat intueri homini, uix subfectura tot uarietatibus rerum ipsa crediderim nomina.

§ 1

a...a INCIPIT . . . ARISTONTELEM] EPISTOLA ALEXANDRI MACEDONIS AD ARISTOTELEM MAGISTRUM SUUM DE ITINERE SUO ET DE SITU INDIAE *B*

§ 2

a statu] de statu *B*

b nouam] nouarum *B*

c coaceruata] uidi *B*

d scribendum] scribenda *B*

§ 3

a subicta] subiecta *B*

b prius] ipse prius *B*

c mater] *om. B*

d...d contemplaris . . . pariens] conceptrix et pariens *B*

e animalium] atque animalium *B*

§ 4. Sed ego de his quae primum cognoui eloquar daturus operam, ne aut fabule aut turpi mendacio dignus[a]. Etiam naturam animi mei, cum fueris praeceptor, non ignorus[b]: solere me terminum aequitatis custodire et partius omnia[c] loqui quam gesta sint[d]. Et nunc spero [e]cognoscis nichil[e] tamquam captantem iactantemque gloriam militiae nostrae [53v] asserere. Quae utinam minus fuissent laboriosa nobis nec tot rebus experimenta necesse esset cognoscere.

§ 5. Ago gratias Macedoniae iuuenum uirtuti et inuicto exercitui nostro, quia in ea patientia perseuerauerunt ut rex regum appellarer[a]. Quod[b] tibi meo titulo misso laetari, carissime praeceptor, si dubito, delinquo, et a mea tuaque aberro pietate, nisi tibi ut Olympiadi matri meae sororibusque meis de singulis regni mei commodis scribam; quae tibi et illis communia esse arbitror, idque nisi feceris, paruum[c] de nobis simpliciter iudicare uideberis.

§ 6. Prioribus litteris significaueram tibi de solis lunaeque eclipsi et de constantia siderum [54r] aerisque indiciis, quae non sine magna cura ordinata tibi misi et has nunc[a] nouas implicaturus historias omnia cartis commendabo. Quae cum relegis, scito esse talia quae cura Alexandri tui complecti decuerant.

§ 7. Mense Maio rege Persarum Dario apud Gangem omnem[a] superato acceptaque in [b]decitione omnem eius regionem[b] ordinarios praeparatoresque nostros praeposuimus orientis prouinciis, multis opibus regalibus ditati, ut in priori epistola significaueram tibi. Et nunc, ne sim scribendi multiplex, priora facta iam praecognita praetereo.

§ 8. Mense Iulio deficiente in India[a] Fassiacen[b] peruenimus, ubi mira celeritate Poro rege deuicto, potiti ingentibus diuitiis [54v] regia gaza repleti sumus. Sed ut cognoscas ea, quae[c] mihi memoriae digna esse uidebantur; quaedem [d]me uoui quia memorabile fiat mirabile et[d] aequum est [e]mihi uisum mihi describere[e] de innumerabili exercitu eius, in quo fuere praeter peditum copias .XVI.[f] milia equitum, .DCCC.tae[g] quadrigae, omnes falcatae; captisque elephantis .CCCC.tis[h] qui

§ 4
a dignus] dignus efficiar *B*
b ignorus] ignoras *B*
c partius omnia] parcius *B*
d sint] sint omnia *B*
e...e cognoscis nichil] quod agnoscis nihil me *B*

§ 5
a appellarer] appeller *B*
b quod] quo *B*
c paruum] parum *B*

§ 6
a nunc] *om. B*

§ 7
a omnem] amnem *B*
b...b decitione . . . regionem] condicionem omni eius regione *B*

§ 8
a India] Indiam *B*
b Fassiacen] Faslacen *B*
c que] quoniam *B*
d...d me . . . et] enim noui que memorabilia fuerunt *B*
e..e mihi . . . describere] uisum mihi scribere *B*
f .XVI.] sedecim *B*
g .DCCC.] octingentae *B*
h .CCCC.tis] quadringentis *B*

superpositas cum armatis iaculatoribus turres gestauerunt[i], ipsam urbem regiam Pori domumque armis inuasimus, in qua columnas aureas solidas[j] ingentique[k] grossitudine atque altitudine cum suis capitellis admodum quadringentas enumerauimus auratosque parietes laminarum[l] digitalium grossitudine. Quos cum aestimare uellem, aliquibus locis intercidi. Uineam [55r] quoque solidam [m]auream argenteamque[m] inter columnas pendentem miratus sum, in qua folia erant[n] aurea racemique [o]chrystallini et lignitis[o] erant interpositi distinguentibus smaragdis. Thalami cubiliaque omnia[p] margaritis unionibus et carbunculis exornata erant, fores eburneae miri candoris fuerunt, et [q]ibino atro[q] lacunaria nitebant et[r] testudinibus [s]cupressinis quibus lauri in insigne loco et in balnearibus erant[s]. Aureae quoque solidae[t] cum crateribus aureis statuae et innumeri thesauri. Fores[u] in domus pariete[v] innumerabilia genera uariis coloribus aberrabant[w] inter aureas platanos unguibus rostrisque inauratis pro[x] inauribus torquibusque quae[y] margaritas et huniones[z] gerentia. Multa gemmea et crystallina electrina[a] [55v] uasa potaria[b] et sextariosa[c], [d]multa aurea[d] inuenimus et [e]rara argentea[e].

§ 9. Quibus in potestatem redactis interiorem Indiam perspicere cupiens cum uniuerso Caspias portas perueneram exercitu. Ubi cum fertilissimarum regionum ammirarer[a] felicitatem, quodam gaudio elatus[b] digna conueneram[c] loca, quamquam praedixerant nobis incolae regionis eius, ne serpentes et rabida ferarum genera incideremus quae plurima in his uallibus et campis siluisque ac montibus habitabant, nemorum saxorumque latebris occulta. Sed ego, ut fugientem ex proelio Porum quam[d] primum assequerer[e], antequam in desertas [f]abiret orbis terrarum[f] solitudines, compendiosa[g] magis quam tuta itinera eligere malui.

[i] gestauerunt] gestauerant *B*
[j] solidas] solidasque *B*
[k] ingentique] ingenti *B*
[l] laminarum] luminarum *corr. in* laminarum *R*
[m...m] auream argenteamque] auro argentoque *B*
[n] erant] *om. B*
[o...o] chrystallini et lignitis] crystallini *B*
[p] omnia] *om. B*
[q...q] ibino atro] ebenina *B*
[r] et] *om. B*
[s...s] cupressinis . . . erant] cypressinis in in signi loco et in balnearibus, quibus lauari erant soliti *B*
[t] solidae] solidaeque *B*
[u] Fores] foris *B*
[v] pariete] pariete auium *B*
[w] aberrabant] oberrabant *B*
[x] pro] cum *B*
[y] quae] *om. B*
[z] huniones] uniones *B*
[a] electrina] electrinaque *B*
[b] potaria] potatoria *B*
[c] sextariosa] sextarios alia *corr. in* sextariosa *R* sextariola *B*
[d...d] multa aurea] multas aureos *corr. in* multa aurea *R*
[e...e] rara argentea] raros argenteos *corr. in* rara argentea *R*

§ 9

[a] ammirer] admirer *B*
[b] elatus] *om. B*
[c] conueneram] cognoueram *B*
[d] quam] *om. B*
[e] assequerer] adsequerer *B*
[f...f] abiret . . . terrarum] orbis terrarum abiret *B*
[g] conpediosa] compendiosa *B*

§ 10. Acceptis igitur .CCCL.[a] [56r] ducibus qui breuitates itinerum[b] nouerant, mense Agusto[c] per feruentes sole harenas et egentia humoris loca profectus sum, pollicitus his praemia qui nos periti regionum ducebant per ignota [d]loca Indiae[d], si me cum incolumi exercitu in Bactriacen perduxissent penitusque[e] ad abditos Seres, quae gens foliis arborum decerpendo lanuginem ex siluestri uellere uestes detexunt. Sed illi maiorem hosti quam mihi fauorem accommodantes efficere pergebant, ut nos in exitiabilia serpentium et rabida ferarum beluarumque[f] genera ignaras[g] regionum inducerent; quae illos cogitasse ex ipsis patebit[h] experimentis. Tum ego cernens ex parte mea[i] accidisse, quo[j] utilia consilia spreueram amicorum pariter et Caspiorum hominum qui perdixerant[k] mihi, ne ita [56v] uincere festinarem, ut nullo[l] interueniente adeunda[m] esset uictoria, imperaui militibus omnibus, ut armis induti agmen sequerentur, propterea quoniam, cum auri ex rapina margaritarumque non paruam secum praedam ueherent, timendum esset, ne occulti[n] hostes sua ablaturi uictoribus insidiarentur.

§ 11. Et sane[a] miles ita [b]erat locupletatus[b], ut uix ferre pondus auri posset. Accedebat quoque armorum non parua grauitas, quia[c] ego [d]laminis omnis aureis incluseram[d]. Ita totum agmen [e]in eo[e] ueluti sidere aut fulgore clarum radiantibus auro insignibusque sequebatur cum signis et uexillis. Eratque inter uarietates spectaculum in conspiciendo talem exercitum, qui[f] ornatu pariter [g]et honoribus[g] ac uiribus inter [57r] gentes ceteras eminebat. Ego certe respiciens felicitatem meam insigni numero iuuentutis inmenso[h] afficiebar gaudio.

§ 12. Sed ut aliquid plerumque in secundis rebus fortuna obstrepit, accidit nobis siti laborare. Quam cum iam uix sustineremus, miles Zeuerus[a] inuentam mihi in lapide concauo aquam galea aurea protulit ipse sitiens, animaeque meae magis quam suae uitae consulebat. Quam ego conuocato[b] exercitu palam effudi, ne me bibente magis sitire miles inciperet, conlaudataque[c] Zeueri[d] erga me beniuolentia[e] dignis eum muneribus ornaui[f]. Quae res cum animaequiorem fecisset exercitum, ceptum

§ 10
[a] .CCCL.] centum quinquaginta *B*
[b] itinerum] iterum *corr. in* itinerum *R*
[c] Agusto] Augusto *B*
[d...d] loca Indie] Indiae loca *B*
[e] penitusque] penitusque remotos *B*
[f] beluarumque] beluarum *B*
[g] ignaras] ignaros *B*
[h] patebit] patebant *B*
[i] mea] mea id *B*
[j] quo] quia *B*
[k] perdixerant] dixerant *B*
[l] ullo] ullo dolo *B*
[m] adeunda] mihi adempta *B*
[n] occulti] occulto *B*

§ 11
[a] sane] sine *corr. in* sane *R*
[b...b] erat locupletatus] locupletatus erat *B*
[c] quia] quia omnia *B*
[d...d] laminis . . . incluseram] aureis incluseram laminis *B*
[e...e] in eo] me *B*
[f] qui] quia *B*
[g...g] *om. B*
[h] inmenso] immenso *B*

§ 12
[a] Zeuerus] Zephyrus *B*
[b] conuocato] uocato *B*
[c] conlaudataque] collaudansque *B*
[d] Zeueri] Zeuere *corr. in* Zeveri *R* Zephyri *B*
[e] beniuolentia] beneuolentiam *B*
[f] ornaui] honoraui *B*

iter institui. Nec longe mihi in desertis locis flumen apparuit cuius ripas [57v] pedum sexagenum arundo uestiebat, pinorum abietumque robora uincens grossitudine, quia[g] Indi materia ad conficienda[h] aedificia [i]incolae uidebantur[i].

§ 13. Tum ego, quoniam quadrupedia et exercitus sitiebant, iussi continuo castra poni a metatoribus. Quae dum ponuntur, ipse sitim leuare cupiens [a]amariore elleborae[a] fluminis aquam gustaui, quam neque homo bibere neque ullum pecus haurire sine tormento possit[b]. Angebar autem magis pro mutis animalibus quam pro nostra necessitate, durabiliorem hominem cunctis in rebus recognoscens quam pecudem; quippe [c]mecum erant[c] qui aurum uehebant elefanti[d] ingentis magnitudinis admodum mille, quadringentae quadrigae equorum, omnes falcatae, bigae uero mille .CC.[e], equi[58r]tum turmae, .XXX.[f] milia, [g].CC.L. milia peditum[g], mulorum castrensium ad subarmilia [h]et sarcinas militum uebendas circiter .II. milia camelorum .D. dromidumque et bubulorum .II. milia sumedumque et boum .II. milia, qui frumenta uehebant, armentorum[h] uero[i] ad usum carnis cotidie[j] ingens numerus sequebatur. Ceterum in equis et mulis [k]et camelis[k] et elefantis[l] aurea quaeque[m] frena luxus parum[n] nobis permiserat uictoriarum. Sed tunc [o]insperata siti[o] ipsa pecora uix se continere poterant. Milites quoque nunc ferramenta lambendo, nunc oleum gustando duram[p] aliquo modo differre sitim[q] auferre conabantur. Uidimus etiam plerosque pudore amisso suam ipsam[r] urinam uexatos ultimis necessitatibus haurientis[s].

§ 14. Quae res [58v] me dupliciter torsit. Primo de statu exercitus magis quam de proprio meo sollicitus fui periculo; iussi[a], ut armati [b]sequerentur agmen[b]; legem dixi me in eum animaduersarum[c] qui non legitimis indutus insignibus in acie deprehensus esset. Quod ipsi quoque mirabantur, quid[d] ita, ubi nullus appareret hostis, necesse esset in tanta siti armatis[e] ingredi. Sed ego sciebam per bestiosa serpentiosaque loca nobis iter esse[f], ac ne [g]ut inprudentes[g] circumueniremur nec opinato[h] periculo uerebamur[i].

g quia] qua *B*
h conficienda] constituenda *B*
i...i incolae uidebantur] utebantur *B*

§ 13
a...a amariore elleborae] amariorem elleboro *B*
b possit] potuit *B*
c...c mecum erant] *om. B*
d elefanti] elephanti *B*
e .CC.] ducentae *B*
f .XXX.] uigenti *B*
g...g .CC.L. . . . peditum] peditum ducenta quinquaginta milia sub armis *B*
h...h et sarcinas . . . armentorum] et ad sarcinas militum uehendas circiter duo milia, camelorum dromedumque et boum duo milia, que frumenta uehebant, et armentorum *B*
i uero] *om. B*
j cotidie] cotidianae *B*
k...k et camelis] *om. B*
l elefantis] elephantis et camelis *B*
m queque] quoque *B*
n parum] non paruus *B*
o...o insperata siti] inasperata *B*
p duram] diram *B*
q sitim] sitim uel *B*
r ipsam] *om. B*
s haurientis] haurientes *B*

§ 14
a iussi] iussi tamen *B*
b...b sequerentur agmen] agmen sequerentur *B*
c animaduersarum] animaduersurum *B*
d quid] quod *B*
e armatis] armatos *B*
f esse] esse ne opposito periculo frangeremur *B*
g...g ut inprudentes] imprudentes *B*
h opinato] inopinato *B*
i uerebamur] feriremur *B*

§ 15. Ripam igitur fluminis sequentes ad horam diei octauam ad oppidum peruenimus quod in medio amne insulae[a] ex his arundinibus quas paulo ante descripsimus, erat aedificatum, paucos[b] Indorum seminudos notauimus homi[59r]nes, qui uisis nobis continuo intra tectorum suorum culmina delituerunt. Quorum ego praesentiam desiderans[c], ut dulcem ignaris aquam demonstrarent, apparente nullo paucas ieci[d] in ciuitatem sagittas[e] imperaui, ut si uoluntate sua nollent procedere, metu [f]belli coacti[f] exhiberentur. Tanto magis cunctis propter timorem abditis, diu apparente nemine .CC.os[g] milites ex Macedonibus leuibus armis misi per amnem nataturos. Iamque [h].IIII.tam partem fluminis pernatauerant[h], cum horrida[i] res uisu subito nobis conspecta est. Maiores elefantorum[j] corporibus hipotami[k] inter profundos aquarum emersi apparuerunt gurgites raptosque in uorticem[l] crudeli poena uiros flentibus nobis adsumpserunt[m]. [59v] Iratus tum ego ducibus qui nos in insidias deducebant[n], iubeo ex his .CL.[o] in flumen mitti. Quibus propulsis natantibusque inuicti [p]hipotami rursum[p] dignos iusta poena affecere; sed [q]maiorum decuplato numero[q] beluarum quam prius affuit. Ad spem inde contingentis cibi ubi[r] cum apparerent, ueluti formicae [s]per flumen efferuere[s]. Et [t]nequati octu[t] cum aquarum prodigiis belua[u] gereremus, iussi dato signo bucino[v] ad iter militem aptari. Quid enim manere in tali sitientibus proderat loco?

§ 16. Igitur ab hora diei [a].X.ma cum horam .XI.mam[a] iter fecissemus, uidimus homines per medium amnem factis ex harundine[b] rotundis praeteruehi nauiculis. Quos cum dulces aquas percunctaremur sua lingua ubi inueniri possint[c], dixerunt [60r] ingens nos stagnum dulcissimae aquae inuenturos, quo et ipsi nos .L.[d] itinerum duces erant deducturi. Et quo[e] facta [f]nobis sunt[f] tot stantia[g] perpeti mala, nocte tota ambulauimus siti et onere armorum confecti. Quibus necessitatibus illa quoque adiciebantur[h] incommoda, quia[i] tota nocte incursantibus leonibus ursisque, [j]et

§ 15

a insule] in insula *B*
b paucos] paucosque *B*
c desiderans] uidere desiderans *B*
d ieci] *om. B*
e sagittas] deici sagittas *B*
f...f belli coacti] bellico acti *B*
g .CC.os] ducentos *B*
h...h .IIII.tam partem fluminis pernatauerant] quartam fluminis partem natauerant *B*
i horrida] horrenda *B*
j elefantorum] elephantorum *B*
k hipotami] hippotami *B*
l uorticem] uertice *B*
m adsumpserunt] absumpserunt *B*
n deducebant] deduxerant *B*
o .CL.] centum *B*
p...p hipotami rursum] rursum hippotami *B*
q...q maiorum . . . numero] maior explicatus numerus *B*
r ubi] *om. B*
s...s per flumen efferuere] efferbuere *B*
t...t nequati octu] ne qua noctu *B*
u belua] bella *B*
v bucino] bucinae *B*

§ 16

a...a .X.ma . . . .XI.mam] decima usque ad undecimam cum *B*
b harundine] arundine *B*
c possint] possent *B*
d .L.] quinquaginta *B*
e quo] quoniam *B*
f...f nobis sunt] sunt nobis *B*
g stantia] instantia *B*
h adiciebantur] adicientur *corr. in* adiciebantur *R*
i quia] quod *B*
j...j et tigribus pardisque] tigridibus pardis *B*

tigribus pardisque[j] ac lincibus[k] pariter resistebamus, quae genera bestiarum[l] promiscua nobis in siluis occurrebant. Tandem ad horam circiter .VIII.[m] postero die, cum iam [n]uere poenae siti[n] defecissemus, ad praedictum nobis stagnum peruenimus quod erat coronatum uetustissima habundantique[o] silua, mille passus[p] patens. Cum ergo dulci aqua potata gaudio[q] alacer pecora et iumenta[r] cum exercitu [s]refecta sunt moxque [60v] cum[s] lassa quadrupedia militem[t] refecissem, meti[u] castra in longum stadia [v].XXII. totidem aeque[v] in latum collocari iussi. Quibus celeriter effectis[w] caedi nemus, ut facilior aquatoribus [x]accessus esset[x] ad stagnum, quia unicum in illis regionibus erat. Igitur inter ipsa tentoria [y]agi gerebantur[y] impedimenta, et [z]elefanti et[z] in media castrorum parte collocabantur, ut aptius contineri possint[a], si quis nocturnus casus[b] oriretur pauor ne[c] tumultusque aliquis nouus, cum iam mille .D.[d] extrinsecus essent ignes accensi sufficienti[e] silua [f]quanta uelimus[f].

§ 17. Hora[a] deinde .XI.[b] testante bucina cibum et ipse cepi et militibus capere imperaui accensis lampadibus aureis admodum duobus milibus, cum ad primos lunae radiantibus[c] ortus subito erectis [61r] caudarum aculeis a pascualibus Indiciis[d] scorpiones consuetam petentes aquationem ad castra innumeri confluxere[e], sed ad nocendum [f]promptissima sunt[f]. Haec prodigia [g]insecunda est inmensa est[g] cerastrarum[h] humidarumque serpentum[i] uariis distincta coloribus, nam quaedam rubentibus squamis[j] erant, quaedam nigri uel[k] candidi coloris, quaedam auri fulgori consimiles[l] inspiciebantur – sibilabat tota regio – non paruum nobis inferens[m] metum; sed frontem castrorum densaueramus[n] clipeis et in manibus longas habebamus[o] hastas, quarum acutissimis spiculis malas pestes configebamus et ignibus plures aliquando necabamus. Quae res nos prope duas horas in eo opere sollicitos tenuit.

[k] lincibus] lyncibus *B*
[l] bestiarum] ferarum *B*
[m] .VIII.] octauam *B*
[n...n] uere . . . siti] siti fere *B*
[o] habundantique] abundantique *B*
[p] passus] passus tamen *B*
[q] gaudio] gaudia *corr. in* gaudio R
[r] iumenta] impedimenta *B*
[s...s] refecta . . . cum] pariter et *B*
[t] militem] militum *B*
[u] meti] *om. B*
[v...v] .XII. . . . aeque] uiginti duo totidemque *B*
[w] effectis] erectis iubeo *B*
[x...x] accessus esset] esset accessus *B*
[y...y] agi gerebantur] aggerebantur *B*
[z...z] elefanti et] elephanti *B*
[a] possint] possent *B*
[b] casus] casu *B*
[c] ne] *om. B*
[d] .D.] quingenti *B*
[e] sufficienti] sufficiente *B*
[f...f] quanta uelimus] quantum uellemus *B*

§ 17
[a] Hora] *om. B*
[b] .XI.] *om. B*
[c] radiantibus] radiantes *B*
[d] Indiciis] Indici *B*
[e] confluxere] confluxere tumultu acciti nostro an siti incertum erat *B*
[f...f] promptissima sunt] promptissimi erant *B*
[g..g] insecunda . . . est] est insecuta immensa uis *B*
[h] cerastrarum] cerastarum *B*
[i] serpentum] serpentium *B*
[j] squamis] suauis *corr. in* squamis *R*
[k] uel] et *B*
[l] consimiles] similes *B*
[m] inferens] inferentes *B*
[n] densaueramus] densabamus *B*
[o] habebamus] habemus *corr. in* habebamus *R*

§ 18. Potata[a] aqua minores [61v] serpentes[b] abire coeperunt[c], maiores cum ingenti gaudio nostro[d] latebras petierunt, cum ad horam noctis tertiam aliquam sperantibus nobis requiem binorum ternorumque capitum cristati serpentes indicio[e] columnarum grossitudine, [f]aliquantulo maiores[f], ad potandum aquam ex uicinis montium speluncis processere oribus squamisque suis humum adterentes[g]; quorum pectora erecta[h] cum trisulcis linguis fauces exercebant[i] scintillantibus ueneno oculis; quorum alitus[j] quoque erat pestifer. Cum his hora non amplius una debellauimus, .XXX.[k] seruis et .XX.[l] militibus amissis.

§ 19. Orabam duces[a] Macedones, ne aduersis casibus cederent nene[b] deficerent [c]animo in periculis[c], quamquam et ipsorum dura[d] patientia. [e]Omnes officiebant[e] operi. [62r] Post serpentes cantri[f] immodicae multitudinis, corcodrillorum pellibus contecti ad castra uenerunt; quae prodigia duritia toracata[g] ferrum respuerunt[h]: multa ignibus usta, multa sese[i] in stagnum receperunt. Iam nos in[j] uigiliis inquietos .V.ta[k] noctis hora bucina ammonebat[l] quiescendum. Sed affuere albi leones taurorum comparandi magnitudine[m]: cum ingenti murmure concussis ceruicibus, stantibus alte iubis in modum fulminum in nos impetum faciunt exceptique uenabulis ruunt. Tantus repentinus oriebatur[n] tumultus cumulante caeca nocte; nec minus apri ingentis formae, iactis[o] ueluti uallo horrentibus metuendi, mixti maculosis [p]lincibus trigribusque[p] et horribilibus pantheris, miscebantur[q] proelia nullae[r] iam pesti comparandi[s]. [62v] Sed et uespertilionum uis ingens columbis[t] corporibus aequales in ora uultusque nostros inferebantur[u], habentes dentes in morem hominum quibus artus militum uiolabant.

§ 18

a Potata] pota *corr. in* potata *R*
b serpentes] *om. B*
c coeperunt] coeperunt serpentes *B*
d nostro] nostras *corr. in* nostro *R*
e indicio] Indici *B*
f...f aliquantulo maiores] aliquantulum proceriores *B*
g adterentes] atterentes *B*
h erecta] et recta *corr. in* erecta *R*
i exercebant] exserebant *B*
j alitus] halitus *B*
k .XXX.] triginta *B*
l .XX.] uiginti *B*

§ 19

a duces] *om. B*
b nene] neue *B*
c...c animo in periculis] *om. B*
d dura] dura esset *B*
e...e Omnes officiebant] Omnes se afficiebant *B*
f cantri] cancri *B*
g toracata] thoracae *B*
h respuerunt] respuebant *B*
i sese] se *B*
j in] *om. B*
k .V.ta] quinta *B*
l ammonebat] admonebat *B*
m magnitidine] magnitudinibus *B*
n oriebatur] oriebantur *corr. in* oriebatur *R*
o iactis] setis *B*
p...p lincibus trigribusque] lyncibus tigridibusque *B*
q miscebantur] miscebant *B*
r nullae] nulli *B*
s comparandi] comparanda *B*
t columbis] columbinis *B*
u inferebantur] ferebantur *B*

§ 20. Una praeterea noui generis bestia maior elephanto apparuit[a], tribus armata in fronte cornibus, quam Indii[b] appellare dentemtyrannum[c] soliti sunt, equo simile caput gerens atri coloris. Haec potata[d] aqua intuens castra in nos subito impetum dedit nec ingens[e] compositis tardatur ardoribus. Ad quam sustinendam cum opposuissem Macedonum manum, .XXVI.[f] occidit, .LII.[g] calcatos inutiles fecit uixque ipsis defixa[h] uenabulis.

§ 21. Ante lucanum deinde tempusculo[a] pestes uenere candido uersecolore[b] in modum zonarum[c], cum quibus mures Indici in castra pergebant [63r] uulpibus similes, quorum morsu uulnerata quadrupedia statim exspirabant[d]; hominibus idem morsus non usque ad interitum nocebat[e]. Appropinquante luce nocticoraces uenere aues uulturibus similes, [f]corpore inmanitate[f] superabant, colore fuluo, rostro pedibusque nigris. Totam stagni[g] compleuere ripam nullam[h] nobis perniciem inferentes[i], sed solitos pisces [j]cum unguibus extrahebant[j]. Quas nos aues neque fugare neque abigere ausi eramus; [k]cum suis[k] unguibus de conspectu nostro abiere.

§ 22. Tum[a] ego locorum demonstratores qui nos semper per[b] insidias deducebant, pessime meritos, crurifragio puniri iussi ut et nocte uiui spirantesque a serpentibus consumerentur, ut nos consumi [63v] uoluerunt. Manus quoque eis confringi imperaui, ut merito pro factis suis uterentur supplicio.

§ 23. Habita deinde contione, ut fortes milites essent neue aduersis ut feminae casibus cederent[a], castra concentu bucinae[b] repente ad Nothi[c] uenti [d]spiramina tendi[d], ubi[e] collectis barbarorum Indorumque uiris noua conspirantes[f] bella cognoueram. Et[g] militibus meis ingentes erant animi, quippe[h] quibus et census uictoriarum suppeditabat et felicibus[i]. Relictis igitur[j] periculosissimis locis munitum

§ 20

[a] apparuit] affuit *B*

[b] Indii] Indii *B*

[c] dentemtyrannum] dentityrannum *B*

[d] potata] pota *corr. in* potata *R*

[e] ingens] ignium *B*

[f] .XXVI.] triginta sex *B*

[g] .LII.] duos et quinquaginta *B*

[h] defixa] defixa est *B*

§ 21

[a] tempusculo] tempus caelo *B*

[b] uersecolore] uersicolores *B*

[c] zonarum] ranarum *B*

[d] exspirabant] expirabant *corr. in* exspirabant *R*

[e] nocebat] nocebit *corr. in* nocebat *R* nocebant *B*

[f...f] corpore inmanitate] corporum immanitate *B*

[g] stagni] sagni *corr. in* stagni *R*

[h] nullam] non *B*

[i] inferentes] ferentes *B*

[j...j] cum unguibus extrahebant] consumebant *B*

[k...k] cum suis] cum siccis *corr. in* cum suis *R* cunctae uero siccatis *B*

§ 22

[a] Tum] Tunc *B*

[b] per] in *B*

§ 23

[a] cederent] deficerent *B*

[b] bucinae] bucinarum *B*

[c] Nothi] Noti *B*

[d...d] spiramina tendi] spiracula tetendi *B*

[e] ubi] ubi a *B*

[f] conspirantes] conspirari *B*

[g] Et] *om. B*

[h] quippe] *om. B*

[i] felicibus] felicitas *B*

[j] igitur] *om. B*

uix tandem iter calcauimus et in loca Bactrianorum auro diuitiisque opulenta peruenimus; benignisque[k] excepti commeatibus[l], cum Persarum uicinia[m] adiacerent agri, in reparando [64r] bello castra .XX.[n] dies statui otio facta[o].

§ 24. Mox dierum [a].IIII.or itenere[a] peruenimus ubi cum collecto Porus[b] consederat exercitu[c] propriae potius[d] deditioni [e]quam proelio[e]. Nam et commeatus nobis palam non ut hostis dedit potestatem, cupiensque[f] me nosse et[g] milites meos subinde comitantes[h] interrogabant[i] ubi ego essem quid[j] agerem. Qui cum incerta responderent, ipse auditis eius interrogationibus – omnia enim regi[k] magno Macedonum referebant[l] – sumpto itaque[m] habitu militari depositoque[n] meo cultu [o]solito perueneram[o] in castra uini[p] et carnis [q]quiddam empturus[q]; casuque Porus sciscitans me interrogauit[r] quid faceret Alexander aut cuius esset aetatis. Quem ludens [64v] mendacio temporis 'Tamquam homo senior', inquam, 'dux noster in tabernaculo [s]accenso ignis calere refecit[s].' Tum[t] gaudio alacer, quia cum decrepito sene esset proelium commissurus, cum esset ipse iuuenis, elatusque[u] tumore 'Quid ergo cur[v]', inquit, 'non respicit aetatem suam?' Respondi ei[w] uno id proposito ignorare me quid faceret Alexander, cum essem gregarius[x] ex Macedonico miles exercitu. Tradidit mihi minis plenam epistolam quam regi Alexandro darem; pollicitusque[y] est praemium. Cui irans[z] dixi futurum, ut in manus eius hae litterae peruenirem[a]; reuersusque protinus in castra et antequam legerem et postquam legi epistolam, magno risu sum dissolutus. Cuius tibi et matri meae sororibusque meis [65r], ut superbam inclinatamque barbari temeritatem miraremini[b], exemplar misi[c].

k benignisque] benigneque *B*
l commeatibus] a commeantibus *B*
m uicinia] confinia *B*
n .XX.] uiginti *B*
o facta] facto *B*

§ 24
a...a .IIII.or itenere] quattuor itinere *B*
b Porus] *om. B*
c exercitu] exercitu Porus *B*
d potius] *om. B*
e...e quam proelio] magis quam proelio se commissurus *B*
f cupiensque] cupidusque *B*
g et] *om. B*
h comitantes] commeantes *B*
i interrogabant] interrogabat *B*
j quid] quidue *B*
k regi] mihi regi *B*
l referebant] referebantur *B*
m itaque] *om. B*
n depositoque] positoque *B*
o...o solito perueneram] perueni *B*
p uini] ut uini *B*
q...q quiddam empturus] quidam emptor *B*
r interrogauit] interrogabat *B*
s...s accenso . . . refecit] se accenso igni calefacit *B*
t Tum] Tum ille *B*
u elatusque] elatus *B*
v cur] *om. B*
w ei] *om. B*
x gregarius] gregorius *corr. in* gregarius *R*
y pollicitusque] pollicitus *B*
z irans] iurans *B*
a peruenirem] peruenirent *B*
b mirarimini] mirareis *B*

c misi] *post* misi *textum epistolae Pori add. B*: Epistola Pori ad Alexandrum. Rex Indiae Porus Alexandro. Miratur prudentia nostra, quod Perside calcata Porum iuuenem senex et regnum Indiae omnibus diuitiis opulentum, armis munitum, nimis populosum, inter alia mundi regna nominatissimum tam parua manu pertinaci temeritate aggredi ausus sis. Sed nec Darium nobis nec Persas Indis ulla ratione aequiperandos credideris. Et quoniam de militibus bellorum periculis innumeros amisisti, datur a nobis licentia reuertendi aut residuis qui tecum sunt, ut maximae aetati tuae parcas, que uix sufficit tibi, si Macedoniam redire disponas, aut deditionem tuam nobis offeras, ne capitis tui damnum incurras.

§ 25. Mox contuli cum Indis manum superatisque his ita ut uolebam erepta armis [a]Poro regna[a] restitui. Qui, ut ei superatus[b] honor datus[c] est, mihi thesauros suos manifestauit quos esse[d] ignorabam; ex quibus me et comites meos et uniuersum ditauit exercitum factusque est[e] amicus ex hoste [f]Macedones ad Erculis[f] Liberique trophea me[g] deduxit. In orientis autem ultimis horis[h] aurea utraque deorum [i]constituta erant[i] simulacra. Quae an solida essent ego scire cupiens, omnia iussi[j] perforari[k] [l]et rursum cum uiderem[l], simili metallo compleui, Liberumque et Erculem[m] deiectis uictimis conplacui[n].

§ 26. Ultra deinde [65v] progressuri, si quid memorabile cerneremus, nihil praeter desertos [a]ad oceanum[a] campos siluasque ac montes audiuimus, in quibus[b] elephanti et serpentes esse[c] dicebantur. Pergebam tunc[d] ad mare nauigare[e] oceanum. Quem quoniam tenebrosum uadosumque mihi locorum nicolae[f] affirmabant, quodque Herculis et Liberi ausus[g] esset temptandi[h], praestantissimorum deorum, tanto maiorem me ipsis uelle uideri [i]uel quanta ultra potentiam[i] mortalium et[j] sacra praeterire uestigia. Quibus honoratis conlaudatisque[k] sinistram partem Indiae perscrutari[l] institui, ne quid mihi in ignotis subtraheretur locis, Poro rege non detractante[m], ne[n] abdita tegere[o] uideretur regni sui bona.

§ 27. Palus erat sicca et canna[a] habundans. Per quam [66r] cum transitum[b] temptaremus, belua noui generis prosiliuit serrato tergo[c], duo capita habens, [d]alterum lunae[d] simile, [e]hippotamo pectore[e], corcodrilli[f] gerens alterum simillimum duris munitum dentibus, quod caput duos milites repentino occidit ictu. Quam ferreis uix umquam comminuimus malleis, quam hostis[g] non ualebamus[h] transfigere. Ammirati[i] diu nouitatem eius.

§ 25

a...a Poro regna] regna Poro *B*

b superatus] insperatus *B*

c datus] donatus *B*

d esse] *om. B*

e est] *om. B*

f...f Macedones ad Erculis] Macedonibus in Herculis *B*

g me] *om. B*

h horis] oris *B*

i...i constituta erant] constituerat *B*

j iussi] *om. B*

k perforari] perforaui *corr. in* perforari *R*

l...l iussi perforari et rursum cum uiderem] perforaui et id ipsum ut uidi solida *B*

m Erculem] Herculem *B*

n conplacui] placaui *B*

§ 26

a...a ad oceanum] in oceano *B*

b quibus] quibus esse *B*

c esse] *om. B*

d tunc] *om. B*

e nauigare] tamen uolens, si possem, orbi terrarum circumfluum nauigare *B*

f nicolae] incolae *B*

g ausus] ultra ausus nemini *B*

h temptandi] temptandum *B*

i...i uel ... potentiam] *post* potentiam *add.* quod patientiam *in marg.*; quam in patientiam *B*

j et] *om. B*

k conlaudatisque] collaudatisque *B*

l perscrutari] scrutari *B*

m detrectante] detractante *B*

n ne] ne qua *B*

o tegere] celare *B*

§ 27

a canna] coeno *B*

b transitum] transire *B*

c tergo] tergo hippotami pectore *B*

d...d alterum lunae] unum leaenae *B*

e...e hippotamo pectore] *om. B*

f corcodrilli] corcodrillo *B*

g hostis] hastis *B*

h ualebamus] ualuimus *B*

i Ammirati] Admirati autem sumus *B*

§ 28. Peruenimus deinde ad siluas Indorum ultimas. Ubi cum castra per .L.[a] in longum et per[b] latum fere .XX.[c] stadia collocauimus[d] iuxta amnem Buemar, coeperamus uelle epulari sub nocte hora diei .XI., cum subito pauolatores[e] lignatoresque examinati[f] omnes simul aduenientes nuntiant[g], ut celerius arma caperemus: uenire [66v] e siluis elephantorum inmensos greges ad expugnanda castra. Imperaui [h]ego Thesalicis[h] equitibus, ut ascenderent equos secumque extollerent[i] sues, quorum grunnitus timere bestias noueram, et occurrere quam primum elephantis. Iussi deinde alios cum hostis[j] armatos subsequi equites, et tubicines omnes in prima adesse acie, equos insidentes praecedere, pedites [k]omnes remanere in castris[k]. Ipse cum Poro rege et equitatu procedens uideo examina bestiarum in nos erectis promuscidibus tendentia. Quarum[l] terga nigra[m] et candida et rubri coloris[n] et uaria[o] quaedam erant[p]. Hos Porus rex[q] capi abillis[r] mihi ad[s] usus bellorum affirmabat facileque auerti posses[t], ab equitibus uerberare[u] sues non desi[67r]sterent. [v]Quod nihilhominus fiebat[v]; nec mora trepidantes elephanti conuersi sunt; quam[w] plures quam pugnae priores saltus petere caeperunt[x] bucinis hominum grunitibusque[y] suum attoniti. Quorum[z] equites caedendo poplites admodum .DCCCC.LXXX. occidimus, detractisque[a] cornibus et dentibus insigni honustus praeda in castra perueni[b]. Quieta nox fuit usque ad lucem omnesque somno refecti.

§ 29. Primum[a] deinde aurorae diluculo in alias Indiae profecti regiones nam[b] in campo potenti[c] mulieres uirosque[d] pilosos in modum ferarum toto corpore uidimus, pedum altos nouenum[e]. Hos Indii[f] faunos appellant; hi assueti fluminibus[g] quam terris erant, [67v] crudo pisce tantummodo et aquarum haustu uiuentes. Quos cum

§ 28

a .L.] quinquaginta *B*

b per] *om. B*

c .XX.] *om. B*

d collocauimus] collocauissemus *B*

e pauolatores] pabulatores *B*

f examinati] exanimes *B*

g nuntiant] nuntiabant *B*

h...h ego Thesalicis] ergo Thessalicis *B*

i extollerent] tollerent *B*

j hostis] hastis *B*

k...k omnes . . .. castris] remanere omnes in castris iussi *B*

l Quarum] Quorum *B*

m terga] terga et *B*

n coloris] caloris *corr. in* coloris *R*

o uaria] *om. B*

p prant] erant uaria *B*

q rex] *om. B*

r abillis] habiles *B*

s ad] in *B*

t posses] posse si *B*

u uerberare] uerberari *B*

v...v Quod . . . fiebat] Qui nihilominus fugiebant *B*

w quam] tam *B*

x ceperunt] coepere *B*

y grunitibusque] grunnitibus *B*

z Quorum] Quorum nos *B*

a detractisque] destructisque *corr. in* detractisque *R*

b perueni] *post* perueni *add. B*: Iussi tunc clipeis et lorica uallum praecingi, ne quid iniurie noctu elephantorum uiolentia ferarumque aliarum afferret.

§ 29

a Primum] Primo *B*

b nam] *om. B*

c potenti] patenti *B*

d uirosque] uiresque *corr.* in uirosque *R*

e nouenum] nouem *B*

f Indii] Indi *B*

g fluminibus] fluminibus nec non et stagno *B*

adire uellemus uicinius, Ebigmaritis[h] fluminis se inmersere uorticibus[i]. [j]Cenocephalis deinde ingentibus[j] plena inuenimus nemora, qui nos adlacessere temptabant et iectis[k] sagittis fugiebant. Iam deserta intrantibus nobis loca nihil dignum spectaculo ab Indis ultra superesse ferebatur[l].

§ 30. Igitur [a]rursus ad occidentem[a] signa conuerti imperaui, ut ex eo loco usque ad duodecimum miliarium castra uicina equationi[b] poneremus. [c]Etiam erecta cuncta[c] tentoria erant largique ignes accensi, cum repente Euri uenti tanta uis flantis exorta est, ut omnia tabernacula principiaque maiorum[d] in modum stupentibus nobis. [e]Quadrupedi atque[e] multo [68r] uehementius uexabantur exitu[f] scintillarum[g] et titionum his[h] in terga uenientibus[i] adurebantur. Tum ortor milites quia noctuali[j] tempore id accidisset, non deorum ira Octobre[k] mense autumnoque urgueret[l]. Uix tandem recollectis sarcinis ex integro in priore[m] ualle sedem castrorum inuenimus[n] ordinatisque rebus omnibus cenare milites[o] iussi. Nam et flatus[p] Euri ceciderat sed[q] frigus ingens uespertino adcrebrescebat[r] tempore. Cadere mox in modum uellerum [s]inmenses niues coeperunt[s]. Quarum aggerationem intueris[t] ne in[u] castra cumularent[v], calcare militem niuem uiuebam[w], ut quam primum iniuria pedum [x]tabescerent, prodebantur[x] et ignes aliquatenus, [68v] qui niue paene erant extincti. Una tunc[y] res fuit saluti, quod momento[z] temporis hae dilapsae sunt[a] imbre superueniente[b] largo. Quem protinus atra nubes subsecuta[c] uisaeque sunt[d] nubes ardentes de caelo tamquam faces decedere[e], ut incendio earum totus campus arderet. Uerebantur dicere ne deorum ira nos[f] premeret, quod[g] homo Herculis Liberique uestigia transgredi conatus essem. Iussique[h] milites scissas uestes opponere ignibus. Nox serena continuo

h Ebigmaritis] marini *B*
i uorticibus] uerticibus *B*
j...j Cenocephalis deinde ingentibus] Cynocephalis ingentibus deinde *B*
k iectis] eiectis *B*
l ferebatur] ferebantur *corr. in* ferebatur *R* referebatur *B*

§ 30
a...a rursus ad occidentem] aditurus Fasiacen, unde ueneramus *B*
b equationi] aquationi *B*
c...c Etiam . . . cuncta] Atque cuncta erecta *B*
d maiorum] nostra conturbauerit euerteritque maiorem *B*
e...e Quadrupedi atque] Quadrupedia *B*
f exitu] exituque *B*
g scintillarum] seintillarum *R*
h his] *om. B*
i uenientibus] uenientium *B*
j noctuali] equinoctiali *B*
k Octobre] quod Octobri *B*
l urgueret] urgeret *B*
m priore] apriciore *B*
n inuenimus] inueni *B*
o milites] militem *B*
p flatus] status *corr. in* flatus *R*
q sed] et *B*
r adcrebrescebat] accrescebat *B*
s...s inmenses. . . ceperunt] immensae coeperunt niues *B*
t intueris] metuens *B*
u in] *om. B*
v cumularent] cumularentur *B*
w uiuebam] iubeo *B*
x...x tabescerent, prodebantur] tabesceret, proderentur *B*
y tunc] tamen *B*
z momento] memento *corr. in* momento *R*
a sunt] sunt niues *B*
b superueniente] ueniente *B*
c subsecuta] secuta est *B*
d sunt] *om. B*
e decedere] decidere *B*
f nos] *om. B*
g quod] quod ego *B*
h Iussique] Iussi igitur *B*

reddita est nobis orantibus. Tunc[i] ignes ex integro accenduntur et a securis aepulae[j] capiuntur et triduo continuo sine sole claro id nobis accidit pendente minaci nubilo.

§ 31. Et ego sepultis admodum .D. militibus qui inter ni[69r]ues perierunt, castra inde mutari imperaui. Nam et edita caelo promuntoria ad oceanum in Ethiopio[a] uidimus [b]Ethneos quoque[b] montes et antrum[c], quo perditos inmisimus, quia dicebantur tertia die febribus mori qui speluncam dei intrauissent[d]. Quod fuisse manifestum[e] mortibus eorum probauimus, quia intrari praeter religionem et[f] muneribus specus[g] non poterat[h]. Supplex orabam numina, ut me regem totius orbis terrarum cum sublimibus tropheis triumphantem[i] in Macedoniam Olimpiadi matri meae remitterent. Quam rem frustra me petere ita cognoui, quoniam dum sciscitor[j], si quid etiam adhuc [k]uideri possim[k] dignum ammiratione aut memoria, omnibus indicentibus[l] [69v] nihil aliud memorabile inueniri[m] posse in illis[n] locis quam quod cognouimus, [o]tunc deuerti[o] signa in Fasiacen imperaui[p], antiohci[q] uenti flatum secutus.

§ 32. Dumque[a] in itinere, sumpto[b] agmen sub signis me ducente, duo senes[c] facti sunt nobis[d] obuiam. Quos cum interrogarem, siquid[e] nossent in illa regione dignum memoria[f] spectaculum, responderunt mihi esse uiam decem non amplius dierum, per quam difficilis [g]esset tunc[g] accessus propter penuriam aque tantisque impedimentis, si cum uniuerso pergere [h]exercitu uellem[h]. Ceterum si commeatus .XL. milia[i] hominum proponerem propter [j]bestiosa satis[j] loca, posse mihi contingere, ut aliquid[k] incredibile perspicerem negotium. Tum ego [l]quo facto[l] laetus [70r] 'Dicite mihi', inquam, 'duo senes', humanitatis lege eos mulcens, 'quid sit illud quod mihi tam illustre et tam magnificum pollicemini'. Tum unus exilaratus blanda me[m] uoce: 'Uidebis', inquit, 'rex, quicumque es, duas solis et lunae arbores Indice et Grece loquentes, quarum [n]una uirile lignum[n] solis, alterum [o]lunae femininum est[o], et ab his quae tibi instent[p] bona aut mala nosse poteris.

i Tunc] Tum *B*
j aepulae] nobis epulae *B*

§ 31
a Ethiopio] Aethiopia *B*
b...b Ethneos quoque] et Enesios quoque uidimus *B*
c antrum] antrum Liberi *B*
d intrauissent] introissent *B*
e manifestum] manistum *corr. in* manifestum *R*
f et] et sine *B*
g specus] *om. B*
h poterat] poterat specus *B*
i triumphantem] triumphantem *R*
j sciscitor] sciscitator *corr. in* sciscitor *R*
k...k uideri possim] uidere possem *B*
l indiscentibus] India discentibus *B*
m inueniri] inuenire *corr. in* inueniri *R*
n illis] his *B*
o...o tunc deuerti] iussi diuerti *B*
p imperaui] *om. B*
q antiohci] antea Noti *B*

§ 32
a Dumque] Tumque *B*
b sumpto] sumptum *B*
c senes] senes nobis *B*
d nobis] *om. B*
e siquid] numquid *B*
f memoria] aliquid ad *B*
g...g esset tunc] tamen *B*
h...h exercitu uellem] uellem exercitu *B*
i milia] milium *B*
j...j bestiosa satis] angustas semitas et bestiosa *B*
k aliquid] aliquod *B*
l...l quo facto] eo responso *B*
m me] mea *B*
n...n una . . . lignum] lignum uirile est *B*
o...o lune femininum est] femineum est lunae *B*
p instent] instant *B*

§ 33. Qua re tam incredibili illudi me a barbaris senibus[a] existimans, poena eos inpingi et aliqua contumelia iussi notari, illa[b] dicens: 'Itane eo usque[c] maiestas mea peruenit ab occidente usque ad orientem, ut a senibus barbaris ac decrepitis[d] posse uidear?' Quibus iurantibus [70v] se nihil falsi comminisci[e], experiri [f]me modo[f] posse an uera dicerent, appariturum in[g] breui id non esse uanum, orantibus quoque[h] amicis comitibusque meis, ne tantae rei experimento fraudaremur, .XL. milia mecum eum[i] equitatu traxi, remissis in Fassiacen[j] copiis cum quibusdam praefectis exercituque cuncto, elephantis[k] et impedimentis omnibus [l]et rege Poro[l]. Mox lecto robore iuuentutis ammiranda[m] uisuri spectacula ducentibus Indorum senibus iter arripuimus; qui nos, ut dixerunt[n], per auia[o] egentia plerumque aquarum [p]et per tot serpentum[p] ferarumque loca deduxerunt usque[q] in proximum[r] oraculi sedem. De quibus feris et serpentibus, quia innumerae et Indica lingua [71r] erant uocitatae, scribendum tibi non putaui.

§ 34. Cum adpropinquaremus regioni a nobis petitae, uidimus feminas uirosque aliquos pantherarum tigridumque pellibus contectos; a quibus cum requireremus[a] quinam hominum essent, Indos se sua lingua esse dicebant. [b]Locus autem[b] erat largus, ture et [c]oppobalsamo inmenso habundabat[c], quae plurima in[d] ramis [e]suorum nascebantur[e] nemorum et uesci incolae eius regionis consueuerant.

§ 35. Et cum sacrarium nobis praedictum et multis incognitum incessissemus, pedum amplius .X. statura altior, nigro corpore, dentibus [a]caninis, antistes[a] oraculi apparuit, perforatis auribus, ex quibus uniones dependebant, et erat pellibus uestitus. Et[b] cum [71v] nos[c] more suo[d] salutaret [e]metum simulatione silentioque texit. Et cum interrogaret[e] quid ego uenissem, dixi me cupientem inspicere [f]arbores sacras[f] solis et[g]

§ 33

[a] senibus] senis *corr. in* senibus *R*
[b] illa] ita *B*
[c] usque] *om. B*
[d] decrepitis] decrepitis illudi *B*
[e] comminisci] commiscere *B*
[f...f] me modo] modo me *B*
[g] in] *om. B*
[h] quoque] *om. B*
[i] eum] cum *B*
[j] Fassiacen] Fasiacen *B*
[k] elephantis] elephantis et rege Poro *B*
[l...l] et rege Poro] *om. B*
[m] ammiranda] admirabilia *B*
[n] dixerunt] diximus *B*
[o] auia] immania et *B*
[p...p] et per tot serpentum] plenaque serpentium *B*
[q] usque] *om. B*
[r] proximum] proximam *B*

§ 34

[a] requireremus] requiremus *corr. in* requireremus *R* quaerimus *B*
[b..b] Locus autem] Lucus *B*
[c...c] oppobalsamo . . . habundabat] opobalsamo abundans *B*
[d] in] *om. B*
[e...e] suorum nascebantur] eorum innascebantur *B*

§ 35

[a...a] caninis antistes] canis antestes *corr. in* caninis antistes *R*
[b] Et] Atque *B*
[c] nos] me *B*
[d] suo] rituque *B*
[e...e] metum . . . interrogaret] interrogare coepit *B*
[f...f] arbores sacras] sacras arbores *B*
[g] et] ac *B*

lunae. Tum barbarus[h]: 'Si a coitu[i] puerili', [j]inquid, 'femineoque tactu[j] uacas, scilicet intrabis diuinum locum[k].' Astantibus mecum[l] amicis et commilitonibus meis circiter trecentis ponere anulos uestesque cunctas calciamentis[m] imperauit per[n] omnia homini, ut paperemus[o] religioni. .XI. [p]hora diei et spectabat[p] sacerdos solis occasum: nam solis arborem loqui ac responsa[q] dare ad primos iubaris ortus affirmabat. Item noctis eadem tempora custodire lunae narrabant[r] arborem. Quae res mihi [s]plus mendacio [72r] quam[s] ueritati similis uidebatur.

§ 36. Igitur perambulare totum [a]incipio nemus[a], quod intra parietem erat non magno aedificatum opere, [b]uideo oppobalsamum[b] cum optimo odore ex[c] omnibus ubique[d] arborum ramis habundantissime manantem[e]; cuius odore captus et ipse clibulis[f] praeuellebam de corticibus et idem comites mei faciebant. In medio[g] autem luco[h] sacrae arbores consistebant diuersis [i]frondium generibus[i] circumastantibus. Hae [j]autem arbores pedum altae centenum erant[j], quas hibrionas[k] Indi appellant. [l]Cum eas[l] mirarer diceremque frequentibus inbribus in tantum creuisse, sacerdos affirmabat mihi numquam in his locis pluuiam neque feram aut auem aut [72v] ullam adire serpentem; [m]illas autem arbores[m] antiquitus ab Indorum maioribus consecratas[n] soli et lunae[o] uberrimis lacrimis commouere[p] de numinum suorum statu timentes. Et cum sacrificare instituerem et uictimas immolare, prohibitus sum a sacerdote, quia[q] negabat licere aut thus in eo sacrario ignorari[r] aut animal ullum interfici, sed uolutus[s] truncis arborum oscula dare orareque solem et lunam praecepit[t] ut ueridica mihi darent responsa. Quod ego cum facturus essem, interrogandum tamen sacerdotem existimaui, Indice an Grece mihi essent arbores responsurae. Tum ille inquit: 'Utraque lingua solis arbor pronuntiat futura, lunae Graeco sermone incipit, In[73r]dico finit[u]'. Dum ista[v] geruntur, uidimus[w] ab occidente iubare fulgente[x] Phoebi radiis

h barbarus] barbaris *corr. in* barbarus *R*
i coitu] coitu inquit *B*
j...j inquid . . . tactu] et femineo contactu *B*
k locum] lucum *B*
l mecum] *om. B*
m calciamentis] cum calciamentis *B*
n per] parui per *B*
o paperemus] pareremus *B*
p...p hora . . . spectabat] hora diei exspectabat *B*
q responsa] responso *corr. in* responsa *R*
r narrabant] enarrabat *B*
s...s plus . . . quam] mendacio magis quam *B*

§ 36
a...a incipio nemus] nemus incipio *B*
b...b uideo oppobalsamum] uideoque opobalsamum *B*
c ex] *om. B*
d ubique] undique *B*
e manantem] manans *B*
f clibulis] clibulas *B*
g medio] media *B*
h luco] parte luci *B*
i...i frondium generibus] generibus frondium *B*
j...j autem . . . erant] pedum altae centum erant arbores *B*
k hibrionas] brebionas *B*
l...l Cum eas] Eas cum *B*
m...m illas . . . arbores] terminos *B*
n consecratas] consecratos *B*
o lunae] lunae affirmabat easque in eclipsi solis et lunae *B*
p commouere] commoueri *B*
q quia] qui *B*
r ignorari] igni uri *B*
s uolutus] uolutos *B*
t praecepit] *om. B*
u finit] fuit *corr. in* finit *R*
v ista] ea *B*
w uidimus] uidemus *B*
x fulgente] fulgentibus *B*

percussa[y] cacumina et sacerdos ait: 'Sursum', inquit, 'omnes intuemini et de quibus quisque rebus consulturus est occulto[z] cogitet silentio, nemo palam pronuntiet.'

§ 37. Tum ego et amici et commilitones accuratius sumus intuiti[a] ne inter nemorum densitatem aliqua seductione in morem uoce[b] docta nos hominum aliquis eluderet. [c]Moxque nullo dolo[c] interueniente ad[d] cacumina [e]arborum ramos[e] perspeximus: stantibus nobis comminus diuina [f]auribus occupamur[f] oracula. Cogitabam enim si deuicto orbe terrarum in patriam triumphans ad Olimpiadem matrem sororesque meas carissimas possim[g] reuerti, cum subito [73v] Indico sermone tenuissimo arbor respondit: 'Inuicte bellis Alexander, ut consuluisti[h] numen[i], unus eris orbis terrarum dominus, sed uiuus in patriam non reuerteris amplius, quoniam fata tua[j] ita de tuo capite statuerunt.' Haec ego audiens mente perculsus sum: displicuit enim[k] quod tam multos adduxi mecum ad sacras arbores. Simul et amici mei et comites mei qui mecum erant[l] fleuerunt ualde et contristati sunt. Quos ego partim minis partim muneribus consolatus sum, praecepique eis ut nemini haec responsa dicerent. [m]Rursus autem[m] lunae oracula[n] auditurus, quae media nocte posse fieri sacerdos affirmabat, quoniam tunc luna erat oritura, assumpsi mecum tres fidelissimos amicos, Perdicam [74r] et Ditanam[o] et Philotamn[p], quia nullum metuebam in illo loco, nec [q]me quisquam timebat[q], ubi neminem fas erat interfici. Iterumque lucum intrantes iuxta [r]seras arbores[r] constitimus et mox solita consuetudine adoramus.

§ 38. Consulens igitur ubi moriturus essem, [a]et cum[a] ad primum lunae ortum percussa[b] cornu splendoreque accepto arbor Graece respondit: 'Alexander', inquit, 'plenum[c] iam aetatis finem habes. Sed sequenti[d] anno mense nono Babilonis[e] morieris: a quo minime speras, decipieris.' Tum [f]ego effudi lacrimas[f] et amici mei circumstantes[g] flebant. Nullumque ab his dolum aut scelus resurrecturum aestimabam[h] sed magis pro mea salute mori paratos, [74v] neque[i] ego quicquam de fidelissimis [j]amicis meis[j] consulerem, aut[k] illos cauendos[l] Alexandro praemoneret

y percussa] percussa arborum *B*
z occulto] occulte *B*

§ 37
a intuiti] intuitu *corr. in* intuiti *R*
b uoce] ueterem *B*
c...c Moxque nullo dolo] mox *B*
d ad] nullo tali dolo usque ad *B*
e...e arborum ramos] ramosque *B*
f...f auribus occupamur] aures occupant *B*
g possim] possem *B*
h consuluisti] consiluisti *corr. in* consuluisti *R*
i numen] unus *B*
j tua] *om. B*
k enim] enim mihi *B*
l erant] uenerant *B*
m...m Rursus autem] Rursum *B*
n oracula] oraculo *corr. in* oracula *R*
o Ditanam] Ditoricam *B*
p Philotamn] Philotam *B*
q...q me quisquam timebat] a me quicquam erat metuendam *B*
r...r seras arbores] arbores sacras *B*

§ 38
a...a et cum] tum *B*
b percussa] percusso *B*
c plenum] plenam *B*
d sequenti] sequente
e Babilonis] Babilonia *B*
f...f ego . . . lacrimas]lacrimas effudi *B*
g circumstantes] circumsistentes *B*
h aestimabam] sperabam *B*
i neque] nec *B*
j...j amicis meis] mihi amicis *B*
k aut] ut *B*
l cauendos] cauendos esse *B*

oraculum. [m]Discessum deinde[m] iam ad epulas reuertimur[n], ego animo aeger ad requiem uado. Rogantibus amicis meis[o], ne me anxietate[p] conficerem, paululum cibi contra animi uoluntatem sumere coepi neque[q], ut praesto essem ad primum solis ortum, in sacrario collocaui[r].

§ 39. Postera[a] die matutinis[b] expergefactus diluculo amicos etiam semisopere[c] somno excitos[d]. Sed adhuc ipse quoque sacerdos uelatus pellibus ferinis quiescebat, positaque ante eum in [e]tabella ebimna[e] ingens clibatura[f] erat, quae illi ex pridiani[g] cena super[75r]fuerat et culter eburneus. Nam aere et ferro et plumbo et argento sed[h] auro abundant, cadentemque[i] riuo puram ex uicino monte potant aquam homines, accubantes et quiescentes sine ullis ceruicalibus stratis[j], tantum pellibus ferarum. His [k]amictis contenti[k] uiuunt ibidem annis fere trecentis.

§ 40. Excitato igitur[a] sacerdote lucum intraui tertio consulturus [b]item mihi[b] sacratissimam solis arborem, cuius mortem [c]manum percussoris habebam cauendam quemue[c] exitum mater mea sororesque meae habiturae sint. Arbor Graece dixit: 'Si matris[d] tuae tibi insidiatorem prodidero, sublato eo facile instantia facta[e] mutabis [f]nam mihi[f] tres irascentur sorores, quod [75v] ueridico oraculo earum pensa inpedierim, Clothos[g] Lachesis Atropos. Igitur ad[h] annum et menses .VIIII. Babiloni[i] morieris, non ferro, quod suspicaris, non auro non[j] argento neque ullo metallo, sed ueneno. Mater tua [k]turpissimo miserandoque[k] exitu sepultura carebit [l]et in uia iacebit[l], praeda auium ferarumque, sororesque tuae felices erunt [m]factae diu etiam tu autem, si breue tibi superest[m] tempus, dominus tamen orbis terrarum eris. Nunc modo caue, ne nos ulterius sciscitaris; unde[n] excede terminos luci nostri et ad Fasiacen Porumque regem[o] reuertere.' Sed et [p]sacerdos emonuit, ut exiremus oboediremus pareremus dicens fletus et ululatus [76r] noster arbores offendit[p].

m...m Discessum deinde] Discessu deinde facto cum *B*
n reuertimur] reuerteremur *B*
o meis] *om. B*
p anxietate] anxietate et ieiunio *B*
q neque] meque *B*
r collocaui] collocari

§ 39
a Postera] postero *B*
b matutinis] matutino *B*
c semisopere] semisopore *B*
d excitos] excito *B*
e...e tabella ebimna] tabula *B*
f clibatura] cliba turis *B*
g pridiani] pridiana *B*
h sed] egent *B*
i cadentemque] opobalsamo et ture uescuntur cadenteque *B*
j stratis] stratisque *B*
k...k amictis contenti] amictibus contecti *B*

§ 40
a igitur] *om. B*
b...b item mihi] eandem *B*
c...c manum quemue] percussoris manu cauendam habeam quamue *B*
d matris] mortis *B*
e facta] fata *B*
f...f nam mihi] mihique
g Clothos] Clotho *B*
h ad] post *B*
i Babiloni] Babilonia *B*
j non] neque *B*
k...k turpissimo miserandoque] miserando turpissimoque *B*
l...l et in uia iacebit] iacebitque in uia *B*
m...m facte . . . superest] fato diu tu autem etsi breue superest tibi *B*
n unde] inde *B*
o regem] *om. B*
p...p sacerdos . . . offendit] monuit sacerdos ut pergeremus fletum et ululatum nostrum sacras arbores dicens offendisse *B*

§ 41. Tum ego [a]continuo accitos[a] uniuersos milites[b], ut Porum Fassiacen[c] ex responso peteremus, et[d] quod nobis faustum felixque esset futurum; de tempore uitae meae[e], ne a comilitonibus [f]desperationi redditis et in alienum genus distruerer locis. Et per eas uoces[f], quas ex responsis una mecum audierunt, [g]comites meos obsecrabam ut[g] ex sua fide et meo [h]consilia silentio tegerent[h]. Iamque a sacris excesseramus arboribus, sed iam odore turis oppobalsamique nares[i] uerberabantur. Indi enim sacra deorum ad oceanum colentes[j] me quoque [k]parum per inmortalem esse dicebant[k], qui usque aeuum[l] penetrare potuissem. Quibus ego, quod de nobis opinarentur insinuans, [76v] gratias agebam. Peruenimus deinde in uallem Iordeam[m], in qua serpentes habitabant, habentes colla[n] lapides qui smaragdi appellantur. Hi[o] lumen in oculis profusum accipiunt, [p]uellemque nulli ad euadendum incolunt; hi serpentes lassere et albo pascuntur pipere[p]: nam super hanc uellem[q] sunt piramides institutae pedum uigenum[r] quinum, ab antiquis Indorum ab hanc causam aedificatae. Sed hi serpentes, quos paulo ante descripsimus, inter se quotannis uere primo depugnant multique morsibus depereunt. Inde nos paucos extulimus ingentis formae smaragdos. Per magna deinde pericula peruenimus[s] ad Seres, que gens iustissima omnium gentium esse perhibe[77r]tur. Ubi nec homicidium neque[t] adulterium non[u] periurium neque ebrietas committi dicitur. Paene [v]tantummodo holeribus et aqua vescitur[v]. Qui nos [w]optimis commeatibus[w] suscipiunt et [x]recto itinere nos[x] per Caspias portas [y]usque in Fassiacen ad Porum regem[y] deducebant. Inde profecti[z] flatum [a]uenti Euri[a] secuti incidimus [b]in aeternas[b] feras, de quarum carnibus[c] uelut gladii a uertice [d]acuti serrataque osso emittebant quae more arietino[d] in aduersos incurrunt homines; [e]ut tunc[e] inuictae ferae plurimorum militum clipeos cornu suo transuerberabant. [f]E quibus ego[f] admodum .VIII.[g] milibus .CCCCL. sic deinde[h] ad Porum regem[i] exercitus meus cum summo tandem labore ac periculo meo metuque [77v] militum peruenit. Ibique legato meo praecepi, quem praesulem[j] praeposueram, nomine [k]Alanem, ut praeciperet Persis et Babiloniis ut[k] pilas solidas aureas duas pedum uigenum[l] quinum [m]altas fecissent praeciperentque ut his omnia gesta mea scriberent posuissentque[m] in ultima India ultra Liberi et Herculis trophea, quorum[n] centum erant [o]quaedam in diuersis regionibus et[o] ego quinque mea aurea eis[p] altiora [q]de his[q] pedibus statui imperaui, quaeque[r] miraculo futura sunt, carissime

§ 41

a...a continuo accitos] contionatus apud *B*

b milites] milites dixi *B*

c Fassiacen] et Fasiacen *B*

d et] *om. B*

e meae] meae reticui *B*

f...f desperationi . . . uoces] meis redditus desperationi in alienis dirumperer locis eas uero uoces *B*

g...g comites . . . obsecrabam ut] qui his nominibus appellabantur: Sermition, Protesilaus et Mistomus et Timotheus et Lacon et Traseleon et Deditus et Macon et Erocles et Silbrus et Sunsiclus et Perdicas et Philotas et praefectus praetorii Coracdas, silentio *B*

h...h consilia . . . tegerent] tegebant consilio *B*

i nares] nares nostrae

j colentes] colentes dicebant *B*

k...k parum . . . dicebant] esse immortalem *B*

l euum] eo *B*

m Iordeam] Diardinis *B*

n colla] in collo *B*

o Hi] Hi serpentes lasere et albo pascuntur pipere hi *B*

p..p uellemque . . . pipere] hi uallem nulli adeundam incolunt *B*

q uellem] uallem *B*

r uigenum] tricenum *B*

praeceptor, posteris saeculis non [s]parua ammiratione[s]. Nouum perpetuumque statuimus[t] monimentum ut[u] inuiuendum[v] mortalibus[w] esset perpetua de[x] nobis opinio [78r] et animi industriae optimae[y].

---

[s] pervenimus] incidimus inscitas talis generis bestias, habentes capita leonum, caudas unguibus binis, late ad mensuram sex pedum, quibus uerberabantur homines, ut inutiles fierent. His erant intermixti grifi, rostra habentes aquilarum et alia parte corporis dissimiles. Qui mira uelocitate in ora oculosque nostros resiliebant et scuta clipeosque nostros caudis pedum binorum ternorumque crudelissime admodum uerberabant. Qui partim sagittis, partim contis militaribus conficiebantur. Perdidi in eo certamine ducentos sex milites bestiarum utriusque generis morsu; occidimus admodum sedecim milia. Inde ad Occluadas fluuium uenimus, qui sine flexu rectus ad oceanum ferebatur, latior stadiis ad ripam alteram uiginti; erant arundines ac trecente per litora, quarum unam uix triginta milites possent ferre: excedebant enim arborum procerissimarum altitudinem. In his arundinbus stratum potentissimo ebore uidimus. Inhabitabant enim locum eundem milia elephantorum innumera, qui nos nescio quo facto lacessere non temptabant; alioquin crudelissime percalcati eramus. Multis collectis dentibus ratibus ex arundine factis transnauigauimus amnem. Inhabitabant litus ulterius Indi beluarum ferarum contecti pellibus; non fuere inhospitales, qui nobis spongias albas purpureasque in manus dedere cum bucinis et genere coclearum, capientes binos et ternos congios, et stragula mollesque tunicas ex uitulorum marinorum pellibus factas. Cocleas praeterea sextariales esce pulcherrimae, item uermes ex ipso flumine extractos, femore humano grossiores, qui nobis omni generi piscium sapore praeferendi sunt et fungos immensos magnitudine uincentes, cocco rubriores, posuerunt nobis et murenas habentes pondera ducentena, affirmantes esse maiores in uicino ipsis oceano, qui erat ad miliarium tertium et uicesimum, pisces praeterea scaros pondus centenum quinquagenum, qui gurgitibus nassis eburneis capiebantur, ne arundines morsu confringerent aut capillatae mulieres, que pisce uiuebant, aquis immerse pranderent. Que ignaros regionum homines in flumine natantes aut tenendo in gurgitibus suffocabant aut tractos in arundineto, cum essent specie mirabiles, inaffectu suo auide uictos rumpebant aut ueneria exanimabant uoluptate. Quarum nos duas tantummodo cepimus colore niueo, similes nymphis, diffusis per tergum capillis. Et in Gange flumine erant mirabilia portenta. De quibus, ne tibi fabulosus uiderer, scribendum non putaui nisi quod aque fluminis et Euphratis Borea uenientes sole ad Noti uenti spiracula exeunt. Quorum fluminum ripe altera ab alia conspicue non sunt earum aquarum latitudine. Inde ad castellum quod Indi colunt peruenimus, deinde *B*

[t] neque] nec *B*
[u] non] neque *B*
[v...v] tantummodo . . . uescitur] tantum et oleribus et aqua uescuntur *B*
[w...w] optimis commeatibus] commeatibus optimis *B*
[x...x] recto itinere nos] itinere recto ducentes *B*
[y...y] ad regem Porum in Fasiacen *B*
[z] profecti] profecti et *B*
[a...a] uenti Euri] Euri uenti
[b...b] in aeternas] externas *B*
[c] carnibus] capitibus *B*
[d...d] acuti . . . arietino] serrata eminebant ossa quae more taurorum
[e...e] ut tunc] et *B*
[f...f] E quibus ego] Quibus ergo occisis *B*
[g] .VIII.] nouem *B*
[h] deinde] inde *B*
[i] regem] *om. B*
[j] praesulem] Persidi *B*
[k...k] Alanem . . . ut] Alconi ut poneret in Persarum et Babiloniorum terris *B*
[l] uigenum] uicenum *B*
[m...m] altas . . . posuissentque] et in his omnia facta mea scriberet atque *B*
[n] quorum] quae *B*
[o...o] quedam . . . et] *om. B*
[p] eis] *om. B*
[q...q] de his] denis *B*
[r] quaeque] que *B*
[s...s] parua ammiratione] paruo *B*
[t] stauimus] statuimus uirtutibus *B*
[u] ut] *om. B*
[v] inuiuendum] inuidendum *corr. in* inuidendum *R* inuidendum *B*
[w] mortalibus] ut immortalitas *B*
[x] de] et *B*
[y] optimae] optime Aristoteles indicium *B*

APPENDIX IIb

The Letter of Alexander to Aristotle

Old English text

SIGLA

V British Library, Cotton Vitellius A. xv, fols. 107r–131v
C Cockayne, *Narratiunculae anglice conscriptae*, pp. 1–33
B Baskervill, 'The Anglo-Saxon Version of the *Epistola Alexandri*', pp. 139–67
R Rypins, *Three Old English Prose Texts*, pp. 1–50
K Klaeber, 'Notes on Old English Prose Texts', pp. 241–7
D Bradley and Sisam, 'Textual Notes on the Old English *Epistola Alexandri*', pp. 202–5
P Pickles, 'Studies in the Prose Texts of the *Beowulf* Manuscript', pp. 100–7

§ 1. [107r] HER IS SEO GESETENIS[a] Alexandres epistoles þæs miclan kyninges 7 þæs mæran Macedoniscan, þone he wrat 7 sende to Aristotile his magistre be gesetenisse Indie þære miclan þeode, 7 be þære widgalnisse his siðfato 7 his fora, þe he geond middangeard ferde. Cwæþ he þus sona ærest in fruman þæs epistoles:

§ 2. Simle ic beo gemindig þin[a], ge efne betweoh tweondan frecennisse[b] ura gefeohta, þu min se leofesta lareow 7 efne to minre meder 7 geswystrum þu me eart se leofesta freond. Ond for þon þe ic þe wiste wel getydne in wisdome, þa geþohte ic for þon to þe to writanne be þæm þeodlonde Indie 7 be heofenes gesetenissum 7 be þæm unarimdum cynnum nædrena 7 monna 7 wildeora, to þon þæt hwæthwygo to þære ongietenisse þissa niura[c] þinga þin gelis 7 [d]gleawnis to[d] geþeode. Þeoh [107v] to þe seo gefylde gleawnis 7 snyttro 7[e] naniges fultumes abædeð[f] sio lar þæs rihtes hwæþere ic wolde þæt þu mine dæde ongeate, þa þu lufast 7 þa þing þe ungesewene mid þe siond, þa ic in Indie geseah þurh monigfeald gewin 7 þurh micle frecennisse mid greca herige.

§ 1

a GESENTNIS] GESENGENIS *V* GESETENID *C*

§ 2

a þin] *om. V* þin *D*

b frecennisse] freonnisse *V* frecennisse *R*

c niura] minra *V* niura *D*

d...d gleawnis to] glengista *V* gleawnis to *D*

e 7] *om. V* 7 *D*

f abædeð] abæded *V* abædeð *D*

APPENDIX IIc

The Letter of Alexander to Aristotle

A translation of the Old English text

§ 1. Here is the text of the letter of Alexander, the great king and the famous Macedonian, which he wrote and sent to Aristotle, his teacher, concerning the situation of the great nation of India, and the extent of his expeditions and his travels, which he made throughout the world. He says as follows in the very beginning of the letter:

§ 2. I always remember you, even in the midst of the dreadful uncertainty of our battles, since you, my dearest teacher, are, next to my mother and sisters, my dearest friend. And since I know that you are well set in wisdom, I thought to write to you about the great nation of India, and the disposition of the heavens, and the countless varieties of serpents, and men, and wild beasts, so that your learning and knowledge might contribute to a certain extent to the understanding of these novelties. Although in you consummate wisdom and erudition and teaching of what is correct require no assistance, yet I wished that you should learn of my deeds, which you love, and of those things which you have not seen, and which I saw in India after manifold struggles and after great danger alongside the Greek army.

§ 3. Þa ic þe write 7 cyþe, 7 æghwylc þara is wyrðe synderlice in gemyndum to habbanne æfter þære wisan þe ic hit oferseah. Ne gelyfde ic æniges monnes gesegenum swa fela wundorlicra þinga þæt hit swa beon mihte ær ic hit self minum eagum ne gesawe. Seo eorðe is to wundrienne hwæt heo ærest oþþe godra þinga cenne, oððe[a] eft þara yfelra, þe heo þæm sceawigendum is æteowed. Hio is cennende þa fulcuþan [b]wildeora 7 wæstma[b] 7 wecga oran, 7 wunderlice wyhta, þa þing eall þæm monnum þe hit geseoð 7 sceawigað wæron uneþe to gewitanne for þære missenlicnisse þara hiowa.

§ 4. Ac þa ðing þe me nu in gemynd cumað ærest þa ic þe write, þy læs on me mæge idel spellung [108r] oþþe scondlic leasung beon gestæled. Hwæt þu eac sylfa const þa gecynd mines modes mec a gewunelice healdon þæt gemerce soðes 7 rihtes. Ond ic sperlicor mid wordum sægde þonne hie mid dædum gedon wærun. Nu ic hwæþre gehyhte 7 gelyfe þæt þu þas þing ongete swa þu me ne talige owiht gelpan 7 secgan be þære micelnisse ures gewinnes 7 compes. For ðon ic oft wiscte 7 wolde þæt hyra læs wære swa gewinfulra.

§ 5. Ic ðæs þoncunge do greca herige 7 swyðost þæm mægene þære iuguþe 7 þæm unforswyþdum urum weorode, for þon on ieþum þingum hie me mid wæron 7 on þæm earfeðum no from bugon. Ac hie on þære geþylde mid me a wunedon þæt ic wæs nemned ealra kyninga kyning. Þara weorðmynta blissa þu min se leofa lareow. Ond ic nu þas þing write to þe gemænelice 7 to Olimphiade minre meder 7 minum geswustrum for þon incer lufu sceal beon somod gemæne. 7 gif hit [108v] oþor bið, þonne æteawest þu læsson þonne ic nu ær to þe gelyfde.

§ 6. On þæm ærrum gewritum þe ic þe sende, ic þe cyþde 7 getacnode be þære asprungnisse sunnan 7 monan 7 be tungla rynum 7 gesetenissum 7 be lyfte tacnungum. Þa ðing eall ne magon elcor beon buton micelre gemynde swa geendebyrded 7 forestihtod. Ond nu þas niwan spel ic þe ealle in cartan awrite. Ðonne þu hie ræde, þonne wite þu þæt hie ealle swylce wæron swa þam gemyndum gedafenode þines Alexandres þe to sendanne.

§ 7. On Maius þæm monþe Persea se kyning Dariun æt Gande þære ea we hine oforcwomon 7 oferswyðdon 7 us þær in onweald geslogon eal his londrice. Ond we þær settan 7 geendebyrdedon ure gerefan þæm eastþeodum[a] 7 monegum cynelicum weorðmyndum we wæron gewelgode. On þæm ærron epistole ic þe þæt sægde 7 þy læs þæt eow seo sægen monifealdlicor bi þon þuhte [109r] to writanne, ic þa wille swa lætan, 7 þa secgon þe nu ðær gewurdon.

§ 3

[a] oððe] odðe *V*

[b..b] wildeora 7 wæstma] *om.* *V* wildeora 7 wæstma *P*

§ 7

[a] eastþeodum] eastþeodum ingemong *P*

§ 3. These things I write and tell you, and each of them is individually worth bearing in mind exactly as I observed it. I would not have believed the words of any man that so many marvellous things could be so before I saw them myself with my own eyes. The earth is a source of wonder first for the good things she brings forth, and then for the evil, through which she is revealed to observers. She is the producer of well-known wild beasts, and plants, and stones and metal-ore, and of wondrous creatures, all those things which are difficult to comprehend for those who look and observe because of the variety of their forms.

§ 4. But now I will write to you about those things that come first to mind, in case I can be accused of empty talk and shameful lies. Look, you yourself know that the nature of my mind is always such as to keep me continually within the boundaries of what is true and right; and I have described things in words more sparingly than they actually occurred. So now I hope and believe that you perceive these things so as not at all to reckon me to boast in telling of the greatness of our struggle and contest. For I often wished and wanted that fewer of them were so severe.

§ 5. In this I give thanks to the Greek army, and especially to the strength of youth and our unconquered troop, because they were with me in the easy things and did not depart during the hardships, but with patience they bore with me always so that I was called king of all kings. Be pleased with these honours, my dear teacher. And now I shall write these things jointly to you and to my mother Olympias, and my sisters, for the pair of you shall share a common love. And if it is otherwise, then you show yourself a lesser man than I previously believed of you.

§ 6. In the previous letters which I sent you, I explained and indicated to you about the eclipse of the sun and moon, and the courses of the stars and configurations, and the heavenly signs. All these things cannot otherwise be arranged and fore-ordained than by a great intelligence. And now I shall write down all this new information for you in a letter. When you read it, be aware that this is all such as seemed appropriate, in the opinion of your Alexander, to send to you.

§ 7. In the month of May we overcame and conquered King Darius of Persia at the river Gande, and there took all his kingdom into our possession. And we set and designated our stewards over the eastern nations, and we were enriched with many royal honours. In the earlier letter I told you about this, and, in case reporting it will seem to you too repetitious to write, I will pass over it, and tell you what has happened now.

§ 8. On Iulius monðe on þæm ytemestum dagum þæs monðes we cwomon in Indie lond in Fasiacen þa stowe. Ond we þa mid wunderlicre hreðnisse Porrum þone cyning ofercwomon 7 oferswyðdon. Ond we ealle his þeode on onwald onfengon, 7 on[a] þæm londe we wæron monegum cynelicum weolum geweorðode. Ac ic wolde þæt þu þa ðing ongeate þa ðe weorðe sindon in gemyndum to habbanne. Ærest ic þe write be þære unarimedlican mengeo his weoredes, þæs wæs buton unarimedlican feþum, sixtene þusend monna 7 eahta hund eoredmanna ealle mid heregeatwum gegerede. 7 we þa þær genoman feower hund elpenda, 7 on þam ufan stodon gewæpnode scyttan, 7 þa torras 7 þa scylfas on him bæron þa elpendas þe ða byrnwigon onstodan. Æfter þon we ða cynelican burh Porres mid urum wæpnum in eodon. Ond his healle [109v] 7 þa cynelican geseto his sceawedon. Þær wæron gyldene columnan swiðe micle 7 trumlice 7 fæste, ða wæron unmetlice greate heanisse upp, ðara wæs þe we gerimdon be þæm gemete .CCCC. Þa wagas wæron eac gyldne mid gyldnum þelum anæglede fingres þicce. Mid þy ic ða wolde geornlicor þa þing geseon 7 furðor eode þa geseah ic gyldenne wingeard trumlicne 7 fæstlicne, 7 þa twigo his hongodon geond þa columnan. Ða wundrode ic þæs swiðe. Wæron in þæm wingearde gyldenu leaf 7 his hos[b] 7 his wæstmas wæron cristallum 7 smaragdus, eac þæt gimcyn mid þæm cristallum ingemong hongode. His brydburas 7 his heahcleofan ealle wæron eorcnanstanum unionibus 7 carbunculis þæm gimcynnum swiðast gefrætwode. Uton hie wæron elpendbanum geworhte þa wæron wunderlice hwite 7 fægere 7 cypressus styde 7 lau[118r]risce hie utan wreþedon, 7 gyldne styþeo[c] 7 aþrawene ðær ingemong stodon, 7 unarimedlicu goldhord þær wæron inne 7 ute 7 monifealdlicu hie wæron 7 missenlicra cynna. 7 monig fatu gimmiscu 7 cristallisce dryncfatu 7 gyldne sestras ðær wæron forð borenne. Seldon we þær ænig seolfor fundon.

§ 9. Siðþan ic þa me hæfde þas þing eall be gewealdum, þa wilnode ic Indeum innanwearde to geseonne. Ða becwom ic on Caspiam þæt lond mid ealle mine herige. Þa wæs ðær seo wæstmberendeste eorþe ðæs þeodlondes. 7 ic swiðe wundrade þa gesælignesse þære eorðan[a] 7 ic efne gefeonde in minum mode geornlicor ða lond sceawigean wolde. Þa sægdon us ða bigengean þæs londes þæt we us warnigan scoldon wið þa missen[118v]lican cynd nædrena 7 hrifra wildeora þy læs we on ða becwomon. Þæra mænego in ðissum dunum 7 denum 7 on wudum, 7 on feldum eardigeað 7 in stanholum hie selfe digliað. Ac hwæþre ma ic wolde þæm frecnan wege 7 siðfatum foeran ðonne þæm gehyldrum wegum, to ðon þæt ðone fleondon Porrum of þæm gefeohte þæt ic hine gemette ær he on þa westenu middangeardes gefluge.

§ 8

[a] on] *om.* *V* on *D*

[b] hos] hon *V* hos *P*

[c] styþeo] styþeo hie uton wreþedon *V*

§ 9

[a] eorðan] eorðan 7 ic swiðe wundrade þa gesælignesse þære eorðan *V*

§ 8. In the month of July, in the final days of that month we came into the land of India to a place called Fasiacen. And with amazing swiftness we overcame and conquered Porus, the king. And we took his entire nation under our control, and in that land we were enriched with many royal honours. But I want you to know those things which are worth having in mind. First I will write to you about the countless multitude of his troop, which comprised (not counting an innumerable number of foot-soldiers), sixteen thousand men and eight hundred cavalry, all equipped with battle-gear. And there we captured four hundred elephants, on whom were there stood armed archers, and the elephants carried towers and platforms, on which the mail-clad warriors stood. After that we entered the royal city of Porus with our weapons. And we saw his hall and his royal quarters. There were golden columns, very great, and mighty, and firm, which were enormously large and tall, of which we counted a tally of four hundred. The walls were also golden, sheathed with gold plates the thickness of a finger. When I wished to see these things more keenly and went further, I saw a golden vineyard, mighty and firm, and its branches hung about the columns. And I was greatly amazed at that. The leaves of the vineyard were of gold, and its tendrils and fruits were of crystal and emerald, and jewels hung among the crystal. His bedrooms and his main chambers were all most highly embellished with precious stones, the gem-stones pearls and carbuncles. On the outside they were wrought in ivory, wonderfully white and fair, and posts of cypress and laurel supported them on the outside, and twisted golden props stood within, and there were countless hoards of gold inside and out, and they were manifold and of various kinds. And many jewelled vessels and crystal drinking-cups and golden pitchers were brought forth there. Seldom did we find any silver there.

§ 9. When I had all these things in my possession, I wanted to see the interior of India. Then I came into the land of Caspia with all my army. There was the most fruitful soil in the country. And I marvelled greatly at the fertility of the soil, and, truly rejoicing in my heart, I wished more eagerly to see that land. Then the inhabitants of the land told us that we should beware the various kinds of serpents and savage wild beasts, in case we came upon them. A multitude of them dwell in these hills and valleys, and in woods, and in open country, and they hide themselves in stony hollows. And yet I wished rather to travel the dangerous paths and ways than the safe paths, so that I could catch up with Porus, fleeing from the battle, before he could escape into the deserted tracts of the world.

§ 10. Ic me ða mid genom .CC. ladþeowa 7 eac .L. þe ða genran wegas cuðan þara siðfato. Ða ferde we in Agustes monþe þurh þa weallendan sond, 7 þurh þa wædlan stowe wætres 7 ælcere wætan. 7 ic mede gehet þæm us cuþlice gelæddon þurh þa uncuðan land Indie 7 mec wolde mid mine herige onsund gelædon in Patriacen þæt lond. 7 swiðast ic wilnade þæt hie me gelæddon to þæm dioglum godwebwyrhtum, ða þonne wunderlice of sumum[a] treowcynne 7 of his leafum 7 of his flyse, þæs [119r] treowes spunnon 7 swa eac to godewebbe wæfon 7 worhtan. Ac hie þa londliode tiolodon ma ussa feonda willan to gefremmanne þonne urne, for þon þe hie us gelæddon þurh þa lond þe þa unarefnedlican cyn nædrena 7 hrifra wildeora in wæron. Ða ongeat ic selfa 7 geseah of dæle þæt me þa earfeðu becwoman. For þon ic ær forlet 7 ne gymde þara nytlicra geþeahta minra freonda 7 þara monna þe me þæt logon þæt ic þæm wegum ferde. Ða bebead ic minum þegnum 7 hie het þæt hie hie mid heora wæpnum gereden, 7 mid þy herige forð ferdon. 7 hie eac swylce þæt min weorod 7 þa mine þegnas 7 eal min here goldes 7 eorcnanstana[b] þæt hie gehergad, 7 genumen hæfdon micel gemet mid him wægon 7 læddon. For þon hie wendon 7 ondredon gif hie hit behindon forleton þæt hiora fynd hit þonne deagollice genomon 7 onweg aleddon.

§ 11. Ond efne swiðe þa mine þegnas [119v] 7 eal min weorod wæs gewelgod þæt hie uneðe ealle þa byrðene þæs goldes mid him aberan 7 alædan meahton. Swelce eac heora wæpena noht lytel byrðen wæs for þon eal heora wæpenu þæra minra þegna 7 ealles mines weoredes 7 heriges ic het[a] hie mid gyldenum þelum bewyrcean. Ond eall min weorod wæs on þa gelicnesse tungles oððe ligite for þære micelnisse þæs goldes. Hit scan 7 berhte, foran swa ymb me uton mid þrymme 7 herebeacen 7 segnas beforan me læddon. Ond swa micel wundor 7 wæfersien wæs þæs mines weoredes on fægernisse ofer ealle oþre þeodkyningas þe in middangearde wæron. Ða sceawede ic seolfa 7 geseah mine gesælinesse 7 min wuldor 7 þa fromnisse minre iuguðe 7 gesælignisse mines lifes, þa wæs ic hwæthwugo in gefean in minum mode ahafen.

§ 12. Ac swa hit oft gesæleð on þæm [120r] selran þingum 7 on þæm gesundrum, þæt seo wyrd 7 sio hiow hie oft oncyrreð 7 on oþer hworfeð, þa gelomp us þæt we wurdon earfoðlice mid þurste geswencte 7 gewæcte. Ðone þurst we þonne earfoðlice abæron 7 aræfndon, þa wæs haten Seferus min þegn funde þa wæter in anum holan stane 7 þa mid ane helme hlod hit 7 me to brohte. 7 he sylfa þursti wæs se min þegn, 7 hwæþre he swiðor mines feores 7 gesynto wilnade þonne his selfes. Þa he þa þæt wæter me to brohte swa ic ær sægde þa het ic min weorod 7 ealle mine duguþe tosomne, 7 hit þa beforan heora ealra onsyne niðer ageat, þy læs ic drunce 7 þone minne þegn þyrste 7 minne here 7 ealne þe mid me wæs. Ond ic þa beforan him eallum herede Seferes dæde þæs mines þegnes, 7 hine beforan hiora ealra onsione mid deorweorðum [120v] gyfum gegeafede for ðære dæde. Ond þa mid þy þe þæt

§ 10
a sumum] sunnan *V* sumum *D*
b eorcnanstana] eorcnanstane *V*

§ 11
a het] *om. V* het *D*

§ 10. I took with me 250 guides who knew the direct routes of that journey. Then we travelled in the month of August through the boiling sands, and the rough places devoid of water or any moisture. And I offered a reward to those who led us knowledgeably through the unknown land of India and were willing to lead me with my army safe to the land of Patriacen And most of all I wished that they would lead me to the secret weavers of precious cloth, who spun it wonderfully from a certain tree, and from its leaves and fleece, and wove and worked it into precious cloth. But those natives strove to fulfil the will of our enemies rather than ours, since they led us through those lands in which there were intolerable varieties of serpents and savage wild beasts. Then I realised myself and saw for my part that these difficulties beset me. For I had discounted and disregarded the useful advice of my friends and of those men who tried to dissuade me from travelling on those paths. Then I gave orders to my thegns and commanded that they kept their weapons to the ready, and proceeded in battle-array. And my troop and my thegns and all my army had brought and carried a great deal with them of the gold and precious stones that they had plundered. For they expected and feared that if they left it behind their enemies would secretly take it and steal it away.

§ 11. And indeed my thegns and all my troop had gained so much wealth that they could only with difficulty bring and carry with them the burden of all that gold. Also their weapons were no little burden because I had commanded that all the weapons of my thegns and all my troop and army be covered with gold plate. And all my troop looked like stars or lightning because of the amount of the gold. It shone and glittered before me and around me in glory, and they led before me war-banners and standards. And so great was the sight and spectacle of that troop of mine in splendour beyond all the other mighty kings there have been in the world. When I myself gazed and saw my prosperity and my glory and the success of my youth and the prosperity of my life, I was somewhat uplifted with joy in my heart.

§ 12. But as it turns out so often in better and sounder things, fate and fortune often change them, and turn them into something else, and at that time it happened to us that we were sorely vexed and afflicted with thirst. We bore and suffered that thirst sorely, when one of my thegns who was called Seferus found water in a hollow stone and poured it into a helmet and brought it to me. And that thegn of mine was himself thirsty, and yet he cared more for my life and health than for his own. And when, as I have said, he brought that water to me, I ordered together all my troop and all my trusted band and poured it away in the sight of them all, lest I should have drunk and my thegn and my army, and all who were with me thirst. And then before them all I praised the deed of Seferus my thegn, and gave him precious gifts for that deed in the sight of them all. And when my troop was heartened and

min werod gehyrted 7 gestilled wæs, þa ferdon we forð þy wege þe we ær ongunnon ða næs long to þon in þæm westenne þæt we to sumre ea cwoman. On þære ea ofre stod hreod 7 pintreow[a] 7 abies þæt treowcyn ungemetlicre gryto 7 micelnyssc þy clyfe weox 7 wridode.

§ 13. Þa we to þære ea cwoman, ða het ic for ðæm unarefnedlican þurste þe me selfum getenge wæs 7 eac eallum minum herige 7 þæm nytenum þe us mid wæron mine fyrd restan 7 wician. Mid þy we ða gewicod hæfdon ða wolde ic minne þurst lehtan 7 celan. Þa ic þæt wæter bergde ða wæs hit biterre 7 grimre to drincanne þonne ic æfre ænig oðer bergde. 7 nowþer ne hit se mon drincan meahte ne his ænig neat onbitan ne meahte. Þa wæs ic swiðe on minum mode generwed for ðæm dumbum nytenum, for þon ic wiste þæt men yþelicor meahton þone þurst arefnan þonne þa [121r] nietenu. Wæs þæra feðerfota nietena micel mænigeo mid me 7 micel mænigeo elpenda þa þe gold wægon 7 læddon ungemetlicre micelnisse ðusend, 7 twa þusenda horsa 7 .CCCC. buton þæm eoreda, 7 .XX. þusenda feþena. Þonne wæs þridde healf þusend mula ðe þa seamas wægon, 7 .XXX. þusenda ealfarena 7 oxna þa ðe hwæte bæron, twa þusenda olfenda, fif hund hryðra þara þe mon dæghwamlice to mete dyde. Wæs unrim getæl eac þon on horsum 7 on mulum 7 on olfendum 7 on elpendum ungemetlicu mængeo us æfter ferde. Ealle þa wæron mid unarefnedlice þurste geswencte 7 gewæcte. Ða men þonne hwilum hie þa iren geloman liccodan hwilum hie ele byrgdon 7 on þon þone grimman þurst celdon. Sume men ðonne of hiora scome þa wætan for þæm nyde þigdon.

§ 14. Seo wise wæs þa in[a] me on twa healfa uneþe [121v] ærest be minre seolfre nedþearfe, 7 mines weorodes. Het ic þa ælcne mon hine mid his wæpnum gegerwan, 7 faran forð 7 þæt eac fæstlice bebead ðæt se mon se ne wære mid his wæpnum æfter fyrdwison gegered, þæt hine mon scolde mid wæpnum acwellan. Ða wundredon hie swiðe for hwon hie þa hefignesse 7 micelnisse ðara wæpna in swa miclum þurste beran scoldon þær nænig feond ne æteowde. Ac ic wiste hwæþre þæt ure for 7 siðfæt wæs þurh [b]þa lond[b] 7 stowe þe missenlicra cynna eardung in wæs, nædrena 7 rifra wildeora. Ond we we ðe þæs londes ungleawe 7 unwise wæron, [c]þæt usic[c] ðonne semninga hwelc earfeðo on becwome.

§ 15. Ferdon we þa forð be þære ea ofre, ða wæs seo eatoðe tid dæges. Þa cwoman we to sumre byrig, seo burh wæs on midre þære ea in anum eglonde getimbred. Wæs seo burh mid þy hreode 7 treowcynne þe on þære [122r] ea ofre weox 7 we ær biwriton 7 sægdon asett 7 geworht. Ða gesawon we in þære byrig 7 ongeaton Indisce[a] men fea healf nacode eardigende. Ða hie þa us gesawon hie selfe sona in heora husum deagollice hie miþan ða wilnade ic þara monna onsyne to gesconne, þæt hie us fersc

§ 12
[a] pintreow] wintreow *V* pintreow *D*

§ 14
[a] in] iu *V* in *B*

[b...b] þa lond] þæt alond *V* þa lond *R*
[c...c] þæt usic] þus ic *V*

§ 15
[a] Indisce] mennisce *V* Indisce *P*

calmed by this, we went ahead on the route we had taken before, and it was not long until we came to a certain river in the wilderness. On the river-bank there stood reeds and pines, and silver-fir trees of huge size and stature grew and flourished on the cliff-edge.

§ 13. When we came to the river, because of the unbearable thirst which was afflicting myself and also all my army and the animals that were with us, I ordered my host to rest and make camp. And when we had camped there I wanted to ease and cool my thirst. When I tasted the water it was more bitter and harsh to drink than any other I had tasted. And neither was any man able to drink it, nor could any animal taste it. Then I was particularly disturbed in my heart for the dumb animals, since I knew that men could more easily bear their thirst than the beasts. There was a great multitude of four-footed animals with me, and a great multitude of elephants, a thousand of huge size who bore and carried the gold, and two thousand four hundred horses (not including the cavalry), and twenty thousand foot soldiers, then there was two and a half thousand mules who carried the packs, and thirty thousand pack-horses and oxen who carried the wheat, two thousand camels, five hundred cattle, of which some were slaughtered every day for food. There was also an innumerable tally of horses and mules and camels and elephants who followed us in countless droves. They were all vexed and afflicted with unbearable thirst. Then the men sometimes licked their iron tools and sometimes they tasted oil and cooled their thirst in its pungency. Then in their shame some men in their need drank piss.

§ 14. Things had then become difficult for me for two reasons: first with regard to my own necessity, and that of my troop. Then I ordered each man to equip himself with his weapons, and set out, and gave a strict command that any man who was not equipped with his weapons in battle-array should be killed with weapons. Then they wondered greatly why they had to bear the weight and size of their weapons in such great thirst when no enemy was in sight. But I knew that our path and journey led through those lands and places in which various kinds of serpents and savage wild animals had their dwelling. And since we were unfamiliar and unaware of that terrain, any disaster might suddenly befall us.

§ 15. Then we went forth along the bank of the river, at the eighth hour of the day. Then we came to a village, built in the middle of the river on an island. The village was built and constructed from the reeds and trees that grew on the river-bank, and which we have written about and described already. When we looked into the village we saw dwelling in it a few half-naked Indians. But as soon as they themselves saw us they hid themselves furtively in their houses. I wanted to catch sight of these men, to find out about clean fresh water.

wæter 7 swete getæhton. Mid þy we ða longe bidon 7 us nænig mon to wolde þa het ic fea stræla sendan in þa burh innan, to þon gif hie hiera willum us to noldon þæt hie for þæm ege þæs gefeohtes nede scoldon. Ða wæron hie þy swyðor afyrhte 7 hie fæstor hyddan. Þa het ic .CC. minra þegna of greca herige leohtum wæpnum hie gegyrwan, 7 hie on sunde to þære byrig foron 7 swumman ofer æfter þære ea to þæm eglande. Þa hie ða hæfdon feorðan dæl þære ea geswummen, ða becwom sum ongrislic wise on hie. Þæt wæs þonne nicra mengeo on onsione maran 7 un[122v]hyrlicran þonne ða elpendas in ðone grund þære ea 7 betweoh ða yða þæs wæteres þa men besencte 7 mid heora muðe hie sliton 7 blodgodon 7 hie ealle swa fornamon, þæt ure nænig wiste hwær hiora æni cwom. Ða wæs ic swiðe yrre þæm minum ladþeowum, þa us on swylce frecennissa gelæddon. Het hiera ða bescufan in þa ea .L. 7 .C. 7 sona þæs ðe hie inne wæron, swa wæron þa nicoras gearwe tobrudon hie swa hie þa oðre ær dydon, 7 swa þicce hie in þære ea aweollon swa æmettan ða nicras, 7 swilc unrim heora wæs. Þa het ic blawan mine byman 7 þa fyrd faran.

§ 16. Þa hit ða wæs sio endlefte tid dæges 7 we forð ferdon. Ða gesawon we men æfter þære ea feran, hæfdon of þæm hreode 7 of þæm treowcynne þe in ðære ea ofre stodon on scipwisan geworht þæt hie onufan sæton. Þa men [123r] mid þy we æfter ferscum wætre hie frunon, þa onswaredon hie us 7 sædon hwær we hit findan mehton in hiora gereorde 7 cwædon þæt we fundon sumne swiðe micelne mere in þæm wære fersc wæter 7 swete genog, 7 þæt we genog raðe to þæm becwoman gif we geornfulle wæron. 7 þa for þæm þingum swa monigra geswencnissa þæt we ealle þa niht ferdon mid þurste gewæcte 7 mid ura wæpna byrþenum swiðe geswencte. 7 ofer ealle þa niht ðe we ferdon þus[a] symle leon 7 beran 7 tigris 7 pardus 7 wulfas ure ehtan, 7 we þæm wiðstodon. Þa ðy æftran dæge ða hit wæs seo eahtoðe tid dæges, þa cwomon we to þæm mere ðe us mon ær foresæde. Þa wæs he eall mid wudu beweaxen mile brædo, wæs hwæþre weg to ðæm wætre. Ða wæs ic gefeonde þæs swetan wætres 7 þæs ferscan 7 þa sona minne þurst ærest gelehte [123v] 7 þa eal min weored, ða het ic wætrian sona ure hors 7 ure nieteno eall wæron hie swiðe mid þurste fornumene ða het ic sioððan[b] sona þa fyrd wician. Wæs seo wicstow ða on lengo .XX.es furlonga long, 7 swa eac in brædo. Sioðþan hie þa gewicod hæfdon, þa het ic ceorfan ða bearwas 7 þone wudu fyllan þæt monnum wære þy eþre to þæm wæterscipe to ganganne, 7 to þæm mere þe we bi gewicod hæfdon. Þa het ic ða gesamnian eall þa ure hors 7 nietenu 7 elpendas 7 hie het gebringan on middum þæm urum wicum, 7 betwih þæm geteldum, þy læs hiora ænig to lore wurde, for þon us wæs uncuð hwæt us on nihtlicum fyrste gesælde. 7 þa het ic eac of þæm wudo þe ðær gefylled wæs þæt mon fyr onælde, sio fyrd þe mid me wæs þa didon hie swa. 7 þa ðær onældon þusend fyra 7 eac fif hund, for þon [124r] ic þæt dyde gif us on niht uncuðes hwæt on becwome þæt we hæfdon æt þæm fyre leoht 7 fullaste

§ 16

a þus] þæt us *V* þus *R*

b sioððan] siodðan *V* sioððan *C*

After we had waited a long time and none of them would emerge, I ordered a few arrows to be shot into the village, so that if they would not come out to us voluntarily, they should of necessity, through fear of battle. Then they were still more greatly afraid, and hid themselves more securely. Then I ordered two hundred of my thegns from the Greek army to arm themselves with light weapons and go over to the village by swimming, and they swum over across the river to that island. And when they had swum about a quarter of the river, something terrible happened to them. There appeared a multitude of water-monsters [hippopotami], larger and more terrible in appearance than the elephants, who dragged the men through the watery waves down to the river bottom, and tore them to bloody pieces with their mouths, and snatched them all away so that none of us knew where any of them had gone. Then I was very angry with my guides, who had led us into such danger. I ordered that one hundred and fifty of them be shoved into the river, and as soon as they were in the water-monsters were ready, and dragged them away just as they had done with the others, and the water-monsters seethed up in the river as thick as ants, they were so innumerable. Then I ordered the trumpets to be sounded, and the army to head off.

§ 16. It was the eleventh hour of the day, and we set forth. Then we saw men coming over the river, and they had made boat-shapes from the reeds and trees that stood on the river bank, and sat on top of them. When we asked the men about fresh water, they answered us in their own language and told us where to find it and said that we would find a very big lake in which there was plenty of clean fresh water, and that if we were keen we would get there fairly soon. And in addition to so many hardships we travelled throughout the whole night vexed with thirst, and greatly afflicted by the burden of our weapons. And throughout the whole night as we travelled, lions and bears and tigers and leopards and wolves attacked us continually, and we held them off. And on the next day, when it was the eighth hour of the day, we came to the lake that had been described to us. It was entirely overgrown with woods a mile deep, but there was a path to the water. I was delighted in this clean fresh water, and immediately slaked my thirst and then that of all my troop, and immediately ordered all our horses and our animals to be watered, since they were all greatly suffering with thirst. After that I immediately ordered the army to pitch camp. The campsite was twenty furlongs in length, and the same in width. After they had camped, I ordered the grove cleared, and the trees felled to make it easier for people to get to the water, and to the lake by which we had camped. Then I ordered all our horses and animals and elephants to be gathered together, and ordered them brought to the middle of our encampment, into the midst of the tents, in case any of them were lost, since we did not know what might occur during the night. And then I also ordered that fires be lit from the wood which had been felled, and the troops with me did so: they lit fifteen hundred fires, and I did that so that if something unexpected should happen to us, we should have the light and comfort of the fires.

§ 17. Þa we þara fyra hæfdon onæled swa fela swa us þa ðuhte, þa bleow man mine byman 7 ic mete þigde 7 eall min fyrd swa dyde. Wæs hit þa an tid to æfenes, 7 þa het ic onbærnan ðara gyldenra leohtfato þe ic mid me hæfde twa þusendo. Ða toforan monan upgonge þa cwomon þær Scorpiones þæt wyrmcyn swa hie ær gewunelice wæron toweard[a] þæs wætersciepes. Wæs þæra wyrma micel mænegeo 7 heora wæs unrim 7 hie swiðe on þa ure wic onetton 7 in þa feollon. Ða æfter þon cwoman þær hornede nædran Carastis þæt nædercyn. Þa wæron ealle missenlices hiwes, for þon hie wæron sume reode, sume blace, sume hwite. Sumum þonne scinan þa scilla 7 lixtan swylce hie wæron gyldne þonne mon onlocode. [124v] Eall þæt lond hleoðrade for þara wyrma hwistlunge, 7 us eac noht lytel ege from him wæs. Ac we þa mid scyldum us scyldan, 7 eac mid longsceaftum sperum hie slogan 7 cwealdon monige eac in fyre forburnon. Þas ðing we þus drugon þæt we swa wið þam wyrmum fuhtan 7 wunnan huru twa tida þære nihte.

§ 18. Sioðþan hie þa wyrmas hæfdon ondruncen þæs wætres þa gewiton hie þonon, 7 ure no ne ehton. Ða wæs seo þridde tid þære nihte, þa wolde we us gerestan, þa cwoman þær nædran eft wunderlicran þonne ða oþre wæron 7 egeslicran. Þa hæfdon tu heafdo 7 eac sume hæfdon þreo. Wæron hie wunderlicre micelnisse, wæron hie swa greate swa columnan ge eac sume uphyrran 7 gryttran, cwoman þa wyrmas of þæm neahdunum 7 scrafum þider to þon þæt hie þæt wæter drincan woldon. Eodon þa wyrmas 7 scluncon wundorlice, wæron him þa breost upgewende 7 on ðæm [125r] hricge eodon, 7 a swa hie hit geforan gelice mid þæm scillum gelice mid ðe muþe ða eorþan sliton 7 tæron. Hæfdon hie þa wyrmas þrie slite tungan 7 þonne hie eðedon þonne eode him of þy muðe mid þy oroþe swylce byrnende þecelle. Wæs þæra wyrma oroð 7 eþung swiðe deadberende 7 æterne 7 for hiora þæm wolbeorendan oroðe monige men swulton. Wið þissum wyrmum we fuhton leng þonne ane tide þære nihte, 7 hie þa wyrmas acwealdon .XXX.tig monna þære fyrde, 7 minra agenra þegna .XX.

§ 19. Ða bæd ic þa fyrde hwæþre þæt hie hæfdon god ellen þara þinga þe us on becwomon swa monigra geswencnissa 7 earfeðo. Þa hit wæs seo fifte tid þære nihte, þa mynton we us gerestan, ac þa cwoman þær hwite leon in fearra gelicnisse swa micle 7 hie ealle swiðe grymetende ferdon. Mid þa ða leon þyder cwoman þa ræsdon hie sona on us 7 we us wið him sceldan þæs ðe we [125v] mihton 7 us wæs swælc geswencnis 7 swilc earfeþo mid deorum becymen in þære sweartan niht 7 in þære þystran. Swelce eac eoforas[a] þær cwoman unmætlicre micelnisse, 7 monig oþer wildeor 7 eac tigris us on þære nihte þar abisgodon. Swelce þær eac cwoman hreaþemys þa wæron in culefrena gelicnesse swa micle, 7 þa on ure ondwlitan sperdon 7 us pulledon. Hæfdon hie eac þa hreaþemys teð in monna gelicnisse, 7 hie mid þæm þa men wundodon 7 tæron.

§ 17
[a] toweard] *om.* *V* toweard *P*

§ 19
[a] eoforas] laforas *V* eoforas *K*

§ 17. When we had lit as many fires as seemed necessary, my trumpets were sounded, and I ate some food, and so did all my army. It was then one hour before night-time, and I ordered two thousand of the golden lanterns I had with me to be lit. Then before moon-rise there came the type of insect called a scorpion, just as they usually did, towards the water. There was a great multitude of these insects, beyond number, and they hastened greatly and scurried into our camp. Then after that there came horned serpents, the kind of serpent called Carastis. They were all of different colours, some red, some black, some white. On some of them their scales glittered and shone as if they were gold when one looked at them. And the whole country resounded with the hissing of the serpents, and we had no little terror of them. But we shielded ourselves with our shields and slew and killed them with long-shafted spears, and many also burned in the fires. We endured these things to the extent that we were fighting and struggling with the serpents for fully two hours of the night.

§ 18. After the serpents had drunk the water they went away, and harmed us no more. When it was the third hour of the night, and we wanted to rest, there came serpents still more marvellous and more fearsome than the others. They had two heads, and some even had three. They were of a fantastic size, as big as columns, and some even bigger and mightier, and these serpents came down from the neighbouring hills and caves to drink the water there. The serpents came and slithered in an extraordinary fashion, with their bellies turned up and travelling on their backs, and as they advanced they ripped and tore the ground with their scales as well as their mouths. These serpents had three-pronged tongues, and when they breathed their breath came from their mouths like a burning torch. The breath and exhalation of the serpents was very deadly and poisonous, and many men died because of their pestilential breath. We fought against these serpents for more than an hour of the night, and the serpents killed thirty men from the army, and twenty of my own thegns.

§ 19. Then I commanded the army nonetheless to maintain good spirits in the face those things that afflicted us in the shape of so many difficulties and hardships. When it was the fifth hour of the night, we intended to get some rest, but there came white lions in the shape and size of bulls, and they all approached roaring mightily. When the lions came closer they immediately attacked us, and we defended ourselves against them as well as we could, but there had been such difficulty and hardship from beasts in that dark and shadowy night. There also came boars of an immeasurable size, and many other wild animals and also tigers kept us busy during the night. There also came bats in the shape and size of doves, and they scratched our faces and pulled at us. The bats had teeth like those of humans, and wounded and tore the men with them.

§ 20. Eac ðæm oþrum bisgum 7 geswencnissum þe us on becwom, þa cwom semninga swiðe micel deor sum mare þonne þara oðra ænig. Hæfde þæt deor þrie hornas on foranheafde 7 mid þæm hornum wæs egeslice gewæpnod. Þæt deor Indeos hatað *dentes tyrannum*. Hæfde þæt deor horse gelic heafod, 7 wæs blæces heowes. Ðis deor mid þy ðe hit þæs wætres ondronc, þa beheold hit þa ure wicstowe, 7 þa semninga on us 7 on ure [110r] wicstowe ræsde. Ne hit for þæm bryne wandode þæs hatan leges 7 fyres þe him wæs ongean, ac hit ofer eall wod 7 eode. Mid þy ic þa getrymede þæt mægen greca heriges, 7 we us wið him scyldan woldon, þa hit ofsloh sona minra þegna .XXVI. ane ræse, 7 .LII. hit oftræd, 7 hie to loman gerenode þæt hie mec nænigre note nytte beon meahton. 7 we hit þa unsofte mid strælum 7 eac mid longsceaftum sperum of scotadon 7 hit ofslogon 7 acwealdon.

§ 21. Þa hit wæs foran to uhtes, þa æteowde þær wolberende lyft hwites hiowes, 7 eac missenlices wæs heo on hringwisan fag, 7 monige men for heora þæm wolberendan stence swulton mid þære wolbeorendan lyfte þe þær swelc æteowde. Þa ðær cwoman eac Indisce mys in þa fyrd in foxa gelicnisse and in heora micle. Ða þonne ure feþerfotnietenu [110v] bitan 7 wundedon 7 monige for hiora wundum swultan. Þara monna hit þonne ælc gedigde, þeah hie heora hwelcne gewundodan. Ða hit wæs toforan dæges þa cwoman þær þa fugelas, Nocticoraces hatton, wæron in wealhhafoces gelicnesse, wæron hie þa fugelas brunes hiowes, 7 him wæron þa nebb 7 þa clea ealle blace. Þa fuglas ybsæton eallne þone ofer þæs meres, 7 þa fuglas us nænige laðe ne yfle ne wæron, ac hie þa gewunelican fixas þe in þæm mere wæron mid hiora cleum uptugon 7 þa tæron. Ða fuglas þa we hie ne onweg flegdon ne him lað dydon. Ac hi him selfe eft gewiton þonon.

§ 22. Þa hit ða on morgen dæg wæs, ða het ic ealle mine ladþeowas þe mec on swelc earfeðo gelæddon, het hie þa gebindan 7 him þa ban 7 sconcan forbrecan, ðæt hie [111r] on niht wæron from þæm wyrmum asogone þe þæt wæter sohton. 7 ic him het eac þa honda of aheawan, þæt hie be gewyrhtum þes wites wite drugon, þe hie ær hiora þonces us on gelæddon 7 gebrohton.

§ 23. Het ða blawan mine byman 7 þa fyrd faran forð þy wege þe we ær ongunnen hæfdon. Foran we ða þurh ða fæstlond 7 þurh þa ungeferenlican eorþan. Þa wæs þær eft gesomnad micel fyrd Indiscra monna 7 þæra elreordigra þe ða lond budon, 7 we þa wið þæm gefuhton. Mid þy we þa us eft ongeaton maran gefeoht toweard 7 mare gewin. Ða forleton we þa frecnan wegas 7 siðfato 7 þa þæm selran we ferdon. Ond swa mid mine werode onsunde in Patriacen þæt lond we becwoman mid golde 7 oþrum weolum swiðe gewelgode, 7 hie us þær fremsumlice 7 luflice onfengon. Mid þy we þa [111v] eft of þæm londe foron of Patriacen, ða becwoman we on þa londgemæro Medo 7 Persa, þa we ðær eft edniowunga hæfdon micle gefeoht. 7 .XX. daga ic þær mid minre fyrde wið him wicode.

§ 20. In addition to the other trials and difficulties which afflicted us there came suddenly one very huge beast bigger than the others. That beast had three horns on its forehead and was fiercely armed with those horns. The Indians call the beast *Dentestyrannus* [rhinoceros]. The beast had a head like a horse, and was black in colour. Once this beast had drunk the water, it saw our camp-site, and immediately attacked us and our campsite. It was not put off by the burning of the hot fire and flame that was in its path, but it went and trod on everything. After I had rallied the force of the Greek army, and we tried to protect ourselves, it promptly slew twenty-six of my thegns in a single charge and trampled fifty-two, rendering them cripples who could be of no further use to me. And we determinedly shot at it with arrows and also with long-shafted spears until we slew and killed it.

§ 21. When it was just before dawn there appeared a pestilential vapour of a white hue, which was also variously tinged with billowing swirls, and many men perished because of the pestilential stench which arose from the pestilential vapour. Then there also came against the army Indian mice the size and shape of foxes, which bit and wounded our four-footed animals; and many of them died from their wounds. Each of the men escaped, although they were all wounded. When it was just before daybreak there appeared birds, called night-ravens, looking like falcons, birds which were brown in colour, but with beaks and claws completely black. These birds sat about round the whole edge of the lake, and caused no harm or ill to any of us, but with their claws they snatched up and ripped to pieces their usual fish which were in the lake. We did not put the birds to flight nor harm them, but they soon departed of their own accord.

§ 22. When it was daylight next morning I ordered all my guides who had led me into such hardships to be tied up and their bones and legs broken, so that they might be devoured that night by the serpents on their way to the water. And I also ordered that their hands be cut off, so that thereby those might experience torment for the torment into which they had knowingly led and brought us.

§ 23. Then I ordered my trumpets to be sounded, and the army to set forth on the journey which we had started. We passed through inaccessible and impassable territory. There was soon once more gathered against us a great army of Indians and other strangers who inhabited that land, and we fought against them. We then further realised that more battles and more struggles lay ahead. Then we abandoned the dangerous routes and paths, and proceeded on the better ones. And so with my troop we came safely into the land of Patriacen, greatly enriched with gold and other wealth, and they received us there in a friendly and generous fashion. When we left the land of Patriacen, we came to the frontiers of the Medes and Persians, and there we fought once again a further great battle. And I camped there with my army for twenty days.

§ 24. Sioðþan we þa þonon ferdon þa wæs hit on seofon nihta fæce, þæt we to þæm londe 7 to þære stowe becwoman þær Porrus se cyning mid his fyrde wicode. 7 he swiðe þæs londes fæstenum truwode þonne his gefeohte 7 gewinne. Þa wilnade he þæt he me cuðe 7 mine þegnas, þa he þæs frægen 7 axsode from þæm ferendum minra wicstowa, þa wæs þæt me gesæd þæt he wilnade me to cunenne 7 min werod. Ða alede ic minne kynegyrylan 7 me mid uncuþe hrægle 7 mid lyþerlice gerelan me gegerede, swelce ic wære hwelc folclic mon 7 me wære metes[a] 7 wines þearf. Þa [112r] ic wæs in þæm wicum Porres swa ic ær sæde, ða sona swa he me þær geahsode 7 him mon sægde þæt þær mon cymen wæs of Alexandres herewicum, þa het he me sona to him lædan. Mid þy ic þa wæs to him gelæded þa frægn he me 7 ahsode hwæt Alexander se cyning dyde 7 hulic mon he wære 7 in hwylcere yldo. Ða bysmrode ic hine mid minum ondswarum 7 him sæde þæt he forealdod wære 7 to þæs eald wære þæt he ne mihte elcor gewearmigan buton æt fyre 7 æt gledum. Þa wæs he sona swiðe glæd 7 gefeonde þara minra ondswaro 7 worda, for þon ic him sæde þæt he swa forealdod wære. 7 ða cwæð he eac 'hu mæg he la ænige gewinne wið me spowan swa forealdod mon, for þon ic eom me self geong 7 hwæt.' Þa he ða geornlicor me frægn be his þingum, ða sæde ic þæt ic his þinga feola ne cuþe 7 hine seldon gesawe ðone cyning, for þon þe ic wære his [112v] þegnes mon 7 his ceapes heorde 7 wære his feohbigenga. Þa he ðas word gehyrde, ða sealde he me an gewrit 7 ænne epistolan, and me bæd þæt ic hine Alexandre þæm kyninge ageafe, 7 me eac mede gehet gif ic hit him agyfan wolde 7 ic him gehet þæt ic swa don wolde swa he me bæd. Swa ic ða þonon gewiten wæs 7 eft cwom to minum herewicum, þa ægþer ge ær ðon þe ic þæt gewrit rædde ge eac æfter þon þæt ic wæs swiðe mid hleahtre onstyred. Ðas þing ic for þon þe secge magister, 7 Olimphiade minre meder, 7 minum geswustrum, þæt ge gehyrdon 7 ongeaton þa oferhygdlican gedyrstignesse þæs eheordgan kyninges.

§ 25. Hæfd ic þa þæs kyninges wic 7 his fæstenu gesceawod þe he mid his fyrde in gefaren hæfde. Ða sona on morgne þæs ða eode Porrus se kyning [113r] me on hond mid ealle his ferde 7 dugoþe þa he hæfde ongieten þæt he wið me gewinnan ne meahte. Ond of þæm feondscipe þe us ær betweonum wæs þæt he seoðþan wæs me freond 7 eallum greca herige 7 min gefera 7 gefylcea. 7 ic him ða eft his rice ageaf 7 þa ðære unwendan are þæs rices þe he him seolfa næniges rices ne wende, þæt he ða me eall his goldhord æteowde, 7 he þa ægþer ge mec ge eac eall min werod mid golde gewelgode. 7 Herculis gelicnisse 7 Libri ðara twegea goda, he buta of golde gegeat 7 geworhte 7 hie butu asette in þæm eastdæle middangeardes. Ða wolde ic witan hwæþer ða gelicnissa wæron gegotene ealle swa he sæde. Het hie þa þurhborian þa wæron hie buta of golde gegotene, ða het ic eft þa ðyrelo þe hiora mon þurh cunnode mid golde forwyrcean 7 afyllon [113v] 7 het þa ðæm godum bæm onsægdnisse on secgan.

§ 24
[a] metes] mete *V* metes *P*

§ 24. Afterwards we journeyed for a period of seven nights, until we came to the land and the place where Porus the king was encamped with his army. And he trusted more in the security of the terrain than in his own martial prowess. Then he wanted to know more about me and my thegns, so that he asked and inquired from people coming from my camp, and I was told that he wanted to know more about me and my troop. Then I laid aside my royal attire, and dressed myself in unfamiliar garb and lowly clothes, as if I were an ordinary man in need of food and wine. When I was in Porus's camp, as I have already said, as soon as he learnt that I was there, and he was told that someone had come from Alexander's war-camp, he had me brought to him immediately. When I was brought to him he asked me and inquired what King Alexander was doing, and what sort of man he was, and of what age. I deceived him with my answers, telling him that he was extremely old, so old that he could not keep himself warm except at the fire and coals. He was at once very glad, rejoicing at these words and answers of mine, since I told him that he was such an extremely old man. And then he said 'So how can he have any success in battle against me, when he is such an extremely old man and I myself am young and fit?' Then he asked me more keenly about his affairs, and I said I did not know many of his affairs, and only saw the king seldom, since I was his thegn's man, and his cattle-herd, and his retainer. When he heard these words, he gave me a document and a letter, and told me to give it to King Alexander, and also promised me a reward if I would give it him, and I said that I would do as he asked. So I left there, and came back to my war-camp, and both before I read the document and also afterwards I was greatly rocked with mirth. I am telling you these things to you, teacher, and to Olympias my mother and my sisters, so that you can hear and understand the overweening brashness of the foreign king.

§ 25. I had spied out the king's camp and the protective surroundings into which he had gone with his army. Early the next morning King Porus came into my hands with all his army and personal retinue, when he realised that he could not fight against me. And after the hostility that had been between us, he became a friend to me and to all the Greek army, and my companion, and ally. And I gave him back his kingdom, and in return for the unexpected favour of the kingdom, since he did not expect any kingdom, he showed me his entire store of treasure, and he endowed both me and all my troop with gold. And he had cast and wrought in gold statues of the two gods Hercules and Bacchus, and set them both up on the eastern edge of the world. Then I wanted to know if the statues were entirely cast as he described. So I ordered holes to be drilled into them, and they were made of solid gold, and then I ordered the holes which had been drilled to be filled up and replaced with gold, and decreed sacrifices to be offered to both gods.

§ 26. Þa ferdon we forð 7 woldan ma wunderlicra þinga geseon 7 sceawian 7 mærlicra. Ac þa ne gesawon we swa swa we þa geferdon noht elles buton þa westan feldas 7 wudu 7 duna be þæm garsecge, ða wæron monnum ungeferde for wildeorum 7 wyrmum. Þa ferde ic hwæþre be þæm sæ to þon þæt ic wolde cunnian meahte ic ealne middangeard ybferan swa garsecge beligeð. Ac þa sægdon me þa londbigengan þæt se sæ wære to þon þiostre 7 se garsecg eall, þæt hine nænig mon mid scipe geferan ne meahte. On ic þa ða wynstran dælas Indie wolde geondferan þy læs me owiht in þæm londe beholen oððe[a] bedegled wære.

§ 27. Ða wæs þæt lond eall swa we geferdon adrugad 7 fen 7 cannon 7 hreod weoxan. Ða cwom þær semninga sum [114r] deor of þæm fenne 7 of ðæm fæstene, wæs þæm deore eall se hrycg acæglod swelce snoda hæfde þæt deor seonowealt heafod swelce mona 7 þæt deor hatte *quasi caput luna* 7 him wæron þa breost gelice niccres breastum 7 heardum toðum 7 miclum hit wæs gegyred 7 geteþed. Ond hit þa þæt deor ofsloh mine þegnas twegen. Ond we þa þæt deor nowþer ne mid spere gewundigan ne meahte ne mid nænige wæpne, ac we hit uneaþe mid isernum hamerum 7 slecgum gefyldon 7 hit ofbeoton.

§ 28. Ða becwoman we syðþan to þæm wudum Indie 7 to þæm ytemestum gemærum þæs londes 7 ic þa het þa fyrd þær wician be þære ea þe Biswicmon hatte. Wæron þa wic on lengo .L. furlanga long 7 swa eac in brædo. Woldon we þa to urum swæsendum sittan, wæs hit þa seo endlefte tid dæges, þa wæs semninga geboden þæt we wæpenu noman [114v] ure tioloden, 7 us wære micel þearf þæt we us scyldan. Þa dydon we swa fengon to ussum wæpnum swa us beboden wæs. Ða cwom þær micel mængeo elpenda of þæm wudo ungemetlic weorod þara diora. Cwoman hie to þon þyder þæt hie on ða ure wic feohtan. Þa het ic sona þa hors gerwan 7 eoredmen hleapan up, 7 het geniman swina micelne wræd 7 drifan on horsum ongean þæm elpendum, for þon ic wiste þæt swin wæron ðæm deorum laðe, 7 hiora rying hie meahte afyrhton. 7 þa sona þæs þa elpendas ða swin gesawon þa wæron hie afyrhte, 7 sona on þone wudu gewiton. Ond we þa niht on þære wicstowe gesundlice wicodon, 7 ic hæfde hie[a] mid fæstene gefæstnad þæt us nowþer ne deor ne oðer earfeðo sceððan meahten.

§ 29. Ða hit þa on morgen dæg wæs, þa ferdon we on oþer þeodlond India, ða cwoman [115r] we on sumne micelne feld. Ða [a]gesawon we[a] þær ruge wifmen, 7 wæpned men wæron hie swa ruwe 7 swa gehære swa wildeor. Wæron hie nigon fota uplonge, 7 hie wæron þa men nacod 7 hie næniges hrægles ne gimdon. Ðas men Indeos hatað Ictifafonas 7 hie of ðæm neaheum 7 merum þa hronfiscas uptugon 7 þa æton 7 be þæm lifdon 7 þæt wæter æfter druncon. Mid þy ic þa wolde near þa men geseon 7 sceawigon, ða flugon hie sona in þa wæter 7 hie þær in þæm stanholum

§ 26
[a] oððe] odðe *V* oððe *C*

§ 28
[a] hie] om. *V* hie *P*

§ 29
[a...a] gesawon we] gesawe we *V* gesawon we *D*

§ 26. Then we went forth and wished to see and witness more marvellous and noteworthy things. But as we travelled we saw nothing but desolate expanses and woods and hills by the ocean, which were impassable for men because of wild beasts and serpents. Yet I still travelled along the sea, because I wanted to know if I could go right round the earth, which the ocean surrounds. But the inhabitants told me that the sea and all the ocean was too dark for any man to travel it by ship. And then I wished to make a trip through the left-hand region of India, in case anything in that land had been hidden or concealed from me.

§ 27. Then all the land through which we passed was dried up and marshy, and canes and reeds grew there. Then there came suddenly out of the fen and fastness a beast, and the beast's back was all studded with pegs like a snood, and the beast had a round head like the moon, and the beast was called *Quasi caput luna* ['moon-head', crocodile], and it had a breast like a sea-monster's breast and it was armed and toothed with hard and large teeth. And that beast slew two of my thegns. And we were unable to wound that beast with spears in any way, nor with any kind of weapon, but with difficulty we beat it and subdued it with iron mallets and sledge-hammers.

§ 28. Then we came to the woods of India, and to the furthermost edge of that country, and I ordered the army to camp there by a river which is called Beswicmon. The camp was fifty furlongs in length and also in breadth. We wanted to sit down to eat, since it was then the eleventh hour of the day, when the order was suddenly given that we should get on and take up our weapons, for there was a great need for us to defend ourselves. We did so, and grabbed our weapons as we had been ordered. Then there came out of the woods a great multitude of elephants, an immense herd of the beasts; they came to attack our camp. Then I ordered the horses to be made ready at once, and the cavalry to mount up; I ordered them to round up a big herd of pigs and drive them on horseback against the elephants, because I knew that pigs were loathsome to those beasts, and their grunting might frighten them. And as soon as the elephants saw the pigs they were afraid, and immediately went into the woods. And we passed the night safely in that camp, and I had securely protected it so that no beast nor any other hardship could harm us.

§ 29. When it was morning, we went into another area of India, and came into a great plain. There we saw shaggy women, and men who were as shaggy and hairy as beasts. They were nine feet tall, and naked, not bothering about any clothing. The Indians call these people Ictifafonas, and they snatch up whales from the neighbouring rivers and lakes, and eat them and live on them, and drink the water afterwards. When I wanted to take a closer look and observe these people, they immediately fled into the water and hid themselves in stony hollows.

hyddon. Þa æfter þon gesawon we betweoh þa wudu bearwas 7 þa treo healfhundinga micle mængeo, ða cwoman to þon þæt hie woldon us wundigan. 7 we þa mid strælum hie scotodon, 7 hie sona onweg aflymdon ða hie eft on þone wudu gewiton. Þa syððan[b] geferdon we in þa westenn India 7 we þa þær noht wunderlices ne mærlices gesawon.

§ 30. Ond we þa eft in Fasiacen þæt [115v] lond becwoman þanan we ær ferdon 7 we þær gewicodon be þæm neahwætrum 7 we þær ure geteld bræddon ealle on æfen, 7 þær wæron eac fyr wel monigo onæled. Ða cwom þær semninga swiðe micel wind 7 gebræc, 7 to þæs unheorlic se wind geweox þæt he þara ura getelda monige afylde, 7 he ða eac usse feþerfotnietenu swiðe swencte. Ða het ic gesomnigan eft þa geteld 7 seamas ealle tosomne, 7 hie mon þa seamas 7 þa þing ðara ura wicstowa earfoðlice tosomne for þæm winde gesomnode. Ond ða on gehliuran dene 7 on wearmran we gewicodan. Mid þy we gewicod hæfdon 7 ure þing eall gearo, þa het ic eallne þone here þæt he to swæsendum sæte 7 mete þigde, 7 hie þa swa dydon. Mid þy hit æfenne nealehte, ða ongunnon þa windas eft weaxan, 7 þæt weder hreogan 7 ungemetlic cele geweox on þone æfen. Ða cwom þær micel snaw 7 swa [116r] miclum sniwde swelce micel flys feolle. Ða ic þa unmætnisse 7 micelnisse ðæs snawes geseah, ða þuhte me þæt ic wiste þæt he wolde ealle þa wicstowe forfeallan. Ða het ic þone here þæt hie mid fotum þone snaw trædon, 7 þa fyr eall wæron forneah for þære micelnesse þæs snawes adwæscte 7 acwencte. Hwæþere us þær wæs anes þinges eþnes, þæt se snaw ðær leng ne wunede þonne ane tide. Ða sona wæs æfter þon swiðe sweart wolcen 7 genip, 7 þa eac cwoman of þæm sweartan wolcne byrnende fyr. Þa fyr ðonne feollon on þa eorþan swelce byrnende þecelle 7 for þæs fyres bryne eall se feld born. Ða cwædon men þætte hie wendon þæt þæt wære goda eorre þæt usic þær on becwome. Ða het ic eald hrægl toslitan 7 habban wið þæm fyre 7 sceldan mid. Þa seoððan[a] æfter þon we hæfdon smolte niht 7 gode siðþan[b] [116v] usic þa earfeðo forleton.

§ 31. 7 we ða sioðþan butan orenum þingum mete þigdon 7 usic restan, 7 ic þær þa bebyrgde minra þegna .V. hund þe ðær betweoh ða snawas 7 earfeþo 7 þa fyr þe us þær in þæm wicum on becwoman þæt hie forwurdon 7 deade wæron. Ond þa het ic of þære wicstowe sioððan[a] þa ferd faran forð 7 we þa foron forð be þæm sæ, 7 þær ða hean hos 7 dene 7 garsecg ðone Æthiopia we gesawon. Swelce eac þa miclan 7 þa mæron dune we gesawon þa mon hateð Enesios 7 þæt scræf Libri þæs godes. Ða het ic þær in bescufan forworhte men þæt ic wolde gewitan hweþer sio segen soð wære þe me mon ær be þon sægde, þæt þær nænig mon ingan mehte 7 eft gesund æfter þon beon nymþe he mid asegendnisseum ineode in þæt scræf. 7 þæt wæs eac æfter þon gecyðed in þara monna deaðe, for þon ðy þriddan dæge hie swulton ðæs þe hie in [117r] þæt scræf eodon. Ond ic eaþmodlice 7 geornlice bæd þa godmægen þæt hie mec ealles middangeardes kyning 7 hlaford mid hean sigum geweorþeden, ond in Macedoniam ic eft gelæded wære to Ollmphiade minre meder 7 to minum geswustrum 7 gesibbum.

[b] syððan] sydðan *V* syððan *C*

§ 30
[a] seoððan] seodðan *V* seoððan *C*

[b] siðþan] siðþan siððan *V* siðþan *B*

§ 31
[a] sioððan] siodðan *V* sioððan *C*

After that we saw amongst the wooded groves and trees a great multitude of Cynocephali who came because they wished to wound us, and we shot them with arrows, and they soon fled away and went back into the woods. Then we went into the Indian desert, and we saw nothing marvellous or extraordinary there.

§ 30. And we returned back to the land of Fasiacen from whence we came, and camped there by some nearby water, and set up all our tents in the evening, and there were also a great many fires lit. Then there came suddenly a very mighty wind and bluster, and the wind grew so fierce that it blew down many of our tents, and also greatly distressed our four-footed animals. Then I ordered all the tents and baggage to be gathered together again, and because of the wind the baggage and camp-belongings were with difficulty gathered together. And then we camped in a milder and warmer valley. When we had camped, and all our belongings were ready, I ordered the whole army that they should sit down and partake of their food, and they did so. When it approached evening, the winds began to swell again, and the weather grew rough, and a hard frost developed in the evening. Then there came much snow, and it snowed as much as if a huge fleece had fallen. When I saw the extent and depth of the snow, it seemed to me that I knew the whole camp would be engulfed. Then I ordered the army to tread the snow down with their feet, and almost all the fires were quenched and put out by the abundance of snow. Yet one thing offered us relief, that the snow lasted no longer than an hour. Immediately after that the sky grew very black and dark, and from the dark sky there came burning fire. The fire fell to the earth like a burning torch, and the whole plain was burning from the fire's flame. Then men said that they thought it was the anger of the gods which had fallen upon us. Then I ordered old clothing to be torn up and used as a protection against the fire. After that we had a quiet and peaceful night, once our difficulties assuaged.

§ 31. And then we took our meal and rested without trouble, and I buried there the five hundred of my thegns who had perished and were dead as a result of the snow and fire and other difficulties that had befallen our camp. And then I ordered the army to set forth from the camp, and we set forth along the sea, and we saw the high promontories and valley and ocean of Ethiopia. And we also saw the high and famous mountain which is called Enesios, and the cave of the god Bacchus. Then I ordered condemned men to be pushed in because I wanted to know whether the tradition was true that I had been told, that no one could enter and emerge afterwards unscathed unless he entered the cave with offerings. And that was afterwards made clear by the men's death, for they perished on the third day after they had entered the cave. And I humbly and eagerly asked the gods that they honour me with splendid victories as the king and lord of the entire world, and that I be led back to Olympias my mother and to my sisters and family.

§ 32. Ða wolde ic eft in Fasiacen þæt lond feran, mid þy ic þa ferde mid mine weorede, ða cwoman us þær on ðæm wege twegen ealde men togeanes. Ða frægn ic hie 7 ahsode hwæþer hie owiht mærlic in þæm londum wisten. Ða ondsworadon hie mec 7 sægdon þæt nære mara weg þonne ic[a] meahte on tyn dagum geferan. Hwæþre mid ealle mine weorede somod ic hit geferan ne mehte for ðara wega nerwette, ac mid feower þusendum monna ic hit geferan meahte, þæt ic mærlices hwæthwugo gesawe. Ða wæs ic swiðe bliðe 7 gefeonde for þæm hiora wordum. Ða cwæð ic eft [117v] to him 7 him spræc liðum wordum to: 'secgað, la, mec, git ealdon, hwæt þæt sie mærlices 7 micellices þæt git mec gehatað þæt ic þær geseon mæge?' Ða andswarode me hiora oðer 7 cwæð: 'þu gesiehst kyning gif þu hit geferest[b] þa tu trio sunnan 7 monan on Indisc 7 on grecisc sprecende. Oþer þara is wæpnedcynnes sunnan trio, oþer wifkynnes þæt monan trio, 7 hie gesecgað þæm men þe hie frineð, hwæt godes oþðe yfles him becuman sceal.'

§ 33. Ða ne gelyfde ic him ac wende þæt hi mec on hyscte 7 on bismer sægdon. 7 ic swa cwæð to minum geferan: 'min þrym is from eastewearde middangearde oþ þæt westanweardne 7 mec þas forealdodan[a] elreordegan nu her bysmergeað.' Mynte ic hie haton yflian, ða sworan hie swiðe þæt hie soð sægdon 7 noht lugen þara þinga. Ða wolde ic gecunnian [126r] hwæþer hie mec soð sægdon, 7 mec mine geferan bædon þæt hie swelcra merþo bescerede ne wæron, ac ðæt we[b] gecunnedon hwæþer hit swelc wære ða hit næs micel to geferanne. Genom þa mid mec þreo þusendo, 7 forlet mine fyrd elcor in Fasiacen under Pore þæm kyninge 7 under minum gerefum ðær abidon. Ða foran we 7 usic þa ladteowas læddon þurh þa wædlan stowe wætres 7 þurh þa unarefndon lond wildeora 7 wyrma þa wæron wunderlicum nomum on Indisc geceged.

§ 34. Mid þy we þa nealehtan ðæm þeodlonde þa gesawon we ægþer ge wif ge wæpnedmen mid panthera[a] fellum 7 tigriscum þara deora hydum gegyryde 7 nanes oðres brucon. Mid þy ic þa frægn hie 7 ahsode hwelcre ðeode kynnes hie wæron. Ða ondswarodon hie mec 7 sægdon on hiora geþeode þæt [126v] hie wæran Indos. Wæs seo stow rum 7 wynsumo 7 balzamum 7 recels ðær wæs genihtsumnis 7 þæt eac of þæra treowa telgan weol 7 þa men þæs londes bi ðy lifdon 7 þæt æton. Mid þy we ða geornlicor þa stowe sceawodon 7 betwih þa bearwas eodon, 7 ic ða wynsumnesse 7 fægernesse þæs londes wundrade.

§ 32

[a] ic] *om. V* ic *C*

[b] geferest] geferest 7 *V* geferest *D*

§ 33

[a] forealdodan] forealðoðan *V* forealdodan *C*

[b] we] we his *V* we *P*

§ 34

[a] panthera] palthera *V* panthera *P*

§ 32. Then I intended to go back to the land of Fasiacen, but as I travelled with my army, there came two old men to meet us on the way. Then I asked them and inquired whether they knew of any noteworthy thing in that land. Then they answered me and said that there was, and could be reached in no more than ten days. But I could not travel there along with all my army, because of the narrowness of the way, but I could travel with four thousand men, and see something extraordinary. Then I was very pleased and delighted by their words. I addressed them again and spoke kind words to them: 'Tell me, indeed, you old pair, what it is of note and importance that you promise me that I can see there?' Then one of them answered me and said 'King, you will see, if you get there, the two trees of the Sun and Moon speaking in Indian and Greek. The tree of the Sun is male, and the tree of the Moon is female, and they say to the people who ask what good or ill shall befall them'.

§ 33. Then I did not believe them, but thought that they spoke to me in ridicule and mockery. And I said to my companions: 'My might extends from the East of the world to the West, and these aged foreigners are now mocking me'. I intended to have them punished, but they swore fervently that they spoke the truth and were not lying about those things. Then I wanted to find out whether they were telling me the truth, and my companions asked that they should not be deprived of such an honour, and that we should go and find out if it were so, since it was not a long journey. I took three thousand with me, and let the rest of the army remain in Fasiacen under King Porus and my companions. Then we set out and the guides led us through a place bereft of water and through lands unbearable with wild beasts and serpents called by marvellous Indian names.

§ 34. When we approached the land we saw both women and men dressed in the skins of panthers and the hides of the beasts called tigers, and wearing nothing else. When I asked them and inquired what kind of people they were they answered me and said that they were Indians. The place was spacious and pleasant, and balsam and incense were there in abundance, and welled out from the boughs of the trees, and the people of that land ate them and lived thereby. Then we took a closer look at that place, and went through the groves, and I was amazed at the loveliness and beauty of the land.

§ 35. Đa cwom se bisceop þære stowe us togeanes. Wæs he se bisceop .X. fota upheah, 7 eall him wæs se lichoma sweart buton þæm toþum ða wæron hwite. 7 þa earan him þurh þyrelode, 7 earhringas onhongedon of mænigfealdan gimcynne geworhte, 7 he wæs mid wildeora fellum gegerwed. Þa he se bisceop to me cwom, ða grette he me sona 7 halette[a] his leodþeawe. Frægn he eac me to hwon ic þider cwome 7 hwæt ic þær wolde. Þa ondswarode ic him[b] þæt mec lyste geseon þa halgan trio [127r] sunnan 7 monan. Đa ondswarode he: 'gif þine geferan beoð clæne from wifgehrine, þonne moton hie gongan in þone godcundan bearo.' Wæs minra geferana mid me þrio hund monna. Þa het se bisceop mine geferan þæt hie hiora gescie 7 ealne heora gerelan him of adyden. Ond het ic æghwæt swa don swa he us bebead. Wæs hit þa sio endlefte tid dæges. Đa bad se socerd sunnan setlgonges[c] for þon sunnan trio agefeð ondsware æt þæm upgonge 7 eft æt setlgonge, 7 þæt monan triow gelice swa on niht dyde.

§ 36. Đa ongon ic geornlicor þa stowe sceawigan, 7 geond þa bearwas 7 treowu gongan, þa geseah ic þær balzamum þæs betstan stences genoh of þæm treowum ut weallan. Þæt balzamum ægþer ge ic ge mine geferan þær betwih þæm rindum noman þæra trio. Þonne wæron ða halgan trio sunnan 7 monan [127v] on middum þæm oðrum treowum meahton hie beon hunteontiges fota upheah, 7 eac þær wæron oþre treow wunderlicre heanisse ða hatað Indeos Bebronas. Þara triowa heannisse ic wundrade, 7 cwæð þæt ic wende þæt hie for miclum wætan 7 regnum swa heage weoxon. Đa sægde se bisceop þæt þær næfre in þæm londum regnes dropa ne cwome ne fugel ne wildeor, ne nænig ætern wyrm þæt her dorste gesecean ða halgan gemæro sunnan 7 monan. Eac þonne he sægde se bisceop þonne þæt eclypsis wære þæt is þonne ðæs sunnan asprungnis oðþe þære monan, þæt ða halgan triow swiðe wepen 7 mid micle sare onstyred[a] wæron, for þon hie ondredon þæt hie hiora godmægne sceoldon beon benumene. Đa þohte ic[b] þæt ic wolde onsægdnisse þær onsecgan, ac þa forbead me se bisceop, 7 sægde þæt ðæt nære [128r] alyfed ænigum men þæt he þær ænig nyten cwealde oþþe blodgyte worhte, ac mec het þæt ic me to þara triowa fotum gebæde, þæt sunna 7 mone me soþre [c]ondswarege ondwyrdum[c] þara þinga ðe ic frune sioððan[d] þas þing þus gedon wæron. Þa gesawon we westan þone leoman sunnan 7 se leoma gehran þæm treowum ufonweardum. Đa cwæð se sacerd: 'lociað nu ealle up 7 be swa hwylcum þingum swa ge willon frinan, þence on his heortan deagollice, 7 nænig mon his geþoht openum wordum ut ne cyðe.'

§ 35

a halette] alette *V* halette *K*

b him] hin *V* him *C*

c setlgonges] setlgongen *V* setlgonges *D*

§ 36

a onstyred] instyred *V* onstyred *P*

b ic] *post* ic *add*. sægde Alexander *V*

c...c ondswarege ondwyrdum] ondsware ge ond wyrdum *V* ondsware geondwyrdum *D*

d sioððan] sioddan *V* sioððan *C*

§ 35. Then the bishop of the place came to meet us. The bishop was ten feet tall and his entire body was black, except his teeth were white. And his ears were pierced through, and ear-rings hung down made of many kinds of jewels, and he was dressed in the skins of wild-animals. When the bishop approached me, he greeted me immediately, and welcomed me according to the custom of that people. He asked me why I had come, and what I wanted. I answered that I wished to see the sacred trees of the Sun and Moon. Then he answered: 'If your companions are pure of the touch of women, they can enter the holy grove'. There were three hundred of my companions with me. Then the bishop ordered my companions that they take off their shoes and all their clothing. And I ordered them to do as he asked us. It was then the eleventh hour of the day. Then the priest waited for the setting of the sun, for the tree of the Sun gave its answer at the rising and setting of the Sun, and the tree of the Moon did so likewise at night.

§ 36. Then I began to take a closer look at the place, and to pass through the groves and trees. I saw plenty of balsam of the finest perfume welling out from the trees. My companions and I gathered the balsam from the bark of the trees. The holy trees of the Sun and the Moon were in the midst of the other trees; they might have been a hundred feet tall, and there were other trees of a remarkable height which the Indians call Bebronas. I was amazed at the height of the trees, and said that I supposed that they grew so high on account of much moisture and rainfall. Then the bishop said that no drop of rain ever came in that land, nor bird, nor wild beast, nor did any poisonous serpent dare to seek out the holy precincts of the Sun and the Moon. The bishop also said that during an eclipse, that is a waning of the Sun or Moon, the holy trees wept greatly, and were stirred with great sorrow, for they feared that their divine power would be taken. Then I thought that I would make a sacrifice, but the bishop forbade me, and said that it was not permitted to any man to kill any animal there or cause bloodshed, but he ordered me pray at the foot of the trees, that the Sun and Moon would give a truthful answer to those things I should ask after this was done. Then we saw the Sun's ray set, and the ray touched the tops of the trees. Then the priest said: 'Look up, all of you, and think secretly in your heart what you want to know, and let no one openly reveal his thought in words'.

§ 37. Mid þy we þa wel neah stodan þam bearwum 7 þæm godsprecum, þa ðohte ic on minum mode hwæþer ic meahte ealne middangeard me on onweald geslean, 7 þonne sioþþan mid þæm siogorum geweorþad, ic eft meahte [128v] becuman in Macedoniam to Olimphiade minre meder, 7 minum geswustrum. Ða ondswarode me þæt triow Indiscum wordum 7 þus cwæd: 'Ða unoferswyðda Alexander in gefeohtum þu weorðest cyning 7 hlaford ealles middangeardes, ac hwæþre ne cymst þu on þinne eþel ðonan þu ferdest ær, for þon ðin wyrd[a] hit swa be þinum heafde 7 fore hafað aræded.' Ða wæs ic ungleaw þæs geþeodes þara Indiscra worda þe þæt triow me to spræc, ða rehte hit me se bisceop 7 sægde. Mid þy hit mine geferan gehyrdon þæt ic eft cwic ne moste in minne eþel becuman, ða wæron hie swiðe unrote for þon. Þa wolde ic eft on þa æfentid ma ahsian, ac þa næs se mona þa gyt uppe. Mid þy we þa eft eodon in þone halgan bearo, 7 we þa eft be þæm treowum stodan ge[129r]bædon us þa sona to þæm treowum swa we ær dydon. 7 ic eac in mid mec gelædde mine þrie ða getreowestan frynd, ða wæron mine syndrige treowgeþoftan, þæt wæs ærest Perticam, 7 Clitomum, 7 Pilotan, for þon ic me ne ondred þæt me þæra ænig beswice, for þon þær næs riht on þære stowe ænigne to acwellanne for þære stowe weorþunge.

§ 38. Ða þohte ic on minum mode 7 on minum geþohte on hwelcre stowe ic sweltan scolde. Mid þy ða ærest se mona upeode þa gehran he mid his sciman þæm triowum ufeweardum 7 þæt triow ondswarode þæm minum geþohte 7 þus cwæð: 'Alexander fulne ende þines lifes þu hæfst gelifd, ac þys æftran geare þu swyltst on Babilone on Maius monðe from þæm þu læst wenst from þæm þu bist beswicen.' Ða wæs ic swiðe sariges [129v] modes, 7 þa mine frynd swa eac þa me þær mid wæron. 7 hie weopon swiðe, for þon him wære min gesynto leofre þonne hiora seolfra hælo. Ða gewiton we to urum geferum eft, 7 hie woldon to hiora swæsendum sittan, 7 ic wolde for þæm bysegum mines modes me gerestan. Ac þa bædon mec mine geferan þæt ic on swa micelre modes unreto 7 nearonisse mec selfne mid fæstenne ne swencte. Þigde ða tela medmicelne[a] mete wið mines modes willan, 7 þa tidlice to minre reste eode for þon ic wolde beon gearo æt sunnan upgonge þæt ic eft in geeode.

§ 39. Ða on morgne mid þy hit dagode, þa onbræd ic 7 þa mine getreowestan frynd aweahte þæt ic wolde in þa halgan stowe gan. Ac þa reste hine se bisceop þa giet, 7 mid wildeora [130r] fellum wæs gegerwed 7 bewrigen. 7 irenes 7 leades þa men on þæm londum wædliað 7 goldes genihtsumiað 7 be ðæm balzamum þa men in þæm londe lifgeað 7 of ðæm neahmunte wealleð hluter wæter 7 fæger 7 þæt swiðe swete. Þonne drincað þa men þæt 7 by lifigeað. 7 þonne hie restað, þonne restað hie buton bedde 7 bolstre, ac on wildeora[a] fellum heora bedding bið. Ða awehte ic þone bisceop. Hæfde se bisceop þreo hund wintra on yldo.

§ 37

[a] wyrd] eþel *V* wyrd *C*

§ 38

[a] medmicelne] micelne *V* medmicelne *D*

§ 39

[a] wildeora] wildeor *V*

§ 37. As we stood very close to the grove and the oracles, I thought in my heart whether I would be able to force the whole world under my power, and then, honoured by those victories, be able to return to Macedonia, to Olympias my mother, and to my sisters. Then the tree answered me in Indian words and said: 'Alexander, unconquered in battle, you shall become king and lord of all the world, but you shall never return to your homeland whence you came, since your fate has so decided it on your head, and so decreed it'. Since I could not understand the language of the Indian words the tree spoke to me, the bishop translated it and told me. When my companions heard that I would not return to my homeland alive, they were greatly sad because of it. Then I wished to ask more that evening, but the moon was not yet up. When we returned to the holy grove, and stood beside the trees, we immediately prayed to the trees as we had done before. And I took with me my three most trusted friends, who were especially loyal; first Perticas, and Clitomus, and Pilotas, for I had no fear that any of these would betray me, and because it was not right to kill anyone there on account of the reverence due to the place.

§ 38. Then I thought in my heart and in my thoughts in which place I should die. When the Moon first rose it touched with its beam the tops of the trees, and the tree answered my thought and said: 'Alexander, you have lived the full course of your life, and in the next year you shall die in Babylon, in the month of May, from a source by which you least expect to be betrayed'. Then I was extremely sick at heart, as were my friends that were with me. And they wept greatly, since my safety was dearer to them than their own health. Then we went back to our companions, and they wanted to sit down to eat, but because of the cares of my heart I wanted to rest. But my companions asked me in such distress and anxiety of heart not to vex myself with fasting. I ate very little food, against my heart's will, and then went early to bed, since I wanted to be ready to go in again at sunrise.

§ 39. In the morning, when day came, I awoke and woke up my truest friends, since I wanted to enter the holy place. But the bishop was still resting, wrapped and covered with the skins of wild animals. And the people of that place are poor in iron and lead, but rich in gold. And the people of that place live on balsam, and from a neighbouring mountain there wells up clear and beautiful water, of great sweetness. The people drink it and live thereby. And when they rest, they rest without any bed or bolster, but the skins of wild beasts are their bedding. Then I woke the bishop. The bishop was three hundred years old.

§ 40. Mid þy he þa se bisceop aras, ða eode ic on þa godcundan stowe 7 þa þriddan siðe þæt sunnan treow ongon frinan þurh hwelces monnes hond min ende wære getiod, oððe[a] hwelcne endedæg min modor oþðe min geswuster nu gebidan scoldon. Þa ondswarode me þæt treow on grecisc 7 þus cwæð: 'Gif ic þe þone [130v] gesecge þines feores yþelice þu ða wyrde oncyrrest 7 his hond befehst. Ac soð ic þe secge þæt yb anes geares fyrst 7 eahta monað þu swyltst in Babilone, nalles mid iserne acweald swa ðu wenst ac mid atre. Ðin modor gewiteð of weorulde þurh scondlicne deað 7 unarlicne, 7 heo ligeð unbebyrged in wege fuglum to mete 7 wildeorum. Þine sweostor beoð longe gesæliges lifes. Ðu þonne ðeah þu[b] lytle hwile lifge hweþre ðu geweorðest an cyning 7 hlaford ealles middangeardes. Ac ne frign ðu unc nohtes ma ne[c] axa, for þon wit habbað oferhleoðred þæt gemære uncres leohtes, ac to Fasiacen 7 Porre þæm cyninge eft gehworf þu.' 7 fer ðy þa weopon mine geferan, for þon ic swa lytle hwile lyfigan moste. Ac þa forbead hit se bisceop þæt hi ne weopon, [131r] þy læs þa halgan treow þurh heora wop 7 tearas abulgen.

§ 41. Ond ne geherde ða ondsware þara treowa ma manna þonne þa mine getreowestan freond, ond hit nænig mon ut cyþan ne moste þy læs þa elreordegan kyningas ðe ic ær mid nede to hyrsumnesse gedyde, þæt hie on þæt fægon þæt ic swa lytle hwile lifgean moste. Ne hit eac ænig mon þære ferde ðon ma ut mæran moste þy læs hie for ðon ormode wæron 7 þy sænran mines willan 7 weorðmyndo, ðæs hie mid mec to fromscipe geferan scoldon. Ond me næs se hrædlica ende mines lifes swa miclum weorce swa me wæs þæt ic læs mærðo gefremed hæfde þonne min willa wære. Ðas þing ic write to þon, min se leofa magister, þæt þu ærest gefeo in þæm fromscipe mines lifes 7 eac blissige in þæm weorðmyndum. Ond eac [131v] swelce ecelice min gemynd stonde 7 hleouige[a] oðrum eorðcyningum to bysne, ðæt hie witen þy gearwor þæt min þrym 7 min weorðmynd maran wæron, þonne ealra oþra kyninga þe in middangearde æfre wæron. *Finit.*

§ 40
a oððe] odðe *V* oððe *C*
b þu] þu þu *V* þu *P*
c ne] ne ne *V* ne *P*

§ 41
a hleouige] hleonige *V*

§ 40. When the bishop arose, I went into the holy place and for the third time I began to ask the tree of the Sun through which man's hand my end was decreed, and what kind of death my mother or my sisters could now expect. Then the tree answered me in Greek and said: 'If I tell you about your life you will easily turn aside your fate and stay its hand. But it is true what I tell you; in the space of one year and eight months you will die in Babylon, killed not, as you expect, with iron, but with poison. Your mother will leave the world by a shameful and lowly death, and she will lie unburied in the street as food for birds and wild beasts. Your sisters will have long and happy lives. And as for you, though you live but a short time you shall be sole king and lord of the whole world. But do not question or ask the pair of us any more, for we have spoken beyond the limit of our light, but turn back to Fasiacen and King Porus'. And because of that my companions wept, because I had so little time to live. But the bishop forbade them to weep, in case the holy trees should be angered by their weeping and tears.

§ 41. And no one else heard the answers of the holy trees except my most trusted friends, and no one was allowed to make it known, in case the foreign kings that I had forcibly brought under my command should be glad that I had so little time to live. Nor was anyone allowed to reveal it further to the army, in case they became dispirited, and more indolent concerning my will and my honour, for which they had to carry me to success. And to me the swift ending of my life was not so much pain as the fact that I had achieved less glory than I would have wished. I write these things to you, my beloved teacher, that you first can rejoice in the success of my life, and exult in the honours. And also my memory shall forever stand and tower as an example for other earthly kings, so that they know the more readily that my power and my honour were greater than those of all the other kings who have ever lived in the world. *Finit.*

APPENDIX IIIa

Liber monstrorum

Latin text

SIGLA

W Wolfenbüttel, Herzog-August Bibliothek, Gudianus lat. 148, fols. 108v–123v
S St Gallen, Stiftsbibliothek 237, pp. 2–6
L Leiden, Bibliotheek der Rijks-Universiteit, Voss. lat., Oct. 60, fols. 1v–12v
R New York, Pierpoint Morgan Library 906, pp. 79–110
Y London, British Library, Royal 15. B. xix, fols. 103v–105v
H Haupt, ed., 'Index lectionum aestivarum 1863', pp. 218–52
P Porsia, ed., *Liber monstrorum*, pp. 126–286
B Bologna, ed., *Liber monstrorum*, pp. 34–154
T Butturff, 'The Monsters and the Scholar', pp. 61–90

[a]INCIPIT LIBER MONSTRORUM DE DIVERSIS GENERIBUS[a]
PROLOGUS

[a]De occulto orbis terrarum[b] situ interrogasti[c] et si tanta monstrorum essent genera credenda quanta in abditis mundi partibus per deserta et Oceani insulas et in ultimorum montium latebris nutrita monstrantur, et praecipue de his tribus orbis terrae generibus respondere[d] petebas quae maximum formidinis terrorem humano generi incutiunt[e], ut de monstruosis[f] hominum partibus describerem et de ferarum horribilibus innumerosisque[g] bestiarum formis et draconum dirissimis serpentiumque ac uiperarum generibus. Et dum sermo de his per multarum scripturarum auctoritatem uelud excelsi[h] sideris fulgore[i] olim humano generi paene ubique refulsit, mendacia[j] ea nemini iteranda putassem nisi me uentus tuae postulationis a puppi praecelsa pauidum inter marina praecipitasset monstra. Ponto namque tenebroso hoc opus aequipero, quod[k] probandi si sint uera an instructa mendacio, nullus

a...a INCIPIT . . . GENERIBUS] *om. WSLR*

PROLOGUS

a...a De . . . fabulae] *om. SLR*
b terrarum] *om. Y*
c interrogasti] rogasti *Y*
d respondere] respondi *Y*
e incutiunt] incutiunum *Y*
f monstruosis] monstruosis *corr. in* monstrosis *W*
g innumerosisque] numerosisque *Y*
h excelsi] excelsis *W*
i fulgore] fulgor *Y*
j mendacia] mendacidam *W om. Y*
k quod] quia *Y*

APPENDIX IIIb

Liber monstrorum

A translation

HERE BEGINS THE BOOK OF MONSTERS OF VARIOUS KINDS:
PROLOGUE

You have asked about the secret arrangement [or 'filthiness'] of the lands of the earth, and if as many kinds of monsters are to be credited as are demonstrated in the hidden parts [or 'births'] of the world, raised throughout the deserts and the islands of the Ocean and in the recesses of the farthest mountains, and you were particularly asking me to answer about these three kinds of the world's area which strike the greatest terror of fear in humankind, so that I should record the monstrous parts [or 'births'] of men, and the horrible and innumerable forms of wild beasts, and the most dreadful kinds of dragons, and serpents, and vipers. And whilst discussion of these things once shone almost everywhere for humankind as if with the brightness of a lofty star through the authority of many writings, I should have thought that those lies were unrepeatable to anyone, if the gust of your request had not cast me from the high poop quivering amongst the monsters of the deep. For I compare this task with the dark sea,

patet accessus eaque per orbem terrarum aurato sermone miri rumoris fama dispergebat, quorum maximam partem philosophorum et poetarum scriptura[l] demonstrat, quae semper mendacia nutrit. Quaedam tantum in ipsis mirabilibus uera esse creduntur, et sunt innumerabilia quae si quis ad exploranda pennis uolare potuisset et ita rumoroso [m]sermone tamen[m] ficta probaret, ubi nunc urbs aurea et gemmis aspersa[n] litora dicuntur, [o]ibi lapideam[o] aut nullam urbem et scopulosa[p] cerneret. Et de[q] his primum eloquar quae sunt aliquo modo credenda et sequentem historiam sibi [r]quisque discernat[r], quod per haec antra monstrorum marinae puellae quandam formulam sirenae[s] depingam, ut sit capite rationis[t] [u]quod tamen[u] diuersorum generum hispidae squamosaeque[v] sequuntur fabulae[a].

[w]Primoque namque de his ad ortum sermo prorumpit quae[x] leuiore discretu[y] ab humano genere distant, daturus operam de singulis quae terra fouet[z] mortalium nutrix, aut quondam[a] [b]fouisse fertur[b], quia[c] nunc humano[d] genere[e] multiplicato et terrarum[f] orbe repleto, sub astris[g] minus producuntur[h] monstra, quae ab ipsis per [i]plurimos terrae angulos[i] eradicata funditus et subuersa[j] legimus et nunc reuulsa[k] litoribus [l]prona torquentur ad undas, quaeque turbine poli uertice[l] sub arduo[m] a[n] totius gyri ambitu et [o]omni loco[o] terrarum ad hanc[p] uastam gurgitis [q]se uoraginem uergunt[q] [w].

l scriptura] scriptara *corr. in* scriptura *Y*
m...m sermone tamen] sermo setam *W* sermone tam *Y*
n aspersa] aspera *Y*
o...o ibi lapideam] ubi lapideum *W*
p scopulosa] scopolosa *W* scropulosa *Y*
q de] *om. Y*
r...r quisque discernat] unus quisque decernat *Y*
s sirenae] sirinae *W*
t rationis] rationabilis *Y*
u...u quod tamen] quot tantum *W* quam tamen *Y*
v squamosaeque] squamose quae *W*
w...w Primoque . . . uergunt] *om. S*
x quae] qui *L*
y discretu] discreto *WLY*
z fouet] fououet *Y*
a quondam] condam *W*
b...b fouisse fertur] fuisse feruntur *Y*
c quia] quae *WY*
d humano] ab humano *Y*
e genere] generi *W*
f terrarum] terra *W*
g astris] alstris *R*
h producuntur] producentur *W*
i...i plurimos . . . angulos] plurimos terra angulos *L* plurimas terrae latebras *Y*
j subuersa] effundit uniuersa *Y*
k reuulsa] reuulsas *Y*
l...l prona . . . uertice] prona torquentur ad undas quaeque turbidine poli uerticae *W* prora torqueatur ad undas quaeque turbide poli uertice *R* pro ira torquentur ad undas quaeque turbide poli uertice *L* insulas assidua celi tempestate *Y*
m arduo] arduo *corr. in* a duo *R*
n a] ac *WR om. Y*
o...o omni loco] omni *W* omnem locum *Y*
p hanc] *om. Y*
q...q se . . . uergunt] uoraginem uertunt *L* se uergere *Y*

since there is no clear way of testing whether that rumour which has spread throughout the world with the gilded speech of marvellous report is true or steeped in lies; of which things the writings of the poets and philosophers, which always foster lies, expound the greatest part. Only some things in the marvels themselves are believed to be true, and there are countless things which if anyone could take winged flight to explore, they would prove that, although they should be concocted in speech and rumour, where now there is said to lie a golden city and gem-strewn shores, one would see there rocks and a stony city, if at all. And first I will discuss those things which are in some part to be trusted, and then let each judge for himself the following material, because throughout these monster-filled caverns I shall paint a little picture of a sea-girl or siren, which if it has a head of reason is followed by all kinds of shaggy and scaly tales.

For first the discussion takes its beginning with those things which differ by a rather trifling amount from humankind, paying heed to the individuals that the earth, the mother of mortals, spawns, or is said once to have spawned, because now, when humankind has multiplied and the lands of the earth have been filled, fewer monsters are produced under the stars, and we read that in most of the corners of the world they have been utterly eradicated and overthrown by them, and now, cast out from the shores, they are thrown down to the waves, and that by the churning from the steep summit of the pole they turn from the edge of the entire circle and from every place on earth towards this vast abyss of the flood.

LIBER I

I.1 Me enim quendam hominem in [a]primordio operis[a] utriusque sexus cognouisse[b] testor, qui[c] tamen[d] ipsa facie plus et pectore uirilis quam muliebris apparuit[e]; et uir a nescientibus putabatur[f], sed muliebria [g]opera dilexit[g], et ignaros[h] uirorum[i] more [j]meretricis, decipiebat[j]; [k]sed hoc[k] frequenter apud humanum genus contigisse[l] fertur.

I.2 [a]Et fiunt monstra[a] mirae magnitudinis, ut rex Higlacus[b], qui[c] imperauit Getis[d] et a Francis occisus est, quem equus a duodecimo aetatis[e] anno portare non potuit. Cuius ossa in Rheni[f] fluminis insula, ubi in Oceanum[g] prorumpit[h], reseruata[i] sunt, et de longinquo uenientibus pro miraculo ostenduntur[j].

I.3 Et ut Colossus[a] qui mole uastissima monstrorum ad instar maritimorum[b] cunctos homines excreuit, quem unda Thybridis[c] uulneratum cooperire [d]non ualuit[d], in quem[e] se dolore[f] marcescens moriturum iactauit et ab ipso usque ad Tyrrheni[g] maris terminum per .XVIII.[h] milia passuum aquam[i] tanto sanguine commixtam[j] reddidisse[k] fertur ut[l] totus fluuius de uulneribus eius manare[m] uideretur[n]. Postquam[o] Romani [p]paene per

LIBER I

I.1 DE UTRIUSQUE SEXUS HOMINE *WPB* DE UTRIUSQUE SEXUS HOMINUM *ST* DE UTRISQUE SEXUS HOMINE *L*

a...a primordio operis] in primo hominis *WS* in pridio operis *R*
b cognouisse] cognosse *R* agnouisse *L*
c qui] quae *S*
d tamen] tantum *WS* tunc *Y*
e apparuit] apparui *S*
f putabatur] putabar *S*
g...g opera dilexit] dilexi opera *S*
h ignaros] ignoras *WS*
i uirorum] uiros *Y*
j...j meretricis decipiebat] meretrices decipiebam *S*
k...k sed hoc] set haec *W*
l contigisse] contiguisse *WS* contingisse *R*

I.2 DE HUNCGLACO MAGNO *WB* DE HUNCGLACO MAGNO *S* DE HYGLACO GETORUM REGE *LP* DE GLAUCO MAGNO *Y* DE GETARUM REGE HUIGLACO MIRAE MAGNITUDINIS *T*

a...a Et fiunt monstra] sunt alii homines *Y*
b Higlacus] huncgacus *corr. in* huncglacus *W* huncglagus *S* huiglaucus *RY*
c qui] quae enim *W* qui enim *S*
d Getis] gentes *W* gentibus *S* gethis *R* getys *Y*
e aetatis] *om. R* aetatis suae *Y*
f Rheni] reni *WLY* reno *R*
g oceanum] oceano *W*
h prorumpit] prorupit *S*
i reseruata] seruata *L*
j ostenduntur] ostendentur *W*

I.3 DE COLOSIO *WSTB* DE COLOSSO CUIUS IMAGO EST ROMAE *LP* DE COLOSSIO *Y*

a Colossus] colosius *WRLY*
b maritimorum] marinorum *S*
c Thybridis] tyberidis *W* tiberidio *S* tibridis *R* tiberi *L* tibiridis *Y*
d...d non ualuit] noualuit *R* non potuit *Y*
e quem] quam *WSY*
f dolore] dolere *WS om. Y*
g Tyrrheni] terreni *WSRY* tyrreni *L*
h .XVIII.] .X. et .VIII. *S* .XIII. *RY*
i aquam] aqua *WS*
j commixtam] conmixtum *WS*
k reddidisse] redisse *Y*
l ut] et *WS*
m manare] manuere *WS* mare *L*
n uideretur] uidebatur *WRL*
o postquam] post quem *L*
p...p paene . . . erexerunt] pene per totum orbem terrarum auditum esse hoc opus erexerunt *S* pene per totum orbem terrarum inauditum opus erexerunt *R* penerant *L*

BOOK I

I.1 Indeed I bear witness at the beginning of the work that I have known a person of both sexes, who although they appeared more masculine than feminine from their face and chest, and were thought male by those who did not know, yet loved feminine occupations and deceived the ignorant amongst men in the manner of a whore; but this is said to have happened often amongst the human race.

I.2 And there are monsters of an amazing size, like King Hygelac, who ruled the Geats and was killed by the Franks, whom no horse could carry from the age of twelve. His bones are preserved on an island in the river Rhine, where it breaks into the Ocean, and they are shown as a wonder to travellers from afar.

I.3 Or like Colossus, who in his huge bulk like that of sea-monsters outgrew all men. When he was wounded the stream of the Tiber could not cover him, into which he had flung himself at the point of death, failing from his wounds. From him right out to the mouth of the Mediterranean (some eighteen miles) the water is said to have been mixed with so much blood that the whole river seemed to flow from his wounds.

totum orbem terrarum auditum est hoc opus erexerunt[p] statuam procerissimae[q] magnitudinis, quae .C. et .VII.[r] pedes[s] altitudinis habet et prope omnia[t] Romae[u] urbis opera miro rumore praecellit[v].

I.4 Et quosdam[a] immensa[b] corporum magnitudine et bellicosissimos[c] fuisse legimus qui [d]in ambis[d] manibus [e]sex digitos[e] et[f] singulis[g] [h]habuerunt pedibus[h]; mente tamen[i] rationabiles erant, et .IIII. [j]tantum augmento[j] digitorum a ceteris discrepuerunt[k] hominibus[l].

I.5 Fauni enim siluicolae[a], qui sicut[b] a fando nuncupati[c] sunt; [d]a capite usque ad umbilicum[d] hominis[e] speciem habent; [f]capita autem[f] curuata naribus cornua dissimulant[g] et[h] inferior pars duorum pedum[i] [j]et femorum[j] in caprarum forma[k] depingitur[l]. Quos poeta Lucanus, secundum[m] opinionem Graecorum, [n]ad Orphei[n] liram, cum innumerosis[o] ferarum generibus, cantu deductos[p] cecinit[q].

q procerissime] procerrimae *LY*
r .VII.] .VIII. *WS* .IIII. *Y*
s pedes] *om. L*
t omnia] omnium *S*
u Romae] Romanae *LY*
v praecellit] precellet *W*

I.4 DE HIS QUI AMBAS MANUS DIGITIS .VI. *WS* DE IPSIS QUI HABENT .VI. DIGITOS *L* DE HIS QUI HABENT .VI. DIGITOS *YP* DE HIS QUI IN AMBIS MANIBUS DIGITOS SEX *BT*

a quosdam] quosdam homines *Y*
b immensa] *om. WS*
c bellicosissimos] bellicosas *R* bellicissimos *L*
d...d in ambis] *om. L*
e...e sex digitos] digitos sex *S post* sex *om. S* et . . . hominibus
f et] et in *Y*
g singulis] singulos *R*
h...h habuerunt pedibus] manibus habuerunt *W*
i tamen] tantum *W*
j...j tantum augmento] tamen aumento *L om. Y*
k discrepuerunt] discernerunt *W*

l hominibus] *post* hominibus *add. R*: Faoni [*corr. in* Fauni] de ueteribus pastoribus fuerunt in principio mundi, qui habitauerunt in locis super quae constructa est Roma et poetae cantica de ipsis cecinerunt. Faoni [*corr. in* Fauni] nascuntur de uermibus nutis [*pro* natis] inter lignum et corticem et postremo procedunt ad terram et suscipiunt alas et eas amitunt, postmodum et efficiuntur hominis siluestres et plurima cantica de ipsis poetae cecinerunt.

I.5 DE FAUNIS *WSLYPB* DE FAUNI *T*

a siluicolae] siluestri *S* siluicolae homines *R*
b sicut] sic *S*
c nuncupati] dicti *Y*
d...d a capite . . . umbilicum] *om. Y*
e hominis] homines *W*
f...f capita autem] caput hoc *WS* caput autem *L* cum capite *Y*
g disimulant] simulant *SL*
h et] *om. Y*
i pedum] peduum *S*
j...j et femorum] femoribus *Y*
k forma] pedibus *W*
l depingitur] depinguntur *Y*
m secundum] per *Y*
n...n ad Orphei] ab orpheo *S*
o innumerosis] innumeris *SL*
p deductos] deductus *WS* ductos *Y*
q cecinit] *post* cecinit *add. R*: De Orpheo. Orpheus citharista erat eneae [*pro* Aenius?] et quantus citharista in Grecia postmodum erudita [*pro* Eurydice] uxor ipsius a serpente percussa mortua erat et pene insanus factus est in siluis liram percutiebat et bestiae ad audiendum lirae [*pro* liram] ipsius ueniebant

Afterwards the Romans erected a statue of the greatest size – this work has been heard of throughout almost the entire world – which stands 107 feet tall and surpasses nearly everything in the city of Rome by its marvellous reputation.

I.4 And we read that there were certain extremely bellicose men of huge bodily size who had six fingers on each hand and six toes on each foot. Yet they were sound of mind, and differed from other people only in the addition of four digits.

I.5 Moreover fauns, who are called thus from their speaking (*fando*), are wood-dwellers, and have human appearance from the head to the navel (although curved horns in their noses disfigure their heads), and the lower part of the two feet and the thighs is represented in the form of goats. The poet Lucan sang that, according to the opinion of the Greeks, they, along with countless other kinds of wild animals, were drawn to the lyre of Orpheus by his song.

I.6 Sirenae sunt marinae puellae[a], quae[b] nauigantes pulcherrima forma et [c]cantu dulcedinis decipiunt[c], et a capite usque[d] ad umbilicum [e]sunt corpore uirginali[e] et humano generi simillimae[f], squamosas tamen[g] piscium caudas habent, quibus semper[h] in gurgite latent.

I.7 Hippocentauri[a] equorum et hominum [b]commixtam naturam habent[b] et more ferarum sunt capite setoso, sed[c] ex parte aliqua humanae[d] [e]normae simillimo[e], quo[f] possunt incipere loqui. Sed insueta labia [g]humanae locutioni[g] nullam [h]uocem in uerba[h] distingunt[i].

I.8 Et quendam[a] hominem in Asia natum ab humanis parentibus [b]monstrosa commixtione[b] didicimus: qui pedibus et uentre[c] fuit[d] genitori compar, sed tamen[e] duo pectora quattuor[f] manus et bina capita habuit[g]. Et ad [h]ipsius mirationem[h] multos[i] rumorosa[j] contrahebat[k] opinio.

I.9 Sunt enim[a] Aethiopes toto corpore nigri, [b]quos sol flagrans nimio ardore semper adurit[b], quia[c] sub tertio[d] zonarum[e] feruentissimo et torrido[f] mundi circulo demorantur[g],

I.6 DE SIRENIBUS *W* DE SIRENIS *SLYPBT*

[a] puellae] belue *S*
[b] quae] qui *R*
[c...c] cantu . . . decipiunt] cantu dicipiunt duclitudinis *W* cantu decipiunt dulcedinis *S* cantu mulcidinis decipiunt *R* cantu mulcendo decipiunt *Y*
[d] usque] et usque *R*
[e...e] sunt . . . uirginali] corpore uirginali *R* habent corpora uirginum *Y*
[f] simillimae] simillimi *S* similia *Y*
[g] tamen] tantum *WS*
[h] semper] *om. S* tantum *Y*

I.7 DE IPOCENTAURIS *W* DE YPOCENTAURIS *S* DE EPOCENTAURIS *L* DE HYPPOCENTAURIS *Y* DE HIPPOCENTAURIS *PBT*

[a] Hippocentauri] ypocentauri *WS* epocentauri *RLY*
[b...b] commixtam . . . habent] habent commixtam naturam *WS* commixtam naturam *L*
[c] sed] *om. Y*
[d] humanae] humano *W* humane locutioni *S*
[e...e] normae simillimo] formae similes *Y*
[f] quo] quae *S* quos *L*
[g...g] humanae locutioni] huma locutione *L*
[h...h] uocem in uerba] in uerbo uocem *S*
[i] distingunt] distinguunt *S*

I.8 DE HOMINE DUPLICI *WSLYPBT*

[a] quendam] quondam *L*
[b. b] monstrosa commixtione] monstruosa commixtiosa *S* commixtione monstrosa *R* monstruosa commixtione *L* commixtione monstruosa *Y*
[c] uentre] uentri *WS*
[d] fuit] sunt *L*
[e] tamen] tantum *WS*
[f] quattuor] et .III. *Y*
[g] habuit] habens *S*
[h...h] ipsius mirationem] ipsa admirationem *Y*
[i] multos] multorum *Y*
[j] rumorosa] rumerosa *S* innumerosa *Y*
[k] contrahebat] trahebat *L* currebat *Y*

I.9 DE ETHIOPIBUS *W* DE ETHIOPIS *S* DE HAETHIOPIBUS *L* DE AETHIOPIBUS *YPBT*

[a] enim] *om. RY*
[b...b] quos . . . adurit] ardore solis *S* fraglans nimio ardore semper adurit *L*
[c] quia] quod *W om. Y*
[d] tertio] quatuor *R* quinto *L*
[e] zonarum] aronarum *R*
[f] torrido] horrendo *WS* orrido *L*
[g] demorantur] demonstrantur *WSL*

I.6 Sirens are sea-girls, who deceive sailors with the outstanding beauty of their appearance and the sweetness of their song, and are most like human beings from the head to the navel, with the body of a maiden, but have scaly fishes' tails, with which they always lurk in the sea.

I.7 Hippocentaurs have the mingled nature of horses and humans, with heads shaggy like wild animals, but in another respect most like the human norm, with which they can begin to speak. But their lips are unaccustomed to human speech, and they cannot form any sound into words.

I.8 And we have heard of a person born in Asia from human parents with a monstrous mixture. He was like his father in the feet and stomach, but had two chests and four hands and two heads. And wide-spread rumour drew many people to marvel at him.

I.9 There are Ethiopians who are black in their whole body, whom the flaming sun continually burns with excessive heat, because they dwell under the third, most seething and torrid circle of the world's zones,

et a uapore ardentissimorum siderum terrarum[h] defenduntur latebris[i]. [j]Sic e contrario, pro[j] frigore niuali, genus quoddam humanum Rhipaeis[k] montibus uicinum in[l] hieme[m] terris defensum[n] legimus[o], ubi niues sub gelido septentrionis arcto[p] in .VII.[q] ulnas consurgunt.

I.10 Onocentauri [a]corpora hominum[a] [b]rationabilia habere uidentur[b] usque ad umbilicum, et inferior pars corporis[c] [d]in onagrorum[d] setosa turpitudine[e] describitur[f], quos sic diuersorum generum uaria naturaliter coniungit[g] natura.

I.11 Et fuit quoddam humanum[a] genus in Sicilia, ubi[b] Aetnae[c] montis incendium legitur, qui[d] unum oculum sub asperrima[e] fronte clipei latitudinis habuerunt[f]. Et Ciclopes[g] dicebantur et procerissimarum[h] arborum altitudinem excedebant[i] [j]et humano sanguine uescebantur[j]. Quorum quidam [k]in suo antro[k] resupinus una manu duos uiros tenuisse[l] et crudos[m] manducasse[n] legitur[o].

I.12 [a]Quis Herculis[b] fortitudinem et arma non miretur[c], qui in occiduis Tyrrheni[d] maris faucibus columnas mirae magnitudinis ad humani generis spectaculum erexit,

h terrarum] *om. S*
i latebris] latebribus *Y*
j...j Sic . . . pro] et sic e contrario prae *W* et sic est contrario *S* sic e contrario prae *RY* sic et contrario prae *L* et sic e contrario pro *H*
k Rhipaeis] ripis *W* ripheis *S*
l in] *om. S*
m hieme] cheme *R* hime *L*
n defensum] defossum *H*
o legimus] *om. S*
p arcto] aracturo *S* arctu *R* artico *L* arto *Y*
q .VII.] *om. WSL* .IIII.or *R*

I.10 DE ONOCENTAURIS *WYPBT* DE MOCENTAURIS *L capitulum om. S. licet titulus adest*: DE ONECEN REM IN FINE LIBRI .XI.

a...a corpora hominum] corpora humanum *R* corpore humano *Y*
b...b rationabilia . . . uidentur] a capite *Y*
c corporis] eorum *Y*
d...d in onagrorum] monstrorum *W* in agrorum *L*
e turpitudine] turpidine *L*
f describitur] describuntur *LY*
g coniungit] confingit *L*

I.11 DE CICLOPIBUS *WST* DE CLYCLOPIBUS *L* DE CYCLOPIBUS *YPB*

a humanum] hominum *W*
b ubi] *om. S*
c Aetnae] athaenae *W* aetheni *S* ethnae *R* aethnae *Y*
d qui] quia *S*
e asperrima] asperissima *W* asperisma *S*
f habuerunt] habuerat *L*
g Ciclopes] clyclopes *L*
h procerissimarum] proceressimum *S*
i excedebant] exercebant *W* exercebantur *S*
j...j et . . . uescebantur] *om. S*
k...k in suo antro] sub anthro *R*
l tenuisse] tenuisset *W*
m crudos] uiuos *Y*
n manducasse] mandicasse *W*
o legitur] *post* legitur *add. R*: De cyclope. Veniens autem Ulixes ab expugnatione Troie inuenit unum ab his in quadam spelunca in Sicilia cum suis capris De familia huius una manu [duos] tenuit et deuorauit et postea dormiuit. Et Ulixes magnum burdillum [*pro* burcellum] iecit in oculum eius.

I.12 DE ERCULE *W* DE HERCULE *SLYPBT*

a...a Quis . . . inuoluit] non mireris scito Erculus post multorum hominum sanguinis effusionem flamma semet ipsum occidit *S*
b Herculis] erculus *W*
c miretur] miraretur *WR*
d Tyrrheni] terreni *W* thyrreni *R* tyrreni *L* tirreni *Y*

and are protected by the recesses of the land from the vapour of the most burning stars. And likewise, on the other hand, we read of a certain race of humans near the Rhipaean mountains protected from the snowy cold by the land in winter, where the snows under the chill Great Bear of the North fall to a depth of seven ells.

I.10 Ass-centaurs seem to have the reasonable bodies of humans down to the navel, and the lower part of the body is represented by the shaggy foulness of wild asses. In this way the diverse nature of different species naturally combines them.

I.11 And there was a certain human race in Sicily, where the flame of Mount Etna is read about; they had a single eye as broad as a shield under the roughest of foreheads. And they were called Cyclops and used to exceed the height of the tallest of trees and feed on human blood. And one of these is said in books to have lain in his cave holding two men in one hand, and to have eaten them raw.

I.12 Who does not admire the courage and weaponry of Hercules, who, at the western entrance to the Mediterranean, erected pillars of an amazing size as a spectacle for the human race,

quique[e] bellorum suorum [f]tropaea in Oriente[f] iuxta Oceanum Indicum[g] ad posteritatis memoriam construxit, et postquam paene[h] totum orbem cum bellis peragrasset et terram[i] tanto sanguine maculauisset[j], sese moriturum flammis ad deuorandum inuoluit[a?k]

I.13 Et[a] quandam[b] puellam[c] in occiduis Europae[d] litoribus, necdum turgentibus[e] mammis[f], repertam didicimus[g], quam[h] undae gurgitum ab Oceano[i] terris aduexerunt[j]; cuius magnitudinem[k] lapidibus designabant. Erat enim ipsius corporis[l] longitudo[m] .L. pedum, et inter[n] humeros [o].VII. latitudinis habuit[o]. Purpureo induta pallio, [p]uirgis alligata[p] et in caput occisa peruenerat.

I.14 Scylla monstrum nautis inimicissimum[a] in eo freto[b] quod Italiam [c]et Siciliam[c] interluit[d] fuisse[e] perhibetur capite quidem et pectore[f] uirginali[g] sicut sirenae[h], sed[i] luporum uterum et caudas[j] delfinorum[k] habuit. Et [l]hoc sirenarum[l] et Scyllae[m] distinguit naturam[n] quod ipsae mortifero carmine nauigantes decipiunt et illa per uim fortitudinis [o]marinis succincta canibus[o] miserorum fertur lacerasse[p] naufragia.

[e] quique] qui *W* quippe *Y*
[f...f] tropaea in Oriente] trophea moriente *W*
[g] Indicum] inditium *Y*
[h] paene] *om. L*
[i] terram] terrarum *W*
[j] maculauisset] maculent *W* maculauit *R* maculant *L*

---

[k] inuoluit] *post* inuoluit *add. R*: De Scylla Scylla forti [*pro* Forci] filia et creditis [*pro* Crataeidis] nimphae amauit Glaucum et Glaucus aliam habuit nomine Circen Solis filiam et haec Circes Scyllam transfigurauit in formam hominis et canis et delfinis simul causa uiri sui et illa bestia inter Italiam et Siciliam fuit ut gentiles aiunt quae deuorabat nautas ut dictum est in Virgilio.

I.13 DE INGENTI PUELLA *WSLYPBT*

[a] Et] *om. S*
[b] quandam] quondam *W om. S* quoddam *L*
[c] puellam] puellam quondam *S*
[d] Europae] eurupe *W*
[e] turgentibus] torquentibus *R*
[f] mammis] mamellis *Y*
[g] didicimus] indicimus *W* didimus *L*
[h] quam] quae *WLY*
[i] Oceano] oceanum *L*
[j] aduexerunt] aduexerat *Y*
[k] magnitudinem] magnitudine *W*
[l] corporis] *om. S*
[m] longitudo] magnitudo *WS*
[n] inter] per *Y*
[o...o] .VII. latitudinis habuit] .IIII.or uel .VII. latitudinis habuit *W* .IIII. latitudinis habuit *S* .VII. habuit longitudinis pedum *Y*
[p p] uirgis alligata] uirginis *S*

I.14 DE SCILLA *WSY* DE SCYLLA *LPBT*

[a] inimicissimum] inimicum *Y*
[b] freto] fretu *R*
[c...c] et Siciliam] *om. L*
[d] interluit] interfluit *S*
[e] fuisse] fons esse *WS*
[f] pectore] pectora *W*
[g] uirginali] uirnali *Y*
[h] sirenae] sirine *W* sirene *S* serenae *R* femine *Y*
[i] sed] et *S*
[j] caudas] caudam *Y*
[k] delfinorum] delphinum *L*
[l...l] hoc sirenarum] hac sirinarum *W* hac sirinarum *S* hoc serenarum *R* hoc sori narum *Y*
[m] Scyllae] scille *S*
[n] naturam] natura *S*
[o...o] marinis . . . canibus] in armis succincta carnibus *W* in armis succincta *S*
[p] lacerasse] lacerare *Y*

and who constructed trophies of his wars in the East by the Indian Ocean, as a memorial for posterity, and afterwards travelled in battles through almost the entire world, and spattered the earth with so much blood, and at the point of death wrapped himself in flames to be consumed?

I.13 And we have heard tell of a certain girl, not yet with swelling breasts, discovered on the western shores of Europe, whom the waves of the sea brought to land from the Ocean; they marked her size with stones. Indeed fifty feet was the length of her body, and she was seven feet wide between the shoulders. She had come dressed in a purple cloak, bound with saplings, and fatally wounded in the head.

I.14 It is reckoned that Scylla has been the monster most hostile to sailors in that channel which washes between Italy and Sicily, having indeed the head and chest of a maiden (like the sirens), but the belly of a wolf and the tails of dolphins. And what distinguishes the nature of sirens from Scylla is that they deceive seamen by their deadly song, whilst she with the strength of her force, girt about with sea-dogs, is said to have mangled the wrecks of the unfortunate.

I.15 Et in India iuxta[a] Oceanum pilosum[b] [c]toto corpore[c] quoddam[d] genus humanum[e] didicimus, qui in[f] naturali nuditate [g]setis tantum[g] more[h] ferino[i] contecti[j] crudis cum aqua piscibus ita[k] uiuere dicuntur. Quos Indi[l] Ichthyophagos[m] appellant[n]. Qui [o]non tantum[o] in[p] terris adsueti[q], sed fluminibus ac stagnis et [r]iuxta amnem Epigmaridem[r] maxime demorantur.

I.16 Cynocephali[a] quoque in India nasci perhibentur, quorum sunt canina capita, et omne uerbum quod loquuntur[b] intermixtis[c] corrumpunt latratibus, et non homines[d], crudam carnem [e]manducando, sed[e] ipsas imitantur[f] bestias.

I.17 Et ferunt[a] [b]genus esse[b] hominum[c] quos[d] Graeci Sciapodas[e] appellant[f], eo quod se ab ardore solis pedum umbra [g]iacentes resupini[g] defendunt. Sunt enim[h] celerrimae naturae. Singula tantum habent[i] in pedibus crura[j] et eorum genua inflexibili[k] [l]conpagine durescunt[l].

I.15 DE HOMINIBUS SETOSIS *WSYPBT* DE HOMINIBUS AETOSIS *L capitulum om. L, licet in indice titulus*

a iuxta] iuxt *Y*
b pilosum] philosum *Y*
c...c toto corpore] totum corpore *WS* toto cor *R om. Y*
d quoddam] *om. R* quod *Y*
e humanum] hominum *WL*
f in] corpore *Y*
g...g setis tantum] setosi sunt tamen *Y*
h more] modo *S*
i ferino] fermo *W* sermo *S*
j contecti] contenti *R* contexti *Y*
k ita] uescuntur et ita *Y*
l Indi] indii *S* inde *Y*
m Ichthyophagos] ictifanos *W* ictifonas *S* ictifaos *R* nati faunos *Y*
n appellant] appelunt *S*
o...o non tantum] *om. S*
p in] *om. WR*
q adsueti] tantum *S*
r...r iuxta amnem Epigmaridem] iuta epiinaridem *W* iuxta epigmaridem *S* iuxta amnem epigrandem *Y*

I.16 DE CYNOCEFALIS *W* DE CENOPHALIS *L* DE CENOCEPHALIS *Y* DE CYNOCEPHALIS *PBT capitulum om. S. licet titulus adest*: CHENOCOFOLI INTER ILLOS

a Cynocephali] Cenocephali *W* Cinocefali *R* Cenophali *L* Shenofali *Y*
b loquuntur] loquentur *W*
c intermixtis] permixtis *Y*
d homines] homine quidem *Y*
e...e manducando sed *L*
f imitantur] emitantur *W* immitantur *Y*

I.17 DE SCINOPODIS *WLB* ITEM DE SCINOPODIS *S om. Y* DE SCIAPODIS *PT*

a ferunt] fertur *Y*
b...b genus esse] esse genus *S*
c hominum] humanum *Y*
d quos] quos appellant *S*
e Sciapodas] scinopodos *W* scinopodes *S* scinopodas *RL* scinopodar *Y*
f appellant] *om. S* appellat *L*
g...g iacentes resupini] supini iacentes *S*
h enim] *om. R*
i habent] *om. S*
j crura] crura habent *S* gcrura *Y*
k inflexibili] inflexibile *W* inflexisibile *S*
l...l conpagine durescunt] durescunt conpagine *S*

I.15 And in India next to the Ocean we have learnt of a certain race of humans hairy in their whole body, who are said to live on water and raw fish, covered in natural nakedness only by bristles like wild animals. And the Indians call them Ichthyophagi ['fish-eaters'], and they are not only accustomed to the land, but dwell in streams and ponds and mostly next to the river Epigmaris.

I.16 Cynocephali are also said to be born in India, who have the heads of dogs, and spoil every word they say with mingled barks, and do not imitate humans but the beasts themselves in eating raw flesh.

I.17 And they say there is a race of people whom the Greeks call Sciapods ['shade-feet'], because lying on their backs they protect themselves from the heat of the sun by the shade of their feet. Indeed they are of a very swift nature. They have only one leg each for their feet, and their knees harden in an inflexible joint.

I.18 Sunt homines in Oriente in cuiusdam[a] heremi [b]uasta solitudine[b] morantes qui, ut[c] perhibunt, barbam[d] usque ad[e] genua[f] pertingentem habent, et [g]crudo pisce et aquarum sunt haustu uiuentes[g].

I.19 [a]Et in his incredibilibus[a] quoddam[b] [c]genus utriusque sexus[c] describitur[d], qui[e] dexteram mammam uirilem pro exercendis operibus et ad fetus nutriendo sinistram habent[f] muliebrem. Quos inter[g] se uicibus coeundo ferunt alternis generare[h].

I.20 Quidam quoque[a] [b]homines Nilo Brixontique fluminibus[b] uicini corpora[c] miri candoris habentes, .XII. pedum altitudinem[d] habentia[e], facie quidem bipertita et naso[f] longo et macilenti[g] corpore describuntur.

I.21 Et[a] sunt homines quos Graecorum [b]historiae ora[b] non habere perhibent[c] ut ceterum genus humanum et nullis[d] eos cibis uesci, sed[e] [f]per nares[f] [g]halitu tantummodo[g] uiuere[h] testantur.

I.18 DE BARBOSIS HOMINIBUS *WLYPBT om. S*

[a] cuiusdam] cuidam *S*
[b...b] uasta solitudine] uasta latitudine *WSLY* solitudine *R* uasta solitudine *H*
[c] ut] *om. W*
[d] barbam] barba *W*
[e] ad] *om. L*
[f] genua] ienua *Y*
[g...g] crudo . . . uescuntur] crudos pisces et aquarum sunt austu uiuentes *W* crudos pisces et aquarum astutia uiuunt *S* crudo pisce et aquarum sunt hastu uiuentes *L* crudis piscibus uescuntur *Y*

I.19 DE COMMIXTO SEXU *WB* DE COMMIXTO GENERE SEXUS *LP* DE COMMIXTO SEXUS *T capitulum om. S hic tituli explicunt Y*

[a...a] Et . . . incredibilibus] et his incredibilibus *R* et in his credibibus *L* Ex his incredibilibus
[b] quoddam] quodam *W*
[c...c] genus utriusque sexus] genus est utriusque sexus *W* genus *R* genus hominum utriusque sexus *Y*
[d] describitur] scribitur *R* ascribitur *L* adscribitur *Y*
[e] qui] quod *L*
[f] habent] habet *L*
[g] inter] per *Y*
[h] generare] genere *L*

I.20 DE MAGNIS HOMINIBUS BRIXONTIS *WSPBT* DE MAGIS HOMINIBUS BRIXONTIS *L*

[a] quoque] *om. Y*
[b...b] homines . . . fluminibus] homines brixonti in niloque fluminibus *W* homines brixonti in nilo flumine *S* nili brixontisque fluminis *R* homines nilo brixantique fluminibus *L*
[c] corpora] corporem *S*
[d] altitudinem] altitudinis *Y*
[e] habentia] *om. S*
[f] naso] nati *Y*
[g] macilenti] macellenti *WL* macies lenti *R* macelenti *Y*

I.21 DE EIS QUI TANTUM VIVUNT *W om. S* DE HIS QUI TANTUM HABITU VIVUNT *L* DE HIS QUI TANTUM HALITU VIVUNT *PB* ASTOMI *T*

[a] Et] *om. S*
[b...b] historiae ora] storiae hora *W* storiae os *S*
[c] perhibent] perhibentur *WS*
[d] nullis] mellis *R* nulli *L*
[e] sed] *om. SR*
[f...f] per nares] semper naris *S*
[g...g] halitu tantummodo] alitantum modo *W* halito tantummodo *S* alitu tantum *L*
[h] uiuere] uescere *S*

I.18 There are people in the East dwelling in the vast solitude of a certain desert who, so they say, have beards reaching right to their knees, and live on raw fish and by drinking water.

I.19 And amongst these incredible things there is described a certain race of joint sex, who have a right male breast for performing work and a left female breast for nourishing babies. And people say they reproduce by alternating sexual roles.

I.20 Also certain people from near the Nile and Brixontis rivers are described as having bodies of amazing whiteness, twelve feet tall, with a split face, long nose, and skinny body.

I.21 And there are people whom Greek tales say have no mouth like the rest of the human race, and eat no food, but are reckoned to live only by the breath of their noses.

I.22 Mulieres, ut ferunt, iuxta montem Armeniae[a] nascuntur pellibus indutae, barbam usque ad mammas[b] [c]prolixam habentes[c], quae[d] [e]sibi, dum[e] uenatrices[f] sunt, tigres[g] et leopardos[h] et rapida[i] ferarum genera pro canibus nutriunt[j].

I.23 [a]Et quoddam inuisum genus humanum[b] in antris et concauis montium latebris nasci perhibetur[c], [d]qui sunt[d] statura cubitales et, ut testantur, aduersum[e] grues in tempore messis bellum coniungunt[f], ne eorum sata diripiant. Quos Graeci[g] a cubito[h] pigmeos uocant[a].

I.24 Sunt quoque homines in insula Brixontis[a] fluuii[b] qui absque capitibus nascuntur, quos Epifugos[c] Graeci uocant[d]; et .VIII.[e] pedum altitudinis sunt[f] et tota[g] in pectore capitis officia[h] gerunt, nisi quod oculos in humeris[i] habere dicuntur[j].

I.25 Et quendam hominem[a] fideli historia lunatas habuisse plantas duorum non amplius digitorum conperimus; cuius quoque manus [b]in huius[b] normae mensuram [c]editae describuntur[c].

I.26 In Oriente quoque, iuxta Oceanum, formosum genus humanum[a] [b]legimus. Et hanc causam amoenitatis[c] eorum[b] esse adserunt quod crudam carnem et mel [d]purissimum manducant[d].

I.22 DE BARBOSIS MULIERIBUS *WPBT* DE MULIERIBUS BARBATIS *S* DE BARBOSIS *L*

a Armeniae] armenta *L*
b mammas] mammam *SL*
c...c prolixam habentes] habentes prolixam *S*
d quae] quadum *S* qui *R*
e...e sibi dum] *om. SY*
f uenatrices] uenatrices sibi *S*
g tigres] tygris *W* tigrides *L* tygrides *Y*
h leopardos] leopardes *S*
i rapida] rabida *L* pida *Y*
j nutriunt] nutriantur *S*

I.23 DE PIGMAEIS *WP* DE PIGMEIS CUBITALES SUNT *S* DE PIGNEHIS *L* DE PYGMAEIS *B* DE PIGMEIS *T*

a...a Et . . . uocant] contra grues pugnant propter sata eorum *S*
b humanum] *om. L* hominum *Y*
c perhibetur] perhibentur *WR*
d..d qui sunt] quis *R*
e aduersum] aduersus *L*
f coniungunt] committunt *Y*
g Greci] grece *W*
h cubito] cubitu *WRY*

I.24 DE EPISTIGIS *WB* DE EPISTOGOS *S* DE EPIFUGIS *LP* DE EPISTIGOS *T*

a Brixontis] brixantis *L*
b fluui] fluii *S*
c Epifugos] epistigos *W* epistogos *S*
d uocant] uocantur *S*
e .VIII.] .VII. *WRY*
f sunt] *om. L*
g tota] tanta *WS*
h officia] efficia *W* effigia *S*
i humeris] humeri *L*
j dicuntur] uidentur *WS*

I.25 DE HIS QUI LUNATAS HABENT PLANTAS *WLP om. S* DE HIS QUI HABENT PLANTAS LUNATAS *BT*

a hominem] *om. S*
b...b in huius] unius *S* in humeris *Y*
c...c editae describuntur] editi describantur *L* aditae describuntur Y

I.26 DE HIS QUI CRUDAM CARNEM MANDUCANT *WLPBT om. S*

a humanum] hominum *WL*
b..b legimus . . . eorum] legimus et hanc causam amoenitatis *L om. Y*
c amoenitatis] amoenitis *S*
d...d purissimum manducant] purum manducant *W* comoedunt purum *S*

I.22 Women, so they say, are born near the mountain of Armenia covered with hair, having long beards down to their breasts, who, since they are huntresses, rear tigers and leopards and swift kinds of wild animals instead of dogs.

I.23 And it is said that a certain hostile [or 'unseen'] race of people are born in caves and the hollow recesses of mountains, who are a cubit in height, and, it is reckoned, join war against cranes at harvest-time, in case they snatch their crops. And the Greeks call them Pigmies, from [the Greek word for] 'cubit'.

I.24 There are also men on an island in the river Brixontis who are born without heads, whom the Greeks call Epifugi. And they are eight feet tall and have all the functions of the head in their chests, except they are said to have eyes in their shoulders.

I.25 And in a reliable [or 'faithful'] narrative we find that a certain person had crescent-shaped feet with no more than two toes, and that their hands also are described as being formed after the measure of this pattern.

I.26 In the East also, next to the Ocean, we read of a beautiful race of people. And they claim that the cause of their pleasantness is that they eat raw meat and the purest of honey.

I.27 [a]Est et[b] aliud genus humanum[c] qui[d] angustissimam metam [e]terminandi uitam[e] habere dicuntur. Quorum feminae quinquennes[f] concipiunt et amplius[g] quam ad annum[a] octauum [h]uitam non producunt[h].

I.28 Sunt mulieres, ut ferunt, speciosae[a], Rubro mari[b] coherentes, quarum[c] corpora marmoreo nitore fulgent, quae[d] .XII.[e] [f]pedes altitudinis[f] et crines usque ad talos[g] defluentes[h], caudas boum in lateribus, et camelorum pedes habent[i].

I.29 Et[a] dicunt esse gentem ab humana natura[b] hoc modo discrepantem: sunt[c] enim [d]integris corporibus[d], sed plantae retro curuatae [e]officia capitis contraria[e] uidentur. Quorum hoc[f] ignorantes uestigia fallunt.

I.30 [a]In quodam quoque deserto montes ignei leguntur, in quibus nascuntur homines toto corpore nigri sicut Aethipoes, quorum nos quendam uidimus carbonea nigredine[b], dentibus et oculis [c]tantummodo et unguibus[c] nitentem[a].

I.31 Erat monstrum quoddam in Arcadia[a], [b]nomine Cacus[b], in antro fluminis Tiberini, flammas de pectore euomens[c], et toto corpore[d] setosus, qui quatuor tauros

I.27 DE FOEMINIS QUAE QUINQUENNES CONCIPIUNT *WPBT om. S* DE FOEMINIS QUAE QUINQUENNES CAPIUNT *L*

a...a Est . . . annum] sunt femine quae quinquennies concipiunt et amplius quam ad anum *S*
b et] *om. R*
c humanum] hominum *WL*
d qui] quod *Y*
e...e terminandi uitam] tantum in amiguitate *W* terminandae uitae *Y*
f quinquennes] cumquinnes *L*
g amplius] non amplius *L*
h...h uitam non producunt] uitam non producant *R* perducant uitam *L*

I.28 DE MONSTRUOSIS MULIERIBUS *WLPBT om. S*

a speciosae] spetiose *S om. Y*
b mari] mare *S*
c quarum] quorum *W*
d quae] qui *R*
e .XII.] .XIII. *LY*
f...f pedes altitudinis] pedebus altitudine *S*
g talos] tales *L*
h defluentes] defulgentes *WS*
i habent] hoc uerbo explicit *Y*

I.29 DE PLANTIS RETROCURVATIS *WLPBT om. S*

a Et] *om. S*
b natura] statura *RL*
c sunt] fiunt *WR*
d...d integris corporibus] in integris corporibus *R* integre *L*
e...e officia . . . contraria] officio capitis contrariae *WR*
f hoc] haec *SL*

I.30 DE MONTIBUS IGNEIS *WB* DE NIGRIS *S* DE NIGRIS HOMINIBUS *LP* MONTIUM IGNEORUM INCOLAE *T*

a...a In quodam . . . nitentem] sunt ignei montes in deserto et homines in eis toto corpore nigri nisi oculis et dentibus et unguibus candescunt *S*
b nigredine] nigritudine *WR*
c...c tantummodo et uinguibus] tantum *L*

I.31 DE CACO ARDIE *W* DE CATO ARCADIE *S* DE CACO ARCHADIAE *L* DE CACO ARCADIAE *PB* DE CACO *T*

a Arcadia] archadia *S*
b...b nomine Cacus] caccus nomen *W* cacasus nomen *S* nomen cacus *R* nomine Kacus *L*
c euomens] euomans *S* uomens *R*
d corpore] pectore *R*

I.27 And there is another race of people who are said to have the briefest of spans to mark their life. Their women conceive at five years old, and they do not live beyond their eighth year.

I.28 There are, so they say, beautiful women living near the Red Sea, whose bodies shine with the brightness of marble, who are twelve feet tall and have hair flowing down to their ankles, cow-tails on their flanks, and the feet of camels.

I.29 And they say that there is a race differing from human nature in the following way: they have complete bodies, but the functions of the head seem at odds to the turned-back feet. And their footprints deceive those who do not know this.

I.30 Also in a certain desert fiery mountains are read about, in which people are born black in their whole body like Ethiopians, of whom we saw a certain one as black as coal, but with shining teeth and eyes and nails.

I.31 There was a certain monster in Arcadia called Cacus, in a cave by the river Tiber, spewing flames from his chest, and hairy all over, who stole four bulls

furto[e] et totidem uaccas abduxit armentario[f] et eos per uim fortitudinis retrorsum, ne inuestigarentur[g], caudis traxit[h] in antrum.

I.32 Et ferunt monstrum aliud in quodam loco iuxta Oceanum fuisse, quod[a] ut [b]barcam adlabi[b] undis[c] [d]de litore[d] cernebat[e] et nautas[f] hesitantes[g] ad terram uenire, uisu eius territos, in medio rapiebat gurgite et nauem cum hominibus [h]in terram[h] [i]aridam deposuit[i].

I.33 Hominum quoque genus inmensis corporibus[a] [b]Brixontis fluminis[b] ab Oriente nascitur[c], corpore nigri[d], et[e] .XVIII.[f] pedes altitudinis accipiunt[g]; et[h], ut ferunt, homines cum[i] comprehendant[j], crudos[k] manducant[l].

I.34 Et dicunt[a] monstra esse in paludibus [b]cum tribus humanis capitibus[b] et sub[c] profundissimis stagnis sicut nimphas habitare fabulantur. Quod[d] credere profanum est: ut non illuc[e] fluant gurgites[f] quo inmane monstrum ingreditur.

I.35 Protheus quoque ceruleo corpore[a] bipedum equorum [b]curru per aequora nudus uehi[b] perhibetur et super omne[c] piscium genus principatum habuisse et in[d] omnium rerum formas [e]se uertere[e] potuisse describitur.

e furto] furtu *S*
f armentario] armento *WS*
g inuestigarentur] inuestigantur *S*
h traxit] extraxit *WS*

I.32 DE QUODAM INMANI MONSTRO *WPB om. S* DE CODAM INMANE MONSTRIO *L* DE QUODAM IN MARI MONSTRO *T*
a quod] qui *L*
b...b barcam adlabi] barbam adlui *WS*
c undis] undas *S*
d...d de litore] et de littore
e cernebat] cernebant *S*
f nautas] naute *S*
g hesitantes] hestantes *L*
h...h in terram] *om. R*
i...i aridam deposuit] aridam disposuit *W* deposuit aridam *S*

I.33 DE HIS QUI MANDUCANT HOMINES *WLPBT om. S*
a corporibus] corribus *L*
b...b Rrixontis fluminis] *om. R* brixanti fluminis *L*
c nascitur] nascuntur *R*
d nigri] nigro *S*
e et] *om. S*
f .XVIII.] .X. et .VIII. *S* .XIIII. *L*
g accipiunt] capiunt *RL*
h et] *om. L*
i cum] *om. L*
j comprehendant] comprehenderant *W* comprehenderint *S* comprehendunt *R* comprehenderint *L*
k crudos] *om. S*
l manducant] deuorant *L*

I.34 DE HIS QUI TRIA CAPITA HABENT *WPB om. S* DE ILLIS QUI TRIA CAPITA HABENT *L* DE IPSIS QUI TRIA CAPITA HABENT *T*
a dicunt] dicuntur *R*
b...b cum . . . capitibus] capitibus humanis *S*
c sub] *om. L*
d quod] quam *L*
e illuc] illic *L*
f gurgites] grugite *S*

I.35 DE PROTHEO *WSLPT* DE PROTEO *B*
a corpore] colore *R*
b..b curru . . . uehi] curru per equora nudus uehi *S* cursu uehi per equora nudus *R* corrumpere equora nudus uechi *L*
c omne] omnem *W*
d in] *om. S*
e...e se uertere] se uerti *WR* reuerti *L*

and the same number of cows from their herdsman, and through force of strength dragged them backwards by their tails to his cave, so that they would not be discovered.

I.32 And they say that there has been another monster in a certain spot near the Ocean, who saw from the shore a boat slipping on the waves, and the sailors, terrified by the sight of him, hesitating to come to shore, and he snatched the ship and its crew from the midst of the sea and placed it on dry land.

I.33 Also a race of people with huge bodies is born in the east of the river Brixontis black in body, and who reach eighteen feet in height; and, so they say, when they catch folk, they eat them raw.

I.34 And they say there are monsters in swamps with three human heads and they are alleged to live like nymphs under the deepest pools. It is a profanity to believe this, since floods do not flow there, where a huge monster enters.

I.35 Proteus also with his azure body is said to have been carried naked through the sea in a chariot of two-legged horses, and to have had dominion over every kind of fish, and is described as being able to turn himself into the shapes of all things.

I.36 Et quaedam insula in Orientalibus [a]orbis terrarum[a] partibus [b]esse dicitur[b], in qua nascuntur homines rationabili statura, nisi quod eorum oculi sicut lucerna[c] lucent[d].

I.37 Fuit quidam homo mirabilis naturae[a] quem Midam appellauerunt, qui, ut fabulae fingunt, omnia quae tetigerat in aurum uertebat. Quod nemo nisi ueritatem spernens credit[b].

I.38 Gorgones quoque [a]in monstruosa mulierum[a] natura tres, quae[b] dicebantur [c]Stheno, Euryale, Medusa[c], iuxta montem Atlantem[d] fuisse et in finibus Libiae[e] describuntur[f], quae[g] suo uisu homines [h]conuertebant in lapides[h]. Quarum unam Perseus scuto uitreo[i] defensus interfecit[j], quae[k] absciso [l]capite suos[l] oculos [m]ita uertisse[m] fertur ut[n] uiua[o].

I.39 Argus[a] multos habuisse[b] oculos numerosae[c] uisionis [d]describitur, quem[d] nihil latere omnino potuisse[e] dicunt quia[f], ut fingitur[g], quibusdam[h] oculis semper uigilauit[i].

I.36 DE HIS QUORUM OCULI VELUT LUCERNA LUCENT *WPBT* QUORUM OCULI UT LUCENA LUCET *WP* DE HIS QUORUM OCULI VELUT LUCERNE LUCENT *L capitulum om. L, licet in indice titulus*

a...a orbis terrarum] *om. S*

b...b esse dicitur] est *S*

c lucerna] lucernae *R*

d *post* lucent *add. WS*: De fabulani [fabulane *S*, *pro* fabula] Proserpine. Fabulani [fabulane *S*, *pro* fabula] Proserpine quam rapuit Idoneus [*pro* Aidoneus], id est Orcus rex Molosorum [*pro* Molossorum], cuius canis ingentis magnitudinis Cerberus [cerborus *S*] nomine Protheum [*pro* Perithoum] deuorauit. Quod ad raptum [raptam *S*] uxoris eius cum Theodosio [*pro* Theseo] uenerat. quem et ipsum iam in mortis periculo constitutum adueniens Herculus [*pro* Hercules] liberauit et ob id quasi ab inferis receptus dicitur [dictus *S*]

I.37 DE MIDA *WSLPBT*

a naturae] *om. W* rationabilis naturae *R*

b credit] credidit *W* creditur *S*

I.38 DE GORGONIBUS *WLPBT* DE GORGONIS *S*

a...a in monstruosa mulierum] monstruosem uero *S*

b quae] qui *W*

c...c Stheno Euryale Medusa] strenue euridice medosa *W* strenue iuridice medosa *S* stenno eurale medusa *R* strenuae eridice medusa *L*

d Atlantem] athlantem *WSR* anthlantem *L*

e Libiae] libie *R* liuiae *L*

f describuntur] describantur *W* desscribuntur *S* scribuntur *L*

g quae] qui *R*

h...h conuertebant in lapides] in lapides conuertebant *S*

i uitreo] uetereo *R*

j interfecit] interficit *WR*

k quae] quam *R*

l...l capite suos] suo capite *R* capite doctus a minerua hoc ut tantum discens suos *L*

m...m ita uertisse] uersisse *WS*

n ut] in *S*

o uiua] *post* uiua *add. R*: quem habere describitur

I.39 DE AR *W* DE ARE *L* DE ARGO *PB* DE ARGE *T capitulum om. S*

a Argus] Ar *WL* Argi *R*

b habuisse] *om. R*

c numerosae] humerosae *L*

d...d describitur quem] *om. R*

e potuisse] posse *L*

f quia] quam *W*

g fingitur] fingunt *L*

h quibusdam] quibus *W*

i uigilauit] uigilant *R*

I.36 And there is said to be an island in the eastern parts of the lands of the world, in which people are born reasonable in stature, except that their eyes shine like lanterns.

I.37 There was once a person of marvellous nature whom they called Midas, who, as the tales allege, turned everything which he touched into gold. And no one believes this unless scorning the truth.

I.38 Three Gorgons are also described with the monstrous nature of women, Stheno, Euryale, and Medusa, who are said to have lived on the borders of Libya next to Mount Atlas, who used to turn men to stone by their sight. Perseus slew one of them, protected by a glassy shield, and she is said, when her head was cut off, to have moved her eyes as though alive.

I.39 Argus is described as having had numerous eyes to see, and they say that nothing could be concealed from him completely, because, it is imagined, he was always on the lookout with some eyes.

I.40 Est gens aliqua commixtae naturae in Rubri[a] maris insula quam linguis[b] omnium nationum[c] loqui posse[d] testantur. Et ideo homines de longinquo uenientes, eorum cognitas[e] nominando, adtonitos faciunt, ut decipiant[f] et crudos deuorent[g].

I.41 Innumerosa[a] quoque monstra in Circeae [b]terrae finibus fuisse leguntur[b], leones[c] et ursi, apri quoque ac[d] lupi, qui cetero corpore in ferarum natura manente[e], hominum facies habuerunt.

I.42 Et dicunt, quod dici nefandum est, monstrum quoddam nocturnum fuisse, quod semper noctu[a] per umbram caeli et terrae uolabat, homines in urbibus horribili stridore[b] territans[c], et quot[d] plumas[e] in corpore habuit, tot[f] oculos, totidem aures et ora[g]. Semper quoque sine requie et somno fuisse describitur.

I.43 Nascuntur[a] homines in Orientalibus plagis, qui, ut fabulae fingunt[b], .XV. [c]altitudinis pedes[c] capiunt et corpora [d]marmorei candoris[d] habent et uannosas[e] aures, quibus se substernunt noctu[f] et cooperint, et[g] hominem cum uiderint, erectis auribus per deserta uastissima fugiunt.

I.40 DE HIS QUI OMNIUM LINGUAM LOCUNTUR *WBT* DE HIS QUI OMNES LINGUAS LOCUNTUR *S* DE HIS QUI OMNIBUS LINGUIS LOQUUNTUR *LP*

a Rubri] rubro *L*
b linguis] linguas *WR*
c nationum] natium *S*
d posse] potuisse *WS*
e cognitas] cognitos *S*
f decipiant] decipiunt *W*
g deuorent] deuorant *WR* deueran *S*

I.41 DE MONSTRA IN CIRCIAE TERRA *W* DE CIRCEA *S* DE MONSTRIS CIRE *L* DE MONSTRIS IN CIRCIA TERRA *P* DE MONSTRIS IN CIRCAEAE TERRAE FINIBUS *B* DE MONSTRIS CIRCAEAE TERRAE *T*

a Innumerosa] numerosa *WL*
b...b terrae . . . leguntur] fuisse terrae finibus leguntur *S*
c leones] leonis *L*
d ac] et *L*
e manente] manentem *L*

I.42 DE MONSTRO NOCTURNO *WSLPBT*

a noctu] nocte *SL*
b stridore] stridorem *L*
c territans] terrens *WS*
d quot] quod *WSL*
e plumas] plummas *R* plumans *L*
f tot] et *S*
g ora] nares *S*

I.43 DE INMENSIS HOMINIBUS *WSLPBT*

a Nascuntur] nascunt *S*
b fingunt] ferunt *W*
c...c altitudinis pedes] pedes altitudinis *S*
d...d marmorei candoris] marmoreae candoris *S* marmorea *L*
e uannosas] uanosas *S*
f noctu] nocte *SL*
g et] *om. L*

I.40 There is a certain race of mixed nature on an island in the Red Sea, who are said to be able to speak the languages of all nations. In this way they astonish people who come from afar, by naming their acquaintances, in order to deceive them, and eat them raw.

I.41 Innumerable monsters are also said in books to have been on the borders of the Circean land, lions and bears, boars also and wolves, who, whilst the rest of their body kept the nature of wild beasts, had human faces.

I.42 And they say what is impious to be said, that there is a certain monster of the night, which always used to fly by night through the shade of the sky and the earth, terrifying people in cities with its dreadful cry, and it had as many eyes and ears and mouths, as it had feathers. And it is always said to have been without rest or sleep.

I.43 People are born in the regions of the East, who as the fables imagine, reach fifteen feet in height and have bodies of marble whiteness, and ears like fans, with which they cover and conceal themselves at night, and when they see a human, they flee through the vastest deserts [or 'most deserted wastes'] with ears outstretched.

I.44 Legitur quod Harpyiae[a] quaedam monstra in Strophadibus[b] insulis [c]Ionii maris[c] fuissent in forma uolucrum, facie tamen[d] uirginali. Quae hominum linguis[e] loqui potuerunt et rabida[f] fame semper insaturabiles[g] erant et cibum uncis pedibus de manu manducantium[h] traxerunt.

I.45 Eumenides quoque quasdam[a] mulieres uana historia depromit[b], quae uipereum[c] crinem habuerunt[d], sanguineis uittis innexum[e], quo[f] caerulei angues per uesanam[g] discordiam scatebant[h]. Quarum ferrei[i] thalami apud inferos incredibilibus finguntur fabulis.

I.46 Item Satyri et[a] Incubones siluestri[b] homines dicuntur[c], quorum pars summa humano corpori simillima et inferior cum ferarum formis et Faunorum[d] depingitur.

I.47 Et quoddam[a] monstrum apud inferos [b]scribitur, hoc est Tityos, quem[b] [c]alumnum Terrae[c] dixerunt. Cuius corpus per .IX.[d] iugera ibi porrectum extenditur[e].

I.44 DE ARPIETIS *W* DE ARBITIS *S* DE ARPIIS *L* DE HARPYIIS *PT* DE HARPYIS *B*

[a] Harpyiae] arpie *WSRL*
[b] Strophadibus] stropadibus *WS* strapodibus *L*
[c...c] Ionii maris] iunii maris *W* maris ionii *S*
[d] tamen] tantum *WSRL*
[e] linguis] linguas *W*
[f] rabida] rapida *WR*
[g] insaturabiles] insaturabilis *W* irrationabiles *L*
[h] manducantium] mandicantium *W*

I.45 DE EUMENIDES *WT* DE EUMENIDIBUS *LPB capitulum om. S*

[a] quasdam] quosdam *L*
[b] depromit] depingit *L*
[c] uipereum] uiperium *R*
[d] habuerunt] *om. L*
[e] innexum] innextum *W*
[f] quo] quod *W* quam *R*
[g] uesanam] insaniam *RL*
[h] scatebant] sactebant *R*
[i] ferrei] *om. R*

I.46 DE SATURIS ET INCUBONES *W* DE SATYRIS ET INCUBONIBUS *LPB* DE SATYRI ET INCUBONES *T capitulum om. S*

[a] et] quoque et *L*
[b] siluestri] siluestres *W*
[c] dicuntur] dicitur *L*
[d] Faunorum] fanorum *W*

I.47 DE TITIONE *WL* DE TICIONE *S* DE TITYO *PBT capitulum om. L, licet in indice titulus*

[a] quoddam] quod *W*
[b...b] scribitur . . . quem] inscribitur hic est ticius quae *W* esse inscibitur hoc est titius *S*
[c...c] alumnum Terrae] terrae alumnum *S*
[d] .IX.] .VIII. *S*
[e] extenditur] ostenditur *S post* extenditur *add. R*: uultorio iecur in epulas prebet quod absumtum die nocte in penas renascitur in uirgilio legitur.

I.44 It is read that there have been certain monsters, Harpies, on the islands of Strophades in the Ionian Sea, in the form of birds, but with the faces of maidens. And they could speak in human language, and were always insatiable with gnawing hunger, and with their hooked feet they snatched food from the hands of those eating.

I.45 A false [or 'empty'] tale also describes certain women, the Eumenides, who had viperous hair tied back with bloody headbands, in which azure snakes were thrashing in mad anger. And their iron bed-chambers are imagined in incredible fables to be in the underworld.

I.46 Likewise Satyrs and Incubi are called woodland folk, of which the top part is very like the human body, and the lower part is depicted with the forms of wild animals and fauns.

I.47 And a certain monster in the underworld is written of, that is Tityos, whom they have called Earth's nursling. And his body extends stretched out there for nine *iugera.*

I.48 [a]Aegeon quoque monstrum aliud[a] uastissima[b] mole et formae incredibilis fuisse[c] narratur. Qui habuit .L. capita et .C. manus et unoquoque ore [d]ignem uomens[d] crepitantes eructabat flammas et ad bellorum[e] instrumenta[f] .L. clipeos[g] et totidem gladios portabat[h].

I.49 Ferunt fabulae[a] Graecorum homines inmensis corporibus fuisse et [b]in tanta[b] mole tamen[c] humano[d] generi[e] similes, nisi quod [f]caudas draconum[f] habuerunt[g], unde et Graece dracontopodes[h] dicebantur.

I.50 Minotaurum[a] autem, illud[b] deforme monstrum in eisdem [c]fabulosis Graecorum fictionibus[c] depingam, qui taurinum caput habuit, et [d]inclusus[e] laberinto[f] tam clamore quam mugitu ingemuisse describitur[d], quia domum[g] illam Cretae[h] egredi non potuit, [i]quae mille[i] parietibus intextum errorem[j] habuit.

I.51 Erycis[a] quoque bellorum instrumenta omnem [b]modum humanum[b] [c]excedentia leguntur[c]; non tamen[d] monstrum, sed homo [e]monstruosa magnitudine fuit[e]. Cuius clipeum[f] [g].VII. coria[g] boum ferro ac[h] plumbo consuta[i] tegebant.

I.48 DE EGIONE *W* DE EGEONE *SL* DE AEGAEONE *PB* AEGAEON *T*

a...a Aegeon . . . aliud] et quodam monstrum aliut *L*
b uastissima] uastisma *S* uastissimum *R*
c fuisse] esse *S*
d...d ignem uomens] ignem euomans *S* igniuomens *R* ignem vocens *L*
e bellorum] belli *S*
f instrumenta] strumenta *R*
g clipeos] crlipeos *S*
h portabat] portauit *WR*

I.49 DE DRAGOPENTIBUS *W om. S* DE DRACONTOPEDIBUS *LP* DE DRACONTOPODIBUS *B* DE DRACONTOPEDES *T*

a fabulae] famulae *L*
b...b in tanta] magna *S* in tanto *L*
c tamen] tantum *W om. SL*
d humano] humani *W* hominibus *S*
e generi] *om. S* genere *L*
f...f caudas draconum] draconum caudas *S*
g habuerunt] habuerant *L*
h dracontopodes] dracontopedes *WLR*

I.50 DE MINOTAURO *WLPBT* DE MENITAURO *S*

a Minotaurum] moenitaurum *S* minataurum *R*
b illud] *om. L*
c...c fabulosis . . . fictionibus] fabulis grecorum fictis *WS*
d...d inclusus . . . describitur] labiis mugiens gemit *S*
e inclusus] indusus *L*
f laberinto] labis into *W*
g domum] dum *L*
h Cretae] cretiae *L*
i...i quae mille] quem ille *WS*
j errorem] errore *L*

I.51 DE ERICII *W* DE ERICE *SL* DE ERYCE *PBT*

a Erycis] ericis *S*
b...b modum humanum] modum humana *W* modum humanam *S* mundum humanum *L*
c...c excedentia leguntur] excedentiam legitur *S*
d tamen] tantum *W om. R*
e...e monstruosa magnitudine fuit] monstruosus fuit magnus *S*
f clipeum] dipeum *L*
g...g .VII. coria] coria septem *S* .VIII. coria *R*
h ac] et *S*
i consuta] conseta *S* consueta *R* consuebantur *L*

I.48 Aegeon also is said to have been another monster with the most massive bulk and of incredible shape. And he had fifty heads and one hundred hands, and from every single mouth he used to vomit fire and spew forth crackling flames, and as instruments of war he carried fifty shields and the same number of swords.

I.49 The fables of the Greeks say that there have been people with huge bodies and of such bulk, similar, however, to humankind, except that they had dragon-tails, whence they were also called in Greek Dracontopodes.

I.50 But I shall depict the Minotaur, that deformed monster in the same fabulous Greek stories, who had the head of a bull, and, when enclosed in the labyrinth, is said to have groaned with both cries and bellowing, because he could not escape that house in Crete, which had a maze surrounded by a thousand walls.

I.51 It is read that the instruments of war of Eryx also exceed all human measure. He was not a monster, however, but a human of monstrous size. And seven ox-hides sewn with iron and lead used to cover his shield.

I.52 Et Tritonem capite humano, pectore semifero, et deorsum ab umbilico piscibus dixerunt similem, [a]qui in Aegyptiorum Carpathio mari[a] et circa oras[b] Italiae uisus fuisse describitur. Et utrum a Tritone Libyae palude[c] an palus ab illo hoc nomen inditum possideat[d], ignoratur.

I.53 Ferunt et hominum genus esse[a] sub orbe quos Antipodas uocant, et secundum illam Graeci nominis interpretationem[b] imum orbis fundum[c] ad nostra uestigia sursum directis pedibus calcant.

I.54 Gigantes enim ipsos[a] tam enormis[b] alebat magnitudo ut eis omnia maria pedum gressibus transmeabilia fuisse perhibeatur[c]. Quorum ossa [d]in litoribus[d] et in [e]terrarum latebris[e], ad indicium [f]uastae quantitatis[f] [g]eorum, saepe conperta leguntur[g].

I.55 Scribunt et geminos[a] Aloidas[b] tam inmensae[c] [d]corporum magnitudinis[d] fuisse [e]ut ter[e] caelum manibus adgressi essent destruere, ut Iouem, pro[f] flammea regnandi[g] cupidine, summo detruderent[h] Olympo[i].

I.56 Orion autem[a] talis fuisse confingitur ut omnia maria transire potuisset et profundissimi[b] quamuis[c] gurgitis[d] undas superare[e] humeris et [f]siquando ornos[f] aut[g]

I.52 DE TRITONE *WPBT* DE TIRTONE *L capitulum om. S*

a...a qui . . . mari] quia eqyptiuorum mari carpatio *W* qui in egitiorum mari carpatico *R* egyptiorum carphiatio mari *L*

b oras] oris *W*

c palude] paludi *L*

d possideat] possedeat *W* possidebat *R*

I.53 DE ANTIPODIS *WPB* DE ANTEPODIS *L* DE ANTIPODAS *T capitulum om. S*

a esse] est *W*

b interpretationem] interpretantur *L*

c fundum] profundam *W*

I.54 DE GIGANTE *W* DE GIGANTIBUS *SPB* DE GYGANTIBUS *L* DE GIGANTES *T*

a ipsos] ipsas *W*

b enormis] inormes *S*

c perhibeatur] perhibetur *W* perhibentur *SRL*

d...d in litoribus] illitoribus *L*

e...e terrarum latebris] latebris terrarum *S*

f...f uastae quantitatis] uasta equitantes *S* tante uastitatis *L*

g...g eorum . . . leguntur] insignum sunt uie recte *S* eorum saepe reperta leguntur *L*

I.55 DE ALLOIDIS *WLP* DE ELAIDIS *S* DE ALIOIDIS *B* DE ALOIDAS *T*

a geminos] geminus *W* gemini *S*

b Aloidas] alleodes *S*

c inmensae] inmensa *R*

d...d corporum magnitudinis] magnitudinis corporum *S*

e...e ut ter] inter *W* ut inter *S*

f pro] per *W*

g regnandi] segregandi *R*

h detruderent] detraherent *WS*

i Olympo] olympho *R*

I.56 DE ORION *WST* DE ORIONE *LPB post* ORION *add. W* FINIUNT CAPITULA MONSTRORUM *post* ORIONE *add. L* FINIT

a autem] hoc *L*

b profundissimi] profundissimos *S*

c quamuis] quam *W om. S*

d gurgitis] gurgites *SR*

e superare] superasse *WS*

f...f siquando ornos] sique normas *WS* sicut ornos *R*

g aut] *om. R*

I.52 And they said that Triton was like a human in his head, a semi-wild thing in his chest, and like fish down below the navel. And he is described as having been seen in the Carpathian Sea of the Egyptians and around the shores of Italy. And it is not known whether he had his name bestowed from the swamp Triton in Lybia, or the swamp from him.

I.53 They also say that there is a race of humans under the globe which are called Antipodes, and according to the interpretation of that Greek name they tread the lowest foundation of the globe with feet directed straight up to our footprints.

I.54 Indeed giants used to grow to such an enormous size that it is said that all the sea were passable to them on foot. And their bones are often found, according to books, on the shores and in the recesses of the world, as a mark of their vast size.

I.55 They also write that the twin Aloidae were of such immense bodily size that they tried three times to destroy the sky with their hands, because of a burning desire to rule, so that they could hurl down Jupiter from high Olympus.

I.56 But Orion is imagined to have been such that he could cross all seas and overtop with his shoulders the waves of even the deepest flood. And thus he dragged mountain-ashes and huge oaks torn up by their roots from the mountains.

ingentia[h] robora de montibus euulsa radicitus[i] traxit. Ferunt eum[j] iuga peragrasse montium et capite[k] sublimia caeli [l]nubila pulsasse[l].

EPILOGUS

Haec[a] sunt inmania monstra de quibus me fluctus[b] tuae postulationis tundebat[c] et ea[d] quae de [e]spumosis fabularum[e] gurgitibus ad haec litora congessi. Adhuc tamen[f] innumberabilia[g] sunt[h] quae et[i] in terris et in mari fuisse dixerunt[j]. De quibus tediosum est plus scribere uelle et id quod[k] de[l] inferis[m] hominibus, quodque[n] [o]de Chirone, Niobe, Daedalo, Triptolemo, Atlante, Coeo, Iapeto, Typhoeo, et ceteris quibusque[o] turpissimis depromunt fabulis[p].

[q]FINIT LIBER DE MONSTRIS[q].

LIBER II

PROLOGUS

Belua nuncupari potest quidquid[a] in terris aut in gurgite [b]in horrendi[b] corporis ignota et metuenda reperitur forma[c]. Sunt ferme[d] innumerabilia marinarum genera beluarum, quae tam inormibus[e] corporibus[f] [g]magnorum ad instar montium uastas undarum moles[g] et deruta[h] funditus contorquent pectoribus maria, dum cursus ad[i] dulcia fluuiorum freta dirigunt et spumosos[j] natando[k] gurgites magno perturbant murmure[l], et in illo uastissimorum agmine monstrorum, turgida dum caerula[m]

h ingentia] ingenti *L*
i radicitus] radicibus *W*
j eum] enim *L*
k capite] capita *W*
l...l nubila pulsasse] nubila pulsasse *S* nebula pulsisse *R* nebila pulsasse *L* *post* pulsasse *explicit S sic*: oremus dominus qui unigeniti domini nostri

EPILOGUS

a Haec] hac *W*
b fluctus] uentus *W*
c tundebat] tondebat *R*
d ea] ea sunt *R*
e...e spumosis fabularum] spinosis fabulosis *L*
f tamen] tantum *W*
g innumerabilia] innumebilia *R*
h sunt] *om. L*
i et] *om. RL*
j dixerunt] dixerant *L*
k quod] quam *L*
l de] *om. W*
m inferis] his inferioribus *L*
n quodque] quotque *W*
o...o de Chirone . . . quibusque] de tirrone moledilato treptolemo adlante coeto lupeto tiphoeo et ceteris quibus *W* de tinore nilo dedalo trptolemo athlante ceto lupeto thiphoeo et ceteris quibusque *R* dese chirone niole dedalo treptolemo athalante coeteo tropeo et ceteris quibusque *L*
p fabulis] fabulosis *R*
q...q FINIT LIBER DE MONSTRIS] *om. RL*

LIBER II

PROLOGUS

a quidquid] quicquid *RL*
b...b in horrendi] inoriendo *R*
c forma] formae *W*
d ferme] fermae *WR* enim *L*
e inormibus] inmanis *L*
f corporibus] corporis *W*
g...g magnorum . . . moles] magnarum uastas undarum moles ad instar montium *R*
h deruta] deseruta *W* diluta *R*
i ad] ac *L*
j spumosos] spumosis *W*
k natando] natanda *L*
l murmure] murmore *W*
m caerula] *om. W* cerulas *L*

They say he crossed the peaks of mountains, and knocked the high clouds of the sky with his head.

EPILOGUE

These are the huge monsters concerning which the wave of your request buffeted me, and those are the ones which I have gathered to these shores from the foaming torrents of fables. But there are still innumerable things which they have said have existed both on land and in the sea, concerning which it is tedious to wish to write more, even that which they say in highly disgraceful fables about hellish people, such as Chiron, Niobe, Daedalus, Triptolemus, Atlas, Coeus, Iapetus, Typhoeus, and certain others.

HERE ENDS THE BOOK OF MONSTERS.

BOOK II

PROLOGUE

Whatever is found on land or in the sea of unknown and fearsome form of terrible bodily appearance can be called a beast. The kinds of sea-beast are almost innumerable, and with their so enormous bodies they churn up vast masses of waves as big as great mountains, and with their chests disrupt seas from the very bottom, whilst they direct their paths to the sweet river-courses and by swimming disturb the foamy depths with a great roar, and in that legion of the most enormous monsters, whilst

trudunt[n], auras marmoreis[o] [p]deuerberant spumis[p] et ita inormi membrorum mole agitata litore tenus aequora tremebundo[q] gurgite uerrunt[r] ut non tam spectaculum intuentibus[s] quam horrorem[t] praebeant. De quibus iam tibi nihil scribendum [u]putaui quia et[u] innumerabilia sunt, et eorum cognitio[v] longe ab humano genere[w], uelut[x] horrendis undarum gurgitis[y] turribus et marino disiungitur muro. Sed tamen[z] ne lucernam uerbi postulantis [a]gurges neglegentiae demergat[a], de his tibi sermo pauca depromet[b] beluis et horribilibus[c] ignotarum[d] formis bestiarum quae in fluminibus uel stagnis paludibusque, siue in desertis[e] orbis terrarum latebris fuisse quondam, [f]poetae ac[f] philosophi aurato sermone in suis litteraturis[g] inaniter depingunt.

II.1 Leonem, quem regem esse bestiarum, ob metum eius[a] et nimiam fortitudinem poetae et oratores cum phisicis[b] fingunt, in frontem beluarum horribilium ponimus. Qui fiunt generaliter colore [c]fuluo, sed tamen[c] albos cum ingentibus iubis[d] leones et in taurini corporis magnitudine habuisse Indus fertur. Et ipse uastissimae leo formae describitur[e] quem Hercules sub rupe Nemeaei[f] montis occidit.

II.2 Elefanti[a] autem, licet sibi[b] leones timeant, omnibus tamen[c] cognitis maiores sunt animantibus. Qui apud Gangaridos[d] et Indos et inter Nilum fluuium et Brixontem[e] nasci perhibentur. Quorum Pyrrhus[f] in Romaniam[g] .XX. primus ad auxilium belli [h]deduxit, quia[h] turres ad bella cum interpositis iaculatoribus portant[i] et hostes erectis promuscidibus[j] caedunt. Quorum quoque Alexander Macedo innumerabiles albo, nigro, et rubicundo, uarioque colore se in India uidisse ad Aristotelem[k] philosophum[l] descripsit[m].

n trudunt] tradant *L*
o marmoreis] murmureis *W* marmorei *L*
p...p deuerberant spumis] deueferant spumeis *L*
q tremebundo] tremebunda *L*
r uerrunt] uergunt *W* ueniunt *R*
s intuentibus] expectantibus *W*
t horrorem] herrorem *R*
u...u putaui quia et] putaui quod et *W* computaui quia *L*
v cognitio] cognito est *W*
w genere] generi *W*
x uelut] uel *L*
y gurgitis] gurgitum *W* gurgites *R*
z tamen] tantum *WL*
a...a gurges . . . demergat] gurgites neglegentia dimergat *W*
b depromet] depromit *WL*
c horribilibus] horroribus *W*
d ingnotarum] ignotorum *L*
e discretis] desertis *L*
f...f poetae ac] poeta hac *W* poctae ac *L*
g litteraturis] litteraturus *W*

II.1 DE LEONE *WLPBT*

a eius] *om. W*
b phisicis] fisitis *W*
c...c fuluo sed tamen] fuluo set tantum *W* fuluoso tamen *R*
d iubis] iouis *W*
e describitur] discribitur *W*
f Nemeaei] nimie *WL* nimiae *R*

II.2 DE ELEPHANTIS *WP* DE ELIPHANTIS *L* DE ELEFANTO *BT*

a Elefanti] elifanti *R* elephanti *L*
b sibi] *om. R*
c tamen] tantum *W*
d Gangaridos] gararidos *W* gargaridos *R* gangaridos *L*
e Brixontem] brisontem *W* brexantem *L*
f Pyrrhus] pyrrus *W* phirrus *R* phyrrus *L*
g Romaniam] romam *W*
h...h deduxit quia] deduxit quot *W* deduxit qui *R*
i portant] portabant *R*
j promuscidibus] promuscedibus *WR*
k Aristotelem] Aristotilem *L*
l philosophum] philosopum *W* philypphum *R*
m descripsit] describit *L*

they thrust aside the swelling sea, they lash the breezes with marbled foam, and thus with an enormous mass of limbs they sweep the stirred-up sea right up to the shore with a fearful flood so that they offer onlookers not so much a spectacle as a source of fear. Concerning these things I have thought nothing worth writing to you, because they are both innumerable, and knowledge of them is far removed from humankind, as if by the terrifying battlements of the sea-waves, and by a wall of sea. But nevertheless, lest the flood of neglect should drown the lamp of the questioning word, a discussion will provide you with a few things concerning these beasts and the horrible forms of unknown beasts which the poets and philosophers emptily depict in the gilded discourse of their writings to have once existed in rivers or lakes and swamps, or in the deserted recesses of the globe.

II.1 We place in the forefront of fearsome beasts the lion, which because of his dread and excessive strength poets and orators, as well as scientists, imagine to be the king of the beasts. They are generally of a tawny colour, but the Indus, however, is said to have had white lions with huge manes and bodies as large as bulls. And the same kind of lion of the most enormous size is described, which Hercules slew under the rock of the Nemean mountain.

II.2 But elephants, even if they themselves fear lions, are however bigger than all known living things. They are said to be born among the people of Gangeris and Indians and between the river Nile and the Brixontis. And Pyrrhus first brought twenty of them to Romania to help in battle, because they carry towers to war with archers interspersed, and strike the enemy with outstretched trunks. Alexander of Macedon described to the philosopher Aristotle that he had seen innumerable ones of white, black, red, and various colours in India.

II.3 Onagri animalia sunt, non bestiae, sed ingenti animo et saepe[a] elata exultantes fortitudine, saxa de montibus[b] euellunt[c]. Sed ipsi in desertis Persarum esse cum incredibilibus quibusdam prodigiis[d] boum[e] habentes[f] cornua[g] et magnis describuntur corporibus[h].

II.4 Tigres sunt ferae horrendae animositatis, quae in India et apud Hyrcanos et in Armoenia[a] nascuntur. Et sunt ualde rapaces et mirae uelocitatis: unde et Tigris, Assyriorum fluuius[b], eo quod rapidissimo cursu ad instar ipsius[c] bestiae a monte Caucaso[d] prorumpit ab ea nomen accepisse describitur.

II.5 Lynces bestiae maculosis corporibus sunt, quae et[a] nimium ferocitatem habent et pantheris uario[b] sunt colore consimiles; [c]quae et in Syria[c] et in India[d] et ceteris quibusque regionibus nascuntur.

II.6 Pardus est fera rapax et toto corpore discolor, qui Alexandro et Macedonibus cum ceteris nocuerunt bestiis, paulo postquam Aornim[a] petram expugnauit in India [b]a qua[b] prius Hercules[c] terrae motu fugatus recessit. Et Indorum rex, quodam[d] tempore, quia[e] ibi maxime nascuntur, ad regem Romae Anastasium[f] duos[g] pardulos misit in camelo et elefanto[h], quem[i] Plautus[j] [k]poeta ludens lucabum[k] nominauit.

II.7 Pantheras autem quidam mites, quidam[a] horribiles esse describunt. quas[b] [c]poeta Lucanus[c] ad liram Orphei cum ceteris animantibus[d] et bestiis a deserto Thraciae[e] per carmen miserabile prouocatas cecinit, dum ipse tristis et[f] maerens ad undam [g]Strymonis, raptam[g] Eurydicen[h] lacrimabili defleuit carmine.

II.3 DE ONAGRIS *WLP* DE ONAGRO *BT*

[a] saepe] sese *R*
[b] montibus] monti *W*
[c] euellunt] uellunt *RL*
[d] prodigiis] prodigus *W*
[e] boum] bouum *R* boi *L*
[f] habentes] *om. RL*
[g] cornua] cornuabentes *L*
[h] corporibus] corporeis *W*

II.4 DE TRIGRIBUS *W* DE TIGRIBUS *LPB* DE TIGRIS *T*

[a] Armoenia] carmoenia *R*
[b] fluuius] fluuios *L*
[c] ipsius] istius *R*
[d] cuicassu *W* caucasso *R* caucasi *L*

II.5 DE LINTIBUS *W* DE LYNCIBUS *LPBT*

[a] et] *om. RL*
[b] uario] uariis *W*
[c...c] quae et in Syria] quae et in tirria *W* qui in tyria *R* quae in tria *L*
[d] India] indos *R* indo *L*

II.6 DE PARDIS *WPBT* DE PARTHEIS *L*

[a] Aornim] urneam *W* ormem *R* ornem *L*
[b...b] a qua] aliquo *L*
[c] Hercules] haerculae *W* hirculis *L*
[d] quodam] quod a *W* quondam *L*
[e] quia] quae *W*
[f] Anastasium] anasthasium *W* anathasium *R*
[g] duos] duas *W*
[h] elefanto] elefante *R* elievantum *L*
[i] quem] regem quem *W*
[j] Plautus] *om. R* plustus *L*
[k...k] poeta . . . lucabum] poeta uidens lucem licabum *W* poeta lucamlium *R* poeta lucabum *L*

II.7 DE PANTHERIS *WLPBT*

[a] quidam] quidem *W* quibusdam *L*
[b] quas] quos *W*
[c...c] poeta Lucanus] lucanus poeta *L*
[d] animantibus] animalibus *WL*
[e] Thraciae] trahiae *L*
[f] et] esset et *R*
[g...g] Strymonis raptam] trimoris raptum *L*
[h] Eurydicen] erudicem *W* eridicen *R* eurindicen *L*

II.3 Wild asses are animals, not beasts, but with great courage and often exulting in proud strength they tear rocks from the mountains. But there are those in the deserts of Persia which are described amongst incredible prodigies, having the horns of cattle, and with large bodies.

II.4 Tigers are wild animals of fearsome hostility, which are born in India and amongst the Hyrcanians and in Armenia. And they are extremely rapacious and of amazing speed; whence also the river Tigris of Assyria is said to have derived its name, since it rushes from Mount Caucasus with the swiftest of currents, just like that beast.

II.5 Lynxes are beasts with spotted bodies, which both have outstanding ferocity and are very like panthers in their mottled body. And they are born in both Syria and India, and in certain other areas.

II.6 The leopard is a rapacious wild beast of mixed colour on its whole body, and they caused harm to Alexander and the Macedonians, along with other beasts, just after he took by storm the Aornis Rock, from which Hercules had earlier retreated, put to flight by an earthquake. And on one occasion the king of India, since they are especially born there, sent two little leopards to King Anastasius of Rome on a camel and an elephant, which the poet Plautus jokingly named a Lucanian cow.

II.7 Some describe panthers as gentle, others as fearsome. And the poet Lucan sang that they were stirred from the Thracian desert along with other animals and beasts towards the lyre of Orpheus because of his sorrowful song. For he himself was sad, and, grieving by the waters of Strymon, he lamented in piteous song for Eurydice, who had been snatched away.

II.8 Ferunt fabulae Graecorum plurima in libris antiquitatum suae philosophiae quondam fuisse quae nunc incredibilia esse[a] uidentur, tam de monstris quam etiam [b]beluis et serpentibus[b]. De quibus partem replicaturi[c] sumus. Inter quae belua Lernae[d] describitur, quam nunc apud inferos esse[e], tam horrendam stridore quam forma[f] terribilem, Graeci cum quibusdam fingunt Romanis.

II.9 Hippotami[a] beluae in India esse perhibentur maiores elefantorum[b] corporibus, quos dicunt in quodam fluuio aquae impotabilis[c] demorari. Qui quondam .CC.[d] homines una hora in rapaces gurgitum[e] uortices[f] traxisse et crudelem in modum deuorasse narrantur.

II.10 Quasdam[a] enim bestias prope ad mare Rurum nasci ipsa[b] fabulositas perhibet, et quod .VIII. pedes duplicibus membris et capita bina habent[c] cum oculis fingunt gorgoneis[d].

II.11 Chimaeram[a] Graeci scribunt quandam[b] fuisse bestiam triplicis[c] monstruosa corporis foeditate terribilem quam flammis dicunt armatam, eo quod tria capita ignem habuisset[d] uomentia[e].

II.12 Et[a] sunt quoque, ut ferunt, in India beluae, quas aeternas, ob[b] uiuidam uirtutem, uocant. Quae in suis uerticibus ossa serrata[c] uelut gladios gestant, quibus arietino, dum aduersus[d] incurrunt, impetu, obpositi transuerberantur[e] clipei.

II.8 DE LERNA *W* DE LUCERNA *L* DE BELVA LERNAE *PT* DE LERNIS *B*

a esse] *om. WR*
b..b beluis et serpentibus] belbuis *L*
c replicaturi] replicati *WR*
d Lernae] lerna *WL*
e esse] describuntur esse *L*
f forma] formae *WL* forme *R*

II.9 DE YPOTAMIS *W* DE IPOTAMIS *L* DE HIPPOTAMIS *P* DE HIPPOTAMIS *BT*

a Hippotami] Ippotami *W* Epotami *R* Ipotami *L*
b elefantorum] elephantores *L*
c impotabilis] inpotabiles *W*
d .CC.] .CCCC. *W* .CCC. *RL*
e gurgitum] paer *R* gurgitorum *L*
f uortices] uertices *R*

II.10 DE HIS QUI BINA CAPITA HABENT *WBT* DE BESTIIS QUAE HABENT BINA CAPITA *LP*

a Quasdam] quisdam *W*
b ipsa] *om. R*
c habent] habebant *L*
d gorgoneis] gurgones *W* gorgones *L*

II.11 DE CIMERICA *W* DE CYMERA BESTIA *L* DE CHIMAERA *PBT*

a Chimaeram] cimericam *W* cymeram *R* cumeram *L*
b quandam] quodam *R* quondam *L*
c triplicis] triplici *R*
d habuisset] habuisse *R*
e uomentia] uouentia *R* formantia *L*

II.12 DE BELVA *W* DE AETERNIS INDIAE BELVIS *LP* DE BELVA AETERNA *BT*

a Et] *om. L*
b ob] ut *L*
c serrata] reserata *L*
d aduersus] aduersus clipeos *R*
e transuerberantur] transuerberant *W*

II.8 The fables of the Greeks tell of very many things in the books of their philosophy from ancient times which now seem to be incredible, as much about monsters as also beasts and serpents. And we are about to unfold a part of these, amongst which is described the beast of Lerna, which is now in the underworld, and which the Greeks, along with certain Romans, depict as being as horrible in its clamour as dreadful in its form.

II.9 Hippopotami are said to be beasts in India greater in body than elephants, and they say that they live in a certain river with undrinkable water. And once they are said to have dragged two hundred men in a single hour into the greedy eddies of the flood, and to have devoured them in a cruel fashion.

II.10 Legend itself holds that certain beasts are born near the Red Sea, and they imagine that they have eight feet on double limbs and two heads, with Gorgon's eyes.

II.11 The Greeks write that the chimaera was formerly a certain terrible beast of triple body with monstrous hideousness, which they say was armed with flames, in that it had three heads spewing fire.

II.12 And there are also, so they say, beasts in India [crocodiles], which they call eternal on account of their lively strength. And they bear serrated bones like swords on their heads, by which, when they attack shields, charging like a ram, the opposing shields are split apart.

II.13 Et in Perside[a] fingunt esse bestias quas[b] conopenos[c] appellant, quibus sub caninis[d] capitibus equina[e] dependet[f] per ceruices iuba[g] et ore naribusque[h] ignem flammamque expirant[i].

II.14 Cerberus autem[a] tria capita[b] habuisse describitur. Quem poetae et [c]philosophi ab ianua[c] inferni mortales perturbare trino arbitrantur[d] latratu. Sed tamen[e] eum trementem ab Orci regis inferni solio[f] [g]famosissimum Alciden[g] in uinculis traxisse turpi[h] depromunt mendacio, [i]et quod eum inritatum[i] ille contumax insanis prouocauit[j] latratibus[k].

II.15 Et[a] inter ipsa quae dicunt inania, ferunt formicas[b] in quadam esse insula, et quod sex pedes et atrum colorem et miram habeant[c] celeritatem, depromunt. Cum quibus incredibilis[d] auri abundantia describitur, [e]quod ipsae[e] [f]sua seruant[f] industria.

II.16 Fuit praeterea quaedam in Indorum finibus bestia maior, ut ferunt, elefanto[a], colore nigro, quam Indi dentem tyrannum uocauerunt[b]. Quae in medio toruae[c] frontis tria cornua gessit, et tantae animositatis erat, ut[d] sibi[e] conspectis hominibus, non tela neque ignes[f], nec ulla uitaret pericula. [g]Quam ferunt Alexandrum[g], mortuis .XXVI. militibus, tandem confixam occidisse uenabulis[h].

II.13 DE COENOPENOS *W* DE CONOPONIS *L* DE CONOPENIS *P* DE COENOPOENIS *B* DE CYNOPENOS *T*

[a] Perside] persida *WR* persidia *L*
[b] quas] quos *W*
[c] conopenos] coenopenos *W*
[d] caninis] cannis *W* annis *R*
[e] equina] aquina *W* equi *L*
[f] dependet] dependit *WRL*
[g] iuba] iuba per cerin munces *W*
[h] naribusque] naribus qui *W*
[i] expirant] exspirant *R* spirant *L*

II.14 DE CERBERO *WLPBT*

[a] autem] haec L
[b] capita] aepita R
[c...c] philosophi ab ianua] philophi a ianua R philosophia ianua L
[d] arbitrantur] arbitrentur W
[e] tamen] tantum W tunc L
[f] solio] solo L
[g...g] famosissimum Alciden] fanosissimum alceden W
[h] turpi] turpide W turbi L
[i..i] et quod eum inritatum] et quod eum inuitatum R adquod deum inritandum L
[j] prouocauit] prouocant R prouocabit L
[k] latratibus] latrantibus L

II.15 DE FORMICAE *W* DE FORMICIBUS MAGNIS *L* DE FORMICIS MAGNIS *P* DE FORMICIS *B* DE FORMICAS *T*

[a] Et] *om. R*
[b] formicas] formices *L*
[c] habeant] habent *W*
[d] incredibilis] incredibilibus *R*
[e...e] quod ipsae] quam ipse *R*
[f...f] sua seruant] suaserunt *L*

II.16 DE DENTEM TYRANNUM *W* DE DENTE TYRANNO BEL VA INDIAE *LP* DE DENTE TYRANNO *B* DE DENTEM TIRANNUM *T*

[a] elefanto] elephanto *WR*
[b] uocauerunt] uocarunt *L*
[c] toruae] turbae *W* torbuem *L*
[d] ut] et *R*
[e] sibi] illi *W*
[f] ignes] ignis *WR*
[g...g] Quam ferunt Alexandrum] proferunt alaxandrum *R*
[h] uenabulis] funalibus *L*

II.13 And in Persis they imagine that there are beasts which they call Conopeni, beneath the dog-shaped heads of which a horse-like mane hangs from their neck, and they breath fire and flame from their mouth and nostrils.

II.14 But Cerberus is described as having had three heads. And poets and philosophers reckon that he deters mortals from the gates of Hell with his triple barking. Yet however they put out in a shameful lie that the most celebrated Hercules dragged him trembling in chains from the throne of Orcus, king of the underworld, and that the defiant hero provoked the enraged beast by mad barking.

II.15 Among the other empty things which they say, they maintain that there are ants on a certain island, and claim that they have six feet and a black colour and amazing speed. Alongside them there is described an incredible abundance of gold, which they guard in their diligence.

II.16 Moreover there was a beast on the borders of India, so they say, larger than an elephant and black in colour, which the Indians call 'Tyrant's tooth' [rhinoceros]. It bore three horns in the middle of its cruel forehead, and it was of such savagery that when it caught sight of humans, it would shun no weapons or fires or any dangers. They say that Alexander at last pierced it with hunting-spears, after twenty-six of his soldiers had died, and slew it.

II.17 Et[a] cum his incredibilibus fingunt execrandae[b] formae hippotamos[c], quos ferunt triplicem habere[d] colorem. Qui oris latitudine[e] uanno comparantur[f]. Sunt autem[g] tam fugaces ut, si quis insequitur, fugiant[h] quousque sanguine[i] sudant.

II.18 Leopardi [a]feri ac[a] terribiles sunt, qui[b] atrocissimarum binae[c] formae ferarum[d] permixtam habent horrendi corporis formam, quia[e] ex leonibus et pardis generantur. Quos ferunt iuxta Rubrum mare et in [f]quibusdam aliis[f] regionibus nasci.

II.19 Fingunt quoque poetae in mari Tyrrheno[a] ceruleos esse canes, qui posteriorem corporis partem cum piscibus habent communem[b]. Ipsis quoque Scylla ratem Ulixis[c] [d]lacerans marinis[d] succincta[e] canibus describitur[f].

II.20 Et dicunt bestias esse nocturnas, et non tam bestias quam dira prodigia, quia[a] nequaquam in luce, sed [b]in umbris[b] cernuntur nocturnis[c]. Quas[d] ferunt in omnium bestiarum formas se uertere[e] posse[f] dum[g] insequentium timore[h] perturbantur.

II.21 Fluuius autem Nilus, qui, in septem ostia discurrens[a], mari [b]Tyrrheno absumitur[b], omnia monstra, ferarum similia, gignit, eo gurgite quo se ad ortum dirigit et [c]quo item flexus[c] a mari rubro ad occasum refunditur[d].

II.17 DE YPOTAMOS *W* DE IPOTAMIS *L* DE HIPPOTAMIS *P* ITEM DE HIPPOPOTAMIS *B* ITEM DE HIPPOPOTAMOS *T*

[a] Et] *om. R*
[b] execrandae] extende *W* exsecrandae *R*
[c] hippotamos] ippotamos *W* ipotamos *R* ipotamus *L*
[d] habere] habuisse *W*
[e] latitudine] latitudinem *L*
[f] comparantur] conparant *L*
[g] autem] haec *L*
[h] fugiant] fugiunt *WL*
[i] sanguine] sanguinem *L*

II.18 DE LEOPARDO *W* DE LEOPARDIS *LPB* DE LEOPARDOS *T*

[a...a] feri ac] fere *L*
[b] qui] quod *W*
[c] binae] laene *W*
[d] ferarum] bestiarum *L*
[e] quia] quod *WL*
[f...f] quibusdam aliis] quibus aliis dam *L*

II.19 DE CERULEOS CANES *W* DE CAERULEIS CANIBUS *LPB* DE CERULEOS CANES *T*

[a] Tyrrheno] terreno *WR* tyrreno *L*
[b] communem] communionem *L*
[c] Ulixis] ulixes *R* ulixi *L*
[d...d] lacerans marinis] lacerant smarinis *L*
[e] succincta] succinctis *W*
[f] describitur] describit *L*

II.20 DE NOCTURNIS PRODIGIIS *LP om. W* DE BESTIIS NOCTURNIS *B* DE BESTIAS NOCTURNAS *T*

[a] quia] quod *WL*
[b...b] in umbris] mbris *L*
[c] nocturnis] quae nocturnis *L*
[d] Quas] quos *W*
[e] uertere] uerti *WRL*
[f] posse] potuisse *W*
[g] dum] *om. L*
[h] timore] more *WL*

II.21 DE NILO FLUVIO *WBT* DE BEL VIS NILI *L* DE BEL VIS NILI FLUMINIS *P*

[a] discurrens] decurrens *R*
[b...b] Tyrrheno absumitur] terreno obsumitur *W* terreno absumitur *R* tyrreno adsumitur *L*
[c...c] quo . . . flexus] coitem flesus *L*
[d] refunditur] refundit *R*

II.17 And amongst these incredible things they imagine hippopotami of awful size, which they maintain to have three kinds of colour. And in the breadth of their mouth they are compared to a winnowing-fan. But they are so shy that, if anyone follows them, they flee until they sweat blood.

II.18 Leopards are wild and fearsome, and have a body of fearsome form mixed from the twin shape of the most dreadful wild animals, since they are produced from lions and panthers. They say that they are born next to the Red Sea and in certain other areas.

II.19 The poets also imagine that there are azure dogs in the Mediterranean, the hind parts of whose bodies they share with fish; also girt round with these same sea-dogs Scylla is described tearing apart the ship of Ulysses.

II.20 And they say that there are night-beasts, and not so much beasts as grim prodigies, since they are never seen in the light, but in the nocturnal shadows. They say that these are able to change themselves into the shapes of all beasts when they are disturbed by the fear of pursuers.

II.21 But the river Nile, which, running into seven mouths, is swallowed in the Mediterranean, produces all kinds of monsters, like wild animals, in that flood where it flows towards the East, and where again, turning from the Red Sea, it flows back into the West.

II.22 Ferunt et in India[a] beluam fuisse[b] quae[c] habuit bina capita, alterum lunae bicornis ut [d]puta imaginem[d], alterum corcodrilli[e] gerebat. Et tergo serrato[f] et saeuis armata[g] dentibus[h] quondam in Alexandri[i] milites prosiliens duos occidisse describitur.

II.23 Bestia autem illa inter omnes beluas dirissima[a] [b]fertur, in qua[b] [c]tantam ueneni[c] copiam adfirmant ut eam sibi leones quamuis inualidioris[d] feram corporis, timeant, et tantam uim eius uenenum habere[e] arbitrantur, ut eo licet ferri[f] acies intincta liquescat.

II.24 Et iuxta Eufraten flumen[a] scribunt esse animal quod [b]nuncupatur autolops[b], quod longis cornibus quae serrae[c] figuram habent ingentia robora praecidens ad terram deponit.

II.25 [a]In Nilo autem[a] flumine ferunt esse corcodrillos[b], beluas[c] non modicae staturae[d], qui[e] ad solis aestum per litus[f] se sternunt. Et humani generis sunt rapaces si quos a[g] somno excitati[h] sibi uicinos persenserint[i]. Quae bestiae maxime in aquis et in[j] oris [k]litorum demorantur[k].

II.26 Balena[a] quoque fera intolerabilis in India nascitur, ubi plurima prope totius orbis prodigia leguntur. De quarum [b]pellibus balenarum sibi[b] gens quaedam apud Indos uestimentorum tegmina[c] conponit[d].

II.22 DE BEL VA QUI ABUIT BINA CAPITA *W* DE BEL VIS INDIAE BINORUM CAPITUM *L* DE BEL VA QUAE HABUIT BINA CAPITA *LPBT*

[a] India] me *L*
[b] fuisse] esse *L*
[c] quae] qui *R*
[d...d] puta imaginem] putae imaginem *W* putei maginem *R* pute imaginem *L*
[e] corcodrilli] corcodrillo *W*
[f] serrato] ferrato *R*
[g] armata] anata *W*
[h] dentibus] dentis *L*
[i] Alexandri] alaxandri *R*

II.23 DE BESTIA VENENOSA *LPB om. WT*

[a] dirissima] dirissimas *R* durissima *L*
[b...b] fertur . . . qua] *om. R*
[c...c] tantam ueneni] tantum uenenum *W* tantum ueneni *L*
[d] inualidioris] inualidiores *W*
[e] habere] *om. W*
[f] ferri] feri *W*

II.24 DE AUTOLOPE *WPB* DE AUTULAPRAE *L* DE ANTOLOPS *T*

[a] flumen] fluuium *L*
[b...b] nuncupatur autolops] nuncupatur autulaps *R* nuncupantur aut laps *L*
[c] serrae] serra *W*

II.25 DE CORCODRILLO *WB* DE CORCODRILLIS *LP* DE CROCODILI *T*

[a...a] In Nilo autem] in illo autem *W* in illo *R* in nihilo autem *L*
[b] corcodrillos] corcodrilos *R*
[c] beluas] bellas *L*
[d] staturae] flaturae *L*
[e] qui] quae *W*
[f] litus] litora *W*
[g] a] ad *L*
[h] excitati] excitat *W*
[i] persenserint] persenserunt *W* senserint *L*
[j] in] *om. RL*
[k...k] litorum demorantur] littoris morantur *L*

II.26 DE BALENA *WBT* DELLENIS *L* DE BALLAENA *P*

[a] Balena] bellina *RL*
[b...b] pellibus . . . sibi] bellibus beluarum sibi *W* pellibus bellinarum sibi *R* ballinarum sibique *L*
[c] tegmina] tegenina *L*
[d] componit] componuntur *L*

II.22 And they say that in India there is a beast which had two heads; it bore one (for example) the image of a two-horned moon, the other of a crocodile. And with its serrated back and armed with savage teeth it is described once as having leapt out on Alexander's soldiers and killed two.

II.23 But that beast is said to be amongst the fiercest of all brutes, in which they assert that there is such a quantity of venom that lions fear it although it is an animal of weaker body, and they reckon that its poison has such strength, that the cutting-edge even of iron, dipped in it, melts.

II.24 And next to the river Euphrates they write that there is an animal which is called antelope, because with its long horns which have the shape of a saw it cuts through mighty oaks and fells them to the ground.

II.25 In the river Nile they say that there are crocodiles, beasts of no mean size, which stretch themselves out in the heat of the sun on the banks, and are greedy for humankind if they sense any near when they are roused from their sleep. And these beasts lurk mostly in water and on the edges of shores.

II.26 Balena, an unbearable wild animal, is also born in India, where most of the wonders of almost the entire globe are read about. And from the hides of these *balenae* a certain race of Indians puts together coverings of clothing.

II.27 Fluuius [a]Indiae Ganges[a], qui aurum cum lapidibus profert[b] pretiosis, mira monstruosae feritatis genera gignit. Quarum scriptores beluarum se[c] de his[d] tacuisse, pro incredibilibus testantur [e]formatis figuris[e].

II.28 Et scribunt Romani cum Graecis per ipsas poeticas incredibilium rerum[a] fabulas, bipedes equos[b] in mari esse Tyrrheno[c], qui[d] parte[e] corporis priore equorum figuras et posteriore piscium[f] habeant[g].

II.29 Alexander[a] Macedo se[b] in India mures uulpium statura[c] uidisse ad Aristotelem[d] descripsit, qui[e] morsibus pestiferis[f] homines et iumenta lacerabant[g].

II.30 Et in uicino Armoeniae[a] montis loco, ubi margaritae nasci perhibentur, leones et[b] tigres[c], lynces et leopardos et cuncta genera ferarum horribilium mons quidam altissimus[d] gignit.

II.31 In Brixonte[a] quoque bestiae quaedam non magnae, sed prope omnibus nationibus ignotae, gigni perhibentur[b], quas celestices uocant. Quem fluuium in quo nascuntur, Nilo uicinum, descripsimus, cuius[c] secundum plurimos ignoratur[d] initium. Qui apud Aegyptios Archoboleta[e], quod est aqua magna, uocatur[f].

II.27 DE BELVIS QUAE SUNT IN GANGE *WP* DE EL VIS QUAE SUNT IN GANTES *L* DE FLUVIO INDIAE GANGETE *B* DE FLUVIO INDIE GANGETIS *T*

a Indiae Ganges] indie gandes *R* ina egantes *L*
b profert] proferet *W*
c se] *om. W*
d his] eis *L*
e...e formatis figuris] formarum generibus *L*

II.28 DE BIPEDES *WT* DE BIPEDIBUS EQUIS *LPB*

a rerum] *om. W*
b equos] et quos *W*
c Tyrrheno] terreno *WR* turreno *L*
d qui] quod *W*
e parte] maiore parte *WR*
f piscium] piscius *L*
g habeant] habent *L*

II.29 DE ALEXANDRO MACEDO *WB* DE MURIBUS VULPIUM STATURA *LP* MURES VULPIUM STATURA *T*

a Alexander] alaxander *R*
b se] *om. R*
c statura] staturas *L*
d Aristotelem] aristotilem *RL*
e qui] quae *R*
f pestiferis] *om. L*
g lacerabant] lacerabunt *W*

II.30 DE GENERIBUS OMNIUM BESTIARUM *LB om. W* DE OMNI GENERE BESTIARUM *P* DE MONTE ALTISSIMO FERIS FECUNDO *T*

a Armoeniae] armonie *R*
b et] *om. RL*
c tigres] triges *L*
d altissimus] *om. W*

II.31 DE BESTIAE CAELESTICAE *W* DE CAELESTICIBUS *LP* DE BESTIIS CAELESTICIBUS *B* CELESTICES *T*

a Brixonte] brixanti *L*
b perhibentur] perhibetur *R*
c cuius] cuiusque *R*
d ignoratur] ignorat *L*
e Archoboleta] anchoboleta *R om. L*
f uocatur] uocat *L*

II.27 The river Ganges in India, which yields gold and precious stones, produces wondrous races of monstrous ferocity. But writers about these beasts claim to have kept quiet about them because of their incredibly-formed figures.

II.28 And along with the Greeks the Romans write in their poetic fantasies of incredible things, that there are two-footed horses in the Mediterranean, which have most of the front part of their body in the shape of horses, and the rear of fish.

II.29 Alexander of Macedon described to Aristotle that he had seen mice in India the size of foxes, and they used to tear men and pack-animals with their destructive biting.

II.30 And in a place near the mountains of Armenia, where pearls are said to be produced, a certain very high mountain yields lions and tigers, lynxes and leopards and all kinds of horrible wild beasts.

II.31 In Brixontis certain beasts called Celestes, not large, but unknown to almost all nations, are said to be born. And we have described the river, in which they are born, near the Nile, the source of which is unknown, according to most. Amongst the Egyptians it is called Archoboleta, that is 'great water'.

II.32 Fingunt enim fabulae Graecorum bestias omnes et terrena animalia cum uariis monstrorum et beluarum generibus[a] in mari esse[b] Tyrrheno[c], cum[d] binis tantum[e] pedibus, eo quod a pectore usque ad caudas squamosa[f] corpora habent.

II.33 Et per [a]quandam picturam[a] Graeci operis didicimus quod homines quos cerulei canes prima[b] laceratione[c] non deuorauerunt in dorso supra dicti generis beluarum [d]uecti sine lesione[d] fuissent, postquam[e] Scylla eisdem[f] circumdata monstris ratem Ulixis[g] spoliauerat[h] nautis, et ita cum marinis leonibus, tigribus[i], pantheris[j], onagris, lyncibus, [k]et leopardis[k], et omni genere[l] ferarum atque[m] animalium per[n] proprias sui maris[o] regiones transierint[p].

II.34 Et fingunt ideo his non nocuisse[a] hominibus quia[b] seminis humanam[c] commixtionem quaerebant, et inde natum genus formae triplicis perhibetur[d]. Et in eiusdem modi[e] fictis[f] cernebam uanitatibus quod infantes ab his hominibus ac feris in mari progenitos lactis mulgendi gratia cum concis natare[g] per undas putabant, ut a suis sibi[h] cibum exciperent[i] parentibus.

II.35 Fuit rex Aeeta[a] qui regnauit in Colchide, quem scribunt tauros ignem flantes[b] habuisse et pellem auream, propter quam[c] [d]Iason Thessalus[d] ad Colchos[e] nauigauit. Cui rex tauros flammantes domare ut pellem mereretur[f] tribuit.

II.32 DE BESTIIS CUM BINIS PEDIBUS *WBT* DE BEL VIS TYRRHENI MARIS *LP*

a generibus] gentibus *R*
b esse] *om. RL*
c Tyrrheno] terreno *WR* turreno *L*
d cum] et cum
e tantum] vel *L*
f squamosa] scamosa *W* qua mora *L*

II.33 DE PICTURAM GRECI OPERIS *W om. LP* DE PICTURA GRECI OPERIS *BT*

a...a quandam picturam] quendam picturam *W* quandam pictura *L*
b prima] *om. R*
c laceratione] lacerationem *L*
d...d uecti sine lesione] uectis in lesione *L*
e postquam] postqua *W*
f eisdem] autem de in *W* hisdem *R* isdem *L*
g Ulixeis] olixis *W* uluxis *R* ulixi *L*
h spoliaueat] spoliauerunt *L*
i tigribus] turgribus *L*
j pantheris] pantegris *W*
k..k et leopardis] et leopardos *W om. R*
l genere] genera *W*
m atque] adque *R*
n per] *om. W*
o maris] manus *L*
p transierint] transierunt *WL*

II.34 DE NON NOCUIS HOMINIBUS *WT om. LP* DE NON NOCITIS HOMINIBUS *B*

a nocuisse] nocuis *W*
b quia] quod *W*
c humanam] humani *W* humanum *L*
d perhibetur] perhibent *WL*
e modi] modo *W*
f fictis] uictis *L*
g natare] nature *L*
h sibi *om. W*
i exciperent] exhiberent *W* exquirerent *L*

II.35 DE REGE ETA *W* DE TAURIS IGNEM FLANTIBUS *LP* DE REGE AEETA *BT*

a Aeeta] heta *W* eta *RL*
b flantes] flantem *L*
c quam] quod *W om. L*
d...d Iason Thessalus] iasonte salus *W* ioron thesalos *L*
e Colchos] cholchidos *W* cholchos *L*
f mereretur] mereret *WR* inereret *L*

II.32 The fables of the Greeks imagine that all beasts and land-animals, along with various kinds of monsters and beasts are in the Mediterranean, and with only two feet, because from the chest to the tail they have scaly bodies.

II.33 And through a certain picture of Greek art we have learnt that men whom the azure dogs did not devour with their first bite, have been carried unharmed on the backs of beasts of the above-named kind, after Scylla, surrounded with the same monsters, had plundered the ship of Ulysses of its sailors, and so with marine lions, tigers, panthers, wild asses, lynxes, and leopards, and all kinds of wild beasts and animals they passed through their own areas of her sea.

II.34 And so they imagine that they did not harm humans because they wanted a mingling of human seed, and from there a race of triple form is said to have been born. And in empty fictions of the same kind I saw that they thought that children produced in the sea by these men and beasts were swimming in the sea with conches for the sake of milking, so that they might take food for themselves from their own parents.

II.35 There was a King Aeeta who reigned in Colchis, whom they write had bulls breathing fire and a golden fleece, on account of which Thessalian Jason sailed to Colchis. The king conceded to him the taming of the flaming bulls so that he might deserve the fleece.

II.36 Et cum beluis Indorum, quoddam genus duplicibus fertur fuisse[a] caudis, quae duplicitas[b] ad sex pedum[c] mensuram in latitudine cum binis patebat[d] unguibus, quibus homines uerberauit[e] pungens[f].
[g]FINIT LIBER DE BELVIS[g].

LIBER III
INCIPIT DE SERPENTIBUS.

III.1 Lerneum[a] anguem poetarum fabulae fingunt dirum fuisse spiramine et tartareo[b] nociuum ueneno et linguis triplicibus terribilem. Cui [c]de media[c] fronte turba ingens monstrorum ac serpentium pullulabat[d], generisque uelut uiperei, Eumenidum crines, circa[e] eiusdem anguis faciem globorum[f] innumerabilibus nodis, horrenda scatebant prodigia. Qui quondam fertur Herculem hac turba serpentium et sibilantibus circumstetisse capitibus atque in eo sibi proditus[g] nihil profecisse[h] perhibetur[i].

III.2 Serpentes quoque Assyriorum in desertis nasci perhibentur, qui habent capita bina et inmensa corporis uolumina torquent quatuorque per umbras nocturnas oculis in modum lucernae lucent.

III.3 Hydra anguis armatus fuisse describitur, quae Euridicen[a], coniugem Orphei, in ripa fluminis capite[b] truncauit et demersit in gurgitem; et sicut Scylla monstris, ita et haec serpentibus praecincta fuisse fingitur. Cuius tale signum Hercules in suo clipeo cum aliis[c] .C. gerebat anguibus[d].

II.36 DE BELVIS QUAE HABENT CAUDAS DUPLICATAS *WBT* DE BELVIS INDIAE QUAE DUPLICES HABENT CAUDAS *LP post* DUPLICATAS *add. W* EXPLICIUNT CAPITULA DE MARINIS BELVIS *post* CAUDAS *add. L* FINIT

a fuisse] efuisse *L*
b duplicitas] duplicatas *WR* duplicitae *L*
c pedum] pedium *L*
d patebat] latebat *L*
e uerberauit] uerberabat *R*
f pungens] pingues *L*
g...g FINIT LIBER DE BELVIS] FINIT DE BELVIS *W* FINIT LIBELLUS DE BELVIS *L*

LIBER III
III.1 DE URNEUM ANGUEM *W* DE LERNAEO ANGUE *PBT*

a Lernaeum] Urneum *W* Lerneum autem *R*
b tartareo] tartaro *W* tanta re *R*
c...c de media] dimidia *W*
d pullulabat] pululabunt *W* pululabat *R*
e circa] *om. W*
f globorum] globosorum *W*
g proditus] perditi *W* perditus *R*
h profecisse] perfecisse *W*
i perhibetur] *explicit R*

III.2 DE SERPENTIBUS ASIRIORUM *W* DE SERPENTIBUS ASSYRIORUM *PBT*

III.3 DE HYDRA *WPBT*

a Euridicen] rudicen *W*
b capite] rabide *P*
c aliis] alis *W*
d anguibus] signibus *W*

II.36 And amongst the beasts of India a certain kind is said to have had two tails which doubled to the size of six feet in length, when it open both claws, with which it used to strike and wound humans.
HERE ENDS THE WORK ABOUT THE BEASTS.

BOOK III
HERE BEGINS THE BOOK ABOUT SERPENTS.
III.1 The fables of poets imagine that a snake of Lerna had dreadful breath, and was poisonous with Tartarean venom, and terrible with its triple tongue. From the middle of its forehead a huge crowd of monsters and serpents used to seethe, and hair of the viperous kind of the Eumenides, like fearsome prodigies, used to bubble around the face of this snake, in countless gatherings of knots. It is once said to have surrounded Hercules with this crowd of serpents and hissing heads, and in that situation nothing is said to have availed him.

III.2 Serpents are also said to be born in the Assyrian desert which have two heads and twist the enormous coils of their body and shine with their four eyes through the nocturnal shadows like lanterns.

III.3 The Hydra is described as having been an armed snake which struck Eurydice, the wife of Orpheus, in the head on a river-bank, and drowned her in the flood; and just as Scylla was girt about with monsters, so too this is imagined to have been girt about with serpents. Hercules used to wear such a sign on his shield, along with a hundred other snakes.

III.4 Stares namque serpentes in India dicuntur gigni inmensi[a] corpore, uario colore terribiles, qui[b] in quibusdam squamis auri fulgore radiabant[c] et in quibusdam candidis ac purpureis coloribus et nigris [d]cernebantur distincti[d]. Cum quibus quondam Alexander Macedo bellum contulisse perhibetur.

III.5 In Calabris[a] quoque saltibus anguis mirae magnitudinis in tempore Caesaris[b] Augusti fuit, qui in uere stagna paludesque colens ranis ac piscibus rabidam[c] repleuit ingluuiem; et postquam solis ardore paludes dehiscebant adustae, tunc pestis[d] irata, cibo potuque carens, agros scintillantibus peragrauit oculis et nimiam dedit mortalibus plagam.

III.6 In confinio Rubri maris et Arabiae serpentes esse perhibentur cum quibus nascitur piper album, quod incenso loco sub terram fugientibus homines nigrum flammis lambentibus[a] deripiunt. Qui serpentes corsia nuncupantur et cornua habent arietina, et ab eis percussus[b] cito moritur tumens.

III.7 Et in India gigni serpentes huius describuntur modi, qui, ut perhibent, columnarum crassitudinem et bina trinaque[a] habent cristata[b] capita et processi[c] de montium latebris ad aquam erectis pergebant pectoribus, et ita sinuosis motibus ac squamis terram reddiderunt[d] adtritam et oculis horrendo scintillantibus ueneno, linguis ora uibrabant[e] trisulcis et mortiferos[f] exalabant alitus[g].

III.8 Fertur et in Sicilia uisus fuisse serpens qui lubrico laterum sinuamine labens septena uolumina globoso corpore traxit et ceruleam fulgore[a] speciem aureo per omnes miscebat squamas[b].

III.4 DE SERPENTES STARES *WT* DE SERPENTIBUS STARIBUS *P* DE SERPENTIBUS STARES *B*

[a] immensi] immensis *W*
[b] qui] quae *W*
[c] radiabant] radiebant *W*
[d...d] cernebantur distincti] cernebant distincte *W*

III.5 DE ANGUIBUS MIRE MAGNITUDINIS *WBT* DE ANGUE MIRAE MAGNITUDINIS *P*

[a] Calabris] lubris *W*
[b] Caesaris] caesauris *W*
[c] rabidam] rapidam *W*
[d] pestis] pestes *W*

III.6 DE SERPENTIBUS CUM QUIBUS NASCITUR PIPER ALBUM *WPBT*

[a] lambentibus] labentibus *W*
[b] percussus] percussi *W*

III.7 DE SERPENTIBUS QUI HABENT BINA CRISPATA CAPITA *WT* DE SERPENTIBUS QUI HABENT BINA CRISTATA CAPITA *PB*

[a] trinaque] triaque *W*
[b] cristata] crispati *W*
[c] processi] proseliti *W* processi Porsia
[d] reddiderunt] redderunt *W*
[e] uibrabant] uiprobant *W*
[f] mortiferos] mortiferis *W*
[g] alitus] saltibus *W*

III.8 DE SERPENTE IN SICILIA *WPBT*

[a] fulgore] fulgure *W*
[b] squamas] auroe *W*

III.4 Now, Stares are serpents said to be born in India with a huge body, terrible in their varied colour, and they used to glitter with the brightness of gold in some of their scales, and were separately seen in white and purple and black colours. And Alexander of Macedon is once said to have waged war against them.

III.5 In the valleys of Calabria there was also a snake of marvellous size in the time of Caesar Augustus, which in spring, living in the pools and swamps, sated its fierce greed on frogs and fish. But after the swamps dried up, burnt by the heat of the sun, then the enraged pest, lacking food and water, roamed the fields with flashing eyes and caused an excessive plague to mortals.

III.6 On the border of the Red Sea and Arabia there are said to be serpents from whom white pepper is produced, which humans gather, blackened by the licking flames, after the place has been burnt and the snakes flee underground. The snakes are called Corsiae and have ram's horns; anyone struck by them swells up and quickly dies.

III.7 And in India serpents of this sort are said to be born which, so they say, have the thickness of columns and have two or three crested heads, and journeying from the mountain hideaways they used to travel to water with puffed-up breasts, and so with curving movements and scales, they rendered the earth worn away, and with their eyes shining with horrid venom their mouths used to quiver with triple tongues and they breathed out deadly breath.

III.8 And it is said that a serpent has been seen in Sicily that sliding on the slippery sinuousness of its sides dragged its sevenfold coils with its rounded body, and mingled its azure appearance with a golden sheen throughout all its scales.

III.9 Quidam quoque serpens horrendae magnitudinis a Romano exercitu in Africa iuxta flumen Bagradam[a] repertus describitur; et, pro ultione militum quos primo deuorauit impetu[b], eum acutis[c] cuncti Romani[d] circumdederunt iaculis et tandem ballistis infixo molari lapide ictus[e] in spinam crepuit, qui[f] prius cuncta squamis tela, uelut obliqua [g]scutorum testudine repulit[g]. Cuius corium trans mare Tyrrhenum[h] ad Romam usque deductum est, quod .CXX. pedes longitudinis habuisse perhibetur.

III.10 Et in excidio Troiae gemini serpentes a Tenedo insula omni populo tuente, fretum sinuosis uerberabant magno murmure[a] motibus et ad[b] terrae litus erectis natabant pectoribus. Qui[c], ut Maro, praecipuus poeta, cecinit, iubas habebant sanguineas et oculi eorum[d] igni horrebant et cruore. Duos quoque primo impetu paruulos et tertium ipsis subeuntem uenenosis diripuerunt morsibus.

III.11 Dicuntur et in India serpentes gigni in ualle que uocatur Iordia, per eorum colla lapides pretiosi ualde nascuntur, nitores quorum[a] zmaragdi nuncupantur; lasere[b] quoque et albo[c] pipere pascuntur. Quorum Alexander Macedo paucos de ualle pyramidibus[d] quingentorum et quinque pedum habentibus longitudinem clausa[e] lapidum extulit[f].

III.12 Est insula quaedam in mari Tyrrheno[a] quam ante homines omnia prope serpentium inhabitabant[b] genera, cum quibus erat dominator serpens setosus et tam uasta corporis mole ut hi qui uidere ipsius speluncam[c] in quibus latuit bouem ingredi posse perhiberent[d].

III.9 DE SERPENTE CUIUS CORIUM .CXX. PEDES LONGITUDINIS HABERE PERHIBETUR *WPT* DE SERPENTE CUIUS CORIUM .CXX. PEDES LONGITUDINIS HABUISSE PERHIBETUR *B*

[a] Bagradam] bragadam *W*
[b] impetu] impetum *W*
[c] acutis] cunctis *W* acutis Porsia
[d] Romani] Romam *W*
[e] ictus] iectus *W*
[f] qui] quae *W*
[g...g] scutorum . . . repulit] scutodorum testitudine repulsit *W*
[h] Tyrrhenum] terrenum *W*

III.10 DE GEMINIBUS SERPENTIBUS IN TROIE *WT* DE GEMINIBUS SERPENTIBUS IN TROIAE EXCIDIO *PB*

[a] murmure] marmore *W*
[b] ad] a *W*
[c] Qui] quae *W*
[d] eorum] eorunt *W*

III.11 DE SERPENTE IORDIA *WT* DE SERPENTIBUS IN VALLE IORDIA *P* DE SERPENTE IN IORDIA VALLE *B*

[a] quorum] eorum *W*
[b] lasere] lasare *W*
[c] albo] alio *W*
[d] pyramidibus] permitibus *W*
[e] clausa] causa *W*
[f] extulit] extollit *W*

III.12 DE SERPENTE SETOSO *WPBT*

[a] Tyrrheno] terreno *W*
[b] inhabitabant] inhabitant *W*
[c] speluncam] saepe loca *W* spelunca Porsia
[d] perhiberent] perhibent *W*

III.9 A certain serpent of horrendous size is also described as having been discovered by the Roman army in Africa near the River Bagrada. And, in revenge for the soldiers whom it devoured in its initial attack, all the Romans surrounded it with all their spears, and finally, struck by a mill-stone thrown from a ballista, its spine cracked, after it had previously repelled all the spears with its scales, like the slanting *testudo* of shields. Its hide was brought across the Mediterranean to Rome, and is said to have been 120 feet long.

III.10 And at the destruction of Troy, as the whole population looked on, two serpents thrashed with a great noise the waves from the island of Tenedos with their curving motion, and swam to shore with puffed-up breasts. As Vergil, the outstanding poet, sang, they had bloody crests and their eyes were grim with fire and gore. They tore apart in poisonous bites two little boys in their first attack, and a third man coming to their aid.

III.11 Serpents are also said to be born in India in a valley which is called Iordia, in whose necks are found very precious stones, and their glitterings are called emeralds. They are fed on laser and white pepper. Alexander of Macedon carried off a few of the stones from the valley, closed off by pyramids with a length of five hundred and five feet.

III.12 There is a certain island in the Mediterranean which, before humans, almost all kinds of serpents used to inhabit, amongst which there was a ruler-serpent which was bristly with such huge bodily bulk that those who saw the places in which it hid assert that a cow could enter.

III.13 Et atram aput inferos [a]Stygem rumoroso[a] sermone gentes, anguem totius mundi maximum, describunt, quae nouem uicibus, ut fingunt, per Stygiam[b] paludem Tartara ululantium animarum atris ingens orbibus modo lacrimabili cingit; et ita uipereo muro Styx ipsa et palus [c]putridae undae, quam nullus[c] audet terribilem adtingere metam, animas, ut putant, rugientes in aeternis fletibus cludunt.

III.14 Salamandra quoque tantae atrocitatis esse describitur ut eam nulla uis[a] flammarum ledere possit, set in ignibus uelut pisces in aqua uiuere posse perhibetur.

III.15 Cerastes autem cornuti serpentes fiunt, sed non tam cornibus quam ore nocent et linguis, quae nimiam atrocitatem habere dicuntur, et in multis regionibus nascuntur.

III.16 Chelydri sunt nigri colore serpentes, qui in algidis et lapidiosis nascuntur terris et [a]glaream ruris[a] pro latebris et [b]tophos sectantur[b] pro cibo. Et rex Aeeta[c], quem superius descripsimus, pater Medeae[d] uirginis, more serpentis tales habuisse dentes describitur ut si quis eos simul conpressos saeuisset, inde armati prosilirent[e] homines ad interfectionem saeuientes. Sed quidam draconis dentes fuisse arbitrantur.

III.17 Coluber genus est diri ualde ac uenenosi serpentis, qui umbris et tecto succedere solet et ita et inprouisus et uenenosis morsibus nocet. Quem Octauianus[a] grammaticus feminini generis colubram[b] nominauit.

III.18 Vipera autem, eo quod ui pariat[a], ita nuncupatur, de qua scribunt phisici quod ignotum[b] genus quoddam[c] humanae formae simillimum usque ad umbilicum habeat, et semen ore concipiat et fracto latere moriens pariat[d].

III.19 Et in India, cum ceteris quibusque [a]prodigiis Ophitae[a] serpentes atrocissimi nascuntur generis, quas omnium prope colorum[b] uarietatibus distinctas[c] esse perhibent.

III.13 DE ATRAM *WB* DE ATRA STYGE *P* DE STYGEM ATRAM *T*

a...a Stygem rumoroso] stigiem rumorose *W*
b Stygiam] stigiem *W*
c...c putridae . . . nullus] putridus unde quam nullam

III.14 DE SALAMANDRA *WPBT*

a uis] uris *W*

III.15 DE CERASTE *WBT* DE CERASTIS *P*

III.16 DE CELEDRI *W* DE CHELYDRIS *PB* DE CHELYDRI *T*

a...a glaream ruris] claria rura *W* glaream ruris *P*
b...b tophos sectantur] domos secantur *W*
c Aeeta] eta *W*
d Medeae] mediae *W*
e prosilirent] prosilerent *W*

III.17 DE COLUBER *WT* DE COLUBRO *PB*

a Octauianus] octaulanius *W*
b colubram] colubrum *W*

III.18 DE VIPERA *WPBT*

a pariat] pereat *W*
b ignotum] tgnota *W*
c quoddam] quaedam *W*
d pariat] pareat *W*

III.19 DE SERPENTIBUS ATROCISSIMI GENERIS *P om. WB* DE OPHITA *T*

a...a prodigiis ophitae] prodigium oditae *W*
b colorum] colore *W*
c distinctas] desinatas *W*

III.13 And the pagans, in their rumour-filled talk, describe the black Styx amongst the underworld as the greatest snake in the whole world, which, they imagine, hugely surrounds nine times with its black rings Tartarus in a piteous manner, through the Stygian swamp of wailing souls. And thus the Styx with its viperous wall, and the swamp with its putrid wave, whose horrible edge none dares approach, seals in souls groaning, so they think, in eternal tears.

III.14 The salamander is also described as being of such fierceness that no force of flame can harm it, but it is said to be able to live in fire like fish in water.

III.15 Cerastes are horned serpents, but they do not harm so much with their horns as with their mouth and tongues. They are said to have excessive fierceness, and are born in many regions.

III.16 Chelydri are serpents black in colour, who are born in cold and stony lands, and they roam the gravel of the countryside for hiding-places and tuff for food. And King Aeeta, whom we have described above, the father of the maiden Medea, is described as having had such teeth of serpent's kind that if anyone furiously forced them together, as a result armed men would leap up, furious to kill. But some think they were the teeth of a dragon.

III.17 Coluber is a kind of very dreadful and poisonous snake, which usually retreats to the shadows and shade and so causes unexpected harm with its poisonous bite. The grammarian Octavianus [Priscian] placed Colubra amongst the feminine gender.

III.18 But the viper is so called because it gives birth by violence. About which scientists write that they have a certain unknown kind most like the human form down to the navel, which receives seed in the mouth and in death gives birth through its split side.

III.19 And in India amongst certain other prodigies the Ophitae serpents are born of the most atrocious kind, which they say are distinguished by shades of almost every colour.

III.20 Hercules namque geminos angues, secundum quod poeta cecinit, in manu [a]premens eliserat[a], quos ille [b]noui et[b] ignoti generis cum quibusdam prostrauit monstris.

III.21 Hydri serpentes sunt aquatici, qui [a]fluuios ac stagna[a] colunt, sicut de aliquibus Indorum uermibus describitur, quos ibi genus quoddam Oceano propinquum, ab amne Occluada[b] sibi uictum humano femore crassiores traxisse et cocco rubriores perhibetur[c].

III.22 Aspis[a] non catulos, set oua fouens gignit et minus uiua quam mortua nocet. Est caput eius sicut turturis [b]rostrum et[b] siquem os eiusdem pupugit[c] serpentis, pro tactu uipereo tumet.

III.23 In his enim poetarum fictionibus describitur quod angues[a] gemini cum monstris et nubes ex aere[b] latrantes Cleopatram ad Nilum fugassent exterritam, que cum Antonio contra Cesarem nauale proelium gessit. Et sicut huic mendacium a tergo reginae monstra et angues finxit aethereos, ita et fallaces poetarum fabulae sibi plurima quae non fiunt uoluntarie fingunt[c].

III.24 Dicunt quoque Tisiphonem[a] aput inferos sanguinea palla[b] succinctam et animabus[c] uipereo flagello nocentem, urbis seruare uestibulum. Quam triplici muro circumdatum et flammeo fulmine [d]Pyriflegethontis Tartarei mentiuntur[d], qui rapidis, ut putant, ignibus saxa murmurantia torquet, et fingunt hydram interius urbis ipsius uestibulum seruare, quae ibi, ut arbitrantur, cum .L. capitibus Tartaream habitat sedem.

III.20 DE ERCULES *W* DE ANGUIBUS AB HERCULE ELISIS *P* DE HERCULE *B* DE HERCULES *T*

a...a premens eliserat] praeminens eleser ad *W* b...b noui et] nouerat *W*

III.21 DE HILIDRIS *W* DE HYDRIS *PB* DE HYDRI *T*

a...a fluuios ac stagna] fluuio ac stagno *W*
b Occluada] occluba *W*
c perhibetur] perhibentur *W*

III.22 DE ASPIDE *WPBT*

a Aspis] aspes *W*
b...b rostrum et] rostrumque *W*
c pupugit] pupungit *W*

III.23 DE ANGUIBUS CLEOPATRAE *P om. WB* DE FICTIONIBUS POETARUM *T*

a angues] anges *W*
b aere] aerae *W*
c fingunt] figunt *W*

III.24 DE SERPENTIBUS APUD INFEROS *P om. WB* DE TISIPHONE *T*

a Tisiphonem] stifonem *W*
b palla] pellea *W*
c animabus] animalibus *W*
d...d Pyriflegethontis . . . mentiuntur] pirefigetonitis tartari mentientur *W*

III.20 For, according to what the poet sang, Hercules strangled and crushed two snakes in his hand, which of a new and unknown kind he destroyed amongst other monsters.

III.21 Hydri are aquatic serpents, who live in rivers and ponds, just as is described of other worms in India. And a certain race near the Ocean is said to have dragged them out of the river Occluada for food, thicker than a human thigh, and redder than scarlet.

III.22 The asp does not produce live young, but nourishes eggs, and causes less harm alive than dead. Its head is like a turtle-dove's beak. If the head of this serpent punctures anyone, they swell with its viperous touch.

III.23 For it is described in these fictions of poets that twin snakes with monsters and clouds barking from the sky chased off to the Nile the terrified Cleopatra, who along with Anthony waged a naval battle against Caesar. And just as a lie has created monsters and etherial snakes on this queen's back, so too do the lying fables of poets wilfully fake very many things for themselves which do not occur.

III.24 They also say that in the underworld Tisiphone is girt round with a bloody mantle, injuring souls with a viperous whip, and guards the vestibule of the city, which (they lie) has been surrounded with a triple wall, and with the flaming flood of Tartarean Pyriphlegothontis, which, they think, dashes resounding rocks with swift flames, and they imagine that a Hydra guards the inner vestibule of the city, which, they reckon, inhabits the Tartarean seat with fifty heads.

EPILOGUS

In his namque serpentibus quos superius descripsimus, quaedam uera, quaedam namque omni ueritate carentia reperiuntur. Sunt quoque plurimi adhuc serpentini generis angues, ut [a]dipsades, reguli, haemorrhoides, spelagi, natrices[a], de quibus iam nihil singulare et admiratione dignum reperri.

FINIT DE SERPENTIBUS DEO GRATIAS AMEN.

EPILOGUS

a...a dipsades . . . natrices] bidsades reguli hemures spelagi nutrices *W*

EPILOGUE

Now, amongst these serpents which we have described above, some true things are found, and some lacking all truth. There are also still very many snakes of serpentine kind, like Dispades, Reguli, Haemorroides, Spelagi, Natrices, concerning which I have now found nothing remarkable or worthy of notice.

THE END OF THE SERPENTS; THANKS BE TO GOD, AMEN.

APPENDIX IIIc

Liber monstrorum

Sources and Analogues

Sources and analogues have been detected for almost every section of the *Liber monstrorum*; a fairly cautious list, ordered by section number, might run as follows:[1]

I.1 Augustine, *De civitate Dei* XVI.viii
I.2 UNCERTAIN[2]
I.3 cf. Jerome, *Eusebii Pamphili Chronici canones*, p. 270
I.4 Augustine, *De civitate Dei* XVI.viii Vergil, *Aeneid* VIII.314–15
I.5 Isidore, *Etymologiae* VIII.xi.87
I.6 UNCERTAIN
I.7 Jerome, *Vita S. Pauli*, PL 23, cols. 22–3
I.8 Augustine, *De civitate Dei* XVI.viii
I.9 *Wonders of the East* § 32
I.10 Isidore, *Etymologiae* XI.iii.39
I.11 Vergil, *Aeneid* III.622–40
I.12 UNCERTAIN[3]
I.13 UNCERTAIN[4]
I.14 Vergil, *Aeneid*, III.424–8
I.15 *Letter of Alexander to Aristotle* § 29
I.16 Augustine, *De civitate Dei* XVI.viii; cf. Isidore, *Etymologiae* XI.iii.15
I.17 Augustine, *De civitate Dei* XVI.viii; cf. Isidore, *Etymologiae* XI.iii.23; Pliny, *Historia naturalis* VII.ii.23
I.18 *Wonders of the East* § 8
I.19 Augustine, *De civitate Dei* XVI.viii
I.20 *Wonders of the East* § 11
I.21 Augustine, *De civitate Dei* XVI.viii; Pliny, *Historia naturalis* VII.ii.25
I.22 *Wonders of the East* § 26

1 With regard to the *Wonders of the East* and the *Letter of Alexander to Aristotle*, see the editions above, pp. 175–82 and 204–23; it is clear, particularly with regard to the parallels with § 41 of the *Letter of Alexander to Aristotle*, that the compiler of the *Liber monstrorum* had access to a fuller version of the text than that preserved in British Library, Royal 13 A. i, as a comparison with the critical apparatus will demonstrate. Other editions used (except as stated) are as follows: Augustine: Dombart and Kalb, ed., *Augustini De civitate Dei*; Isidore: Lindsay, ed., *Isidori Etymologiarum sive Originum libri XX*; Jerome/ Eusebius: Fotheringham, ed., *Eusebii Pamphili Chronici canones*; Orosius: Zangemeister, ed., *Pauli Orosii historiarum aduersum paganos libri vii*; Ovid: Anderson, ed., *P. Ovidi Nasonis Metamorphoses*; *Physiologus*: Carmody, ed., *Physiologus Latinus*; Pliny: Jan and Mayhoff, ed., *C. Plinii Secundi Nauralis historiae libri XXXVII*; Quintus Curtius Rufus: Müller, ed. and trans. *Geschichte Alexanders des Grossen*; Servius: Thilo and Hagen, ed., *Servii Grammatici in Vergilii Carmina Commentaria*; Vergil: Mynors, ed., *P. Vergili Maronis Opera.*

2 See above, pp. 109–12.

3 See above, pp. 114–15.

4 See above, pp. 107–9.

I.23 Augustine, *De civitate Dei* XVI.viii; Isidore, *Etymologiae* XI.iii.7; Pliny, *Historia naturalis* VII.ii.26

I.24 *Wonders of the East* § 15; cf. Augustine, *De civitate Dei* XVI.viii; Isidore, *Etymologiae* XI.iii.17; Pliny, *Historia naturalis* VII.ii.23/ 5.8.46

I.25 Augustine, *De civitate Dei* XVI.viii

I.26 *Wonders of the East* § 28

I.27 Augustine, *De civitate Dei* XVI.viii; Isidore, *Etymologiae* XI.iii.27; Pliny, *Historia naturalis* VII.ii.30

I.28 *Wonders of the East* § 27

I.29 Augustine, *De civitate Dei* XVI.viii; Isidore, *Etymologiae* XI.iii.34; Pliny, *Historia naturalis* VII.ii.2

I.30 *Wonders of the East* §§ 32 and 36

I.31 Vergil, *Aeneid* VIII.193–267

I.32 UNCERTAIN

I.33 *Wonders of the East* § 13

I.34 UNCERTAIN

I.35 Vergil, *Georgics* IV.387–9, 394–5, 441–3

I.36 *Wonders of the East* § 22

I.37 Servius, *In Aeneidos* X.142; cf. Ovid, *Metamorphoses* IX.119–33

I.38 Vergil, *Aeneid* VI.289; cf. Servius, *In Aeneidos* II.616

I.39 Servius, *In Aeneidos* VII.790; cf. Ovid, *Metamorphoses* I.625–7

I.40 *Wonders of the East* § 20

I.41 Vergil, *Aeneid* VII.10–20

I.42 Vergil, *Aeneid* IV.173–88

I.43 *Wonders of the East* § 21

I.44 Vergil, *Aeneid* III. 209–35

I.45 Vergil, *Aeneid* VI.280–1; cf. *Georgics* IV.482–3

I.46 UNCERTAIN

I.47 Vergil, *Aeneid* VI.595–600; cf. Isidore, *Etymologiae* XI.iii.7

I.48 Vergil, *Aeneid* X.565–8

I.49 cf. Augustine, *De civitate Dei* XV.9; Tertullian, *De resurrectione carnis*, PL 2, cols. 854–5; Rufinus, *Recognitiones S. Clementis*, PG 1, col. 1223

I.50 Vergil, *Aeneid* V.588–95, VI.24–7; cf. Servius, *In Aeneidos* III.74,VI.14

I.51 Vergil, *Aeneid* V.404–14

I.52 Vergil, *Aeneid* X.209–12

I.53 Servius, *In Georgica* I.235; Augustine, *De civitate Dei* XVI.viii; Isidore, *Etymologiae* IX.ii.133

I.54 UNCERTAIN

I.55 Vergil, Servius, *In Aeneidos* VI.582–4

I.56 Vergil, *Aeneid* X.763–67

II.1 *Letter of Alexander to Aristotle* § 19

II.2 *Letter of Alexander to Aristotle* §§ 8 and 28; Orosius, *Aduersum paganos* IV.i.6 *Wonders of the East* § 10

II.3 *Wonders of the East* § 6

II.4 Isidore, *Etymologiae* XII.ii.7

II.5 Vergil, *Aeneid* I.323

II.6 Letter of Alexander to *Aristotle* § 16; cf. Quintus Curtius Rufus, *Historia Alexandri* VII.ix.2

II.7 UNCERTAIN

II.8 Vergil, *Aeneid* VI.286–7

II.9 *Letter of Alexander to Aristotle* § 15

II.10 *Wonders of the East* § 4

II.11 Vergil, *Aeneid* VI.288, VII.785–8

II.12 *Letter of Alexander to Aristotle* § 41

II.13 *Wonders of the East* § 7

II.14 Vergil, *Aeneid* VI.392–6, 417–18; Georgics IV.483

II.15 *Wonders of the East* § 9

II.16 *Letter of Alexander to Aristotle* § 20

II.17 *Wonders of the East* § 12

II.18 Isidore, *Etymologiae* XII.ii.11

II.19 Vergil, *Aeneid* III.432

II.20 UNCERTAIN

II.21 UNCERTAIN

II.22 *Letter of Alexander to Aristotle* § 27

II.23 UNCERTAIN[5]

II.24 *Physiologus* 106

II.25 Isidore, *Etymologiae* XIII.vi.19–20

II.26 *Letter of Alexander to Aristotle* § 41

II.27 UNCERTAIN

II.28 Servius, *In Georgica* IV.389

[5] See above, pp. 111–12.

II.30 *Wonders of the East* §§ 25 and 26
II.31 *Wonders of the East* § 11
II.32 UNCERTAIN
II.33 UNCERTAIN
II.34 UNCERTAIN
II.35 UNCERTAIN
II.36 *Letter of Alexander to Aristotle* § 41

III.1 Vergil, *Aeneid* VIII.299–300
III.2 *Wonders of the East* § 5; *Letter of Alexander to Aristotle* § 41
III.3 Vergil, *Aeneid* VII.655–8
III.4 *Letter of Alexander to Aristotle* § 17
III.5 Vergil, *Georgics* III.425–39
III.6 *Wonders of the East* § 6; *Letter of Alexander to Aristotle* § 41; Isidore, *Etymologiae* XVII.viii.8
III.7 *Letter of Alexander to Aristotle* § 18
III.8 Vergil, *Aeneid* V.84–9
III.9 Orosius, *Aduersum paganos* IV.viii.10–15
III.10 Vergil, *Aeneid* II.204–17
III.11 *Letter of Alexander to Aristotle* § 41
III.12 UNCERTAIN
III.13 Vergil, *Aeneid* VI.439; *Georgics* I.242–5; IV.480
III.14 Isidore, *Etymologiae* XII.iv.36
III.15 Isidore, *Etymologiae* XII.iv.18
III.16 Vergil, *Georgics* II.212–15
III.17 Vergil, *Georgics* III.418–19
III.18 Isidore, *Etymologiae* XII.iv.10–11
III.19 UNCERTAIN
III.20 Vergil, *Aeneid* VIII.288–9
III.21 *Letter of Alexander to Aristotle* § 41
III.22 Servius, *In Georgica* III.48
III.23 Vergil, *Aeneid* VIII.696–701
III.24 Vergil, *Aeneid* VI.550–56, 570–2

BIBLIOGRAPHY

ADRIAEN, M., ed., *Gregorii Magni Moralia siue Expositio in Iob*, 3 vols., CCSL 143, 143A and 143B (Turnhout, 1979–85)

ANDERSON, Earl R., 'Treasure Trove in *Beowulf*: a Legal View of the Dragon's Hoard', *Mediaevalia* 3 (1978 for 1977), 141–64

ANDERSON, Earl R., 'Beowulf's Retreat from Frisia: Analogues from the Fifth and Eighth Centuries', *English Language Notes* 19 (1981), 89–93

ANDERSON, Earl R., 'Grendel's *glof* (*Beowulf* 2085b–88) and Various Latin Analogues', *Mediaevalia* 8 (1982), 1–8

ANDERSON, W. S., ed., *P. Ovidi Nasonis Metamorphoses* (Leipzig, 1977)

ANDERSSON, Theodore M., *Early Epic Scenery: Homer, Virgil, and the Medieval Legacy* (Ithaca, NY, and London, 1976)

ANDREW, M., 'Grendel in Hell', *English Studies* 62 (1981), 401–10

ARENT, Margaret, 'The Heroic Pattern: Old Germanic Helmets, *Beowulf*, and *Grettis saga*', *Old Norse Literature and Mythology*, ed. Edgar C. Polomé (Austin, TX, 1969), pp. 130–99

ASSMANN, ed., B., *Angelsächsische Homilien und Heiligenleben*, Bibliothek der angelsächsischen Prosa 3, repr. with a supplementary introduction by P. A. M. Clemoes (Darmstadt, 1964)

BACKX, S., 'Sur la date et l'origine du *De monstris, beluis et serpentibus*', *Latomus* 3 (1939), 61

BAIRD, Joseph L., 'Grendel the Exile', *Neuphilologische Mitteilungen* 67 (1966), 375–81

BAMBERGER, Bernard J., *Fallen Angels* (New York, 1952)

BAMMESBERGER, A., 'Five *Beowulf* Notes', in *Words, Texts and Manuscripts: Studies in Anglo-Saxon Culture Presented to Helmut Gneuss on the Occasion of his Sixty-Fifth Birthday*, ed. Michael Korhammer (Cambridge, 1992), pp. 239–55

BANDY, Stephen C., 'Cain, Grendel, and the Giants of *Beowulf*', *Papers on Language and Literature* 9 (1973), 235–49

BARTELINCK, G. J. M., 'Les dénominations du diable chez Grégoire de Tours', *Revue des études latines* 48 (1970), 411–32

BASKERVILL, W. M., 'The Anglo-Saxon Version of the *Epistola Alexandri ad Aristotelem*', *Anglia* 4 (1881), 139–67

BATELY, Janet M., ed., *The Old English Orosius*, EETS SS 6 (Oxford, 1980)

BATELY, Janet M., 'Old English Prose Before and During the Reign of Alfred', *Anglo-Saxon England* 17 (1988), 93–138

BAZIRE, Joyce, and James E. CROSS, ed., *Eleven Old English Rogationtide Homilies*, Toronto Old English Series 7 (Toronto, 1982)

BECKER, G., *Catalogi Bibliothecarum Antiqui* (Bonn, 1885)

BENEDIKTSSON, Jakob, ed., *Landnámabók*, Íslenzk fornrit I (Reykjavík, 1968)

BERG, Beverley Joan, 'Tales of Alexander and the East: Wonders and Wise Men' (unpublished PhD dissertation, Stanford University, 1972)

BERGIN, O. J., R. I. BEST, Kuno MEYER, and J. G. O'KEEFFE, ed., *Anecdota from Irish Manuscripts*, 4 vols. (Halle, 1910)

BERKHOUT, Carl T., and James F. DOUBLEDAY, 'The Net in *Judith* 46b–54a', *Neuphilologische Mitteilungen* 74 (1973), 630–4

BERNARD, J. H., and R. ATKINSON, ed. and trans., *The Irish Liber Hymnorum*, 2 vols. (London, 1898)

BEST, R. I., and Osbern BERGIN, ed., *Lebor na Huidre* (Dublin, 1929)

BETHURUM, Dorothy, ed., *The Homilies of Wulfstan* (Oxford, 1957)

BIELER, Ludwig, ed., *Anicii Manilii Severini Boethii Philosophiae Consolatio*, CCSL 94 (Turnhout, 1957)

BIELER, Ludwig, ed. and trans., *The Patrician Texts in the Book of Armagh*, Scriptores Latini Hiberniae 10 (Dublin, 1979)

BIGGS, Frederick M., *The Sources of 'Christ III': a Revision of Cook's Notes*, Old English Newsletter Subsidia 12 (Binghamton, NY, 1986)

BIGGS, Frederick M., Thomas D. HILL, and Paul E. SZARMACH, *Sources of Anglo-Saxon Literary Culture: a Trial Version*, Medieval and Renaissance Texts and Studies 74 (Binghamton, NY, 1990)

BLAKE, N. F., 'The Heremod Digressions in *Beowulf*', *Journal of English and Germanic Philology* 61 (1962), 278–87

BOBERG, Inger M., *Motif-Index of Early Icelandic Literature*, Bibliotheca Arnamagnaeana 27 (Copenhagen, 1966)

BOER, R. C., *Zur Grettissaga*, Zeitschrift für deutsches Philologie (Halle, 1898)

BOER, R. C., ed., *Grettis saga Ásmundarsonar*, Altnordische Saga-Bibliothek 8 (Halle, 1900)

BOER, W. W., ed. *Epistola Alexandri ad Aristotelem*, Beiträge zur klassischen Philologie 50 (Meisenheim am Glan, 1973)

BOESE, H., ed., *Thomas of Cantimpré: Liber de Natura Rerum. Teil I: Text* (Berlin, 1973)

BOLOGNA, Corrado, 'La tradizione manoscritta del *Liber Monstrorum de diversis generibus*, Appunti per l'edizione critica', *Cultura Neolatina* 34 (1974), 337–46

BOLOGNA, Corrado (rev. of Whitbread), *Cultura Neolatina* 35 (1975), 366–9

BOLOGNA, Corrado, ed., *Liber Monstrorum de diversis generibus: Libro delle mirabili difformità* (Milan, 1977)

BONJOUR, Adrien, *The Digressions in Beowulf*, Medium Ævum Monographs 5 (Oxford, 1950)

BONJOUR, Adrien, 'The Problem of Dæghrefn', *Journal of English and Germanic Philology* 51 (1952), 355–9

BOSWORTH, Joseph, *A Literal Translation of King Alfred's Anglo-Saxon Version of the Compendious History of the World by Orosius* (London, 1855)

BOYLE, Leonard E., 'The Nowell Codex and the Poem of *Beowulf*', in *The Dating of 'Beowulf'*, ed. Colin Chase (Toronto, 1981), pp. 23–32

BRADLEY, Henry, and Kenneth SISAM, 'Textual Notes on the Old English *Epistola Alexandri*', *Modern Language Review* 14 (1919), 202–5

BRADY, Caroline, 'Weapons in *Beowulf*: An Analysis of the Nominal Compounds and an Evaluation of the Poet's Use of them', *Anglo-Saxon England* 8 (1979), 79–141

BRAEGER, Peter C., 'Connotations of *(earm) sceapen*: *Beowulf* ll. 2228–2229 and the Shape-Shifting Dragon', *Essays in Literature* (Western Illinois University) 13 (1986), 327–30

BRASWELL, Laurel, 'The Horn at Grendel's Mere: *Beowulf* 1417–41', *Neuphilologische Mitteilungen* 74 (1973), 466–72

BRAUN, A., *Lautlehre der angelsächsischen Version der 'Epistola Alexandri ad Aristotelem'*, Würzburg diss. (Borna, 1911)

BRIDGES, Margaret, 'Empowering the Hero: Alexander as Author in the *Epistola Alexandri ad Aristotelem* and its Medieval English Versions', in *The Problematics of Power: Eastern and Western Representations of Alexander the Great*, ed. Margaret Bridges (forthcoming)

BRIGHT, James W., 'An Idiom of the Comparative in Anglo-Saxon', *Modern Language Notes* 27 (1912), 198

BRITTON, G. C., 'Unferth, Grendel and the Christian Meaning of *Beowulf* ', *Neuphilologische Mitteilungen* 72 (1971), 246–50

BRODEUR, Arthur Gilchrist, *The Art of 'Beowulf'* (Berkeley, CA, 1971)

BROOKE, Stopford A., *English Literature from the Beginning to the Norman Conquest* (London, 1898)

BROWN, Alan K., 'Bede, a Hisperic Etymology, and Early Sea Poetry', *Mediaeval Studies* 37 (1975), 419–32

BROWN, Carleton, '*Beowulf* and the *Blickling Homilies* and Some Textual Notes', *Proceedings of the Modern Language Association* 53 (1938), 905–16

BRYNTESTON, William I., '*Beowulf*, Monsters, and Manuscripts: Classical Associations', *Res Publica Litterarum* 5.2 (1982), 41–57

BUDGE, E. A. Wallis, trans., *The Contendings of the Apostles* (Oxford, 1935)

BUTTS, Richard, 'The Analogical Mere: Landscape and Terror in *Beowulf*', *English Studies* 68 (1987), 113–21

BUTTURFF, Douglas R., 'The Monsters and the Scholar: An Edition and Critical Study of the *Liber Monstrorum*' (unpublished PhD dissertation, University of Illinois, 1968)

BUTTURFF, Douglas R., 'Style as a Clue to Meaning: A Note on the Old English Translation of the *Epistola Alexandri ad Aristotelem*', *English Language Notes* 8 (1970–1), 81–6

CAIE, Graham D., *The Judgment Day Theme in Old English Poetry* (Copenhagen, 1976)

CAIE, Graham D., 'The Old English *Daniel*: a Warning against Pride', *English Studies* 59 (1978), 1–9

CAMERON, Angus, Ashley Crandell AMOS, and Gregory WAITE, with the assistance of Sharon BUTLER and Antonette di Paolo HEALEY, 'A reconsideration of the Language of *Beowulf*', in *The Dating of 'Beowulf'*, ed. Colin Chase (Toronto, 1981), pp. 33–75

CAMPBELL, Jackson J., 'Schematic Technique in *Judith*', *ELH* 38 (1971), 155–72

CARENS, Marilyn M., 'Handscioh and Grendel: the Motif of the Hand in *Beowulf*' *Aeolian Harps: Essays in Literature in Honor of Maurice Browning Cramer*, ed. Donna G. Fricke and Douglas C. Fricke (Bowling Green, OH, 1976), pp. 39–55

CARLSSON, Signe M., 'The Monsters of *Beowulf*: Creations of Literary Scholars', *Journal of American Folklore* 80 (1967), 357–64

CARMODY, F. J., ed., *Physiologus Latinus* (Paris, 1939)

CARNEY, James, *Studies in Irish Literature and History* (Dublin, 1979)

CARRIGAN, E., 'Structure and Thematic Development in *Beowulf*', *Proceedings of the Royal Irish Academy* 66C (1967), 1–51

CARY, G., *The Medieval Alexander*, ed. D. J. A. Ross (Cambridge, 1956)

CHADWICK, Nora, 'Norse Ghosts: A Study in the *draugr* and the *haugbúi*', *Folk-Lore* 57 (1946), 50–65 and 106–27

CHADWICK, Nora, 'The Monsters and Beowulf', *The Anglo-Saxons: Studies in Some Aspects of their History and Culture Presented to Bruce Dickins*, ed. P. Clemoes (London, 1959), pp. 171–203

CHAMBERLAIN, David, '*Judith*: a Fragmentary and Political Poem', *Anglo-Saxon Poetry: Essays in Appreciation*, ed. Lewis E. Nicholson and Dolores Warwick Frese (Notre Dame, IN, 1975), pp. 135–59

CHAMBERS, R. W., *Beowulf: An Introduction to the Study of the Poem with a Discussion of the Stories of Offa and Finn*, third edition, with a supplement by C. L. Wrenn (Cambridge, 1959)

CHAPMAN, Richard L., 'Alas, Poor Grendel', *College English* 17 (1956), 334–7

CHASE, Colin, ed., *The Dating of 'Beowulf'* (Toronto, 1981)

CIKLAMINI, Marlene, 'Grettir and Ketill Hængr, the Giant-Killers', *Arv* 22 (1966), 136–55

CIZEK, A., 'Ungeheuer und magische Lebewesen in der *Epistola Alexandri ad magistrum suum de situ Indiae*', in *Third International Beast Epic, Fable and Fabliau Colloquium*, ed. Jan Goossens and Timothy Sodmann (Munster, 1979)

CLEMENT, Richard W., 'Codicological Considerations in the *Beowulf* Manuscript', *Proceedings of the Illinois Medieval Association*, ed. Roberta Bux Bosse *et al.* (Macomb, IL, 1984), pp. 13–27

CLEMOES, Peter, 'Style as a Criterion for Dating the Composition of *Beowulf*', in *The Dating of 'Beowulf'*, ed. Colin Chase (Toronto, 1981), pp. 173–85

COCKAYNE, Thomas Oswald, ed., *Narratiunculae anglice conscriptae* (London, 1861)

COFFIN, R. N., '*Beowulf* and its Relationship to Norse and Finno-Uguric Beliefs and Narratives' (unpublished PhD dissertation, Boston University, 1962)

COLGRAVE, Bertram, ed., *Felix's Life of Saint Guthlac* (Cambridge, 1956)

COLGRAVE, Bertram, and R. A. B. MYNORS, ed., *Bede's Ecclesiastical History of the English People* (Oxford, 1969)

COLKER, Marvin L., ed., *Galteri de Castellione Alexandreis* (Padua, 1978)

COLLINS, Rowland L., 'Blickling Homily XVI and the Dating of *Beowulf*', in *Medieval Studies Conference Aachen 1983*, ed. W-D. Bald and H. Weinstock (Frankfurt, 1984), pp. 61–9

COOK, A. S., ed., *Judith: an Old English Epic Fragment* (Boston, MA, 1889)

COOK, Robert, 'The Reader in *Grettis saga*', *Saga-Book of the Viking Society* 21 (1984–5), 135–54

COOK, Robert, 'Reading for Character in *Grettis saga*', *Sagas of the Icelanders: A Book of Essays*, ed J. Tucker (New York, 1989), pp. 226–40

COX, Betty S., *Cruces of 'Beowulf'* (The Hague, 1971)

CORNELIUS, Roberta D., 'Palus Inamabilis', *Speculum* 2 (1927), 321–5

CRAWFORD, Samuel J., ed., *The Old English Version of the Heptateuch*, EETS OS 160 (London, 1922)

CRAWFORD, Samuel J., 'Grendel's Descent from Cain', *Modern Language Review* 23 (1928), 63

CRAWFORD, Samuel J., ed., *Byrhtferth's Manual*, EETS OS 177 (London, 1929)

CROSS, J. E., 'The Ethic of War in Old English', in *England Before the Conquest: Studies in Primary Sources Presented to Dorothy Whitelock*, ed. Peter Clemoes and Kathleen Hughes (Cambridge, 1971), pp. 269–82

CROSS, J. E., 'Towards the Identification of Old English Literary Ideas – Old Workings and New Seams', in *Sources of Anglo Saxon Culture*, ed. Paul E. Szarmach, Studies in Medieval Culture 20 (Kalamazoo, MI, 1989), pp. 77–101

CRYSTAL, David, ed., *The Cambridge Encyclopedia* (Cambridge, 1992)

CULBERT, Taylor, 'The Narrative Function of Beowulf's Swords', *Journal of English and Germanic Philology* 59 (1960), 13–20

CURTIUS, E. R., *European Literature and the Latin Middle Ages*, trans. Willard R. Trask (New York, 1963)

DANIELLI, Mary, 'Initiation Ceremonial from Norse Literature', *Folk-Lore* 56 (1945), 229–45

DAVIDSON, D., and A. P. CAMPBELL, 'The Letter of Alexander the Great to Aristotle: The Old English version turned into modern English', *Humanities Association Bulletin* 23 (1972), 3–16

DAVIDSON, Hilda R. Ellis, 'The Hill of the Dragon: Anglo-Saxon Burial Mounds in Literature and Archaeology', *Folk-Lore* 61 (1950), 169–85

DAVIDSON, Hilda R. Ellis, *The Sword in Anglo-Saxon England* (Oxford, 1962)

DAVIS, Norman, ' "Hippopotamus" in Old English', *Review of English Studies* 4 (1953), 141–2

DEKKERS, E., ed., *Tertulliani Opera*, 2 vols. (Turnhout, 1954)

DIANE-MYRICK, Leslie, *From the De Excidio Troiae Historia to the Togail Troí: Literary-Cultural Synthesis in a Medieval Irish Adaptation of Dares' Troy Tale* (Heidelberg, 1993)

DIETRICH, Franz, '*Hycgan* und *hopian*', *Zeitschrift für deutsches Altertum und deutsche Literatur* 9 (1853), 214–22

DILLON, Myles, 'Notes on Irish Words', *Language* 17 (1941), 249–51

DOANE, A. N., ed., *Genesis A: a New Edition* (Madison, WI, 1978)

DOANE, A. N., ed., *The Saxon Genesis* (Madison, WI, 1991)

DOBBIE, Elliott Van Kirk, ed., *Beowulf and Judith*, ASPR 4 (1953)

DOMBART, B., and A. KALB, ed., *Augustini De civitate Dei*, 2 vols., CCSL 47–8 (Turnhout, 1955)

DONAHUE, C., 'Grendel and the *Clanna Cain*', *Journal of Celtic Studies* 1 (1950), 167–75

DONNER, Morton, 'Prudery in Old English Fiction', *Comitatus* 3 (1972), 91–6

DOUBLEDAY, James F., 'The Principle of Contrast in *Judith*', *Neuphilologische Mitteilungen* 72 (1971), 436–41

DRAGLAND, S. L., 'Monster-Man in *Beowulf*', *Neophilologus* 61 (1977), 606–18

DUMVILLE, David N., 'Biblical Apocrypha and the Early Irish: a Preliminary Investigation', *Proceedings of the Royal Irish Academy* 73C (1973), 299–338

DUMVILLE, David N., '*Beowulf* and the Celtic World: the Uses of the Evidence', *Traditio* 37 (1981), 109–60

DUMVILLE, David N., 'English Square Minuscule Script: the Background and the Earliest Phases', *Anglo-Saxon England* 16 (1987), 147–79

DUMVILLE, David N., 'Beowulf Come Lately. Some Notes on the Palaeography of the Nowell Codex', *Archiv für das Studium der neueren Sprachen und Literaturen* 225 (1988), 49–63

EARL, James, 'Beowulf's Rowing-Match', *Neophilologus* 63 (1979), 285–90

EHWALD, Rudolf, ed., *Aldhelmi Opera Omnia*, MGH AA 15 (Berlin, 1919)

EINARSSON, Stefán, 'Beowulfian Place-Names in East Iceland', *Modern Language Notes* 76 (1961), 385–92

EINARSSON, Stefán, 'Bjólfur and Grendill in Iceland', *Modern Language Notes* 71 (1956), 79–80

ELIASON, Norman E., 'Beowulf's Inglorious Youth', *Studies in Philology* 76 (1979), 101–8

EMERSON, Oliver Farrar, 'Legends of Cain, Especially in Old and Middle English', *Publications of the Modern Language Association* 21 (1906), 831–929

EMERSON, Oliver Farrar, 'Grendel's Motive in Attacking Heorot', *Modern Language Review* 16 (1921), 113–19

ETTMÜLLER, Ludwig, ed., *Carmen de Beovulfi Gautarum regis rebus praeclare gestis atque interitu, quale fuerit ante quam in manus interpolatoris, monachi Vestsaxonici, inciderat* (Zurich, 1875)

FADDA, A. M. Luiselli, ed., *Nuove omelie anglosassoni della rinascenza benedettina*, Filologia Germanica Testi e Studi 1 (Florence, 1977)

FALK, A., *Altnordische Waffenkunde* (Copenhagen, 1914)

FARAL, Edmond, 'Une source latine de l'histoire d'Alexandre: la lettre sur les merveilles de l'Inde', *Romania* 43 (1914), 199–215 and 353–70

FARAL, Edmond, 'La queue de poisson des sirènes', *Romania* 74 (1953), 433–506

FELDMAN, T. P., 'Grendel and Cain's Descendants', *Literary Onomastics Studies* 8 (1981), 71–87

FINNBOGASON, Guðmundur, 'Hallmundarkviða', *Skírnir* (1935), 172–81

FOOTE, Peter, ed., and QUIRK, Randolph, trans., *The Saga of Gunnlaug Serpent-Tongue* (London, 1957)

FÖRSTER, Max, 'Zur altenglischen Mirabilien-Version', *Archiv* 117 (1906), 367–70

FOTHERINGHAM, J. K., ed., *Eusebii Pamphili Chronici canones, latine uertit, adauxit, ad sua tempora produxit S. Eusebius Hieronymus* (London, 1923)

FOX, Denton, and Hermann PÁLSSON, trans., *Grettir's saga* (Toronto, 1974)

FRANK, Roberta, 'Some Uses of Paronomasia in Old English Scriptural Verse', *Speculum* 47 (1972), 207–26

FRANK, Roberta, and Angus CAMERON, ed., *A Plan for the Dictionary of Old English* (Toronto, 1973)

FRANK, Roberta, 'The *Beowulf* Poet's Sense of History', in *The Wisdom of Poetry: Essays in Early English Literature in Honor of Morton W. Bloomfield*, ed. Larry D. Benson and Siegfried Wenzel (Kalamazoo, MI, 1982), pp. 53–65

FRANKIS, Peter J., 'The Thematic Significance of *enta geweorc* and Related Imagery in *The Wanderer*', *Anglo-Saxon England* 2 (1973), 253–70

FRASER, J., 'The Passion of Saint Christopher', *Revue Celtique* 34 (1913), 307–25

FREDERICK, Jill, ' "His ansyn wæs swylce rosan blostma" ': a Reading of the Old English *Life of St Christopher*', *Proceedings of the Patristic, Medieval and Renaissance Conference* 12–13 (1989), 137–48

FRIEDMAN, John Block, 'Thomas of Cantimpré: *De Naturis Rerum*, Prologue, Book III and Book XIX', in *La Science de la Nature: Théories et Pratiques* (Montreal, 1974), pp. 107–54

FRIEDMAN, John Block, *The Monstrous Races in Medieval Art and Thought* (Cambridge, MI, 1981)

FRIEDMAN, John Block, 'The Marvels-of-the-East Tradition in Anglo-Saxon Art', in *Sources of Anglo Saxon Culture*, ed. Paul E. Szarmach, Studies in Medieval Culture 20 (Kalamazoo, MI, 1989), pp. 319–41

FRY, Donald K., 'Type-Scene Composition in *Judith*', *Annuale Medievale* 12 (1972), 100–19

FRY, Donald K., 'The Cliff of Death in Old English Poetry', in *Comparative Research on Oral Traditions: a Memorial for Milman Parry*, ed. John Miles Foley (Columbus, OH, 1987), pp. 213–33

GAIDOZ, H., 'Saint Christophe à tête de chien en Irlande et en Russie', *Mémoires de la Société Nationale des Antiquaires de France* 76 (1924), 192–218

GARMONSWAY, G. Norman, and Jacqueline SIMPSON, *Beowulf and its Analogues* (London, 1971)

GARRAD, Barry L., 'The Anglo-Saxon Prose Translation of The Wonders of the East from the Cotton MS Vitellius A. xv, Collated with the Text of the Cotton MS Tiberius B. v, vol. I' (unpublished PhD dissertation, University of London, 1925)

GERING, Hans, 'Der *Beowulf* und die isländische *Grettissaga*', *Anglia* 3 (1880), 74–87

GERRITSEN, Johan, 'British Library MS Cotton Vitellius A.xv – a Supplementary Description', *English Studies* 69 (1988), 293–302

GERRITSEN, Johan, 'Have with You to Lexington! The *Beowulf* Manuscript and *Beowulf*', in *In Other Words: Transcultural Studies in Philology, Translation and Lexicography Presented to Hans Heinrich Meier*, ed. J. Lachlan Mackenzie and Richard Todd (Dordrecht, 1989), pp. 15–34

GIBB, Paul Allen, '*Wonders of the East*: a Critical Edition and Commentary' (unpublished PhD dissertation, Duke University, 1977)

GILLAM, Doreen M.E., 'The Use of the Term *æglæca* in *Beowulf* at Lines 813 and 2592', *Studia Germanica Gandensia* 3 (1961), 145–69

GILLIES, W., 'Ffigur Alexander: tystiolaeth o brydyddiaeth farddol Aeleg', in *Beirdd a Thywysogion: Cyfrol i Gyfarch yr Arthro R. Geraint Gruffydd*, ed. Morfydd E. Owen and Brynley F. Roberts (forthcoming)

GLENDINNING, Robert, '*Grettis saga* and European Literature in the Late Middle Ages', *Mosaic* 4 (1970), 49–61

GLORIE, F., ed., *Aenigmata Bonifatii*, in *Variae Collectiones Aenigmatum Merovingicae Aetatis*, CCSL 133 (Turnhout, 1968), pp. 273–343

GNEUSS, H., 'A Preliminary List of Manuscripts Written or Owned in England up to 1100', *Anglo-Saxon England* 9 (1981), 1–60

GODDEN, Malcolm, 'Biblical Literature: the Old Testament', in *The Cambridge Companion to Old English Literature*, ed. Malcolm Godden and Michael Lapidge (Cambridge, 1991)

GODMAN, P., ed., *Alcuin: The Bishops, Kings, and Saints of York* (Oxford, 1982)

GOLDSMITH, Margaret E., *The Mode and Meaning of 'Beowulf'* (London, 1970)

GORDON, E. V., 'Old English Studies', *The Year's Work in English Studies* 5 (1924), 66–72

GORDON, I. L., ed., *The Seafarer* (London, 1960)

GRAFF, Eberhard, ed., *Diutiska: Denkmäler deutscher Sprache und Literatur, aus älten Handschriften* (Stuttgart, 1827)

GREEN, Peter, *Alexander of Macedon, 356–323 B.C.: a Historical Biography* (Oxford, 1991)

GREENFIELD, Stanley B., 'Attitudes and Values in the *Seafarer*', *Studies in Philology* 51 (1954), 15–20

GREENFIELD, Stanley B., 'The Formulaic Expression of the Theme of "Exile" in Anglo-Saxon Poetry', *Speculum* 30 (1955), 200–6

GREENFIELD, Stanley B., 'Grendel's Approach to Heorot: Syntax and Poetry', *Old English Poetry: Fifteen Essays*, ed. Robert P. Creed (Providence, RI, 1967), pp. 275–84

GREENFIELD, Stanley B., 'Old English Words and Patristic Exegesis – *hwyrftum scriþað*: a Caveat', *Modern Philology* 75 (1977), 44–8

GREENFIELD, Stanley B., 'A Touch of the Monstrous in the Hero, or Beowulf Re-Marvellized', *English Studies* 63 (1982), 294–300

GREENFIELD, Stanley B., *Hero and Exile: The Art of Old English Poetry*, ed. George H. Brown (London, 1989)

GREENFIELD, Stanley B., and Daniel G. CALDER, *A New Critical History of Old English Literature* (New York and London, 1986)

GRIMSTAD, Karen, 'The Giant as Heroic Model: The Case of Egill and Starkaðr', *Scandinavian Studies* 48 (1976), 284–98

GRINSELL, Lynne V., 'Barrow Treasure in Fact, Tradition and Legislation', *Folk-Lore* 78 (1967), 1–38

GUNDERSON, Lloyd L., *Alexander's Letter to Aristotle about India*, Beiträge zur klassischen Philologie 110 (Meisenheim am Glan, 1980)

HAARDER, Andreas, *'Beowulf': the Appeal of a Poem* (Viborg, 1975)

HABER, Tom B., *A Comparative Study of the Beowulf and the Aeneid* (Princeton, 1931)

HAHN, Thomas, ed., 'The Middle English *Letter of Alexander to Aristotle*', *Mediaeval Studies* 41 (1979), 106–60

HALL, Thomas N., 'Jamnes and Mambres', in *Sources of Anglo-Saxon Literary Culture: a Trial Version*, ed. Frederick M. Biggs, Thomas D. Hill, and Paul E. Szarmach (Binghamton, NY, 1990), pp. 27–9

HALLDÓRSSON, Oskar, 'Goðsögnin um Gretti: nokkrar athuganir', *Sjötíu ritgerðir helgaðar Jakobi Benediktssyni*, 2 vols. (Reykjavík, 1977), I, pp. 627–39

HALLDÓRSSON, Oskar, 'Tröllasaga Bárðdæla og Grettluhöfundur', *Skirnir* 156 (1977), 5–36

HAMILTON, Marie Padgett, 'The Religious Principle in *Beowulf*', *Publications of the Modern Language Association* 61 (1946), 309–31

HANSEN, Elaine Tuttle, 'Hrothgar's "Sermon" in *Beowulf* as Parental Wisdom', *Anglo-Saxon England* 10 (1982), 53–67

HARF-LANCNER, Laurence, *Métamorphose et bestiaire fantastique au moyen âge* (Paris, 1985)

HARICH, Henriette, *Alexander epicus: Studien zur Alexandreis Walters von Chatillon* (Graz, 1987)

HARRIS, Richard L., 'The Deaths of Grettir and Grendel: A New Parallel', *Scripta Islandica* 24 (1973), 25–53

HARTEL, W., ed., *Magni Felicis Ennodii Opera Omnia*, CSEL 6 (Vienna, 1882)

HASTRUP, Kirsten, 'Tracing Tradition: an Anthropological Perspective on *Grettis saga Ásmundarsonar*', *Structure and Meaning in Old Norse Literature*, ed. John Lindow, Lars Lönnroth, and Gerd Wolfgang Weber (Odense, 1986), pp. 281–316

HAUPT, M., ed., 'Index lectionum aestivarum 1863', in his *Opuscula*, 2 vols. (Berlin, 1876; rptd Hildesheim, 1967), II, pp. 218–52

HAYCOCK, Marged, ' "Some Talk of Alexander and Some of Hercules": Three Early Medieval Poems from the Book of Taliesin', *Cambridge Medieval Celtic Studies* 13 (1987), 7–38

HEALEY, Antonette di Paolo, ed., *The Old English Vision of St Paul*, Speculum Anniversary Monographs 2 (Cambridge, MA, 1978)

HEINEMANN, F. J., '*Judith* 236–291a: a Mock-Heroic Approach-to-Battle Type Scene', *Neuphilologische Mitteilungen* 71 (1970), 83–96

HEIST, W. W., *The Fifteen Signs before Doomsday* (East Lansing, MI, 1952)

HENNESSY, W. M., ed., *Chronicon Scotorum* (London, 1866)

HERMANN, John P., 'The Theme of Spiritual Warfare in the Old English *Judith*', *Philological Quarterly* 55 (1976), 1–9

HERMANN, John P., *Allegories of War – Language and Violence in Old English Poetry* (Ann Arbor, MI, 1989)

HERZFELD, George, ed., *An Old English Martyrology*, EETS OS 116 (London, 1900)

HESSELS, J. H., ed., *An Eighth Century Latin-Anglo-Saxon Glossary* (Cambridge, 1890)

HEUSLER, Andreas, *Die altgermanische Dichtung* (Wildpark-Potsdam, 1923)

HILKA, A., ed., 'Ein neuer (altfranzösischer) Text der Briefes über die Wunder Asiens', *Zeitschrift für französische Sprache und Literatur* 46 (1923), 92–103

HILL, Joyce, ed., *Old English Minor Heroic Poems*, Durham and St. Andrews Medieval Texts 4 (Durham, 1983)

HILL, Thomas D., '*Hwyrftum scripað*: *Beowulf*, line 163', *Mediaeval Studies* 33 (1971), 379–81

HILL, Thomas D., 'The Old World, the Levelling of the Earth, and the Burning of the Sea: Three Eschatological Images in the Old English *Christ III*,' *Notes and Queries* 19 (1972), 323–5

HILL, Thomas D., 'The Return of the Broken Butterfly: *Beowulf* Line 163, Again', *Mediaevalia* 5 (1979), 271–81

HINTZ, Howard W. 'The "Hama" Reference in *Beowulf* 1197–1201', *Journal of English and Germanic Philology* 33 (1934), 98–102

HOLDER, A., 'Collationen zu angelsächsischen Werken I. *De rebus in oriente mirabilibus*', *Anglia* 1 (1878), 331–7

HOLDER, A., 'Collationen zu angelsächsischen Werken II. *Epistola Alexandri ad Aristotelem*', *Anglia* 1 (1878), 507–12

HOLLÄNDER, Hans, 'Alexander: *Hybris und Curiositas*', in *Kontinuität und Transformation der Antike im Mittelalter*, ed. Willi Erzgräber (Sigmaringen, 1989), pp. 65–79

HOOPS, Johannes, *Kommentar zum Beowulf* (Heidelberg, 1932)

HORGAN, E., *The Irish Nennius from Lebor na Huidre*, Royal Irish Academy Todd Lecture Series 6 (Dublin, 1895)

HUFFINES, Marion Lois, 'OE *aglæca*: Magic and Moral Decline of Monsters and Men', *Semasia* 1 (1974), 71–81

HUGHES, Kathleen, 'On an Irish Litany of Pilgrim Saints', *Analecta Bollandiana* 77 (1959), 328–31

HUISMAN, Rosemary, 'The Three Tellings of Beowulf's Fight with Grendel's Mother', *Leeds Studies in English* n.s. 20 (1989), 217–48

HUME, Kathryn, 'The Thematic Design of *Grettis saga*', *Journal of English and Germanic Philology* 73 (1974), 469–86

HUME, Kathryn, 'The Theme and Structure of *Beowulf*', *Studies in Philology* 72 (1975), 1–27

HUME, Kathryn, 'From Saga to Romance: The Use of Monsters in Old Norse Literature,' *Studies in Philology* 77 (1980), 1–25

HUPPÉ, Bernard F., *The Web of Words* (Albany, NY, 1970)

IRVING, Edward B., *A Reading of 'Beowulf'* (New Haven, CT, 1968)

JACKSON, Kenneth H., *A Celtic Miscellany: Translations from the Celtic Literatures* (Harmondsworth, 1971)

JACKSON, Peter, 'Palladius Helenopolitanus', in *Sources of Anglo-Saxon Literary Culture,* ed. Frederick M. Biggs, Thomas D. Hill, and Paul E. Szarmach (forthcoming)

JAMES, M. R., ed., *Apocrypha Anecdota: A Collection of Thirteen Apocryphal Books and Fragments,* Texts and Studies: Contributions to Biblical and Patristic Literature II.3 (Cambridge, 1893)

JAMES, M. R., *The Lost Apocrypha of the Old Testament* (London, 1920)

JAMES, M. R., *Marvels of the East, A Full Reproduction of the Three Known Copies* Roxburghe Club Publications 191 (Oxford, 1929)

JAN, L., and C. MAYHOFF, ed., *C. Plinii Secundi Nauralis historiae libri XXXVII* (Leipzig, 1892–1900)

JÓHANNESSON, Jón, ed., *Fljótsdæla saga,* Íslenzk fornrit XI (Reykjavík, 1950)

JOHANSEN, J. G., 'Grendel the Brave? *Beowulf,* Line 834', *English Studies* 63 (1982), 193–7

JONES, C. W., ed., *Bedae Venerabilis Libri quatuor in Genesim,* CCSL 118A (Turnhout, 1967)

JONES, C. W., ed., *De temporum ratione,* in his *Bedae Venerabilis Opera: VI, Opera didascalica 2,* CCSL 123B (Turnhout, 1977), pp. 263–460.

JÓNSSON, Finnur, ed., *Alexanders saga. Islandsk Oversættelse ved Brandr Jónsson (Biskop til Holar 1263–4)* (Copenhagen, 1924)

JÓNSSON, Guðni, 'Drangey', *Lesbók Morgunblaðsins,* 26 August 1934, 277–81

JÓNSSON, Guðni, 'Tvö Grettisbæli', *Árbók Fornleifafelags 1936,* 49–60

JÓNSSON, Guðni, ed., *Grettis saga Ásmundarsonar,* Íslenzk fornrit VII (Reykjavík, 1936)

JÓNSSON, Guðni, ed., *Ketils saga hængs,* in his *Fornaldar Sögur Norðurlanda,* 4 vols. (Reykjavík, 1954), II, 151–81

JORGENSEN, Peter, 'Grendel, Grettir, and Two Skaldic Stanzas', *Scripta Islandica* 24 (1973), 54–61

JORGENSEN, Peter, 'Beowulf's Swimming Contest with Breca: Old Norse Parallels' *Folk-Lore* 89 (1978), 52–9

JORGENSEN, Peter, 'The Gift of the Useless Weapon in *Beowulf* and the Icelandic Sagas', *Arkiv för nordisk filologi* 94 (1979), 82–90

JOST, Karl, ed., *Die 'Institutes of Polity, Civil and Ecclesiastical',* Swiss Studies in English 47 (Bern, 1959)

KÅLUND, K., *Bidrag til en historisk-topografisk beskrivelse af Island,* 2 vols. (Copenhagen, 1877)

KASKE, R. E., '*Sapientia et fortitudo* as the Controlling Theme in *Beowulf*', *Studies in Philology* 55 (1958), 423–57

KASKE, R. E., 'The Sigemund-Heremod and Hama-Hygelac Passages', *Publications of the Modern Language Association* 74 (1959), 489–94

KASKE, R. E., 'Weohstan's Sword', *Modern Language Notes* 75 (1960), 465–8

KASKE, R. E., ' "Hygelac" and "Hygd" ', in *Studies in Old English Literature in Honor of Arthur G. Brodeur,* ed. Stanley B. Greenfield (Eugene, OR, 1963), pp. 200–6

KASKE, R. E., 'The *eotenas* in *Beowulf*', in *Old English Poetry: Fifteen Essays,* ed. R.P. Creed (Providence, RI, 1967), pp. 285–310

KASKE, R. E., '*Beowulf* and the Book of Enoch', *Speculum* 46 (1971), 421–31

KASKE, R. E., '*Sapientia et fortitudo* in the Old English *Judith*', in *The Wisdom of Poetry: Essays in Early English Literature in Honor of Morton W. Bloomfleld,* ed. Larry D. Benson and Siegfried Wenzel (Kalamazoo, MI, 1982), pp. 13–29

KEMBLE, John Mitchell, *The Dialogue of Salomon and Saturnus, with an Historical Introduction* (London, 1845–8)

KER, N. R., *Catalogue of Manuscripts Containing Anglo-Saxon* (Oxford, 1957, rptd. 1990)

KERMODE, P. M. C., *Manx Crosses* (London, 1907)

KIERNAN, Kevin S., *'Beowulf' and the 'Beowulf' Manuscript* (New Brunswick, NJ, 1981)

KIERNAN, Kevin S., 'The Eleventh-Century Origin of *Beowulf* and the *Beowulf* Manuscript', in *The Dating of 'Beowulf'*, ed. Colin Chase (Toronto, 1981), pp. 9–21

KIERNAN, Kevin S., 'Grendel's Heroic Mother', *In Geardagum* 6 (1984), 13–33

KLAEBER, Frederick, 'Notes on Old English Prose Texts', *Modern Language Notes* 18 (1903), 241–7

KLAEBER, Frederick, 'Die christlichen Elemente im *Beowulf*', *Anglia* 35 (1911–12), 111–36; 249–70; 453–82; 36 (1912), 169–99

KLAEBER, F., ed., *Beowulf*, 3rd ed. (Boston, 1950)

KLEGRAF, Josef, ed. and trans., *Die altenglische 'Judith': eine Ausgabe für den akademischen Unterricht*, Ausgewählte Texte aus der Geschichte der christlichen Kirche 3 (Stuttgart, 1987)

KNAPPE, Fritz, *Der angelsächsische Prosastück Die Wunder des Ostens. Überlieferung, Quellen, Sprache und Text nach beiden Handschriften* (Berlin, 1906)

KNOCK, Ann, 'The *Liber Monstrorum*: An Unpublished Manuscript and Some Reconsiderations', *Scriptorium* 32 (1978), 19–28

KNOCK, Ann (rev. of Bologna), *Medium Aevum* 48 (1979), 259–62

KNOCK, Ann, 'Wonders of the East: a Synoptic Edition of the Letter of Pharasmenes and the Old English and Old Picard Translations' (unpublished PhD dissertation, University of London, 1982)

KOSKENNIEMI, Inna, *Repetitive Word Pairs in Old and Middle English Prose* (Turku, 1968)

KOTZER, Günter, ed., *Das altenglische Martyrologium*, Bayerische Akademie der Wissenschaften, Philosophisch-historische Klasse, Abhandlungen, Neue Folge 88.1–2 (Munich, 1989)

KRATZ, Dennis M., *Mocking Epic: Waltharius, Alexandreis, and the Problem of Christian Heroism* (Madrid, 1980)

KRISTJÁNSSON, Jónas, *Eddas and Sagas: Iceland's Medieval Literature*, trans. Peter Foote (Reykjavík, 1988)

KÜBLER, B, ed., *Iuli Valeri Alexandri Polemi Res Gestae Alexandri Macedonis* (Leipzig, 1888)

KUHN, Sherman M., 'Old English *aglæca*—Middle Irish *ochlach*', in *Linguistic Method: Essays in Honor of Herbert Penzl*, ed. I. Rauch and G. F. Carr, Janua linguarum series maior 79 (The Hague, 1979), pp. 213–30

LANE FOX, Robin, *Alexander the Great* (London, 1973)

LAGARDE, P. de, ed., *Hieronymi Liber quaestionum hebraicarum in Genesim*, CCSL 72 (Turnhout, 1959), pp. 1–56

LAPIDGE, Michael, '*Beowulf*, Aldhelm, the *Liber Monstrorum* and Wessex', *Studi Medievali*, 3rd series, 23 (1982), 151–92

LAPIDGE, Michael, '*Beowulf* and the Psychology of Terror', in *Heroic Poetry in the Anglo-Saxon Period: Studies in Honor of Jess B. Bessinger, Jr.*, ed. Helen Damico and John Leyerle, Studies in Medieval Culture 32 (Kalamazoo, MI, 1993), pp. 373–402

LAPIDGE, Michael, and Michael HERREN, trans., *Aldhelm: The Prose Works* (Cambridge, 1979)

LAPIDGE, Michael, and Andy ORCHARD, 'Aldhelm', in *Sources of Anglo-Saxon Literary Culture*, ed. Frederick M. Biggs, Thomas D. Hill, and Paul E. Szarmach (forthcoming)

LAPIDGE, Michael, and James ROSIER, trans., *Aldhelm: The Poetic Works* (Cambridge, 1985)

LAPIDGE, Michael and Richard SHARPE, *A Bibliography of Celtic-Latin Literature 400–1200* (Dublin, 1985)

LAWRENCE, William Witherle, 'The Haunted Mere in *Beowulf*', *Publications of the Modern Language Association* 27 (1912), 208–45

LAWRENCE, William Witherle, *'Beowulf' and the Epic Tradition* (Cambridge, MA, 1928)

LAWRENCE, William Witherle, 'Grendel's Lair', *Journal of English and Germanic Philology* 38 (1939), 477–80

LAXNESS, Halldór Kilján, 'Litil samantekt um útilegumenn', *Tímarit máls og menningar* 10 (1949), 86–130

LEAKE, Jane, A., *The Geats of 'Beowulf': a Study in the Geographical Mythology of the Middle Ages* (Madison, WI, 1967)

LECOUTEUX, Claude, ed., *De rebus in Oriente mirabilibus (Lettre de Farasmenes). Edition synoptique accompagnée d'une introduction et de notes*, Beiträge zur klassischen Philologie 103 (Meisenheim am Glan, 1979)

LECOUTEUX, Claude, *Les monstres dans la littérature allemande du moyen âge. Contribution à l'étude du merveilleux médiéval*, Göppinger Arbeiten zur Germanistik 330 (Göppingen, 1982)

LECOUTEUX, Claude, *Kleine Texte zur Alexanderssage*, Göppinger Arbeiten zur Germanistik 388 (Göppingen, 1984)

LECOUTEUX, Claude, *Fantômes et revenants au moyen âge* (Paris, 1986)

LEHMANN, Winifred, 'Atertanum fah', *Studies in Historical Linguistics in Honor of George Sherman Lane*, ed. W. W. Arndt (Chapel Hill, NC, 1967), pp. 211–32

LEINBAUGH, Theodore H., 'St Christopher and the *Old English Martyrology*: Latin Sources, and the Phrase *hwæs gneaðes*', *Notes and Queries* 32 (1985), 434–7

LENDINARA, P., 'Un'allusione ai Giganti: versi gnomici exoniensi 192–200', *Annali, Sezione Germanica* (Naples) 16 (1973), 85–98

LEYERLE, John, 'The Interlace Structure of *Beowulf*', *University of Toronto Quarterly* 37 (1967), 1–17

LIBERMAN, Anatoly, 'Beowulf-Grettir', *German Dialects: Linguistic and Philological Investigations*, ed. Bela Brogyanyi and Thomas Krömmelbein (Amsterdam, 1986), pp. 353–91

LIEBERMANN, Felix, ed., *Die Gesetze der Anglesachsen*, 3 vols. (Halle, 1903–16)

LIEBERMANN, Felix, 'Grendel als Personenname', *Archiv* 126 (1911), 180

LINDOW, John, *Comitatus, Individual and Honor: Studies in North Germanic Institutional Vocabulary*, University of California Publications in Linguistics 83 (Berkeley, CA, 1975)

LINDOW, John, *Swedish Legends and Folktales* (New York, 1978)

LINDOW, John, '*Þorsteins þáttr skelks* and the Verisimilitude of Supernatural Experience in Saga Literature', *Structure and Meaning in Old Norse Literature*, ed. John Lindow, Lars Lönnroth, and Gerd Wolfgang Weber (Odense, 1986), pp. 264–80

LINDSAY, W. M., ed., *Isidori Hispalensis Episcopi Etymologiarum sive Originum libri XX*, 2 vols. (Oxford, 1911)

LLOYD-JONES, H., and N. G. WILSON, ed., *Sophoclis Fabulae* (Oxford, 1990)

LOCHERBIE-CAMERON, Margaret A. L., 'Wisdom as a Key to Heroism in *Judith*', *Poetica* (Tokyo) 27 (1988), 70–5

LÖFSTEDT, Bengt, 'Notizien zum "Liber Monstrorum" ', *Orpheus* 11 (1990), 117

LOGANBILL, Dean, 'Time and Monsters in *Beowulf*', *In Geardagum* 3 (1979), 26–35

LÖNNROTH, Lars, 'Hetjunar líta bleika akra. Athuganir á Njáls sögu og Alexanders sögu', *Skírnir* 144 (1970), 12–30

LÖNNROTH, Lars, *Njáls saga. A Critical Introduction* (Berkeley, CA, 1976)

LOTSPEICH, C. M., 'Old English Etymologies', *Journal of English and Germanic Philology* 40 (1941), 1–4

LUCAS, Peter J., 'The Place of *Judith* in the *Beowulf*-Manuscript', *Review of English Studies* 41 (1990), 463–78

MAC AIRT, Seán, ed., *The Annals of Inisfallen (MS Rawlinson B. 503)* (Dublin, 1951)

MAC AIRT, Seán, and Gearóid MAC NIOCAILL, ed., *The Annals of Ulster (to AD 1131), Part I: Text and Translation* (Dublin, 1983)

MAGENNIS, Hugh, 'Adaptation of Biblical Detail in the Old English *Judith*: the Feast Scene', *Neuphilologische Mitteilungen* 84 (1983), 331–7

MALMBERG, L., 'Grendel and the Devil', *Neuphilologische Mitteilungen* 78 (1977), 241–3

MALONE, Kemp, 'Hygelac', *English Studies* 21 (1939), 108–19

MALONE, Kemp, 'Hygd', *Modern Language Notes* 56 (1941), 356–8

MALONE, Kemp, 'Grendel and Grep', *Publications of the Modern Language Association* 57 (1942), 1–14

MALONE, Kemp, 'Grendel and his Abode', in *Studia Philologica et Litteraria in Honorem L. Spitzer*, ed. A. G. Hatcher and K-L. Selig (Bern, 1958), pp. 297–308

MALONE, Kemp, 'Readings from Folios 94 to 131, Cotton Vitellius A xv', in *Studies in Medieval Literature in Honor of Professor Albert Croll Baugh*, ed. MacEdward Leach (Philadelphia, PA, 1961), pp. 255–71

MALONE, Kemp, ed., *The Nowell Codex, British Museum Cotton Vitellius A. xv, Second MS*, EEMF 12 (Copenhagen, 1963)

MALONE, Kemp, 'An Anglo-Latin Version of the Hjaðningavíg', *Speculum* 39 (1964), 35–44

MANITIUS, M., 'Liber monstrorum de diversis generibus', in his *Geschichte der lateinischen Literatur des Mittlelalters*, Handbuch der klassischen Altertums-Wissenschaft IX.2.1 (Munich, 1911), pp. 114–18

MANITIUS, M., *Geschichte der lateinischen Literatur des Mittelalters*, 3 vols. (Munich, 1911–31)

McCONCHIE, R., 'Grettir Ásmundarson's Fight with Kárr the Old: A Neglected *Beowulf* Analogue', *English Studies* 63 (1982), 481–6

McCREESH, Bernadine, 'Structural Patterns in the *Eyrbyggja saga* and Other Sagas of the Conversion', *Mediaeval Scandinavia* 11 (1978–9), 271–80

McGURK, P. M. J., D. N. DUMVILLE, and M. R. GODDEN, ed., *An Eleventh-Century Anglo-Saxon Illustrated Miscellany (British Library Cotton Tiberius B. V Part I)*, EEMF 21 (Copenhagen, 1983)

McNAMARA, Martin, *The Apocrypha in the Irish Church* (Dublin, 1975)

MELLINKOFF, R., 'Cain's Monstrous Progeny in *Beowulf*: Part I, Noachic Tradition', *Anglo-Saxon England* 8 (1979), 143–62

MELLINKOFF, R., 'Cain's Monstrous Progeny in *Beowulf*: Part II, Post-Diluvian Survival', *Anglo-Saxon England* 9 (1981), 183–97

MENNER, Robert J., 'Nimrod and the Wolf in the Old English Solomon and Saturn', *Journal of English and Germanic Philology* 37 (1938), 332–54

MENNER, Robert J., ed., *The Poetical Dialogues of Solomon and Saturn* (London, 1941)

MERONEY, Howard, 'The Early History of *down* as an Adverb', *Journal of English and Germanic Philology* 44 (1945), 378–86

MEYER, Kuno, 'Die Geschichte von Phillip und Alexander', *Irische Texte* II.2 (1887), 3–5

MEYER, Kuno, ed., *Rawlinson B 502, a Collection of Pieces in Prose and Verse in the Irish Language, Compiled during the Eleventh and Twelfth Centuries* (Oxford, 1909)

MEYER, R. T., 'The Sources of the Middle Irish Alexander', *Modern Philology* 47 (1949), 1–7

MEZGER, F., 'Goth. Aglaiti "Unchastity", OE Aglæc "Distress" ', *Word* 2 (1946), 68–72

MICHAEL, Ian, *Alexander's Flying-Machine: the History of a Legend* (Southampton, 1974)

MORRIS, R., ed., *Old English Homilies, First Series*, 2 vols., EETS OS 29 and 34 (London, 1868)

MORRIS, R., ed., *The Blickling Homilies of the Tenth Century*, EETS OS 73 (London, 1880)

MOTZ, Lotte, 'Withdrawal and Return. A Ritual Pattern in the *Grettis saga*', *Arkiv för nordisk filologi* 88 (1973), 91–110

MOTZ, Lotte, 'The Hero and his Tale', *Arkiv för nordisk filologi* 93 (1978), 145–8

MÜLLENHOFF, Karl, 'Die innere Geschichte des *Beowulfs*', *Zeitschrift für deutsches Altertum und deutsche Literatur* 14 (1869), 193–244

MÜLLENHOFF, Karl, *'Beowulf'. Untersuchungen über das angelsächsische Epos und die älteste Geschichte der germanischer Seevölker* (Berlin, 1889)

MÜLLER, K., ed. and trans. *Geschichte Alexanders des Grossen* (Munich, 1954)

MÜLLER, Wolfgang G., 'Syntaktisch-semasiologische Analyse des Grendel-Kampfes im *Beowulf*', *Literaturwissenschaftliches Jahrbuch* 29 (1988), 9–22

MURPHY, Gerard, trans., *Duanaire Finn: The Book of the Lays of Fionn*, Irish Texts Society II (London, 1933)

MUSHABAC, Jane, '*Judith* and the Theme of *Sapientia et Fortitudo*', *Massachusetts Studies in English* 4 (1973), 3–12

MYNORS, R. A. B., ed., *P. Vergili Maronis Opera* (Oxford, 1969)

NAPIER, Arthur S., ed., *Wulfstan: Sammlung der ihm zugeschreibenen Homilien nebst Untersuchungen über ihre Echtheit* (Berlin, 1883)

NECKEL, Gustav, 'Altnordisch *draugr* in Mannkenningar', *Beiträge zur Geschichte der deutschen Sprache und Literatur* 39 (1914), 189–200

NELSON, Marie, '*Judith*: a Story of a Secular Saint', *Germanic Notes* 21 (1990), 12–13

NEWTON, Sam, *The Origins of 'Beowulf' and the Pre-Viking Kingdom of East Anglia* (Cambridge, 1993)

NICHOLLS, Alex, 'Bede "Awe-Inspiring" not "Monstrous": Some Problems with Old English *aglæca*', *Notes and Queries* 38 (1991), 147–8

NIETZSCHE, Friedrich, *Jenseits von Gut und Böse* (Berlin, 1886)

NILES, John D., 'Ring-Composition and the Structure of *Beowulf*', *Publications of the Modern Language Association* 94 (1979), 924–35
NILES, John D., *Beowulf: The Poem and its Tradition* (Cambridge, MA, 1983)
NITZSCHE, Jane C., 'The Structural Unity of *Beowulf*: the Problem of Grendel's Mother', *Texas Studies in Literature and Language* 22 (1980), 287–303
NORDAL, Sigurður, ed., *Egils saga*, Íslenzk fornrit II (Reykjavík, 1933)
NORDAL, Sigurður, and Guðni JÓNSSON, ed., *Bjarnar saga Hítdœlakappa*, Íslenzk fornrit III (Reykjavík, 1938)
NORDAL, Sigurður, and Guðni JÓNSSON, ed., *Gunnlaugs saga*, Íslenzk fornrit VII (Reykjavík, 1938)
NORDAL, Sigurður, *Sturla Þórðarson og Grettis Saga*, Studia Islandica 4 (Reykjavík, 1938)
NORDAL, Sigurður, ed., *Flateyjarbók*, 4 vols. (Reykjavík, 1944)
Ó CRÓINÍN, Dáibhi, ed., *The Irish Sex Aetates Mundi* (Dublin, 1983)
O'BRIEN, John Maxwell, *Alexander the Great: the Invisible Enemy. A Biography* (London, 1992)
O'DONOVAN, J., ed., *Annála ríoghachta Éreann: Annals of the Kingdom of Ireland by the Four Masters* (Dublin, 1851)
OGILVY, J. D. A., *Books Known to the English, 597–1066* (Cambridge, MA, 1967)
O'KEEF[F]E, Katherine O'Bri[e]n, '*Beowulf*, Lines 702b–836: Transformations and the Limits of the Human', *Texas Studies in Literature and Language* 23 (1981), 484–94
O'KEEFFE, Katherine O'Brien, 'The Geographic List of *Solomon and Saturn II*', *Anglo-Saxon England* 20 (1991), 123–41
OMONT, Henri, ed., 'Lettre à l'empereur Adrien sur les merveilles d'Asie', *Bibliothèque de l'Ecole des Chartes* 74 (1913), 507–15
OPLAND, Jeff, 'A *Beowulf* Analogue in *Njálssaga*', *Scandinavian Studies* 45 (1973), 54–8
ORCHARD, A[ndy] P. McD., 'Some Aspects of Seventh-Century Hiberno-Latin Syntax: A Statistical Approach', *Peritia* 6–7 (1987–88) [1991], 158–201
ORCHARD, A[ndy] P. McD., 'Crying Wolf: Oral Style and the *Sermones Lupi*', *Anglo-Saxon England* 21 (1992), 239–64
ORCHARD, Andy, 'Tolkien, the Monsters, and the Critics: Back to *Beowulf*', in *Scholarship and Fantasy: Proceedings of the 'The Tolkien Phenomenon', Turku May 1992*, ed. Keith Battarbee, Anglicana Turkuensia 12 (Turku, 1993), pp. 73–84
ORCHARD, Andy, *The Poetic Art of Aldhelm*, CSASE 8 (Cambridge, 1994)
PÁLSSON, Hermann, 'Drög að síðfræði Grettis sögu', *Tímarit máls og menningar* 30 (1969), 372–82
PÁLSSON, Hermann, '*Sermo datur cunctis*: A Learned Element in *Grettis saga*', *Arkiv för nordisk filologi* 94 (1979), 91–4
PÁLSSON, Hermann, *Úr hugmyndaheimi Hrafnkels sögu og Grettlu*, Studia Islandica 39 (Reykjavík, 1981)
PÁLSSON, Hermann, and Paul EDWARDS, *Legendary Fiction in Medieval Iceland*, Studia Islandica 30 (Reykjavík, 1971)
PANZER, Friedrich, *Studien zur germanischen Sagengeschichte I. Beowulf* (Munich, 1910)
PELTOLA, N., 'Grendel's Descent from Cain Reconsidered', *Neuphilologische Mitteilungen* 73 (1972), 284–91

PETERS, E., 'Die irische Alexandersage', *Zeitschrift für celtische Philologie* 30 (1967), 71–264

PETERS, F. J. J., 'The Wrestling in *Grettis Saga*', *Papers on Language and Literature* 25 (1989), 235–41

PETSCHENIG, M., ed., *Iohannis Cassiani Conlationes*, CSEL 13.2 (Vienna, 1886)

PETTITT, Thomas, 'The Mark of the Beast and the Balance of Frenzy', *Neuphilologische Mitteilungen* 77 (1976), 526–35

PFISTER, Friedrich, 'Auf den Spuren Alexanders des Grossen in der älteren englischen Literatur', *Germanisch-romanische Monatsschrift* 16 (1928), 81–6

PFISTER, Friedrich, *Kleine Schriften zum Alexanderroman*, Beiträge zur klassischen Philologie 61 (Meisenheim am Glan, 1976)

PFISTER, Friedrich, *Der Alexanderroman mit einer Auswahl aus den verwandten Texten*, Beiträge zur klassischen Philologie 92 (Meisenheim am Glan, 1978)

PICKLES, John Drayton, 'Studies in the Prose Texts of the *Beowulf* Manuscript' (unpublished PhD dissertation,University of Cambridge, 1971)

PIETERSMA, Albert, ed., *The Apocryphon of Jannes and Jambres the Magicians* (London, 1994)

PITRA, J. B., ed., *Analecta Sacra Spicilegio Solesmensi Parata* (1884)

PLUMMER, C., ed., *Vitae Sanctorum Hiberniae*, 2 vols. (Oxford, 1910)

PLUMMER, C., ed., *Bethada Náem nÉrenn: Lives of Irish Saints*, 2 vols. (Oxford, 1922)

POGATSCHER, Alois, 'Altenglisch *Grendel*', *Neusprachliche studien: Festgabe Karl Luick zu seinem sechzigsten Geburtstage* (Marburg, 1925), p. 151

PORSIA, Franco, 'Note per una riedizione ed una rilettura del *Liber Monstrorum*', *Annali della facoltà di lettere e filosofia, Università di Bari* 15 (1972), pp. 317–38

PORSIA, Franco, ed., *Liber Monstrorum* (Bari, 1976)

PRINGLE, Ian, '*Judith*: the Homily and the Poem', *Traditio* 31 (1975), 83–97

PRITCHARD, R. Telfryn, trans., *The Alexandreis* (Toronto, 1986)

PUHVEL, Martin, 'The Melting of the Giant-Wrought Sword', in his *'Beowulf' and Celtic Tradition* (Waterloo, Ontario, 1979), pp. 39–44

PUHVEL, Martin, *'Beowulf' and Celtic Tradition* (Waterloo, Ontario, 1979)

PUHVEL, Martin, 'A Scottish Analogue to the Grendel Story', *Neuphilologische Mitteilungen* 81 (1980), 395–8

PURDIE, E., *The Story of Judith in German and Old English Literature* (1927)

QUIN, E. G., 'Ochtfæochlach Choluim Chille', *Celtica* 14 (1981), 125–53

RAFFEL, Burton, '*Judith*: Hypermetricity and Rhetoric', *Anglo-Saxon Poetry: Essays in Appreciation*, ed. Lewis E. Nicholson and Dolores Warwick Frese (Notre Dame, IN, 1975), pp. 124–34

RENOIR, Alain, '*Judith* and the Limits of Poetry', *English Studies* 43 (1962), 145–55

RENOIR, Alain, 'Point of View and Design for Terror in *Beowulf*', *Neuphilologische Mitteilungen* 63 (1962), 154–67

RENOIR, Alain, 'The Terror of the Dark Waters: a Note on Virgilian and Beowulfian Techniques', in *The Learned and the Lewed; Studies in Chaucer and Medieval Literature*, ed. Larry D. Benson (Cambridge, MA, 1974), pp. 147–60

RICHARDS, Mary P., 'A Reexamination of *Beowulf* ll. 3180–3182', *English Language Notes* 10 (1973), 163–7

RIGG, A. G., '*Beowulf* 1368–72: An Analogue', *Notes and Queries* 29 (1982), 101–2

ROBERTS, Bryley F., 'Rhai o Gerddi Ymddiddan Llyfr Du Caerfyrddin', in *Astudiaethau ar yr Hengerdd (Studies in Old Welsh Poetry) cyflwynedig i Syr Idris Foster*, ed. Rachel Bromwich and R. Brinley Jones (Cardiff, 1978), pp. 281–325

ROBINSON, Fred C., 'Two Non-Cruces in *Beowulf*', *Tennessee Studies in Literature* 11 (1966), 151–60

ROBINSON, Fred C., 'Lexicography and Literary Criticism: a Caveat', in *Philological Essays: Studies in Old and Middle English Literature in Honour of Herbert Dean Meritt*, ed. James L. Rosier (The Hague, 1970), pp. 99–110

ROBINSON, Fred C., 'Elements of the Marvellous in the Characterization of Beowulf', *Old English Studies in Honour of John C. Pope*, ed. R. B. Burlin and E. B. Irving, Jr (Toronto, 1974), pp. 119–37

ROBINSON, Fred C., *Beowulf and the Appositive Style* (Knoxville, TN, 1985)

ROBINSON, Fred C., 'Why is Grendel's Not Greeting the *Gifstol* a *Wræc Micel*?', in *Words, Texts and Manuscripts: Studies in Anglo-Saxon Culture Presented to Helmut Gneuss on the Occasion of his Sixty-Fifth Birthday*, ed. Michael Korhammer (Cambridge, 1992), pp. 257–62

ROBINSON, Fred C. *The Tomb of Beowulf* (Oxford, 1993)

ROBSON, E. Iliff, ed. and trans., *Arrian: Anabasis Alexandri*, 2 vols. (London, 1949)

ROGERS, H. L., 'Beowulf's Three Great Fights', *Review of English Studies* n.s. 6 (1955), 339–55

ROSENFELD, Hans-Friedrich, *Der Hl. Christophorus, seine Verehrung und seine Legende*, Acta Academeiae Aboensis X.3 (Åbo, 1937)

ROSIER, James L., 'The Uses of Association: Hands and Feasts in *Beowulf*', *Publications of the Modern Language Association* 78 (1963), 8–14

ROSIER, James L., 'The Two Closings of *Beowulf*', *English Studies* 54 (1973), 1–6

ROSIER, James L., 'What Grendel Found: *heardran hæle*', *Neuphilologische Mitteilungen* 75 (1974), 40–9

ROSS, D. J. A., *Alexander and the Faithless Lady: a Submarine Adventure* (London, 1967)

ROSS, D. J. A., 'A Check-List of three Alexander Texts: the Julius Valerius *Epitome*, the *Epistola ad Aristotelem* and the *Collatio cum Dindimo*', in his *Studies in the Alexander Romance* (London, 1985), pp. 83–8

ROSS, D. J. A., '*Parva Recapitulatio*: An English Collection of Texts Relating to Alexander the Great', in his *Studies in the Alexander Romance* (London, 1985), pp. 156–68

ROSS, D. J. A., *Alexander Historiatus. A Guide to Medieval Illustrated Alexander Literature*, Beiträge zur klassischen Philologie 186 (Frankfurt, 1988)

RYPINS, Stanley I., 'Notes on *Epistola Alexandri ad Aristotelem*', *Modern Language Notes* 32 (1917), 94–5

RYPINS, Stanley I., 'The Old English *Epistola Alexandri ad Aristotelem*', *Modern Language Notes* 38 (1923), 216–20

RYPINS, Stanley I., ed., *Three Old English Prose Texts in MS Cotton Vitellius A. xv*, EETS OS 161 (London, 1924, rptd. 1971)

SAINT-DENIS, E. de, *Le rôle de la mer dans la poésie latine* (Lyons, 1969)

SALMON, John, 'St Christopher in English Medieval Art and Life', *Journal of the British Archaeological Association* n.s. 41 (1936), 95–6

SANDBACH, Mary, 'Grettir in Thorisdal', *Saga-Book* 12 (1937–8), 93–106

SAWYER, Peter H., *Anglo-Saxon Charters: an Annotated List and Bibliography*, Royal Historical Society Guides and Handbooks 8 (London, 1968)

SCHACH, Paul, 'Tristan in Iceland', *Prairie Schooner* 36 (1962), 151–64

SCHACH, Paul, 'Some Observations on the Influence of *Tristrams saga ok Isöndar*', *Old*

Norse Literature and Mythology, ed. Edgar C. Polomé (Austin, Textas, 1969), pp. 81–129

SCHICHLER, Robert Lawrence, 'Heorot and Dragon-Slaying in *Beowulf*', *Proceedings of the Patristic, Medieval and Renaissance Conference* 11 (1986), 159–75

SCHMIDTKE, D., *Geistliche Schiffahrt* (Tübingen, 1969)

SCHNELL, Rüdiger, 'Der "Heide" Alexander im christlichen Mittelalter', in *Kontinuität und Transformation der Antike im Mittelalter*, ed. Willi Erzgraber (Sigmaringen, 1989), pp. 45–63

SCHRADER, Richard J., 'Sacred Groves, Marvellous Waters, and Grendel's Abode', *Florilegium* 5 (1983), 76–84

SCHRÖER, Arnold, ed., *Die angelsächsischen Prosabearbeitungen der Benediktinerregel*, Bibliothek der angelsächsischen Prosa 2, rptd. with appendix by Helmut Gneuss (Darmstadt, 1964)

SCHRÖER, Arnold, ed., *Die Winteney-Version der Regula S. Benedicti* (Halle, 1888)

SCHÜCK, Hans, *Studier i Beowulfsagen* (Uppsala, 1909)

SCRAGG, D. G., 'The Compilation of the Vercelli Book', *Anglo-Saxon England* 2 (1973), 189–207

SCRAGG, D. G., ed., *The Battle of Maldon* (Manchester, 1981)

SCRAGG, D. G., ed., *The Vercelli Homilies*, EETS OS 300 (London, 1992)

SEDGFIELD, W. J., ed., *King Alfred's Boethius* (Oxford, 1899; repr. Darmstadt, 1968)

SETTIS-FRUGONI, Chiara, *Historia Alexandri elevati per griphos ad aerem: origine, iconografia e fortuna di un tema*, Istituto Storica Italiano per il medio Evo, Studi Storici 80–2 (Rome, 1973)

SHEPHARD, G., 'Scriptural Poetry', in *Continuations and Beginnings*, ed. E. G. Stanley (London, 1966), pp. 1–36

SHIPPEY, T. A., *Poems of Wisdom and Learning in Old English* (Cambridge, 1976)

SIMS-WILLIAMS, Patrick, *Religion and Literature in Western England. 600-800*, CSASE 3 (Cambridge, 1990)

SIMS-WILLIAMS, Patrick, 'The Early Welsh Arthurian Poems', in *The Arthur of the Welsh: the Arthurian Legend in Medieval Welsh Literature*, ed. Rachel Bromwich, A. O. H. Jarman, and Brynley F. Roberts (Cardiff, 1991), pp. 33–71

SISAM, Celia, *The Vercelli Book*, EEMF 19 (Copenhagen, 1976)

SISAM, Kenneth, 'The Compilation of the Beowulf Manuscript', in his *Studies in the History of Old English Literature* (Oxford, 1953)

SISAM, Kenneth, 'Beowulf's Fight with the Dragon', *Review of English Studies* n.s. 9 (1958), 129–40

SKEAT, Walter William, ed., *Ælfric's Lives of Saints*, 4 vols., EETS OS 76, 82, 94, and 114 (London, 1881–1900; rptd. as 2 vols, 1966)

SKEAT, Walter William, 'On the Signification of the Monster Grendel in the Poem of *Beowulf*; with a Discussion of lines 2076–2100', *The Journal of Philology* 15 (1886), 120–31

SMITH, C., 'Beowulf Gretti', *The New Englander* 4 (1881), 49–67

SMITHERS, G. V., 'The Meaning of *The Seafarer* and *The Wanderer*', *Medium Ævum* 28 (1959), 1–22

SPARKS, H. F. D., ed., *The Apocryphal Old Testament* (Oxford, 1984)

STANFORD, W. B., 'Monsters and Odyssean Echoes in the Early Hiberno-Latin and Irish Hymns', in *Latin Script and Letters A.D. 400–900: Festschrift Presented to Ludwig Bieler*, ed. John J. O'Meara and Bernd Naumann (Leiden, 1976)

STANLEY, E. G., 'Old English Poetic Diction and the Interpretation of *The Wanderer, The Seafarer* and *The Penitent's Prayer*', *Anglia* 73 (1955), 413–66

STANLEY, E. G., 'Hæthenra Hyht in *Beowulf*', in *Studies in Old English Literature in Honor of Arthur G. Brodeur*, ed. Stanley B Greenfield (Eugene, OR, 1963), pp. 136–51

STANLEY, E. G., 'The Date of Beowulf: Some Doubts and No Conclusions', in *The Dating of 'Beowulf'*, ed. Colin Chase (Toronto, 1981), pp. 197–211

STANLEY, E. G., *In the Foreground: 'Beowulf'* (Cambridge, 1994)

STEDMAN, D., 'Some Points of Resemblance between Beowulf and the Grettla (or *Grettis saga*)', *Saga-Book* 8 (1913), 6–28

STEVENSON, Jane B., '*Altus Prosator*: a seventh-Century Hiberno-Latin Poem' (unpublished PhD dissertation, University of Cambridge, 1985)

STIENE, Heinz Erich, and Jutta GRUB, *Verskonkordanz zur Alexandreis des Walters von Chatillon* (Hildesheim, 1985)

STOKES, W., *Lives of Saints from the Book of Lismore*, Anecdota Oxoniensia (Oxford, 1890)

STONEMAN, Richard, trans., *Legends of Alexander the Great* (London, 1994)

STORMS, G., 'Grendel the Terrible', *Neuphilologische Mitteilungen* 73 (1972), 427–36

SVEINSSON, Einar Ól., and Matthías ÞÓRÐARSON, ed., *Eyrbyggja saga*, Íslenzk fornrit IV (Reykjavík, 1935)

SWAEN, A. E. H., 'Is *seo hiow* = "Fortune" a Ghost-Word?', *English Studies* 71 (1936), 153–4

SWANTON, Michael, trans., *Anglo-Saxon Prose*, rev. ed. (London, 1993)

SWEET, Henry, ed, *King Alfred's West-Saxon Version of Gregory's 'Pastoral Care'*, 2 vols., EETS OS 45 and 50 (London, 1871–2)

SWEET, Henry, ed., *King Alfred's Orosius. Pt I: Old English Text and Latin Original*, EETS OS 79 (London, 1883; rptd. 1974)

TANGL, M., ed., *S. Bonifacii et Lulli Epistolae*, MGH Epistolae Selectae I (Berlin, 1916)

TAYLOR, A. R., 'Two Notes on *Beowulf*', *Leeds Studies in English and Kindred Languages* 7–8 (1952), 5–17

TAYLOR, Paul Beekman, and Peter H. SALUS, 'The Compilation of Cotton Vitellius A XV', *Neuphilologische Mitteilungen* 69 (1968), 199–204

THACKERAY, H. St. J., ed. and trans., *Josephus, Jewish Antiquities, Books I–IV* (Cambridge, MA, 1967)

THILO, G., and H. HAGEN, ed., *Servii Grammatici Vergilii Aeneidos Commentarii*, 2 vols. (Leipzig, 1881–4)

THILO, G., ed., *Servii Grammatici qui feruntur in Vergilii Bucolica et Georgica* Commentarii (Leipzig, 1887)

THOMAS, A., 'Un manuscrit inutilisé du *Liber monstrorum*', *Archivum Latinitatis Medii Aevi (Bulletin du Cange)* 1 (1924), 232–45

THORSSON, Guðmundur Andri, 'Grettla', *Skáldskaparmál* 1 (1990), 100–17

TIMMER, B. J., ed., *Judith* (Exeter, 1978)

TOLKIEN, Christopher, ed., *The Saga of Heidrek the Wise* (London, 1960)

TOLKIEN, J. R. R., '*Beowulf*: the Monsters and the Critics', *Proceedings of the British Academy* 22 (1936), 245–95

TOLKIEN, J. R. R., *The Monsters and the Critics and Other Essays*, ed. Christopher Tolkien (London, 1983)

TRAUBE, Ludwig, *Vorlesungen und Abhandlungen*, 3 vols. (Munich, 1909–20)

TRIPP, Raymond P., Jr, 'A New Look at Grendel's Attack: *Beowulf* 804a–815a', *In*

Geardagum: Essays on Old English Language and Literature, ed. Loren C. Gruber and Dean Loganbill (Denver, CO,1974), pp. 8–11

TRIPP, Raymond P., Jr, *More about the Fight with the Dragon: 'Beowulf' 2208b–3182, Commentary, Edition, and Translation* (Lanham, MD, New York and London, 1983)

TRIPP, Raymond P., Jr, 'Did Beowulf Have an "Inglorious Youth"?', *Studia Neophilologica* 61 (1989), 129–43

TRISTRAM, Hildegard L. C., 'Stock Descriptions of Heaven and Hell in Old English Literature', *Neuphilologische Mitteilungen* 75 (1976), 102–13

TRISTRAM, Hildegard L. C., ed., *Sex Aetates Mundi: Die Weltzeitalter bei den Angelsachsen und den Iren. Untersuchungen und Texte* (Heidelberg, 1985)

TRISTRAM, Hildegard L. C., 'Der insulare Alexander', in *Kontinuität und Transformation der Antike im Mittelalter*, ed. Willi Erzgräber (Sigmaringen, 1989), pp. 129–55

TRISTRAM, Hildegard L. C., 'More Talk of Alexander', *Celtica* 21 (1990), 658–63

TURVILLE-PETRE, Joan, '*Beowulf* and *Grettis saga*: An Excursion', *Saga-Book* 19 (1977), 347–57

TYLER, Elizabeth M., 'Style and Meaning in *Judith*', *Notes and Queries* 39 (1992), 16–19

UNGER, C. R., ed., *Alexanders saga. Norsk Bearbeidelse fra trettende Aarhunddrede af Philip Gautiers latiniske Digt Alexandreis* (Christiania, 1848)

VENEZKY, Richard L., and Antonette DiPaolo HEALEY, *A Microfiche Concordance to Old English* (Newark, DW, 1980–3)

VICKREY, John F., '*Egesan ne gymeð* and the Crime of Heremod', *Modern Philology* 71 (1974), 295–300

VÍGFÚSSON, Guðbrandur, ed. *Sturlunga saga*, 3 vols. (Oxford, 1878)

VÍGFÚSSON, Guðbrandur, and F. York POWELL, *An Icelandic Prose Reader. With Notes, Grammar, and Glossary* (Oxford, 1879)

VÍGFÚSSON, Guðbrandur, and F. York POWELL, ed., *Corpus Poeticum Boreale*, 2 vols. (Oxford, 1883)

VILMUNDARSON, Þórhallur, and Bjarni VILHJÁLMSSON, ed., *Harðar saga*, Íslenzk fornrit XIII (Reykjavík, 1991)

VISWANATHAN, S., 'On the Melting of the Sword: *wæl-rapas* and the Engraving on the Sword-Hilt in *Beowulf*', *Philological Quarterly* 58 (1979), 360–3

VLEESKRUYER, R., *The Life of St Chad* (Amsterdam, 1953)

WACHSLER, A. A., 'Grettir's Fight with a Bear; Another Neglected Analogue of *Beowulf* in the *Grettis Sag[a] Ásmundarsonar*', *English Studies* 66 (1985), 381–90

WARNER, Rubie D-N., ed., *Early English Homilies from the Twelfth Century MS. Vesp. D. XIV*, EETS OS 152 (London, 1917)

WATANABE, H., 'Monsters Creep?: the Meaning of the Verb *scriðan* in *Beowulf*', *Studies in Language and Culture* (Osaka Univ.) 14 (1988), 107–20

WEBER, Robert, ed., *Biblia sacra iuxta vulgatam versionem*, 2 vols. (Stuttgart, 1969)

WEISSMANN, Chaim Bell, 'Giants and Giantism: Jewish Sources of the Manuscriprt Cotton Vitellius A.xv' (unpublished PhD dissertation, Purdue University, 1978)

WENISCH, Franz, *Spezifisch anglisches Wortgut in den nordhumbrischen Interlinear-glossierungen des Lukasevangeliums* (Heidelberg, 1979)

WENISCH, Franz, '*Judith*: eine westsächsische Dichtung?', *Anglia* 100 (1982), 273–300

WENTERSDORF, Karl, 'Beowulf's Withdrawal from Frisia: A Reconsideration', *Studies in Philology* 68 (1971), 395–415

WHITBREAD, L. G., 'The *Liber Monstrorum* and *Beowulf*', *Mediaeval Studies* 36 (1974), 434–71

WHITELOCK, Dorothy, *The Audience of 'Beowulf'* (Oxford, 1950)
WICKHAM, L. R., 'The Sons of God and the Daughters of Men: Genesis VI.2 in Early Christian Exegesis', *Oudtestamentische Studiën* 19 (1974), 135–47
WIELAND, Gernot, '*Manna mildost*: Moses and Beowulf', *Pacific Coast Philology* 23 (1988), 86–93
WIERSMA, Stanley Martin, 'A Linguistic Analysis of Words Referring to Monsters in *Beowulf*' (unpublished PhD dissertation, University of Wisconsin, 1961)
WILLARD, Rudolph, *Two Apocrypha in Old English Homilies*, Beiträge zur englischen Philologie 30 (Leipzig, 1935)
WILLARD, Rudolph, ed., *The Blickling Homilies*, EEMF 10 (Copenhagen, 1960)
WILLIAMS, David, *Cain and Beowulf: A Study in Secular Allegory* (Toronto, 1982)
WITTKOWER, Rudolf, 'Marvels of the East: a Study in the History of Monsters', *Journal of the Warburg and Courthauld Institutes* 5 (1942), 159–97
WOOLF, Rosemary E., 'The Lost Opening to the *Judith*', *Modern Language Review* (1955), 168–72
WORMALD, Patrick, 'A Handlist of Anglo-Saxon Lawsuits', *Anglo-Saxon England* 17 (1988), 247–81
WRIGHT, Charles D., '*Docet Deus, docet diabolus*: a Hiberno-Latin Theme in an Old English Body-and-Soul Homily', *Notes and Queries* 34 (1987), 451–3
WRIGHT, Charles D., 'Hiberno-Latin and Irish-Influenced Biblical Commentaries, Florilegia, and Homily Collections', in *Sources of Anglo-Saxon Literary Culture: a Trial Version*, ed. Frederick M. Biggs, Thomas D. Hill, and Paul E. Szarmach (Binghamton, NY, 1990), pp. 87–123
WRIGHT, Charles D., *The Irish Tradition in Old English Literature*, CSASE 6 (Cambridge, 1993)
WÜLCKER, Richard Paul, *Grundriss zur Geschichte der angelsächsischen Litteratur* (Leipzig, 1885)
XIVREY, J. Berger de, ed., *Traditions Tératologiques, ou Récits de l'Antiquité et du Moyen Age en Occident* (Paris, 1836)
ZACHRISSON, R. E., 'Grendel in *Beowulf*', in *Festschrift Otto Jespersen* (Copenhagen, 1930), pp. 39–44
ZANGEMEISTER, K., ed., *Pauli Orosii historiarum aduersum paganos libri vii*, CSEL 5 (Vienna, 1882)
ZIMMERMANN, Günter, 'Vorbildisches Verhalten? Zum Thema der Grettis saga', *Sagnaskemmtun: Studies in Honour of Hermann Pálsson* (Vienna, 1986), pp. 331–50
ZUPITZA, Julius, *Beowulf: Autotypes on the Unique Cotton ms Vitellius A.xv in the British Museum, with a Transliteration and Notes*, EETS OS 77 (London, 1882)

GENERAL INDEX

Material in footnotes is included in the general page reference. Norse names are given by first name, rather than by patronymic. Figures in bold type are line-references for passages from Old English poems cited or discussed.